T

ROOTS

ROCK

REGGAE

ROOTS

An Oral
History of
Reggae Music
from Ska to
Dancehall

ROCK

REGGAE

CHUCK
FOSTER

BILLBOARD BOOKS
An imprint of Watson-Guptill Publications/New York

Senior Editor: Bob Nirkind
Edited by: Amy Handy
Book and cover design: Areta Buk
Production Manager: Ellen Greene

First published 1999 by Billboard Books,
an imprint of Watson-Guptill Publications,
a division of BPI Communications, Inc.,
1515 Broadway, New York, NY 10036

Library of Congress Cataloging-in-Publication Data for this
title can be obtained from the Library of Congress

Library of Congress Catalog Card Number: 98-89965

ISBN: 0-8230-7831-0

Manufactured in the United States of America

First printing, 1999

1 2 3 4 5 6 7 8 9/07 06 05 04 03 02 01 00 99

Contents

Introduction

From the early manifestations of ska and rock steady to the stylistic variations of rockers, steppers, lovers rock, roots, Nyahbingi, dub, dj, dancehall, ragga, jungle, drum and bass, and beyond, reggae has had a profound influence on the music of our time. Though reggae has never had the exposure in America it received on the radio in England, it bubbled underground and seeped through, creating change while many remained unaware of its existence. All that is changing now.

For early enthusiasts the only way to really know reggae was on Jamaican 7-inch vinyl pressings, later album and 12-inch. The CD is new to reggae but already a nearly overwhelming amount of music is available and being added to daily. Reggae's time has come.

The artists interviewed here have each contributed uniquely to the development of reggae. I have tried to let them tell their stories in their own words. In many cases those words are in Jamaican patois. It is a language meant to be understood and misunderstood at the same time: designed to reveal and conceal. "You got to see and blind, hear and deaf" is an old Jamaican proverb as well as a song lyric. I have attempted to retain as much of the individualized forms of speech and include as much of each artist's recording history as possible.

I've also included sketches of artists not treated in full-length interviews, though some contain interview material. These are intended to be referenced in relation to the selected discography. As with the records listed, no claim is made to completeness.

For the past ten years I've written a column called "Reggae Update" for *Beat* magazine. Many of these interviews were done as features and cover stories for *Beat,* edited by C.C. Smith. Some of them appeared in the now defunct *L.A. View* and were edited by Bob Remstein. Thanks go to these brave souls and to Keith Scott, who interviewed Desmond Dekker with me. The transcript of that interview first appeared in *Dub Catcher.* Thanks go also to John Skomdahl, who interviewed Admiral Tibet and brought his transcript—and Tibet—to me. That interview was published in *Reggae Nucleus* and *More Axe 8* and appears with kind permissions.

Thanks are also due to Hank Holmes, my longtime partner on *The Reggae Beat,* a radio show that aired for many years on KCRW in Santa Monica, California. Some of the interview material in the non-interview sections is from that show and some from *Reggae Central,* the show I now host on KPFK Sunday afternoons in Los Angeles. I owe a major debt of gratitude to Hank, whose knowledge of the music I have always drawn on.

I would also like to thank Hank's former radio partner Roger Steffens. On many occasions Roger has either opened doors for me or left them open in passing. Neither they nor anyone else mentioned is in any way responsible for errors of fact or opinion in this work.

Thanks are also owed to Chris Wilson, who participated in the Michael Rose interview, and to the label heads, reps, and artists' managers who made some of the interviews possible. I am also grateful to the photographers John Skomdahl, Bob and Jan Salzman, Dave Wendlinger, Ade James, and Anne Marie Staas and to Eric Olson, who edited my contributions to Billboard Books' *Encyclopedia of Top Producers.* Writing twenty-five biographies of reggae producers for that work caused me to suggest this book to Eric, who presented it to Bob Nirkind, Senior Editor of Billboard Books. I thank both of them for their encouragement and support.

The world of reggae is vast and broad and encompasses many unique styles, production techniques, time periods of varying duration, and some of the greatest artists of any kind of music ever made. Respect is owed to all singers and musicians interviewed and not interviewed, mentioned and not mentioned, who have contributed to this great and enduring form of music. Reggae is a positive force that set out to change the world and has already accomplished much toward this goal. As we enter the twenty-first century, I sincerely believe the high ideals it represents will continue to have a profound effect on us all.

CHAPTER 1

Ska-Ba-Doo-Ska-Ba-Day:

Skatalites Bandleader Tommy McCook

Ska. Even the name is a sound—the sound of a strategically placed rhythm guitar upchop transforming a rhythm and blues–based Latin jazz shuffle into a new musical order. Before ska, Jamaican music is mainly derived—the burro drumming from Africa, the quadrille from England, and mento, second cousin to Trinidad's calypso, all contain Jamaican elements grafted onto other music. It can be argued that even those elements that seem the least Jamaican, like mento's banjo, have early roots in African instruments and musical styles.

For most the beginning of ska is represented in one premier early studio band. Though not the first to play the style as a group, the Skatalites became Jamaica's number one ska band in the early sixties and a series of reunions led to a version of the group that is still playing today. They celebrated their thirtieth anniversary only a few years ago, but it's also been thirty years since the band first broke up. A resurgence of interest in ska has the Skatalites in orbit again and the band shows no signs of slowing down. Though some original members have passed and some have stepped aside, the band plays a breakneck series of shows throughout the world and records and releases new albums at a rigorous pace.

For many fans the Skatalites have come to represent the entire era of ska in Jamaica and subsequent revivals in England and America. Amazingly, considering their recorded output and continued influence, the Skatalites had only been together for fourteen months when they disbanded in 1965. A continual interest in the music and those who began it has rekindled careers for many who originated ska, making this early sixties band one of the top draws of the eighties and nineties.

The name *Skatalites* reflects the spirit of the early sixties when they formed, conjoined with the new style then sweeping Jamaica. The forward-looking, hopeful spirit of the early space age they punned off was a fitting metaphor for the new Jamaican spirit that emerged in their music.

The story of reggae rightly begins with ska. But oddly the roots of ska, like the calypso of the 1930s, point in a completely different direction. For founder and longtime bandleader saxophonist Tommy McCook, the roots of ska lie in America. "We used to play orchestrated music from the U.S. from the Big Band era, like Woody Herman, Count Basie, and Duke Ellington," says the venerable musician whose own contributions span the ska, rock steady, and reggae

TOMMY McCOOK. Photograph by Jan Salzman; © 1989 Phantom Photos

eras. The blend of sophisticated jazz with the wild rhythms of ska is part of what makes this music so appealing to young and old.

His personal influences as a soloist included Coleman Hawkins, Sonny Rollins, Lester Young, and Ornette Coleman, names that might fly right by many of today's ska fanatics. "Jazz was my first love," McCook emphasizes. "I love jazz music."

Like many of Jamaica's greatest musicians, McCook attended the Alpha Boys School in Kingston. "It was a Catholic school for the poorer kids of JA," he explains. "I grew up without a father, and it was tough on my mom. I attended this school because of that and to learn music." Graduates of Alpha's school band program fueled Jamaican music from the earliest Big Band era through reggae and included vibist Lennie Hibbert, drummer Leroy "Horsemouth" Wallace, and singers like Leroy Smart and Leroy Sibbles of the Heptones.

McCook graduated to the hotel circuit, playing in large combos and small, then played for many years in the Bahamas. He was a major figure in Jamaica's Big Band scene of the early 1950s, a largely unsung era from which few recordings have surfaced. Many of the legendary players of this early era, like McCook and fellow Skatalite Roland Alphonso, made significant contributions to the music that was to follow. "I left [Jamaica] in '54, came back in '62," recalls McCook. "When I came back the ska was shaping up."

For the horn section, this revolutionary music was closely related to the swing style except that, according to McCook, "The rhythm was going a different way from the American style. [The Skatalites] injected the mento or calypso-type guitar [played then by Jerome "Jah Jerry" Hines] and keyboards [supplied by a young Jackie Mittoo] with a regular walking-bass-style rhythm." Lloyd Brevett played the bass and Lloyd Knibbs played drums. The latter two are still in the band's lineup, along with saxophonists Roland Alphonso and Lester Sterling.

Newer members of the group—though often longtime players themselves—include Nathan Breedlove (who replaced original trumpeter Johnny "Dizzy" Moore), trombonist Will Clark, guitarist Devon James, Bill Smith (who has played keys since Jackie Mittoo's passing), and early singer Doreen Schaeffer. Others who have been in the band or played on recordings under their name include trumpeters Baba Brooks (in the very early days) and the late Roy Harper, guitarists Lynn Taitt and Ernest Ranglin, saxophonists Karl "Cannonball" Bryan and "Ska" Campbell, and trombonist Ron Wilson.

One of the true innovators of the ska era (and a founding member of the Skatalites) was visionary trombonist Don Drummond. On cuts like "Far East" and "Addis Ababa," Drummond helped introduce the practice of playing minor-key leads against major chord progressions, which later became the trademark reggae style championed by Augustus Pablo, Bob Marley, Hugh Mundell, and hundreds of vocal groups from Burning Spear to Israel Vibration. This modal approach reaches back to the African roots of black music: "way back," McCook says.

"Don Drummond was so far ahead of his time," he elaborates. "He was so progressive in his day. He was a great person once you know him. He was skeptical—he's not somebody that would get too cozy with you the first time you met him, but once he knows you he's a very nice person and he talks very intelligently."

Musically brilliant, Drummond was mentally unstable, and he was sometimes incarcerated in mental institutions. "We were playing without Don on a number of occasions when he was in Bellevue, but he was always able to come out periodically and join the group for recordings and play with the band." One of the earliest of Jamaica's great musicians to achieve international acclaim—even winning a "Best Trombonist" slot in a mid-sixties Playboy Jazz poll—Drummond was a musical genius who combined the extemporaneous free style of players like Miles Davis and John Coltrane with the African roots of Jamaica's Rastafari movement in a series of breathtaking records backed by the band.

Much of his finest work is available on the Studio One albums *The Best of Don Drummond, In Memory of Don Drummond,* and the Treasure Isle collection *Don Drummond Greatest Hits.* Early Skatalites collections on these same labels and others also feature his unique trombone leads and insightful arrangements. Some of his major records were "Man in the Street," "Addis Ababa,"

"Green Island," "Schooling the Duke," "Don Cosmic," "Stampede," and "This Man Is Back." Many fine 7-inch sides, tracks on anthologies, and instrumentals originally released as early B-side singles remain uncollected.

The Skatalites were among the first in a long line of house bands for Clement "Coxsone" Dodd's Studio One label. Though they began hitting big on the charts in the early sixties, McCook had a contract with an uptown hotel and so couldn't play with them live for several months. "But by this time some hot instrumentals were out there and people were goin' crazy over the recordings! So the group was formed, we went down the road, and everything looked rosy for fourteen months."

Individually and in combination, for years preceding and after their breakup, the Skatalites were Jamaica's most in-demand studio band and backed the cream-of-the-crop vocalists from the early Wailers and Derrick Morgan to hundreds of up-and-coming young singers, some of whom went on to become the big names of the rock steady and reggae eras. Between these sessions the band cut blistering instrumentals like "Guns of Navarone," "Eastern Standard Time," and "Phoenix City" that created a musical firestorm when played at sound system dances across the island.

Even though their music celebrated Jamaica's then recent independence from England (one of their big sellers was "Independence Anniversary Ska," oddly an instrumental version of a Beatles tune), they scored in Europe. The Skatalites didn't earn much in the way of royalties, says McCook, but "We could live off the regularity of recording and [their music] was played in dancehalls all over the island. As far back as Germany, people were buying ska, so we had something coming in regularly. The promoters would pay us to record, so we were making a living from it." During this time they also recorded for Top Deck, Randys, King Edwards, and a plethora of other producers.

But at this point tragedy struck. Drummond's fragile psyche shattered and in 1965 he killed his wife, Marguerite, a singer best known for the tune "Woman a Come," found on a number of ska anthologies. He was incarcerated, this time permanently, in Kingston's Bellevue Hospital, where he died in 1969. "And that," McCook says succinctly, "was the end of that era. 'Cause they put him away indefinitely, so he couldn't come out again as before. We went on a few months after he got himself in trouble, but every time the band play, people keep lookin', hopin' that he would show up and now they know that he won't show up, so we may as well call it a day."

Mittoo, Alphonso, and trumpet player Dizzy Moore stayed with Coxsone to form the Soul Brothers, who cut many hits for Studio One both under that name and as a backing band. McCook moved over to competitor Duke Reid's Treasure Isle label (the Skatalites had cut many hits for Reid as well), calling his band the Supersonics. There they helped create the sound that replaced ska, the short-lived but brilliant rock steady. Like ska and later reggae, rock steady was originally the name of a dance— they were the Ska, the Rock Steady, and the Reggae in early days.

Several collections from Studio One gather essential Skatalites material, including *Ska Authentic, Celebration Time,* and *Best of the Skatalites.* They are the featured backing band on anthologies such as *This Is Jamaica Ska* and among those featured on the ground-breaking *Jazz Jamaica* from the same label. Their recordings for Duke Reid can be found on *Treasure Ska* and *Skatalites Plus* (both on Treasure Isle). Some are also available on European various-artist CD releases like *Tribute to the Skatalites* and *Skatalites and Friends.* A double-CD set from Heartbeat called *Foundation Ska* collects thirty-two of their finest performances for Studio One.

As premier studio musicians the group also recorded for other producers. Two albums worth of material recorded for Justin "Philip" Yap's Top Deck label between 1962 and 1966 are *Ska Boo-Da-Ba* (WIRL) and *Ska Down Jamaica Way* (Top Deck). The former is mainly an instrumental album and the latter also features vocal groups like the Deacons and singers like Ferdie Nelson, all backed by the Skatalites. Recently VP issued *Skatalites at Randy's,* containing previously unissued backing and solo work.

At a promotional appearance in a reggae record shop in Long Beach a few years back, Roland Alphonso was surrounded by teen and preteen fans decked out in classic ska style. A young fan pointed to the Studio One Wailing Wailers album on the wall and asked "Did you know those guys?" Alphonso smiled and patiently replied, "We are the backing band on that record. That's our album."

Alphonso originally played with Clue J and the Blues Blasters, with whom he recorded "Shuffling Jug" (often credited as the first ska record) before joining the Skatalites. His solo contributions are featured on Studio One albums like *Ska Strictly for You* and *Best of Roland Alphonso.* An early eighties solo release, *Roll On* (Wackies), was produced in New York by Bullwackies' Lloyd Barnes before the long-running Skatalites reunion.

McCook, Alphonso, and the others played on many classic reggae cuts as well. "I was fortunate," says Tommy. "I had the ideas that the guys needed on their sessions and they respected my compositional skills to put music to the rhythms." Check the musicians on some of your favorite rock steady and reggae releases and you'll be amazed how many players from the ska era (particularly the horns) are responsible for the tight sound of the later music.

McCook also had solo instrumental releases like *Tommy McCook* (Treasure Isle), *Tommy McCook Superstar* (Weed Beat), *Brass Rockers* (Striker Lee), and *Cookin'* (Horse), the first produced by the legendary Duke Reid and the others all produced by Bunny Lee and featuring

the Aggrovators. In the late seventies and early eighties a groundswell formed in England that eventually became the "two-tone" movement or first ska revival. From the earliest days ska held sway in the U.K., where Jamaican music got the airplay it never received in America.

The marriage between punk and reggae was strong, and the young white or mixed-culture ska bands—often including a smattering of second generation Jamaican kids raised in England—were dedicated to the narrow black ties, pork-pie hats, rude-boy ideology, and above all the music of singers Laurel Aitken, Prince Buster, Derrick Morgan, and the Skatalites. Groups like Madness (named after a Prince Buster song), the Specials, Selector, and Bad Manners emulated the songs and styles of ska and blended them with themes of racial harmony, delivering it all up with a staccato punk attitude that glossed over some of the jazz elements but retained the youthful energy of original ska. Something in this music spoke to the young, who kept it alive and relevant.

The band briefly reunited in 1975 for a Lloyd Brevett solo project, which has been released in various forms over the years. It came out in 1978 on United Artists as *The Legendary Skatalites,* and later on the Jam Sounds label. It is now available as Lloyd Brevett and the Skatalites' *African Roots* on the Moon Ska label. It could also have been called "The Skatalites Play Reggae" since the players mix musical influences for a sound at once more relaxed and more modern than their early work. The new release contains four otherwise unavailable bonus tracks from the ska days.

By 1983 succeeding waves of ska bands from England, Japan, and the U.S. had drawn such attention that the founders of Jamaica's Reggae Sunsplash asked the Skatalites—by then scattered across the globe in England, Canada, and the United States—to reform and open that year's show. "We disbanded in '65, regroup up in '83, and Sunsplash was the one who brought us back," McCook remembers. "They wanted the people to know where this music was coming from."

A recording of that show was issued by ROIR as *Stretching Out* in 1983 (recently reissued as a two-CD set with bonus tracks from the last rehearsal) and the band began a grueling touring schedule that hasn't stopped yet. Their first post-reunion studio recording was 1984's *Scattered Lights* (Alligator). Almost ten years later they began a trilogy of releases that showed their power undiminished with 1993's *Skavoovie,* followed in short order by 1994's *Hi-Bop Ska, the 30th Anniversary Recording* (for which the group received its first Grammy nomination), followed by *Greetings from Skamania* (1996), all on the Shanachie label.

How does it feel to experience such appreciation after all these years? "In the '90s when we started touring Europe and Japan, I was mostly in a state of shock to see the way the young kids reacted to the music," McCook says. "Especially when we did 'Guns of Navarone' in Berlin, the place was rocking up and down, the people would be singing the song with us and would go actually crazy. I've never had the reaction I've had there and in California back in the early '90s. And in Japan it's the same thing. So the reaction was really shocking. Because we had never dreamt that the music would have such an effect on the young people of today."

This effect can clearly be heard in ska music itself, currently enjoying its second and strongest revival. Moon Ska has issued hundreds of new ska releases in the last few years by bands from New York to California. A newer label, Jump Up!, focuses exclusively on Midwest ska. And all this interest has led to the reissue of scarce sides. Early tracks from Coxsone and Duke Reid have become anthology staples and a series of European and American releases have made much of the Skatalites early work available again.

Triple-bypass surgery kept Tommy from appearing on the latest Skatalites release, *Ball of Fire* (Island Jamaica Jazz). He seemed particularly pleased that the band was nominated for two Grammys. "Although we didn't win, it shows the band is looking toward better things all the time. We look forward to the future, to continue the music as it is. Right now the future looks bright for the group because everywhere we have played, people want us to come back." And coming back is something the Skatalites have always done well.

McCook passed away in May of 1998 at the age of seventy-one. But his attitude had remained amazingly upbeat. As he said of himself and fellow players, "The older the wine is, the more vintage. The older the guys get is the more mellow they become and [they] play better."

Sadly Roland Alphonso collapsed while performing on stage with the Skatalites at the House of Blues in Los Angeles in late 1998. He was diagnosed with a brain embolism and passed away November 20, 1998. It seems likely that some version of the band will continue to record and perform.

CHAPTER 2

Baked Beans for Breakfast:

Desmond Dekker, King of Ska

Though ska made huge inroads in England in the sixties, many Americans remained completely oblivious to it through lack of local airplay. Hints and influences filtered through—Millie Small's "My Boy Lollipop" was a hit (and is still played on "oldies" stations today) and Prince Buster's "Ten Commandments" saw American release and airplay. Jimmy Cliff played New York with Byron Lee and the Dragonaires and Annette Funnicello covered Lee's "Jamaican Ska" here, resulting in some strange hybrids like Billy Strange's "Tennessee Ska" with vocals by

American DJ Lloyd Thaxton, on an album that included ska versions of Beatle tunes.

By late 1966 a new style was developing in Jamaica and rock steady moved to the fore, a slower style with emphasis on picking guitar fills and achingly restive vocals, fewer horns, and a general reconfiguration that eventually led to the sound we now call reggae. Many Americans received their first exposure to this music—albeit unknowingly—through the pop records of American singer Johnny Nash, who recorded a series of rock steady classics in Jamaica that included "Hold Me Tight," a cover of Sam Cooke's "Cupid," and later the early reggae of Bob Marley's "Stir It Up" and Nash's own "I Can See Clearly Now."

In 1969 Desmond Dekker and the Aces scored the first major undoctored Jamaican hit in America (even "My Boy Lollipop" had been over-dubbed in England, with harmonica solos by a young Rod Stewart) with the then-unclassifiable though instantly identifiable "The Israelites." Dekker's career spans the ska, rock steady, and reggae eras with the bulk of his earliest and best work produced by Chinese-Jamaican Leslie Kong and issued on his Beverley's label. Dekker's major hits included cuts like "007 (Shanty Town)" and "It Mek," the latter appearing along with cuts like "Intensified" on his first American album, *Israelites,* on Uni. Dekker's story parallels the rise of Jamaican music.

In those days it wasn't at all easy for a new singer to be heard by a producer of Kong's stature. "Jimmy Cliff and Derrick Morgan was Leslie Kong's two big acts," recalls Dekker, "and they come first. I was a kid—fifteen, sixteen. So when I went there they tried to give me a hard time about 'try a likkle rehearsal and come back' and all dem ting." Competition was stiff from other youths. Keith Scott, who worked for Federal Records during the period in question and was an associate of Kong's (and who joined me for this interview), remembers that when word got around that Kong was recording there were "hundreds of little kids who said they could sing and want to record." Dekker agrees: "Other kids have got songs and want to be heard and there wasn't any time more or less according to the Chinaman [Kong] when he wasn't working with Jimmy Cliff and Derrick Morgan on new singles. He reckons he's gonna get these over first and then hear what we've got."

This created a special problem for Dekker, who was one of the few youths in Kingston with a steady job at the time. "I was learning engineering and welding. [Kong] was telling me to come back, come back, come back and I keep on asking my boss to give me a day off or half a day off and my boss was getting fed up with me." He laughs. "I passed all of my tests in engineering-welding and I started to do underwater welding but [because of success in music] I didn't finish it." Eventually, says Dekker of Jamaica's fledgling music business, "I bluffed my way in."

In those days, Scott reminds us, Beverley's Records was known as Beverley's Record and Ice Cream Parlor. Dekker nods. "Here's the ice cream parlor, you can go into the restaurant, sit down, have a meal, then you have to go past the cigarettes through some staircase upstairs and then you can get through to see him. And then you go upstairs again! So I go in there."

"Is Leslie Kong here?" Dekker is talking to Kong's brother Lloyd. "'Yes, but he's having a private rehearsal with Jimmy.' I said, 'Well, I've got an appointment.' Him say, 'Well I'm afraid you can't go in now, you know. He's busy.'" At this point Dekker took fate into his own hands. "He walk away from the door and went down fe go get something so I just walk in, walking through, go upstairs. What I find is the two giants at the door: Jimmy and Derrick, and I say, 'That's all I need!'"

The established artists who had been figuratively blocking his way now literally blocked it. "I just said, 'Look—I want to see Leslie Kong and one way or another I'm going to see him.'

But they close the door. And when they open the door I just hold it and push everybody aside and just go in. And when I go in the room it was 'Hey, hey, why?' So I went to Leslie Kong and I said, 'Look, you told me to come back a couple of times and I did and nothing. So if you want to hear the songs I've got fair enough, and if you don't want to fair enough.' And he said, 'All right, let me hear what you've got.' And I sing 'Honor Your Father and Your Mother.'"

In the studio that day was pianist-arranger Theophilus Beckford, called "Easy Snappin'" for his huge Jamaican instrumental hit of that title. Dekker continues, "When he come with Jimmy and Derrick—that is a special and private thing you know . . . I started to sing the song and I reach halfway through when he stop playing the piano and start laughing. Yeah. Theophilus Beckford, we call him "Snappin'," he stop in the middle of the song and start laughing and I said, 'What's up?' You know, 'What's goin' down?" Him say, well him hear some nice little song a couple of times but him never hear one like this! And Leslie Kong laugh also and say, 'Sing it again.' And when I sing it he say, 'Sing it again,' and I sing it again. And when I sing it again he say, 'You have any more?' And I said yes—I have another one called 'Madgie.' And I sing it and him say, 'Yeah mon, that is good. I tell you what, next week, next

DESMOND DEKKER. Photograph by Jan Salzman; © 1996 Phantom Photos

Wednesday,' I should come down by him for a proper rehearsal and let him get the feel of these.

"And I went. It was okay. The following day we went to the studio, Derrick Morgan, Jimmy Cliff, Frank Coslo, Eric Morris, Andy and Joey. It was quite a few of us, really. About ten of us, because that's the way they cut in them days."

Scott lays out the musician lineup for us. Australian guitarist Dennis Cindry on guitar, Lloyd Mason bass, Beckford on piano, Stanley Webbs and Deadly Headly on horns. "Those musicians are for his top artists," says Dekker. Some of today's musicians and singers, used to spending months in the studio working on one song, might be interested in the day's results. Besides Andy and Joey and others, "Derrick do about four and Jimmy did the same. And when my turn came I sing the one I've got, 'Honor Your Mother and Father,' and I cut the B-side 'cause the A-side is the hit—he [Kong] knows this! Because he have a very good ear for music. So he can say well, 'Honor Your Mother and Father,' that's the one. 'Madgie' is nice, but no [hit].'"

Waiting for the record's release, Dekker went back to his welding. Working as a trainee in the same shop was young would-be welder Robert Nesta Marley. "He told me he have a song. I was still there at the shop and then he said he have got some songs he would like to bring down." Dekker introduced Marley to Kong and Marley's first single, "Judge Not," backed with "One More Cup of Coffee" resulted. "He did all right with that one," smiles Dekker. "It didn't make a number one, but he made his mark."

Dekker's first single, on the other hand, was an immediate hit with the public. He grins. "Jimmy Cliff and Derrick was a bit surprised." Still, it was a friendly rivalry. "I admired all a them guys actually, because it was like a competition, you gotta be strong to keep on the top, otherwise they would just throw you off. So therefore it was a battle of the giants."

Dekker's American influences include Nat "King" Cole and Sam Cooke. His next recording was "Sinners Come on Home," although "It might sound a bit gospelly" today. "And I sing another one called 'Labor for Learning." I don't know if you remember that: 'Labor for learning before you grow old/For learning is better than silver and gold/Silver and gold it vanish away/But a good education will never decay.'"

In those days, he says, you went in with an idea—"I always have an idea what I want" and "just sing and they find the rhythm and everything and, is you that. I sing it to Theophilus, who play the piano. And as long as I give them the melody then everybody just start to play what they feel they should play to make this work."

The potent combination of Dekker and producer Kong created a ska and rock steady archive that is still being mined to this day. Tracks like "Rude Boy Train," "Intensified," "Nincompoop," "Pickney Gal," "Wise Man," and "Pretty Africa" have been reissued so many times in so many combinations that a reasonable album discography of Desmond Dekker is impossible. At least a dozen albums titled *Israelites* feature some of these songs. The licensing of Leslie Kong product became so murky after his death that most of his early productions of Marley and Dekker were widely and openly bootlegged.

I asked Dekker about one of the more gripping tracks from the rock steady era, a once obscure single called "Fu Manchu" that appears on a couple of recent anthologies, including Rhino Records' recommended *Rockin' Steady: The Best of Desmond Dekker.* Musically menacing and lyrically sparse, it lays out a brief story and repeating refrain: "This is the place of Fu Manchu." It's a song that could have been written only for a voice like Dekker's, which soars, dramatically hovers, then plunges to the heart of the material. On mention of the song he cries, "Golly Miss Molly!" and laughs.

"I wrote this in a bar. I was sitting down inside and some guys was there—big men who was talking away. I was about to go out and I heard them say a couple of things and I said well—very interesting. So I go back in and sit down and I listen to the conversation. They were more or less talking about where they used to work and what happened is them didn't get any breads from there so how much them used to, and I said hmmm, and immediately things started happening in my mind and they are talking away and I am talking away and then it just come up well, 'it make no sense at all,' because seeing them guys talking about 'I used to be this' and 'I used to be that' and 'how much I used to have' and I said, 'Yeah . . . that is that day.' But again what I tried to tell him— I couldn't tell him at that time—but in my record I said, 'It no make no sense to say what you used to do and how much you used to earn.' You see? It's what you keep that makes you a man. That song was a very strange song."

And where does Asian bad guy and Sax Rohmer villain Fu Manchu come in? "Well, I saw a movie about Fu Manchu and the way how he run his thing. You know, he's very careful of certain things and of course if he have got something that is of value he makes sure 'This is mine.' You know, it's what you keep that make you a man. So therefore that make him Fu Manchu."

Keith Scott asks what it was like working with Kong in the early days. "He was easy to get along with," Dekker responds. "He used to treat me well in the beginning. Robert—Bob Marley, which was of course with him at the time, and myself—everything used to be run cool. He treated us all right." Then Jackie Opel, a singer from Barbados, hit Jamaica like a storm. "He just come and dominate the scene. And we can't get even one song in [Kong's] studio—not even one day. All we want a go twenty minutes because I mean, musician go deh dat time from dem hear the song one time them just go into it and do it and get the feel."

Opel had a striking talent apparent on his two albums for Coxsone and Studio One singles like "Solid Rock" and "The Lord Is with Me," though interestingly none of his work with Kong is available today while Kong's productions of Marley and Dekker have been continually in print since that time. "So it was Jackie Opel, all the time Jackie Opel. So Robert said to me, 'Look, I'll a dig up.' I said, "Where you goin'"? Him say, 'Watch out. I'll leggo dis Chinaman y'unno. I'll go up ah Coxsone. Yuh a come?' 'Well, I shouldn't be speakin' this way, I mean—that's a Jamaican—is a way how we say. He said he's goin' up to Coxsone and he asked if I'm comin'. I said, 'Well, I gonna wait and see what happen before I make a move.'"

Bob Marley's move to Coxsone eventually resulted in a huge output as well as some formative years with Lee Perry, then Coxsone's engineer and arranger and later on a producer of some of the Wailers' best work. As for Dekker, "After a while I was getting fed up myself, and I go down by Duke Reid and I said, "Duke, I've got a couple of songs here." He was a bit shocked because he know that I'm a person who, even if I don't sign a contract with you if I say I'm gonna stick by you, then you don't have to sign nothing. I will stick there.

"And when I find that Jackie Opel's number one on the scene and nothing is happening for me, I decide to go to Duke Reid. And Duke Reid said, 'Well, Des, if you want. . . .' Because they are all good friends. You know? They're all good friends! Heh-heh. You can't go up by Coxsone and Beverley's don't know seh you have been up by Coxsone." He laughs. "So Duke Reid tell me, 'All right, meet me 'round by my place and go in my car. I'll take you by the studio,' which was Dynamic. After we reached the studio, Duke Reid and myself, about fifteen minutes after that Leslie Kong drive and come up and said: 'Look Des, don't leave me, man. I've got good intentions for you. I've got something good going for you now, I'm planning things for you.' I said: 'You said you was gonna give me a break, you was gonna give me three days in the studio or two days. Y'unno wha' I mean? And you haven't done anything like that so I wanna do something because I'm writing and I can't really make more music and progress without getting some of them out of the way."

Some of the songs at that time were "Get Up Adina" and the original "King of Ska," sung with his backup group the Aces. Eventually, says Dekker, "He did convince me [to return]. 'Look, all right. I'll get you the studio next week, so come back.' So I went back with him. I went to Duke Reid and Duke Reid look at me and he laugh. Believe me, I think he knew it all along. And when I look at Duke Reid, Duke Reid say, 'All right, I know." I didn't have to say anything to him because he know."

This surprising spirit of cooperation among producers we normally think of as rivals is explained simply by Dekker. "Duke Reid don't take on more than he can handle." Just as Kong ran a combination stationery store and ice cream parlor, Reid had his own liquor store "and that take up a lot of his time." Another complication is that at the time Leslie Kong was not just Dekker's producer, but his manager as well.

One of Dekker's all-time biggest hits and one of the best-known reggae songs in the world is "007 (Shanty Town)." It defined the spirit of Jamaica at a crucial time musically and historically, and was anthologized on the seminal *Harder They Come* soundtrack album. "The reason why I write that song was because of what was happening at that time," he recalls. "The students had a demonstration and it went all the way around back to Four Shore Road and down to Shanty Town. You got wild life and thing like that there because it went down near to the beach. And the higher ones wanted to bulldoze the whole thing down and do their own thing and the students said no way! And it just get out of control. And whatsoever you

hear on the record, that is what was going down. Man take a stone and throw through a window, lick after somebody, and you read it as somebody just kick it and it gone! Is just a typical riot 'cause I say, "Them a loot, them a shoot, them a wail." It was wild."

Besides being number one in Jamaica, "007" reached number 15 on the British charts. "That song was the one that give me my first international recognition." After winning the 1968 Jamaica Festival song competition with "Intensified," Dekker and the Aces toured England, with a group consisting of Barry (Barrington Howard) and James (Winston Samuel, the one with the deep voice); by this time early members Clive Campbell and Patrick Johnson had already left the group. But Barry balked at so much travel. "I tried to convince him but he just wouldn't fly to promote the record."

Eventually Dekker went on without the Aces, but not before they recorded "The Israelites," a monster hit first in Jamaica, then in England, and even in America. Dekker and the Aces' first gold record was a win for all Jamaica. "This guy Cliff Richards was on top . . . Mick Jagger was a giant. You have Tom Jones. . . . You have the Beakles [Beatles]—giants there. So many giants. And of course 'Israelites' just create wonders. I think that song surprised all the British big-name singers."

"Israelites" was a smash in America too, although few understood the lyrics. "Until this day people still asking me. I heard people say, 'Well what do you say, Dekker? Get up in the morning, bake beans for breakfast? Get up in the morning, same thing for breakfast?' And mostly I have to just correct it and say it's 'slaving for breads.' Breads is money. Get up in the morning, slaving, go out there to get some dough, we call it breads." Although it was treated in the U.S. as a "novelty record" like "Tie Me Kangaroo Down, Sport," "Israelites" dealt with "how you feel, and what you are going through." It's still strong today because "It is brutal. It is reality."

Another big hit with Leslie Kong was "A It Mek." Although it's hard to believe after seeing him perform it (with bumps, grinds, and arched eyebrows) that it wasn't all double entendre, Dekker insists, "It's a little story I wrote off my kid sister. She wouldn't hear what her mom say and she scolded them and gone to play with her friends and gamble and all kind of thing. I talk with her and whenever time she see me come in she make a run for it. And anybody who knows that her mother [is coming], she make a run for it. So one day I just passing by and I seen her playing marble or something and she decide to make a run for it and then she fall over. I say, 'You think I never see you with your back against the wall/You think I never see you when you accidentally fall.' You see, most of the songs I sing, is the way how I sing them—if I don't interpret them sometimes you won't get the understanding of them. Because when somebody asks me what 'A It Mek' means I said, 'that's why.'"

Around this time Jimmy Cliff released "You Can Get It If You Really Want," Dekker recalls, "and it didn't do anything for him. Kong asked me to sing it, to have a go at it. And I didn't want to. I told him no. Because I had a record in Jamaica—every other singer sing a version of maybe American song done reggae version or sing other people's record—I was the only one [doing all originals]. I didn't want to break that record—I said no. But [Kong] was a very convincing guy," he laughs, "so I did it and got a silver [record] for it."

As one of the originals, Dekker is pleased to see the ska revival and proliferation of U.S. and English reggae bands. "Because, for instance, UB40, they've done some very nice versions. They do it their own way and the people love it. And of course if you're going to cover something and you do it well then you find the reaction you get from the public is they really support it. I never work with those guys but it make me feel good reggae music is so big that the UB40's and many others said, 'Yes! I love this music! I love this rhythm here,' and they can do something about it, which of course they did and it works for them, although it's not exactly . . ." He smiles. "But they have done a good job."

Dekker's work for Leslie Kong has been anthologized in many forms with major reissues from the Trojan label including live and "rare" cuts. In the early eighties he recorded two albums for Stiff. Most recently he has returned to ska with a vengeance in his live shows, and his 1989 release *King of Ska* reprises that era while updating the sound with contemporary guitar effects and tones. And what does he think of the modern dancehall and DJ business in Jamaica? "Well, today's music is the music that—I wouldn't in no way criticize the music that is going down now. Because it's something different." As is Dekker himself.

CHAPTER 3

Ken Boothe:

Mr. Rock Steady

From his early hit-making days as "Mr. Rock Steady" (his very first recordings were in the late ska era) to his current status as "Reggae Legend" (the subtitle of an album produced by Jammys), Ken Boothe continues to be one of the most soulful, classic reggae singers of all time. His grit-and-gravel delivery matches the power of American soul stars like Wilson Pickett and Otis Redding. One of Jamaica's finest songwriters, he has delivered some of the best originals, like "Freedom Street," which he co-wrote with the Gaylad's B.B. Seaton; "Home,

Home Home," co-authored by Stranger Cole; and hits like "Without Love," later a chart-topper for Leroy Smart as well. In Jamaica's grand musical tradition he has often covered a worn or previously lukewarm tune with such gripping intensity that his version far outstripped the original. And in Jamaica and England in the early '70s he had hit after hit with originals and cover tunes.

In fact, many thought in those heady days when reggae first burst upon the world that it would be Boothe, not Jimmy Cliff or Bob Marley, who would take Jamaica's rhythmic message to the world. He seemed poised to do just that when he scored a major U.K. hit with a cover of Marley's "I Shot the Sheriff," which preceded both Marley's own entry into international charts and Eric Clapton's later hit with the same song. Then his career seemed to falter on the brink. As far as he's concerned, this "misfortune" saved his life. Interviewed at the time his remake of "Train Is Coming" with DJ Shaggy (featured in the movie *Money Train*) was moving up the American charts, Ken tells the whole story of his bout with fame and glory, and the trials and triumphs encountered along the way.

Born Ken George ("like in King George") Boothe in Kingston, Jamaica, on March 22, 1946, Boothe started out listening to gospel

KEN BOOTHE. Photograph by Jan Salzman; ©1995 Phantom Photos

music. "Me mother, she was a singer, right, but she never used to do it commercially. Is when she wash, when she washing our clothes—and she hangin' clothes on the line, she would be singing. The first child from my mother was a big star in Jamaica when I was young. Her name is Hyacinth Clover. She's my biggest sister." Hyacinth is the oldest child of his mother and Ken the youngest, or as he says, "She's the first and I'm the last."

Boothe's oldest sister provided his introduction into show business. "She sing with Bim and Bam, some comedian. You know these comedian in Jamaica years ago. One of them was her husband. They used to have pantomime, they have a lot of production company." Their 1970 underground hit "The Pill" (released in England on the Crab label) was in the tradition of Max Romeo's "Wet Dream."

Bim and Clover recorded together for years, at least through 1975 when they did "Sweet Heart," issued on the Dawn label in Jamaica, where they were mainly known for their stage shows. "I used to act at ones with her," says Boothe, "live performance on stage. Before I start singing I used to love dancing. Most singers start dancing before you sing you know. Most entertainers start dancing. 'Cause I remember I used to go to the dancehall on the street, a lot of children would be competing, dancing close around you, all of us competing. I was a good dancer. And then me and my sister, my last sister, both of us used to dance on stage. And we used to win. They called us Jack and Jill. That's when I was about twenty years old I used to do that."

Still, says Boothe, "I loved singing even before that. That was what take me to dancing. I used to love singing but dancing was the craze in Jamaica in those days. While I was going to school—which we call secondary now, in those days it was elementary school—we guys used to compete in singing. At lunch time, different classes. Like for instance Delano Stewart, the Gaylads that used to sing for Sir Coxsone of Studio One. He's living in New York now but we all attend the same school. And so, the Richard Brothers—my school consist of a lot of entertainers, people who love entertainment and at lunch time we all would gather around at some class or something and compete, you know, sing."

From this competitive milieu grew the unique mix that makes up Jamaican music. Hundreds of great singers competed against and learned from one another. "The first time that I go up on stage is my mother took me to YMCA when I was about seven years old to sing onna concert. In those days I was so young I didn't know the words of the songs. But I still sing whatever comes to me and it work, you know? When school give holidays they used to have concerts and they would mek all the classes compete, the teachers would keep a concert when you go on a holiday. Every year the contest would be between me and the same Delano Stewart. No one can win us. Every year that school goes on holiday is either he runs first I second or I run first and he second."

A fateful encounter began his recording career. "While coming from school those days I used to go Trench Town. I am from Denham Town. And Denham Town and Trench Town they are very close. So when I come from school during the day [to] play ball in the evening at Boys Town I have to pass Stranger Cole's house and I'd be hearin' these guys singin' around the corner and I'd go up there and stand up like, don't know who to approach then but when I was there, many evenings I stop there, listen them singing, and I just find myself singing with these guys. It was a group, Stranger had a group of four and then two of them drift and then I just find myself singing with Stranger Cole. It was Stranger Cole that really led me into the business. He's the one that actually took me into the commercial part of it, into the studio."

The studio was Duke Reid's and the era was ska. "The first time I'm singin' [in the studio] was a duo with Stranger Cole. And then while I was doing this duo with him he was still a solo singer on his own. He would record with Patsy, he would record on his own, and he would record with me. So he took me to Duke Reid and we did a song and up till now that song doesn't come out. Yeah. 'Mo Sinwa,' a lot of Chinese language.

"While we were at Duke Reid now, me and Stranger was singin' so good as a group, and in those days you have Higgs and Wilson, you have Blues Busters, Alton and Eddy—well, when me and Stranger come was, we sound so new to the whole scene that the people in Jamaica think that we were the baddest duo around, you know? They thought we were

Bob Andy and Marcia. That was the last part of the ska."

Boothe began recording in late 1966 ("Goin' up into '67"), just as the driving rhythms of ska began to give way to the slowed-down, soulful lilt of rock steady. In fact, some of Boothe's earliest records helped define the change in sound. "I came in at the last part of ska just like Bob Marley too you know. Ca' if you listen some of our songs like 'Simmer Down,' that's ska, right? 'Simmer down—uhnk, uhnk, uhnk,'" he sings, making a ska guitar sound. "Ca' I have a song too, 'You're No Good—uhnk, uhnk,' it's ska but it's the last part of it. But the privilege that—while Sir Coxsone sendin' me to the studio, right, I get to meet Wailers and all these guys and then we start to associate. And what he [Dodd] did for us is to give us the premises of Studio One."

Talking about those early days Boothe grows philosophical. "When I look at songwriting today I wonder. Because Bob Marley, all of us used to write same place you know? Like that's Bob, I'm over here, Delroy is over there, the other singers are over there," he gestures, "and all of us is writing songs and nobody's disturbing anybody! I can look at Bob Marley right now him used to love—know him did have a van, right, a old van that he got rid of but it was on the premises. That's where Bob Marley used to sit down with a guitar. But this guitar, right, was loaned to all of us. Loaned to me, you know? It was his guitar but if I want to come with it today I get the privilege to go to my house with it."

According to Boothe a lot of great songs were written "with that same guitar. Bob go home with it, Peter Touch [Tosh] go home with it, Delroy go home with it, but Bob was the one that actually loves guitar so he used to be the one that have guitar most of the times. And he would be in that same van I'm telling you about, he doesn't leave that van, I can remember that." Obviously moved by these

me in the studio. During those days you know you have the Wailers, Bob as you know. You have Clarendonians. You have Delroy Wilson.

memories Ken looks up and says simply, "I've been under big tree."

Duke Reid and Coxsone both recorded on old-fashioned two-track decks. "All these songs you're hearin' with us were just two-track songs. At first we have to record the same time, everybody. So you have to really click up here. Because everybody recording in the same time. Singer, musicians. And the musicians in those days if you make a mistake they don't like it because is each songs they get paid for. Right? So the first time I'm gonna do that, man, I pray to the Lord, I say God, let me go through. And I did go through you know! One cut! I tell you because I was so scared of the musicians y'know sayin' hey! 'Cause they're so great!"

From his earliest days in the studio, "Downbeat, Sir Coxsone, didn't think I should sing ska, he want me to sing soul music. So he started me off with two soul songs, that's the first songs I ever did on my own. One was 'Oo Ee Baby' and um, 'Teardrops on My Pillow.' Two adapted songs." (In JA rather than credit the original writer the label often says "Adapted"—making it possible for the producer to haze copyright infringement— and often as not it's misspelled "Adopted" in a bit of unconscious poetry.) "One done by Jackie Wilson and one done by another guy I don't remember his name." This could be Fats Domino; Boothe's version of his "Sick and Tired" appears as "Oh Babe" (along with "Lonely Tear Drops," although interestingly not the Jackie Wilson song of the same title) on the '80s-issued roundup of tracks *A Man and His Hits* (Studio One). "But Jamaican people was into ska so much that they didn't even want to hear that. Sold a few copies and he sent me back in the studio again. And I keep recording. Then I did 'You're No Good'." Boothe's powerful delivery on this song made many sit up and take notice.

Placing the relation between artist and producer in this era in context, Boothe explains,

"What Sir Coxsone done first right is to free us up in the studio. That we just do a lot of songs and what you do in the night now you sit down and you choose which one of the songs to release. So I was recording a whole other songs and from now we get the train—'Train Is Coming'—that's the first song won a hit with me, really been a big seller, and then after that it was just hits after hits no turning back." Interestingly, Ken points out that "Train Is Coming" features "the Wailers doing the background voices. Most of my songs was between Gaylads and Wailers background voices.

"Hits after hits take me right down to 'Puppet on a String,' [included on his first Studio One album, *Mr. Rock Steady*]. Then 'Puppet on a String' went to England, that's the first time—gonna travel, that was '67 now— that's the time when the music changes to the rock steady. That's the first time on the chart there. They invite me to England because of that song. That song was originally done by Sandy Shaw, that's an English girl, and Downbeat [Coxsone] carry one of her records to Jamaica." Elvis Presley also had a respectable chart hit with the song in the U.S., peaking at number 14 in 1965.

"You know how I get to do 'Puppet on a String?' The first song that took me internally? I was in Studio One deh, Jackie Mittoo, the keyboard player who died, he used to make a riddim ahead of us and then he would choose who him thinks the riddim suits. So one day I was leavin' the studio and when I reached the gate to turn down Brentford Road to go to my home, I saw Jackie Mittoo runnin' down the street sayin', 'Ken, come here, I have something for you, right.' I go back, it was the riddim 'Puppet on a String." He said to do it and right away I did [that] night. I can remember that Sir Coxsone told me to meet him at a dance in Greenwich Farm. He made a dub plate of it and he took it to the dance and would you believe that 'Puppet on a String' was a song that played the whole night? Whole night. After they play one song they have to touch it again. And from that now youth start to know Ken Boothe as a solo singer."

Interestingly for a vocalist whom many consider in the main a soul singer, Boothe has always had an ear for adaptable songs from all sources. You would expect him to cover Roy Shirley's magnificent "Hold Them" (he and Shirley sang together in the early days), Otis Redding's "Try a Little Tenderness," or Wilson Pickett's "Mustang Sally," all of which he did for Studio One. But it's a bit surprising to hear his enthusiasm for the authors of "(Come) Tomorrow": "You know this tune 'Come Tomorrow.' It was an adapted song, a white group. Manfred Mann. Remember that band? Sweet singers, man. Sweet."

Boothe's Studio One output alone is impressive. Besides the two albums mentioned it includes *Live Good,* the second disc in the UA *Anthology of Reggae Collectors Series,* later briefly reissued by EMI. *Live Good* includes vintage conscious reggae tunes "This Is the Time," "Thinking," and his monster version of "Moving Away," an obscure American record discovered by Dodd. "Downbeat him have it, but not for sale. A not-for-sale recording, he gave me to sing it." Another early album, *More of Ken Boothe* (Studio One) includes "What This World Is Coming To" and "This Is the Time" (retitled "Decision"), but focuses more on the soul or love songs Dodd encouraged him to record. This album leads off with "Just Another Girl," remade in the 1980s by UB40.

Boothe's ability to "get ahold of" a variety of styles is shown on his pumping version of Simon and Garfunkel's "Richard Cory." And as is typical for this period, many recordings issued on singles have yet to be anthologized to LP much less CD. "Crying Over You" and "Without Love," for instance, both appear on *A Man and His Hits* but "I Am a Fool," flip-side of the Supreme (an early Studio One label)

7-inch does not, even though it was reissued later as the other side of Delroy Wilson's hit "Riding for a Fall."

"I didn't even remember that I did this!" Boothe exclaims when he sees the single, then sings, "'I am a fool/To love someone who don't love me.'" "You know we don't remember some a dem, didn't remember I did this song, man. A wicked tune to do, that tune that! 'I'm a fool/Keep me in the right,'" he recites. "Man, is Stranger [Cole] write this song. He's the original writer. He's the first one that did it, with Patsy. Him do it for Downbeat." "Without Love" is likewise flipped with an otherwise unreleased tune (although only on early pressings, it was reissued with a dub on the reverse in the '70s), the delightfully strange cigarette ad "Swinging King" sung with Boothe's natural exuberance.

Exploitation was the name of the game in the Jamaican record industry. To the producers it was a straight-up business deal: they offered studio time to get hits, and the enormous level of competition and talent insured them. But recognition inevitably increased the awareness of the exploitation that made it possible in the first place. "During that period of time while we start getting fame, Gaylads, all of us, start to get famous in the Caribbean and in some places, America and England, we start to know what's up, our rights, what we're entitled to." Of his first record Boothe says, "Man, this album sell. Sir Coxsone, he's something else. We're getting ready to sue him, you know. All of us." On seeing the American pressing of *Live Good* he asks, "Who put out this album? I get nothing from it. That's why I'm gonna sue him. Leroy just sued him, you know. Leroy Sibbles. Yeah, when we start to realize [what is happening] we made offer [to] Sir Coxsone to get better treatment and he refuse. So we all leave Studio One at one time and find ourself at Beverley's."

Among the artists who made this move were the Wailers (then consisting of Bob Marley,

Peter Tosh, and Bunny Wailer) and Boothe. At Beverley's they cut records for Leslie Kong. For Bob it was a return since, as mentioned in the Desmond Dekker interview, he had previously left Kong for Dodd over similar issues. "Bob did an album. I did one, *Freedom Street*." The disc is essential canon in Boothe's catalog. Rock steady gives way to early reggae right before your ears with cuts like Ken's dramatic rendering of B.B. Seaton's "Now I Know" and his rave-up of Mungo Jerry's "In the Summertime." Boothe explains Seaton's involvement: "'Freedom Street' deal with crisis in Jamaica. At the time there was a prime minister saying this, saying that, so is just like Jah just give me that thought, 'Freedom Street.' And when I start to write the song I realize it was so big that I alone couldn't

raise this song. So I called B.B. Seaton and both of us finish the song. And that song kept me going many years, that song 'Freedom Street.'"

It kept this writer and a lot of other people going as well. When Boothe opened his supercharged set with the song at Bob Marley Day in Long Beach in 1995 it still had the punch that grabbed me nearly twenty years earlier:

Let's not quarrel
Let's not fight
Let's get together
We all can unite
And take off these chains
That are binding we
'Cause we gonna walk, we gonna walk
Down Freedom Street.

KEN BOOTHE. Photograph by John Skomdahl

"I sung that song in Hammersmith, probably, in England, yeah?" Boothe reminisces. "A lot of South Africans were there, white and black. And I take the song down and I said—during that time it was a tribal business between the black—I said, 'Our brothers and sisters fighting each other in England. That's not gonna solve the problem. What we all should do is come together and it don't matter what color you are, choose what is right for us—you understand what I'm saying?' And so said so done, Mandela, they vote him in for president! And that's what I think needs to be done. Ca' he's not a fascist, he's not a racist. But this song can bring over so much things, 'Freedom Street.' Serious thing. You know I've sung that song so many times I forgot. It so relevant at times that you don't know when it gonna take off."

Kong's production style helped ease the transition from rock steady to reggae for Boothe—and for the Wailers, Maytals, and others. But despite the label switch nothing had changed in a record industry where record sales add little return to the singer's pocket. "And," continues Boothe, "in a while we were there again, famous, don't have anything financially. We realize that they were still joking too. So we leave Beverley's again and went to [Sonia] Pottinger. And we find that they were joking too! Well, she got a couple of hits out of me, 'Lady in the Starlight' and 'Say You,' and then we leave again." Boothe shakes his head when he sees Pottinger's name on the latter single where the writer's credit would be on an American record. "Christ, them wicked. See where she put her name now? Like as if she wrote the song!"

At this point the artists grabbed the reigns of production themselves—for a while. "We start branching out and doing our own thing. That's when we—Tuff Gong now, Bob Marley Tuff Gong—that's from when most of us start to aware that it's better to produce tunes ourselves. 'Cause at one time I used to own a company in Jamaica,

Links was the company, consist of Ken Boothe, Gaylads, Delroy Wilson, Melodians—four of us have this company. And then you have Tuff Gong with the Wailers. And what I respect with Tuff Gong is that they didn't give up. But [the big producers] break us up, Links. In those days recording, executive producers, the men who have the money, when they realize that we breaking off from them what they did was come together and start to pressure us. Our songs aren't playing on the radio anymore. When we go to the radio station they don't wanna see us. So we were forced, some of us were forced to go back and sing with these people." From this period comes the album *The Great Ken Boothe Meets B.B. Seaton and the Gaylads* (Jaguar), produced by Pete Weston and featuring their own Now Generation band with Boothe on organ and Seaton on first guitar.

After leaving Pottinger and trying his hand at self-production Boothe hooked up with producer Lloyd Charmers whose early hits with his group the Charmers include the sublime "Rasta Never Fails," with Charmers and Boothe providing the harmony. Charmers' solo career included pop covers like "A Lover's Question" and "Mr. Bojangles" and eventually reached an all-time low with Lloydie and the Lowbites' silly sexist slackness. "After they [the Charmers] break up he start to produce different artists. Ca' at one time he was in [the] Techniques too, y'know. Yeah, he used to sing with them after [the] Charmers break up."

The association with Charmers was long and musically fruitful, ultimately resulting in the albums *Black Green and Gold,* which runs the gamut from gospel ("Hallelujah") to lovers rock (the very quirky "Second Chance"), *Let's Get It On* (featuring Boothe's stirring version of Marley's "African Lady" as well as the Marvin Gaye title track), *Everything I Own* (more about that one later), *Blood Brothers* (with the the outstanding "Silver Words," co-written by Niney the Observer, who produced a separate version for Boothe), and the later compilation of singles called *The Ken Boothe Collection,* all issued on the Trojan label in England. Besides the Trojan connection, Charmers was one of the few reggae producers in the mid- to late seventies who actually got singles released in America, on the New York Clocktower, Wild Flower, and Splash labels.

Charmers also had the savvy displayed earlier by Coxsone to let the artist develop his own material. For instance, "I'm Singing Home" from *Blood Brothers* is an American Negro spiritual that Charmers heard Boothe singing for some people at the back of the studio and told him he wanted to record. With Charmers in the producer's chair Boothe maintained his edge in Jamaica and was the first reggae singer to break big time in England. The single "Everything I Own" went to number one in Europe.

In Ken's own words, "Comin' up the '70s Lloyd Charmers took me up and he produce some song like 'Is It Because I'm Black,' 'Ain't No Sunshine,' a whole heap of song he done with me and out of this comes 'Everything I Own.' Let me tell you a story about 'Everything I Own.' I did a show in Canada and I went to this friend's house and he was playing an Andy Williams album and I heard 'Everything I Own' [actually a song written by David Gates and sung with his group of the time Bread, which Williams had covered] and I fall in love with the song. Somebody in the house said to me, 'Ken, as you go home to Jamaica, do this song.'

"So while I was in the studio during this album with Lloyd Charmers, we had nine songs and I didn't have any more songs in hand. And I remember that song! And when I sing it everybody in the studio, everybody, musicians say, 'This is number one.' The Khouris, that own Federal Records, Ken Khouri, his son Richard Khouri, heard that song, said he's gonna sell the studio, the whole thing, if it doesn't go number one. So it go number one a Jamaica, right, and after that I left to do a mini-tour in England. This mini-tour is some little clubs you have to

stand up on tables like this one," he gestures a a very unsturdy motel "breakfast" table, "to sing to the people.

"But every club that I go to I sing 'Everything I Own.' Every time that I sing it, the people in the clubs, you note the changes that it really took onto them. So I left England and I went back home and one day I was on my veranda sittin' down havin' a reefer and the postman came up with a telegram sayin' that the song is 58 on the disc charts. So I went to England the same week I went at *Top of the Pops.* From *Top of the Pops* it went to something like 10. Next week another *Top of the Pops.* number one! People like the Beatles, Garry Glitter, all these big acts was on the charts at this time. It was a big write-up in Europe at the time that a Jamaican came and took all these people out at the charts. 'Cause it was top 10. And I was really proud because Beatles was one of my favorite groups.

"So I was really glad to know that I was up there with these great guys, you know! But the unfortunate thing about 'Everything I Own' after all that glamour, 'Cause I really get a lot of promotion out of it—I've done shows that transmit through the whole Europe. I've done shows with Michael Jackson, Barry White that like they have a Christmas show every year in England that they have the number one song on satellite broadcast. And I can remember that I feel proud to know I'm around these kind of people. It wasn't the money so much as the privilege. And do you know the unfortunate part of it, it was when I thought I was gonna make some money. They [Trojan Records] went bankrupt!"

Before Trojan's balloon burst Boothe was set to take America by storm as well. At a time when the only reggae singer, if any, most Americans had heard of was Jimmy Cliff, Boothe—on the strength of his English hits— had sold out Carnegie Hall. "The first act in Jamaica getting this kind of recognition," explains Boothe. "I-Threes with Rita Marley, they was my up-front [opening] act on the show. But up to now I don't reach the show. You know Earl Chin? He's the one that kept the show. What I think is that the Lord saved me. That's what I think. I was going into this rich and decadent way of life, I don't really talk about it.

"A lot of things that happened to me in the past in this business, I know that God has saved me. They would do me just like what they did to Bob. Ca' we were coming from Jamaica as a poor people, we don't know much about these rich sophisticated 'real' life, we weren't used to some of the things and don't know how to approach it. I for one I would say it's because of my, I don't wanna say ignorance. It's because of my force I have inside me as an entertainer that kept me alive. 'Cause I don't take bull crap. I would leave millions of dollars just to have comfort within me. So is not money I sing for. I sing for the love of singing, to entertain people."

Boothe's last album for Trojan was 1979's *Who Gets Your Love,* produced by Phil Pratt and Bunny Lee. Somehow Trojan emerged from bankruptcy with their debt to artists wiped out and their catalog intact. "You see what they're like? They're so big—it awful. It still going on, you know?" says Boothe.

For his next two albums, Pratt produced the somewhat lackluster *Disco Reggae* for his own Phil Pratt label and Bunny Lee produced *I'm Just a Man* for the Bunny Lee label. When Bunny Lee's name comes up all Boothe will say is, "A dem mash up the business, you know. Is dem mash up the business." Both albums featured updated versions of Boothe hits like "Tears from My Eyes" and "Artibella," and some of Jamaica's top session players. Other producers he recorded for include Keith Hudson (the classic "Old Fashioned Way" versioned by Hudson, Alcapone, and U Roy) and Jack Ruby. For Ruby he cut six tracks including two of his best message tunes, "Christopher Columbus"

(he recently kicked off a 1997 "Old School" jam set with a burning acapella version of this) and "Namibia," which make up his side of a combination LP with Tyrone Taylor released as *2 of a Kind* by Tuff Gong.

When success in America eluded Ken, "It go right to Bob. You no understand what I really feel for Bob Marley, really felt for him. This man do so much good thing for the music, bring it to us and shine it to a stage where—and never him [get to] enjoy it. Like Moses goes to the promised land but never get there, that's how I check Bob. Promised land is there but him never get to reach there. And I felt for Bob, I felt for him there. That's life, because all generations have to pass one day, every generation have to pass, all of us.

"And it doesn't matter what color you are ca' I don't deal with color. Color is not the answer. God—Jah Rastafari—life in all of us. It doesn't matter if you're blue, you're pink, or white. So this is my motto in life now so— love the music, love God first, music, people— that's where my head is now. Is not riches. I sing now for the love of singing. I've got the chance to get luxury out of it. Riches. And I see that Jah didn't want it to happen that way. He just wanted me to be independent, normal person, you know? And I thank him for that 'cause probably I wouldn't be here now. All these riches would destroy me so young, don't know anything. I'm glad. I feel good, man."

Suddenly Boothe opens up on a subject most artists are reluctant to discuss. "I don't want to tell you the nice part of things and not tell you the bad part of things. At one time I used to take drugs. I find myself taking cocaine, you know? Um, the environment, entertainment environment, you don't know what you're doing, you get caught up in a lotta things. But Jah Rastafari was so good to me that I realized that it was something that I'm not supposed to do. And [I haven't used for] over some twelve, thirteen, fourteen years now.

And Jah show me that he listen to my prayer. Because I'm singing better now and I'm feeling more nicer in every way since I stopped doing those things.

"I used to do it in L.A. here, remember you tell me that you saw me at that club [The Silver Fox] in the late '70s. That was during that time I was taking drugs, you know, and I realize I'm Aries, the ram, and I'm strong in my head and my feet so there's nothing I do that I don't look at. And I look at it and I say, what's this? I look at my body, I see it's going down. You see people stop respecting you. But I was strong enough so I could look and see this and I said no, I'm gonna make a stand and I see that God see that I really want to do that. And he helps me, you know?

"No one is perfect. Only Lord God is the perfect one. And I find indeed that the drug business in Jamaica—all over the world people know that I was taking drugs. When I went back to Jamaica to go on a stage show, Babsy Grange that is managing me now, Specs, one of the reason I want you to write these things, one of the reason why I respect her is she have [made] a new name for me ca' when I went back to Jamaica I was broke. I went to Jamaica to get strong in myself. Eventually I was and I went to her and she started putting on shows. And backstage artists don't look up to me, they don't speak to me.

"You know what saved me? My talent. When I went on stage and sing they realize that I still have that power. And you know, people is funny. If you're not doing the thing that they're pleased with at the time, they ignore you. And when you start to do the thing that they're pleased with they start smiling again and I'm really glad for that. A lot of people who used to say things about me like I take drugs, now they're saying good things, they're saying like how I can be good. I can't forget that woman, Babsy Grange. And here I am, you know."

The self-produced *Reggae for Lovers* (1979), released by Generation Records in Canada, seemed to signal a turnaround for Boothe's career, a realignment of positive direction, with good new songs like "I Know It" and "No More War," and a powerful remake of the still timely "Time of Decision." "After I go to Jamaica I do a couple of shows and Tappa Zukie came to me and we did 'Don't You Know' that go number two and then we did a video and after that Jammys check me out and I did two albums for Jammys." One of them, *Call Me,* was released in America by Rohit. "I did some songs for Bobby Digital too and some for Sly and Robbie that they don't release yet. All these songs, they're still out there. But this was when God was showing me now that yes I'm ready because these people probably wanted to know if I was messin' around still. Respect that, man, this is it. I'm with Specs now, they manage Shabba and Lady Patra, a whole lot of us they manage now."

In recent times Ken has also recorded and released the albums *Imagine* (Park Heights), *Talk to Me* (VP), and *Power of Love* (New Name) and issued singles on Blue Mountain, Anchor, and other labels. Two of my favorites from the last decade are his masterful reworking of U2's "Still Haven't Found What I'm Looking For" for Chinna Smith's High Times label and 1995's pumping "Iron Heart" on Mister Tipsy. Since this interview a number of Ken Boothe albums have been released on CD including a reissue of *Blood Brothers* (K & K) and a compilation called *Memories* (Abraham).

Ken Boothe Sings Hits from Studio One and More and *Say You,* both on Rhino U.K., reprise early works in new versions produced by Bunny Lee and his Now Team and a new album *Acclaimed* has been issued by Upstairs Music out of Miami. Another new collection, *Everything I Own* (not to be confused with the original album of that title), has been issued by Trojan and contains an excellent selection of twenty-eight tracks from his best work for that label, including a previously unreleased version of the Penn-Oldham standard "You Left the Water Running." For those unfamiliar with his work, it's a good overall introduction to his distinctive voice and delivery. He's back on the international charts with the new version of "Train Is Coming" and tirelessly touring; after an absence of nearly twenty years he's played California three times in the last two years. Still at his peak as a performer, he is disturbed by today's approach to recording.

There's a "generation gap at work" he says when asked about reggae in the '90s, "but the musical content not saying nothing. The people get so hooked on listening to the same riddim over and over again that if you go into the studio and create some new riddims, brand-new bass-lines, everything, the people don't want to listen so it frustrates me. Even me did turn to that kind of situation where I sing on a lot of riddims too, you know, that a lot of people's on.

"Sometimes at a dance I hear introduction the same riddim I do, I think is my song—but is not my song, is another man song. It don't nice. Because is the same riddim everybody sing different songs on. So you be at the dance and listen you think it's your song you don't know if it another guy's song or what until you hear the word, the voice. Beca' can be any guy on the same riddim. Frustration! Don't like it! Even Freddie McGregor, I was watchin' him on television the other night, he had a press conference and he told them this is new and give it a break. 'Cause they don't want to give what is new a break. Everything you hear, everybody doing the same thing, that's what they think is music now. Ten different singers with one riddim. They did not create the riddim. Well, that creativity lacks in Jamaica now."

Still, when asked about new young singers he says surprisingly, "I like all of them—a lot of them. Right now I like Luciano, I think his songs are nice. I like Sanchez too but the people that produce Sanchez don't know how to produce him. And I love Beres Hammond. A couple of them really I love who I think really trying to do something for the music. But [producers] are still doin' what they want to do with them too. 'Cause even Beres Hammond, all these songs that is hit songs the same kind of thing where ten people sing and if they're lucky they're lucky. That's their own hit. But a lot of nice entertainer, man. And I don't tell you about my little baby yet. I have a seven-year-old baby. Is gonna be a giant. Remember I told you this.

"His name is Chadan. Everything about him is nice. He was born for music. He's playing keyboards. You see him on stage sing with me, if he was inside here today the whole place [would] mash down. When he comes as a performer at seven years old you'd think he is a man of twenty-five. At seven years old—not because he's my child, let me tell you this. The last time that him perform in Pegasus in Jamaica a man come up to me say, Ken, give me him, me can make him rich, and me say no. Him a go school first. Him good, real good. Him don't fear stage."

"When I was young if you ask me to sing I have to wait about fifteen minutes because I used to kind of fright. Not my baby. I just say sing, really him deep. Him no joke. If I came on a show and said I want you to sing two songs, I'll call on you. He say, you're crazy! I'm comin' on with you now! And just a mash the place! And not only him singin' alone but just his action, the place just a bruk down. Watch this! Did a show again and I think the girls are screamin' for me and it's him, some movement he's doin', man. But him good. We did a show again and his mother, my wife, she look over and kiss him because she didn't know he was so good. A whole lot of them out there in his age bracket love entertainment but him have to finish school first."

Ken Boothe has come full circle, from the young dancer who wanted to sing to the proud father of a son with the same aspirations. Boothe, whose first album was recorded when he was seventeen, whose first brush with fame nearly drowned the young Icarus, looks out to see that his own son doesn't stray too close to the sun.

One of a generation of distinctive vocalists that included the likes of Slim Smith, Leroy Sibbles, Delroy Wilson, Bob Marley and Peter Tosh, he represents an era that will never again exist in Jamaican music, a time of compassion, enlightenment, unity, and strength from which the rest of the world still draws hope and sustenance.

CHAPTER 4

John Holt:

Reggae Classic

John Holt is reggae's golden boy, a classic singer and melodic songwriter who penned some of rock steady's finest entries for his group the Paragons. As rock steady turned to reggae Holt went solo, cutting some of the earliest international hits for the new style. His supper club image gave way to the dreadlock look of the new era and his music also moved with the times, from early love tunes like "Fancy Make Up" and "Only a Smile" to the burning confrontational stance of "Police in Helicopter" and "Up Park Camp." Holt's strong, clear delivery put him in the ranks of reggae's best singers and his prolific writing and recording career have kept him on top, whether delivering his hits from the past or his latest songs today.

Though his work with the Paragons introduced him to most of us, Holt says, "I started out on my own as John Holt during *Opportunity Hour* with Joseph Vere Johns, a great man who developed most of the talent in Jamaica. He's got sort of forgotten but we don't forget him 'cause he was the one who took the shakes, like the nervousness, out of our knees, like Alton Ellis, Bob Marley and the Wailers on a whole, Dennis Brown, Ken Boothe, Marcia Griffiths, and many other artists. He's the man who really groomed Jamaican talent during that time. That was from about 1958."

The American equivalent, for those who grew up in the 1950s, would be Ted Mack, whose Amateur Hour radio and TV program introduced a wide variety of talent to the states. Live shows in Jamaica at venues like the Ward Theater in Kingston put on by Vere Johns took the best of the talent from the high school and local shows and brought them to a wider audience.

"I really got involved in it in 1962," explains Holt, "that's when I won the *Opportunity Hour* finals. These were live theater shows: Majestic Theater, Ambassador Theater, Palace Theater, and so forth. They also had *Opportunity Knocks* on RJR radio, Saturday, one o'clock, different acts, but sometimes some of us get involved in that because we need the prize—and the prize was money and trips. And if you win the finals, the guys will say, 'Well, John Holt, from tonight you are now a professional singer.'

"'Just Out of Reach' was the song I sang that night, it was done up originally by Solomon Burke, and it do me some good. Then I made a song for Leslie Kong's Beverley's records, which was titled 'Forever I Will Stay.'" This was Holt's first single; the flip-side was "I Cried All My Tears." He then recorded songs with Alton Ellis, for Coxsone and formed the Paragons after that.

Holt sang lead and did the bulk of the writing for the Paragons, who in the rock steady era were Jamaica's quintessential group. Songs like "On the Beach," "Wear You to the Ball," and their versions of standards "Yellow Bird" and "Island In the Sun," all recorded for producer Duke Reid and backed by Tommy McCook and the Supersonics, defined not only Jamaican but Caribbean music as a whole in the late sixties. The trio's clean, crisp harmonies accentuated simiplicity and directness with an "island feel" popular among tourists and Jamaicans alike.

"I was the main writer and arranger," says Holt, "the dedicated one." The other members of the group "used to really work during the course of the day. They were working at different companies. Tyrone Evans, he used to work at a bauxite company as a tool technician. And Howard Barrett, he's still working at the telephone company, he's workin' in New York [now] but he used to work at Jamaica telephone company.

"The Paragons started out with Duke Reid," explains Holt. They utilized Reid's Treasure Isle recording studio. "We were together for approximately six years. Bob Andy was involved in the Paragons as well, he was the backup music—the backup man. He left for a period of time because he always wanted to lead . . . he decided to go on his own to do things for himself. And after, the Paragons split, 'cause the guys got scholarships to come to America and work, 'cause they're brainy guys, you know, so they took that opportunity and left and I was left on my own again."

In a country where new styles and trends wash the old away so quickly—the rock steady "era" actually lasted about two and a half years—the Paragons might have been quickly forgotten had it not been for the early DJ U Roy, who cut a series of smashes over Duke Reid's Paragons productions. "I was the one who discovered U Roy," says Holt. "I remember on

JOHN HOLT. Photograph by Jan Salzman; © 1992 Phantom Photos

Gold Coast Beach one night the sound system Tubby's, U Roy was the DJ for Tubby's sound system, and used to go at a beach party every Sunday at Gold Coast beach in St. Thomas [parish], where I heard him doing 'Wear You to the Ball.'"

Sound system DJs had long appropriated an American radio DJ style (hence the name) to "talk over" instrumental cuts, haranguing the crowd to bolster the energy and interest in the dance. On the night, says Holt, that he saw U Roy, "He was talking on the rhythm. So while he was talking, it sounded like a song to me. So I went to him and I said, 'Could you do that again, that same talking you was doing on the rhythm?' And he did it exactly the same way. Yeah! So I said, 'Wow, this is great! I'm gonna let Duke Reid know about you and what you're doing, right, and then I'll contact you and maybe he will make you record it.

"Well, I told Duke, that was a Monday, I told Duke Reid and by Tuesday he went with a brother by the name of Edward to pick up U Roy and by Tuesday night the song was on tape. That was why he started out with 'Wear You to the Ball,' 'cause that was the track that really had me going." The resulting string of hits—at one time U Roy held five of the top ten spots in Jamaica, all as DJ over John Holt-penned Paragon tunes—opened the door to a new style of recording that spawned dozens of seventies DJs like Big Youth, Dennis Alcapone, Dillinger, Trinity, and others and survives today in the work of "dancehall" DJs such as Shabba Ranks, Buju Banton, Mad Cobra, Capleton, and hundreds of others.

Duke Reid himself was a legendary producer, an ex-policeman who owned a liquor store above which he mounted one of Jamaica's most influential recording studios. A sound system operator of the first rank, Reid made his name with a series of "record hop" dances, had a radio show (on which he played American rhythm and blues, long a staple of his sound

system dances), and consolidated his reputation as one of Jamaica's earliest and premier producers first in the ska era and later as the master of rock steady.

Reid's reputation as a kind of mythic Western badman, complete with cowboy hat, bandalero, and weaponry, is the stuff of Jamaican legend. "He used to act crazy sometimes," laughs Holt, "not that he was really crazy but I think because he's so involved in music that sometimes it sort of hit him like a bomb 'cause he's one of the man that started up the music and sound-system business in Jamaica. He used to travel to America to buy blues songs, he used to have a box downstairs in the store so he could hear exactly what's going on upstairs in the studio. So if anything is goin' that he doesn't really appreciate then he would come upstairs and fire a lot of blank shots! He used to wear two guns, and a Winchester 73, what's the name of that gun, across his shoulder and a big hat, cowboy lookin' hat. He was really a different person but I like him very much.

"He is a type of man who really help Jamaican music to get where it is right now. He's a good man, because he used to record actually everybody that comes in, never refuse a talent, and he was the sort of man who sort of encourage you as a youth to do good things with whatsoever you're earning now so you could be a man when you get much bigger. And he used to pay you for your work. Not like most producers. He was one that paid up everything. He was a very kind and generous man, God bless his soul." The classic Paragons album is the Treasure Isle release *On the Beach*.

This early period in Jamaican music was pretty well locked up by two major producers and sound system operators, Treasure Isle's Duke Reid and Clement "Coxsone" Dodd of Studio One. "I was more with Treasure Isle than Studio One," says Holt, "It was just two producers working. Duke Reid and Coxsone.

You find that soon as one gets sort of fed up coming down by Duke Reid he just drift by Coxsone place and do some record for Coxsone. Then he drift back to Duke Reid—he's just to and from—you can't go no further until Federal Records starting doing some recording. The Paragons did two number one recordings for Federal as well, 'Talking Love' and 'Stagger Lee.'"

After the breakup of the Paragons, Holt went on to record cuts like "Tonight" for Treasure Isle. He did "Love I Can Feel" for Coxsone, then songs like "Anywhere You Want to Go," "My Satisfaction," and "Left with a Broken Heart." Much of Holt's best work for Studio One is collected on the early seventies albums *A Love I Can Feel* and *Greatest Hits.* As more studios opened up, more producers came onto the scene and Holt went to different studios and labels, cutting deals with different producers. "As long as the deal was right then I would go ahead and work. But I also produced albums and singles for myself."

"And I did songs like 'Stick by Me,' the longest number-one song ever in Jamaica. It was number one for twenty-three weeks." "Stick By Me" was cut for producer Harry Mudie and appears on the album *Time Is the Master* (Moodisc). Mudie was one of the few Jamaican producers who used strings in his arrangements (the title track is a perfect example of this) and the sophisticated arrangements coupled with Holt's melodic delivery struck a chord in England, where executive producer Tony Ashfield cut the disc *John Holt Sings for I* and 1974's seminal *1,000 Volts of Holt* (originally released as *Sings for I Volume Two,* both issued by Trojan), breaking Holt big in England with his hit rendition of Kris Kristofferson's "Help Me Make It Through the Night."

The latter album spawned a nearly endless series of discs on which Holt covered pop ballads on a reggae style, with titles like *Two Thousand Volts of Holt* and *Three Thousand Volts*

of Holt, eventually surging to five and ten thousand volts with no power outages. But by the mid-seventies Jamaican music was undergoing another amazing transformation as the militant stylings of the film *The Harder They Come* and the first international releases from Bob Marley and the Wailers redefined reggae for all time. Not one to be left behind in the dust, Holt recast his own career in the mode of the day.

Beginning with the album *Holt* he set a new direction. "This was when I was really in a more revolutionary style, because that was the scene. But I always still like to sing love songs. My favorite song on this album was 'There's a Jam in the Streets,' and this song came right back in JA just after the storm Gilbert, it became a black anthem: 'People going here/people going there/people talking this/people talking that'—it started selling again, this album. It just pick right up after [Hurricane] Gilbert." Once again Holt made the musical transition, though he admits to a reluctance to record his first militant broadside, "Up Park Camp."

"I really didn't want to record that song. It took them about five weeks to get me in the studio to record that. It was a terrible thing going on in Up Park Camp [a police roundup site for violent offenders]. Violent days in Jamaica in that time. You have to be careful of what you say to even your best friend. It was some really terrible days. The gun was overpowering the brothers. They didn't know how to control the gun."

Up Park Camp was a detention center. "I was afraid of singin' that song 'cause I was afraid that the brothers who are involved in Up Park Camp maybe come to try to ask me a few questions, even try to hurt me, you know? So it took about five weeks to get me in the studio. Until I finally went there and I was glad afterwards because it was a big shot, it actually brought me back into the dancehall scene, 'cause during that time you have Channel One disco going and we're doing songs like 'Anywhere You Want to Go,' 'My Satisfaction,' and those songs, so when I did 'Up Park Camp,' it brought me right back into the dancehall crowd, and from that we went on to Junjo Lawes and started doing songs like 'Police in Helicopter.' This is a different kind of album. This is a roots album. A lot of people say they don't like some of the songs on this album."

To many this was a real change for John Holt, whom they had grown to think of as a romantic singer and writer of great love songs. Staring out from the cover of albums like *Police in Helicopter* was a newer, militant John Holt, with dreadlocks and a big spliff burning. "Because of the image that I used to wear as a youth and coming up with Byron Lee's Dragonaires," some were amazed. "Oh my God, yeah!" laughs Holt. "During that time I was Rasta in my heart, I was dread in my heart. But because of the image that everybody expect John Holt to really portray—they expect him to shave, put nice trim at the barbers, and comin' in cool."

"'Police in Helicopter'—well, I was inspired really to do it when it comes to that song. I was traveling from Montego Bay to Kingston and there was a helicopter circling over the land, you know, police in helicopter, so in my mind I said, wow, they must be looking for the herb, so I says, wow, Babylon guys is searchin' people's fields and immediately I took my pen out and just write: "Police in helicopter/search for marijuana/and soldiers in the street/searching for collie weed/If you continue to burn up the herb/we gonna burn down the cane fields.

"And it started to happen in Jamaica, that song—the planters of herb started to burning cane fields down in Orange Hill and Lucia, they were burning the fields too strong and they banned the song because of that. They said it was too strong and the guys was takin' it too serious, the lyrics. They used to sing the song in the streets and in the jailhouse. That song was a very serious song in Jamaica. I think we make that song before its time. Whenever they legalize herb throughout the world then

that song will just find its right place. Just like Peter Tosh, bless his soul, 'Legalize It.' Because of the banning of the song it made it stronger 'cause it sold a lot in England. 'Cause it's strong. It's a protest song, and it's wicked out there.

"Once, the police stopped me driving and smoking herbs and they pull you over, 'Hey, John Holt?' 'Yeah, John Holt.' 'Police in Helicopter,' they start singing the song. Shit, what is this? And then they say, 'We're the police, but we're not in helicopter. We're in a car today.' It's a serious thing going on, a very serious thing. And I wrote another one, one I know they're gonna ban, one that's not released yet, called 'Bad Minded People.' But I don't care, they can always ban it. Anytime a song is full of too much truths and rights, they ban it."

Though records like this put artists on the front line, Holt says, "That's best. If you really take the struggle, then you know the sweet part of it. Now when you struggle with the music sometimes you say, what am I doing this for, I wonder if it's through God or man or it's a habit of mine—but it's for a purpose why everyone do things. Everything that we do, you, everybody, it's for a purpose, sometimes you don't even know why, sometimes you say what am I doing this for really? What am I gettin' out of it? But look, it's a work that you doin' and it's through the inspiration of Jah the Almighty why you do such a work, you understand? It's true, my brother, I tell you the truth. Bob Marley and myself used to say that.

"Because during that time, everything was young, everybody was young, no responsibility, you just want to sing and hear yourself playing back on the radio or see yourself on television even one time. And Bob and myself used to say, the next twenty or thirty years, man, we gonna be recognized somehow. So let us go on, don't bother watchin' the goings on, because we used to wonder why our songs is not being recognized internationally when we're doing our best. So I used to say and Bob used to say, let's not watch that, let's just go on because this is God work we're doing. None of us was involved in any kind of responsibility, we were still living with our parents.

"So it was just like singing to hear ourselves sing on the radio. But I didn't know that it was through God and inspiration of God coming through man, that the works as we were writing would manifest and take unto itself flesh and live unto this day. So therefore no regrets. Because even when I and I was coming up, those were the questions that I and I asked ourselves, and out loud too, ask each other. We had to encourage each other to come to the studio the following day. It was fun though. Because you had nothing else to do but just sing, no responsibility, you're young and you just wake up in the morning, hit the beach and exercise, get up, studio. You have some money, you have some herb, you have a little car, sometimes when you really check it out, it's wild. Records not going international, wonder what's the reason, they would say nothing done before the time."

International success returned to John Holt in the early eighties with the release of a cover of an old Paragons tune, "The Tide Is High," by the new wave group Blondie. A major pop radio hit, it also spawned a reunion of the original Paragons. "Island Records decided to get us back together to do a new rendition of the same Paragons album. And it went very well in England and Europe and some parts of America. It was very good for me and the rest of the guys as well. And Blondie.

"'Cause everything takes time, even to walk through that door takes time, and now is the time and the time is not fulfilled as yet. It's still takin' some more struggle. But the struggle is a higher struggle now. 'Cause the foundation has been laid for reggae music. So the struggle is on a higher level now. To get it into the proper market and played on major stations on a daily basis, just like any other music. The music is really

sort of proving itself little by little 'cause they say a million miles start with one single step.

"First it was ska, rock steady, then reggae, now it comes down to rappin', so it's different forms of reggae music now. It's taken its own form. So you can love reggae any way you want now. You can love the DJs, lovers rock, you can take up ska, you can love rock steady, so you have a choice right now. That is good for the music. But the reason why I make a song like 'Ghetto Queen,' 'Fat She Fat,' 'Sweetie Come Brush Me,' 'Police in Helicopter,' songs of reality, chanting these songs, is because I-man get jealous over what is going on in Jamaican music with Yellowman and the talking DJs. Seriously speaking, I know that every song has its place in the world. It's just that sometimes a song is in the wrong place. So therefore when I made 'Police in Helicopter' I know that there's millions of people who love 'Police in Helicopter' and they don't like 'Help Me Make It Through the Night.'"

Similarly a large audience weaned on the lovers rock style were offended by the changes. "So therefore it's like, Jah, you can't please everyone all the time. You can only please them some time. I had to show the guys that was talking, the DJs, like Yellowman, you name them, Lieutenant Stitchie and all the rest of those guys, because they was sort of carrying reggae music in a different direction. And the direction was okay because it was selling and it was good for reggae and another set of people started liking reggae. So it sort of make a new generation now hold on to reggae.

"Then, Jah made about seven of us meet one day in New York City. We had a meeting . . . Alton Ellis, Freddie McGregor, Ken Boothe, Bunny Wailer, myself, Delroy Wilson, and Leroy Sibbles. And we had a meeting that we were all gonna start makin' any kind of reggae song just to compete with the DJ system, that we were gonna flood the market with vocals, 'cause that was what was really keepin' the DJs on top—dancehalls—because they stopped playing the vocal side of the records and played the dubs and talked on top of it. So we decided to put some sort of change to that. That's why Dennis Brown came through with the song 'Stop Your Fighting So Early in the Morning.' We had it all planned, because we had to do something."

But of the DJs Holt says, "They still have their seat in reggae music. They really kept it going strong during that time and even now." In recent years Holt has recorded and issued a massive amount of new product for many producers and labels. "What I-man really do," he explains, "is write the songs I've got at the time, what's going on now. Love songs is different because love is everyday in your heart, regardless of the circumstance. You love your shirt, you love your car, you love your lady, what have you, love is an everyday thing. Love flows on and on, love keeps life going but the things that happen . . . it's not everyday the same

thing happens to you so you have to sort of have that recorded and registered that these things took place.

"That's how I go about writing most of these protest songs like 'Every mouth must be fed.' That was U Roy and myself. That was what the Good Book says, 'Equal Rights and Justice,' that's the name of the song. Lloyd the Matador I made that one for. They had a bad situation and that song helped to sort of cool it down. It wa' during a heavy political changeover, one of those stupid things that they keep up in Jamaica.

"Yes, stupidness! Y'know, 'cause just the same thing on and on every time. Well, you have songs that really keep the war down, and songs that built it up. You find that most songs that were banned, Babylon banned all over the world, is songs which tell you the truth. And most times people don't want the massive to know the truth 'cause then we gonna start fight wi' dem. Yeah. But one o' these days, man, the power with us rise to the fullness of His Majesty, Selassie I."

CHAPTER 5

Johnny Clarke:

Rockers a No Crockers

By the mid-seventies in Jamaica a new style called Rockers was the rage. Like a number of artists interviewed here Johnny Clarke's work spans more than one era, but his music will always be associated with the militant Rockers era in which he made his mark. I interviewed Clarke in the late eighties on his first visit to Los Angeles.

Johnny Clarke today is a classically underrated artist; only a few of his many albums are available in the CD format. The collections *Don't Trouble Trouble* and corresponding dub release *Johnny in the Echo Chamber* (both issued by

Trojan in the U.K.), *Reggae Archives* (RAS), and *Authorized Rockers* (Virgin) cull hits from his work with Bunny Lee, as do reissues of *Rock with Me Baby, Sings in Fine Style* (both on Abraham), and *Don't Stay Out Late* (Rhino U.K.). Other great releases not currently available on CD include *Johnny Clarke Superstar* (Dynamic), *Showcase* (Third World,) *Enter into His Gates with Praise* (Attack), *Rockers Time Now* (Virgin), and more recent discs like *Think About It* (Jammy's).

A natural singer, Clarke first recorded right out of high school, cutting "God Made the Sea and Sun" for producer Clancy Eccles. Here began a twisted tale of Jamaican recording industry tactics that provides insight into the entire music business. "In those days all he did was just put a white label on the record and write 'Johnny Clarke,'" says the singer. "They don't go and print labels and things like that. So I say, if a man deal me so, me just shift him and move to a next man. Clancy could a get 'Everyday Wondering' [Clarke's first hit] too but him wasn't promoting my name by not putting it on the record. People say, 'Who dat? Him sound like John Holt.' I mean, I want a name. Because I have a voice.

"So I moved to Rupie Edward and did 'Everyday Wondering.'" Rupie's label wasn't exactly blank—he printed "Success," the name of his label on it. "But what him didn't do, him didn't put 'Johnny Clarke, Everyday Wondering.'

JOHNNY CLARKE. Photograph by John Skomdahl

Just Success label. Those were days things was kinda out of order certain way." Just like Eccles, Edwards "wasn't putting my name under the title. Just put Success label and every time I go inna shop and the man go press records, take one up and is the same. In those days I was just comin' as a youth. So I move on to Bunny Lee and do 'None Shall Escape the Judgment in This Time.'"

Originally, "None Shall Escape the Judgment" was an Earl Zero song. "I went into the studio to record a song by the name of 'My Desire.'" Bunny Lee asked me to sing with a group what have Earl Zero and two more guys I don't really know. Zero have a nice voice but true in those days a man always check for a crisper voice. I think nowadays the voice level in music kinda drop.

"But what happened was, we did it as a group on tape at Duke Reid's studio, Treasure Isle, on Bond Street. Him and his brothers and me, we all sang it. It was recorded on a four-track tape and we just run a rough voice in those days. It was Errol Brown, Bob Marley's engineer, that put the song on tape. Leavin' the studios I was listening in the car and change up a certain part of the lyrics and put it in my form. They compare the both of dem, the one between the group and the one with me alone, and they decide that mine was better." The final song "was written between both of us, because I change up certain sections to put into my style."

"None Shall Escape the Judgment" got Clarke the recognition he sought. The tune was a sensation, and they finally had to put his name on the record. "And Rupie Edwards was getting crazy!" laughs Clarke. "Because I went and did a hit song for Bunny Lee and he feels that mebbe that song could be done for him, because I was with him. But Rupie just get crazy and go inna studio playin' around ca' him have the rhythm of 'Everyday Wondering,' him run it back and wanna know what him can do with that tune. And he used the rhythm and

some of my voice and all he say is 'Skanga! Skanga!' Him was just jokin', people was laughin' even when him was doin' it in the studio.

"Normally in those [pre-DJ] days," Clarke continues, "if a man sing a tune, a man expect him to really just sing a tune, you know, verse, chorus and like. A man don't expect to go inna studio and just hear rhythm and use a mouth like a piano and a guitar! But him just joke it out and people was laughin' away that evening and him release it in England as 'Irie Feelings,' and it go to number six in the British charts! Top of the pops in England, 'Everyday Wondering,' my tune! And that," Clarke claims, "is the first original reggae tune really go in the international chart!"

In fact in 1990 Trojan released an entire album of *Irie Feelings: Rupie Edward and Friends* featuring the original Johnny Clarke hit "Everyday Wondering," the Rupie Edwards version and fourteen other vocal, DJ, and dub versions of the same cut. One of the first producers to see such an "opportunity" to utilize a backing track in such a foresighted— and, from a producer's point of view, thrifty— manner (after all, he only had to pay the backing musicians to record one track), Edwards prefigured what has become a Jamaican industry standard. Though the complaint that a rhythm is being to put to too much use is common in the nineties it's been going on since the early seventies.

For five consecutive years in the seventies Clarke was elected best male vocalist in Jamaica and they were the same five years he worked with producer Bunny Lee. As the early Aggrovators sound paved the way to the Rockers era the singer was backed by one of the best bands in Jamaican studio history. His songs of this time included "Enter into His Gates with Praise," "Move out of Babylon Rastaman," "Jah Jah We Are Waiting," "Disgraceful Woman," "Blood Dunza," "Roots Natty Congo," "Cold I Up," and "Rebel Soldiering." Like all of Lee's stable of artists, he also sang cover tunes, doing tracks from the Abyssinians, Burning Spear, the Mighty Diamonds, John Holt ("As a youth me love to sing his songs!"), American soul hits, and—oh yes—Bob Marley tunes.

Clarke's recording of "No Woman, No Cry" sold more than 40,000 copies in JA. But sometimes in life the same things that create the greatest success also cause the greatest problems. Songwriting credits to some of Marley's songs were contractually tangled in those days, although Clarke knew nothing about this at the time.

"Bob Marley did that song originally in his early days with Island Records," recalls Clarke. "The song was a very, very great song. A lot of people in JA loved that song. The album was taking a gradual step toward popularity and a lot of people recognize the song and love it. It was in great demand in JA but the song was on an album, not a 45. Maybe it was beca' of a contract and him didn't want to go and do things without orders from who he's in contract with. Everyday people wanted the song and couldn't afford to buy the album. Bob wouldn't just take it off the album and put it on a 45.

"So what Bunny Lee do now, he got me to sing over that song and release it on a 45. And the song just run away, man! Sell out the whole place, yeah! Them can get it on a 45 and that is much cheaper. And Jamaica is not really a very big country. Even the city of Kingston. People influence other people. And from people in Kingston start say 'Ray!' [Hooray] to a song people in country gonna start say 'Ray!' too. So from [Bunny Lee] get to know the people in Kingston, possible him heard that this is the one song on the album dem did like and didn't want to buy the album for that one song. Him see that from far out, him see the vibes and know that people is after this song so if Johnny Clarke do this song, it gwaan run away.

"So him just rope me in an' call me ca' the man just love doin' things that way, him love to have people around him; him use it as a certain advantage, y'know. Him is a type of man make people vex ca' him like to use you and come play you against other artists, go all against the next man and say"—doing a Bunny Lee imitation—"'Ooooh, Johnny Clarke is the *best*.'"

Lee pushed Clarke as his number one artist so hard that other artists began to resent the publicity and attention. "When him say these things certain people don't like me, they feel like the man talk too much good things about me. He had a interview on the big Capital radio station in England with Dave Rodigan, shouting 'Johnny Clarke is the best artist in Jamaica' all over England. I don't know if him do it unaware ca' sometimes you have people different way smart. If you doin' it just to make a man hate me so people who might not like him might not like me first. So you see the formula that is maybe even causin' a whole heap of problems right now with the competition business.

"All of them longtime business wha' certain man do, certain man a keep it an' not leave it, ca' things don't come out of people that easy. You do a man something from a long and him still remember. Like some ten years ago Bunny Lee used to go on and talk up him mouth. You find the table turn now, today we're up, tomorrow down and every day younger youth born and develop and grow up, is not like yesterday when youth did small. So man find himself on a certain position over you and him will just remember you and try fe keep you down 'pon the floor.

"Is a whole heap a things happen in the business still," complains Clarke. "That's why I find the business nah really gone too far an' the whole a we are in one position because not many really gone a West. 'Nuff people really love reggae worldwide but reggae not at a great I and I standard beca' we have to more come together and live good with love amongst ourselves still. And stop the fight 'gainst a man there and a man a fight 'gainst the next man

JOHNNY CLARKE. Photograph by John Skomdahl

and watch what he have. Dem little rat race business. You have people who could mebbe give a helping hand but if him don't see you deserve the help, him might don't give it.

"Beca' the only one man who really reach in a position is just Bob Marley, nobody else. I mean, Bunny Wailers, even Peter Tosh, Jimmy Cliff, them still never really reach Bob's stage. And Bob still have even further to go still. Through we no know weself and be more spiritual in ourselves and mek God love we and respect we an' check for we. Too much evil vibes, man and man too evil within demself privately, ca' you have certain man evil against man privately and just keep it to himself or maybe just have a syndicate 'cause all dem things not s'pose to happen."

The musical rivalries of the past still cause Johnny Clarke problems today. "Bunny Lee brings off a vibes the way him used to go on, ca' you know it all the same, do over a lot of Bob Marley stuff an' you see, them tend to give me a direct fight. You heard about Sunsplash in Jamaica, is a big profile, a lotta people talk about that history music vibe and a man like me—you know I never did do Sunsplash yet! A man like me have so much albums, six tunes in the top ten, a man like me wha' won the best singer five years straight in a row—is a vibe ca' I say weh really happen, Bunny Lee covering versions of other people's songs, Bob Marley's and certain boasts, so when they get the chance there, the first chance they get was to start the Sunsplash at Bob Marley Entertainment Center in Montego Bay and from that's been hosted there I will never be granted a Sunsplash.

"I won't say it was Bunny Lee alone beca' me sing the songs still. But the vibes weh him bring off, it cause the family, Bob Marley Syndicate of Family, to give me an eternal, everlasting fight. Whereas dem just feel like seh as far as food, if there is food to be eat, I must not eat. Up till Bob Marley's death it still go on like that—they don't want me to do no Sunsplash. Every Sunsplash if you look on the screen in back you can see the image of Bob Marley and his guitar. So maybe to their look of way an artist like Johnny Clarke on the same stage with a portrait of Bob Marley and his guitar, it would bother the organizers."

Clarke sees nothing wrong with doing cover songs and wonders why some still hold a grudge against him. "Is nothin' for a man to do over another man's song. You still recognize and respect the original, it just a different version of the song for you to just blend with. So why they don't think that way and stop fighting against?

I want to tell you something. Even in those days, Bob Marley never like dem thing there."

"When you're young and you deal with a producer, he picks the tunes. And when Bunny Lee do that, Bob Marley never used to like it. Ca' you have certain people knockin'. I redo a song, one of your song, right? Your voice is good still, everybody respect you and check for you still but then again now me do it and might feel like my own is nicer. But is people in Jamaica who come and talk and say I do your song and people keep knockin' it that my own is better still. You might dislike me slightly when is not really me sayin' that but I'm the one that did the song. These people are the ones causin' it 'cause they're knockin' you for you to fight against me and them give me an everlasting fight up till the year even when you are dead it must go on still, even your children must go on fighting me too and everybody who's around they just come and do the same."

One of Jamaica's most indelible forms of music is dub, and Clarke is an artist to whom the style's originator, King Tubby, returned again and again to version. Some of his best-known dubs are of Clarke's songs. What does the singer think of dub and of the JA music scene today?

"Dub develop a different vibes now," Clarke explains. "A man can play one version six times and find six different songs on the same rhythm, a DJ, possibly a singer connected with the sound system, just a juggle a thing upon it as well as maybe a professional inside the dance. You see, long ago you never had professional singers singing inna dance, but artists like Sugar Minott, Cocoa Tea, Barrington Levy, Little John, and Tenor Saw after my time develop a dancehall thing. Before those days if you heard about an artist and you go an' watch him, you definitely goin' see him perform with a band on a stage. But in the later days you could just pay your money and go to a dancehall and see an artist with a name who possibly might be on a album cover singin' around a mike on some boxes. Is a difference. Nowadays the level of the price drop to go see a man on a card, that might cost you five dollars. Normally you wouldn't see a man performing on a stage with a band for that."

The onslaught of the DJ style had an adverse effect on singers of Clarke's caliber. "DJ bring down the artist to their level ca' bein' on a mike at a dancehall is normally the work of a DJ, created from the days of King Stitt, U Roy, Big Youth, and man like Prince Jazzbo, I Roy, all the older DJ. But nowadays some a dem level drop that call themselves singjay. They sing like a soul tune on a rhythm with only two or three chords and make the changes and everything, the musicians not following but it still work out. Seh rough, you know.

"All manner of American listen a dem tune and disrespect it ca' him a look to hear the chords and a different changes. But Jamaican him don't really mind, him just go through it same speed ca' him say well, people buy it! And you have ones who make a name, even like Sanchez, Frankie Paul dem do it on the basis, if you're going to go to D [chord] you go to D and then D7 or Gm—they don't do it that way."

This simple approach to music making does not bode well for reggae, Clarke believes. "It don't do nothing good for the reggae. It might make them earn a money and put on the pot that them can eat. But wha' dem a go do for the young generation, for the little one that are born every day? So if we have to do certain things fe dem fe keep dem on the right track, don't go astray, ca' every youth have to have a period with someone older than you that you can learn from."

With nonmusical forces controlling the music scene, the more serious music is set aside so that artists who can be controlled more easily are promoted. Clarke sees a parallel with the horse-racing game in JA. "But what they're really doing, they are fronting the D classes as A class, just like a horse race; even in Jamaica you have a horse run in A class, B, C, and D. You have tricks. The country is small, and sometimes you know the jockey and things. Sometime you know what is happening in the stable. Sometimes they have a horse that really belongs to B class, that is a fit horse and they're just trickin' the people and have him runnin' as a D class horse, and mek him losin' too, ca' they are holding him. And then one day him just run away and leave the whole a dem.

"Him coulda do that every time him run, him coulda beat dem, but it's true the jockey's holdin' him. Ca' he don't really belong in that class. Him should be in the A! A-1! But when him ready to win, nobody not gonna catch him. Even at 99 to 1. And whosoever know win a whole heap a money. So is just so the runnings go in the record business, y'know!"

But Clarke knows that not everyone is corrupt. "There is good and there is bad. Everyone is not bad. You have good people, and boy, sometimes they're hard to find! Just like a woman. You have man who blame woman every day and say woman this and woman that. Well, you have good woman! You have woman who is faithful and won't cheat and won't do certain things.

And that's why I say when a man is fighting against you, you just keep on doing the work. Because the man may be fighting in the east but the man in the west is not. Why stop doing your work to please who is fighting against you? Please him who is not fighting against you!

"So, boss, we nah go stop, ca' the truth is that truth," Clarke says defiantly. "I-man don't just try a thing, I was born to do it. I know you have certain people, is a survival thing fe him ca' mebbe him really can DJ and sing and must eat food. So him goin' find something to see the next day. But me no just come by luck or a man sorry fe me. Me come fe do it spiritually through the powers of God ca' God make me in a form and say boy, this is what you're supposed to do. So who God bless no man curse, ca' so it go."

In 1998 Blood and Fire issued *Dreader Dread 1976–1978*, an excellent compilation of Bunny Lee/Aggrovators tracks. Crucial cuts like "Age Is Growing" join extended mixes of "Love Up Your Brothers and Sisters," "Play Fool Fe Get Wise," and others. The inclusion of hard-to-find cuts like "Top Ranking" and "Fire and Brimstone A Go Burn the Wicked" make this a vital selection.

CHAPTER 6

Skylarking:

A Chat with Horace Andy

Horace Andy's distinctive high tenor is one of reggae's most unique and appealing sounds, the instrument of a legendary artist who wrote and sang a series of captivating Rasta tunes that became part of the bulwark of Studio One. Averaging nearly an album a year over a quarter-century career, he continued to have hits for Bunny Lee, Tappa Zukie, and other Jamaican producers, as well as Lloyd Barnes of New York's Bullwackies label. He has also released several excellent albums recorded in England, where he presently lives. A recent spate of releases includes a collection of tracks from all eras, *Skylarking Volume One* (Melankolic), a greatest hits gathering from the seventies, *Prime of Horace Andy,* and *Roots and Branches* (Blood and Fire), his second CD for England's Neil "Mad Professor" Frazier.

Born Horace Keith Hinds on February 19, 1951, Horace is first cousin to another great Jamaican singer, Justin Hinds. "Is him inspire me," says the man friends call Sleepy, who readily admits to American soul influences as well. "I tell you the truth, you know, I listen to all of them, man. Especially Otis Redding." Of Jamaican singers besides Hinds he says, "Ken Boothe was my favorite. Delroy Wilson was my favorite Boy Wonder." Those familiar with Delroy's youthful ska chargers will see why Horace, whose voice stayed in the upper range where Delroy's started, would like his work so much.

It may surprise some to learn that Horace Andy's first record wasn't cut at Studio One, since those early Coxsone hits helped define his sound and style for most longtime fans and collectors. It was Sun Shot's Phill Pratt who first took him into the studio, cutting the single "Black Man's Country" way back in 1966 at Dynamic, though "At that time it was name West Indian Recording Studio." *Get Wise* (Hot Disc) collects Pratt productions of Andy.

It was four more years before he recorded again, because, according to Andy, "I couldn't sing, man! I could sing anybody's song but when it comes to mine. And Pratt was the one who teach me to play the instrument from I was sixteen." The instrument in question was the guitar. It was Coxsone Dodd who gave him the name Horace Andy in deference to an earlier Studio One star, Bob Andy. Horace's first record for Dodd was the ethereal "Something on My Mind."

Andy's Studio One output was phenomenal, whether romantic ballads such as "Love of a Woman," "Just Say Who," or "Got to Be Sure," social consciousness like "Skylarking" and "Oh Lord, Why Lord," or all-time great early '70s Rasta tunes like "See a Man's Face (But You Don't

See His Heart)" and "Every Tongue Shall Tell." He also had a big hit for Coxsone with a cover of Cat Stevens's "Where Do the Children Play."

The inspiration for many of his songs came from the burgeoning Rasta movement that gripped Kingston like a fever in the late sixties as it had in the mid-thirties. "Before I start even singing I used to go to the Ethiopian World Federation meetings. One of my friend for a long time told me that we must come to the Rastafarian church, come to the meeting and I went and that was 1968, 1969, right up to 1970, '71, '72, yes, where I got my inspiration before I start singing. It was the Rastafarian faith that really open my eyes forming a consciousness, and that's why I sing those songs. 'Cause I know what was happening before I sing those songs. My eyes were open, you know? Before I even—when I was with Studio One I was a Rastafarian and I was singing, was creating my own Rasta songs."

Coxsone's studio functioned as a musical school for the brightest and best and the line-up. "Drums, bass, piano . . . they had the best," Horace says simply. "Horsemouth Wallace was playing drums, and Leroy Sibbles, he is my favorite bass player, man. That's why I made 'Mr. Bassie' offa him. Leroy played bass on 'See a Man's Face,' 'Just Say Who,' all a dem songs man. 'Got to Be Sure,' 'Every Tongue Shall Tell.' Leroy Sibbles, man. When I was at Studio One then I start learning the bass, piano, organ. And I learn a lot from Alton Ellis, too, playin' a instrument. Me and Dennis [Brown] used to take away his guitar. He used to show us a lot."

Besides the two Studio One albums (the original *Skylarking,* issued in America as *The Best of Horace Andy* on United Artists, and *Best of Horace Andy,* a completely different collection of tracks), Heartbeat has recently issued the collection *Mr. Bassie,* which gathers hit singles like "Fever" and "Just Don't Wanna Be Lonely" and includes previously unreleased material as well. Still, there are numerous uncollected

HORACE ANDY. Photograph by Jan Salzman; © 1989 Phantom Photos

Studio One singles from Horace Andy as well as later cuts he recorded for Coxsone in New York. "Yeah, I wish he would put out a new [Horace Andy] album you know. I don't know why he hasn't done that."

Unreissued Coxsone singles include the self-penned "Wanna Be Free," "Christmas Time," and covers of "Just Don't Wanna Be Lonely," "Casanova," "Show and Tell," and a remake of Dave Allen and the Arrow's "Nite Owl" with a burning Prince Jazzbo chat on the flip-side, as well as one he cut for Coxsone in New York, "One More Night."

After his main stint with Studio One Horace turned to Bunny Lee for some classic singles issued on Jackpot, including a remake of "Money Money (The Root of All Evil)," "A Serious Thing," and the album *You Are My Angel* (issued by Trojan in 1973). Another Bunny Lee collection, issued on Clocktower in New York and World Enterprises International, was the much sought-after *Sings for You and I.* This included cuts like "Better Collie," "I Don't Want to Be Outside," and Horace's reworking of a Bob Andy tune he retitled "We've Got to Forward Home."

Crucial cuts from 1974 backed by the Wailers—including the title song—were finally gathered with work from Winston Jarrett in 1988 as *Earth Must Be Hell* (Atra U.K.). Like most Jamaican singers Horace recorded for a multitude of producers. During his career he issued singles on Harry J's Roosevelt label, Winston Riley's Techniques, and labels such as Labrish, Kaya, Music Master, Giant, Rockers, Melrose, and others. Two outstanding singles from the '70s are "Who's to Be Blamed" on Mr. Big and "Love Jah" on Don't Crowd I. Another great one from the late '70s is "Rastaman" on Movements.

There were English 7-inch releases too, on labels like Chanan-Jah, Terminal, Tops, Attack, Atra, and more. In the U.S., New York labels Clocktower and Labrish were among those issuing Horace Andy singles. In 1977 he co-produced the reggae milestone *In the Light* with Everton DaSilva in New York. It and the concomitant *In the Light Dub* were for years two of the most difficult to find albums on the collectible market. They were combined on one crucial CD by Blood and Fire in 1995. The 1978 album *Natty Dread a Weh She Want* was produced by Tappa Zukie and issued on New Star. The title song was a massive hit in the U.K. In the early '80s he began a lengthy association with Lloyd Barnes' Bullwackies label in New York. The first album, *Dance Hall Style* (Wackies) was issued as *Exclusively* on Solid Groove in England.

"Was there I finished learning to play more better," he says. "The organ, everything. With the Bullwackies. Lloyd is a very good person. We eat and sleep in that studio. We eat, sleep, cook, we do everything, man, and never go home. That was the start of the beating down of my first marriage." Horace and his family had relocated to Hartford, Connecticut, at the time. "Through hours dedicated to the music I wasn't looking on the other side. I'm always in New York doing music, music, music." This association also produced the 1988 album *Everyday People*. In New York he also recorded the album *Don't Stop* in 1985.

Back in Jamaica Horace split a disc with Patrick Andy (*Clash of the Andys,* produced by Kenneth Hoo Kim) and recorded albums for Sonny and Jackal (*Confusion*), King Jammy (*Haul and Jack Up,* 1987), and Jah Thomas (*Shame and Scandal,* 1988). His self-productions were issued on his labels Rhythm and Horace Andy.

Three cuts recorded in London for Phil Pratt surface on a showcase album with John Holt called *From One Extreme to Another,* on which two of the songs are written by roots favorite Junior Byles. "Junior Byles is a good bredren, man" he says reflectively. Though one of the brightest stars of the seventies, homelessness, hunger, and mental turmoil reduced Byles to street-level survival throughout much of the eighties and nineties. "Yeah, it just sad to know what happen to him but you know I love how him write, Junior Byles is a very good writer. Very very good writer, you know?"

Throughout his career Horace Andy has also been well represented on 12-inch singles. The Studio One extended mix of the aforementioned "Mr. Bassie" is essential, as well as the later "Gimme Little Soul Oh Jah" issued on Dub-Tune. The U.K. Fashion recording of "Gateman" tore up the sound systems; he also did a nice cover of Bob Marley's "Hypocrites" for the same label. New York 12-inches on Tad's, Wackies, Bullwackies, Checkmate, and Mobsters, among others, kept a steady stream of his music in the shops. One of the best was "Love Is the Light" with Big Youth on Techniques. Two early albums on U.S. labels Brad's and Tad's, respectively (though recorded in JA), well worth checking out are *Showcase,* containing his classic remake of Lloyd Robinson's "Cus Cus" on the original Harry J rhythm, and *Pure Ranking.*

As the digital age dawned in Jamaica in the '90s Horace Andy cut singles for Jammy's, Digital B, Scorpio, African Star, Mister Tipsy, and a host of modern labels. His penetrating delivery seems at home in any era. Released in 1993, *Rude Boy* (Shanachie) features a set of songs produced by Black Scorpio that included the singles "Kuff Dem" and "That's How I Feel" with Third World's Bunny Ruggs. *Hits from Studio One and More* appeared in 1995 on the Rhino U.K. label. In the mold of "hit after hit" records it was a return to the Bunny Lee umbrella with twenty-five cuts reprising his own hits like "Zion Gate," "Better Collie," and "Thank the Lord," as well as a few first made famous by his early hero Delroy Wilson.

Living in London he explored new territory with some of the roots revival producers like Mad Professor and Blackamix as well as producing the album *Elementary* himself. "The Blackamix one [1995's *Seek and You Will Find,* also released in dub as *Seek and You Will Find: The Dub Pieces*] is very good," he says proudly, as if he's talking about one of his seventeen children. "I say to myself long time I haven't done a real roots album, y'know?" Equally rootsy are the Mad Professor productions *Life Is for Living* from 1995 and 1997's *Roots and Branches* (RAS). "I did quite a lot of songs with Mad Professor. We have some leftovers that he put together. So we will be comin' out with another one soon. From the mystery vaults, heh."

Recently he's been working with Madonna's pals Massive Attack; two examples of their very forward-sounding collaborations appear on the new *Skylarking* CD. Through all of this he's managed to keep that hypnotic throbbing interface with the tracks that defined his best early work. "I try my best to mek it stay roots music. But I enjoy working with Massive! I really do. I've always wanted to do something like that but I've never known how to approach it 'cause [people] are always sayin'"—here he imitates a somewhat stuffy middle-class Jamaican—'Oh, you a reggae singer, you can't sing dem kinda song deh.' If I was to go and try and do it in Jamaica they would have said no. Don't do it, you know? But it really good. It really, really good."

In fact his work with Massive Attack has created a whole new set of fans in England and Japan. "That's why that album [a brand-new disc recorded with Massive Attack soon to be released on Melankolic] with all these songs gon' be good." As a result his early singles are trading for high prices on the current collectors market in Japan.

Horace is also proud of the *Skylarking* set. "My fans who know about Massive will get a charge to know what I was doing in my young days." Besides Massive Attack cuts "One Love" and "Spying Glass" the disc includes the original 1981 Bullwackies version of the latter, mid-seventies U.K. smash "Natty Dread a Weh She Want," and early '70s classics like "Don't Let Problems Get You Down," "Children of Israel," "Girl I Love You," and "Money Money," as well as Studio One hits "Every Tongue Shall Tell" and of course the original "Skylarking."

One delightful tune from 1975 included on the disc is the lullaby "Rock to Sleep." "I was swinging my friend's daughter," he explains, "and I was sayin' 'Rock a bye baby' and she went to sleep!" Among friends and family Horace has been known as "Sleepy" since he was a kid. "Anyone who seh them know me and you ask him what they call me and they can't tell you, they don't know me. 'Cause for most people who I know, I'm Sleepy." He imitates someone calling him. "Sleepy! They don't bother with Horace. All my friends call me Sleepy, man." The reason? "If I sit down comfortable ten minutes ah gone!"

I had the great pleasure of seeing Horace Andy live a few years back at the Kingston 12 in Santa Monica for a rare West Coast appearance. Living up to his nickname he wandered out like he was walking in his sleep. When he raised the microphone to his lips the ineffable Horace Andy voice wafted out over the crowd, barely assayed by his half-lidded glance around. The show had been booked late and the house wasn't full but the people got the show of a lifetime from this unique and (though many have attempted) inimitable performer.

Horace has put his stamp on generations of young Jamaican singers. A couple he mentions are Barrington Levy and one close to the heart of roots lovers today, the late Garnett Silk. Says Sleepy, "If you hear Garnett Silk you can hear me. It is the living style from me." Any questions about this can be answered by Silk's loving rendition of "Skylarking." Far from bothering him, such imitation finds appreciation in this original. "I love that, you know." And for all these singers who've made an impression on him and on whom he has made an impression—Alton Ellis, Junior Murvin, and others—his praise is high. "Some wicked styles, mon. Respect all a dem, y'know! Respect all a dem." Just issued on Heartbeat Europe, *See and Blind* is a brand-new Horace Andy disc recorded at Record Factory in Jamaica. Produced by Bunny Gemini, it mixes familiar territory with contemporary production. In late 1998 he toured with Massive Attack.

For Horace's next album he says, "I have a wicked track with me and Joe Strummer from the Clash. Wicked, man, wicked. The new album is gonna be real excellent. And you know you can look for more roots—I will still do more roots music, man. I have an album that's never been released, more than one. So I will be goin' down in the vaults too."

If you're just getting introduced to Horace Andy and this all seems like a lot of music to process, start with Studio One or the Melankolic *Skylarking* selection; it spans all time periods and many producers for a broad sampling of his work. Once you find which period or production you prefer you can zero in on that, though if you're like me you'll eventually want them all. Another good bet is the recently released *Prime of Horace Andy* (Music Club) collecting twenty Bunny Lee productions from the '70s, including crucial works like "Just Say Who" and "Collie Weed." From his early work with Coxsone through his latest tracks with Massive Attack, Horace Andy is one of Jamaica's most inviting and accessible vocalists.

CHAPTER 7

Marcia Griffiths:

Mark My Word

From the early days of ska to the dancehall divas of today, reggae has produced some great female vocalists. One of the best-known Jamaican singers at home and abroad is Marcia Griffiths, who, along with Rita Marley and Judy Mowatt, formed the I-Threes. The trio recorded on their own as well as backing Bob Marley and the Wailers on tour and in the studio. Marcia's long and distinguished solo career preceeded and ran concurrently with her work in the group. She had some of reggae's earliest hits, shared in some of its finest moments, and still charts nearly every record she puts out.

Marcia Griffiths began recording in 1964 at age sixteen under the guidance of the legendary C.S. Dodd, Studio One's founder and producer. "Studio One is like Jamaica's Motown, where all the great stars grew," she explains. "When I went there, Bob Marley and the Wailers was there. Ken Boothe, the Gaylads, just about every Jamaican entertainer you've ever heard of." The label, she says, was "like a university you graduate. We would just all go there like going to work and do recordings every day. We still have [unreleased] songs on tape there!"

Her first hit single for Dodd was "Feel Like Jumping," a genuine reggae standard still covered and played in clubs today. A string of hit 45s also penned for her by the prolific Bob Andy included "Truly," "Tell Me Now," "Mark My Word," and "Melody Life." They can be heard on the first of her dozen albums, *Marcia Griffiths at Studio One*. The rhythms of these songs have been continually re-recorded and reused by the Jamaican recording industry in the intervening years and have propelled literally hundreds of hits.

In addition, "Being a young and upcoming singer then, what Mr. Dodd usually do [was] to couple me with almost every male singer there for a hit song," she recalls. "So I did a song with Tony Gregory, the late Free-I, Bob Andy, and Ken Boothe. I did one with Bob Marley

MARCIA GRIFFITHS. Photograph by Bob Salzman; © 1994 Phantom Photos

that is still on tape. I hear it's gonna be released soon, a love song called 'Oh My Darling' that Bob Marley wrote." In fact, though some date back nearly thirty years, "there are enough songs right now at Studio One to give me another album, which I hear he [Dodd] is getting ready to do."

After her stint with Studio One, Griffiths again joined forces with Bob Andy on three albums for producer Harry J. Their cover of "Young Gifted and Black" was her first international hit and spent an extended period on the British charts. Her next album was produced by Lloyd Charmers for the Federal label, but she soon moved on. "If you see return from your work, then you would just stay one place," she sighs. But in those early days "you work for all these producers, but there's never a payday. It's just the satisfaction [of the music] that you get."

Griffiths then recorded for Sonia Pottinger's High Note label, where she had such hits as "Dreamland"—written, like her later smash, "Electric Boogie," by Bunny Wailer—and the sublime "Peaceful Woman." Two albums of material from this period were big sellers in Jamaica as well. Mrs. Pottinger's pop production style blends seamlessly with Griffith's professional delivery, making these some of her most enjoyable records.

Griffiths first reached America not as a solo singer but as a member of the I-Threes, a female trio who sang backup for Bob Marley and the Wailers on their albums from *Natty Dread* on. The trio also performed as part of the Wailers in concert throughout their later career. How she and her cohorts came to join forces with this legendary musical outfit is an interesting story in itself. Griffiths had won Jamaica's coveted Female Singer of the Year award several times, and was performing at a club in Kingston called House of Chan.

"I invited Sister Rita [Marley] and Sister Judy [Mowatt] to come and give me some backing vocals," she recalls. The two singers provided "harmonies during my performance for the weekend, and at the end of the show we came together and did a little jam doing some [American Gospel group] Sweet Inspiration songs. The audience loved it and that was where we decided we would form a group."

At the time, she says, "I think Bob and the Wailers [original members Peter Tosh and Bunny] were having some differences. And he just decided that he was gonna work along with us. So we went in the studio and did the single 'Natty Dread,' for Bob, and 'Jah Live.'" Previously Griffiths and Rita Marley had provided backgrounds on the tune "Rock It Baby" that included Peter and Bunny. "Rita and myself was friends before we met Sister Judy," she explains.

Her years touring and recording with Marley are clearly standout memories for her. "Nothing compares to the tours with Bob over the years." Anyone who experienced these shows with their combination of music, poetry, politics, religion, and dance—with the colorfully costumed I-Threes as a major part of the shows—will understand. Spiritually uplifting, musically satisfying, and visually stunning, the shows were among the greatest performances ever witnessed by those who attended.

Her obvious love and admiration for Marley is apparent in her voice when she talks about him. Every day working with the Wailers, she says was "a new experience, fresh and interesting. It never stop—it's just like a new heaven opening up every day from the fact that Bob himself was one of a kind and truly a prophet sent. I was one of the persons who knew who this man was while he was with us. I didn't wait until he passed to give him flowers. I knew who I was among."

Marley's presence, which hypnotized audiences on stage throughout the world, had the same effect on those around him. It was, says Griffiths, "one big phenomenon being with him. He captivates everyone with the magic and everything that he commands. When he comes on stage everything is just different energy. Everyone is mesmerized. A lot of times on stage we got carried away just watching him, forgetting certain spots to come in."

Since Marley's passing the I-Threes and Wailers have toured together but Griffiths has also returned to "working out front as a solo singer. I was fortunate to have some international exposure before I started touring with Bob. Even when I was with the I-Threes I never did relinquish my solo career."

A series of strong Jamaican releases for the Penthouse and Taxi labels—some pairing her with modern singers such as Beres Hammond and DJs Cutty Ranks and Tony Rebel—have kept her in the forefront of reggae singers in the eighties and nineties. Her early albums include *Sweet Bitter Love* (produced by Lloyd Charmers for Trojan), *Naturally* and *Steppin'* (produced by Sonia Pottinger and released originally on her High Note label), *Rock My Soul* (co-produced by Marcia herself and Sydney Crooks and issued on Marley's Tuff Gong label), and *I Love Music* (produced by Chris Stanley for Mountain Sound). More recent discs include *Carousel* (produced by the Jerks for Island) and three produced by Donovan Germain, *Marcia* (VP), *Indomitable,* and *Land of Love* (Penthouse).

Though her music has changed with the times, her message hasn't. For her, "music have no class nor creed. I still maintain that music is pure and whosoever thinks he or she has that God-given talent to do this work and communicate to the people through the medium of music, I feel they should contribute in a positive way." She has headlined two Sunsplash tours and performed extensively in Europe and Japan.

Music is valid, she believes, when it deals with "truth and reality. We're all brothers and sister in this world and we experience the same things in life. This is why a singer is so important: we talk about the things people suffer and the things they enjoy. And love is what we have to generate and portray more than anything else. Of all that is happening throughout the world that is bad and on the negative side, we have to remind people that the one main thing is living together in peace and unity and love, regardless of what the situation is. It all boils down to: we have to live together. Animals can live together. Why can't we?"

CHAPTER 8

Bob Marley and the Wailers:

For the Record

Bob Marley has achieved legendary status even among the people who knew him best. "As Bob said to me . . ." begin half a dozen singer's comments scattered through this book. Joe Higgs, who schooled the Wailers in harmony, calls Marley "the most successful exponent of this music and the most conscious person to establish this awareness that Garvey has started."

Marcus Garvey, like Bob Marley and Burning Spear, was born in St. Ann's Bay, Jamaica. His United Negro Improvement Association based in Harlem in the '20s and '30s instilled pride and encouraged a unity that so frightened the governments of the world he soon found himself tried, convicted, imprisoned, and deported to Jamaica where he was again imprisoned. From his cell he ran for and won a seat on Parliament. "Marcus Garvey is the one who really took that light and extend it," says Higgs. "And as I reason we are here to say, Jamaica is the only island in the world who has maintained that connection to Africa through two great M's, Marcus and Marley."

More than any other reggae artist Marley has come to represent reggae in most people's minds. His international presence is huge. The Wailers are the preeminent reggae group and yet—or perhaps precisely because—they are unlike any other group. They were in fact the melding of three groups.

Peter Tosh (born Winston Hubert McIntosh and called "Peter Touch" on early records), Neville O'Riley Livingston (who came to be known as Bunny Wailer), and Robert Nesta Marley—along with tenor Junior Braithwaite (who can be heard singing lead on some early Wailers records), as well as Beverly Kelso and Cherry Smith in the early days and Judy Mowatt, Marcia Griffiths, and Rita Marley in the late—are only part of the Wailers story. The first version of the vocal group had a run of hits for Coxsone Dodd in the mid-sixties. Bob, Peter, and Bunny all issued solo records as well. They traded off leads, unusual for most reggae trios who feature one lead and two back-up singers. Their early records are characterized by a brilliance that runs like a golden thread through their recordings.

Since full-length biographies of all three either exist or are pending (many, in the spirit of this work, in the words of the singers themselves), it seems wiser to focus here on the records they made. Desmond Dekker and Ken Boothe tell about Marley's early career—he cut sides for Leslie Kong before the Wailers worked for Coxsone. They woodshedded at Studio One and Dodd even moved Marley in as they learned the basics of recording. By all accounts, Joe Higgs had a formidable influence on their harmonies before this. The records they made for Coxsone made them stars in Jamaica.

The essential Studio One works are available on a forty-track double-CD from Heartbeat titled *One Love,* or separately issued as *Simmer Down at Studio One* and *The Wailing Wailers at Studio One.* The latter is not the same as their original album *The Wailing Wailers* on Studio One. Though much of it appears on the larger collection, a few legendary cuts like Bob's crooning cover of Tom Jones's "What's New Pussycat" make the original worth seeking out as well.

Early on, a budget line album called *Birth of a Legend* appeared from CBS. Also from Coxsone Dodd Studio One productions, there was both a ten-track single and twenty-track double album issued under this title. The second disc in the set sometimes shows up as *Bob Marley and the Wailers: The Early Years* featuring Peter Tosh. Only one song from the latter appears on the same label's *Best of Bob Marley and the Wailers,* which repeats no tunes from the original Wailing Wailers. Only a couple of these are on the later *One Love,* making this also worth hunting for. It was later reissued in the U.S. with a completely different cover.

Now it starts to get hairy. Studio One released another *Best of Bob Marley and the Wailers* in conjunction with Buddah in 1975 and guess what? It's not the same as any of the above, though it features a couple of cuts from the first album. It also has several songs like "Where Is My Mother" that don't show up anywhere else. *Marley, Tosh, Livingston and Associates,* whose cover is easy to confuse with one of the Studio One "best ofs," had some of its one-time rarities plucked for *One Love* (like the Wailers incorporation of Dylan's "Rolling Stone") or the Tosh set *The Toughest* on Heartbeat (like his delicious "Hoot Nanny Hoot") but it does contain Bunny's original

"Dreamland," which also shows up on some English releases from Trojan.

Marley cut a few songs for Leslie Kong before the Wailers went to Studio One. "Judge Not" and "One Cup of Coffee" were released on single and both are now much anthologized. The work the Wailers did with Kong after leaving Dodd has been reissued so many times in so many forms it seems to be in the public domain. They were initially issued in Jamaica as—oh, great—*The Best of the Wailers.*

Early or dependably complete versions available here were titled *Shakedown* or *Soul Shakedown Party,* but the material has shown up under so many titles it's better just to check for the songs, which include "Caution," "Soul Captives," and a surprising number of Peter Tosh vocals including early versions of "Stop That Train," "Can't You See," "Soon Come," and an arrangement of "Go Tell It on the Mountain" right out of the Simon and Garfunkel songbook. The Leslie Kong material has joined other non-Island Wailers work in a brilliant example of how to make two hundred albums out of four.

And then there's the material Marley—with and without Peter and Bunny—recorded when signed to a songwriting contract with Johnny Nash, Arthur Jenkins, and Danny Sims's JAD organization. Though little of it was released during his lifetime the market has been flooded with material since his passing. If you're a Bob Marley completest you'll want them all, but since the material is very different (they were aiming for a pop-soul crossover feel), Marley fans who love his better-known work might want to dip a toe cautiously before deciding to plunge.

Albums like *Chances Are, Jamaican Storm,* and the generically titled *Bob Marley* mix soft ballads, "uptown" arrangements (often over-dubbed to update), and alternate versions of songs from the Wailers canon with rare uncut gems that are genuinely integral to understanding his evolution. *Soul Almighty* from 1996 also

functions as an interactive CD with hours of Marley material available to those with the proper software. In 1998 JAD issued the first volume of *The Complete Wailers, 1967–1972,* a three-CD set that includes, often for the first time, un-updated versions and many previously unreleased recordings. Non-JAD material, including scarce releases on the Wailers' own Wail-M-Soul-M label and others, make this set vastly different from previous JAD releases.

That set includes some cuts previously available only on *In the Beginning,* which Trojan issued in 1983, including tracks like "Adam and Eve" and "This Train." The song "Wisdom" appears on both, with vocals by Marley. It was later separately recorded by Peter and Bunny; Peter's version was titled "Fools Die." "Destiny," a recent hit by Buju Banton, draws liberally from it as well. The second *Complete Wailers* set, also containing three CDs, covers the Lee Perry productions. These releases may eventually supplant the need to find all the early variants for all but the most obsessed vinyl junkies.

The Wailers as they became known internationally were much more than a vocal group. Visionary producer Lee "Scratch" Perry paired the hardest studio outfit of his day—dubbed variously the Upsetters when cutting for him at Black Ark, the Hippy Boys on their own, and eventually (with the ever-present permutations) the Wailers Band in later years. When teamed with Bob, Bunny, and Peter they made international history. The result, captured on two of reggae's most revolutionary discs, paved the way for their Island recordings and later success.

Of course in the world of the Wailers, two albums are not two albums and the Lee Perry sessions have also been reissued in countless packagings and later blended with those of Kong and Coxsone. *African Herbsman* and *Rasta Revolution* (which was really *Soul Rebels* with the addition of one track) supply the basic Upsetter-Upsetters-Wailers recordings, though additional tracks (like the brilliant "Keep on Skanking") appear here and there and *Soul Revolution 1 and 2* supplies a dub disc for about half the songs.

The version of the Wailers that flowered in the Lee Perry era didn't last too long but left a continuing legacy that shaped the lives of all the principals. By the time they left Perry, the Wailers—now a tightly knit unit that included the Upsetters' former backing band as well—were well capable of producing their own work and, with Island's Chris Blackwell bankrolling their recording, began to rack up an impressive series of albums.

Though many musicians contributed to the Wailers sound from the Skatalites in the Studio One days to Leslie Kong's All-Stars and the open-ended loose-knit group of Upsetters that might include Glen Adams or Winston Wright on keyboards, the lineup that moved on to record at Harry J's for Island included Bob, Peter, Bunny, and two brothers who were instrumental in the sound we've come to know as reggae, Carlton Barrett and his brother Aston "Family Man." Wire Lindo played keys.

Burnin' (1973) recycled some songs from Coxsone, Kong, and Perry, including "Put It On," "Small Axe," and "Duppy Conqueror," done in a new militant style. It also contains a couple of Peter Tosh's magnificent volleys, the stark harmonic convergence of "One Foundation," and the only song credited to Marley and Tosh, the uncompromising "Get Up, Stand Up." Besides the "Rasta Man Chant," something that had not yet been heard in America, there was a little tune called "I Shot the Sheriff."

It was Eric Clapton who took that one to number one on the charts, paving the way for a better reception for the Wailers' second Island album of 1973, *Catch a Fire*. Released originally in a sleeve disguised as a giant lighter with an unfortunately weak hinge, it was quickly reissued with an even bolder cover of Bob choking back a huge spliff (something he also did on the back cover of *Burnin'* and at every available opportunity in interviews). But by the time of

the tour for this LP the Wailers of old had begun to disintegrate.

First Bunny, then Peter "went solo" or left the group, though interestingly the same players back Tosh on his earliest solo album, including Bunny on vocals. Marley reconfigured the group without his longtime companions but with the I-Threes—Judy Mowatt, Rita Marley, and Marcia Griffiths. He took front and center for the rest of his days with the Wailers. *Natty Dread* (1974) was full of the fiery invective that fueled the first two international albums and cuts like "Rebel Music" and "Revolution" made it seem that he had lost none of his outsider credentials.

By the time of 1975's *Rastaman Vibration*, the Wailers band sound was beginning to emerge. Earl "Chinna" Smith, Donald Kinsey, and Al Anderson (who went on to be a mainstay with the Wailers for nearly twenty years) all played on this one. The faux-burlap cover—with a revolutionary Marley looking for all the world like a Che who got away—went well, with cuts like "Rat Race," "Night Shift," and "War," whose lyrics were taken from a speech by Ethiopian Emperor Haile Selassie I, the original Ras Tafari.

That same year's *Bob Marley and the Wailers Live* captured the group at the London Lyceum. "Trenchtown Rock," "No Woman No Cry," and "Lively Up Yourself" were among the songs given full and satisfying live treatment. Marley was laying the foundations for the empire to come with record releases and constant touring. The reggae scene as it exists today from local bands to dancehall owes a large part of its existence to these tours. At their best the festivals of today are a reminder of the power of those shows.

Exodus (1977) opened the door a little more on the man who had "So Much Things to Say." Marley always knew how to reel them in (for every "Heathen" or "Concrete Jungle" there was a corresponding "Jammin'" and "Rock It Baby"). The guileless ("Three Little Birds"), the contemplative ("Natural Mystic"), and the all-inclusive (his reworking of "One Love") were always in his reach.

Marley took a break from saving the world with the release of *Kaya* in 1978, a softer album whose focus was on enjoyment of life, spiritual growth, and inner calm. "Time Will Tell," "Crisis," and "Running Away" pointed toward the reinvigorated Wailer who would reappear on tour and on the double live set *Babylon by Bus* that same year. The Wailers band had gone through some changes over the years, with Bernard "Touter" Harvey replacing Wire Lindo on keys and Junior Marvin, who became the band's lead singer after Marley's death, joined Donald Kinsey and Al Anderson, who incidentally both played for Tosh as well.

Marley's final three Island albums form a set that moved his sound into the international arena. *Survival* (1979), with cuts like "So Much Trouble (In the World)" and "Africa Unite," returned to the militant themes of the early Wailers releases. *Uprising* (1980) contained crossover cuts "Coming in from the Cold" and "Could You Be Loved," as well as the acoustic "Redemption Song." *Confrontation* (1983) gathered final recordings like "Buffalo Soldiers" with Jamaican singles such as "Rastaman Live Up" and the 12-inch "I Know" issued soon after his death from cancer in 1981.

Island issued the Wailers *Reggae Greats* set in 1984, drawing from the Marley-Tosh-Livingston days and *Legend,* which went on to become the best selling Marley catalog item in 1984 as well. *Rebel Music* gathered a slightly different but equally satisfying selection in 1986. *Talkin' Blues* from 1991 includes interspaced interview sections and rare cuts like Tosh's "You Can't Blame the Youth" and the unusual "Am-A-Do."

Natural Mystic (1995) is volume two of *Legend* and issued "Iron Lion Zion" for the first time. In 1997 Island issued the poorly received *Dreams of Freedom: Ambient Translations of Bob Marley in Dub,* on which Material's Bill Lasswell

tinkers with Marley's oeuvre, splicing in passages of easy-listening music with the abandon of a hash-house restaurant watering down orange juice. It came as a slap in the face to longtime Wailers fans, who had waited patiently for the release of the "real" dubs that backed the 7-inch singles and were in every way superior to to this attempt to turn revolutionary music into background noise.

Peter Tosh cut a distinctive post-Wailers path for himself with two revolutionary solo releases on Columbia. *Legalize It* (1976) and *Equal Rights* (1977) were followed by three impressive albums for short-lived Rolling Stone Records, *Bush Doctor* (1978), *Mystic Man* (1979), and 1981's *Wanted Dread and Alive.* His band on the discs and on tour was Word, Sound and Power featured Sly Dunbar and Robbie Shakespeare. A bootleg titled *Island Zoro* that shows up now and then was taped from a live radio broadcast in Southern California in 1979.

Beginning with 1983's *Mama Africa* and the following year's *Captured Live,* Fully Fullwood and Santa Davis took over bass and drums and also played on Tosh's final album, 1987's *No Nuclear War.* After his death in a home invasion robbery some see as a disguised assassination, the unavailability of much of his material caused later reggae fans to miss his crucial place in the scheme of things.

All that began to change in the late nineties. A 1996 collection from Heartbeat called *The Toughest* gathers thirteen Coxsone productions, some with the Wailers and some without but all featuring Peter Tosh singing lead, with a half-dozen Lee Perry productions. Included are rare cuts like "Jumbie Jamboree" and "Rasta Shook Them Up," as well as "Rightful Ruler," which is also U Roy's first record. Don't mistake the above for the 1988 CD *The Toughest,* issued by Capital, which collects songs mainly from the currently unavailable discs issued on Rolling Stone Records. EMI also released a greatest hits in the mid-nineties called *Dread Don't Die.*

The 1997 three-CD boxed set titled *Honorary Citizen* will hopefully return Tosh to his rightful dominant position in reggae. It contains scarce singles like "Pound Get a Blow," "Arise Blackman," and "Mark of the Beast," recorded before, during, and after his tenure with the world's best-known reggae group. One live disc of previously unissued material and one disc of favorites like his duet on "Don't Look Back" with Mick Jagger, his burning version of Joe Higgs's "Stepping Razor" as featured in the movie *Rockers,* and the contemplative "Fools Die" (aka "Wisdom") round out the set.

Peter Tosh was uncompromising in his music and his life, and his career took the blows that missed his body. Beaten and jailed in Jamaica for what amounted to a political offense in directing comments to the prime minister at the One Love "Peace" concert, he had the scar photographed for an album cover. In his music and his life, change was demanded—not requested—and the world was held accountable for its shortcomings in a head-on manner that few who don't seek martyrdom would attempt. His intelligence is demonstrated over and over in his songs, in his frontal attack on linguistic inconsistency, and in the surprising humor he sometimes displayed.

After leaving the Wailers, Neville Livingston—henceforth known as Bunny Wailer—released the legendary *Blackheart Man* album on Island in 1976, featuring the unique combination of Carlie Barrett and Robbie Shakespeare on drum and bass. His reputation as a mystic grew; he was said to have left the Wailers because he couldn't get ital [natural] food on tour, and his steadfast refusal to tour only strengthened the anticipation of his late seventies releases, such as 1977's *Protest,* also for Island. His third album, *Struggle,* was on his own Solomonic label.

Numerous 12-inch (or disco singles, as they're called in Jamaica) were issued on Solomonic in the early eighties. *Bunny Wailer Sings the Wailers* (Mango, 1980) prefigures the rash of Marley tribute albums that have flooded the market since his death. Bunny Wailer himself issued three more such albums, 1981's *Tribute,* 1990's *Time Will Tell,* and 1995's superlative double-CD set *Hall of Fame;* he won Grammys for the latter two.

In I Father's House (1980) gathered some of the 12-inch releases, as did 1983's *Roots Radics Rockers Reggae.* Though he was at this time recording with Sly and Robbie, Bunny's future studio band took their name from the title song. On 1982's *Hook Line and Sinker,* "Jah B" as he became known attempted to reach a black American audience with an experimental rap-reggae release that left American reggae fans confused and dismayed. The same year's live performance at Kingston's National Stadium was a magnificent demonstration that the Wailer could still wail. It was released as an album, predictably called *Live,* the following year.

The mid-eighties also saw the return of Bunny Wailer to the international concert stage, beginning with a mind-blowing show in Long Beach, California, in 1986. Performing with three different bands, including the Roots Radics and Sly and Robbie, he poured out everything his fans had waited for all those years, the entire *Blackheart Man* album included. He went on to play Madison Square Garden the same year.

The year 1986 saw two very different releases: *Marketplace,* which seemed made for it, and *Rootsman Skanking,* which for the first time mainly featured the Radics. The group was even featured in a back cover photo with Bunny on 1987's *Rule Dance Hall. Gumption,* however, from the same year, featured electronic drum programming from Chris Meredith and Danny Browne, as well as some unusual covers including two from Toots Hibbert and one from Johnny Osbourne. In 1988 Bunny turned out one of his finest albums, *Liberation.* With Sly, Robbie, and the Roots Radics on board he burned through tracks like "Rise and Shine," "Botha the

Mosquito," "Bald Head Jesus," and "Serious Thing." It remains one of his tightest works.

In the early '90s an event that would have been inconceivable in the preceding decades occurred: Bunny Wailer was booed offstage in Jamaica and had bottles thrown at him when he attempted to perform at a dancehall show. One of the low points of the change in styles, this showed how far the music had fallen. To his credit he responded with one of his best albums, *Dance Massive,* in which he addressed in song after song—"Conscious Lyrics," "Dance Ha Fi Gwan," "Veteran," and "Still the King" among them—the event and the issues that surrounded it.

A project many years in the making was released in 1993 as *The Never Ending Wailers.* Taking early Wailers tracks with the voices of Bob Marley and Peter Tosh, adding contemporary harmonies by himself, early Wailer Junior Braithwaite, former Tosh back-up singer (and Rita Marley's cousin) Constantine "Vision I" Walker, and Peter's son Andrew, he created a disc that both was and wasn't a Wailers release. Certainly it had more integrity than some of the material available after Marley's death, including ancient vocals with tracks electronically processed into ghosthood with disco backing added and other monstrosities. The disc is something of any anomaly in the Wailers canon.

Across the ocean Marcia Griffiths had an East Coast hit with "Electric Boogie," a song Bunny wrote and produced for her. He included his own version of it on an album, *Just Be Nice,* that was essentially *Hook, Line and Sinker* revisited, including covers of "Sitting in the Park" and "Family Affair" and the James Brown-ish "Hit Back the Crack," all wired into "the new American dance craze" the Electric Slide inspired by "Electric Boogie."

Crucial! Roots Classics (1994) was more to the liking of reggae fans and garnered another Grammy. The mid-nineties saw the *Hall of Fame* set on RAS and *Retrospective* from Shanachie.

These two labels have been mainly responsible for issuing Solomonic product in the U.S. since Bunny Wailer parted with Island. In 1998 Bunny Wailer made his first appearance at Southern California's annual Bob Marley Days event and put on a triumphant show.

The I-Threes issued a number of uncollected singles, including "Many Are Called," "Music for the World," and "Neighbor," as well as a Bob Marley medley and a version of "No Woman No Cry." They issued one album together, 1986's *Beginning,* and Rita Marley, Judy Mowatt, and Marcia Griffiths all continued their solo careers with excellent records in the decades following Marley's passing.

The Wailers Band regrouped with guitarist Junior Marvin taking over lead vocals, playing shows that were often tributary in nature. Though the murder of drummer Carlton Barrett broke up one of reggae's greatest and longest-running rhythm sections, the band would not be stopped and issued several albums of original material. On 1987's *I.D.,* a version of the group included Aston "Family Man" Barrett, Junior Marvin, Wire Lindo, and Al Anderson, as well as keyboardist Martin Batista, drummer Michael "Boo" Richards, and former Third World percussionist Irvin "Carrot" Jarrett; they still seemed to be reeling from the blows. But 1991's *Majestic Warriors* was on more solid footing.

By 1994's *Jah Message* the band—now consisting of Junior Marvin, Aston Barrett, "Wia" Lindo, Martin Batista, Alvin "Seeco" Patterson on percussion (he played with the Wailers during Marley's tenure and guested on the Wailers Band's previous discs), and the returned Tyrone Downie—turned in their best effort yet. At this writing there are again lineup changes in the group, with Junior Marvin said to be out of the band.

By the mid-nineties Marley's children, both with Rita and others, had stepped forward to claim their own place in reggae. Ziggy Marley and the Melody Makers, also featuring Sharon,

Cedella, and Stephen Marley, were first out of the gate and have established themselves as a major international pop-reggae crossover group with albums for EMI, Virgin, and others. Critical acclaim, Grammy nominations (and three wins), radio play, and chart action to a degree their father never saw testify to his legacy and their talent. "The music continues, the message continues," is how Ziggy put it to me recently. "We keep going." Stephen Marley has formed his own production wing, Ghetto Youth, working with his brothers and others. Recently Marley sons Julian, Damian (aka Jr. Gong), and Ky-mani have stepped forward with albums that continue and extend the Marley domain.

Peter Tosh's son Andrew issued his first single, "Vanity Love," produced by DJ Charlie Chaplin, on the Gorgon label. The first album, *Original Man,* he says, "Came about after my father died." Niney the Observer produced. They released the single "Same Dog" (a Peter Tosh song). Later, says Andrew, "Me and Fully (Fullwood) got together" for the album *Make Place for the Youth.* He also sings on the *Never-Ending Wailers* CD. Looking and sounding incredibly like his father, he has appeared on a number of Peter Tosh Tribute shows in the '90s.

A wealth of the best work from Bob Marley, Peter Tosh, and Bunny Wailer remains unissued in the United States. Early Jamaican singles containing some of their finest singing together have yet to be anthologized. A great deal of Tosh's solo material is simply not available on CD; even some of his most popular albums are currently in limbo. Bunny Wailer, who set up his own Solomonic label, has provided us with a great deal of his solo work but there are still some tantalizing and legendary singles uncollected. In an age of reissues and outpouring of archival material of all types of music, we have much to look forward to from Bob Marley and the Wailers.

CHAPTER 9

The Meditations:

Deepest Roots

The Meditations were in the vanguard of reggae's first wave, a mid-seventies rush of artists and groups that prepared the way for Jamaican music around the world. Their first album, *Message from the Meditations,* contained songs originally released as singles by the individual members of the band, Danny Clarke, Winston Watson, and Ansel Cridland. These include some of the earliest records the three sang on together in various combinations. It also collects many of the first records released under the name the Meditations.

Though all the members of the trio write and sing lead, that job has mainly been handled over the years by Ansel Cridland. Cridland started his musical career as lead singer for a group called the Linkers. Their hits include the brilliant "Nyah Man Story," cut for Sir J.J. Most of the rest of their recordings were done for producer Fud Christian's La-Fu-Del label, including "What a Bam Bam" cut over the same track as Winston Heywood and the Hombres' "I Will Never Fall in Love with You Again," for which Ansel also did harmonies.

Their first recording, in 1969, was for Lloyd "Matador" Daley. "A song called 'Say, Say,'" Ansel elaborates, singing, "'Don't mix me up in your say-say.' But I don't know if him did release that song," he goes on to explain. He's a little hazy about the rest of the group, but the line-up included "Donald—forget what his last name was but Donald and Oswald Grey. And uh, Louie—forgot his last name also—and Constantine Brown."

In the beginning the driving force for the Meditations was much the same as for many other Jamaican vocal trios—a love of the rootsy American rhythm and blues sound blasting over the radio from Miami. Says Ansel, "We used to listen to groups like the Impressions—

THE MEDITATIONS (LEFT TO RIGHT): ANSEL CRIDLAND, WINSTON WATSON, AND DANNY CLARKE.
Photograph by David K. Wendlinger; © 1997

Impressions was really the main group we listen to in those times, because we listen the harmony." Probably, when all is said and done, Curtis Mayfield and the Impressions, with hits like "People Get Ready" and "Amen," are the one American band all the seventies Jamaican vocal groups emulated. "Impressions and Temptations," adds Winston, "and [Jamaican] singers like Jimmy Cliff. Most of those Motown [groups]—that's how we develop our type of harmony."

Danny Clarke's roots lay in gospel. Also, explains Ansel, he "used to sing with the Rightous Flames them long time ago. With Alton Ellis, him used to do one and two songs with them in that time. Winston is a man coming from the church also, that's why he have that dynamic voice now." Watson at various times also worked with both the rock steady vocal group the Termites and Lloyd Parks's We the People Band. Danny Clarke was the first to use the name the Meditations, for a song ("The Great Messiah") he cut with two of the Hombres (one of whom was the above-mentioned "Louie"), who sang with Ansel on the Linkers' "Nyah Man Story."

Ansel, Winston, and Danny loved to sing together and eventually they joined forces. Although they've split up and re-formed more than once over the years they always seem to drift back together for harmonies, as Winston says, "Because we are so good at it. If I achieve money as a necessity to take care of material things, understand, it's fine, but this is my life! I mean, this is what I am about, this is me, music, the message, the chant and the culture."

"The three a we, we know it," Ansel adds, "we really know the harmony and sometimes we even end up a quarrel over the harmony beca' one seh him want a go up deh one seh dem want—you know, three people, really, you mix a flavor." For Ansel, "Is the work of the most high, you know? Jah. The three of us, is nothing that we learn. Is an inborn concept."

With the exception of one track produced by Ansel and one by JoJo Hookim, their first album was produced by Dobby Dobson. Two cuts, "There Must Be a First Time" and "Rastaman Prayer," were recorded at Lee Perry's Black Ark studio with Perry engineering: they are generally considered to be Perry productions because of the readily identifiable Black Ark sound. This classic album contains such critical tracks as "Woman Is Like a Shadow" (originally cut for Channel One), Cridland's self-produced "Tricked," and Danny Clarke's "Rome" and "Running from Jamaica."

Although the Meditations sang for other producers, they continued to record for Dobson and released a second album called *Wake Up!* It contained gems like "Fly Natty Dread," "Turn Me Loose, and a remake of "Nyah Man Story." After this they went to work for Lee "Scratch" Perry, one of reggae's most fascinating producers. Says Winston, "Lee Perry heard our harmony when we doing "Running from Jamaica" and all those songs and decided that he would like us to do some harmony for him. We went over there to do backup vocal but we end up working with Lee Perry as a producer after the *Wake Up!* album did finish."

"That is late '78 running to '79," Ansel indicates. "This is the time we started working with Scratch. Lee Perry was the connection with we and Bob Marley during that time. I think that is the time when Bob just came back to Jamaica. We do [background vocals on] 'Blackman Redemption' and 'Rastaman Live Up.' And then after that we did 'Punky Reggae Party.'"

Working with Marley was, says Ansel, "Great inspiration, man. Working with Bob and Scratch, I have to link [the two]. Whenever time people ask me about working with Bob I have to include Scratch because I gained knowledge from both those two, how to go about producing a song and what it really takes, determination. Is not like a thing that is just run in there and look at the clock and trying to get it done in a fifteen or ten minute, I mean an hour or something. It's a time. And when you spend time on your work you get better result. But working with Bob Marley it's a great experience." One Meditations single from this period, "Miracles," came out on Marley's Tuff Gong label.

The Meditations also provided backing vocals for other artists, including Jimmy Cliff. Explains Ansel, "We did that one 'Bongo Man a Come.' And we did also '(Cool Down) Mr. Cop' with Gregory Isaacs. We back up a lot of artist, some of them I can't remember, not even myself."

A song called "Man Find It," cut at Channel One in 1979 remained unreleased until the 1994 collection *Deeper Roots* was issued by Heartbeat."That song come a weh that things that was really taking place in the ghetto," says Ansel, "suffering. Even what I been through [in] my life. I was coming on the bus one day from my home and these feelings of depression came down on me while I'm on the bus. So when I get to Three Mile now, me, Winston, and Danny, I was telling them about the song and we started to jam it around. Winston's mother did love that song but it happened that when we go the studio to record we change the style. We have it in a more pocomania style, but we put it in a different style. But I regret changing it and I not even can't find back the feel of that the way I used to have it, sir."

Despite his dissatisfaction this poetic response to the sufferer's life as it stands is really quite beautiful. After fifteen years in the vault it emerges as one of the group's more interesting efforts. "There's a lot of song that we have that really don't come out yet."

He's not talking about songs that were on singles that never made it to album—although there are an astonishing number of those—but songs recorded on now-deteriorating twenty-year-old magnetic tape. "It's on tape and some of those tapes is sticky now. I don't know how we gonna get them played."

With what they'd learned from their association with Perry and Marley (the Wailers even get a "special thanks" on the back cover), the Meditations produced 1980's *Guidance.* Again each member contributed good songs, including Danny Clarke's "Jungle Feeling" and "Play I," Winston Watson's charming "Senorita," and Ansel Cridland's "Hard Life" and "Life Is Not Easy."

Linval Thompson produced some early '80s releases for them like "Sit Down and Reason" and the 1983 album *No More Friend,* which contains the excellent "Book of History." The Roots Radics supplied the backing for the album as well as their subsequent first American tour.

During this tour agreements were reached resulting in *Greatest Hits* (Shanachie), which solidified "some of the old material" as Cridland puts it, for a changing reggae audience. The early eighties brought a new sound and sway to the music as the production styles of the seventies were improved upon by new equipment and ears. A 12-inch single issued in 1984, "Quiet Woman" backed with "Reggae Crazy," was the end of an era for the Meditations, their last release for a while as a trio.

"You see," explains Ansel, "I didn't like [it] up here at all. My thing was to stay in Jamaica. And you know, the group have a little disagree beca' them up here and I'm in Jamaica. So while I was there I was doing material and they was doing their own thing up here." Ansel's solo work from Jamaica (as Ansel Meditation) included mid- to late eighties singles "Lookout Lookout" and "Competition" as well as lead singing on two albums issued by Sky High and the Mau Mau, *Thunder on the Mountain* and *African Vengeance.* Later work featuring Ansel and young singer Yami Bolo was released as *Tribute to Marcus Garvey* for the same label.

During the same period Winston and Danny were not only touring as the Meditations but recording as well. The group's first LP for Heartbeat, 1988's *For the Good of Man,* features this version of the Meditations. *Return of the*

Meditations (1992, also issued by Heartbeat) and subsequent tours heralded Ansel's return to the group, a revitalized trio comfortable with love songs and the social consciousness that made them stand out in the first place.

It included remakes of the Cable's "What Kind of World" and Curtis Mayfield's "Choice of Colors." Of the latter Ansel says, "We go on and do it in a different way." The man who left the band because he didn't like to tour says, "We been on the road all over since." And, as Winston Watson points out, the years of singing together bring an ease some groups can't afford: "Lot of people don't know when we go onna show sometime we not even rehearse because is just one person do the rehearsal and you go out deh and it just dynamic same way."

Of the changes in reggae since the mid-seventies Ansel says, "We sing about things that happening and the way we feel, what we see taking place and the changes that we would like to see happen between mankind. But the younger generation now—it carry a different vibration. You can't put them down. Some of them you cyaan [can't] go with them and some of them it make you think. You see our time in singing, we was doing it for the joy and the pleasure of getting our message across. We never too thinking about money business. But this young generation now it's more a money thing for them now, so how them really see delivering the message now, they just do it for the pledge and the money. Is not basic for them a think how they waan see this earth really run."

But in the case of the Meditations, "Our writing is to bring unification to each and every one. Like that tune I wrote called 'Tricked,' I write about the system that was going on in my time, the politics, we call it politricks, that was taking place there. And when I looked, even some of my bredren end caught up in it. But when I talk to them and show them certain thing and say bwoy, this thing is a using thing, don't [go] to the Persian Gulf, some of them

laugh at me." Another song written by his partner Danny Clarke contains a similar message showing the group's consistency from the '70s to the '90s—"Babylon Trap Them."

One of the strongest elements of the earlier reggae missing for some time in the dancehall, although recently resurfacing, is the influence of Rastafari. Says Ansel, "Those changes no really bother I you know. Beca' hear what. We come here to do a certain thing." "A work," interjects Winston, "and a heap a jump jump up with . . ." Watson continues the thought, "Them little DJ and girl business, but that is just for now. I like all today music but our music will last forever because it's strictly roots and culture." Ansel goes on, "We like singing something that's teaching the people so another twenty years, another hundred years we may not be around but it will teach the children children children." As Winston says, "It have a message about it."

Cridland continues, "Something that spoil kids and tell kids about a discipline thing and 'shot the one and kill the other'—we nah deal with that. We deal with something constructive." Again Winston picks up the thread of thought: "We deal with humanity and the unification of humanity. That's what our music is about. Our message is telling you we should love mankind. You don't have to be black to be wicked or white to be wicked but that's what we're really beating on is the wicked ones. Fighting against the wicked. I know that righteousness must stand continually and we come to exalt Rastafari to the fullest."

Although many have picked up the trappings of Rastafari, the Meditations have always gravitated toward the deeper roots, the Nyahbingi. "That's because," Ansel explains, "our ghetto that we really come out a, we have a lot of that playing down there, the Nyahbingi drum beating and thing, so we have the revival sound." Winston agrees, "The chant, yeah, the chant. We grow up in the chant but we mek ourselves become universal, like we associate with several other other areas which deal with the other kind of reggae, not just Nyahbingi reggae but other reggae music and we combinate them, we combine them so we could get a sound out of it, to get this sound that we have. So that's how we develop the Meditations sound. We're coming from a ghetto where we hear this chant sound every day and a lot of drums, stuff like that, and then we uptown. We are the uptown kind of reggae and then we have in ourselves already a deeper roots."

Another thing that's changed in the last twenty years (besides the music) is the world it's played in. I asked Ansel in 1994 what he thought of recent changes in South Africa. "Well you see, 'nuff of those song that we sing it really fulfill. The long suffering that we been singing about, it really manifest now in certain way. And not even we alone but there are many artist out there like Bob Marley, that song that him sing 'War' all those freedom fighter song that was out there, it manifest now. So it's a joy, you know? And me have it in mind to work on another song coming here: 'Great Change Needs to Be Happening Still.'"

The message of hope in the face of oppression they and others put forward years ago has borne fruit in the real world. As Winston says, "I feel like I've done a work and I've done it well and I'd like a chance to go to South Africa now to chant and celebrate it. It would be my pleasure to be there now."

This same spirit of unification is apparent in the Meditations themselves, who joined their separate careers into one in the beginning and have reunited after years in the end. Waxing philosophical for a moment Winston says,

"You have to be strong. It takes strong forces to have a togetherness like this so long. Some can handle it and some cannot deal with endurance with all the ignorance and all that kind of thing. But I guess we have the determination to put up a resistance against any negativeness that come up against us."

Since their opening salvo was *Message from the Meditations,* it seems only natural to ask what the Meditations' message is today. Says Winston, "My message is telling all humanity to stand firm and keep the faith because if God didn't love us we wouldn't be around. God love everybody. God loves the Chinaman, God loves the white man, God loves the black man. The [black] Muslim religion they just preachin' 'bout black Muslim, you know? But I'm a Rastaman. I am universal.

"You see, black and yellow red and white, all is precious in God's sight. The white man is wicked and you have black man is wicked too. So if he didn't love the white man he would kill them. If he didn't love the black man he would kill them. Put it like this: if he didn't love the devil he'd kill him already too! So you gonna have to portray and influence the force of love, unificate love so that ones and ones which is us could see that God exist. Once you respect humanity you respect life itself and once you respect life you respect God. Life. That's the real message of Rastafari. So just stand firm and keep the faith 'cause all the while you'll be great."

The year 1997 saw the release of *Reggae Crazy* (Nighthawk), which gathered classics like "Stoning Me Away" and "Really Have to Worry" to the mix. The group continues to tour and record their own brand of roots rock reggae.

CHAPTER 10

The Itals:

Jah Glory

The Itals are one of the best vocal groups to have come out of the '70s, the golden age of the Jamaican vocal group. Stinging insightful Rasta lyrics and crisp harmonies brought them to the attention of Nighthawk records, which released a number of impressive albums and kept them touring and visible during reggae's "first wave." Their roots harmony sound helped to define an era.

Keith Porter, who penned the bulk of their material and sings lead for the band, discusses the trio's musical origins. "We start out in earlier days, calling ourselves the Westmorlites. There was Ronnie Davis and I and a couple more guys like Roy Smith, Lloyd Ricketts, we go back to a guy, Lee White, he's no longer in the musical business, but he's coming from way back in time. We started doing some early recordings on our own, but the first Westmorlites tune that come out was on the Studio One label—we do 'Hitey Titey.'"

By this time Davis had left the Westmorlites to join the Tennors, another of Jamaica's incredibly fine early vocal groups, which had hits like "Ride the Donkey" and "Weather Report." Other members of the Tennors were, according to Davis, "A guy named Murphy and another guy named Fats Brown." Davis sang lead for

most of the rock steady trio's recordings. Their song "My World" is a favorite early reggae single and Ronnie burst into the first verse on seeing the single. Davis has also had a distinguished solo career that covers more than thirty different 45s and such albums as *Crucial, Wheel of Life,* and *The Incredible Ronnie Davis Sings for You and I,* as well as a "clash" album with Gregory Isaacs. Among the singles are such essentials as "The Same Folks (Who Put You Where You Are Today)" (as "Ramney" Davis), "Won't You Come Home," "Hungry People," and "No Weak Heart Shall Enter Zion."

After cutting "Hitey Titey" for Coxsone, Porter went to other producers and studios,

THE ITALS (LEFT TO RIGHT): DAVID ISAACS, KEITH PORTER, AND RONNIE DAVIS. Photograph by John Skomdahl

including Clancy Eccles. "I was in the midst of the happenings from a longer time in Kingston," Porter says, "because that's where most of the studios are. When I left to go back to being in the country where I love most I find myself singing in different bands, entertain people on the coast, hotel circuit, things like that. Finally I think more or less it's time for me to move forward to recording."

A street-corner meeting with old singing mate Davis helped move things forward fast. "While I was doing my solo career Keith was back in Westmoreland," recalls Davis. "I did a song by the name of 'Won't You Come Home,' and I remember one morning I was down on Orange Street and I saw Keith just comin' from country. Probably him was there a couple days before I saw him the Monday morning. I remember it's like him have decided he want to get back in the record business and all that so at the time the easiest way was this rhythm track of 'Won't You Come Home.' I told Keith that if he could get some lyrics together for that it would be a nice move. And he went back to the country and come back with 'Ina Dis Ya Time.'"

Porter picks up the story. "I was so anxious to get back in the business that song only take me about two days to complete—serious work, ya know, 'cause when I get the rhythm I went straight back and decide it. It take me two days—not the complete two days but hours out of the day because I say well, this is a chance, I am going to do it."

"Actually," interjects Davis, "it wasn't intended to be a group." (The original 45 came out as by Porter and was later reissued as the Itals.) "It was the producer [Lloyd Campbell] and some other guy, hearing Keith for the first time and knowing me they guessed it would be nice to have us singing together. 'Ina Dis Ya Time' was a boom [a success] and that encourage us, 'cause we used to sing together before and know we sound good, but in doing 'In a Dis Ya Time,' we more courage to keep the group."

"Ina Dis Ya Time" was a profound song during one of reggae's liveliest periods, a musical and lyrical burst of reality much needed then and now. This parable grips you from the opening "whoa whoa yeah" with lyrics like "Birds tangle by their feet/Man a go tangle by them tongue/So it was written, so it must be done/In a dis ya time." If there are modern Psalms—and the Rasta music of the seventies brims with them—this qualifies as one. The song is delivered with an intensity that leaves no doubt about its sincerity. Many sing about consciousness but few display it to the degree Porter does in these lyrics.

"Definitely that's what I believe in," Porter affirms, "consciousness every time, and that's all I-man try to write about, conscious stuff. Even if it's shifting into the love direction, it's still on the conscious line. I try to get it over to the people as much as I can because I definitely know that culture will forever rule."

After this single Porter and Davis were joined again by Lloyd Ricketts, forming one of Jamaica's most formidable trios. During the mid-seventies Jamaican music thrived on 45s, and the Itals released some great ones. Spiderman, the Lloyd Campbell label that released "Ina Dis Ya Time," also put out "Time Will Tell," "Don't Wake the Lion," and "Brutal." "Temptation" on the JA Man label, "Jah Glory" on Top, and "Beware" on Joe Frazier were also among their best.

On many of these tracks you can hear the tight backing sounds of the Roots Radics. "Roots Radics was producing a good sound at that time, man," relates Porter, "so there was no reason not to go with it." This may be one reason the albums produced by Nighthawk sound so consistent when compared with these early singles. These early American albums captured the flavor of Jamaican recording in a way few U.S.-funded projects did at the time.

"Ina Dis Ya Time" and "Don't Wake the Lion" were included on Nighthawk's *Wiser*

Dread anthology, and the group's debut album, *Brutal Out Deh,* came out on the same label in 1981. The LP showcases such permanent standards as "Brutal," "Herbs Pirate," "Run Baldhead Run," "Rastafari Chariot," and "Smile Knotty Dread." The group also appeared on two label anthologies, *Calling Rastafari* and *Knotty Vision,* and released *Give Me Power* in 1983, featuring cuts like "Material Gain," "Roll River Jordan," and "Me Waan Justice." Around this time a 12-inch version of "Jah Glory" and "In Deh," both including dubs, was issued to coincide with a U.S. tour.

The 1985 EP *Rasta Philosophy* continued the Itals' run of quality with standout tracks like "No Call Dread Name" and "Don't Blame It on Me." Their capacity for serious reasoning, tight harmonies, and lively music (still provided by the Roots Radics) was never more evident. Though the Jamaican music scene was changing by the mid-eighties, the Itals held to their roots and culture.

At this point band member Lloyd Ricketts ran into legal problems in Jamaica, resulting in his incarceration and removal from the music scene. David Isaacs replaced him, first on tours and then in the studio. A planned reunion of original members in which Isaacs would have been the opening act had to be scrapped when Ricketts was prevented from entering the States because of visa problems after his release. He has his own band in Jamaica, and remains friends with the group.

Isaacs too has had a solo career encompassing singles and albums in Jamaica and the U.K. His LP *Just Like a Sea* was released in the U.S. as *More Love* (J & M). "Me have a long solo career," Isaacs says. "When they wanted somebody in the Itals because Lloyd was unavailable at that point they both asked me to start up with them. I know both of them for a very long time. I've been working with them for about five years, touring and recording. It's a good experience because I love singing. I love my work."

Why would two singers with solo careers put their individual aspirations aside to sing backup? The answer lies in the distinction between backup and harmony singing. The blending of voices in harmony is one of music's highest forms. And it's one the Itals learned early. Says Isaacs, "I grew up in Kingston but even though Keith and Ronnie grew up in Westmoreland, Kingston is where the record action was. In Jonestown, in the ghetto, part of all the good reggae singers come from the ghetto. Bob Marley came from Trenchtown. Jonestown had a lotta singers too." Keith adds, "Although I-man really born in Westmoreland I live some of my life in Kingston and always kept returning." Other Westmoreland singers include Hopeton Lewis and Peter Tosh.

The retrospective *Early Recordings, 1971–1979* (Nighthawk) anthologizing some of their first 45s, was released in 1987. It also includes early work by Porter and Roy Smith and the Westmorlites. In 1988 *Cool and Dread* was issued by the same label, featuring tracks like "Heathen," "Peace and Love," "Chat with My Woman" and "Jah Help Those Who Help Themselves." Whether bidding good-bye to Babylon ("Sing Farewell") or delivering a lesson in positive economics ("Material Competition"), their message remained unchanged by time.

Of recent Jamaican music changes Isaacs says, "Not to discredit anything but really some of the music now what's coming out of JA, to me, if I was producing, I wouldn't produce some of those records. Hate fe state which one or what producer. I try to keep up with the current as I can but a lot of the lyrics and tracks are disappointing. We are in the business so we must have a favorite, like the [Mighty] Diamonds, keep up the pressure a long time. But now, a generation of vipers has arrived. A different generation taken up this dancehall, you can't really get rid of it but we haffe continue."

"It will forever continue," adds Porter. "It will forever be like in the beginning until even this time. Because right now you can see the people are reaching out for the cultural music all over the world. The cultural music is what the people really want right now, it's what they really need. 'Cause even some of the current stuff they're putting out—okay, as a DJ you play it like five or six times and there it is—some people don't ever wanna play it again."

The lyrical content was one of the first things that attracted many people to reggae music. Groups like the Itals showed a spiritual consciousness, an awareness of what was going on in the world, talking about things in a positive way, even in love songs. Says Porter: "That's why I-man really take the step [of] writing these songs because definitely now love songs are nice, I'm impressed by a lot of love songs, but it reach down to the bottom line, which is the cultural. It's the bottom line and it's also the top, the rest of the other stuff is in the middle."

Davis offers some recollections of the way the music business was and what it's become. "In the '70s when we first started to do recording, we'd have to walk to Duke Reid, to Coxsone, to Lee Perry, to Joe Gibbs, to all the auditions. It would always be a Sunday. They have auditions for artists and I would have to leave from 130 miles to come to Kingston from Westmoreland, and we would come with all our songs and a man say, "Bwoy, I don't like that, come with a next song with that,' and have to go back a country. Until him get to record ya haffe do that a couple of times well before a man decide. Or he's gone or tell you seh well, 'Come mek a record on Monday,' an' we come Monday no recording, him say, 'Bwoy we change recording date—Wednesday probably.' That was a trend in the '70s.

"Now what happen is that a producer just go a the dance and him hear a guy toast on a mike and him just call him fe go inna studio—these guys go into the yard and pick them up now! And most of them now don't respect the older artists, them kinda show off to them artists who set the pace with a little gold chain around them neck and all o' that. Him don't bother or care about the original people.

"It's just a hustling," David continues. "The producer hustle, and even the likkle guy wha' fe sing. A producer dem prefer record an' dancehall singer haffe sing 'cause as it comes out it a hit for three months and it done. Nobody nuh hear about that again. You hear the rhythm but you no hear the lyrics again. There's different lyrics upon the same rhythm.

"So it's a hustling that no help the industry. It helps the producer. And less to the artist 'cause him no get much. A guy give him three or four hundred dollars to just do that an' it sell 10,000 and the producer makes all the money. Him hustling, look here. But weh the money want neither me nor you nor the Itals can't afford to do that 'cause we lost we whole quality an' everything, but that is what is happening in Jamaican music. Them nah check how far the music go."

"Some producers now just want a quick 2,000 sales, nothing more," says Isaacs. "They don't think about what comes next and record comes out and him say well, dancehall man buy a couple, France buy 2,000 copies an' thing, and just dead there. Certain dancehall tunes they just last three or four weeks or a months and they're done. You no have like in the '70s you could hear a good Paragons, a good John Holt, a good Alton [Ellis], Dennis Brown, Delroy Wilson, Ken Boothe, and still you play those things again for years."

But Jamaica's classic music is not dead. According to Isaacs, "In Jamaica now you have people who keep these oldies sessions and play a lot of these '70s artists, tunes like Prince Buster, and good respectable people go to those places and they enjoy themselves! Yeah, and you don't got any fights and all o' dem things going on there. But as soon as you go a dancehall a man bruk up. This thing carry a whole lot of guys who love to make trouble. So these artists like Ken, Alton, these guys will ever stay because their music can always play."

"Right now cultural music is what I really stand for," Porter explains. "'Cause from the time I write 'Ina Dis Ya Time' until this time, whenever time that song start playing anywhere it capture the attention of everybody. It's like you no say blood run through vein 'cause anytime it started it ring a bell in me and the feeling I get from it, I can see other people also in high gear and I respect that and love that. For me doing cover versions of love songs and things like that, it's not saying that Itals wouldn't do a couple cover versions but it's not the Itals way," although they did record one nice one, the 12-inch "What About Me" sung in an American soul style.

In the late '80s the Itals released an original love song on 45 called "Want It Want It" on the On Top label. "That song, when it came out, it never really did get the push," says Davis, "the drive behind it to make it go, from the DJs in JA. It's like a gamble: sometimes you win, sometimes you lose putting out a single to get it establish[ed] the right way. 'Cause some o' dem DJs you have to be in some business with them to really get the record where it needs to go. They got to be 100 percent behind it even if the song is still good."

One advantage the Itals have had over other groups is U.S. distribution. Notes Davis, "We break into the market right off Jamaica into America. Lotta artists go through England, Europe." Has this been one of the things that kept the group together? "Is just Jah still why the group have hold up. You know the ups and downs and changes." "It just come that I'm dedicated to the Itals," Isaacs adds. "Solo work—it don't make sense. I don't really wanna spread out 'cause I'm comfortable singing with them."

As the nineties began the Itals released the CD *Easy to Catch* on the Rhythm Safari label. Again Porter sang the bulk of tunes, including originals "Blood (Thicker Than Water)" and "Hallelujah." Ronnie Davis contributed two tunes, "Play Your Part" and the striking "Too Much Religion." The disc also contained a contemporary reworking of Bob Marley's "Could You Be Loved" including samples and background vocals from the I-Threes.

"The whole intention is to move forward and reach more people," said Keith Porter, "more audience every time, and come with a strong message just the same. I and I stick to the culture. Even if we do a couple of love songs, it's gonna be love directed through culture. I have to give thanks to the Almighty every time, because in every walks he taught me new songs. Every time there's more lyrics comin' in and I really love that so I keep give thanks and praises through time. Every time until this time always have song through the inspiration of the Most High—like He said, just open up your mouth and He will fill it with words—and that's what I believe in every time."

Of the new work he said, "I'm confident in it so much—nobody can hold much more confidence in yourself than you. It's like we comin' strong but we haffe mek it polished because we don't want Philistines to get us down. That's why we have to put it over so we no get in a war with society that would fight with the sound. We put it over clean and decent so the power of it really to brawl it out, but then make them take it 'cause them gon' cursing ya for being very intelligent and getting it over."

"Right now I-man want to encourage listeners and readers," says Porter, "to let them know that this is the time when you can't only listen to the beat of reggae music. You got to listen to what it's saying also you know, 'cause when you get right down to it it's what it's sayin' is really gon' help you. The beat helps—keeps you movin,' 'cause people like to be movin'. But people need to listen more attentively to the lyrics—the words of the song. Yeah, really, I'm appealin' to people 'cause you see, that's how you learn."

A song can be a form of education, "a combination between the rhythm and the lyrics," believes Porter, "so you need to pay more attention to the lyrics. 'Cause the beat is there, you can feel the beat going, right? But to really have that smooth touch of everything going you need to get the lyrics going down also."

More changes came in 1996 when Ronnie Davis formed a new backing group, the Idren, and returned to Nighthawk Records for the solo disc *Come Straight.* Remaking his early hit "Won't You Come Home," he contributed a new set of songs, all in the serious Rasta vein, like "Jah Is My Light" and "If You Conscious." The group was made up of Davis, Robert Doctor, and Roy Smith, an early member of the Westmorlites. Original Itals singer Lloyd Ricketts contributed harmonies. The Itals' *Modern Age* (RAS, 1998) features the trio of Keith Porter, David Isaacs, and the Itals' first female voice, Kada Porter. Lloyd Ricketts adds harmonies to two songs on this disc as well. The band includes old friends like Flabba Holt and Dwight Pickney from the Radics. Although there are more love songs, serious originals such as "Almighty" and "Happen Before the Time" as well as a straight-up ska remake of "Ina Dis Ya Time" make it an Ital delight. In 1998 both the Itals and Ronnie Davis and Idren were on the road, effectively doubling the roots quotient to the delight of their many fans.

CHAPTER 11

The Wailing Souls:

Soul and Fire

One of the most impressive of the early reggae groups was also one of the youngest: the Wailing Souls. The Souls immediately stood out from the crowd for a couple of reasons. Like the Gladiators, whose career in some ways parallels theirs, they had a lead singer who, without trying to imitate, could sound incredibly like Bob Marley. Another striking feature of the original band was that, unlike most others, they were in those days a quartet, not a trio. In most Jamaican vocal groups a lead singer is answered by a two-part harmony in classic call-and-response fashion, occasionally (in the chorus) breaking into three parts. The Souls went one better: a lead vocal answered by a three-part harmony, combining four parts in the chorus. This created a fullness of sound that matched the fullness of their message and helped bring them interest and attention.

Because they were so young when they started—and because of their own determination—the Souls' career spans more than twenty-five years. Like most bands, they've been through some changes. After almost two decades as a quartet they emerged first as a trio and then slimmed down to a duo. But original members Winston "Pipe" Matthews and Lloyd "Bread" McDonald have come through it all with consciousness and direction. They've been at the top of the heap more than once. Their sound ruled the mid-seventies when Channel One was king, and their 1979 Mango LP *Wild Suspense* helped break the music through in the U.S. They reclaimed their position after years of struggle with two Sony albums, returned to their Jamaican roots for a yard-style release, and recently issued an amazing crossover.

From their earliest days in the ghetto of Kingston, surrounded by luminaries like Bob Marley, Peter Tosh, Bunny Wailer, Jimmy Cliff, and Joe Higgs, through their lean years "stranded in L.A.," the Souls have known triumph and tribulation. Pipe and Bread put together their first band, the Renegades, in the mid-sixties. They did several of their earliest recordings for Coxsone Dodd at Studio One, as well as doing some sides for Marley's Tuff Gong label. It was as a quartet they made their name, with members George "Buddy" Haye and Rudolph "Garth" Dennis, a founding member of Black Uhuru who left that group before their first album for a ten-year stint with the Souls that included their classic Channel One recordings. Even the Studio One albums, because they were issued later, picture the quartet of Pipe, Bread, Buddy, and Garth. Nine other albums were recorded and released with this lineup.

In 1985 Buddy and Garth left the band, with Garth subsequently rejoining Black Uhuru and appearing on that group's Mesa releases with original members Don Carlos and Duckie Simpson. Pipe and Bread went on to record four albums with former Earth Disciples member Winston "Ziggy" Thomas and did some U.S. shows with female backup singer Maisha. On *All Over the World* and subsequent releases they appear as a duo with a new sound and direction but a message as timeless as the Bible and more relevant than the daily news.

Lead-voice Pipe began singing when he was just a boy and his earliest recording was ska. "The first record I ever do is a song called 'Little Dilly.' That was when I was first going to school—when I was around twelve years old. I did it for Prince Buster [with a group called the Schoolboys]. And it take a long period of time—about five or six years—before I started again." That was when Pipe and Bread along with Buddy Haye first got together as the Renegades. It was 1965 when, says Bread, "we did our first record [together]. It was called 'Lost Love.'"

Kingston was a hotbed of musical activity in those days. As they moved from the Renegades to the Wailing Souls, official membership remained in flux; like many studio groups they sang with whoever was around at the time. In the yard they might easily have sung with Marley, Simpson, Higgs, Buddy, or Garth in various combinations. As Pipe says, "There was so much music going on. Everybody was doing music and Duckie was like a brother who could come on more time. When we're jamming, is like anybody come in and sing. But those days wasn't any seriousness."

As youths the Souls received support from Higgs, Marley, Tosh, Wailer and others. One singer who Bread particularly reveres is Ken Boothe. "He is a brother, Ken Boothe—he give us good encouragement. Those guys used to travel, tour, even in America from those early days.

THE WAILING SOULS (LEFT TO RIGHT): LLOYD McDONALD ("BREAD") AND WINSTON MATTHEWS ("PIPE"). Photograph by Jan Salzman; © 1995 Phantom Photos

They always used to come back and tell us, boss, don't stop singing. Ken Boothe always give us that type of encouragement and Jimmy Cliff too. Jimmy Cliff know us from before us really tight up as a group, we used to jam with him and Joe Higgs. With the Wailers and all o' them thing. People always come and say one thing: Don't stop sing."

Rastafari was another encouragement for Kingston youth. "Rasta mean righteousness," witnesses Pipe. "Just righteousness you haffe deal with. Rasta is just love, peace, and happiness with everyone. Rasta live happy with everyone. Peace and love, man. We is the people that really look 'pon the real things of life. And deal with the real things of life. See it? [Babylon] deal with the imaginary things. And that can't work. Because them tell you seh go a school to have some sense. They can't tell you that! The youths them a go to school, have them education and still can't find a job. They feel like they gonna do everything for you— make you like a robot! Them say do as I say but don't do as I do." Pipe looks at Bread and they both laugh.

"But you know, is just life. And all you have to know seh—all wha' go on earth can finish right now if everybody just come together. All of the famine, all the separation. Just respect love, man—just look into it and know what love is."

Yard-style singing created informal relationships that stayed informal into the Souls' early studio work. Two elements that remained constant were Pipe and Bread. On the early Studio One recordings they were sometimes joined by Norman Davis and Oswald Downer on harmonies. These recordings, done for producer Coxsone Dodd, first made the group known in Jamaica.

Pipe and Bread still hold Coxsone in high regard. "We always have a good relationship with him," says Pipe. "Cause him always say we have the talent. From the first time we go record for him he always deal with we good." In those days when a new group went to Coxsone, "he usually say come back in a week. But the first day we went, we never even go fe record. We go to audition. But he wanted us to record that same day! We said no, we didn't come to record." Dodd had them return the following Monday. "We just did 'Back Out with It' right away. 'Row Fisherman Row' and 'Mr. Fire Coal Man.' First session that."

Not bad for a first session. "Mr. Fire Coal Man" is a sharp glimpse of a defining moment. "Police are wailin' in the streets now/Jackie, get up off the floor. . . ." The "fire coal man" is a Jamaican fireman. "We a look 'pon fire coal man as a black man," clarifies Bread. "Fire coal is black. So is kinda all a vision that we have at that time." The vision comes from "just what's takin' place. The youths are wailing, fire burning; it's reality. The message is: live on, 'cause these things happen every day. Always happen. The kids them was taught that them must believe in make-believe. So when the reality comes and the real McCoy face them, they don't know what to do. And we is the group that always a try to sing to soothe people mind, put them thoughts in a right dimension, think positively.

"Right now we don't feel like no youth out there who a grow up now pass through anything like we a been through in our time in the ghetto o' Trenchtown. So we can tell any youth about anything them doin' out there. We have been through that. How you mean? We have been through worse."

The early recordings are collected on their first Studio One album, *The Wailing Souls*. This and another albums' worth of material, later issued as *Soul and Power* on the same label, "were recorded in a twelve-month period," says Pipe. "I was goin' to trade [school] and all o' that," Bread smiles. "Teenage days."

"Mr. Fire Coal Man" was cut over the same rhythm that the Silvertones used for "Burning in My Soul." To avoid a confusion of names with label-mate Bob Marley's Wailers (not to mention the Wailers early Wail N Soul M label), some of their singles were issued under the names the Classics and Pipe and the Pipers. Finally, says Bread, "the Wailing Souls is the original name, so we have to get right forward to that."

Besides recording for Coxsone, the Souls did a couple of songs on Bob Marley's fledgling Tuff Gong label, including the classic "Harbor Shark" and a one-off for Micron. But, says, Bread, "We

GARTH DENNIS. Photograph by John Skomdahl

really started professionally at the time Buddy and Garth joined us. That's when we really started. That's when we said: This is our life. Stopped doing other stuff. 'Cause we all working and stuff like that. All the recording before that was just like something that we could do and liked doing."

In 1976 a new studio—Channel One—was making a name for itself doing new rockers-style versions of classic Coxsone rhythms, a practice that still feeds that Jamaican recording industry today. The Souls jumped in with a remake of their "Back Out with It," adding a new melody and lyrics and calling the tune

"Things and Time." "It was a comeback song," says Pipe. "A number one song." Another track from these sessions was "Jah Jah Give Us Life to Live." This was also at the point, says Bread, 'we're bringing Garth in.'"

"Channel One was really the breaking point," continues Pipe. "That was really where we had some great number one singles." The 12-inch single was just beginning to boom in Jamaica then, and "Very Well," "Fire a Mus Mus Tell" and remakes of their Studio One 45s "Back Out" and "Fire Coal Man" were in great demand as was one of their best songs from this period, "War."

According to Pipe, "'War'—that song was written about a thing just like what just go on in L.A." (the riots after the acquittal of the police who beat Rodney King). "But more people died. More than a hundred people died in Trenchtown. Bombing and shooting and burning. That's how we get that inspiration at that time to write that song."

The popularity of their Channel One work, in Bread's words, "made other producers, even Coxsone who had that *Soul and Power* album, re-release those songs." The tunes sold so well that the Souls were able to set up their own label, Massive, and release their own productions. "That's when we split from Channel One." Using the same musicians and the same studio, they issued a series of singles, including "Bredda Gravalicious" and "Feel the Spirit," every bit as powerful as their Channel One sides.

By this time reggae was putting pressure on the international music scene. Yard-mates Marley, Tosh, and Wailer carved out individual careers for themselves, and early friends and mentors like Higgs and Cliff were touring. The Souls made a deal with Island and remixed songs from this period—adding in some horn parts not on the original singles—and released the album *Wild Suspense* on Mango. Says Pipe, "We were there in London while they were doing that. We mixed that album *Wild Suspense*. We produced it also. We just want it sound different."

After the Island period the foursome joined forces with Sly and Robbie for a few releases on their Taxi label, and then began working with producer Junjo Lawes. Junjo was a massive force in the early eighties, with a direct connection to the English Greensleeves label. Some of the Wailing Souls' hardest-hitting recordings resulted, including the 12-inch "Kingdom Rise Kingdom Fall."

"Political struggle and political uprising don't stop till now," says Pipe of this prophetic track. "Babylon back still against the wall. 'Cause them trying to find a solution now to solve this catastrophe which them haffe face right now! With these young generations that the Bible was telling them about, generation of vipers. Them never make the plan. Them try to keep hiding things. The truth is standing and the lie is running. From we made 'Kingdom Rise Kingdom Fall,' them no leave offa the Earth yet."

During this period the group recorded the albums *Fire House Rock, Inchpinchers,* and *Baby Come Rock* with Junjo Lawes, most of which were released in England on Greensleeves. "They have a wide collection of our music," Pipe says. "They were our main distributor in Europe and we did about five albums with them." Material from this period is also included on three similarly titled LPs: *Best of the Wailing Soul* (Empire, 1984), which reissues JoJo Hookim's Channel One productions; *The Best of Wailing Soul* (Sunset, 1985), produced by Junjo Lawes; and *The Very Best of the Wailing Souls* (Greensleeves, 1987), which combines tracks from these producers, the Wailing Souls themselves, and Linval Thompson.

With Thompson they also recorded an album released on Jah Guidance titled *Wailing*. "We haffe do these things to let the people know we are still here," Pipe explains. "Keep the music going. Because what really happen most of the time we found that things might not be going right with we and the producer. 'Cause like there is more things that the producer could do that he is not doing. So we take a break, we try somebody else. Ca' you haffe trust some one and you mostly have the talent and you want it reach out there. And ya do want it to go out there, so you haffe keep doing these little things. At the same time it's a form of survival inna those period, you haffe maintain yourself by eating food, wearing clothes, have a likkle fun more time—an' you have all your family to take care of."

A hit record in Jamaica doesn't make the same kind of money it does in America, and as Pipe says, "It just go right back into something. Something is there waiting for it. To take it out. There is no loose ends. Something always there waiting to take out a likkle money. So you just have to go back and try something. I know struggling, boss. I'm a struggler. Any day you call upon the name of Jah, remember seh take up the cross, you gonna have to deal with it."

"Through all o' that we know the money may not be comin' right now," says Bread, but later on it will 'cause we doin' the work we a want to do. We write these songs. These songs will always be ours." Pipe nods. "That's why we never promote a bad song. People have told us, 'Bwoy, you never wrote a bad song.'"

In 1981 the Souls set off on a tour that landed them in a place that has had a major effect on their lives from that point on—California. Their first appearance in L.A. was at a converted Safeway market called the Country Club. "That was our first year in the United States," recalls Pipe. We had never been here before. As Jah said, 'Some man will have to search and seek them food in desolate places.' So we have to come out to California."

Seeing the group live was an incredible experience. Each of the quartet had a distinctly different style of moving. Instead of dancing in choreographed steps like the Temptations or Four Tops, they seemed to writhe like one creature with four separate bodies. The buzz of their harmonies was overwhelming.

All the Souls would eventually live for awhile in Los Angeles and sometimes they seemed like lost angels. "Stranded in L.A.," the title track of their 1984 LP *Stranded* (Greensleeves/Shanachie), extended beyond the automotive breakdown that originally inspired the song. The group split in two, with Garth and Buddy staying in Southern California as Pipe and Bread returned to Jamaica. "Two of our original members just went on ahead," says Bread. "That is what they have to do. This is what we have to do." Buddy eventually returned to Jamaica, and Garth for a lengthy period to his previous band, Black Uhuru. "Every man have his own message to spread, remarks Pipe. "Him have to carry it in a different form, different dimension."

Back in Jamaica, Pipe and Bread joined forces with the young singer Ziggy Thomas. They cut three albums for producer Delroy Wright, released on Live and Learn in Jamaica: *Lay It on the Line, Kingston 14,* and *Reggae Inna Firehouse.* The release of the latter album in 1987 on the eve of their first Sony release (on the short-lived subsidiary Chaos) caused some consternation for Pipe and Bread. They had, they said, attempted to contact the producer regarding its status many times in the intervening years.

"We try over and over to get in touch with them," reasons Pipe. "We write him a letter. No reply. First of all, we don't have a written contract with them for nothing. And the law of this country say a man must not put out no production with you unless you and him have a contract. Is America, a no like in Jamaica.

"Me no live in Jamaica no more. Them things are over. Them have a company with lots of stuff and this is America with lots of laws," he sighs. "Every way you can talk about it, boss, I been ripped off by these producers in Jamaica. All these years I been singing I was getting really ripped off." Adds Bread, "Some of them even got ripped off themselves." Pipe reasons, "They sell the music short." This is why many

Jamaicans refer to producers contemptuously as "reducers." Of course, they also refer to lawyers as "liars."

"We always put our trust in people and they always let we down," laments Pipe. "Is one of the main things to our career, we always trust these guys who come and say all right, him sound like him have a clear mind how to make things work. And yet when him see the record start sell, him just start taking everything for himself."

Between the final Live and Learn album and *All Over the World* the Souls recorded *Stormy Night* in Jamaica (issued by Rohit in the U.S.) with Prince Jammy. The title song is a perfect example of the Souls' own natural mystic. "We wrote that song in February [1987] and the storm [Hurricane Gilbert] came in October," Pipe recalls.

The beginning of the '90s found Pipe and Bread again in California. They did some shows and recorded some demos. Then, as Pipe tells it, "We just get the opportunity. We always know the day would come. All those works were not in vain! We know the only thing that could stop us from getting this opportunity was if we give it up. And we nah give it up!"

To be signed by a major label like Sony meant more to the Wailing Souls than a hefty retainer would have, Bread relates. "We come to see a day like today when you can turn on your radio and they have reggae music on their playlist. On all these big commercial stations. Every day! Not just special time for a couple of hours. In the mainstream. So the music can reach the widest possible audience. This is what we been working for—opportunity to really reach the masses."

All Over the World rendered reggae music in the state-of-the-art American studio style of the nineties. "This music gonna reach a broader section of people now," said Pipe. "We still have some old kinda songs on there like 'Shark Attack' and so on. But a song like 'All Over the World' is geared to really everybody. This is what we

want to do and it was no mistake. It have to evolve. Things have to be done to the music to get it from the stage that it is. 'Cause every music evolve. They still have that roots but you still have to go somewhere else. And it stay where it is now for a very long time, so we kinda try to move in another direction right now."

"We were always thinking of doing this," adds Bread, "but the opportunity never really arise until we made the demo and CBS became interested. The music is getting there. It's gonna get there. Maybe we are the ones to really put it there. Bob took it certain places and Peter and all them other great Jamaican artists.

"Jah will it that it is our time to do it, take it a little further. Just like a lot of people take consciousness and bring it out in the street. A lot of people are saying now is really the time to stand up. All these different countries breaking off from Russia. Every tub have to stand on its own bottom. Every vine have to find its own fig tree. Them made the Berlin Wall sound like it was such an invincible thing. But it gone."

Pipe agrees. "Music reach every corner of the world. Can never end. One thing we always say: the best is yet to come. So we always have a song to come. You see, we don't make music just for a minority. We make music for everyone."

"And now we bring a kind of music they haven't heard in a while," continues Bread. "They've been played one type of music right now. Dancehall music is irie, cause we dancehall same way. Dancehall still. We're trying to move this in a new direction. And you can't leave out the DJ." On *All Over the World* I do some DJ and we have another rapper called [Papa] Juggy." The original Jamaican DJ U Roy also joins in on "You Ain't Leaving." So even with a modern sound, as Pipe puts it: "We not forgetting the roots. 'Cause anytime you forget your roots you gone. If a tree lost its roots it die."

All Over the World was nominated for a Grammy in 1993. "That was one of the most exciting moments of my life," says Pipe. With a broad smile Bread adds, "After all these years in the music business." "It was an experience to see what really take place," continues Pipe. Bread adds, "We have a space now. It's nice to see some recognition for some longtime artists who are trying to keep the music conscious."

The Wailing Souls were the first reggae act to play on *The Tonight Show.* Videos from the album were featured on MTV. The group contributed to the soundtrack of the Disney film *Cool Runnings* and opened shows for 10,000 Maniacs, Santana, and Bob Dylan, spreading their roots harmony sound to a whole new audience. What a stretch for two singers from Trenchtown!

"When we had our first box guitar," remarks Pipe, "what we call acoustic guitar, is seven of us put the money together. Because we were such a unified set of youth coming up. One guitar, and everybody learn to play from that one guitar." Still, for reggae, "is still a long way to go but we have to keep plugging. Reggae gonna come so big that you find every time you turn you gonna hear reggae music."

"And not just underground," Bread says, again picking up the thread. At a recent Bill Graham show the crowd—"pure rock people"—piled on the band so heavily "we had to put our back against the wall." Signing autographs with lightning speed, the duo literally write their way out of a tough spot.

The Wailing Soul's next album, *Live On* (Zoo International), reflected these changes. They covered tunes from both ends of the rock spectrum ("Mother and Child Reunion" and "Na, Na, Hey, Hey") but updated their sound on originals like "Bandits" and "O.K. Corral" to include elements of rock, R&B, rap, and dancehall. To critics of these changes Pipe carefully explained their attitude.

"We have these elements from long ago," explains Pipe."Even with Bob, me and Bob sit down in my doorway, ca' Bread and I have a song called 'One Day the World Will Know' and 'Who No Waan Come Can Stay' and Bob start say, 'Boy, you have fe go international because them music too big for the people them here.' You see, Jamaica is a little small place. To really get the demands out of the music you have to take it out there international. When you is a music man the door a open, no boundaries. You play music, if you lock up the house it creep out somewhere, somebody hear that. So you can't stop the music, man, you have to explore different corners of the world 'cause everywhere in the world, every corner of the world you have people a suffer and a struggle."

"I tell you all the while, I don't partial. I deal with everyone. 'Cause is my Father make everyone. The earth is the Lord and the fullness thereof, they that dwell therein, I and I. Everybody. The people are not blind anymore. The time will come when the people all realize [and say], 'You can't tell me that no more.' 'Cause the same thing you tell me over and over again. The whole thing is livity. Any time we can know fe live with each other, that's when things nice. Respect each other. Me respect every man."

"That's why music is so important in this time," explains Bread. "'Cause music is like the background for the whole thing in life. You see a movie without background music— is like the movie dead. This is what keep most of the people from really flaring up most of the time. Soothe the heart. Its very important to be puttin' out the right type of message in music."

And reggae music in particular brings "all people together like no other music. Rock music bring a certain selection of people, folk music bring a certain section of people, soul music, country and western and so on. But reggae—everybody! You bruk up some people at a reggae concert—this man is into Grateful Dead or Rolling Stone but him still into reggae! Time, boss, the music a come to unify.

The people music—simple little music, is not no professor going to no room and draw up nah scales or nothin'."

"The thing about it," according to Pipe, "is it's your own everyday rhythm. When you're walking you keep the rhythm and your heart keep the beat. To play reggae, you haffe clean the system altogether, man. Come up with a different vibe. Don't go too fast now, just go with the flow of the heartbeat."

The world has changed a lot since the early days of reggae, but as Pipe says, "Nah make it change you. You have to stand strong and change it back. 'Cause you know is destruction that Babylon head towards. We call it beating. A sometimes people see things happening to them, and them wondering why it's happening. And is now Jah decide to beat you. You get a beating from your father for certain things you do. Like them people them a come out and preach the gospel and then diggin' out the people around the corner. That can't work, man. 'Cause most people don't know the creator not sleepin'. 'Cause him no sleep. Him see everything a guy do.

"A guy feel like him can just do anything and get away with it, think nobody sees it. But there's always been an unseen eye. Every man say him is the stronger man but every man on Earth is a man. Every man is equal. Every man carry the same amount of parts. A lot of people think is them alone to live. One set o' people. I want them to realize God make up this Earth with a pair. You have a day, you have night. You have sun, you have moon. You have stars. You have the elements. Man, you have woman, male and female in all species. So wha' you a run talk about you alone? God no partial, boss, 'cause if God was partial he wouldn't make all o' this type o' people."

Although they come with all the trappings of modernity, the Wailing Souls carry an ancient thought. "As I say to Bread sometimes," observes Pipe, "I say Bread, is the Almighty preserve we.

To do His work. So now is the time. I don't feel like nothing can go wrong. 'Cause all these years we been through, there's a lot of people get frustrated and give it up. Some die."

"We don't believe we come 'pon earth to die,' says Bread.

Pipe continues, "You have a man in every generation come and say peace and love. That can never die. You always got somebody say peace and love. So it gon' get stronger and stronger if you just speak the word and live it."

In 1995 Island Jamaica reissued the Wailing Souls' ground-breaking *Wild Suspense* LP, including a half dozen dubs previously available only on 7-inch single B-sides. The Sony buyout of Columbia eventually eliminated the sub-labels Chaos and Zoo International and the Wailing Souls made an independent move, returning to Jamaica to record their rootsiest album in years, *Tension* (Pow Wow) with co-producers Freddie McGregor and Noel and Dalton Browne. Once again the disc ran the gamut from tender ("Holding on to Your Embrace") to teacher (the Nyahbingi-inspired anti-violence anthem "Son of a Gun").

On the disc they recut several of their own classics for the new age, including "Back out Wid It" and the early "Mr. Fire Coal Man." Their international approach was not neglected; witness the inclusion of "Fukuoka," aimed directly at the growing group of Japanese reggae fans. The sound is nineties digital but much closer to the "yard style" than their two previous major label releases.

As Bread says of the latest trends in Jamaica, "The dancehall and the slackness out there running, but we have to keep the pressure." Pipe picks up the beat as if one voice speaks through the two of them: "Well, there's a pure in everything. You must have good and bad because you keep the world in balance." Bread goes on, "Rough and smooth. Still we glad to see that the music is being promoted. So all power to Jah."

As to why the Wailing Souls have survived so long and continue to reach new plateaus, the two again speak as one. "We write about what we see and know and sing about it. We don't write no false thing about people yet we know a lot of people like them things more time. All these years we a struggle for the reggae music. And look how much come and drop out. Wailing Souls is still here at the right time now. 'Nuff a dem come in this music red-eye business them say we'll try that too, and some a them get lucky but as you get their first album then you don't hear about them again 'cause them can't come up with a second one, and if you check their first album them don't write one song on it. But me give thanks and praise to the Almighty every day him give me the artistic ability to write and sing songs. No bother try and fool the people, ca' if we a fool the people all these years we wouldn't be here today. Music, Rasta! The race is not for for the swift but for he who can endure it."

In 1998 the Wailing Souls released *Psychedelic Souls* (Pow Wow). Produced again by Richard Feldman, who helmed their work for Sony, the duo romps through a rock-reggae fusion of their Jamaican roots with songs from the sixties delivered in a nineties style. Who but the Wailing Souls could add a triple-time jungle riddim to the Beatles ("Tomorrow Never Knows"), completely revamp the Doors ("Love Her Madly"), the Who ("My Generation"), and Bob Dylan ("Like a Rolling Stone") and make you like it? Bud and Eric from Sublime guest and the disc is experimental (check out their take on Hendrix's "Waterfall") and, best of all, fun.

CHAPTER 12

Black Uhuru:

Uhuru Means Freedom

From their inception Black Uhuru has been a strong voice for freedom and justice. They are a major part of the revolutionary and inspirational vibe that reggae has spread throughout the world. From classic songs like "General Penitentiary," "What Is Life," "I Love King Selassie," "Party Next Door," and "Emotional Slaughter" through incendiary mid-period productions like "Great Train Robbery" to later works like "Iron Storm" and "Genocide," they have helped to define the sound of their time. In the words of longtime member Duckie Simpson, "Whatever I'd like to say is in the music. It's through the music I and I talk still."

When Bob Marley died in 1981, many saw Black Uhuru as the band best positioned to lead reggae's continuing assault. Internal problems caused a series of setbacks, but after many changes Black Uhuru is still one of the best-known names in reggae. When I talked with the seldom-interviewed Duckie Simpson in 1992 the band had recently re-formed in their original lineup—Garth Dennis, Don Carlos, and Derrick "Duckie" Simpson. The story of Black Uhuru—changes and all—is one of reggae's most interesting object lessons. Although his version is at times at variance with others, he has seldom gone "on record" to this degree.

"From I was young I was conscious," Duckie says of his early days before the band. "I start playing some football . . . soccer. Then I realize that this ain't gonna pay off. That was something I make an early choice of. Then I met Garth. And Garth had just come from Trenchtown, from that whole Bob Marley area, to Waterhouse."

Garth's sister Joey was a member of the duo Andy and Joey, whose ska song "You're Wondering Now" was a hit for Coxsone and was later versioned by the Specials, a major U.K. two-tone group in the first U.K. ska revival.

BLACK UHURU. Photograph by Jan Salzman; © 1992 Phantom Photos

"And Garth was really from that musical background, Bob Marley, even Ken Boothe—he knew all of them. He came to live on my road and I was sayin', 'Hey, let's do some singing.' And then we recruited Don Carlos."

Another version has Garth and Don forming the group before Duckie came in. What is certain is that the trio recorded together, releasing the first records under the name Black Uhuru. "We did a couple of songs together," recalled Don Carlos in an earlier conversation. "We recorded one for Dynamics, the name of it was 'Folk Song' [a Curtis Mayfield song, released on the Top Cat label], and another one for Randy's, 'Time Is on Our Side.'" "After that," says Duckie, "we went our separate ways."

"What really happen to those records," according to Don Carlos, "in Jamaica, lotta piracy. Eventually we don't even know what become of that. Once we get a little money a man just buy we out—him don't even release it too tough in Jamaica, him just send it over far country."

By this time the underside of Jamaica's recording industry should have been no surprise to Don. His first recording, "Please Stop Your Lying, Girl," was co-written with Errol Dunkley. But the version that was released later as an Amalgamated 45 featured Dunkley alone.

After the split of the original Black Uhuru, Don began a long and distinguished solo career. His first record was produced by Bunny Lee. After that he recorded for Gregory Isaacs's Zairena label. "Me and Gregory walk around and sell it," he explains. "It was a version of a Drifters' song, 'Magic Moment.' It's comin' from a long way." His solo works include clash albums (in which each artist does one side) with Anthony Johnson and Gladiators, two albums with his partner Gold, and at least seven solo albums produced by the like of Flaco Palmer, Bunny Lee, Junjo Lawes, and RAS Records' Gary "Dr. Dread" Himmelfarb. Don himself produced 1987's *Deeply Concerned*.

GARTH DENNIS. Photograph by John Skomdahl

Garth gained fame as one of the Wailing Souls. His "Slow Coach" is a classic early solo 45 that has also been anthologized as a Wailing Souls record. He was a member of the band for ten years and appears on much of their mid-period material beginning with their early work for Channel One. As Duckie tells it, Garth wasn't the only crossover between the two bands.

"For that whole time we start hanging out in Trenchtown with Bob Marley and the Wailing Souls—I learned most of my music from the Wailing Souls and Bob Marley—that was my university. I sang with the Wailing Souls before Garth. I did two songs with them, one of them by the name of 'Liberty' and a next one. That was after me, Don, and Garth . . . were still hangin' out but we weren't singing together." Of the Wailing Souls he says, "We were kinda like close—I learned a lot from their music."

After Don and Garth left, Duckie re-formed the band with Anthony "Michael" Rose and Errol Nelson of the Jayes. "Me and Michael was rehearsing at the time that I did these songs with the Wailing Souls. Because I was always planning on having my own group. So Garth was the first one we had approached to be the next third member, but Garth had already give his commitment to the Wailing Souls. So we recruit Errol."

This version of the band recorded the first Black Uhuru album, variously released as *Love Crisis* (Jammy's, 1977) or *Black Sounds of Freedom* (Greensleeves, 1981). These tracks also inspired one of the hottest dub albums of all time, first released as *Jammy's in Lion Dub Style* (Jammy's, 1981) and remixed and re-released as *Uhuru in Dub* (CSA, 1982).

After the first album Errol returned to the Jayes and was replaced by Puma Jones. A perky American woman who won the hearts of thousands of fans with her freestyle dancing, she added to Uhuru's distinctive harmony sound live and on records. Puma provided continuity through the band's Michael Rose and Junior Reid periods (more about those in interviews to follow with these two former lead singers of the group). She appeared on most of their best-known albums and was an important part of the trademark Uhuru sight and sound from the mid-seventies through the mid-eighties.

If the tension of egos propelled the band during its mid-period (as was often rumored at the time), it was the presence of Puma, who seldom sang lead but added her talent to the overall blend, that seemed to resolve and dissipate the tension. Her presence signified the revolutionary role of women in the new order that reggae attempted to bring about. I first saw her before she joined Black Uhuru, singing back-up for the American-born reggae singer Jack Miller (she also performed with Ras Michael and the Sons and Daughters of Negus in her pre-Uhuru days). In interviews she was articulate and effective, and as an artist she was always musically engaging.

The lineup of Michael, Puma, and Duckie was probably the band's most famous, due in part to backing support and production from drummer Sly Dunbar and bassist Robbie Shakespeare. The Riddim Twins produced *Showcase* (1979, released on Virgin simply as *Black Uhuru*) before the group signed with Island. *Showcase* contained several of the Jamaican 45s that made the band so accessible, like "Guess Who's Coming to Dinner" and the almost melancholy "Leaving to Zion." The latter version, which included the hit single "Shine Eye Gal," was reissued as *Guess Who's Coming to Dinner* by Heartbeat in 1983.

The first Uhuru album on Island, 1980's *Sinsemilla,* introduced the fast-paced, modern sound that became the band's trademark as the combination of Sly and Robbie and Michael, Puma, and Duckie cut a new path out of the '70s for reggae. At one point Sly and Robbie were treated by Island almost as members of the band. They got back-cover photos on 1982's *Chill Out* and the live release *Tear It Up* from the same year, and by the time 1983's *Anthem* came out they even posed with the trio for the U.S. release's front-cover photo. Uhuru seemed like one big happy family, but success brought problems of its own.

One of the problems, according to Duckie, had to do with Michael Rose and writing. "Writing caused a lot of rifts. He [Michael] wanted to do all the writing. So we just allowed him. Instead of making, of causing a problem, you know? That was the only reason why he wrote so many songs." It should be noted here that both his work with Uhuru and later solo releases show Rose to be one of reggae's finest singers and songwriters.

Duckie referred to Black Uhuru's long stint at Island in two succinct words: "That's history. The Island period was very rough." He says the band had "no financial benefits from that period. They tricked us into signing a bad contract. . . . So we had to work all those years for nothing, paid no royalties from all those CDs, albums, I've not gotten a cent royalties. Yet, they say we still owe them! I don't know for what. When we were with Island CD wasn't invented. So you can imagine."

Red (1981) was nominated one of the top twenty-five albums of the decade by Rolling Stone magazine. It also gained the group a coveted cover story from *Musician* magazine, and many rock critics considered it a high point for reggae. But according to Duckie, it brought no money for the band. A live video accompanied the following year's *Tear It Up*. A greatest hits album (*Reggae Greats*) in 1983 and *Anthem* and *Dub Factor* in 1984 closed their association with Island. A double-CD compilation titled *Liberation: The Island Anthology* from 1993 selects from the period and adds scarce 10- and 12-inch mixes.

Just as the contract Duckie claims they were tricked into signing expired, "Michael left the group. And after that, then everything fall down.

DUCKIE SIMPSON. Photograph by John Skomdahl

That period was not what you have seen on the outside." While to many inspired by their revolutionary music the band exemplified the epitome of their Little Steven-penned hit "Solidarity," there was, as Duckie recalls, "a lot of fight within the group."

When Uhuru left Island, producer-musicians Sly and Robbie stayed with the label, yet the group and duo have no hard feelings. As late as 1991's *Iron Storm,* Sly sat in on drums and according to Duckie, Robbie planned to as well. "He was in Miami, he came the day we finish. What happened with Island, I didn't really blame those guys. It was the lead singer who really mess everything up." (Michael Rose tells his own version of this conflict in the interview that follows.) "Because we already had known that we got swindled. But our contract was still there and it was a seven-year contract. And things was gonna happen now and then the guy walk."

How is it Duckie wound up with the name instead of Michael? "Well I'm the founder and original member," claims Duckie. "I formed the band." But he didn't control it. "When we were working we didn't work in that sense that I was the controller. It was like a free-for-all thing. Like whatever we got [from concerts and the like], we split fifty-fifty between me, Puma, and Rose. And at that time Sly and Robbie was the producer. Plus the musicians, right? So like we just used to go on the road, we used to like take orders—do whatever we're told." In the early days, he says, they were young and naive, they "didn't understand the business and thing, and thought there was maybe some benefit in there for us. But at the end, there was a lot of madness."

Despite the craziness, some great music was recorded. Ducky freely admits, "That stuff was my best musical career." And even if they didn't make a lot of money they certainly became well-known worldwide. "That's where the money went, to make our name." The Black Uhuru sound—mystical, Far Eastern, haunting—influenced groups and singers as diverse

as Foundation and Eek-A Mouse. One singer who drew from the sound and then became a part of it was Black Uhuru's next lead-man, Junior Reid.

"Junior Reid was from the same background," says Duckie, "he hangs out on the same corner. And he was younger than us, a younger singer, he always admire and imitate us. Over the years he got to know the sound. 'Cause he was from nine years old growing up with the sound."

In 1986, with Reid taking the lion's share of lead vocals (Puma and Duckie sang lead on one song each), Sly and Robbie again backed the band on *Brutal* (RAS). Reid brought a renewed energy to the band and songs like "Great Train Robbery," "Fit You Haffe Fit," and "Dread in the Mountain." He also took the helm for 1987's *Positive.* Dub albums of both records—logically titled *Brutal Dub* and *Positive Dub*—were released by RAS.

This era of the band closed out with two releases on the American Rohit label, *Live in New York* and *Love Dub.* The latter gathers remnants of what appears to be an aborted album mixed with Prince Jammy (one song, a recut of their classic "I Love King Selassie" surfaced as a single) sans vocals. It's possible some of these tracks were never voiced—no album corresponds to these dubs—and it stands as an Uhuru album that might have been.

Positive was the first Uhuru album after their first (with their second lineup) without Puma Jones. She left the band for health reasons just before it was recorded and was replaced by Jamaican singer Olafunke. Sadly, Puma died of cancer in 1990. In some later versions of the band Garth, Don and Duckie (and later Garth and Don) have been joined on stage by female singers as if to acknowledge Puma's contribution as a part of the "original" Black Uhuru sound.

Like Michael Rose, Junior Reid eventually left the band to pursue a solo career. Says Duckie somewhat dismissively, "They thought they'd made it." Both have successful solo careers.

Rose and Reid's solo careers are detailed in the interviews that follow, as are their own views of their days with the band.

As Don Carlos says of the split of the original lineup, "The more spread out is the more people hear the sound. Instead of a group of people come together and just spread one sound—it's like it kind of narrow. When me spread it, him spread it, Garth spread it, and other people spread it, it will keep on coming over instead of a group of people say it and it just die out. The more we do it separate, the more it keep on keeping on."

Garth, in the same early interview with Don Carlos, likened the split to the Wailers. "Bob was there most of the time doing most of the lead vocals and other people, like Bunny Wailer, such great performers in their own right." These changes give the individual artist the chance to work in a different environment. "Sometimes," said Garth, "things just happen for the best."

The way Duckie sees it, "This sound, it's a unique sound that I got with the sound. And whosoever I put together, that sound comes out. I'm like the backbone of the sound. I know the sound. At first when we started people used to say, 'I don't think you guys are gonna make it—your sound, well, I never heard people singin' that way. It's original, you know? Can't be copied. That vocal style was a killer."

And who originated it? "Don [Carlos] was the first," claimed Duckie when I interviewed him. "A lot of people think that Don imitate Michael. But Michael imitate Don! We were the first guys in the neighborhood as singers. Michael and Junior were there as young singers. So they learned from us."

I asked Duckie what it was like to have his original band back together after all these years. "The original is always the best. These guys— no ego trips and things. Man just cool and we're all in the same age bracket and comin' through the same environment. So I don't get that egotistic attitude."

The regrouping came about by virtual coincidence. Don and Garth were both booked for an awards show in California to be headlined by Black Uhuru, which at that point was Reid, Simpson, and Olafunke. Reagan-era visa laws, which barred Jamaican performers who had played regularly in the States, kept Reid out and an instant reunion of original members was put together to save the show. This led to a series of meetings and eventually 1990's *Now*, their first of several albums for Mesa.

Now was a definite experiment," explains Duckie. "We went to Europe and toured all those songs before we had even recorded them and saw this vibe that we get and then came in and recorded them." Naturally, a dub album of the same tracks—*Now Dub*—followed. The dubs were unusual in the canon as they included a great deal of vocal in the mix.

The following year they released *Iron Storm*. The title song "Is about America and Iraq and about what happened to Puma Jones and Peter Tosh. Because she really did get a raw deal. So young and thing and drop out of the running and . . . [the song] go back to talk about the whole concept of America oppressing Third World countries and people."

Iron Storm also contained 'Breakout,' "that's Garth's song. It's about the day when South Africa free. Like he said, he wanna be the first to sing freedom songs in South Africa. When Africa free, Black Uhuru wanna be the first. But you know what's amazing, people talkin' about apartheid and Africa bein' free—it's not that simple. Because when South Africa free that means that the world's free. And they gotta be free in America first because America is the one who's holding apartheid, America, Britain, and France. They are the main upholders of apartheid. So a lot of people don't know how deep it is.

"The African, they blaspheme, because they fight against their king. Them fight against king Emperor Haile Selassie I. So it's just tribulation.

That's why in this modern time you see all this vicious suffering happening in Africa, man, tribulation. No one can help them. A lot of people say to me how can Africa be Zion and all these people be dyin'? That's un-understandable. A different thing. The Western world will never understand that. That was predicted by the emperor in his Geneva speech."

Iron Storm begat *Iron Storm Dub* and was followed by 1992's *Mystical Truth.* The Mesa albums signaled another new direction for Black Uhuru as they worked new elements into their music and tinkered with their always-forward sound. Rapper Ice T guested on Iron Storm's "Tip of the Iceberg" and DJ Louie Rankin was featured on one tune on *Mystical Truth.* A cover of "Hey Joe" snagged airplay for *Now* and *Mystical Truth* featured covers of War's "Slippin' into Darkness" and Peter Gabriel's "Mercy Street." *Mystical Truth Dub* followed.

In 1994 the band returned with a set of all originals titled *Strongg,* and the nearly simultaneously released *Strongg Dubb.* Duckie began singing more and all three singers trade off vocals inside the songs. "That is because we are cool," says Duckie, a fascinating remark from an entertainer known for seldom removing his sunglasses. "Most lead singer, they just wanna sing lead. A lot of guys feel like when they're singin' lead, they're up front. Up front don't necessarily mean singin' lead.

"That was the problem with the past groups. These singers don't care if I sing lead or what. The other guys they felt, 'You're tryin' to take away my spot.' If I say, 'Let me lead two tunes,' it will cause an argument and bad vibes, and so I was easy going. I didn't mind leading or whatsoever. At first, the Uhuru before, if they didn't even want me to sing lead I didn't mind. It was my band, so if they wanna pay me for not working I told them I'll just stand here and get paid, no problem. It was a lot of running fight."

Of Jamaican music Duckie muses, "They're having this controversy down there, which music is better, DJ or singers. To understand the politics of it you have to come down and surmise for yourself. And all these little amateur singers . . . you see, it's a business. And the less you put in and the more you take out, then your business is [successful]. So they go for the little amateur artist, make five cents here and a five cent there.

"It's still a quick hustling. They promote the DJ because the DJ have a different consciousness from us. Most of these veteran singers are dreadlock Rastas. These young little DJs are some fashion dressed-up guys with smart haircuts and earrings."

And the music itself? "A lot of the music is mumbo-jumbo," complained Duckie. "I used to listen to music a lot. I don't really listen that much now. Or if I listen, I listen to old stuff. Maybe it's because I'm getting older still, but a lot of the music nowadays is unfinished, not properly done. Production low, off-key.

Since the mid-eighties, he says, "A lot of the music scene has slipped. You have a lot of hustlers now into the music business. They have the money but they don't really know how to go about doin' it so they just record this guy here, that guy there, and put out an album then start gettin' popular and pretty soon he's the biggest producer around and he makes a bag of off-key music."

On the positive side, he says, "My artist is Culture. Me like Culture and one or two artists like Admiral Tibet, Macka B, [Charlie] Chaplin. You see, in Jamaica, the way it's run here, a lot of people don't even know that Black Uhuru exist. Yet we are one of the leading reggae groups in the world! They promote certain artist on the radio every day. People don't know you have local artists here who come to America and can't even draw two humdred people. When they go there and do a little concert they come back home and talk a lot of bullshit. I'm more low profile. When you see me in Jamaica, you don't even think or know that I'm a singer or anything. When I reach outside of Jamaica, then I have a musical voice."

Sometime after this interview Black Uhuru entered another transition. A rift developed between Duckie and Don and Garth that resulted in Duckie playing Europe with dub poet Yasus Afari as Black Uhuru, and Don and Garth touring as Black Uhuru without Duckie, sometimes adding a female singer to the lineup in an eerie reminder of the days of Puma Jones. Legal wrangling kept this version of the group from recording, though Don and Garth were featured live on concert compilations such as *RORX: The Tenth Annual Reggae on the Rocks,* which interestingly also features Michael Rose.

In 1997 Duckie issued a single in Jamaica as Black Uhuru (and singing a rare lead); it was a version of Michael Rose's "General Penitentiary." Don and Garth were said to have won the rights to the name for performance in Jamaica. In early 1998 Duckie won a court case against the two in L.A. Shortly thereafter, Don Carlos released his first new solo album in years, *7 Days a Week* (RAS). In October of 1998 the first Black Uhuru album in years appeared. On *Unification* (Five Star General) the group consists of Duckie Simpson, Jennifer Connally, and their latest lead singer, Andrew Bees, whose debut CD, *Militant* (RAS), created a stir in 1995. Produced by King Jammy, the sound is in the tradition of the Uhuru of old, with Duckie himself reprising the band's early "Wood for My Fire" as "Babylon Fall with John Paul." Whether the new band will strike a chord with their old audience remains to be seen.

CHAPTER 13

Michael Rose:

By Any Other Name

Michael Rose—who is given to Africanized spellings of his name such as Mykal Roze and variants—is for many the quintessential lead singer of Black Uhuru. It was he who penned and sang many of their best-known records like "Guess Who's Coming to Dinner," "Party Next Door," and "Sinsemilla," songs both Rose and the alternate lineups of Black Uhuru have continued to perform live. His songs and style helped catapult the band from an obscure yard roots trio to international renown, redirecting and revitalizing reggae with a breathtaking forward motion.

With Rose up front, ethereal harmonies from Puma Jones, and Duckie Simpson and the pulsating human rhythm machine constructed, primed, and driven way over the limit by drummer Sly Dunbar and bassist Robbie Shakespeare, the group became an awesome live and recording unit that moved from the ghetto of Trenchtown to the cover of *Musician* magazine and, within a few years, bagged the first reggae Grammy. And then Rose seemed to disappear.

The group went on to continued success with Junior Reid at the helm and later re-formed with Garth Dennis and Don Carlos. Duckie Simpson presented his view of the band in the previous interview. In 1995 I sat down with a Michael Rose who was just beginning to emerge from ten years that saw plenty of recording activity in Jamaica but no American releases, a situation which has since been greatly altered.

Michael Anthony Rose was born in and grew up in Kingston 11. "In the ghetto they used to call me Tony Rose, before it [the name Michael Rose] build up so big." He was drawn to music early because, he says, "My brothers

MICHAEL ROSE. Photograph by David K. Wendlinger; © 1997

used to sing. They used to sing the harmony music and end-of-year like Christmas carol and all these things. But my older brother had an accident and he died and we start deal with the music after that. I used to listen to like B.B. King, you know, Temptations, Tavares, Smokey Robinson—a whole bunch of harmony artists."

His first recording was a song called "Woman a Gineal Fe True" by "Tony." "Actually," he says, "that song was a DJ—it was a B-side—the A-side was 'Woman a Gineal Fe True,' the flip-side was with the DJ [Rose] singing." He identi-fies the singer of the A-side as Andel Forgie, who "writes for a paper now in New York." The record was produced by "A guy called Newton Simmons" and issued on SRS, which stands for Simmons Recording Studio. Except for his tone of voice, the record is hardly identifiable as the Michael Rose we know today.

At this time, "I used to do talent shows in Jamaica and then after that—this is like singing now, right? Solo, I used to be on the North Coast entertaining tourists and all this where you sing like calypso, dinner music, R&B—everything. And then after that I left the coast, came back to the city where Sly dem—we grew up in the same neighborhood, Waterhouse. So check Sly and tell him say me want to do some recording."

This took place "in about '72. But I recorded 'Guess Who's Coming to Dinner' [the original recording, issued under the title "Dreadlocks Coming to Dinner"] in that time with Niney the Observer." Other early recordings include "Love Between Us," "Freedom Over Me," and "Clap the Barber." "And is like then Sly realize say that 'you can do the singing thing,' so him say fe get an album ready. But at the time he was touring with Peter Touch [Tosh], so by this now they went on a long tour and when they came back we check Jammy's. And Jammy's say, 'Bwoy, well, do the album with me, man.' You know, okay. Me, Ducky and this guy called Errol— Errol Nelson. He used to sing with a group named the Jayes."

The resulting album was Black Uhuru's first, variously titled *Love Crisis* and *Black Sounds of Freedom*. On the cover, Duckie, Michael, and Errol can be seen in front of "a little house next door a Channel One studio. On the same hand. Right beside it." The album was an instant roots classic with tracks like "African Love" and "I Love King Selassie," all written by Rose. The latter he says was written with "inspiration by bredren, still. Friends tell us bwoy, you should do a song about King Selassie." The album had such a different sound it seemed to signal a new direction for reggae. "But," says Rose, "we never mek no money and such so Errol get fed up and we had to start look for another singer. That's how we run into Puma. We saw Puma singing to a Bob Marley album an' we ask her if she would be interested to sing with us. She said fine."

When I ask about Puma, Michael grows meditative. "Yeah, well, Puma. Mmmmm. Puma played a great part in Black Uhuru because she had the sound, you know, particular sound and it meshes [in] combination. Me always respect her vibes all the while as a person. You know, I-man respect that. It's just that unfortu-nately she died young. After I left the band they were still going on and then all of a sud-den I heard that she was sick. She used to call me a couple of times—I used to like introduce her to bush doctor [herbalist] she can go to get help [from] but like, she go one time and she don't go back. Maybe it just get to her, maybe she was just sick."

Michael, Puma, and Duckie recorded a series of 7- and 12-inch releases that became *Showcase* (issued with early photos of the trio including Errol) and later in America as *Guess Who's Coming to Dinner*. Rose confirms the line-up looking at the cover: "This guy wasn't the guy who sing on this thing you know—that is Puma." "General Penitentiary," "Plastic Smile," and "Leaving to Zion" are among the outstand-ing cuts, all written by Rose. "This was a good album too, you know," says Michael, "but hear what happened: it come ahead of its time."

The cutting-edge sound nonetheless led to a contract with Island Records and 1980's *Sinsemilla,* one of reggae's defining discs. When I went to Jamaica in 1981 you couldn't walk past three or four houses without hearing this album booming from doors and windows of houses and shops. Cab drivers, old women in bars, kids on the street—everybody in Jamaica was listening to Black Uhuru.

The group opened that year's Reggae Sunsplash, a tribute to the recently deceased reggae superstar Bob Marley, and by the end of that year the album *Red,* with cuts like Rose's "Youth of Eglington" and "Sponji Reggae" was big in England and making inroads in American airplay and sales as well. "The Red album came out in like the top 100 thing wha' them did have Bruce Springsteen, Michael Jackson. It was rated as, like rock album," Rose says proudly. "I think it was number 20 or something." *Chill Out* broke new ground in 1982 as well, taking the sound in newer, futuristic directions. And 1983's *Anthem* won the band the first reggae Grammy.

Michael maintains there was no blow-up when he left the band. "We didn't have anything verbal. It's just that we couldn't do business anymore and I decided to do my own thing and they decided to continue and that was just it." He says today there are no hard feelings. "Even Sly and Robbie, nuff respect due to them because you know them guys are genius at work. Even Niney, have to give Niney credit because he's one of the man that start the business. It's just that I decide to do my thing and I'd like to see my, whatever I'm doing, I'd like to see it established."

At the time of the interview Rose had just recorded a new single with Junior Reid, long rumored to be his musical nemesis. "The reason for that song, to tell you the truth, a lot of people feel because Junior Reid was in Black Uhuru and I wasn't there they feel like there was a vibes like we don't talk or we have things personal. So I do 'Burn Down Rome' [produced by Junior Reid and issued on his JR label] to show the public that there's no chip on our shoulders."

Trying to escape identification with the band has been a kind of albatross for Rose. Some of his best known early work is indelibly identified with Black Uhuru. But Rose is moving forward on his own and clearly bears the band no ill will today. "We used to smoke chalice together. I think Black Uhuru is nominated for the Grammy this time too. So things is happening for them." He smiles. "So it's time for things to happen for Michael. When I left the group it's like me did decide to cool out and do a little farming, you know. So, ten years later me decide to start doing some recording."

Although very little of it was commercially available in America, Rose has actually done a massive amount of recording since leaving Black Uhuru. Singles and 12-inches (strangely called disco singles in Jamaica, though they aren't what we would call disco) were released on Observer, his own Michael Grammy Rose label, and Sly and Robbie's Taxi. A 1990 English album, *Proud* (RCA International, not picked up in the U.S.) balanced yard-style cuts like "Demonstration" with pop experimentation.

"When you sign to record companies sometime your manager start telling you you should do this, you should do that, and sometimes you end up doing the wrong thing—but it's music and people love music so I'm versatile so this is why you hear these things," Rose explains. Another album, *Bonanza,* was issued only in Japan. "You have to take the plane" to get that one, he says with a laugh. Recently a disc recorded in the early nineties with Sly showed up in New York as *Mykall Rose: The Taxi Sessions* (on Taxi, though I've only seen it as a pre-release), and a mid-nineties LP *Last Chance* (Ruff Cut), produced by Junjo Lawes, charted in the U.K. While Rose was farming he was sowing and reaping a bumper crop of music, cultivating an advanced style and sound that built on his Black Uhuru days.

None of this material was available commercially in America, but that began to change with the 1995 release of *Michael Rose,* produced by Niney the Observer, on Heartbeat. The sound of this disc was uncompromising and uncompromised, putting Rose back in the arena. Among the outstanding songs were the 7-inch releases "Short Temper," "Don't Play with Fire," and a joust at Duckie Simpson titled "Duck Duck, a Who You" reclaiming Rose's Uhuru works. Once again Rose came with a stepped-up beat and delivery that touched his early Black Uhuru sound while pointing to the future.

Michael Rose kicked off a flood of new releases. The self-produced *Be Yourself* (1996, also on Heartbeat) contained the hip-hop crossover "Rude Boys (Back in Town")," remakes of classics like "Guess Who's Coming to Dinner" and "I Love King Selassie," and quirky tunes only Rose could write, such as "From Babylon to Timbuktu." A corresponding dub album, *Michael Rose in Dub: Big Sounds Frontline* for the same label, dubbed up the *Be Yourself* LP with bonus tracks dubbing from the previous disc as well.

In typical Jamaican fashion, though this time from an American label, a career resurgence opened the gates to previous work "in the can" and new interest from other producers. *Nuh Carbon* (1996, RAS) was produced by Jah Screw and included cuts like "Once Bitten" and "Ordinary Man" that featured a raw and engaging delivery over Screw's bare nineties tracks. Singles and 12-inches poured from Jamaica including powerful cuts like "Eden"

MYKAL ROSE. Photograph by Jan Salzman; © 1995 Phantom Photos

on Tappa Zukie's Tappa label that haven't yet found their way to LP.

In 1997 Rose delivered what could be his most powerful disc to date, *Dance Wicked*, released simultaneously with the dub version *Dub Wicked*, both again on the Heartbeat label. Taking his style to new heights in cuts like "See and Blind," "Reality," and "Life in the Ghetto," he incorporates today's dancehall flavor while keeping his lyrics firmly in a cultural mode.

"What I notice is that most of the DJs are going to reality right now," he says of the music today. "So like the sort of arms house thing is cutting down. Most of the youths them a see Rasta right now, like Capleton and Tony Rebel, as before he is strong, and Buju Banton. So the DJ now, even Beenie Man, it's the same kinda dancehall style but it's more reality." Three years down the line this assessment is still right on the money.

For Rose this is not just a return to consciousness, but to Rastafari. "The time now, it's like the table don't stay firm, you know. It turns. So it's just one a them thing that the table turn right now. You have a lot of good singers as you know, [the late] Garnett Silk. We have tragic—we lost a good youth. Yeah mon." Other singers he mentions are Wayne Wonder and Sanchez: "He's singing reality now—a whole bunch a young youth. Is like Jamaica's a eyeball that people has to watch. 'Cause a lot of great thing's going on. As you notice Ini Kamoze has his "Hotsteppers," so reggae is massive right now. Big." He also mentions American groups Arrested Development and N.W.A. And where does he fit into the picture?

"Michael Rose, if you're listening, it's like a new sound presently. Most of the old slangs, I have like new ones now: 'Tu chu chwang!'" he illustrates. "As time goes on I always have new ones.

I come up with new vibes." New vibes for new times, but Michael doesn't see the times as any less dread. The music and the slang may have changed, but as to the message, "Well, as you notice, nothing has changed. Things get worse but people just ha' fe live with it. You know 'cause it's a system where you just can't get away from it. Today you have a president and in the next six years you have another president—it's just one a them thing that everything just go round and round. It's just that the sound wha' you hear now you wouldn't get to hear them three years ago. And the lyrics them you can't say you hear the same lyrics wha' you hear upon *Red*. Is different now."

"So even though they may know his music, a lot of people don't know Michael Rose. They know Black Uhuru." With his new music, says Michael, "I think a lot of people will get to know who Michael Rose is." And the Michael Rose they're going to get to know is, in his own words, "Badder than you. 'Cause in early time when I used to play, if you see a youth in the street in New York or whatever you say to him you're an African they say no, I'm an American. They believe in the American dream. But of recent a lot of the street youth them start to like the hip-hop reggae and sing about Africa and these things. So we know that the music— they're listening the music. The music a reach."

The year 1997 saw the release of *Selassie I Showcase* (Melodie), containing cuts recorded in England from producers Frenchie and Fashion. Standout tracks include "Rush on the Tonic" and "Jah Is My Shepard," the latter featuring guest DJ Cutty Ranks. Late in 1998 Michael issued his first live solo CD, *Party in Session— Live* (Heartbeat). He continues to thrill audiences around the world.

CHAPTER 14

Junior Reid:

The Strong Survive

If you wanted to sum up Junior Reid in one word it would have to be "independent." From his first vocal group Voice of Progress and early solo work as "Little" Junior Reid through his stint as lead singer of Black Uhuru in the mid-'80s and his later career as artist, producer, and label head, Reid has done things his own way, creating a sound like no one else's. If influenced by singers like Michael Rose and Don Carlos, he has also influenced an upcoming generation of singers like Yami Bolo and others. As a producer his work has a sound all its own—no matter who's singing there's a Junior Reid feel.

JUNIOR REID. Photograph by Jan Salzman; © 1997 Phantom Photos

Born Delroy Reid in Kingston, Jamaica, in 1963, the man called Junior began recording at an age when most of us were just listening to music. "My first record was at the age of fourteen, produced by Hugh Mundell" he explains. The song, "Speak the Truth," was issued on Augustus Pablo's Rockers label. "This is the record that make me up till now. That's how it start."

Previous to this Reid considered himself more of a DJ than a singer. "I used to DJ first and I used to sing, but mostly I used to penetrate the DJ." But Mundell "him hear me DJ and him hear me singing and tell me that this singer must really sing." Reid's friend from the Waterhouse area, singer Locksley Castell, cut his first record ("Babylon World") for Pablo. "When I see my friend coming to the area with a song and a vine him now, it motivate me even more to know that I can do it. Because we all hang out together, you know? So when I sing, Locksley Castell tell me that I'm singin' in the same air. Same melody. So him kinda teach me about air. 'Speak the truth and speak it ever cause it what it will.' 'Bye Saint Peter, bye Saint Paul,' 'Jah is the true and living God,' see, is actually the same air. So him let me know what is the difference between air and air."

Mundell asked Castell to bring Reid by the studio "and him is asking me about the songs that we was workin' out in the back of the yard. But I was givin' him the DJ style and him was saying no man, not that one that. We sing 'Speak the Truth' and him seh, yeah, that one there. So we did a rehearsal with Augustus Pablo." Pablo, by this time a seasoned studio pro, bluntly told Reid he was singing flat. "Which at the time I really didn't understand what is flat. I leave to come back but before I even come back I get a call that Hugh Mundell is working at Harry J Studio and to meet him. I come round there, they laid a rhythm. And then I get a next message saying you will be working at King Tubby's, which King Tubby's Studio is just down the road where I live in Kingston 11 [Waterhouse]."

When he went to sing on the track, "I just take one take and that song was voiced. I find myself doing the intro, taking the solo and coming back in, doing everything that was supposed to be done besides never knowing the difference between solo, intro or bridge or nothing was called because I was doing everything. So it amaze them. To see well naturally he just a do it." With Mundell producing, Reid, on other sessions, also cut the flip-side of a Mundell disco 45 titled "Can't Pop No Style." "My song was on the B-side titled 'Know Myself.' Mundell also "did a song called 'Run Come Come Inna the Dance,' and [in a talking intro] me seh like, 'the man have some faith and wait man, so whe the man a deal I-man can pay my rent."

Mundell and Reid went on to become close friends. Mundell helped guide his career and was to produce an album for him but his own life was cut short by gunfire—a tragedy to which Reid was witness. "After losing him I had to go out there and sing for different producers and then when I build myself up to a certain level I just start to do me things more independent."

That first single hit number six on the English pre-release charts and Reid began to get attention from other producers. "Negus Roots [a U.K. label] come into Jamaica and I did two singles for them, 'Sister Dawn' and 'If I.' Then now they want me to do a album because the vibes was good for Junior Reid in England. I did have some guys that I hang out with called my friends and they used to like the music and they wanted to join up with me. So we true link through the love of a friend. They want to be involved so I just say all right, I will involve them. We name ourselves as Voice of Progress. So when the guy from Negus Roots come back to do the album I change my name from Junior Reid to Voice of Progress." Negus Roots released the album, titled *Mini Bus Driver,* in 1981.

In what became a career trend for his involvement with groups, Reid relates, "I was writing the material and singing the songs." The album was released to moderate success but when it came time to record a follow-up record the group had problems. "They wasn't singing how they was supposed to sing. And I don't know how this [first] album get done, but the second album—they couldn't get it right. So it just kind of sway me away from things. I just decided to go forward as Junior Reid." The salvageable tracks from the botched second Voice of Progress album were later issued as one-half of *Firehouse Clash: Junior Reid and Don Carlos* on the Live and Learn label.

Reid returned with "A-1 Lover" with Sugar Minott and his first solo album, *Boom Shak-A-Lak Rock,* produced by Jammy and released by Greensleeves in 1983. It was later re-released as *Big Timer* (VP) with a few changes. His next song was "Junior Nature." "Then I get some rhythm tracks from Jammy's so I voice some songs on them for myself and take them to Sugar Minott and we together produce *Foreign Mind* and just compile the album." *Original Foreign Mind* was issued on Sunset in JA and Black Roots in the U.K. in slightly differing mixes.

A hyperactive period of touring and recording followed. His first trip to England had been a promotional campaign with Negus Roots in 1981. After returning to Jamaica he toured again with Sugar Minott and Don Carlos (as Worry Struggle and Problem) in '83. A flurry of recordings for various producers between tours resulted in singles like "Youth Man" (issued on Sunset), "Poor Man Transportation (Rockers Forever)," and others, some of which have recently been collected on two combination albums released on Tamoki Wambesi, *Two of a Kind: Junior Reid and Teezy* and *Double Top: Junior Reid and*

DON CARLOS (LEFT) AND SUGAR MINOTT (RIGHT). Photograph by John Skomdahl

Cornell Campbell. "After that I did a U.S. tour." The tour featured Reid, Sugar Minott, Michael Palmer, and Half Pint.

On returning to Jamaica, "I hear that Black Uhuru having problems with the group and they want me to lead the group. They are from the same area [as Reid] and at the time Black Uhuru is the group that is at the forefront of reggae and the first reggae group to win the Grammy award. So to keep up the standard of reggae music, knowing that Bob Marley wasn't around anymore and ting, I see Black Uhuru as the group that was keeping the front line." Rather than see the group break up and knowing "that they respect me and I could strengthen it, I just link with them and we work together." Black Uhuru was at the height of their power when Rose split from the band. They were playing large halls and getting unheard of press in Europe and America. With Reid at the helm the reconstituted Black Uhuru issued *Brutal* on RAS.

Reid says he was unintimidated by the stature of the group. "I just know that it's my job and I have to do it and I'm comfortable and confident in the victory. So maybe Sly and Robbie [then powering the band's rhythm section] them did have doubts but I didn't have any doubts 'cause I know what I can do, and even the lead guy for the band, Duckie Simpson, he know that I'm capable of accomplishing the job that's why he requested me." Todd Simpson said in an interview he'd known Reid since he was "a kid," Reid smiles. "Yeah. So is a long time him been watching me. Because he know that somewhere down the line he gonna have a problem with Michael Rose. So him know that was him next resort to go to Junior Reid."

"Even when I was doing this album *Mini Bus Driver*," relates Reid, "is Sly and Robbie them produce the album. When I leave the studio they want to get back in touch with me to come and work with the Taxi label and they say they couldn't get ahold of me because they didn't know how to contact me. They always telling Duckie that they want to see Junior Reid, like to do some work with him but Duckie didn't let me know. Him keep me away because him know that him gon' need me down the line and if I did go and tie up with them and sing a lot of tracks, maybe when him ready him couldn't get me. When we on the tour bus now [with Black Uhuru] we talking, that's the way the conversation come up. Sly them say long them want to get in touch with me and Duckie say well me couldn't mek you go tie up me artist and me know say me go have problem down the line."

Reid had recorded but not released an early version of his song "Fit You Haffe Fit." When approached it seemed like the perfect song to begin the new association with. The band began working on other Reid tunes as well. He describes an eerie feeling of pre-déjà vu. "When I was on the road touring with Don Carlos and Sugar Minott I saw a lot of posters for Black Uhuru, looking for Black Uhuru coming next month or whatever and at the time I really didn't know that it was me they were gonna request to come back to do me show! So I find myself just leaving the show touring in the States go back to Jamaica work onna album. Within a month we finish the album and then I was back on the road touring now as Black Uhuru."

His first gig with the band was intense. "Normally we start a tour out a state or whatever. That tour Black Uhuru just start right in the middle of everything in New York, in Manhattan. We did four shows at the Ritz, two tonight and two the following night and fans that came for the first shows they stay and watch the second show so one that was out there waiting for the second show have to come back the second day.

"A lot of people they was expecting it not gonna work and don't see how me fit in the band but I already see myself in the band because I already have certain songs which is song of freedom. Because I sing song of freedom which is like 'Babylon Release the Chain' and when I come to Black Uhuru now I bring those song in the group and work them in on stage with Black Uhuru singing harmony behind. Then now sing my song like 'Let Us Pray,' 'Fit You Haffe Fit,' 'Brutal,' 'Great Train Robbery,' with some [already established Black Uhuru tunes written by Michael Rose like] 'General Penitentiary' and some other songs. So the fans who love those songs don't miss from hearing them."

One of these shows was later issued as *Live in New York City* on Rohit, interestingly featuring Santa Davis (formerly of the Soul Syndicate, the drummer who replaced Sly Dunbar in Peter Tosh's Word Sound and Power band and currently drumming for the American reggae group Big Mountain) and Chris Meredith on bass. Like *Brutal,* the vocal lineup featured Junior Reid on lead, harmonies from anchor man Duckie Simpson, and the mystical vibrations of Puma Jones.

"Puma Jones is part of the influence that influence me to go into Black Uhuru" says Reid of the late legendary female vocalist. "I like her performance and how she sang. I like how she present herself, the way she come over in her interviews. I admire those things like that about her and I admire how she dance on stage. I just imagine those movements behind me moving. Is special, you understand? That support my energy. Because anytime I look around and I see Puma is more a right mood because she's pushing me, you know? And when Puma leave the band, when Puma pass away now is like I no feel the same about the band anymore. Although we get a new girl, 'cause Olafunke replace her, but I didn't feel Olafunke any way."

Although *Positive* (RAS), the album recorded with Olafunke (and again backed by Sly and Robbie) was well received, for Reid the vibe just wasn't the same. "On stage and off stage, everything was changed. Olafunke is a nice girl and thing but away from that I think that Puma

have a better vibes, you know." For Reid the band had lost its magic "and the feelings and everything." Interestingly aside from 7-inch single B-sides the dub albums of *Brutal* and *Positive* issued by RAS are the only Junior Reid dubs available to date.

The story of Black Uhuru seems riddled with a vague apprehension of dread. Reid, for instance, is suspicious of the graphics on his three Uhuru albums. Noting his face is masked by a scarf on the cover of *Brutal,* he elaborates, "They use the wrong picture them all the while when nobody know nothing. If you notice this again: I'm covered in a lot of photos. Why they use the one of me with glass hiding my face and just a little piece like that [on the cover of *Positive*] and with this now [*Live in New York City*] they didn't feature me on the front of the jacket. What is going on here is some likkle—permission that they mustn't feature me too much. So you can see that they can't take the vibes of Junior Reid in Black Uhuru, is like them try to hide that from the world."

Reid shakes his dreadlocked head and gazes through the window philosophically. "Well, this is history because in the fields of music you always find lead singer leave band and go solo. But I leave solo and go into a band then leave the band and go back solo. I enter the band with hit song and I leave the band with hit song. I enter with 'Fit You Haffe Fit' and I leave it with 'One Blood.' So you know me know what the people want."

At the time Junior Reid left Black Uhuru, visa problems complicated his ability to tour with the group. By way of explanation Reid says, "There's a lot of politics going on with this group right now, right? You see? I didn't have a problem traveling as Junior Reid before I went into Black Uhuru. When I leave my solo career and go into Black Uhuru, Black Uhuru was the next group behind that get promote 'longside Bob Marley."

In many people's expectations Black Uhuru was the group poised to fill the gap left by the death of Bob Marley. "So they didn't want no one there to fill no gap. Ca' they want to keep that kingdom. The industry didn't want no other man that have the influence of the people as how Bob Marley have the influence of the people. Me shouldn't call them name still—you can gather, but through music politics they seh now we're gonna work on Junior Reid and we can market this, we can sell this, we have this and can do this and we don't have anyone to come to us to ask any publishing or royalties, we can just do whatever we want to do with this."

The plotline is straight out of noir fiction, like Kenneth Fearing's *The Big Clock*. The threatened music monolith creates division within the group through money problems, ego problems, visa problems—"I don't know, but I just know them send a lot of confusion within the band. So the band did mash up and stay so and dem don't care about that cause them didn't want to go no further with the reggae music. 'Cause where it reach where them have it them must know them can sell it there and keep it so.

"So if they're producing, like seh Bob Marley's selling ten million a year, them don't want no competition against no living man. So Black Uhuru can capable a selling ten million and so around there them no really want it because what we are doing, we are educating people and teaching people but they are spending millions

JUNIOR REID. Photograph by Jan Salzman; © 1997 Phantom Photos

to lead the people astray. While we just utter and sing some songs and keeping some people together. And so on. All these people getting together on a positive and a conscious level. They don't want it like that, they want fe just mess up the world! The evil spirit and wicked people dem ting so."

When Reid joined Black Uhuru he dreamed of signing with Island Records. "Then after, I get to find out that there wasn't any backing from the Island. This was just me, Duckie Simpson and Puma! There wasn't even Sly and Robbie. We did have to pay Sly and Robbie to come on the road at that time. A large salary. To be on the road. But not me. Duckie. 'Cause Duckie want to save the band. So he put out that money. But I don't think no man have a money that the band could a go on. Me never see much money but me never really a do it for the money, me just do it for the love. When I get in the band I was on the road paying some old bills for the band that they leave on the road."

Despite financial setbacks, on return to Jamaica they began to work on *Positive*. Ca' we no watch nobody, me tell them right now me believe in doin' the right thing for us and for people have to come after us and thing." Touring behind *Positive,* "The bus alone that we have on tour, how massive it was, with the first album nominated for Grammy and this little RAS Record comin' a independent and at the time we and Black Uhuru bigger than RAS Records. We was the first artist to take RAS to the Grammy awards."

But on returning to JA "of a sudden me just having visa problem. Police come to my house and take over my visa problem. And I owe them nothing. I'm not a criminal, I don't have any conviction! I have a clean record. I never murder no one, I never do nothing against the law that I go up to prison and spend any time for or anything like that. Any likkle thing was a misdemeanor like a likkle joint smoking or— you know? And a lotta time the police come

up and seh that they hold me a smoking joint, when it's a lie. Is not saying don't smoke joint, you understand me, but they tell lie on you."

The root of the problem is clear to Reid. "It's just to mash up the band why them take away my visa. I didn't realize it at that time but growing up and looking back now in the business I can see everything, is like a book before me. Them wanna stop the band. When I couldn't get no visa and I go to the embassy, just telling me they suspect me as involved in things. And poor little me who is a little guy who don't buy a house and don't have a car!"

Reid says he took out bank loans to buy his father a house and purchase a car when he joined the group, "just to make Black Uhuru look good. I didn't get any advance going to Black Uhuru but people in Jamaica they're expecting big things so me just profiling big 'cause I have ambition. A lot of people saw me, because when I was Junior Reid I wasn't driving. But since I'm in Black Uhuru I just went and there wasn't any backative [support] behind it, getting a deal or something so I just make it be a deal for myself."

With Black Uhuru Reid played Sunsplash Europe and toured "Italy, Greece, all over. While I was in Europe now the 'Great Train Robbery' was number 40 on the British chart and that is the biggest Black Uhuru song ever go into international chart is 'Great Train Robbery,' Junior Reid." While in England Reid cut what was to have been a one-off 12-inch for Big Life Records after meeting its head, Charles Summers, then having great success with the group Wham (from which singer George Michael later emerged). The track was "Stop This Crazy Thing." "They want to sign me but I tell them I will sing on this one track and I won't be able to perform it on live show. I'll do one and two things solo but if you want to see me live you have to see me with the band."

As Reid continued touring with Black Uhuru, "Stop This Crazy Thing" moved up the British charts. "But when I reach Berlin the company contact me in East Germany and tell me that the song is number 20 on the British chart and they're gonna need me to fly in to do *Top of the Pops*. While I was in Europe on the television I saw this song following us around. And Duckie didn't know about that song." When he found out "him kind of feel upset a way," admits Reid. "So I don't know if"—and here emerges a familiar shadow cast by the dim glow of suspicion—"them just a plan it so to mash up the band because people could a just get Charles Summers [Big Life's head] to try to get me to do a track and then big up all over Europe just to cause jealousy in the band to mash it up beca' we were penetrating Europe and all. But we never did even get to penetrate Japan, a did just tour 'pon Canada and America."

The Berlin show was rescheduled and "Them did send in a girl to get me on the flight to London." The scene and the inexorable fate it inches toward seem drawn from '40s film noir. "When I reach to London now I was supposed to go and do *Top of the Pops* [but] they did seh that the song did a stop at 20 but if it go to 19 I would get to do *Top of the Pops*. So them just stop it at that one. Yes sir, them people a play a game with people. Them a sabotage a tour upon the road same time. And a play with my head. 'Cause them have the power to do anything them want you know. If a song get to number 20 there's no way they can't hike it up to get it to 19.

"But they know me talent a good, cause if I was in Black Uhuru up till now and singing hit song people demand me to come in. But when I lose my visa I wasn't getting any support from Duckie Simpson or member from the band. They be acting like is not their problem is like me alone was trying to get back my visa to get to come and work for the band. So I find when I need them, them wasn't there for me but when they did need help I was there for them still. And I must show them seh right now you a hear me, me a go trod on, me a go just do my thing."

After returning from London and finishing his Black Uhuru tour, "When we a go back a Jamaica, the vibes didn't right as how it was before." First there was Reid's independent streak. "Me is a man who no wait upon no company fe do nothing. From me have the money me have a telephone, me a book some studio time. Seh [to] Duckie them, just come round we do an album.

"All those days when I was there in the studio Duckie didn't show up. So we get to find out seh the only time them show up for the work is unless a company send down the money and is a company work. Anytime them see like I am trying independent mek something happen they think I am trying to produce for myself." His final singles with the band, he says, "Is I record independently hoping that them come in and we work together and have a album we can give it to any company and getting the money so we can work on new things again. Well, 'Nah get Rich and Switch,' now that release with Black Uhuru, me and dem, and 'Pain the Poor Man Brain' [one of the first records issued on his own JR label in 1987] is really my production."

Without the other members of the group Reid simply set up his sessions and voiced the tunes himself, "and them no come me no care, me a go work on my 'One Blood' and them nah know what them missing by not coming in the studio. So by the time me a come out and find out where them really at—Duckie say him a cool and right now the whole thing get social without the visa." Reid felt he could work solo and be in the band as well. Duckie's response, according to Reid was, "'Well, right now Black Uhuru just a Black Uhuru.' So I say by losing this visa my name's gone down in quality so me need to take more things and to wait on the group, how long it take to work on a song when you work with a group? I'm not saying right now it can't work but so I just say my name Junior Reid, me love my name and me know say me gotta really set up my vineyard and plant my seed and seed just keep on growing."

Perhaps Reid's is the kind of talent that just can't be contained in a group format. "When I find out with the Uhuru thing that they don't agree for me to work as a solo artist and work for the band too, doing my solo thing, my work in the band, performing on stage with the band, I just go ahead and put out my first song release." The song was "Worried Life" on his own JR label.

"When I go solo as Junior Reid, then Big Life [know] me have a [album titled] *One Blood* [and] wanted to sign me, Island wanted to sign me and they come to my house and give me an offer for the album and say that they will give me a certain amount of money. And then when me have a visa they will give me a certain amount more. And I say if you want to sign me just sign me without the visa beca' me no have no visa right now."

Reid's suddenly elusive visa became a sticking point in contract negotiations. "Most companies approach me like I have a problem when is them with the problem you know. Them is the one who caused the problem. So me just say well Big Life give me a number 20 song already so me a go just try them. Fly back over to sign a deal with Big Life, which wasn't really a good deal though me young at the time and not knowing nothing 'bout deal and them thing and soon get 'pon them case man, get smart, a get rights." A collaboration with a group signed to the same label, the Soup Dragons, was issued and reached number five in the British charts. Ironically the song was a version of a Rolling Stones classic, "I'm Free." But one of Reid's most stirring and enduring works was about to emerge.

One Blood was issued on Big Life. But the cosmic wheel of the record industry continued to spin. "Didn't sign the deal with Island, signed with Big Life. Then while I was with Big Life, Big Life now get a deal from Polygram for millions of dollars. So we all feeling good—now maybe some good attention paid to Junior Reid, and just when them get the deal them claim they spend a million pounds on me. How can you spend a million pound and nobody don't know you? So a get to find out is a game a play and the money them, the deal they get it wasn't in order to work on my career, this is a just put me in debt." The irony of Polygram's purchase of Big Life—and of Polygram's subsequent acquisition of Island Records—is clearly not lost on Reid.

One Blood was one of the most striking reggae anthems of the 1980s. The album itself stands as one of the best out of Jamaica in that decade. But for Junior Reid, the frustration of no financial gain on a hugely popular track had been his before, and obviously still stings. "So and even they do a great Jamaican hits or something like that they didn't use 'One Blood,' which is one of the songs that do it. I wonder why they hide it from the people. I don't know what is their plan. To have such a great works and not giving it to the people! That was the thing that make me not even to want to deal with certain record company because I know they're playin' games with certain works."

In typical fashion he returned to the studio for an album that was a natural progression musically and artistically. The original title for the album was *Progress,* which was how it was issued on Reid's JR label in Jamaica. When released worldwide by Big Life it became—with the addition and deletion of one or two songs—*Long Road.* Reid draws the distinction about as finely as it can be drawn: "I was looking for progress when I was with this company Big Life. But for me they were seeing a long road. Them do the *Progress* album and change it up to *Long Road.* No progress. Yeah. Because when I really track it and check it back now I see why them make the change. You see then, they did tell me that is a long road, y'know, but when I see it, I don't see it as a long road. I see it as a short road."

The original idea for the song came from former Wailers keyboard player Tyrone Downie. "Him write that song and me help co-write it. Me and him put in lyrics together. And after me really sing that song there and check it back, is an all right song and is a song with an all right tune. Wha' the song a say still? It say Marcus try, Martin Luther King die, and a lot of people die along the wayside and it's a long road, a long way. So it a mek a man feel like it don't even mek sense to even try and live up right 'cause it no come to no good and it no really survive 'cause it's a long road. Y'unnerstan? Ca' me tell you 'bout that song there now. At the time when Tyrone bring it to me him a say Marcus die and Martin Luther King try. But me say Marcus can't die. Well, it's a good thing me did a sing it so Marcus try and Martin Luther King die," he laughs. Still, this struggler's tune has the potency of one of Marvin Gaye's "reality" songs like "What's Goin' On" or "Mercy Mercy Me." But the point—especially since it's his road we're talking about—is well taken.

Reid's next album, *Visa* (JR) lacked U.S. distribution but contained hot-shot singles like "Friend Enemy," "Cry Now," "All Fruits Ripe," and "Hospital, Cemetery or Jail" (co-written with DJ Native Wayne Jobson). It was followed by 1995's *Junior Reid and the Bloods* (RAS), a collection of combination tracks with artists Reid had produced including Gregory Isaacs, Dennis Brown, and DJs Roger Flames, Captain Thunder, Ricky General, Gringo, Fragga Rocks, and Snaggapuss, to name a few. The album's standout track pairs Reid with former Uhuru alumnus Michael Rose, though they attended in different semesters. "'Burning Down Rome' is a real Black Uhuru song," Reid says proudly, a sound unheard "since Michael Rose and me quit the group. When me hear the Black Uhuru sound, 'Burning Down Rome'—I like how him [Michael Rose] sound on that track."

Producing and recording at a feverish pace, Reid next issued *Listen to the Voices* (RAS, 1996)

which incorporated Jamaican singles like "Rasta World Dance" and "Rise and Shine" and new material such as "Cross Fire." Though he says Tappa Zukie still has an album "in the can" from this period, he returned to his own studio for the self-produced *True World Order* in 1997 with cuts like "Crime Monster," "Vision," "Rose Where Is Your Clothes," which isn't about Michael Rose, and "Madonna," which is about the superstar trying to find Reid to sign him but being unable to tell him from the other dreads in his neighborhood.

It seems Junior Reid's visa problems are finally resolved, though in his words, "Me no really have a problem, and them make it look like a problem for a longtime." He got a one-week work permit to do a Bob Marley Day appearance in the mid-nineties. "From that time I'm always trying to get a work permit and they're always turning it down and denying it like I'm a wrongdoer. Is work I want to work. That's my livelihood and they're playing with my livelihood.

"So I come to America and I apply for my work permit. And they give me a year to work! So is not really America the problem coming from. It coming from the music politics. And the island too. Jamaica is a little island so them hold me down suffer for nine years. But through nine are the finishing number ca' a nine months it take to bring forth life, so it couldn't be no more than nine. So through the power of His Imperial Majesty them have to release the chain—but still them use them brain. So I'm out here and I'm gonna get to work for the people. So give thanks to the life-giver because that is life, and me can go out there and share. Share what you have with people."

His live shows here in the late '90s have been impressive. The boundless energy he emitted when whirling across the Black Uhuru stage still seems to know no bounds. Those who missed him for years always get a high energy show from Junior Reid.

Although reggae has been on a commercial upswing in the U.S. Reid says, "I don't really see them pushing the kind of music that I want to put out to the people. So you have to be a rebel in the system. So now I stay independent in my company. Most people want to sign you for like a six-album deal. Well, I don't wanna caught myself so long because I've just been through several deals." It's Reid's feeling that the problems the majors have had "breaking" reggae artists are caused by their intent to "break" them in a far different sense. "Is not that they can't break, they're just playing a game with the artist that limit them. Nobody no limit me ca' I'm a free man now."

No one is more qualified than Reid to sum up his own career and he does it succinctly and not quite like anyone else. "Junior Reid love the people them. The songs that I sing is in order to comfort the people, them mind and them soul. Me no lead them down, [but] bring them up and educate them. And all I have to say is just give thanks to the life-giver for life 'cause life is the greatest.

"Each day you get up and you have place to be, you have your two arm and your two foot or your bed, Jah know you have to give thanks you still have a chance. 'Cause some man can't get up and have him hand, him head and his foot and everything. Him nah live no life, him exist but him can't get up on his foot in the morning and use him head in the right way. I know so well, man have right now God in flesh and God move through man. 'Cause everything you ask God for you get—but you better make sure, man. Him a move through man to accomplish everything you fe accomplish. Just like your mother say she would like some vegetable in her vineyard and God knows she would appreciate that. And it a go happen from her little grandson put the seed in her garden. So I give praise to God. God move inna her servant and make it possible."

CHAPTER 15

Reasoning with the Ras:

Ras Michael and the Sons of Negus

The ancient African origins of Jamaican music are most apparent in the Nyahbingi drumming that lays the foundation of the music of groups like Count Ossie and the Mystic Revelation of Rastafari and Ras Michael and the Sons of Negus. The funde, repeater, and big bass drum blend with chanted lyrics, often biblical in nature, in the up-in-the-hills Grounation or gathering. Count Ossie was the first to bring this sound into the studios of Kingston in the late fifties and in ska-era recordings of the Folkes Brothers, Bunny and Skitter, and others. Several albums show

RAS MICHAEL. Photograph by Jan Salzman; © 1989 Phantom Photos

Count Ossie's innovative and experimental approach. After Ossie's passing it is Ras Michael and the Sons of Negus more than any others who have kept this tradition alive.

Today the influence of Nyahbingi is more prevalent than at any other time. Contemporary DJs like Beenie Man and Anthony B. and singers such as Cocoa Tea have returned to the ancient drum patterns, played today on drum programs and digital synthesizers. The chant style may have once been viewed as a "folk tradition," but make no mistake about it, Nyahbingi—the term translates to "death to black and white oppressors"—is dread serious music and no folly business. Its main progenitor in this time, Ras Michael, born Michael George Henry, is an uncompromising figure in the world of reggae, a teacher and elder looked up to and respected by other artists and legions of fans internationally.

"My parents were from St. Mary, 'The Fruitful Parish,' on the North Coast." The Parishes in Jamaica, explains Ras Michael, are "like the different cities you have here. We call a Parish the country part. But I was really born in Kingston and grow up in Trenchtown. Maxfield Avenue, Salt Lane, Cockburn Pen, and up in a Waterhouse. Those were the areas that I lived and grow up, and my school days were there. I went to the All Saints School, Jamaica. My mother used to send me to All Saints Church as a little boy."

Among the youth he knew growing up were "Duckie Simpson and Garth [Dennis] and all a those brothers. Bob Marley. We know them from the early concept because I tell you Bob Marley mother and my mother they knew each other. Like for instance Bunny Wailer. Is a vibes with us all. We grew with that form of solidarity, that African philosophy that was within us."

Ras Michael is a musician in the tradition of Nyahbingi drummers reaching back to African roots. His band uses a basic lineup of four drums (augmented by bass, guitar, keyboards, and kit-drums), a high and low funde, a repeater, and

RAS MICHAEL. Photograph by John Skomdahl

a big bass drum. His introduction to the music came from some legendary early Rastas in Jamaica. "I was born in the area of the ghetto and grow up down there in Salt Lane with Mortimer Planno and Skipper, Charles Napier and Alan, all those brothers."

His musical education began with "just drums, just pure playing drums. As I tell you I involve mostly in the drumming, just stepping out. We call any works that is right or can be—we just say we ah step out of Babylon, leave Babylon and come. So we just step from all likkle works whe' we think is Babylonian works." He mentions, "Our brother again Prince Immanual. Ca' I remember when deh was back-a-wall, all kinds of people when them did hear the drums boom them did get frighten. Africa you chant 'bout, the drums of Africa, people get bummy. At their own culture through the system poison them minds!"

With the same vision that sights the birth of mankind in Africa Ras Michael sees the birth of all music in the drum. "Man used to use drums and talk to each other civilized in Africa. Hear a man deh 'boom boom' a next one 'bim bim bim' a next one 'bing bing bing.' Is like telepathic communications within drums sounds. After awhile see a man come and put a little guitar or a little hand [clap] or a little shakin' to it like a little percussion thing, but the first instrument in creation was an African drum."

But for Ras Michael the drum is more than a beginning. It is a foundation. As he says, "Until right now I'm still doin' it. I remember we used to have a shed on the gully bank where also Bunny [Wailer] used to come down there. For Peter Touch [Tosh] him did live a little further down on the other side. If we did all tape dem song wha we a sing together, man! It would [be] priceless to people a deal with the monetary aspect a things. We had Nyahbingi there whe we sing and chant, Bunny, the said Mr. Marley, the said Peter with Ras Michael and some other elders chanting iya."

From such sessions came the impetus for the earliest formation of the Sons of Negus. Members have come in and out of the band over the years but Ras Michael has remained the central figure. In the mid- to late sixties he broke new ground in other ways, with the first Rastafarian radio program, "The Lion of Judah Time." The program featured music and cultural teachings.

Sons of Negus cut their first Jamaican 45 in 1967. The studio "was known first as the West Indies. Now it's called Dynamics, Seen? The first 45 I did was known as 'The Lion of Judah.'" The single and several others were issued on Ras Michael's own Zion Disc label and are highly prized collector's items today. They include a Nyahbingi version of the Ethiopian National Anthem and all feature hand-drumming and cultural chants.

A major influence on the reasoning of the early Rastafarians was the philosophy of Jamaican-born Marcus Garvey, whose United Negro Improvement Association inspired the black power movement of the 1960s— Malcolm X's father was among its active members. It was Garvey who introduced the concept of black pride internationally. "In Jamaica where I born and grow up," says Ras Michael, "the U.N.I.A. was a very powerful force."

Another back-to-Africa influence was the Ethiopian World Federation, "which was really brought together for the people in the West through his Imperial Majesty. That's why the land of Shashamane [in Ethiopia] was granted to all the people who want to come and according to you come through His Majesty. Those organizations were prominent in Jamaica."

Ras Michael mentions Jamaican liberation figures, "Paul Bogle and William Gordon and all those man." Another central influence he notes is a preacher who provided a historical link between the teachings of Marcus Garvey and the concept of the divinity of Haile Selassie I. "Leonard Howell him was really the first man that spoke about this back-to-Africa movement [saying], you will see a king crowned [who brings] redemption. So when His Majesty was coronated in 1930 it started to be more progressive to where it reach now."

The movement began in the 1930s and included many elements we now think of as Rastafarian—the divinity of Haile Selassie I, natural living, allowing the hair to grow naturally into locks, and increasing cultural awareness. "They go way, way back. So therefore at times I love to speak 'bout the foundation, for if you don't have the roots you can't have the branches.

"So this is a concept that has been going on through the years. Through the ages. For you have ancient elders Brother Time, Brother Irie Iron, Brother Silver, Sam Clayton. All those brothers is ancient man who bore a lot of the concept of this Rastafari movement, some older than me. So this concept is going way back from that time where we as Rastafarians always think of this back to Africa movement. Brother Sam Brown. All them elders there. We have come so far."

After recording a handful of Sons of Negus singles in the mid- to late sixties, Ras Michael concentrated on perfecting his unique and formidable approach to the music. He released three albums in 1975, the seminal *Dadawah* (produced by Lloyd Charmers and said to have been recorded in one continuous session), *Nyahbingi* (also issued by Trojan in the U.K. and produced by Tommy Cowan), and *Rastafari* (Grounation). All feature Ras Michael on vocals and what he calls his "drum core."

The following year brought *Freedom Sounds* (Dynamic), which mixed the Nyahbingi drum and chant music with some wild guitar leads provided by Earl "Chinna" Smith. This experimental approach, though also well within the tradition of the music—just listen to Count Ossie's work with Cedric "IM" Brooks—was a startling departure for critics who had come to think of Ras Michael's work as a kind of Jamaican folk music. The same year saw the release of an album, *Tribute to the Emperor,* in which Ras Michael's music was coopted by horns overdubbed in England by Jazzboe Abubaka.

The year 1977 saw the appearance of the hard-to-find Jamaican release *Irations of Ras Michael* (Top Ranking). Two strong albums issued in 1978, *Kibir Am Lak* (recently reissued in England and America) and *Movements,* revealed a pattern of experimentation and return to

tradition that has continued throughout his career. On the latter album he was joined by the first in a series of Daughters of Negus (some of his later recordings list the band as Ras Michael and the Sons and Daughters of Negus). The singer was Puma Jones, who worked with Ras Michael before she joined Black Uhuru.

Of this American sister who left an indelible mark on the world of reggae, Ras Michael reminisces, "Puma Jones, she came to Jamaica and I knew some sistrens who used to dance with me. For my group used to have dancers." The dance troupe wasn't a permanent part of the group for financial reasons; as he puts it, "The lack of support mek me ha fe cut down on the band. So she came and she danced and she sang, man she was a very nice sistren. They all dance and choreograph out my music and it was a lovely time.

"That time Puma was just irie, innocent. With my music, the people really deal with it, them find themself more on a uplift consciousness. For is like you know of the glitter out there but it doesn't really mean anything to me. That is where I and I music, is like you can see farther. So Puma Jones used to dance and sing 'long with some other sistrens who used to dance also." Another early member of the group was Congo Ashanti Roy.

The Sons of Negus, he says, "was a mystic group but it was the historical part of the music in Jamaica along with my brother, who has also passed Count Ossie." Though Ossie recorded before Ras Michael (and played for Haile Selassie I on his trip to Jamaica in the early sixties) their eras overlapped and, says Ras Michael, "We played [together] but we used to live in two different parts of Jamaica. We kinda rest in the dung hill, and him was in Wareika Hill."

Ras Michael closed out the seventies with one of the most unique dub albums ever issued, the uplifting *Rastafari in Dub.* Issued originally on the Grounation label, it was a brilliant concept album melding Nyahbingi rhythms with the stripped-down back-to-basics dub approach. For many years a scarce and collectible vinyl album (with a cool cover drawing that resembled a Frankenstein Tiki), it was picked up in the nineties by the ROIR label, reissued first on cassette with the original cover and later on CD with new graphics.

In his conversation as in his music Ras Michael returns again and again to the themes of repatriation, righteousness, judgment, and redemption. *Kibir Am Lak*'s "New Name" is a case in point as he intones over a hypnotizing drum rhythm:

A new name Jah got and it terrible and
   dreadful
Heathen no like Jah name . . .
For when we call him Rastafari
Watch how weak heart tremble
Heathen no like Jah name.

"Jamaica," he explains, "is like a cradle of the Rastafarian repatriation movement. Rasta was speakin' so much of goin' back to Africa a lot of people in the government didn't understand what was goin' on. They thought like say you want overtake. No, Rasta no want no place inna the West. Him want go home back to Africa! That is not his concept to come overthrow no government, no. His own concept is going back to Africa. That is him birthright."

"This Rastafari movement as Bob me know would a say, a no Bob Marley in deh alone. A the whole a we, you know. Ca' one time Bob say to me early on when him went to Africa and come, him say Ras Michael, hear me now man. Your music dem a play down in a Africa the poco-shan drums and ting deh. Me gone on all Nigeria and see the man seh them jump it 'pon the bass. So wha' happen when you go a Africa, him say when you reach Africa iya you're like God deh, the music whe' you play and the vibe whe you have.

"Bob was a brother who me love spirituality, not fe no material nothin'. Ca' me and Bob and Bunny, the said whole a we, is like certain vibes that was there. No one can come in between deh sir. It was no likkle funny love, we have the real love. Me love all the man dem who me and dem did associate from me a youthful. Ca' my love no change. For Jah love no change from no one. But people would change. Material things would make people change and go wide and strayin' from the biblical roots."

"Him say if a man dead him can't carry none a him riches with him and as you know if a man dead and them bury him with it you have them grave robbers what call themselves anthropologists. They go get things and get rich offa it. So is like when ya talk, people no like the vibes but how long can you hide from the truth and the rights in your heart?

"So many thing weh the Rastaman philosophy show you that His Imperial Majesty, the King of Kings and the Lord of Lords, the 225th man out of Solomon dynasty come of the lineage of King David and King Solomon line right down to Menelik. And that is the gospel. We deal with the Bible. His Majesty say the Bible is a rallying point for humanity. Him never say just for certain humans. For all. So is a reality. You have to love.

"History show you the system put so much things in front of the people and them not put the right thing in front of them. The words of the Rastaman nah divide no people man. The real Rastaman words a bring the people together. The Rastaman word nah tell you to chop up white man. No. The Rastaman word a tell you seh the whole world is a garden and all the people in it is his flowers. And we a beautify this garden. Weh you wan' fight in that? You see any hatred in that? No hatred is in that. A pure love inna that.

"That is what the Rastaman philosophy is based upon. And a nuh bad man thing. A no drugs peddling thing like how some people want to put for our lives, Rasta a nuh posse. Rasta people ain't no posse people. Rasta people a God-fearin' people. For Him say the fear of the Lord is the beginning of wisdom. For you know as a wise man, we know all power is subjected to a higher power. I really hope we can try to work together to bring peace and love universally. Or else Jah shall come and judge the earth with lightning, thunder, earthquake."

"Alas, Alas! The great city Babylon burn and her smoke rose up forever. House on a rock back shall take heed. Whole of the buildings have them skyscrapers holy night and rock back. But before that time everyman can step within Jah glory for *H.I.M.* is there for every individual one. Just humble yourself. That is the philosophy of the Rastaman. Ca' the queen of civilization is mother Africa, Ethiopia. Not like them a seh Ethiopia is a little beenie 'pon the map. The whole continent was Ethiopia!

"You can't speak every language in the world. You can't do that. You a go dead man or a mad man. Can't. You don't know everything. You can't make life. You know how much doctors try fe do that? The essence of the breath whe you blow and breathe—you can make that? No doctor! No man. Can't do nothin like that my bredren, none. Can't give you gift of life. That is within the powers of the Almighty God. Them no want to deal with God. Them no even want the children a read the Bible in school. What kinda thing you a bring up, them no heathenism that? If you nah bring the tree from it young that it can grow upon the biblical words of the Almighty—so whe you a bring up?

"They come with our rights not to learn. You have rights not to read the Bible. Weh you see a rights not to read the holy scrolls? What kinda right that? That no right, that a wrong! You wrong nah fe wan' read the holy scroll of the Bible! Don't tell me you have right.

Right to what? You must use your rights with righteousness, not with devil corruption fe say you have right not fe this and you have right not fe that. You know you wrong fe do it and say you right. Right can never be wrong and wrong can never be right. Is a whole different vibes completely."

The impact of the Rastafari movement on reggae and through reggae on the world is immeasurable. The themes that underline Ras Michael's comments are the same ones embedded in his music, and much of the great reggae music from its point of origin. As Ras Michael says, "That's a Rastaman vibration we a come with. All dem brother dem you know, all Big Youth, Joe Higgs, brother U Roy same way. Culture. Burning Spear. Skatalites. Brothers them thing there. Stranger Cole. Earl Chinna Smith, Robbie Shakespeare, and all dem man there, official Negus man dem, Sons of Negus."

By 1980 Ras Michael had begun a nearly endless tour of the globe, bringing the Nyahbingi sounds to the world. That year he released another experimental live album, *Promised Land Sounds* on the Lions Gate label out of Canada. Periodic returns to Jamaica resulted in the Trojan albums *Revelation* (1982) and *Disarmament* (1983). *Love Thy Neighbor* (1984, Live & Learn), though produced by Delroy and Hyman Wright along with Ras Michael, incorporates a very dubby sound. In 1985 Shanachie issued *Rally Round*, a collection of crucial singles and otherwise unavailable cuts.

Zion Train, a 1988 collaboration with Bad Brains' HR, is a very different kind of Ras Michael album. The following year he gathered a new set of Negus Sons around him for an album, *Know Now*, that showed his strength and vision undiminished while incorporating new rhythms and lyrics. Crisp recordings of traditional themes like "Jah Giveth Life," "Rastaman Gives Thanks and Praise," and "Marriage in Canaan" were augmented by the tender "Sister Lilac" performed on acoustic guitar with a vocal that reveals a gentle side.

Mediator (1993, High Times) was recorded in Jamaica with Earl "Chinna" Smith. Again mixing a blend of traditional concepts and experimental elements, Ras Michael presented a new set of songs on an album that unfortunately has never seen wide distribution. The music was in stark contrast to that which then held sway in Jamaica. But the new wave of consciousness that swept Jamaica in the mid-nineties began to pick up on the ancient Nyahbingi style. Says Ras Michael, "A lot of those brothers and people them never used to use the drums but I love to know that the awareness of their historical order is coming to some of them. If a man promote dancehall music and don't promote the culture then it come like dancehall music is the music and it come like it suffer. So when the I-thems go fe hear them hear pure dancehall music most of the time and them can't hear the culture. So them must promote the real thing which is the culture."

In 1997 Ras Michael, along with Joe Higgs, the Wailing Souls, and many others, contributed to the two-volume set *Fire on the Mountain,* a reggae tribute to the Grateful Dead. His version of "If I Had the World to Give" gently restates Garcia/Hunter's song. He also recorded with some of the artists keeping the cultural fires burning in Jamaica, including one of reggae's freshest voices, Luciano. "He and I work together on a wonderful 45, which I haven't seen come out yet, I think it's 'Come Pray with Me.' I hope him know that I appreci-love him a very lot." He also recorded an unreleased single with reggae poet Mutabaruka.

Just back from touring Europe, Ras Michael is preparing to release a new CD titled *Lion Country.* As on many previous recordings Sly and Robbie, Robbie Lyn, and Chinna construct the rhythms, this time aided by Squiddly Cole, Chris Meredeth, David Madden, and others.

A remake of his earliest single, "Ethiopian Anthem" kicks off the set, which also includes new songs like "Visioning" and one track cut with the original Wailers band including the Barrett brothers. Once again his message is a cultural one.

"People have to wake up now," he says emphatically, "and the only way you can wake up is dealing with truth. I'm trying to build a culture center which has been started in Jamaica. That's my main goal, to really see that project completed in my lifetime through the power of the Almighty."

The Ras Michael Cultural Center "will be in Kingston 11, that's on the gully bank, the said place where I tell you that Bob and Peter them and Bunny and the whole a the Rastafarians dem used to come. Our culture center will have classrooms where youths can learn. We intend to also have a computer center to teach the youth deh. I have a lot of teachers already who has volunteered to assist us." The plan includes instruction on African drumming and dancing, a recording studio, a stage for shows, and a cafeteria.

"I-man have a personal mission, a special mission. I even look and I see some of the elders in Jamaica, they need a home for the aged where they can be taken care of until the time come when we repatriate them. But right now they need programs where we can help them, doctors who can come an administer to them. It's a movement within a movement, a culture within a culture. It's an Ethiopian righteous African government within a government. Our mission is going back to Africa as the Bible say and as Marcus Garvey say. Me just have a work to bring people together.

"When I go down Jamaica at times I wish and I hope I could do even more for the people on a whole, not just Rasta, but as I tell you, the Rastaman him go through great tribulations through his concept and people not having a great understanding of what he really is defending.

Knowledge is increasing. As we say the DJ now them start listen back to songs now and hear the real truth fe themselves. Jamaica is a blessed island. Jamaica is the first place where we got our independence through the slave trade emancipation. We are the island that couldn't deal with this slave chattel. Went up in the hills and start to resist.

"The real Rastaman nah just deal with man who have beard and longie dread. No tek side against this or that. You have to set yourself in order. We fight against spiritual wickedness in a high or low places. We nah fight 'gainst flesh and blood. And when it come to politician them a kill people and a murder people and all kinda thing. But I and I ride on."

CHAPTER 16

Steel Pulse:

Stayin' with the Rastaman

International reggae began in England, where reggae gained airplay as "homegrown soul" for the United Kingdom. Singers like Delroy Washington, who moved to England as a child with his parents, made careers in reggae and bands, often mixing first- and second-generation Jamaicans with other island influences. Local musicians, played live and recorded, working to try and capture the elusive Jamaican sound. Visiting Jamaican singers recorded in English studios, engineers and producers from the island emigrated, and slowly a specifically English reggae sound began to emerge.

The diversity of English reggae is as astonishing as its Jamaican counterpart. From the pop stylings of Aswad and Maxi Priest to the heavy thump of Misty in Roots to a whole generation of lovers rock singers who in turn influenced Jamaican vocalists like Dennis Brown, Gregory Isaacs, Johnny Osbourne, and others, "English reggae" flourishes with new voices like Peter Hunningale and Sylvia Tella. For collectors one great benefit of the U.K. reggae scene was English pressings of Jamaican releases. After the oil crunch of the seventies, during which hundreds of thousands of ska and rock steady records were melted to press new records in Jamaica, the U.K. issues were sometimes the only chance to get a classic song on vinyl.

Just as happened with ska, U.K. bands and reggae singers redefined the sound in their own style. The international success of UB40 with reggae covers, reggae-fied pop songs, and original material with a pop-reggae feel brought a reassessment of the music. Though some heard their style as watered-down reggae or reggae lite, they brought many new listeners an awareness of reggae and contributed to its eventual acceptance. Whether pop or reggae, they helped create a mainstream respect for Jamaican roots.

In later years a new roots movement emerged from the work of Jah Shaka and Mad Professor (who also has recorded his share of lovers rock singers like Kofi and Deborah Glasgow) to spawn hundreds of recording groups, the best of which, like Dub Syndicate, Zion Train, and Alpha and Omega, took reggae into uncharted territories as fascinating as that of Jamaica's own reggae—and new roots singers like Trevor Hartley, Barry Isaacs, Tena Stelin, and Steven Wright held true to the conscious foundation of reggae when dancehall moved Jamaican reggae into an entirely different direction.

Among the most influential and longest lasting of the British-based bands, Steel Pulse took on the mantle of premier U.K. reggae group by the late seventies, long before UB40 or "new roots."

Their blend of punk ethos and energized rock-reggae gave them a crossover appeal that resulted in early albums issued by Island, the label nearly all reggae artists aspired to be on at the time. It's hard to imagine where the music would be today without their patented brand of reggae.

From their first album, 1978's *Handsworth Revolution,* Steel Pulse struck a path all their own, mixing elements of rock and jazz guitar with the reggae sound and concentrating on social themes in their lyrics. Cuts like "Ku Klux Klan" and "Macka Splaff" made it clear this was not the soft and gentle "lovers rock" previously popularized in the U.K. Lead singer "Congo Dread" David Hinds (so named for the way he wore his dreadlocks tied straight up in the air) eschews the "second-generation" tag, saying, "We call ourselves the first generation because we were the first generation of blacks born in England."

According to co-founder and keyboardist Selwyn Brown, "Most of our parents came to England in the '50s and they brought a lot of their culture with them food-wise, attitude-wise, and even [in terms of] music. The original music we heard when we were growing up was blue beat and ska and goin' into rock steady and what later became known as reggae. We as kids were just growing up and expressing a part of the culture we feel close to: the music. I think you see the fruition of that in ourselves, Aswad, Maxi Priest—even to a certain extent through UB40."

What made Steel Pulse's sound so different from other reggae groups, even other English bands of their day was, according to Brown, "When we were younger and first starting out, we got caught right in the middle of the punk rock movement. A lot of people see it as a big joke, but we don't. We were young black kids growin' up in Britain protesting against the system. Punk rock is basically young white kids growin' up in England—and they're doin' the same thing. Basically we were comin' from different backgrounds from the punk rock guys—the way they grow up, the food they eat, the things they do—but the one thing we have in common, we're livin' within a system that's unjust."

Hinds reminisced about those early days: "For a long time we were called Jah Punk or punky reggae when we first started hittin' the London scene. We were opening for bands like XTC, Ultravox, Generation X, the Stranglers. A lot of the West Indian community used to see us in line with these people and had no idea we were playing reggae music." Adds Brown, "We were the first reggae band to go on that circuit because most of the reggae bands—it wasn't their fault, but they were fearful to play

on that circuit. So were we! But we took a chance and it worked and since then other bands said, 'Maybe we can do it too!'"

"The Rock Against Racism movement started out of that as well," continues Brown. "We played with the Police, the Clash, Graham Parker and the Rumor, the Sex Pistols, and all the rest of those guys. Sid Vicious—they used to come to our gigs, and what's his name, Billy Idol. And they didn't used to come down with an attitude like 'We're comin' from a middle-class background,' they used to come in on a level with us."

This is not to deny the influence of Jamaican reggae on the band. "When we were kids growing up in England, Rastafari came to England through Bob Marley and Ras Michael and the

STEEL PULSE (LEFT TO RIGHT): DAVID HINDS, STEVE NESBITT ("GRIZZLY"), AND SELWYN BROWN. Photograph by Jan Salzman; © 1995 Phantom Photos

Sons of Negus, and numerous other people," Brown relates. "The media made it appear Rasta came back, and all of a sudden there was dreadlocks, everybody stopped eating meat and started smokin' herb—but it didn't happen like that. We know it's been part of our culture for a long time. Growing up in England, we tried to push the positive side of the Rasta movement. They say Steel Pulse is a political band—which we are in a certain way. But if I were a politician I wouldn't be in power very long. 'Cause I notice any politician that's for the people, they don't last long."

The second Steel Pulse album, *Tribute to the Martyrs* (1979) added to the band's militant credentials. A live version of "Sound System" from the first album made it clear this was a playing band and cuts like "Babylon Makes the Rules" displayed an uncompromising stance. By the following year's *Caught You,* released as *Reggae Fever* in the U.S., they were mixing cuts like "Drug Squad" with more "commercial" cuts like "Caught You Dancing." Island released a "greatest hits" package in their *Reggae Greats* series in the mid-eighties with ten tracks drawing from these three discs.

Their English upbringing has a lot to do with the sound of the band. According to Hinds, "We were comin' from a British viewpoint, things were a lot more uptempo, there were a lot more mid-range melodies happening in the music, as well as basic drum and bass rhythm. We were featuring a lot more harmonies than was normally heard of in reggae and also a lot of counter melodies against the vocal. All that helped to enhance our music."

The lineup of the group featured Hinds, Brown, and Steve "Grizzly" Nesbitt on drums, all still playing in the band today. Other players—Basil Gabbidon on guitar and vocals, bassist Ronnie McQueen, percussionist Fonso Martin, and vocalist Michael Riley—who were there in the early days dropped out one by one, leaving the core trio and a series of support

DAVID HINDS. Photograph by Jan Salzman; © 1995 Phantom Photos

musicians. Riley was the first of the originals to go. Gabbidon's last album with them was their first for Elektra, *True Democracy* (1982), McQueen's was 1984's *Earth Crisis.*

The band remained a foursome through their final Elektra release, *Babylon the Bandit* (1985), and their first two for MCA, 1988's *State of Emergency* and 1992's *Victims.* They continued to tour behind each of these releases. In the years that passed between the latter two discs the band built their own studio, where they cut the basic tracks for *Victims* and later releases.

Meanwhile much had changed in reggae, particularly the growth in popularity of the "dancehall" style. Typically Steel Pulse listened to and incorporated this and other new elements into their music. "I'm very impressed with the dancehall sound," Hinds said at the time, particularly with "the syncopation on the drums, the bass lines."

As he explains it, "In the old days we tried to get as much bass on the track as possible, and the more laid back the track sounded, the better. But that's not the issue now. [It's] tempo, they're goin' into as much as a hundred beats per minute on some of these tracks. The thing that disappoints me, number one, is there's too many versions of one song; and secondly, there's too much cover versions. Apart from that, it's still the greatest music in the world, as far as I'm concerned."

Elements incorporated in their new sound included sampling, the DJ style, rap, and a bit of drum programming. Like many "old school" groups who tried to move into the new era, the mix muddied their uniqueness, though on cuts like "Gang Warfare" their old "message music" style was still apparent: "The kids are killing each other for next to nothin'," said Brown, "and something's got to be said about it!" On a slightly lighter note, "Taxi Driver" accused New York cab drivers of refusing service to dreads, West Indians, and blacks in general. In a move that may have been as much record promotion as protest, they filed a suit in New York over the matter.

Victims was Fonso Martin's last album with Steel Pulse, and the band, now generally pictured as a trio, snapped right back with *Rastafari Centennial* (MCA, 1992), recorded live in Paris and reprising many of their best and best-known songs. "A lot of people don't understand that Steel Pulse is not really a set of guys like the Drifters or the Temptations where if you take so and so away, that's the end of the Temptations," Hinds said. "Steel Pulse was based not on

people but on a philosophy, a concept. So— the force must still go on."

Vex (1994, MCA) signaled a return to their earlier sound and style as exemplified in "Back to My Roots," with Hinds's poignant lyrics clearly stating his intention to stray no more in the commercial arena and return to the Steel Pulse sound of old. This reaffirmation continued with their first release on the Mesa label, 1997's *Rage and Fury*. Still, being Steel Pulse they could mix militant cuts like "Settle the Score" and "The Real Terrorist" with a cover of Van Morrison's "Brown-Eyed Girl" and a "jungle" remix of a new version of their early classic "Ku Klux Klan."

The year 1997 also marked the time Island issued a massive double-CD set containing all the tracks on the original three albums as well as 12-inch mixes and unreleased live performances. *Sound System: The Island Years* captures the early band in its entirety and returns us to the early roots of this rocking reggae band. Together with their newest work it shows a continuity few bands have achieved over two decades of recording. A kind of alternate history of the band is available on *Rastanthology* (Wise Man Doctrine), which draws from both their Island catalog and later labels as well.

"When Steel Pulse started," said Selwyn Brown, "we couldn't even play an instrument, but we had to have a concept. When I heard [Bob Marley and the Wailers'] 'Catch a Fire' my concept was, if I can make music that inspires other people the way that music inspires me, that's what I want to do. I feel fortunate to have grown up in an era when people love roots music, not money.

"The world has changed, but as far as the whole government thing, it's getting worse. But as far as Rasta and as far as what the Rastaman is sayin' in the beginning, the Rastaman is still sayin' the same thing. So I have to just stay with the Rastaman. He's one of the few people that's sayin' the truth."

CHAPTER 17

Alpha Blondy on the New Generation of Africans

The man who today calls himself Alpha Blondy was Born Koné Seydou in Dimbokru on what is chillingly still referred to by the world as the Ivory Coast. His stage name, which actually means "first bandit," came to him in later years. As a young man he fell in love with music, but not traditional African music.

"This African generation is more rock and roll than African," he says simply. "People ask me, 'Why as an African, don't you play African music?' They don't ask Guns n' Roses to play country music! This African music they relate to is a lot of tom-toms and Tarzan yodels. I call this touristic; this is not the reality today."

Alpha Blondy is not one to romanticize his African roots. "I was born in 1953, so I cannot really say that I'm gonna be fighting for my roots. I was born in a modern hospital with electricity. You hear electric guitar, you go to nightclubs—you don't wanna be like the man who sings in your backyard every day. You wanna be Mick Jagger. You wanna be Woodstock. How many nights I spent dreaming of Woodstock! When I came to America I had to see Woodstock—that was a personal challenge.

"So when they say, 'Play African music,' I say, 'Now wait a minute.' Don't get me wrong.

I'm a black man with a white brain. And I want them to understand that. This pure, wild young African cannibal is over. The coconut tree is over. Now, no matter where you come from, there's got to be a school, a radio. There's got to be a young friend you meet, you talk, smoke a joint together and you dream together. We're part of that dream, that universal big American dream."

"So people ask why don't you sing like Salif Keita? I say, 'I wish I could!' But I grew up listening to Mick Jagger. He doesn't sing African music. But the one he plays, we love it! We come out of that new generation. That's how I got into reggae music."

ALPHA BLONDY. Photograph by Ade James

Alpha Blondy's music presents a broad cultural mix. He speaks—and sings in—five languages fluently, and presents Muslim, Judaic and Christian themes side by side in his work. "I sing in African tongues, American tongues, French tongues." He also sings in Hebrew and Arabic. "But my secret aim is to give the two-coated dimension to the cake: reggae and rock. That's the culture I have in my head."

He first started playing rock and rock in a high school band, playing Creedence Clearwater Revival and other "sixties" rockers. He and his friends saw reggae as a natural extension of '60s music. "The Rastas," he says, "are really black hippies."

As a young man he attended college in New York but ran out of money and got sick. In New York he also began playing reggae, then returned to the Ivory Coast where—to his parents' dismay—he put together a band and appeared on a TV talent show. "What I'd seen in America is that people don't mess around with the job. Even the musicians who play in the park tend to really try to be perfect. Because there's so much competition you cannot afford to be second." The TV appearance led to his first African reggae LP, *Jah Glory* (Syllart).

On this album he was backed by the Natty Rebels and most of his other records, like 1987's *Apartheid Is Nazism,* feature his touring band the Solar System, but on the 1987 LP *Jerusalem* and the song "Cocody Rock" (collected on the 1988 LP of the same name) he was backed by the original Wailers band. All three of these albums were released in America by Shanachie. Working with the Wailers was a great experience for him, which he encapsulates in his own characteristic way. "It's like working with Bruce Springsteen. No matter how the song works, you're learning."

Alpha Blondy's material has always dealt with international issues. Of the current Mideast situation he says, "I think that there is hope of peace between Israel and the Arab countries, but I also think that some Arab countries have to stop throwing oil on the fire. The victims of the system are the Palestinians and the Jewish people, the Israelis. The Arabs are telling the Palestinian, 'Go and get your land: we're behind you.' It's a very subtle way to say 'get out.' So French people say, 'With one stone they make two strikes.'"

In 1989 he issued the LP *Revolution* (Shanachie). Many of the songs were in his native language and one contained an entire speech by the president of the Ivory Coast, but there was also a cut called "Rock and Roll Remedy." In 1990 Shanachie put out *The Best of Alpha Blondy,* which included "Rasta Poue," a song cut with the Wailers and not appearing on any of his previous releases.

That same year saw the release of *The Prophets* on Capitol with cuts like "Black Men Tears," "Coup d'etat" and "Jah Music." It was followed in 1992 by his most stunning release to date, *Masada* (EMI). Drawing from Middle Eastern, African, and European cultural concepts and skipping from language to language like James Joyce after tea, he chastises the war makers of the world on cuts like "Peace in Liberia" and "Desert Storm" while mixing musical elements in a manner that helped to define the concept of world beat. Highlights from this and other discs were featured on the following year's *Live Au Zenith (Paris),* also on EMI.

The young man, sometimes dread and sometimes bald head, also takes a pan-religious view on the song "God Is One," and has been known to perform with a Koran in one hand and a Bible in the other. "My parents are Moslem," he explains. "In Africa, the Christian man marries a Moslem woman. He goes to church, she goes to mosque. You don't brutalize people to make them go into heaven. Ayatollah Khomeini wants to kill everybody who smokes a joint. What is that? I don't understand. You don't use the name of God to kill."

On 1994's *Dieu* (World Pacific) he restates his major themes on songs like "La Guerre," continues his world tour with "Goree (Senegal)," "Afrique—Antilles," and "Soukeina (Nangnele)" but still manages to squeeze in "Rocking Time." Outspoken, multicultural, and definitely off the wall, Alpha Blondy draws crowds wherever he goes. His Los Angeles show at the Music Machine in the early nineties packed more people in that club than any show ever played in that venue. In 1998 he issued one of his most political statements to date, *Yitzhak Rabin* on Bob Marley's Tuff Gong label. On it he attacks "Les Imbeciles" and "Hypocrites" and points the way to a "New Dawn."

Alpha Blondy is optimistic about technology, using the movie *2001: A Space Odyssey* as a point of departure. "See the monkey in the beginning? Now the monkey has his plane, goes to school. The monkey with time goes on the moon. Hey, that's a big step, dread. When I see that and I see what we are living today, it is not so bad— it could have been worse. If I wanna call Abijan, I just pick up a plastic box, push a few numbers, and I talk to Abijan. So many positive things have been done, it's now how to control everything that God has given to us and to use it on the wise purpose." He extends this

even to nuclear power: "Might as well try to control the power that God has given to us. If we control it good it might be positive. If we miscontrol it, then we'll pay for it."

Since politics figures prominently in his music, it's interesting to note what this Ivory Coast "now generation" African thinks of the political situation in the U.S. today. "I like Clinton because he looks like John Kennedy," he says disarmingly. "I was very much in love with Kennedy. The only American president who really cared for we Africans is John Kennedy. He is the one who sent us the Peace Corps. So the English I'm speaking today, you should be thanking John Kennedy, man. I would have been speaking Mandingo or French to you."

He pauses for a moment and a playful gleam springs into his eye. "I was very much in love with Marilyn Monroe, too. It's too bad she couldn't wait for me to come marry her. I was too young. If she could just hold the time for me to grow up and become famous in America! And then we could play in the White House! It's a nice dream, man! Rasta in the White House. Hey dread! Give me democratic system."

CHAPTER 18

South Africa's Lucky Dube:

What Good Is a Song Without a Message?

Although it was the harder-edged militant reggae of the 1970s that initially attracted a larger audience for the music, from the late '80s reggae in Jamaica turned its back on the international activism of the Wailers, Culture, and Burning Spear and returned the music to its dancehall origins. Paradoxically Lucky Dube, a singer from South Africa, is one of the major figures leading reggae again toward the concerns that first made it a rallying point for forward-thinking people around the world.

Dube set the reggae world on its collective ear with 1988's *Slave*

LUCKY DUBE. Photograph by Jan Salzman; © 1990 Phantom Photos

(Shanachie), though by this time he had released seven albums in his homeland. The first five were in a style referred to as "Zulu soul," African pop productions that revealed his ability to sing but not to reach a worldwide audience. His first two reggae albums, *Rastas Never Die* and *Think About the Children* were reissued on Polygram International after the success of *Slave*.

The year 1989 saw the release of the outstanding album of his early period, *Together as One* (Celluloid). Songs like "Jah Save Us," "Eyes of the Beholder," and "On My Own" showed that Lucky Dube was an artist who could not be stopped, a singer whose lower range echoed the thunderous qualities of mentor Peter Tosh and whose upper reaches challenged the high harmonies of some of America's outstanding soul groups like the Impressions and the Temptations. In fact, Dube is one of the few singers who could probably sing all the parts on a Temptations record.

With 1990's *Prisoner,* Dube moved to the head of the pack, surpassing many roots releases from reggae's home turf in Jamaica. *Captured Live* (1991) showed the vibrancy of his impressive stage show. His band, dubbed the Slaves, played Wailers-style reggae as if caught in a time warp and his incredible backup singers were outdistanced only by Dube's own incredible vocal prowess.

His performance at Jamaica's Reggae Sunsplash festival in 1991 was so impressive that he was chosen one of the headliners of the following year's traveling Reggae Sunsplash, with which he toured the U.S. A series of top-quality releases have kept him on the reggae charts and constant touring keeps him in the public eye. Though he is among the upper echelon of international reggae singers, his work continually returns to themes and subjects that deal directly with oppressed people and the land of his birth.

"Changes are taking place in South Africa," he says with the degree of understatement that makes his lyrics so powerful. "The oppressive laws that they had are being removed and the people are getting to know each other better. They get to understand each other better now."

Unlike many writers who deal with topical subjects, Dube's work always seems pertinent to today's events. "Maybe that's because when I write my music I write about real things, things that I have personally experienced, and things that the people around me have experienced."

House of Exile (1992) was a case in point. One of the strongest songs was "Group Areas Act." According to Dube, "The Group Areas Act was one of the oppressive laws that they had in South Africa—a black man couldn't buy businesses in town, a black man couldn't buy a house in town, a black man was just a black man. But when these acts were scratched from the books, I mean, to me, it was about ten steps forward. We could now see the light at the end of the tunnel. At least we could see that we're getting somewhere! And then, by that act being removed, people in South Africa would get to know and understand each other because they won't be living 3,000 miles apart from each other."

Circumstances since then hint that the light at the end of the tunnel may have been the next train coming. The bipolar swing of hope and frustration is a prominent feature in Dube's music. For every hopeful cut like "Group Areas Act" there's a song of despair like "Mickey Mouse Freedom" from the same LP. Still, the positive vibration predominates, as on cuts such as "Different Colours/One People" and "Soldiers for Righteousness" from 1993's *Victims*. All these albums, from *Prisoner* through *Victims,* were issued by Shanachie. In 1995 Dube issued one album, *Trinity,* on Tabu, a Motown subsidiary. The following year Shanachie released a "greatest hits" package called *Serious Reggae Business*.

In 1997 Dube returned to Shanachie with the release of *Taxman*. His roots and culture sound predominated as track after track—

LUCKY DUBE. Photograph by Jan Salzman;
© 1994 Phantom Photos

tion: reggae music. "When I started in Africa, South Africa, the people and the government were somehow against reggae. The people didn't love reggae, they didn't understand reggae so much as they do now. I had to find a way to introduce it to them."

Outstanding among his early songs is the cut "Rastas Never Die." Though he has recorded two versions of this song, the one on *Together as One* is a powerful musical affirmation of the Rastafarian faith. When originally released, he says it "didn't do no good. People didn't love it, you know? Now that they understand it's time I do what I wanted to in the past." Reggae's all-consuming lifestyle is beautifully captured: "The bed I'm sleeping on/Is a reggae bed/The food I'm eating/Is reggae food/I'm walking reggae/Talking reggae/Living reggae." For so many lovers of the music, this describes exactly how they feel.

Though he played on the name in his first film, *Getting Lucky* (he also appears in the film *Voice in the Dark*), he says of his moniker, "It's no nickname. That's actually my real name. My mother didn't have children for a long time and then when she finally got me she considered herself to be very lucky."

Speaking of names, I asked how his band feels about being called "The Slaves." "Well, the name came about with the success of the album *Slaves*. Before that, they didn't have a name. They were just called Lucky Dube's band." He laughs. "You know? With the success of the album the band had to have a name, and we thought up a lot of names. But there's only one name that came out tops and that was 'Slaves.' As in the album. And they feel very comfortable about it 'cause they know we don't mean 'Slaves' as in 'slaves.'" The band has recorded and released two albums of their own material, *Talkin' Reggae* (Celluloid) and 1992's *Temperature* (Flame Tree), with lead vocals by keyboardist Thuthukani Cele.

Dube is refreshingly candid about the new deejay and dancehall style coming out of Jamaica.

"Well Fed Slave/Hungry Free Man," "Is This the Way," and "Take It to Jah"—brought home an undiminished message delivered in an unflagging style. Though many of his songs are incredibly personal (he has sung about his mother, his father, his girlfriend, his wife, and personal problems, as well as taking on countries and corporations), his best work views the world through the perspective of his own origins.

One small but tangible sign of change in South Africa is the new acceptance there of one of the world's most viable symbols of revolu-

"Some of it don't have a message at all and I personally don't like it. Not to say it's bad, but that's what music is all about. What good is a song without a message?"

Lucky Dube's message is a simple yet timeless one: "It's the message of coming together of the people. Unity is the message. We're not talking unity, say, amongst the black community, we're talking unity amongst everybody. You know? Because we've got to be together as one. God didn't create white men or black men. God just created men in his image. We are his children. There's no reason to be separated like we are. So the basic message is the coming together of the people."

And what will it take to get that message across? "I think that all depends on the people. Because we are the people that are directly involved in this. The government in all the countries can make adjustments. Peace treaties can be made, but it all depends on us, the people involved. A change of attitude towards one another, that what will make a difference, not the peace treaties and everything they do."

What appeals to new and old reggae fans alike in the music of Lucky Dube is the very commitment to the high ideals that established reggae music in the first place. That an artist from Africa, the land to which reggae music called out initially for inspiration and repatriation, should be the one to come with such a message is at once edifying and right. Though reggae music was born in Jamaica it has always been rooted in Africa, and in the words of Lucky Dube, "We are bringing the roots."

CHAPTER 19

Majek Fashek of Nigeria:

Prophet Without Margin

Nigerian reggae singer Majek Fashek blends traditional African music, seventies reggae, and sixties rock, stirring it all with a personal perspective that is both diverse and innovative. His African roots mix well with his reggae stylings and his rock influences add an accessible edge. Still, it's Majek's ability to capture a spiritual vibe and express his social concerns in varied musical styles that give his work international appeal.

Nigeria, he says, is "a beautiful country, full of nature and a good vibe, and humble and loving people." The country has also had its share of political problems, been locked down for years under military rule and, as witness the treatment of Fela Kuti, has not always treated its artists with the greatest respect. Though songs such as "Police Brutality" from his first album may not be appreciated by the Nigerian government, he notes they are "well accepted by the people."

As a boy Fashek started out playing traditional (or, as he calls it, "ritualistic") music, creating all sorts of different sounds and rhythms on percussion instruments. Later he found himself drawn to reggae. He grew up listening to R&B, blues and rock.

"In the late sixties, early seventies," he explains, "we listened to Joe Cocker, Jimi Hendrix, and the Beatles—that's on the rock level." In reggae, he says, "We listened to Jimmy Cliff, Toots and the Maytals, Bob Marley, and Peter Tosh." By high school he had his own reggae band, Jah Sticks. They played live shows and concerts in the city of Benin where they lived (not to be confused with the country of Benin, which lies just to the west of Nigeria along the coast).

While still in Benin, he remembers, "I worked for a recording company called Tabansi Records as A&R manager. I was also a producer at that time. I worked with the company for three and a half years, producing African music and all different kinds of music. I moved to Lagos and invited my group—Lagos is like New York City, and the capital of Nigeria."

Fashek's label wanted him to record as a solo artist, but he wanted to make it as a group. His band signed with a label and recorded, but the recordings were never released. "I wanted to come as a group first, but as destiny would want it everything was slow. They wanted me to record so I took the chance. So I did *Prisoner of Conscience,* my first album.

The album was issued in Nigeria on the Tabansi label and picked up for release in America by Mango in 1990. Its impact—first in his homeland, and then internationally, was initially tied to one particular song. Its success— and not just commercially—made Fashek seem a kind of modern prophet.

Nigeria had long been suffering the effects of an extended drought. "When this album was released there was no money for promotion. But the mystical power of the song 'Send Down the Rain' promoted this record. In Nigeria, in Africa, in Ethiopia, there was rain. Wherever I did this song there was rain. So they started calling me 'Rainmaker,' 'Rain Prophet'—this was the beginning of I." His explanation for the phenomenon is simple: "God blessed the record. There was so much rain! That's the rain I'm still reaping today. It never stops falling; the rain falls every season, the message continues."

Some might argue the same power was operating on his hit single "Free Afrika, Free Mandela" from 1989's *I and I Experience* (CBS International). The album also contained "Religion Na Politics," which he remade as "Religion Is Politics" on his next disc. In it Fashek calls for pan-religious unity. Unfortunately this is one prophecy that has not yet been realized.

Songs such as "Send Down the Rain" can't really be planned out in advance. "That is why I try to write by inspiration, not just writing. It can come anytime, in your sleep, while driving, even just sitting." And Fashek has another unique approach to his music: "My songs never finish. I don't finish my music." An alternate version of "Send Down the Rain" appears on his third album, 1991's complexly textured *Spirit of Love* (East/West). "I don't finish that yet again," he says smiling. "An original song is never finished, it has no end. It lingers on. It's a continuation."

Unlike most who listen to his work, Fashek doesn't refer to his own music as reggae. "I call it African music," he says. "And that's the definition of reggae music. It's Africa music, although they have a name, they call it reggae. But I call it African music: that is the fullness of the sound. The vibe is the same. African music is the inspiration for all. Africa is roots. Rhythm and blues and reggae come from Africa. The spirituals."

"My brothers from Africa and African Americans," he continues, "we wail. You must come to Benin one time, it's incredible. They use maracas, they make—it's the kind of music they play for the dead. Music of the dead. It's too heavy—deep music. It's used to send the soul of the dead peacefully. You can feel that music in my music, too. It's like wailing or crying."

To Fashek, specific labels serve only to place boundaries on the potential of his music. "Just to call my music reggae or rock music is limiting.

The most high have no limit. Music is God, Jah has no limitation, so why should I limit myself? I play Africa music 'cause everything is African—rock music, rhythm and blues—you can feel it in my music. It's a full marriage of the music which is a consciousness and a unification for the white race and the black race. I don't deal with black music or white music. Why should I deal with color? Jah has no color, Jah is everything. When you say African, it means roots. It means beginning. Because we come from Africa, all of us—you and I."

One example of his international approach is *Spirit of Love*'s "Majek Fashek in New York"

MAJEK FASHEK. Photograph by Jan Salzman; © 1995 Phantom Photos

in which he decries the plight of the homeless in the land of the free. "I was surprised when I got down to New York and there was beggars in the street. The brothers over here always send up pictures of limousines, beautiful women, different houses, say they have a good time. So every Nigerian growing up today wants to come to America. It's good to travel! But they don't tell us about the tribulation we go through here too. Definitely, life's a struggle. It's a struggle everywhere. Same thing in Nigeria, you have homeless everywhere. So I wrote this song. As I walked down the street, I was getting the inspiration."

On his latest album, *Rainmaker* (Tuff Gong) he talks of his experience in Los Angeles in the song "L.A." "One thing I don't like about L.A.," he says, "too much police brutality." On the disc he also sums up his feelings about reggae and African music with the song "Kpangolo." "In America they call it rock and roll, rhythm and blues/In Jamaica they call it reggae/In Africa we call it Kpangolo."

"Everything is going back to Africa again," says Fashek, "and that is why we need each other. The Armageddon war almost came through Iraq and the Americans. The only land that's gonna survive after the Armageddon war is Africa. We're gonna receive the European people in Africa because that's the prophecy. We must unite. There will be no bad blood, no bias. I think by God's grace there won't be no second slavery because there's no use to go backward— you gotta go forward. We know they have the ammunition and everything, but we are one— we need each other. So I am using music to propagate this message."

In person as in his music, Majek Fashek is self-confident and inspired. "It's only me that can free myself. Reggae music is a powerful African music that has to be completed. Bob Marley took it to a level—but I have to take it higher, man." And his message is not to be taken lightly. To people of all races he says, "I think we need each other, and that's why we must unite. I just say peace and love, so we can make a better world for our children and the future of the Earth. Because the Earth is a great planet. It was given to man. So man should not abuse it—man should use it well."

CHAPTER 20

Raymond Myers:

Reggae from Nicaragua

It's a smoky night in L.A. as Belizian Pupa Curley wraps up a DJ segment on one song from Raymond Myers's forthcoming debut CD. At the mixing board is Jamaican-born ex-Bullwackies hand Fabian Cooke. The singer and songwriter hails from Nicaragua, making this a truly international endeavor.

It might surprise many to know that Nicaragua has a black population. Raymond Myers, who co-founded the Nicaraguan reggae band Soul Vibrations with his friend Phillip Montalvan, is of African descent via the Caribbean population of the country's

North Coast. "My dad was a Jamaican, says Myers, "So I think it's one scene. We are on the Atlantic Coast (of Nicaragua) so we have the whole Caribbean."

The band recorded a remarkable CD and was featured in a documentary that brought international interest. Whittled down from a seven-piece to a duo the band eventually split, but Raymond Myers has continued to record and perform solo, headlining a Caribbean festival in Los Angeles in 1997 broadcast live on KPFK.

"I was born in Bluefields," Myers says, "that's like the capital of the Atlantic Coast. The population is 40,000 people. It's more populated since the new government. Other people from the Pacific came over after the hurricane."

Hurricane Joan brought unprecedented destruction in Nicaragua. "Who really had a home, the hurricane blew down everything and everyone was running trying to find something," recalls Myers. "A lot of people was running through the rain picking up things like TV, and after that people just take their own piece of land and build their houses. So everything change in that sense."

The makeup of Nicaragua's population is complex. The Atlantic coast's diversity historically included free blacks and former slaves, Afro-Nicaraguan Creole, British-influenced local culture, Spanish, and several Indian languages. "Spanish is the dominant language," Myers explains. "Through the colonialism what we had down there. British they come and enslave the Indian dem. Well, the African side of Bluefields is people who came in from the Caribbean [mixed] with the Indians in Bluefields and that is what formed the black culture down there."

Unlike Jamaica, where the Spanish fled when the British arrived, Myers explains that these two dominant European cultures operated independently in Nicaragua "at the same time." This resulted in a sort of dual colonialism. "The Spaniard was on the Pacific and the British was on the Atlantic. So the influence of the English, their custom, their way of life—we adopt some of that style."

He first became interested in music in church through his devout grandmother, who played the accordion. "Always in church I would be the one to lead the singing and clapping and things like that. We had a pastor who used to play keyboards. He didn't teach me anything, but I continue. Growing up I had the chance to be with some older musicians—they didn't want me to hold their instruments but I only wanted to put my hand on it."

One form of music Myers grew up listening to was ska. Along with this healthy dose of early Jamaican sounds, he heard "rock 'n' roll and all dem things. My grandpa had a lot of that. A lot of Caribbean. I like some from B.B. King. Jimi Hendrix have some good one. Muddy Waters—real old-time blues. But as a child I couldn't imagine what it would be like to really put it to the music. I remember first time I was gonna write a song I didn't even have idea how to do that. I didn't have structure, form, nor nothin'. I used to want to do it always. I like American music. The influence is Latin and America."

But the dominant influence on Soul Vibrations' 1991 CD *Black History/Black Culture* (Redwood) is reggae. The disc contains the song "Rock Down Central America," which became the title of a documentary covering the area of Bluefields, the band, and their music. The aural equivalent is the album's "Journey Through El Salvador," in which this unique reggae band displayed their own unlikely roots.

In the early nineties Soul Vibrations participated in an album called *Chicken Made of Rags* (also released on Redwood), singing and serving as backing band for Holly Near and others. In 1993 the band played one of their final gigs at the prestigious Long Beach Bob Marley Days Festival with a restructured lineup that included Jamaica's legendary Santa Davis, drummer for the original Soul Syndicate and longtime member of Peter Tosh's band Word, Sound and Power.

For a while Raymond played under the Soul Vibrations banner with a handpicked team of L.A. musicians, but eventually he decided to record and perform under his own name.

In a series of shows up and down the coast he mixed his own special blend of salsa, Latin rhythms, and occasional rock influences, holding it all together with a pounding reggae rhythm and an energized vocal delivery, alternating between guitar and timbales as he dominated the stage. Commuting to Los Angeles from Managua, where he lives with his family, he recorded his first album, the soon-to-be-released *Nicaribbean Man*.

Inspired by reggae's positive message of change, Myers, like his Jamaican musical forebears, comes with a style that takes the percussive sound of Latin music together with ska, reggae, and rhythm and blues, to create a unique and inspired sound unlike any other on the reggae scene. Myers continues the work today, playing international festivals and spreading the new vibe at home and abroad. His multicultural performance warms the hearts of audiences and his message of peace and inner strength reaches across cultural barriers to point the way to a better world.

RAYMOND MYERS. Photograph by Anne Marie Staas

CHAPTER 21

International Explosion

The eighties and nineties have seen an explosion in international reggae. Reggae from inside and outside the U.S. mixing Latin elements include the Cuban reggae of Arawak Jah and Johnny Dread, and the Latin dancehall style of El General. A quick listen to Mexican radio shows a great influence of reggae on the music being made there today, even by nonreggae groups.

Brazil's Cidade Negra melds smooth, relaxed vocals with dancehall. Skank plays an entirely different style with raw horn-dominated vocals. Toaster Eddie is a Brazilian DJ who waxes "Paz

Universal" in "Espanglish." Nomad blends carnival with dancehall and a healthy dose of electric guitar. One of the best reggae discs from Brazil is Tribo de Jah and Fauzi Beydoun's *Ruinas Da Babilonia*. Bantus feature a smooth pop sound and Jah Mai mix Brazilian reggae with hip-hop. Rogelio Mitchell utilizes a sophisticated mix of jazz, Caribbean, and Brazilian elements.

Peruvian reggae? Leave it to the visionary Adrian Sherwood to record Tierra Sur, a dub-drenched reggae band from Peru in his London studios. Few opening cuts have the power to grab like Argentina's Pericos, whose CD *Pampas Reggae* (EMI International) features "Mucha Experiencia," a free translation of Bob Andy's "Too Experienced" (though probably learned from Barrington Levy). The disc also boasts titles like "Cabeza de Policia" and "La Cienega Blvd."

Recently the group Roots Afrika from Israel released their first CD, *Rise Oh Israel* (NMC, Israel). Serious in tone but backed by lilting rhythmic melodies and power-punch bass and drums, it blends music and culture from Africa, Jamaica, and Israel. The themes of repatriation, Zion, and biblical references that dominate reggae take on a special vibration with this group.

Reggae from Africa is one of the largest growing segments of the international explosion. Along with Lucky Dube, Alpha Blondy, and Majek Fashek artists like Innocent from Tanzania (who led the Nebraska-based African reggae band Les Exodus for years) have helped to blend the African and Jamaican styles. From Zaire in 1992 came Elijah with *Rastaman Is Never Angry,* mixing elements of his own Central African heritage—particularly African rumba—with roots reggae. Singing in Swahili and Lingala, along with some French and English, Elijah's scope is indeed international.

The Mandators released a half dozen albums in Nigeria that led to 1994's *Power of the People* on Heartbeat. Band leader Victor Essiet explains that the band has "a mandate of one love and overstanding for peace, love, and justice to the people. I play reggae music," says Essiet, who has done so since the late seventies. Majek Fashek was his lead guitarist "way back in time."

"Reggae music is an African music" is the way he sees it. "Jamaicans are Africans." Another Nigerian who gives a whole new meaning to the concept of roots is Ras Kimono, with several fine releases including *What's Gwan* on Polydor. Other Nigerian reggae singers include Orits Williki (Kole-Man Revolutionaire), Sam Thio, Endy Rasta, and Prince Chyke Jonathan. Nigeria's Jerri Jhetto is based in L.A. and his music features themes of social conscience and unity, African roots and gritty reggae rhythms. It's roots and culture with an African vibe.

Ethiopia's Dallol recorded and toured on their own, then backed Ziggy Marley and the Melody Makers for two albums and tours. Recently Zeleke from Dallol unveiled a solo CD. Released out of Switzerland, Jah Olela African N'Koy Band's *New Exile* (Uhuru), with liner notes in French and band members from Ghana and Cameroon, is a good example of the international feel of much African reggae. Adbloyt Abashi, also on a Swiss label, serves up a mix of English, French, and African dialect in a dancehall DJ style on his CDs *Love Is Equal* and *Survival Is the Game,* recorded in Kingston and Zurich. Ivory Coast's Soweto Soleil and the Flames of Fire operate out of New York.

African reggae in general and the South African variety in particular retain the revolutionary vibe of early Jamaican groups. South Africa's O'Yaba has two CDs available, *The Game Is Not Over* and *One Foundation,* both issued in the U.S. by Shanachie. Sounding like eight Lucky Dubes, the harmonies are truly amazing, a blend of roots themes and African elements. Also from South Africa, Sons of Selassie display militant roots while always maintaining their African edge on *Changes* (Rhythm Safari), and Ras Dumisani adds his own "Universal Message" on *Zululand Reggae* and *Mister Music* (both on the Blue Silver label). Rocky Dawuni from

Ghana has two reggae releases, the most recent of which is 1998's *Crusade* (Who Dun It?).

Massilia Sound System's *Parla Patois* (RAS) is French reggae. Stasha Bader's award-winning short film *Paris Rap* shows the influence of dancehall in France. Metal Sound melds rap, hip-hop and ragga. Sophia Asher spews rapid-fire French with intensity over digital riddims. Good Morning Babylones feature a ragged horn section and feel-good vocal style. Sauri offers pop arrangements sung in French and African. Also of interest is Niominka-Bi Diaxas Band. The Declic label in France has a whole roster of ragga acts, including Trio Bad who aren't.

Roadblock (1989, Nubian) was an impressive debut for West Germany's Three Dimension, who were schooled by former U.K. Reggae Regulars Tony Benjamin and garnered raves from Capital Radio's David Rodigan. Germany is also home base for the Lions, Mighty V., and Ras Perez. Originally from Dominica, Perez has recorded in Martinique and Guadaloupe, jammed in Boston and Salt Lake City, and lived and worked in Paris, Berlin, and London (he sings in English and French). Poland is represented by Baksysz, a rockin' reggae band who've been together for ten years and sing in English and Polish.

One of the most experimental reggae records ever recorded is *Higher Heights* on the Twinkle label. Twinkle Brother Norman Grant and bassist Dub Judah provide a reggae backing for a Polish string trio and Grant translates their Polish folk lyrics into Jamaican patois, weaving intricate melodies through the already densely lush tracks. By "discovering" this European music and giving it back to us in the form of reggae, Grant teaches a simple lesson disguised as a brilliant musical creation.

Papa Jube brings a special intensity to his Haitian reggae as evinced on his 1993 Melody Makers CD *Liberasyon*. Declic's *Haiti Rap and Ragga* samples several artists. Condition 4 from Guam, Tropical Depression from the Philippines, and the Maori reggae of New Zealand's Herbs are but a few of many. The Middle Eastern dub of Badawi, the Zydeco reggae of Ras Cloud and the Sons of Selassie-I, and bands in which all cultures collide emerge daily. Helsinki, Finland, is home to Ron Hardy's No Explanation whose music "ingested via sound vibrations travels to brain."

The Netherlands have become home base for the raggamuffin stylings of Ragga Frankie and the roots vibe of Jamaica Papa Curvin, Militant Irie, and the heavy riddims of Twilight Circus in Dub. Easy Chanting melds sweet harmonies and simple themes with a modern dancehall vibe. Gracy and the Herbman Band and a dub-vocal conglomerate known simply as the Vision have issued several CDs. One-Style MDV actually fuse several. Roots Syndicate from Holland play a style they refer to as "rude and gentle." Sundance Kid stirs Bob Marley, the Beatles, '50s croon tunes and hip-hop. Panache Culture issues product on RUNNherlands, one of several labels that release and distribute international reggae via the Netherlands.

Nowhere has reggae had greater impact than Japan. Japanese buyers are among the most active collectors of "golden age" reggae 7-inches. Mute Beat, a ska-dub band from Japan, has mastered both styles live and on record with stunning authenticity. Their discs *Still Echo* and *Flowers* are hard to find but essential listening. *In Dub* (ROIR) selects from both and may be easier to find. Among other Japanese reggae outfits of note is Tokyo's the Highest Region, with *Vibes from Jah Jah Mountain* (Afjah-Japan). They play top-flight reggae with deep bass-and-drum grooves and generous portions of saxophone.

Canada has long provided a second home for transplanted Jamaicans. Major reggae singers like Stranger Cole, Johnny Osbourne, and Leroy Sibbles and such musical luminaries as Lynn Taitt and Jackie Mittoo stretched out beneath her maple leaf. From Canada come roots artists like Selassie I Power's King of Kings, Kali and Dub, and Pressure Drop. The Canadian posse includes Reggae Cowboys, who exclude no element from dancehall, roots rock or popular. And of course Canada has Snow.

A collective called Young Lions groups a heap of singers and DJs under producer Trevor (Napthali) Phillips' wing. Shuggy Milligan produces, records, and releases his own work and that of others including veteran Yabby You. One of the more recent Canadian phenomenons is the runaway reggae of Candice Robinson. Candice was born in Canada but spent her high school years in Barbados, where she records. Also from Barbados, Soca star John King adds reggae to his crown on *Yard Style* (Mesa, 1996).

Switzerland's Ganglords took the international *and* local band concept one step further, living in Kingston for six months to get the vibe, then recording as backing band for a series of Jamaican singers and DJs, including Spanner Banner, Courtney Melody, Captain Barkey, and Lady Patra. These and other tracks are available on a 1992 CD called *Kingston Confidential* on their Gangproductions label. Among the 7-inch Jamaican releases included on the disc is Frankie Paul's "Thanks and Praises," one of the best singles of his career.

Recording in Switzerland, Mickey Tuff offers "Geneva Ragga" in "Dancehall Roots" style on *Nah Lef Jah Jah.* The music is provided by the Rough House Crew; the CD is on the Rootsman Records label. One track was also recorded at Mindsearcha's Studio in London. Winchester is another good example of international independence. I have two albums and one CD of all original material from him: one recorded in Caracas, Venezuela, one in Zurich, and one in Holland.

Island reggae is no longer limited to the island of Jamaica. Crucial Bankie and Al G from the Virgin Isles, Rashani from Grenada, Inner Visions from St. Thomas, and Tonka from St. Maarten, Netherlands Antilles, join releases from Barbados, Cuba, Hawaii, and other bodies of land surrounded by water all over the world. Check out Llwybr Llaethog's *Mewn Dub* (ROIR) for reggae from Wales.

I've reviewed these and many other international releases along with reggae from England, Jamaica, and America for over a decade and I'm continually amazed at the wide variety. Reggae takes root in the most unlikely (and most likely) places because it has a purpose and a message that seeks to unite diverse people. A good cross-section sampler is RAS Record's *MNP: Reggae from Around the World,* including Sweden's Reggae Team, Ruina De Moda from Uruguay and Italy's Different Stylee.

CHAPTER 22

Eek-A-Mouse:

One of a Kind

Eek-A-Mouse holds a unique position in reggae, as you might imagine from his fanciful name. On his earliest records he has a rough "country" sound reminiscent of a young Don Carlos—the Waterhouse "Black Uhuru" style seems to be where he breaks off from—but by his first hit he had created a style all his own. He's gone on to be, along with Mikey Dread and Yellowman, something of an international phenomenon quite apart from the rest of the world of reggae.

His style, surely one of the oddest to come from Jamaica, is a universal blend of accents and rhythms, even without the trademark string of "biddy biddy bong bong" that punctuates his songs. The smile-a-minute stream of consciousness of his lyrical word-play leaps from subject to subject, returning continually to that most unusual topic, himself (something a few other hit-makers, like England's Pato Banton, have also made work for themselves) and his unusual name.

"In Jamaica in the late '70s," he explains, "there was a racehorse named Eek-A-Mouse—back in them days I liked to bet on the horses. I always bet on him and he always lose. So once I didn't bet on Eek-A-Mouse, and he won. My friends them like it so they called me Eek-A-Mouse. And we seh love it now 'cause it's making me dough!"

His first few singles were recorded under his real name, Ripton Hylton, and released by him on the Eek-A-Mouse label. Not only were they waxed while he was going to college, they were produced by his math teacher, Mr. Dehaney. "Even when I was in high school, if there's a concert or a dance going on they gotta call Eek-A-Mouse."

Those early tunes have a far different sound from the serio-comic "Far East" style Eek-A-Mouse is known for now. "At the time I didn't find Eek-A-Mouse style with the "bang bang didley bang bang." That came up natural singing

EEK-A-MOUSE. Photograph by John Skomdahl

in dancehall, just start make some new sound. My friend say, 'Man, you sound like a Japanese Indian Mexican!' So I keep it up and that's the Mouse today."

"Wah Do Dem" was the 1980 single that made his name in Jamaica. "When I made 'Wah Do Dem' I sing 'She too short and me too tall,' because my chick, she kinda short—you know, me tall. So I make a song about it. Right away they wanted more!" To simply say he's tall is as close to modest as Mouse gets. At six foot six he's easy to spot in a crowd. As he puts it, "I'm the tallest mouse in the world."

"Wa-Do-Dem" (or "A Wha Do Dem" in alternate spelling) was produced by Douglas Boothe. It was followed by "Modeling Queen," another JA hit single that appeared on his first album, *Bubble Up Yu Hip*. Both were produced by singer Linval Thompson and issued on his Thompson Sound label in Jamaica.

But it was his hookup with rising star producer Henry "Junjo" Lawes that took the Mouse man international. *Wa-Do-Dem* (Greensleeves, 1981) remade the JA single but included two tracks, "Operation Eradication" and "Ganja Smuggling" that got plenty of U.K. airplay. A distribution deal with Shanachie also put these records in the hands of American reggae fans. With Lawes Mouse also cut the album *Mouskateer* (Shanachie, 1984), containing the brilliant "Anarexol" and the self-explanatory "How I Got My Name."

The early eighties also saw two more albums produced by Linval Thompson, 1982's *Skidip* (Shanachie) and *The Mouse and the Man,* (Shanachie, 1983). Nearly all these discs were cut at Channel One with the Roots Radics backing. *Very Best of Eek-A-Mouse* (Shanachie, 1990) draws from the Greensleeves/Shanachie LPs. Other albums include *Live at Reggae Sunsplash 1982,* issued on the Sunsplash label (one side is Eek-A-Mouse and one side Michigan and Smiley), *Assassinator* (1983), *King and I* (1985), *Mouse-a-Mania* (1987, which collects

tracks from the two preceding discs), and *Eek-A-Nomics* (1988). These last four albums were all issued by the RAS label.

With these albums to his credit Mouse branched into movies, playing Fat Smitty in *New Jack City*. "I do seven or eight minutes in the movie but they cut me down to one minute and I was pissed. Lost my Oscar! I'm a born entertainer and when I'm singing on the stage I'm a more actor because you gotta do it all in one take. [In Hollywood] they [say], 'Cut! Cut! Stop! Stop!' On the stage you can't stop. I'm a born actor! I'm just like Clark Gable"—he pauses for effect—"but a me, I'm Dark Gable."

When I spoke with him in 1993, Mouse had just replaced Shabba Ranks as co-headliner with Maxi Priest at a human services charity benefit for disadvantaged youths in Pasadena. Ranks's controversial remarks in support of Buju Banton's gay-blasting "Boom Bye Bye" cost him the spot (as well as a scheduled appearance on *The Tonight Show*). The controversy seemed to have a sobering effect on both Shabba's and Buju's careers, however, as they emerged in the following year with some of their best material.

Of the controversy Eek-A-Mouse says, "In this world you can't judge nobody. To each his own: I don't wanna downplay nobody. Everybody come to the Mouse show, straight guy, married guy, they love the Mouse. Gay loves Eek-A-Mouse, drag queen loves Eek-A-Mouse, and Eek-A-Mouse love them."

In fact he's been known to perform in some outrageous costumes himself, touring and stepping out on stage dressed as a pirate, one of the Three Musketeers (a natural), in a prison outfit complete with ball and chain, and other variations. He's also been known to write a song at the drop of a hat, surreally juxtaposing concepts and images till your head spins. Brash, outspoken, inherently comedic, it's no wonder he finds intolerance intolerable.

It's something he has experienced firsthand. "Anywhere in the world when they see a

Jamaican passport they wanna pull you over. I got a beard, I got the hair, they think I'm a ganga-smoking gangster from Jamaica. Two weeks ago me and my friend was coming into Miami and the [drug-sniffing] dog stay right beside me. The guy say we smokin' something. I guess if you come from Jamaica you smell of weed."

From his point of view, dogs and Hollywood producers share similar traits. "They want Jamaicans to play gangster all the while, like a gunman or a lawyer." He passed on a part of Steven Seagal's *Marked for Death* after reading the script. It had "some bad vibe about Jamaicans. It have Rastaman doing all kinda voodoo and drugs."

Despite show biz tribulations he feels at home in movieland. As he puts it, "I own L.A. I'm the mayor." (He also admits to being president of the United States and prime minister of Jamaica.) Still, he seems a bit sensitive about Orange County and Anaheim in particular. "I'm the only real Mouse, man, so Mickey Mouse better watch it. I am a Disneyland outcast."

Where does Mouse's music fit in reggae music today? "I'm roots and I'm dancehall," he says expansively. "Dancehall style was there from way down: Dennis Alcapone, U Roy, I Roy, Scotty, King Stitch. And those kinda style was introduced in America as the rap. Talk over sound system—we Jamaican introduced that first and [it] was underground until it just blew up."

He likes some of the modern Jamaican stylists like Ninjaman and Shabba Ranks because of the diversity in their work. "Some talk about reality and some talk about sex." His own style is harder to define. "There was no influence," he says. "That's why I'm so unique. Only got influence by the likes of Natty King Cole, Marty Robbins, Sam Cooke, the Rolling Stones, and the Who, and all them band.

"Back in Jamaica we listen to all them records in the '60s. Millie Jackson and all that gospel stuff." His real education, he maintains, came from "The sound system, because the

sound system is like the roots. If you can't go to music school you go to the sound system. They teach you tempo, timing, like school but more hard-core."

Having established his acting credentials, Eek-A-Mouse returned to recording in 1991 with *U-Neek*, his first album for Island Records. The standout song from this album, "Rude Boys a Foreign," he says, "is about all the bad boys in Jamaica who wanna come to America and do drugs or rob. They find that's the wrong attitude, so they're in prison, some die, some get mad. For them, America ain't no dream. It's a nightmare."

A far different style was offered in "D'yer Maker," his version of the Led Zeppelin standard that appears on the same disc. "Back in the early '70s when Bob Marley was kicking up, all them big rock and roller was doin' kinda reggae stuff and that song was like some good shit. So I thought I could give it a try—I think Robert Plant love it." Still, some may balk at his surprising theory: "Reggae music is most like heavy metal. If you take down heavy metal slow, it's the reggae. You take reggae, speed it up, you get heavy metal rock and roll."

Mouse rode back into town in 1996 with *Black Cowboy* (Sunset Boulevard). Though his voice seemed to have dropped an octave, the breadth of subject matter—"Bi-Racial Baby," "Shopping," "Local Fisherman," and the very Mouse-ical "Isn't Life a Trip"—as well as his patented "bingy-boingy" style indicate that Eek-A-Mouse is still "in the house."

From some of his earliest work, Eek-A-Mouse has used a mix of his special brand of wit and current events to produce a surprising twist on things. "When I'm in Jamaica," he says, "I'm like CNN. Guys come around saying, 'Mouse man. Tom Jones got shot and Harry Sue got pregnant.'" In his hands this material takes on universal themes from a slightly skewed perspective. As he says in nontypical understated fashion, "I go after a different style."

CHAPTER 23

Wicked Inna Dance:

The Dancehall Invasion

Reggae music started in the dance. "In Jamaica," says DJ originator U Roy, "this is like one of the major enjoyment for poor people. Nothing to them like a sound system dance 'cause is not everyone can find this big money to take in some big ball at the Sheraton or someplace like that. So a lot of people enjoy coming to the dance." The "dancehall" style as we know it today opened up the field to thousands of young singers and DJs too.

The DJ or "deejay" has been around through all of this—the earliest, like Count Machuki, Sir Lord Comic and King Stitt were live MCs who called the crowds to the dance over thumping rhythms. Dub and the DJ style led to a whole new approach to music. The new styles of the early eighties brought in a whole new crop of DJs like Peter Metro and Kojak. Already by 1981 a Junjo Lawes album heralded a *Whole New Generation of DJ,* though few of those anthologized as such sustained their careers into the mid-eighties much less the nineties.

Perhaps the most successful Jamaican dancehall DJ internationally was Winston "Yellowman" Foster, an alumni of the famed Alpha Boy's School. That his star began to rise just as Bob Marley passed is perhaps no coincidence. Yellow represented a 360-degree spin from the social concerns of the seventies and helped kick off the "new" dancehall era with songs replete with sexual braggadocio, misogyny, and violent imagery, pandering to concerns earlier reggae artists might call "Babylonian." His success generated scores of imitators. He continues to be a popular live draw and was nominated for a Grammy as recently as 1998.

The real key to what constitutes dancehall and what doesn't is not the artists but the producers. As the eighties dawned, one who moved to the head of the class was Henry "Junjo" Lawes. Working with singers like Barrington Levy and a heap of dancehall's top DJs, Lawes and his studio band the Roots Radics recorded at Channel One, mixing at King Tubby's with Scientist on the board (at least in the early days). The dancehall sound began a slow march away from the era of the Revolutionaries and the Aggrovators into the present.

Lawes issued his product on Greensleeves in England and many a DJ and singer went from the sound system to the studio and out into the world at a pace that would have amazed the earlier generation. One of the first of the newcomers was Toyan, whose lyrics followed the lead of "second generation" DJs like Dillinger and Trinity and moved away from the concerns that had dominated the seventies.

DJs were becoming entertainers. Up until then they had been social commentators.

Each decade seems to cleave Jamaican music in a different way. The year 1967 saw ska giving way to rock steady and the beginnings of reggae, while 1977 is a cut-off point for many collectors of Jamaican 45s who confidently buy anything recorded before that year, suspiciously finger any record dated '77 or later. Another watermark year is 1987, whem digital recording innovations first put forth by Prince Jammy in 1986 took hold of the dancehall style, which had always been around, and new artists moved to the fore.

Among them were DJs like Admiral Bailey, whose shotgun-gravel voice laid down a line in the sand for lovers of "old school" reggae. His singsong hit "Two Year Old" and fat guy fave "Big Belly Man" were massive. You gotta love a guy who's not concerned about his weight! Major Mackeral, whose real name is Garfield Dixon, is another DJ who burst on the scene in 1987, a key year for changing styles and dancehall music.

Lieutenant Stitchie, a high school teacher who turned an attempt to make an anatomy lesson more interesting into an international hit ("Body Body") scored in '87 with "Broad Hips" and "Wear Yuh Size" and continued to make exciting DJ records like 1993's "Bun It Down." Two albums for Atlantic and a strong collection of '90s singles on Shanachie well attest to his powers, and his live performances are not to be missed.

DJ duos locked in with Michigan and Smiley, who started the old fashioned way—at Studio One. Clint Eastwood paired up with General Saint, Papa Finnigan banked on Junior Ranking, and everybody got to breathe now and then until Chaka Demus and Pliers hit so big that DJ duos were out and every DJ went looking for a singer to "double up" with. The combination records turned out to be some of the strongest in dancehall as wise producers used the best of both styles and no one voice was stretched to the limit.

One DJ who made it on his own was Papa San, who has worked with producers like Gussie Clarke, Jack Scorpio, Mikey Bennett, and Danny Brownie. He picked up on the super-speed style of the English MCs and delivered it in a Jamaican manner that could well be called (as was one of his releases) *Fire Inna Dance Hall.* He wowed crowds at the traveling Reggae Sunsplash shows and can truly say with his 1990 hit single, "Dance Hall Good to We." His brother Pan Head was also building a career when he was shot down in a still unsolved murder.

King Kong is another Jamaican performer who grappled with the change in sound and won. A singer who incorporates some of the DJ in his delivery, he rode Jammy's new riddims with a flair. Though many of his songs are of the "sound boy" variety (boastful put-downs of his competition), he contributed cuts like "Trouble Again" that demonstrated there was room for political awareness, cultural considerations, and conscious vibes even in the changing times that encapsuled the late eighties.

The line between dancehall and reggae proper is so fine as to be at times nonexistent. What makes Ranking Joe one of the last of the "classic" DJs and Ringo one of the first dancehall DJs may simply be the former's cultural approach. Though Ringo's 1982 album *Eye Witness* (Esoldun, produced by Tommy Cowan) includes "Cleanliness" and his *Riding West* (Jah Guidance, from the same year, produced by Junjo Lawes) contains "Jah Jah Guide Over Me" the song that made him was the ultra-crude single "Two Lesbians Hitch" on the Mic label.

The term *slackness* covers a range of material that runs the gamut from the naughtiness of General Degree's "The Pianist" to General Echo's "Bathroom Sex." Dancehall embraced the sexuality society tries to mask and by the time of Shabba Ranks, "slackness" was being called "yard style," a term once denoting roots.

"Killing" another "sound boy" seemed less a metaphor than a daily activity.

Still, there's more to dancehall than its lowest common denominator. As Michigan of Michigan and Smiley says, "We ha fe have the culture in it! We cannot mislead the people, we must be directing them at all times. We protest against things that we don't like. We lick out against the system. We ha fe educate the youth!"

Sugar Minott, Barrington Levy, Sanchez Robert French, Michael Palmer, and Spanner Banner have all been dubbed dancehall singers. Gold Teeth, Million Teeth, Singing Teeth, Singing Sweet, and Singing Melody could be nothing else. Other dancehall singers include Thriller U, Echo Minott, Anthony Red Rose, Courtney Melody, Pinchers, and Anthony Malvo. Singers from the same era considered roots include Andrew Bees, Icho Candy, Ed Robinson, Jesse Jendau, and Everton Blender and newcomers like Stanrick, Mikey Roots, and Mikey Spice.

For many in the U.S., dancehall has come to mean simply "inna DJ style." Singers like Junior Tucker and Wayne Wonder veer close to lovers rock but Jamaican fans have "no problem" considering them dancehall. Dancehall has, in the words of one of its first and best singers, Little John, "Found a New Sound." Interestingly, when a young singer begins to hit it big—like the late Garnett Silk or Luciano—he often ceases to be classed as dancehall and becomes a reggae singer. This is in keeping with the dancehall's earlier function as a testing ground for recording careers.

Among the DJs who mix dancehall with roots themes are Brigadier Jerry and Charlie Chaplin. Both served lengthy sound system apprenticeships and issued CDs backed by the Roots Radics that contain none of the negative elements of dancehall and all of the positive elements of reggae. They can be claimed by either camp.

In England the DJ was called an MC, and a completely different dancehall style developed, most recently dubbed "ragga." Asher Senator, Papa Face, General Levy, and Macka B. are just a few of the diverse toasters who plied their trade in the U.K., many recording for the progressive Fashion label.

When I visited in 1994 it was Top Cat who was on top. Among the major U.K. DJ hits were Papa Levi's early eighties rapid-fire paen "Mi God Mi King." Levi returned in the '90s with a good CD produced by Mad Professor. Smiley Culture's hip "Cockney Translation" was one of a wave of such records that included Peter Metro and Dominic's "Yardee and Cockney." DJ/MCs Tippa Irie and Tippa Lee and Rappa Robert all weighed in via the U.K.

One of the first heard in America was Ranking Roger of the Beat (if you were from England), the English Beat (for Americans), and later the ska-flavored International Beat. Gifted with the ability to make up lyrics to anything (I once heard him riff on some airplane music), he livened up the two-tone movement. He in turn discovered and recorded Pato Banton, who went on to become a kind of pop-MC phenomenon in the U.S., gaining airplay in a market few of his contemporaries could scratch. His witty themes and bright delivery made him a recognized reggae figure here, though the focus was often on only one aspect of his career.

"I believe that everyone's got a whole heap of different sides," says Pato. "We like to laugh, sometimes we like to play, sometimes we need love and companionship. But there's also a time when we have to really take time out for Jah and show him the respect. Some people tend to take a part of Pato Banton that they can relate to the most."

Today the diversity of Jamaica's dancehall DJs is truly astonishing. Bounty Hunter, Bounty Killer, Terror Fabulous—each has his own sound. Fans can easily identity and separate Louie Culture, Shaka Shamba, Spragga Benz, Risto Benji, Benjie Miyaz, Jigsy King, Baja Jedd, Red Dragon, Flourgan, Bananaman, or a host of

military men like Mikey General, General Trees, General Plough, General TK, Major Damage, Major Worries, Major Trouble, Captain Barkey, or England's Sargent Pepper.

One unusual name or style inspires a dozen, especially a successful one. Delroy "Pinchers" Thompson had the field clear until the success of "Agony" for Jammy's and later "Bandalero." Then there was a run on the toolbox with Pliers, Screwdriver, Grip Wrench, Scissors, several Saws, a couple of Hammers, and, as long as we're stretching it, Ruler. Ray Hurford of Small Axe recently called my attention to the proliferation of reggae rodents including John Mouse, White Mice, Black Mice, Country Mouse (who later became Simple Simon), and godfather Eek-A-Mouse. Red Rat, formerly known as Mice, the hottest new sensation of early '98, shaves whisker streaks into his eyebrows to enhance his ratlike appearance.

In the seventies the names of gangsters predominated with the likes of Al Capone and Dillinger and cowboys—especially movie cowboys—have always been popular; witness Lone Ranger, Clint Eastwood, Josey Wales, Trinity, John Wayne, Lash La Rue, and Lee Van Cliff. Movie stars supplied stage names for Charlie Chaplin, U.K.'s DJ team Laurel and Hardy, dancehall singer Tony Curtis, and DJs Gregory Peck and Burt Lancaster. There has even been a tendency toward intellectuals in the dancehall with artists like Professor Nuts. Professor Frisky, Professor Grizzly, and Professor Short Hair had less tenure.

For a while it seemed the nineties would bring a kinder, gentler time as cartoon character names like Goofy, Shaggy, and the irrepressible Snaggapuss emerged. The latter, who began his career as Dicky Ranking, actually DJs in the voice of the cartoon character. Lately there's been a darker trend as can be seen by the emergence of Vicious, Vicious Irie, Merciless, Chrome Nine, Poison Chang, Monster Shack, Scare Dem Crew, and others. Most recently a new wave of yard-yuppies has emerged with names like Mr. Vegas, Mercedez, Lexxus, and Rolex.

None of this explains Chuckleberry, Jamalski, Chicken Chest, Super Black, Gospel Fish, Ghost, or the late Pirate (formerly Bionic Steve). One eighties DJ who lived up to his name was Tiger, whose wild performance live and on record invigorated the scene. A motorcycle accident has his career presently on hold. For every Big Joe of the seventies there are a dozen singers such as Little Kirk or DJs like Likkle Wicked's in the '90s. One of the biggest (if fastest fading) was Little Lenny, a seventeen-year-old DJ who couched sexuality in a safe-sex message with "Gun in a Baggy."

Everything irritating to "traditional" reggae lovers—and innovative to dancehall fans, at least briefly—can be summed up by the career of Ninjaman, whose bad-boy posturing (he went so far as to have the image of a gun stamped on his front tooth) and rapid-fire lyrics came to represent for some an attack on music itself. He first charted in 1987 with the Jammy production "More Reality" but it was the early '90s single "Ting a Ling a Ling" that made him. He contributed some of the best (like "Pastor Come Out of the Church") and worst (like "Hollow Point Bad Boy," "My Weapon," and "Kill Dem and Dun") records of his time. He recently resurfaced in a new incarnation as Brother Desmond.

COCOA TEA (LEFT) AND CUTTY RANKS (RIGHT). Photograph by John Skomdahl

Ninjaman inspired Ninja Kid, Ninja Force, Ninja Ford, and Ninja Turtle. Tenor Saw, whose mid-eighties "Roll Call," "Pumpkin Belly," and "Ring the Alarm" helped usher in the age, inspired the late Nitty Gritty in style and begat Tenor Fly and later Lady Saw. Buju Banton—himself inspired by Burro Banton—inspired Lefty, Mello, Lenny, and Mega Banton. Most were preceded by England's Pato. It should be noted "banton" is an old Jamaican term for a storyteller and thus a natural DJ title.

More than just Bantons abound. There's Silver Cat and Alley Cat, Super Cat and Junior Cat, who put out a CD with Junior Demus and Nicodemus—presumably Chaka Demus couldn't make it. In this case it's the late Nicodemus who led the pack—his early eighties hits like "Natty Sell a Million" on TR and "Boneman Connection" showed flair and humor. His final CD *Dancehall Giant* found him still in excellent form.

Shabba Ranks, who inspired a flood of imitators both in name and style, was himself repeating a motif from the seventies that included Ranking Dread, Ranking Ann, Ranking Trevor, and others. After Shabba came Sluggy Ranks, June Ranks, Killer Ranks, Nardo Ranks, Mackie Ranks, and Cutty, Fleshy, Fragga, and Squitty Ranks. And then there's Nut Head Irie.

Ska, rock steady, and reggae all began as popular dances. The early '90s saw the Bogle and the Butterfly and sometimes the DJs and singers who take the day are the ones who ride these brand-new rhythms best. What is puzzling about the "riddim" being the star today is that the riddims of the nineties are generally much blander versions of rhythm tracks reworked from the mid- to late seventies, often themselves "updates" of original Studio One riddims from years before. Still there are some incredible bursts of genius—witness the sudden influx of classical music in the dancehall in the late nineties resulting in tracks like Beenie Man's "Maestro" or Buccaneer's wild "Bad Boy Sonata."

For many reggae fans the distinction between reggae and ragga or dancehall is drawn with the word "digital." When Prince Jammy and others began programming tracks, the writing was on the wall for the "old school," though to this day an interesting mix of the two styles survives and many of the musicians who played on ska, rock steady, and reggae tracks still find work today. Jamaican music has never spurned technological advance. It has triumphed by absorbing each wave from the phasers and bounce-back echo of the sixties in the seventies to the programmed machine rhythms from disco to hip-hop today.

Some DJs in the eighties and nineties came with a style so unique they can't be lumped together. Tony Rebel's high art application mixes strong melodies (often based around old "pop" songs like Jackie De Shannon's "Son of a Preacherman" for 1992's "God of Abraham" on Sky High) with conscious cultural lyrics. Rebel has contributed some of the best tunes of the dancehall era with cuts like "War and Crime," "Guns and Ammunition," and the brilliant "If Jah (Is By My Side)" as well as combination records with Garnet Silk and Cocoa Tea. Terry Ganzie has done some great cultural DJ tunes for producer Donovan Germain, including a mid-nineties album on Profile. Kulcha Knox DJ's cultural lyrics and 1997's *Praise Jah Again* (Karaing) is recommended.

Lest the movie *Dancehall Queen* cause you to think women serve a mainly decorative function in the dancehall, it should be noted that some of the more interesting DJs of the eighties and nineties are of the feminine gender. One of the first was Sister Nancy. Another early female DJ is Lady Ann who worked with producer Leon Symone and recorded the album *Vanity* for Alvin Ranglin's GG's label in 1983. In the late eighties Shelly Thunder received unheralded attention with *Fresh out of the Pack* but seemed to fade from the public's eye just as fast. A good record could bring her right back.

The early nineties saw the emergence of Lady Saw, who could out-nasty the nastiest male DJ with cuts like "Find a Good Man" and "Bad Inna Bed" (both collected on her Diamond Rush LP *Bare as You Dare*), and still come back with cuts like "Thank You Lord." Her live performances scandalized the Jamaican press but brought her to the forefront of the DJ movement. *Give Me the Reason* and *Passion* on VP and *Collection* from Diamond Rush all display her talents. Her showbiz savvy suggests she'll be around a long time.

Similarly styled Lady Shabba made less impact. A few other ladies include Lady English, Lady Junie, Lady Mackerel, and Lady Patra, who dropped the Lady to become a commercial success mixing hip-hop and dancehall. Slightly less successful was Lady Levi whose 1991 Motown CD *Legend of Lady Levi* sank without a sigh. More yard style, Lady G came with pure consciousness in the nineties (her first single, "Dem Things No Right," was issued by Music Works in 1989). "Mi or the Gun" and "Too Much Violence" are a couple of her major mid-nineties hit singles. The VP CD *God Daughter,* produced by Xterminator Fatis Burrell, is recommended.

A good dancehall singer who took her name from a Pam Grier film is Foxy Brown. She hit with a cover of Tracy Chapman's "Fast Car" and issued two lovers-style albums on the RAS label. Her VP LP *Whip Appeal,* also produced by Burrell, is more in the dancehall mode. Tanya Stephens is another dancehall singer who isn't taking any guff. When she sings about a "Big Ninja Bike" it has about as much to do with a motorcycle as Robert Johnson telling you he wanted to check your oil. "Handle the Ride" turns the DJ's boasts back around. Her "Big Heavy Gal" shows woman-of-size pride, a far step from the Heptones' "Fatty Fatty" of old. Interestingly, she is not herself a big woman.

Major American labels love hybrids, and New York's Shinehead has probably come closer than anyone to joining hip-hop with dancehall. He's a highly energetic performer and his super-speed lyrics made him a favorite of the touring Sunsplash show. On record he's at his best when he draws on his Jamaican roots, as on "Buff Bay" from the CD *Troddin'.* Born Jamericans are another example of reggae joined with black American influences.

It was Rexton Gordon, aka Shabba Ranks, who more than anyone since Yellowman led the assault on conscious reggae with dancehall slackness. "Wicked Inna Bed" and "Trailerload of Girls" were major hits as the '90s dawned in Jamaica. "Mr. Loverman" put him over the top and soon you couldn't turn on BET without seeing Shabba in his Hammer hand-downs frolicking on screen. The end result was Shabba Ranks taking two Grammys in a row in 1991 and 1992, cementing dancehall as "today's reggae" and Shabba as its biggest star.

Despite his early lowest-common-denominator approach Shabba is an incredibly talented performer whose subtle shift in lengthening the melodic structure of the music created a ripple effect on the style of dancehall that has yet to diminish. And he's capable of making great records as "Stop Spreading Rumors" and "Respect" reveal. But those aren't the records he's been rewarded for, so we can probably look forward to more wickedness from the ranking Ranks.

Shabba's rise on the American charts created a feeding frenzy as major labels scrambled to sign the Next Big Thing. The Jamaican talent pool has always been wide and deep, and a host of DJs rose to the occasion, some genuinely innovative and some just hopping aboard. Among the DJs who signed on the dotted line and released product were England's Apache Indian who put out two CDs mixing English, Indian, and Jamaican roots on Mango.

Jamaica's Cobra (later to become Mad Cobra) parlayed major U.S. label interest in the DJ phenomenon into a series of albums for a number of labels. He grabbed an international smash when he cut "Flex" over a half-time dancehall riddim that nearly did to dancehall what rock steady did to ska. Redd Foxx, Johnny P., and Louie Culture all had major label releases.

A lot of good music and vibes made it to American record bins in the '90s through a more open attitude to distribution as a result of the greater acceptance of dancehall via rap channels, making available artists such as Determine and Prezident Brown.

A new generation of dancehall artists like Buju Banton, Capleton, and Beenie Man led a DJ return to righteous Rasta reasoning (though to more beats per minute) and new young DJs like Anthony B. and Sizzla began to change the music again. New artists like Mikey General (whose autobiographical "Miss Taylor Bwoy" and "Babylon Cake" are among the best singles of the late nineties), Jah Mason, Jah Cure, and others are melding the sound of the late nineties with the concerns of the mid-seventies to make conscious dancehall reggae viable today.

CHAPTER 24

Cutty Ranks:

"No Shabba, Nor No Other DJ"

Cutty Ranks is perhaps the prototypical dancehall DJ. In no other period of Jamaican music could he have risen to prominence. Though many like Admiral Bailey preceded him by a half-dozen years and some like Shabba Ranks rose higher on the international charts, his success has been undeniable. By his late twenties Cutty was on the cutting edge of reggae. Cutty calls this "stirring up." And before he's through, he growls, "I'm gonna stir up this music business some more."

The proudly displayed scars apparent on the cover of his album *In My Heart* (Shanachie) might

CUTTY RANKS. Photograph by Jan Salzman; © 1997 Phantom Photos

lead you to assume they are the origin of his stage name. But according to Cutty, whose real name is Phillip Thomas, the jagged snakelike wound on his stomach is from an operation he had when he was 14. His nickname, he says, was conferred while working in a meat shop. "And then when I really get start in the music, I put on the Ranks."

His first release was 1985's "Gunman Lyrics" on Techniques, followed swiftly by "Fishman Lyrics" and later "Culture Fe Lick." He's also released singles on Music Works, Two Friends, Star Trail, Top Ranking, and other Jamaican labels. He had an early album (*Discovery,* 1986) on the stateside Skengdon label and two hot tunes for Outernational, "Money Money" and "Truths and Rights." The lyrical content of the latter rose well above most DJ records of the time.

But it was the Fashion 45 "The Stopper" and the album that resulted (*The Stopper* on Profile) that took him international. The abrupt, stark, trend-altering track interruption added to the power of the lyric line and the music itself. The 45s released afterward on Jah Life, Wild Apache, and Taxi, as well as an album of previously recorded tracks (*Retreat,* VP) hit the market on the heels of his success. "They sit on it (the album) until I bust in the music business and start to get big," he elaborates. "It never reach too far because they never put it out at the right time."

Much more impressive, a series of fine singles and 12-inches on Penthouse had him DJing over "new classic" tracks by Beres Hammond and Marcia Griffiths, revealing him to be one of his days most innovative reggae rappers. Unlike some DJs, Ranks has not been content to repeat himself. This, he says, is "because the other DJ used to pirate my style and eventually I have to switch, leave them and create a new style. I don't want to sound like Buju Banton and I don't want to sound like any other person. I am original person. That mean, anybody following anybody is must somebody following me, not me following

them. This is no Shabba nor no other DJ, this is Cutty Ranks, this is a totally different DJ with different ideas."

Cutty grew up listening to "Bob Marley, Bunny Wailer, Daddy U Roy, Big Youth, and them guys there, and the whole time American soul music with Diana Ross and most of them big guys. When I was a kid I listen all a dem songs. Also Nat 'King' Cole." But amazingly he has no latent desire to be a singer. He prefers to "fit myself in between" the singers' phrases, to "pick out some positive message from the lyrics those singers write and learn from it and create something new in reggae style."

In this regard he's had the opportunity to work with some of his favorite singers, including Ken Boothe, Dennis Brown, and Beres Hammond. Other artists he admires include John Holt, Cocoa Tea, and the late Garnett Silk, as well as reggae rockers Third World. Of the contemporary DJs he's worked in combination with he says, without mentioning any names, "We get along well but everything has its ups and downs."

"The Stopper" was Cutty Ranks's biggest hit and he seems cautiously outspoken when discussing gun lyrics. "My gun songs don't really promote guns. I don't tell people to shoot people. I just talk about what's going on. Because the same big guy in Jamaica who lick out against gun and talking about 'him promoting violence,' they are the same guys who bring the guns and give the youths to fight and do their dirty works.

"Now, the kids and the younger guys are getting wise up and find up that politics don't really put them anywhere—now they start to turn it around on the guy who bring it to them and go at their home and rob them, shot them, kidnap, so now they try to blame it on the Jamaican artists, say that we are promoting violence. It's not we—they are the guys who start it. They should try to do something about it from long time. When the guys them killing off them one another in the ghetto they never used to do anything about it. But now that it reach them they don't want to take the blame."

Warming to the subject, Cutty rips into it like a new riddim. "What about all these gun movie what's showing all about and the kids watch it and dress like the guy in the movie and go out and sling them big gun and shoot you? The gun movie promoting violence more than what we say and nobody complain about it. To tell you the truth, the guys who DJ about gun, is not every one of them promote it. They just talking about what's going on."

Reality lyrics are prominent in Ranks's work. "I focus my lyrics on the system," says Cutty, "that certain corruption that go on in the system and the big guy's not doing anything about it. Like people who's sleeping on the sidewalk, homeless, no food, nothing, and you see this guy come and look for this kid and him give him some food or find somewhere to put him, he just ready give him a coke pipe to finish messin' up his life." His repertoire includes "love songs and hard-core songs" as well as reality lyrics.

"My message is about things that go on in the street. Like poverty, crime, people who fight for freedom and stand up for their rights. It have whole heap of different meanings. It's about slavery, using people, poverty." It's his goal, says Cutty, to "make sure I'm comin' with even more positive stuff. And I would like to say 'nuff respect to the American kids and also my Jamaican people, all the yardman, the Jamaican girls and the American kids, girls and boys. I just wanna send this message to them: just live up irie, and make sure they love another. I want them to unite, both white and black, all a dem get moving together."

CHAPTER 25

The Strange Case of Ini Kamoze

In the early eighties Ini Kamoze was the hottest thing happening in roots reggae, a young lion with so much push that he captured the masters Sly Dunbar and Robbie Shakespeare as his producers and backing band at the height of their international acclaim. Born October 9, 1957, by the seventies Kamoze was a committed Rastafarian, vegetarian, and poet. His early singles like "World Affairs" and "Mer Tel Ler" on the Mognu Naba label signaled great promise.

A demo passed to Sly Dunbar brought him to Channel One, where he cut the stirring "Trouble

INI KAMOZE. Photograph by John Skomdahl

You A Trouble Me," "World a Music" and "General," released as Taxi singles (Sly and Robbie's label) and on a six-song 1984 EP titled *Ini Kamoze* by Island. This was followed by a full-length album, 1984's *Statement* for the same label. The disc included several very forward-sounding cuts like "Call the Police" and "I Want It Ital" and Kamoze hit the ground running with a Taxi tour backed by the studio band including Sly and Robbie and keyboardist Robbie Lyn.

In 1986 the same team with additional musicians like Danny Brownie on guitar and sax-man Dean Fraser on horns recorded his third release in Kingston and London. Though *Pirate* lacked the standout songs of the first two discs, the sound was again at the forefront of change and the songs—like "Gunshot" and "Rough"—prefigured changes to come. Following a split with Island, Kamoze made an album for RAS in 1988. *Shocking Out* featured the new digital sound of Steely and Clevie on synth bass and programmed drums, sometimes with Wailer Tyrone Downie on keys and Danny Brownie again on guitar.

Singles from this album were released on Kamoze's own label, Selectra, in the late eighties. A series of 45s issued on the same label in 1990 seemed to portend a very different direction, particularly "Another Sound" and the controversial "Me and Mi Gun." The following year he cut singles for Phillip "Fatis" Burrell's Exterminator label, the fiery first version of "Hotstepper" and the chilling "Hardware." Rumors flew that he had been arrested in New York on gun- and drug-related charges.

"Yeah, well, rumors and rumors, you know" he says. But it's a fact that this rising star disappeared from the scene and several years went by during which young singers Ed Robinson and Anthony Red Rose had hit singles that were blatantly derivative of Kamoze's early style."We just say yeah, we went through, um, some personal confinement, yeah. And that was basically

INI KAMOZE. Photograph by John Skomdahl

the reason for the people not hearing anything from I during that period of time."

Upon his reemergence he garnished a hit song and video ("Here Comes the Hotstepper," featured in Robert Altman's film *Prêt à Porter* (Ready to Wear) that signaled a change of direction in his career as well as his style. Kamoze returned to the scene with *Lyrical Gangsta* (Elektra), a CD that attempted to blur the boundaries between hip-hop and reggae. As often happens when an artist tries to straddle categories, the move alienated some of his core audience without gaining him the massive welcome in the rap community the new sound obviously aimed for, and within a year he was leaning in the other direction on a series of Jamaican singles that constituted his true musical comeback.

It was never his intention to drive away those who loved his early work. In Ini's own words, "The longtime fan we want to be forever." Still it's obvious even in his new work that his music has evolved and in truth even his earliest work had all the earmarks of the often sought-for cutting edge.

"Sound changes," is how he puts it. "Different sound, different times—now [the nineties] is a whole different thing. You can play the music you been playin' from 1981 the same way or you can play some other thing too." Labels are confining and in Kamoze's case records recorded at different times but released simultaneously have caused confusion as well. Just as "Hotstepper" broke—it spent two weeks at number one on *Billboard's* Hot 100 pop singles chart, a major feat for reggae, and the video received heavy rotation on MTV—Columbia rush-released a repack of his Island work (including an early version of "Hotstepper") disguised as a new album. It's just this kind of music business machination that sometimes causes a reggae singer to think the deck is stacked against him.

"The Jamaican artist should have that kinda opportunity to sell as much records as Prince or Madonna because we're writing good music," he says. "It appear a lot of times we're writing better music! So why we're not having all the kinda facility too, you know? We're not saying we have to be categorized here or there, we're just playing music and we expect to be dealt with like any artist on the American market."

To Kamoze his new sound is "beyond any music form. This is a different element now. This not just you can play reggae or you can play hip-hop or this is R&B or something—this is just music. World music. People that listen to 'Here Come the Hotstepper,' some a dem people just listen to opera. Some a dem only listen to R&B, but they still tune in to that

song. So we really wanna bridge that kinda thing now where anybody who hear that gonna check for what Ini Kamoze do. But we know we are from Jamaica. Reggae is the music that we know—what we are, you know?"

Of the change in style he says, "The voice is me, so if it was on a Far East riddim it would be me still. And if the fans are really checking, they're checking for the vibe. That's what make you become a fan. You like what this voice is doing over this music."

But though the voice is the same the vibe is very different on *Lyrical Gangsta,* from the collaged urban intros cutting fast to the digitally programmed feel of the tracks (mostly recorded in New York) to the "gangsta" pose of the lyrics. To him, there's no pose involved. "My style is not really a style. Is the style that is not a style, is just what is real. Is just how we describe as 'real-core.' And we're not saying hard-core now, we're saying 'real-core,' 'cause this is not a condition that you're trying to do. Is just a core, that realness about what you're hearing."

What is especially odd about all this is that it comes just at the time when dancehall, which changed the direction not only of Jamaican music but of reggae's message from the spiritual and revolutionary to prurient sexuality and violence, seems to be having a change of heart. By the mid-nineties DJs like Buju Banton, Capleton, and Beenie Man were tailoring their tunes to a return to the messages of peace and love that were predominant in the seventies. Ini seemed to be traveling on the same road but going in the opposite direction.

He explains, "Before now, you had a lot more metaphysical expression" in reggae. "But that's not what we do. Now we're just expressing more direct than alla that metaphysical so that they don't have to sit and think about it. A lot of the people don't really want to spend time to sit down and meditate about what you're saying and what does that mean. You're speaking in parable. So we just givin' it direct now."

It doesn't get more direct than "Ballistic Affair" (the retitled "Me and Mi Gun") or "Hole in the Head" ("What they need is hole in the head/In the motherfucking head"). And Kamoze sounds less like a vegetarian Rastafarian and more like an NRA activist, calling his gun the "regulator," though he says in the same song "Trigger happy I'm not/I protect my flock." It's still a pretty far stretch for a guy who says his early influence was the gentle-voiced U.K. prophet Ijahman Levi, though come to think of it, Levi himself is said to have spent some time in jail in London on weapons charges early in his career.

"A lot of times, too, you'll find when you record songs, people don't really listen and get the message exactly," he explains when asked about the seeming contradictions between his early work and the violent images of today. "We usually have a different meaning to the things we say, even back in the '80s. So like we say now, the approach that we're taking is more direct. So it's hard for you to make a mistake with what we're saying now. Yesterday I listen to a song Ziggy Marley have that Stephen Marley doing where they saying, 'Can't let bygones be bygones, we nah laugh at all.' So it is the same kind of approach. This is not a new thing, is the same thing in a more direct form. Is a new day. Is a real-core day now."

Kamoze postulates a straight line from his early work through the latest. "If you listen back to the first couple of things that we did like 'Trouble Me No Trouble You,' where we said: 'Down in the region where I live/It's the survival of the hardest/One man well cool, the next man tense/And sound like these [gunshots] across the fence.' Now this was way back in the '80s, and at that time nobody was talking about hardest or being hard or anything. That was just me describing that real situation that I was in. So there's not any new emphasis on anything else as far as I am thinking or feeling or writing."

In fact, says Kamoze, the direct approach is "what we've been always known for. Tomorrow morning if you need to hear something from the Bible, yeah, we can quote that too. It don't mean that we're gonna walk down the street and turn the other cheek, neither. Don't mean any of that kind of thing. We just represent what is the real core. What is real. If everything is good, then everything is good. But things can be bad too. Yeah? Rain create a flood. Some people get drown in that flood. But is good, is rain. That is just the real thing."

He bristles when questioned about the influence of lyrics like "make love to my automatic" (from "Listen Me Tic," a single from *Lyrical Gangsta*) or "finger on the trigger" ("Hole in the Head") on young listeners. "I don't know how many people wonder about influence of *Bonanza* and the *Sundance Kid* or *High Chaparral*. We don't find that people really wonder about that. But they tend to pressure the music into explaining or into justifying this kind of expression." He wonders why the young black songwriter, whether a rap or reggae artist, is taken to task for the same kind of violent imagery Hollywood has gotten away with "from the first movie that they made till the last one, which is the same."

"When we're talking about 'Me and Mi Gun'—um, 'Ballistic Affair'—is not a situation where we're telling you how much hundred people we shot yesterday and how big my gun is or anything like that, that kind of situation where mothers and babies gonna have to be runnin' up and down. We're talking about a regulatory kind of situation. This is the regulator. This is nothing different from that. So you have to be comfortable with it—if you can't be cool with it."

To Kamoze the gun is "as much a solution as the pen. The pen is a solution. How much less dangerous is the pen than the gun? You don't have to shoot me now, but you can go to your typewriter and your notepad and can create such a situation that might as well I was shot."

"Picking up the gun or not picking up the gun," he continues, "is not the problem. That is not where it's at. The situation is, if you're picking that up, what you're gonna do with it? 'Cause that's all we're talking about, what you're doing. Am I preventing you from killing me or do I want to kill you? So it go a much further than just the act of, or just that three-letter word *gun*."

The inclusion on *Lyrical Gangsta* of the song "Haile Selassie" shows that Kamoze sees no inconsistency between his current approach and his Rastafarian roots. 'King Selassie himself some time in his life have to deal with ballistic affair," he points out.

And even though this "direct approach" might stir up as much controversy among old fans as his new sound, that might not seem so bad for an artist who has his eye on the coveted pop stardom of the artist formerly known as Prince or Madonna. "Basically, we want the people to be listening, and yeah, if we're creating a situation where people gon' be raisin' their eyebrows and sayin', well, what is he sayin' and why is he sayin' that, then we're doing something good. We're wanting that kind of situation. We want to make music that rustle the trees and make the birds fly out. We want to create that kind of situation. With music."

CHAPTER 26

Shaggy:

The New Breed

Born in Jamaica and raised in Brooklyn, dancehall sensation Shaggy hit the top with his debut single "Oh Carolina," a remake of a Prince Buster production many consider to be the very first reggae record. Shaggy and producer Sting International turned the song on its ear and caused both the reggae and pop markets to sit up and take notice as it topped the British charts and made inroads in the U.S.

Disarmingly soft-spoken for someone who made his mark as a gravel-voiced shouter, Shaggy's youthful diffidence belies his international success. It could be partly

SHAGGY. Photograph by Jan Salzman; © 1996 Phantom Photos

a result of his military background—he spent four years in the U.S. Marines, serving in the Persian Gulf. He learned his DJ chops not in Jamaica but in the sprawling Jamaican section of New York City.

Born Orville Richard Burrell in Kingston, Jamaica, he got his nickname when he was "just a little skinny kid with a lot of hair on my head. I reminded them of Shaggy from the cartoon character—you know, Scoobie Doo and Shaggy." In the '70s, DJs projected a tough image and named themselves after gangsters such as Al Capone and Dillinger, but by the early nineties some of the hottest names in reggae were Goofy, Snaggapuss, and Shaggy himself.

Shaggy moved to New York in 1985, though he's returned often to the island where most of his family still lives. Almost immediately he began "chatting the mike" and released his first record in 1989. "I was always a music listener," he says. "I'm nonathletic. I don't run and kick soccer, I don't watch TV much. I'm mostly into music."

Shaggy got his start on the Gibraltar sound system in New York, and cut some early 12-inch singles for the Don Juan label, the first of which was "Bulletproof Buddy." As he began to develop his own style he had the good fortune to hook up with Sting International, producer and co-founder of then-tiny Signet Records. "We're a wicked combination, man," Shaggy says proudly.

Around this time Shaggy joined the Marines. "When I went into the military," he says, "that was my only way out. I live in the Flatbush area [of Brooklyn], which isn't too much of a crime-ridden area. I got out of high school and tried to get a job."

Jobs were few and far between in Flatbush. "I'm not gonna spend the rest of my life at McDonalds. I tried to go to college—I got accepted to the Pratt Institute for Art and Design. But I needed money to support myself and the most legal way to do it was to join the military."

Why did he choose the Marines? He smiles sheepishly. "Well, their uniform looks good, I guess." Still a Jamaican citizen, Shaggy was able to enlist with the help of a resident card. While stationed in North Carolina, he continued his recording career. "I used to drive down from North Carolina to New York for recording. Two of my records became hits in the reggae charts when I was in the military."

While in the Marines Shaggy also spent five months in the Persian Gulf as part of Operation Desert Storm. "I was a cannoneer," he says, "an artillery man. I was at the border of Kuwait and Saudi Arabia. I was working on the one-nine red Howitzer, an artillery piece." Of the situation there now he believes, "As far as the Saddaam thing, man, I just think they should have finished the whole job from day one. We would have been relieved of the whole ordeal. But what can I say? I'm not trying to run for office."

"Oh Carolina" was cut on his return from the Gulf. Originally written and recorded by the Folkes Brothers in the early '60s, "Oh Carolina" is the earliest known Jamaican record to meld pop singing with the Nyahbingi drumming, provided on the original by the legendary Count Ossie and the Mystic Revelation of Rastafari. It is this style of drumming that formed reggae's basic structure: to this day the bass and drum syncopation take their cues from the funde, repeater and big bass drum of the Nyahbingi arrangements. The song has often been called the first reggae tune.

The original "Oh Carolina" was produced by the inimitable Prince Buster and was also remade in the seventies by roots singer Junior Byles. Shaggy says the Prince Buster version was still popular in the dancehall when he was a kid. In fact, Shaggy says, "I grew up on this old tune. Peacemaker was the sound that used to play it, because the kids used to sing 'Raas Bumba Claat' [a coarse Jamaican insult] to it. They would curse to it, so it was a hip thing."

Remaking this Jamaican standard in a dancehall style was the result of a series of events. "It wasn't like I planned to remake this record. Sting came up with the Peter Gunn sample [a riff the track is built around and for which Henry Mancini received a healthy portion of the proceeds] and the first thing that came to my mind was 'Oh Carolina.' The only thing I actually used from it was the actual 'Oh Carolina' and part of the melody. The lyrical content [of the Shaggy song] is totally original. We didn't expect any major success from it but it came and I obviously welcomed it."

The new version first went to number one on the reggae charts in New York. "Then it went to number one in London [for] sixteen weeks, then it crossed over to the pop charts and went number one there too. We definitely kicked something off, some sort of revolution or whatever." The song hit big in Japan, Europe, and South Africa but the samples and copyright ownership of the original delayed release in the U.S. Some of the offending samples were stripped from the U.S. release, though not the intro which harks back to the original Prince Buster track or the Peter Gunn theme that snakes through the basic track.

Shaggy's first CD, 1993's *Pure Pleasure* (Virgin), contained the hit, as well as a remixed "Raas Bumba Claat" version, and a selection of wide-ranging themes from "Bedroom Bounty Hunter" to "Give Thanks and Praise." Produced by Robert Livingston (aka Sting International) and Ben Socolov, it mixed hip-hop groove and reggae rhythms to show that Shaggy was no one-hit wonder. Backing vocals were supplied by label-mate Rayvon, who later issued a solo album of his own.

He toured widely and his pumped-up bump-and-grind delivery pleased crowds and won over new fans. He followed up with 1995's *Boombastic* (also on Virgin), again featuring Rayvan (on a version of Mungo Jerry's "In the Summertime," which tried to recapture the momentum of "Oh Carolina"), as well as Jamaican lovers rock stylist Wayne Wonder and others. The standout track was a remake of Ken Boothe's "Train Is Coming," featured in the movie *Money Train,* with Ken himself providing vocals.

In 1997 Shaggy issued his third disc, *Midnite Lover,* on the same label, this time with Robert Livingston, Gemma Corfield, and Ashley Newton producing. Jamaican hit-makers Brian and Tony Gold, U.K. pop phenomenon Maxi Priest and Bob Marley's son Ky-mani provided backing vocals. In the succeeding years there had been numerous attempts by Jamaican and U.K. DJs to duplicate his formula—Jack Radics, Chaka Demus, Pliers, and many others dusted off oldies from Fats Domino and others and treated them to the rolling bass line and post-Shabba inflections of the nineties. None was as successful as Shaggy's hit.

Shaggy's own work shows versatility while staying strictly in the dancehall groove. "You won't find any diluted, watered-down tunes 'cause I'm not into all of that," he says. "You won't find no R&B feel, you won't find no hip-hop type of feel on there. You might get a hip-hop thing of Shaggy on a remix, but [from Shaggy you get] reggae . . . in a dancehall style. That's me, that's what I'm into." Though he respects Jamaican DJs such as Buju Banton and Tony Rebel, for Shaggy, "What's coming out of Jamaica all basically have the same sound. You might have different patterns in the beats, but even when they come out with a new style it's the same drum machine tone."

The international success of "Oh Carolina" cleared the way for the first number one for reggae in the U.S., yet it came not from Shaggy himself but from Canadian Snow in the form of his one-off hit "Informer." Shaggy bears him no malice. "I know Snow personally and it's pretty great what he's doing," he said at the time. "He's introducing this music, my music, dancehall music, to a mainstream audience.

Right now my record is going into territories and getting played on pop stations that normally never play reggae."

Surprisingly for an artist who is credited with helping bridge the gap between reggae and contemporary American black music, Shaggy doesn't listen to much rap. "I'm not a rap fan at all," he admits. "I listen to the commercial rap, which is the Naughty by Nature, the Ice Cube, you know, but to sit here and say I'm really deep into it wouldn't be fair." And as to the tendency of the DJs to cross over to singing, he is blunt: "I'm a reggae dancehall artist. I don't want to go sing or be a Luther Vandross or whatever. I'm a reggae dancehall raggamuffin chatter. I might fling my style a little bit, but that's my style, that's the way Shaggy drops it."

CHAPTER 27

Buju Banton:

Inna Heights

Little in Buju Banton's early career would prepare you for the artist he has become. Born Mark Myrie, Buju has been a dancehall favorite since the late eighties and his early records reflected then-current dancehall concerns. By the early nineties he was firmly established not only as a dancehall favorite but as a major artist in Donovan Germain's Penthouse stable with hits like "Woman Nuh Fret," "Love Me Browning," and "Batty Rider," gathered on the album *Mr. Mention*. Around the same time these were breaking, earlier recordings produced by Winston

Riley were issued on his Techniques label as *Stamina Daddy*.

He started out, says Buju, "On Rambo International Sound Station, Whitehall Avenue" and has DJed since he was about eleven years old. He cut his first single, "The Ruler," when he was seventeen. Music has always been the paramount concern in his life. "Just the love for the music, man, I know you can do something a the music, you can really make sense beca' other things you deal with nuh really mek sense, y'unno?"

Linking with Germain was a major turning point for the young DJ. "Donovan Germain, him have him mood. Y'know wha me a seh? But just like the devil you ha fe tell him to get behind you sometimes." Buju laughs at his own joke. "Him all right man, Him a good producer and him know the music and that is what I want. Him know the music too much too much. When I born the man have record shop in New York in a 1973, eh? So wha? The man nuh did learn before I come forth man? What happen, we got chemistry now is just pure music and a find the riddim deh man and me no baddah, me no worry my mind me just do me fe do."

He also did some recording for Digital-B and others. A one-off 12-inch for C. Specialist Dillon on the Shang label, distributed in the U.S. by VP, plunged Banton into a controversy that still has repercussions on his career. The song, "Boom Bye Bye," was violently anti-homosexual and cost Banton a spot on *The Tonight Show* as well as some canceled gigs just as he seemed ready to break through to American radio. He issued an apology and a safe-sex single with proceeds donated to AIDS research.

In his own words, "Fear is the beginning of wisdom. What is to fear but fear itself." His trial by media fire seemed to cause a reassessment of his career and his next release, *Voice of Jamaica* (his first on the American Mercury label), was one of the strongest dancehall releases of the early '90s. It contained the songs "Deportees

(Things Change)" and "Operation Ardent," both Jamaican hits that immediately went international. It was followed in 1995 by *'Til Shiloh* for the same label, and also produced by Germain and Lisa Cortez. This was not only the best dancehall album of the year, it was one of the best reggae albums.

Buju Banton became one of the few DJs who moved into the international arena without having left the dancehall. In his later incarnation he was defender of the oppressed and upholder of the faith, a far cry from the early recordings, all without losing his dancehall credentials.

Til Shiloh and the new Buju Banton have been major forces in changing the direction of dancehall from the slackness of the eighties to the conscious roots vibration of an earlier generation of reggae that includes Peter Tosh, Bob Marley, and first-generation DJs like U Roy. "Till I'm Laid to Rest" and "Murderer," a song written about the death by gun of his friend and fellow DJ Pan Head, along with "Complaint" featuring the late Garnett Silk, returned the high standards of seventies reggae to the grassroots yard-style music of the dance. As a new Buju—now sporting dreadlocks and espousing a Rastafarian perspective—took center stage, the entire dancehall movement seemed to follow.

Suddenly instead of sex and guns, DJs like Capleton and Beenie Man were joining Banton in working serious themes into the raggamuffin style. New DJs like Anthony B and Sizzla, who echoed the conscious themes Buju espoused, moved to the fore. A DJ chatting about punany and pistols was more likely to be booed offstage in Kingston than lauded. Dancehall, which had become a dirty word to many international reggae fans of the roots-and-culture dominated reggae of the seventies, was earning a new respect.

Buju sees all this as an "elevation in the music. The music have to move from one stage to another. It can't just one thing, you know?

And there's so much things happen in reality that if one choose to speak on one particular subject you find yourself trapped. So you have to be broad-based like a book, mon, from A to Z, y-nuh so?" From his point of view it's not so much change as evolution. "Just use the term *evolve,* mon."

Buju's latest album, *Inna Heights* (Penthouse/VP), is a culmination of all these elements and more. Though he's lost none of his dancehall edge, songs like "Hills and Valleys" and "Circumstances" show a surprising maturity for a twenty-four-year-old dancehall

DJ. The disc—and his recent live shows—encompass every element of reggae from ska to ragga, and the subject matter rolls from the hit "Love Sponge" to pro-woman concerns like "Mother's Cry" and "Single Parent," themes no one would have imagined as dancehall subject matter a few years ago.

One of the disc's high points is the song "Close One Yesterday." Though his voice retains the rough edge that marked him as the successor to Shabba Ranks, the song is a surprisingly gentle reminder of the fragility and importance of life. Another standout track is "Destiny,"

BUJU BANTON. Photograph by David K. Wendlinger

recently issued as a Jamaican single. Taking off from a song called "Wisdom" recorded separately by Bob Marley, Peter Tosh, and Bunny Wailer, it moves in a new direction with an ancient wisdom. "There was good and evil," he intones at the beginning. "We chose good."

Inna Heights, says Buju, "give it a more higher form a meditation inna the music and a more upliftment. It begins with a little thing called 'Our father who art in Zion, hallowed be thy name.' I mean the objective musically is to bring forth a quality within the music where all one and one can enjoy it. No matter who you are or what color, class, or creed. Just natural vibe goin' through the music that all soul can succumb to it and feel it."

On the disc Buju is joined by some of today's hottest artists including Beres Hammond, Red Rat, Jah Mali, and Ras Shiloh. Two of the finest cuts feature performers much better known to previous generations of reggae lovers: King Stitt, who trades vocals with Buju on "Small Axe," and Toots Hibbert of Toots and the Maytals.

"Working with Toots Hibbert is great," explains Buju. "As you know, Toots is a reggae legend. Personally the man is a genius." Though the vocals were recorded separately, the artists have worked together on stage shows in the past. King Stitt, according to Buju, is "one of the musical icons, musical legends. Many people don't remember them, you know, and it our duty to keep them in the face of people. And keep them in the hearts and minds of ones and ones."

In fact the tracks are two of the liveliest on the disc. "My generation don't know too much about dem man deh," he continues. "So the music put those tracks from generation to generation from generation so anyone can get a handful of what was happening." The disc contains several "inter lingua" portions where Buju explains his feelings about the music and life. Though each of his albums has gotten successively better, Buju says, "Feel no fear, man. The best is yet to come. The most important thing is you find favor in the songs and what is in you for you to do so another person see it as upliftment."

This surprising maturity of talent and attitude in an artist so young might affect other performers in a different way but Buju remains humble and guarded in his expression. "Jah guide and protect you know. At earlier age than that there have been apostles and greater man than I ruling the world and making more significant impact." Perhaps this attitude is partly based on earlier perceptions of him by others.

"When I am in my early stage no one no want to do no combination with I too tough, them a say I too bad. Some man like Beres Hammond and Marcia Griffiths did always want to sing with I and them never too too hold I back. But they had a preference so me grateful for that, so you find we have good songs together."

Few contemporary artists have exhibited this kind of growth. But for Buju, "I don't really change, you know, I say the music evolve and as a man you must evolve too. So with everything you do you can't do it one way all all day every day of your life. You must try and improve on the way you understand things every day to make it better. And this is improvement fe I and I in terms of what I a do. And this is what Jah want I to do. It have to be done because a Jah will. Within I."

Where once Buju might have been outspoken about girls or guns he is now outspoken about "Selassie I, the Lord that live. You know that. The Lord live man and I and I have fe make sure the music manifest that beca' too much things a go on right now, deception and a bagga rey rey and a bagga a rey rey. And me a seh hold firm to it beca Jah live."

In concert Buju's high-energy performance is a nonstop wonder. Powered by a very tight traveling band, his performance is comparable to that of international reggae star Lucky Dube, with solid backing and tightly woven harmonies.

"The Shiloh band is my personal band," says Buju. "We try to mek the music enjoyable from coast to coast. East Coast, West Coast. It's a music composed of different different dimension. My band strive professionality. We rehearse a lot and what they get from practicing is perfection."

For the future Buju sees more of the same. "I want evolve as a writer too. Really and truly I see the time I able to translate what I feel in words. So through the positivity of time all dem t'ings may [happen], wha we a seh."

A major element in his work with Donovan Germain has been studio whiz Dave Kelly, with whom he's also done some recording on the side. A recent 12-inch is produced by Dave and Tony Kelly. "Tony and Dave Kelly are brothers," he explains. "The riddim twins dem you know? Tony Kelly play everything mon. Drums, keyboard." With such strong support—Germain is now managing and touring with Buju as well—the future looks bright for the young dancehall DJ who has turned the genre on its ear.

Says Buju, "Right now the positiveness in the music whe I and I bring forth I say to the man them, open them eyes and view all the time for you have eyes and don't see the time is indeed blind. With these few words I leave you, seek ye first the kingdom of Jah and everything else must be added." It will be interesting to see what comes next from Buju Banton.

CHAPTER 28

Sister Carol:

Return to the Roots

Many lifelong reggae fans who loved the conscious, uplifting music of Jimmy Cliff, Bob Marley, Peter Tosh, Bunny Wailer, and groups like Culture, the Mighty Diamonds, Itals, and others found dancehall deeply disappointing. Though the DJs of the seventies had some low points (like Dillinger's "Cocaine in My Brain") and slackness was not unknown in the sixties (Prince Buster) or the eighties (General Echo), the massive outpouring of sex and gun lyrics of the early nineties—as well as the general lowering of musical standards brought on by the digital revolution—caused many to step away from a music that had held its own for a long run.

The role of woman in reggae seemed more in question than ever as the struggle of the early pioneers like Marcia Griffiths opened the door for many female singers who too often found themselves forced to sing material that was suggestive if not downright pandering. The dancehall era, where misogyny ran rampant and women were expected to be obscene and not heard, was challenged by a few, significantly in England where the likes of Ranking Ann and new roots singers like Aisha stepped forward. In Jamaica even the rootsy Lady Ann was often paired with Yellowman and the mid-nineties brought forth Lady Saw, who out-crotch-grabbed Madonna to achieve notoriety, though once she had achieved it she did something with it, challenging the objectification of women by reversing the roles.

One woman who bucked all the trends years before was New York's Carol East, better known as Sister Carol. One of the most outstanding of the first wave of female DJs, she hit with roots-and-culture dancehall in New York and stood her ground to become one of the most significant female DJs. Besides a series of uncompromising albums on the RAS and Heartbeat labels she obtained a teaching credential from the City

SISTER CAROL. Photograph by Jan Salzman; © 1997 Phantom Photos

University of New York and made appearances in the Jonathan Demme films *Something Wild* and *Married to the Mob*. She is a woman who walks with dignity through an undignified world.

Music was a part of Sister Carol's life even as a child. "Where we lived in Kingston the ghetto was very, very, very poor but yet very rich with music, a lot of jukeboxes and a lot of sound systems. Music was just there every day. Because of the music I didn't realize we were really poor at the time. We went to school, church, and then you come home, and just expose [to] a lot of music there."

The music she heard was "All kinda music, you know. We got music from America, music from England, jazz, rhythm and blues, pop music, soul music, gospel, but most of the time we hear reggae too. So I grow up listening to a lot of music. A lot of American artist. The Jamaican artist music was influenced by the American artist that they used to play. I try and incorporate it right now in some of my songs, some of the songs I knew way back then, modified a little by my own style and creativity too."

When Carol was fourteen her parents moved the family (she has five sisters and four brothers) to Brooklyn. "I came to this country as a teenager because my parents were here. They thought they would have a better life because jobs were more available here and alla that." Upon arrival, "I started school, at the start I went to Prospect Heights High School. After that I went to City College in New York." She has a degree in education but right now her focus is on the music.

In 1981 she met roots DJ Brigadier Jerry through a friend. "I saw Brigadier Jerry deejaying on a sound system at that friend's house one day. At the time I was pregnant and a couple of days after that I delivered. So I actually started singing the songs during my delivery, you know? After I had the baby I just started writing and singing my own style and building up my image for myself because I used to imitate Brigadier Jerry a lot. After that I just started to build and create and write and from there I'm here now."

"The first song I did was called 'Black Cinderella.'" Another 12-inch single, "Jamaica Little Africa," was done around the same time. "Those were my first records, they came out about 1982." Her first album, *Liberation for Africa,* was issued by a small label called Serious Gold. "It really was a limited amount of copies that brother let out. We've been trying to find him to get that album on CD 'cause a lot of people still want to hear it but we haven't gotten to him yet." Two albums for Jah Life, *Black Cinderella* (1984, reissued by Heartbeat in 1995) and *Jah Disciple* (circa '85 and reissued on the RAS label in 1989) followed.

During this period she issued 7-inch 45s on Jah Life and self-produced singles on her own Black Cinderella label in New York. Some of these were released on the Spiderman and Fameous [sic] labels in Jamaica. She recorded a rendition of Bob Marley's "Screwface" with Judy Mowatt. "She had asked me at the time if I would like to do a song with her and I did my version called "Them Vex." She produced the song and it came out in Jamaica on her label, Ashandan, and in New York it came out on Jah Life. A 12-inch cut with Scion Success (which Sister Carol also produced) called "Mandela's Release" celebrated that historic event and was included on her 1991 RAS release *Mother Culture*.

"When you're an independent producer," she confides, "trying to produce the material, sometimes it's hard to get out there. So what I do, I more fe work on an album to get it out there to a company so a company will pick it up. That's the thing I do here with *Call Mi Sister Carol* (Heartbeat, 1994). I produced the album myself and I was shopping for a [major] label and I didn't have any success. So I try a more smaller label. And I was fortunate that Heartbeat pick it up because we got a good thing going now."

The relationship was solidified with the 1996 release *Lyrically Potent* for the same label. Newcomer Junior Jazz joins her on "Gimme Mi Freedom" and longtime producer and singer Sugar Minott sings with her on "Sell-Out." Like the previous album the disc is built around a combination of original and preexisting rhythms from Bob Andy, Coxsone Dodd, and Bob Marley. Among the most striking songs is one called "Herbal Affair."

"I want to stay on the cultural side of things," says Carol, "lettin' the youth be aware of the power of reggae music and how it could be distributed in different ways, not necessarily the same gun, punanny, drug thing, you know? If we're gonna celebrate the medicinal purposes of the natural herb—we don't see herb [marijuana] as a drug, but basically I was more focusing on penetrating the youth and I really took the opportunity to incorporate the different beats that would attract the younger listening audience like the hip-hop and some of the hard-core dancehall style, but I still keep my style focused, my type of lyrics and the way how I put them together."

One of the most fascinating things about Jamaican music from the earliest days has been the way it presents an ancient, biblical message in an extremely contemporary form, whether it be ska, rock steady, reggae, or raggamuffin dancehall. According to Carol, "If I'd done just the new thing to attract the younger audience then I would lose my original audience. What I do is make everybody be represented. I have a lot of hard-core roots and culture, strong tracks on the album. But my main focus was to get to the youth because I've found it necessary to step up and do something about all what's going on."

"I'm just expressing all that I grew up knowing," she continues, "and I'm actually bridging the gap between that time and this time of the dancehall artist. A lot of people take the time out to define dancehall, they think dancehall is a separate thing from reggae. But it's part and parcel of reggae music. Dancehall music is sometimes viewed as just some computers with a DJ talking about guns or drugs—that's not it, because you can have the same rhythm with a DJ talking something quite edifying. So sometimes I like to clear up the confusion between dancehall and reggae because they don't separate. It's one thing. Dancehall is not a new thing. It's something recycled from my time growing up in Jamaica. So what I try to do, I try to bridge the gap, let them know what was happening through the rock steady reggae era."

She has words of caution for those who are trying to adjust to a new culture while maintaining one of their own. "A lot of people wanting to go the fast way and they start to dealing the drugs and get in trouble with the law and they lose a lot of money that they had acquired and they get deported. Let them know that, hey, it's not bad being deported after all! 'Cause [Jamaica] needs people like you to build up the country too. If everybody run away and leave the country then you won't have as strong a country, that strong backbone. Everybody will be building up America!"

One of her earliest hits was the anti-sexist "A No Me Name Peggy." Of the sexual exploitation rampant in dancehall lyrics she says, "A lot of people want to tell you, oh yes, sex sells, sex sells, but then people like me, I can't follow the same pattern because I have children and I'm sometimes not able to screen what they listen to and what they watch on the video. So if I can do something about it by letting somebody else's child hear something that's not about drugs or guns, then I know I'm doing the right thing. And besides, people can talk about sex, but I think they should be more glorifying the act of something sacred as opposed to being derogatory or degrading to women."

Strong musical backing has long been a hallmark of Sister Carol's own productions. In 1996 *Lyrically Potent* received a Grammy nomination, a fact of which she's clearly proud. In 1997 RAS Records released *Potent Dub,* a dub version of the *Lyrically Potent* CD. To date this is Sister Carol's only dub release.

From the beginning there's been a strong link to Africa in Sister Carol's work and though the "Ital Jacuzzi" she speaks of in the song of the same name on *Call Mi Sister Carol* is in Jamaica, she says excitedly, "And now I just found a bigger one! I just found a bigger one 'cause I just recently had the opportunity to visit Ethiopia, Africa. And I found a bigger ital jacuzzi there than the one I'm accustomed to in Jamaica!" Her visit to Ethiopia was "an experience that I cherish for a lifetime. The most uplifting, most spiritually rewarding, educationally benefiting—all the things that I've aspired over the years to accomplish in my studies of Ethiopia and Africa."

During the visit, "I managed to actually hunt down experiences of the things that I've been studying through the years, like I had the opportunity to visit place like Axum, where the Queen Sheba was. I also had the opportunity to visit the rock churches in Lalabela. That was an experience totally out of this world. Unbelievable. And like I said, most rewarding, spiritually uplifting, rejuvenate my vibe and my spirit. I also visit Gondor, a province in Ethiopia once ruled by Falashas. And of course I was in Addis Ababa, and Shashamane."

This last stop was especially significant for her because "Shashamane is where most of the people who repatriated from Jamaica now reside. And it's just wonderful over there, just life in natural state. Not a lot of refrigeration, you know, livestock, fresh things, you just go out and you pick your fruit for your breakfast, type of living that I knew growing up in Jamaica. The whole experience was very nice for me. The political side of things, there's still a lot of uncertainty, but in time I know that it will work out."

I mention news reports of the discovery, right outside of Addis Ababa, of human bones more than a million years older than those previously discovered. "Oh yes, oh yes," she exclaims. "First cradle of civilization. Those things are fact and they'll be finding more fact." But even with her fascinating mix of traditional perspective and contemporary sound, Sister Carol balks at being characterized as a "'90s Rastawoman." "I don't represent a '90s Rastawoman, you know, 'cause I know myself, I'm always conscious of Rastafari." To her Rastafari is a reality beyond time. "Rastafari's an innate concept, a born concept, you know? From birth. So it's something from creation until now. That meant to say God permit if I'm still around in the year 2000 or 3000 I'm still a Rastawoman."

CHAPTER 29

Foundation:

Ever Firm

The TV, sound off, flickered with the early reports of the 1989 San Francisco earthquake, which took place about two hours before I sat down to interview Foundation. "Earthquake in big city," they sing on "Sign of the Times" from their second Mango album, *Heart Feel It.* The title song of their first album, *Flames,* seemed chillingly appropriate as well. Due to play San Francisco in two days, they had been causing a rumble of their own in the reggae world.

The roots harmony sound that was once reggae's mainstream and fueled groups like Culture, the Gladiators, Mighty Diamonds, and those interviewed here like the Itals and the Wailing Souls, seemed to dim with the rise of slackness and the computer DJ style of the '80s. The classic groups were still classic, but where were the conscious young people?

To get across the ancient message the music seemed to need to take new forms. Foundation, a roots trio in every sense of the word, flew against reggae's new face when they first appeared on the scene and seem today to stand in stark contrast to the sound, if not the new vision, of the "new" reggae. They are not the last harmony group—a few new outfits like Brown, Eagle and Spear, and Fire Facts have come up behind and alongside them—but they come in a traditional style at a time of change.

Their first two albums, produced by the late Jack Ruby, were a step forward for a music that had occasionally faltered but never fallen. The return to militancy, strong and simple tracks and arrangements with penetrating lyrics added up to songs that stuck with you and spoke for this time as Black Uhuru's "Sinsemilla" or Bob Marley and the Wailers' "Exodus" did for theirs.

Errol "Keith" Douglas's voice is one of those unique and abiding sounds for which Jamaica is rightly famous. Like an Albert Griffiths or a Justin Hinds, Douglas doesn't have to try to sound like anyone but himself. Emilio "Pupa" Smiley and Euston "Ipal" Thomas lay a bed of harmonies for Douglas's animated and heartfelt delivery. The back-and-forth blend of harmony and lead weave a textured sound for the lyrics to cascade over. In live shows Foundation exhibits a bold intensity and a writhing, expressive presence.

The trio grew up in the Port Maria area of Jamaica, also home base for the group Earth Messengers. The two groups, and a third from the area, Link 'n Chain, have traded members around so that each band has members who have been in both other bands at one time or another. Other people that come from or passed through Port Maria in their formative years include Johnny Osbourne, Ini Kamoze, and

Admiral Tibet. The members of Foundation grew up listening to rock steady and later groups like the Diamonds and the Wailers. Soon enough they moved on to their own songs.

Says Ipal, "In Port Maria, we have a little band we call Black Brothers Roots. That was our real main development in the music. I used to play a little drums, and Donovan played the bass. Keith play a rhythm guitar, Pupa did play the guitar, one of the harmonies in Earth Messengers did play, and our next brethren played melodica."

Pupa originally sang with the Revealers, which first became Earth's Last Messengers and later became Earth Messengers. A few years later they changed their name again to Jah Messengers. "I and I grew up and come see music as a powerful force in Port Maria," he says. "Port Maria is a very musical vibe. Some man a play wicked bongo there, and I and I come see mento strong. Is like we grow up with just the vibes there. Singing in the churchyard vibes."

Adds Keith, "Music is a thing you have to born with. If you no really born with it, you can't really keep it up and work together so long. Is just music inside the three of us. You'll see the time an album come out with a group called Link and Chain (it has since been released), the final album that Jack Ruby produce. Culture same as Foundation, Donovan, and Earth Messengers."

Like many young singers Keith's first studio session did not survive intact. "Me is a man who pass through Joe Gibbs' studio," he notes of his early days, "doing solo and do a song already, but I would say in a dem young days there, we probably nah ride the rhythm the right way, so a next singer take it and do it."

The singer was Dennis Brown and the song was "Jah Can Do It," but, says Keith, "That's passed by. I would say normally that happens by producer. Producer say, well, is just a country youth. So after that now we just come together, work with this man [Ipal] first. After work with Joe Gibbs, me say me nah work with no more uptown producer, because him might change me mind if me have to think to be like some deadly man to them or something. Them think them would change we mind or reduce we down from really positive. So we just thrown out with those things and start work with a group now.

"Jack Ruby do music with the Revealers, so me just check Jack Ruby. First start out with a next brethren before Pupa, but we never ready, you know. We go inna studio, but song nah live up to a standard the man show we have to work on it. And we realize that because we know positive heights. So we work along with it for many years till we build it to the heights, seen?"

Tracks from the Revealers and the early version of Earth Messengers (then called Earth's Last Messengers) are available on an early Clappers anthology called *Jack Ruby Hi-Fi*. Clappers was one of the first New York reggae labels and though their releases are now difficult to find they are, like the releases of New York's Bullwackies label, among the best. It's obvious from his own modest output that Ruby sought a conscious sound and his music was always edifying and uplifting. There's no such thing as a slack Jack Ruby tune.

"Most people love the rhythm section more than the lyrics," explains Keith. "You have people

FOUNDATION (LEFT TO RIGHT): EUSTON THOMAS ("IPAL"), ERROL DOUGLAS ("KEITH"), AND EMILIO SMILEY ("PUPA"). Photograph by Jan Salzman; © 1997 Phantom Photos

KEITH DOUGLAS. Photograph by John Skomdahl

who listen to the lyrics more. The two of them go along, but the lyrics are the main thing still, you know. Jack Ruby is a man that typical upon the lyrics. No matter what rhythm go on, him always want to have good lyrics—conscious vibration. With Jack Ruby, you have to have something positive. Something you know will live on. Is a man cool still. Not a man operate like some brethren! Mostly him can joke and steady yourself. Not rushing towards it. A man really nice to work with. Some men dem money a go buy Mafia bread. But with Jack Ruby, just relax back yourself and study life."

The passing of Jack Ruby left a hole in the fabric of roots reggae production. Keith summed up the loss for the band. "We, it's like, can't look beyond the future. Make we just relax. I and I come fe do a certain work. We can't really stop, you know. We just hafta continue."

Of the militant cultural attitude Foundation shares with their reggae forerunners like Peter Tosh, Bob Marley, and Jacob Miller, Keith says simply, "Not all man can do it. Most men are afraid. Who wants to die?" At this remark the entire band, in typical Rasta fashion, laughs. "Yet you have man who never think about that, just do positive works. Whether it hit the white man or it hit the black, we have to spread the message." I wondered aloud that the group laughed so easily but always appeared unsmiling in photographs. Keith explained it as "Vibes. If you're serious inside, you can't laugh outside."

One of their best songs, "Beverley Hills," has recently been recut with a wicked DJ part by conscious rapper Prezident Brown. Keith declares, "We a reach here [Los Angeles] but we don't, like, tour upon dem [Beverly Hills]." "I want to take a look," Ipal rejoins. "I get a little glimpse on Beverly, but I don't get no glimpse on Watts inna the ghetto yet."

"The idea of the song work out like the rich and poor," Keith explained, "because the poor man down at the bottom would like to get rich. So him just start looking upon the rich, and the rich one looking down at the valley." In the song he names the places "rich people live—Beverly Hills, Sweden, Buckingham—and most of the wealth come from Africa . . . we built Beverly Hills," then names "Harlem, Brixton, inna the Ghetto/Where poor people live." He doesn't even try to tell you what to do about it.

As the images of the earthquake and aftermath flooded the screen, I asked about their upcoming appearance in the Bay Area. "San Francisco, that's in trouble now?" mused Keith. "Sign of the times." It's a song title from *Heart Feel It.*

"Lot of trouble down there, we don't even know what's going on. Symptom and sign [the title of another Foundation song], that's the truth. Certain areas get certain lick. Still, if you even nah live the right way, said the Almighty in it. Whether black or white, if him nah hear and nah live right, him father will just divide and wash away anything him want, y'know. If Father nah struck them tomorrow with earthquake, them would a gone back in them badness, too."

As we spoke of earthquake and fire, Haile Selassie I, Rastafari himself, moved to the fore of the conversation. "To me," said Keith, "I see H.I.M. as a great king. In myself me check that the Almighty is in everyone. The Almighty is life. The Almighty can't dead. No man can destroy the Almighty. But we see him as a great king in our time."

Ipal put forward his point of view as well. "The I is the King of the whole universe! All heights still, you know. A man live on the basis of how you think of him. A man can't be living any if I and I don't see him at the heights.

So spiritually within the I, I see life. If it wrong, I say it live for you. But is I say life. So the I is the greatest king of earth, 'cause life maintain all things. Life keepeth all flesh."

In 1996 Foundation released their third album, *One Shirt* (Island Jamaica). When I first interviewed the group I called Foundation "the future of reggae." Predicting the future has never been easy, as Keith himself pointed out in the interview, and reggae took a far different direction in the nineties than the resurgence of the roots harmony trio I hoped for or envisioned. And still by the late nineties there was a return to the themes, if not the sound, that drove the reggae of the mid-seventies.

And on their new album Foundation continues to manifest that better future for us all. Songs of substance like "Universal Unrest" and "Set the People Free" have never been more needed and sweet harmonies have seldom sounded sweeter.

Redefining the crisp roots sound of their early work (the disc included the new version of "Beverly Hills" with Prezident Brown as well as reality tunes like "Struggling Man," "Serious Time," and "Leaders of the World"), Foundation continues a tradition of roots trios that brought us such gifted vocal groups as the Melodians, Meditations, and many others. The subtle use of horns, heavy bass, and drums (on about half the album provided by Island's two-man tourist board Sly and Robbie), and the likes of old-time production hands Errol Brown and Clive Hunt, hold to Jack Ruby's original vision of the group. The thoughtful lyrics, intricate melodies, and plain old good singing make Foundation today essential listening.

CHAPTER 30

Soul Stirrer:

The Beres Hammond Story

Lovers of roots reggae have had much reason to despair as the music they fought so hard to break into the mainstream finally "crossed over," leaving behind much that drew them to it in the first place—melody, harmony, and conscious lyrics. Many of today's young singers and DJs lack those basic elements—the ability to stay on pitch and sing in key (or in some cases to sing at all) and the DJs of much of the '80s and early '90s were talking about a whole different world than the Rastafarian themes of peace and love that dominated the '70s.

One artist who bucked this trend is Beres Hammond, a singer who can hold his own with the best of previous eras, whether delivering a soulful love song or a message to the world. His story is unlike that of any other singer from Jamaica. Beres (originally Beresford) Hammond first made his name in Jamaica in the '70s as a singer of ballads, and he can still tear up a ballad like no other singer around. His twenty-year "overnight success" is a story of feast or famine that offers some insight into the changes in the world of music—and the world in general—as well as a Horatio Alger-style moral tale of the benefits of remaining true to yourself no matter what the world does or says.

Born in Annotto Bay in the province of St. Mary, he was gripped early by the love of music. "When I was about eleven I started going between Kingston and Annotto Bay just to see the artists. I'd go to Kingston weekends and walk past the record shops, walk down Beeston Street and come back and see Peter Touch and walk down King Street and see Scotty and dem guys—it was a thrill! Alton Ellis was on the same street,

BERES HAMMOND. Photograph by Bob Salzman; © 1995 Phantom Photos

Niney, Upsetter, and all those people, so I just go on a weekend and pick up a vibe. I went to school in the country too. After primary school I got my university education on the streets. When I was very little I knew I could sing 'cause folks around me, this is the one thing everybody knew me for, or thought that I should like to do."

In music Beres inclined toward the soulful singers like Alton Ellis and Ken Boothe. "Long before I came in the business Ken was amongst my favorites, Leroy Sibbles from the Heptones was another, and the main person for me was Alton Ellis. He reassured me that I should use melody. When I listen to him in those days, say yeah.

"On the conscious side now Bunny and Bob really had me. I liked what Peter stood up for in his own way. Some people tend to think that he came on too strong, the statements that he made. But whichever way he made the state-ment—if something is red I don't see why you should tie ribbons to it before I tell you it's red. You know what I'm saying? So I really admired these three guys. They gave me strength. So I took a little from all of them. But mainly now when I was growing up and going to school my father was a collector of records, he was a great collector of song. He used to mostly collect rhythm and blues and jazz and all a that. So I got this sort of rhythm and blues, maybe that's where the soul came out of. Sort of grew up under that influence."

"My favorites were Otis Redding and Sam Cooke. Sometimes Sam Cooke used to be with a gospel group name Soul Stirrers. I used to lis-ten to him singing Christian songs." "Songs like 'If I Could Just Touch the Hem of His Garment'?" I asked. Hammond sits bolt upright and looks me straight in the eye. "You know those songs, man?" He stands up, paces halfway around the room, then stretches out on the bed completely relaxed. Suddenly this doesn't seem like an inter-view. We both feel like we're talking to a friend.

"I loved those guys," he says. "But after they passed away the only people who sort of fit in for the two of them was Marvin Gaye. There was something about not just his voice but how he delivers—he blew my mind. I started listening to Marvin Gaye all day. All these were happening when I was still in school. He came to Jamaica quite a few occasions. I saw him about twice in Jamaica. Not on concerts. Just came by because he used to visit Bob Marley.

"Yeah, Marvin. I saw him up there one day and saw the guy sitting down out in the yard y'know? He was just like me, [wearing a] tam, and was just cool and say yeah, the guy sings like that and behaves like that. This [talent] happen to be God-given and you shouldn't brag about that. Just observing how he was behaving, easy, like nothing was happening, I said to myself, I was asking—is Marvin Gaye that? Say yes, it look like him. And I turn to the next guy and say, is Marvin that? He say yeah. 'What's Going On?' Him say yeah. 'Let's Get It On?' He say yeah. I don't believe you!"

Soul music was part of the Beres Hammond sound from the beginning. His very first record-ing effort surfaced over twenty years after it was recorded on a Clancy Eccles anthology. The song, "Wanderer," was sung in a distinctly Alton Ellis style very different from the Beres Hammond of today. "But I never did hear that song after I did it until recently," says Beres, "so even when I heard it one night—I was doing a little interview with some radio guy and to be very honest with you I didn't even know it was me. To be honest!" He laughs. "Yes, I say don't play no more cause it sounded so different." Recorded in the very early '70s, the track gives no hint of the vocal power Hammond was later to capture and control. The session was promptly forgotten, though not the desire to sing.

Friends encouraged Hammond to use his own God-given talent. "When I got that real heavy push from a friend was in about '72, '73.

I was passing some place they were doing audition for Merritone Amateur shows." Winston Blake's Merritone was a classic early Jamaican label and such talent shows were a staple of the music scene. "Yes, he used to have some good stuff on his label. I was just passing the place they were doing the auditions and a friend, was one of them pushy guys, said, 'Stop by and sing down them guys'—it's a Jamaican term—sing down the guys! 'You can do much better than this brother over deh, suh. Let's just a stop and mek some trouble.'

"We stopped and asked what was going on. They told us they were doing audition for a show that was coming up the following week. So I just trouble some and ask them to write my name down so I could fall in line with those guys. When I went inside the man who was doing the audition made me sing about a dozen songs, different kinds of songs, reggae, ballad, jazz, was just testing me and I thought he liked what he heard."

In December 1975 he joined the band Zap Pow as lead singer. The band had already made a name in England with a hit record, "This Is Reggae Music," which became the title song for a three-volume anthology series (later five volumes) issued by Island. "I stayed with Zap Pow for about four years." He sang lead on the single "The System," and the albums *Zap Pow* (released on Mango in 1978) and *Reggae Rules* released by Rhino in 1980. Both albums are now long out of print. Beres laughs when he sees the photo of the group on the back of the later LP. "This picture is very, very, very old!" He indicates himself in the photo, referring to the wide-flared pant bottoms as "Inna bell-foot! And that's how old this picture is!" Also in the band in those days were Roots Radics member Dwight Pickney, Cornell Marshall, Mike Williams, and horn men Glen DaCosta and Dave Madden.

Beres's solo career took off about the same time. "It was during the period I was with them

that I took some time off to go do my recording, so when the name Beres Hammond broke I was still with Zap Pow. I was performing as a member of Zap Pow, not Beres Hammond. When I was with them I performed as Zap Pow and then on the other side too, Beres Hammond. Until I realized that you can't serve two masters."

He recorded his first solo album, *Soul Reggae* (Aquarius), in 1976. The album "took off in the shops in Jamaica. I realized that something was happening big. They said, we want to do a 45 so could you release one of the songs off the album? I said no, you're not touching the album. If you really want a 45 we have to go back in the studio and make one. So we went back in the studio, Willie Lindo and myself, he was my producer and a very good friend, and did a 45 and it was an instant hit. It went to number one and stayed there for three and a half months." The song was called "One Step Ahead" and it was a ballad, kicking off his first solo career.

A second single, "I'm in Love," was cut for producer Joe Gibbs in 1978 and also went to number one. But after two number one singles, "I wasn't making any money and I knew that I was doing something wrong. Maybe it was the business side of it that I wasn't taking care of properly. I decided to cool off a little" because "this business weren't too right."

He wrote and produced a song ("Life Is a Rainbow") for the soundtrack of the 1979 film *Children of Babylon,* which also includes cuts from the Mighty Diamonds and Delroy Wilson and featured the acting talents of singer-songwriter Bob Andy. Then Beres shifted gears and began making his living doing backup vocals for other singers in the studio. "They always seem to find me when it came to arranging harmony parts and stuff like that because that's the kind of stuff I really and truly love. Singing harmony is like—in those days I much prefer singing harmony than the lead. I enjoy singing harmonies."

After a break from solo recording, "I came back and did another album—I did an album with Joe Gibbs and from the album they took two 45s and they went number one." Called *Just a Man,* this early Joe Gibbs LP was, according to Beres, "A very good album, too. I didn't make any money off that either."

Anyone familiar with Joe Gibbs's reputation as a producer would not be overly shocked by either of these observations. Beres laughs again, "True man, everybody know him for that, right? We were all subjects of Joe Gibbs. Yeah, we all feeling the pain. He did everything there was to Dennis Brown. This brother was like his little pet, like his little lollipop he could come and lick him anytime. He was just constantly recording Dennis." Determined not to let this happen to him, Beres again stepped out of the scene for a while.

"I laid back for about a year. Then I did another album with Willie Lindo, like a joint thing. We did it, Dynamics distributed it. It's called *Comin' at You.* Just recently I see them re-releasing it as *Red Light.*" The album was recorded in 1981, although the version out now was released with "more recent pictures—they're long after." The photos were taken during a visit to England a few years ago when Beres did a duet with Maxi Priest called "How Can Music End."

An emerging pattern in his career is reflected in his comment "I still was not satisfied with the business." The problem was "Money—money more than anything else because in those days I was much more interested in surviving than to actually think first in my head about promotion or career. I was thinking about hey, I want to live until next week, then I want to live until next month." Nonetheless Beres sought no employment outside the music business. "That's what I knew, I started from school. When I left school I was already singing."

Besides recording, he says, "I had a group for myself. Three of us, three guys. We called ourselves Tuesday's Children. Don't ask me

why, because I never stopped to think whether this person was born Monday, Tuesday, or Wednesday. We just called ourselves Tuesday's Children. We didn't record but I made quite a few dollars with the group, just ordinary shows like doing a guest spot on a amateur show and quite a few promoters would come and say, wow, harmonies! We want you! So we right away got on some very good shows like Miss Jamaica and all of that."

Also in the group was another classic Jamaican singer named Calman Scott, whose song "One Teacher, One Preacher" is one of the outstanding anthems of the '70s. "He's the brother of Scotty, the DJ" whose work with producer Derrick Harriot helped define that genre. Scotty has cut some excellent modern tunes in the nineties as well, and today, says Beres, his brother Calman Scott "lives in Japan. He's been there for quite some time now—really about ten years."

The third member of the group was "a young accountant named Ferris Walters." Between the group and session work, "I was able to survive a little bit better with a few dollars coming in from there, a few from my harmony singing and I was sorta in balance but [from] my actual records I still was not seeing any form of compensation. I was just hustling all around."

For his next recording, "I went into a joint thing again with another accountant friend of mine because I figured I have talent, I have a few dollars that I've saved up, he has a talent of taking care of business, let's do it. We went in and we recorded this album *Let's Make a Song.* We formed a little company and we named it Brotherhood. This was between he and I.

"It worked out and it did well and I still did not see anything much—at this point I did not know who to blame because this bredren was my very good friend. I did not want to say he was the one—although I was feeling that kinda way still. It just wasn't working out. After that time I laid low for a while, wondering how much more wrong moves am I gonna make. I decided to save some money and this time do something for myself, me and me alone.

"So I formed this little label called Harmony House. I said whatever happens this label will always be here. This is going to be me. No matter what label I go on, I'm always going to have something here on Harmony House. Then I made another single name "Groovy Little Thing." To be truthful that was the only time I saw some good returns from recording. Besides the fact that the record took off—this is in '85."

Around this time, "Willie Lindo and myself were still doing recordings and he put out another single tune called "What One Dance Can Do." A smash hit for Beres, this tune was later contested by Prince Buster, who claimed the rhythm as his own. "I heard about that but I'm not sure what he's talking about," Beres observed. "There was a song called 'Pressure and Slide' [by the Tennors, and not a Buster production]—I think it was a little closer to that. So maybe he should be checking himself. Personally I think it's something similar to 'Pressure and Slide' but it's not the same. It's a different set of chords completely, it just has that familiarity about it. So I don't know what's his problem." Still, he says somewhat philosophically, "If he thinks he's got some rights it's all right with me [if he] can prove it."

These two singles "was creating waves" not only in Jamaica but abroad, "particularly in England because both of them entered the international charts. But because they just entered on their own merit with nobody pushing it I guess they just came back. So we followed up with 'She Loves Me Now,' which was on Willie Lindo's label." An album simply titled *Beres Hammond* was issued by VP containing these Willie Lindo productions. "Things were going nicely, neatly and I decided I was going to put another single on Harmony House now. This one was 'Settling Down' and it got up and started moving now also in Jamaica."

At this point the harsh nature of reality reared its ever-ugly head. As his latest tune was climbing near the top of the charts, Beres was the victim of holdup men in his own home. "I got robbed by some"—he laughs—"some dangerous guys in Jamaica, right? This was in '87 now. Thieves came down, had me tied up. I was tied up. It wasn't something that I expected. To be truthful it was the farthest thing from my mind.

"After that ordeal I decided to cool out because I was figuring to myself, well, the reason why this thing happened is because these guys think I'm making some money now. So I must retreat and see what I was doing wrong again or how I should place myself. I went to New York [where family, including brothers and sisters, live] and I was like in between New York and Jamaica not doing anything, not working. I decided gotta cool out a little bit, see what I was doing wrong, see what I could correct and come again. This lasted about three years."

During this "cooling off" period, "I spent most of my time in New York, just thinking about the business and how come I have some hit songs going on presently and not doing anything about it and how should I approach it because that was a time that I should be making some money, but then being, not really scared but more concerned as to how I should position myself in life itself, it took me about three years sorting out myself and sorting out my head and sorting out all the violence."

"In that time," he continues, "Willie Lindo got sick also—he had some nervous breakdown. He was in New York about two years and in that two years I was in New York so I managed to get him to go back into the studio in Long Island. So both of us, sick in the head really, went in the studio and we recorded an album called *Have a Nice Weekend* (VP)—that one had about three covers on it. I personally don't like cover songs—I like making songs. That was 1989, 1990."

During the time these sessions were taking place, Hammond traveled back and forth to Jamaica, "Tappa Zukie was a friend of mine and he's always in my skin about doing recording. Each time I was down there he would come check me and every now and then we'd go down and lay two, three tracks of an album called *(Putting Up) Resistance*," later issued by RAS.

So at the same time he was recording a very ballady crossover LP in America, Beres and Tappa Zukie were cooking up one of his rootsi-est albums in Jamaica. "I was in between two different places and I couldn't get the studio out of my blood, out of the system. It was really after we had this big hurricane [Gilbert]. When the hurricane was down there I was in New York and I went back to Jamaica about a week and a half [later], when electricity was restored in most of the places so that's the time [Tappa] grab onto me and we finish [the album]." Of '70s DJ and '90s producer extraordinaire Tappa Zukie, Hammond says, "He is a good producer. Unorthodox or whatever one want to call it but he gets the right sound."

As the finishing touches were being put on the *Resistance* LP, *Have a Nice Weekend* was released and a couple of tracks were issued off of it by Chrysalis Records in Europe. "It was doing its own thing neatly, but then this wasn't really what I wanted if you understand." The difference in sound and vibe between the two discs is readily apparent. The latter one "is Beres Hammond but I wasn't as relaxed in my mind as I would have been if I was in Jamaica, so that was nice album but *Resistance* is much more militant. Take it for what it is and [*Weekend*] is another chapter in my life.

"The real thing I wanted to do was my hard-core Jamaica thing so when 1990 came around I decided, must go back to Jamaica now and put the past behind you. It's time enough to get over that because the guys who did it, I understand that they paid for their wrongdoings. I went back to Jamaica decided that I'm going to

set my life straight once and for all." It was then Hammond made possibly the best career move of his life. He connected with a friend from his harmony-singing days, a producer named Germain.

"I went to Donovan Germain at Penthouse records, 'cause I was looking for some studio time to do my own thing. All the studios were booked and because he's a good friend of mine I decided to check him if he could squeeze me in at an early date. They were all booked up for three weeks and month and alla dat so I figured if I knew Germain well and he say is my friend then must can find some space early up, like another two days or so.

"When I check him, him say he is full up too, three weeks of booking and all that. The only thing he could probably work out was, he has some time for himself there. So if he gives me some time in return could I do a song on a riddim he's got. This has nothing to do with payment, it was just you granting me a favor of getting an early time. I said gosh, if this is what I have to do to get my time, you know, man, well, play the rhythm!

"He put it on right away, he stop whatever session was going on deh, play the rhythm for me and I listen to it. Yeah, I do this for you, man. I do this for you sometime down in the week. Can get the time tomorrow, my time? Yes, you can get time tomorrow, but Beres—like how you listen the rhythm already—sing it now, mon!" He laughs. "Can't manage this now man! I'll come back and do it for you [this] weekend but just let me have my time tomorrow. Him say you have a time tomorrow, Beres, but just do it for me now, now that you are here. He had me in a spot."

After trying to talk his way out of it Beres "went in the studio and listen the rhythm over and over until a lady pass. A little suggestively dressed lady. Because in the studio you have people always walkin' and when she passed she had on this shorts that looked kinda like, as I said, suggestive, and I just started humming." He sings, "'Hey little girl, each time you pass my way, I'm tempted to touch.'"

"I found myself singing that and in about half an hour the song was done. I wanted to finish it fast and get it up there, make sure I have my time. And them seh, 'Beres, you finish, sing the harmonies too man.' I went back in and I did the harmonies and say, satisfied? Yes. All right, I have my time tomorrow? Say yes, my lord. Come tomorrow at five o'clock you have from five o'clock until. So okay, and he gives me a little discount on the rates too. So that's fine with me. All right? Came back the following day and I did my recording, all a that, and left for New York again.

"Germain called me in New York. He called me about a month after and asked me if I can come and do an album for him. I said, can't do no album now, my thing I wan' tek care of. He said Beres, you have to do it because the song, the 45 you did for me it start creating some storm. And I, to be truthful, I couldn't remember anything about it because I was doing it because I wanted my studio time. So I said which 45, he said 'Tempted to Touch.' I said 'Tempted to Touch.'" He laughs. "I don't even remember the name of the song! So I went out to the record shop [VP in New York] and asked them for 'Tempted to Touch.' They say yeah mon, it a go like hot bread! Said yeah, for real? And before I know it within the next two weeks it was in the top five record charts in New York."

If "What One Dance Can Do" created a stir, "Tempted to Touch" was the song that put Beres Hammond on the map—twenty years after he first charted the territory. The timing was perfect. After years of no respect for Jamaican music on the radio in Jamaica, a little station called Irie-FM was making waves with the first twenty-four-hour reggae programming ever, and they were hungry for tunes to match the times.

"By the time I go back to Jamaica it was the ruling song all over, everybody was into 'Tempted' and it just blew up. And then when I heard from England now it lodge as the number one song in Europe. So I said okay, I'll finish your album for you. So I did an album for him, he had a whole lotta riddims you know, cover riddims and t'ing, and I just went in the studio and every time they played them I make a song."

Although singing over existing rhythms is standard practice in Jamaica it hadn't been standard practice for Beres Hammond up to this time. He felt "completely out of my form but then I must survive. So we finish the album and the album sounded good. As far as Germain is concerned it's his first number one album."

The album was called *A Love Affair* and featured several other songs destined to be big hits on the new Jamaican radio, like "Respect to You Baby," "Is This a Sign" and "Feeling Lonely," as well as duets with guest vocalists Freddie McGregor, Dennis Brown, and Marcia Griffiths. "And then during that time I teamed up with Buju, did something with Cutty Ranks . . . it's been going on like that.

"All the different producers now who were my friends from long time now all dem come down on me one time—you give to Germain a 45, you must give me one—and everybody come down now and I did records for each one of them, you know. Blackbeard from Sonic Sounds, for him I did a song name 'Step Aside' [Richie Stevens had a career-making hit on the same rhythm with a version of Dennis Brown's "Should I"]—fixed up all a dem." Later he returned to Tappa Zukie to cut the 45 "Distress," because, he says with a laugh, "Tappa Zukie won't let go."

The Penthouse sound controlled the early '90s like Gussie Clarke's Music Works studio ruled the late '80s. As Beres says, they "could do no wrong. That was the time when reggae came back on its feet in my estimation because it was sort of down for awhile and the business started getting back interesting [in] '91, '92. Lots of stage shows started happening again and all dat because there was a time when not much of that was happening. Records were not selling for a period of time and then after that everything just started to be good and I started making money now! And almost starting to forget the guys who didn't want to pay me or the guys who still owe me. I could maybe forget them, hey, keep that, keep that. Nineties been some of the best for me."

Hammond himself represents a great element of that return because he bases his sound on melody, harmony, and the conscious lyrics of groups like Bob Marley and the Wailers. "And that was lost for a while," he notes. "But you see, even with Bob—Bob and Peter—Bob was a good friend. Peter was a much closer friend of mine, you know, and being around them guys for the main time I been around them I learned a lot, not say musical, but about the business and about what people appreciate on a more international level. So experiences like that kinda support me to what's the right even though I told myself what was the right thing from the start."

Although many might think of Hammond as primarily a "lovers" or romantic singer, you don't have to search too far in his work for examples of the conscious roots sound on which reggae was founded. Check out "Preacherman," for example, a neglected single from the album *Full Attention*. Hammond's soulful delivery is here matched by hard-hitting social lyrics of an uncompromising nature. Not surprisingly, the song was not that well received on the island.

"In Jamaica if you sing this type, tut-tut because they have too much false preachers down deh. It's an international thing but in Jamaica, because Jamaica is so much smaller, songs like this is much more pronounced— it's kinda more individual now. Everybody takes it personal. So it got some play but I don't think it enjoyed the kind of play that the other songs I did enjoyed. And I tend to know the reason why. I knew that before but this is just one of the songs I have to do because I sing about things that affects me and my immediate surroundings. I don't sing about what I don't know."

Hammonds eyes flash as he warms to a subject he clearly feels strongly about. "This is one of the things that I hate sometimes to see, churches packed and the people who go to churches are poor—and the preacher's always living lavishly. There's something wrong and I couldn't figure out why every Sunday you have something to preach, every Sunday it's like you prepare, 'Hey,'" he says in imitation of a pretentious preacher, "this is how I'm gonna take their monies. Tell them about Joshua today.' Yeah, uhm, you know? So."

He says there are "lots more civic concerns like those I would like to approach but these songs don't get across in Jamaica if you don't put a hell of a promotion behind them. Like I could sing 'Step aside now, another man wants to take over' and that just get up and go because it doesn't affect the system. Because I know this, with revolutionary songs I tend to incline myself more [toward] love [songs] but it doesn't mean I don't want to speak out certain other things. I just don't want to pressure myself because you can't help the weak if you are weak, you have to be strong in order to be able to help the weak. So when I regain my original strength that I thought I had when I was just coming I'll address what I think deep in my heart, properly from a stronger foundation. True, and it's not that I'm afraid of being targeted by society because they're gonna target you for one thing or another, it's just that I think in order for one to target me I should be able to have enough ammunition to counter you or to stand on my own in defense if you try to break me right up."

The nature of the Jamaican recording industry—artists record for myriad producers and much of this work doesn't see the light of day until they make a name for themselves—has caused a flood of releases for Beres since his Penthouse hits. Two compilations, *Soul Reggae and More* (VP) and *Irie and Mellow* (Rhino U.K.) collect tracks from the Willie Lindo discs *Soul Reggae* and *Comin' at You* (even a track from the Joe Gibbs album winds up on the former). This adds some confusion for collectors but as Beres says, "I prefer him [Willie Lindo] to do this than the other guys because the other guys made so much and to be honest we didn't earn anything off it. And we suffered along the way."

Sweetness (VP) is an excellent collection of hits including "Double Trouble" and the aforementioned "Step Aside," which controlled the radio in Jamaica in 1991. *Full Attention* (VP) is another powerful group of songs from producer Fatis Burrell's Exterminator label. "Fatis is one of the best producers in terms of freedom. I got freedom with all of them because I do what I want to do. If I can't get the freedom I leave. I want to know I have total control of what I am doing and don't be telling me this and that if you can't do it. This is just how I am, so I get freedom with all of them, but with Fatis, he doesn't have to say anything to me. he would not cough if he knows its gonna disturb me, if you know what I mean, so you call that total freedom and I respect him for that. So with that kind of a behavior he must end up with good product."

Two combination albums are available too, the first with Derrick Lara called *Just a Vibes* on Heavy Beat. "This happened during the time when 'Tempted to Touch' was hitting. Derrick Lara, he's a member of the Tamlins. He sings the falsetto lead. And he's a very good, very close friend of mine as a singer, right? And I just wanted to make something happen for him so I figured if I do a team-up on an album with him—he approached me and I said no sweat."

Another, called *Beres Hammond/Barrington Levy* (Live & Learn) was never intended (at least by Beres) to be an album. "It started out as two tracks long before 'Tempted to Touch.' The guy asked me to do two tracks for him and when I actually went in the studio he had a change of mind like he was thinking album and I wasn't thinking in that direction. I was thinking of a two song, three or four at most. I went to do two and I ended up doing two more and said hey, call it a day. No album thing. So I think what happened after is he made Barrington—because they actually laid the tracks before, he just laid some rhythms and I said, oh, so you're planning for me? No, not never. So I did about four and left. I think he got Barrington Levy to come and do the other tracks and just put them together.

"But I wasn't even there when Barrington was working, don't know nothing 'bout it. But we have a way of hustling. Jamaicans. I respect Jamaicans for that. Because Barrington is a very good singer also. Good voice."

Like Sugar Minott, Barrington Levy is often considered a "dancehall" singer, but Beres brushes off the distinction between reggae singer and dancehall singer. "I think of myself as a singer. I never try to place a label on me, never. I started out, I made my name in Jamaica as a balladeer. It wasn't reggae. Talking ballads, like Lionel Richie, that kinda stuff. That's what they knew Beres Hammond in Jamaica for in the '70s. All of the number ones in the '70s were ballads.

"That's what they knew me before I just decided, hey, let's try another rhythm. This time, goin' do some reggae. As far as I'm concerned when the inspiration comes, the kind of music I hear in my head, that's the form I'd like the music to take. Don't necessarily have to be reggae. If it feels like reggae to me it's reggae. Feels like a ballad, let it be. I don't wanna put a restriction on what rhythm this should be under. I prefer me and the musicians feel a vibe. You know, this is what its all about."

A reputation as a balladeer caused Beres some unexpected problems. "They didn't like how I was dressing. In Jamaica they criticize me badly, tore me down. Because when I was singing them ballads they were brainwashed into thinking that people who sing this kinda way should be attired in suit, nice gold watch, and alla that. So when I am on the street, because I was very popular in them ballad days, I was on the street and somebody say, Beres Hammond that, and they look past me! Push me out of the way, right, where is he? Them said no, you just touch him! That was the kind of attitude and it went on for years, years, years."

This misperception continued "even until the '90s because they wanted me to dress [the part] and I couldn't find myself comfortable that way. Finally, I told myself if this gonna cost me my career it gonna ha fe go cost me, because I am not changing! This is me and this is how I got my inspiration, was in the street and making them songs, so I can't see why you can't accept me like I am, easy feel free, everything, and they wouldn't accept me."

Beres's "everyday attire"—the same street style he so admired as a young man in singer Marvin Gaye—brought him not only fan censure but media criticism. "They write all sort of things about me: Beres is great, has a good voice and he could be this and he could be that but he needs to take more interest in his attire and in spite of his singing and voice and lyrics and thing the person you see is not the same person—and even early '90s!

"It could have been about '91, '92 in Jamaica at the end of the year they put me into a parade in the Gleaner and said I'm—amongst the ten worst-dressed, not entertainers, you know, *people!* Yeah, the ten worst-dressed, and in the same lineup they categorized Shabba amongst the ten best.

"So I said to myself, life is so funny because here I am singing love songs, joining people together making them feel good about each other, and you call me worst-dressed and here comes Shabba—with no disrespect—telling you about or disrespecting the lady that you're amongst and they classify him as amongst the best dressed. So where your priorities lie, and how we measure how far one should dress? How does one measure that, and me tell myself again, I say a worry for them, not for me."

As with his music, Beres saw such concerns began to turn around. "Since that time that they made the description I've had about six number one songs in Jamaica and they're the ones that put them hits. Number one after number one after number one and when they reach they say we're pleading to Beres and they can't change me, that's how I am, and finally when they couldn't do better one year they just turn around and give me all the awards on every award show. They even give me award that I was not guilty of! And I asked them about it, I said hey, on one of the award thing, I say, you're sure you didn't give me somebody else's own? Because I'm not accustomed to even collecting one! Much more four at one, please, three at one, please, but I finally said to myself, I wasn't wrong, they're wrong! Because they're trying to apologize in all sorta different ways.

"It's been interesting! It's been [an] interesting life. The fight that I got from society, really, Bob Marley suffered much more than that in Jamaica. Suffered far more than that. It was not until people from America, Europe, and all over the world started accepting Bob Marley—as a matter of fact, it was when Bob died! The rest of Jamaica started respecting him. For real. They didn't know him. They used to call hey, little Rasta boy—these society people they never respected him until they heard what was happening in foreign land. So—he's the same little Rasta boy? Oh, Bob. Hypocrites we call them. Bob did talk about that too. Hypocrites and parasites."

Whether you call it ska, rock steady, reggae or dancehall Jamaican music has had its ups and downs over the years, but many see a return to the conscious vibe that brought it to the international fore. Says Beres, "We Jamaicans are a talented people in all walks of life. If we are con people, we are very good at conning. In the music business, if you're gonna sing we have some a the nicest voices. And if you really do want to make songs we can make some wonderful songs.

"If you're going to copy something we could be like the Japanese, very good. In the music business then, the younger artists tend to follow wha' they see going on—in other words, if slackness is what they hear going on they will follow that trend but once you set up a good precedence they will follow that too. If it seem like it gonna work—and give thanks that we have some real good ones out there that they're sorta inclined to follow now—I trust we'll be getting some better music now the singers are coming back and you have some of these conscious DJs.

Still, says Beres, "I personally I am not here to judge what the next hand does. I know what I am doing or what I intend to do and I hope that's the right thing. I'm not saying that they should follow me as the right thing because I'm still not sure what I am doing is the right thing, I am only telling myself that it is."

In 1994, after two decades of Jamaican hits, Beres Hammond released his first album on a major U.S. label. On *In Control* (Elektra), he seemed to sum up all the elements and styles covered in this interview. Album opener "Reggae Calling" set the pace as it first asked, "What's wrong with the world?" and then attempted to set it straight. Though he delivered a full serving of the romantic ballads that first made his name, he filled the disc with some militant gems like the brilliant "Another Day in the System" and the uplifting "Motherland." The understated video for "No Disturb Sign" gained regular rotation on BET (Black Entertainment Television) in the States and seemed to signal a breakthrough

for Jamaican music here. That year Hammond headlined the prestigious Reggae Sunsplash tour as well.

A flood of repackagings poured forth, including *Beres Hammond and Mikey Zappow Meet in Jamaica* (Rhino U.K.), containing many of his Zap Pow hits, and a few that weren't. Heartbeat picked up the Star Trail combination LP with Derrick Lara, retitling it *Expression,* and RAS put out *Putting Up Resistance* adding the single "Distress" and "Heroes Die Young" as bonus tracks. Heartbeat next issued *Getting Stronger,* a collection of Beres's best recordings for Richard Bell's Star Trail label, including such imperative singles as "False Preacher" and "Fight to Defend It."

In 1997 Hammond emerged again with the uplifting *Love from a Distance* (VP), containing his own productions for Harmony House. Highlights include "Black Beauty," "Sing Glory," and "Sweet Lies." Jet Star UK issued a Beres compilation in their *Reggae Max* series that gathered singles and combination records and in 1998 VP released an all-new set called *A Day in the Life.* "Can You Play Some More," "It's Not Official," and "Victory" are among the outstanding selections on this set. As we've seen in this interview, it's second nature for him to "haul and pull up" every once in a while to realign his course. This holds true for his career, but, he says, "Not musically. When I'm finished with the music I'm finished with the music and no regrets.

"You know something? I never really try to study how this thing come about. I don't even want to know how these songs come about, how the whole a these come about. These things just keep comin' out and I don't strain it! I never stop to study and I don't think I want to. 'Cause it's working! Definitely working. I know, I know. Me no really wanna know at all. But in terms of livity now, I always stop and look back to check my progression. Yeah mon, every year I look back at the year before and how much progress I've made this year against last year and it's good to do that because if you don't do these kinda things then you wouldn't know where you're headed."

At this point in his career things must look pretty good for the man who likes to stop and check his progress. With a twinkle in his eye and a laugh he says, "Yeah, well, they shape up nicely and neatly and I take shape with it too. Yeah man, everything seems to be working out nicely. But I don't want people to get carried away by overexpecting this or that of Beres. What I want is for people to see me for the simple person that I am, respect me for the simple things that I do. I can make mistakes too. Don't jump on judgment, just take time to sort yourself out when I do make a mistake. If this one is not your favorite song, don't worry. I have another one coming."

CHAPTER 31

Admiral Tibet:

Serious Singer for a Serious Time

Admiral Tibet is a roots singer who came up in the dancehall era and helped bridge the Rasta music of the '70s and the revitalization now being enjoyed in reggae with the new roots singers like Everton Blender and the return of conscious themes to the dancehall. At times in the late '80s and early '90s it seemed Tibet was one of the only voices of reason in a music that was losing its own. With the renewed focus on uplifting the youth in reggae the time has come for this uncompromised artist to get his due.

Born Kennell Allen in the Parish of St. Mary's in Jamaica, Tibet came from a large family—five brothers and two sisters—and now has a large family of his own (seven children, the oldest eleven years of age). His unusual stage name came from a cousin to whom he pointed out the country of Tibet on an atlas in grade school, where things that might not normally seem funny can provoke unbridled hilarity. From that day forward, he was known as Tibet among his friends. He picked up his Admiralty from friend Glen Douglas, who also produced his first single, "Too Many Violence," at King Tubby's studio in 1982.

"It's like we press about a hundred copies as I can remember," says Tibet. "It was on the Melody Rocks label. But that song didn't break me to the public. I was just getting experience in the studio from that song." It wasn't until 1985 when Tibet returned to the studio and recorded "Babylon War" (released as a 7-inch on the Arabic and Kings International label) that Tibet gained recognition in Jamaica.

Like a lot of young singers his eagerness to record sent him to a variety of producers and studios in Jamaica, recording a lot for little or no financial return. Over the years, Tibet singles were issued on Power House, Redman, Kings and Courage International, Time 1, and a host of other labels. His first two albums, *War in a Babylon* (RAS, produced and arranged by Ivor Broderick) and *Time Is Going to Come* (Rhino U.K., for producers Winston and Melvin Dakin and Donna Johnson), were recorded around the same time and *Come into the Light* (Live and Love—Jamaica, produced by Prince Jammy) was issued in 1987. "I was doing a lot of work," says Tibet in something of an understatement, though as usual in the dog-eat-dog record world the rewards were not great.

Tibet also cut an album for Winston Riley's Techniques label, *Leave People Business*. He recorded extensively with Bobby Digital. Three albums have now come out, *Reality Time,*

Separate Class, and *Weeping and Mourning,* the first two on VP and the third on the French Melodee label. He also split a combination album with Thriller U called *Two Good to Be True* on Digital B. He issued singles on a variety of new labels like Kingston 11, African Star, Supply de Beat and Cannon Music in the early nineties. His 1996 CD, *Excitement* (VP) was produced by Bunny Gemini. There's also a CD produced by King Jammy, *Things That You Do* (Super Powers). Reportedly, full-length releases produced by Phillip Burrell and Record Factory are "in the can." As a writer, he says, "I concentrate on the riddim and I concentrate on the lyrics—to get them to blend together."

As you might imagine from the lyrics of tunes like "Call on Jah Name," "Burn in Flames," "Seek Jah First," "Rich Man Pressure," and "Serious Time," Tibet sees a guiding hand in his own work. "I find it easy still to create my style. When saying so I've always been telling people that the Almighty Father is with me doing my work so that is why it can come easy. Because if it was me alone, nothing. So I have to ask the Father to guide me."

In explaining his style, he says, "It's not that anyone tell me to sing conscious songs, it come like it was just born in me—I couldn't do nothing else but conscious songs. Because there is so many things I need to sing about—even in the ghettos around Jamaica is many youths come to me and say "'nuff respect," because I am the one who may prevent them from getting involved in certain things. They say when they listen to some of my songs even if they were thinking of picking up a gun they're not gonna do it. So these are the main things I'm focusing on right now. That's why I sing conscious songs. It doesn't make sense I sing songs without meaning. I have to sing to protect my brother and sister."

Though music with a message is on the rise in Jamaica again, Tibet recalls when "It was just like me, Edi Fitzroy, and a few others maintaining the consciousness and music. It was pure

ADMIRAL TIBET. Photograph by John Skomdahl

slackness and gun lyrics around us by other entertainers dem." Encouraged to do some cover tunes or sing over an American song, Tibet says, "Right now it's a message that me a deal with. . . . Even people, because the slackness have a hold on them, it's like them become accustomed to it, like they wanted the slackness. Now that was in those times but not right now because right now I can see the vibes change."

Tibet's brush with international fame came in 1990 when he penned the title tune for the movie *The Lunatic*. The soundtrack was released on Island Records. That the movie—and thus the song—was not the most successful fazed him not in the least. "I just enjoy writing my songs and the message going out there to the people. Going to Germany, England, America, Japan—that's the greatest thing to me." He sees himself as a man with a message and adds, "I still feel like time to come. Then you have more people want to hear consciousness. The more rougher the times getting, the more them will want to hear consciousness."

A sign of this growth he sees in the changes happening in Jamaica right now. "Violence is going on but it's not like in the '70s or the '80s. Political violence was very big, but ya see, is like, even the youths dem and the people dem is getting wiser now to know that the politicians are just using them. So them getting wiser." He headlined a show in L.A. in 1996, his first visit to the West Coast. This positive artist who has contributed so much to keeping reggae on the right track continues to help set the standard for reggae performers at home and abroad. In 1998 Tibet racked up a series of cultural singles like "Brave and Bold" (Mafia & Fluxy), "Hard Time" (Henfield), and releases on Techniques and Record Factory that show his talent is stronger than ever.

CHAPTER 32

Luciano:

Sending Out a Message

With a series of trend-defying Xterminator singles launched throughout the course of 1994, Luciano and producer Phillip "Fatis" Burrell helped shake the reggae world to its original foundation—roots music. "Forward to Africa," "Black Survivors," "One Way Ticket," "Jah Is Alive"— each release seemed to get better and better, cresting with "It's Me Again Jah." This visionary booming vocalist, who had just begun to record two or three years earlier, rose to the top of Jamaica's charts. Four albums issued on three different U.S. labels by this prolific team—as well as two discs worth of material recorded earlier for other producers—brought him to the States for a series of stunning live shows with the Firehouse Crew, led by Dean Frazer.

For an artist who's only been making records for four years to suddenly find himself signed to Island with major distribution and marketing the likes of which many reggae singers can only dream about, Luciano seems a remarkably humble and straightforward artist. He exudes a spiritual presence others only sing about. Dressed a little like a military man, with nubby dreads poking out of his cap, his manner is that of a friendly bear with a viselike grip who misses little if anything that goes on around him but inhabits higher ground. As positive and uplifting in person as on record, Luciano is just that shot in the arm reggae needs—a return to center for a music whose very core is an emotional support system for the disadvantaged, underprivileged, and downtrodden of the world.

The man now called Luciano was born Jepther Washington McClymont in Clarendon, Jamaica, on December 20, 1964. His early life was hard. "My father moved on when I was eleven years old," he recalls. "My mother had to struggle with nine of us. She doesn't have a skill, she doesn't have a trade. So she have to be washing clothes on the weekend and so on. Now, when I left Manchester High School with three subjects, math, English, and biology, I thought that I had the qualifications to make it through life. But when I went back to Kingston to look a job it was like walking for many weeks without. I said to myself I should go back to the country."

At this point he took up his first trade. "I started selling oranges in the marketplace," he says. "After a while the drought set in and then we couldn't get no orange. So we started selling ice cream cakes. I used to sleep in the marketplace. Through these stages of development I identified an essence in myself which kept me going and gave me the fuel to push on through in life even though it can be real tough. It gave me a reassurance that there was better to come at a different time and at the end of the tunnel a light would be shining. So I kept on with the spirit of long endurance and with the love of the Almighty abiding with me in my heart and my soul reassuring me at all time. I kept pushing forward."

Returning to Kingston, he recalls, "I learned a skill. Upholstery. I used to do the upholstery and a lef' upholstery an a go to the studio and sound system dances, singing sound systems weekends. But through all this something, some inner prompting kept telling me that there is really more to life and this is what I really keep seeking for."

Like many Jamaicans, music was a prominent part of his life as a young man. But his early attempt to sing with a group was a dismal failure. He recounts, "I tried to put together a group with one of my sister and my brother-in-law but the first appearance we made, which was on Tastee's contest, I tell you the truth man, it didn't work out so well. We flopped big time that night, you know?" He laughs. "And when we came off the stage there was a stampede. And I was so frightened that I stayed away from music in that sense for a long while. But this inner prompting kept taunting me all the while. 'Cause my father moved on, leaving a guitar he built and played. Through those early years of my life I, hearing the melody, fell in love really with the guitar. I started learning to play."

An industrial accident interrupted his playing for some time. He displays a wicked-looking scar and explains, "While working in upholstering I got a finger caught in the crosscut saw—the left index finger. So I thought I couldn't play the guitar again but recently with this new reassurance of spirit I bought a guitar and I'm playing very well. I look forward to playing a different dimension of music on my next albums to come."

LUCIANO. Photograph by Jan Salzman; © 1996 Phantom Photos

In 1992 he recorded a couple of tracks for producer Earl Hughes, then "met up with Sky High from Mau Mau Productions." His work for Sky High was released under the name Luciana. A combination album with another young singer was issued as *Luciana and Presley: Stuck on You* (Mau Mau, 1993).

In what he calls the "preliminary stages," he recounts, "I wasn't serious or knowledge[able] about my name." Advised that Jepther McClymont might be a cumbersome name for a popular singer and that he needed a name "that people were willing to call," he and a friend "had a selection of name from which we derive Luciana. At one time I thought about finding a name that would be more in harmony with my message and thought. Long after becoming involved and seeing how much the music required of me I investigate my name to find the true meaning and the root. *Luci-* is a prefix which means 'light'— Luciano means 'the bearer of light.' The word has seven letters and it coincide with my lucky number, which is seven." Over time, as his self-knowledge evolved, Luciana became Luciano.

Right after working with Sky High, he says, "I moved on to Castro Brown, to New Name, which is owned and run by Castro Brown. Still seeking to find a stadium in which I could do some constructive work. There I did songs like 'Slice of the Cake' and 'Give Love a Try.'" Another burning 7-inch issued on New Name was "Jah Jah Never Fail I," along with "Give Love a Try," a foretaste of the conscious music to come. But "Noel Browne was so busy— he was the engineer at that time and he was always going on tour."

The young singer then hooked up with Freddie McGregor. During a lengthy career that spans four decades McGregor's smooth style and professional attitude made him one of the most dependable artists on record and live. A major hit—"Big Ship Sailing on the Ocean"—allowed him to form his own Big Ship label and produce other artists as well.

"He invited me over to one of his studio sessions and I did the first thing, 'Shake It Up,' and realizing the potential we went on to do other tracks and come forth with an album which have the same title." *Shake It Up Tonight* was released by Big Ship in England and Jamaica in 1993. Co-produced by McGregor and Dalton Browne, it was issued in the U.S. by VP in 1995 as *After All,* with one additional track and an added remix of one song. But "even then I realized I was a second." Just as before, "the engineer was always on the road with another band."

It should be pointed out that Dalton Browne (sometimes spelled and always pronounced Brownie) is the brother of Noel Browne, the engineer for Castro Brown (Dennis Brown's cousin) who was also always on the road. Both were at the time in the band Bloodfire Posse. Another brother, Cleveland Browne, is one half of the rhythm section/production team Steely and Clevie. The three keyboard-playing engineer-producers are all major factors in the digital music explosion of the '90s.

Still seeking a better working situation, Luciano explains, "I had to find a very serious producer who would be willing to work with my ideas. So I heard of Xterminator. I did the first song, 'Chant Out.' Meeting Fatis [producer and Xterminator label head Phillip Burrell] I realize how serious he is and then I realize he have the apparatus and the facilities for the work, so I just decided to work along with Fatis and from that day I haven't been drifting. I've done a couple tracks for Sly and Robbie and the Taxi and a couple other tracks for other producers that was previous to Sly." These include singles on Pickout, Mixing Lab and Star Trail, as well as those previously mentioned.

In fact, he says, "Sly is very instrumental in my records and songs." Even on the Xterminator productions, "he is actually the man with the drum." Robbie Shakespeare, the Firehouse Crew, and Dean Frazer also share responsibility for the hard steady rhythms his powerful voice glides over. "So having these expertise around me I said to myself I have to stick to Xterminator 'cause I have no problems so far."

The Exterminator (who dropped the E or moved the X forward in the early '90s) seems to have the mid-to-late '90s locked up like Penthouse did in the late '80s, putting out crucial records with great singers and DJs voicing sturdy tracks that, like Channel One in the '70s, are often original Studio One riddims played in a modern style. And though Burrell has worked with new and renewed talent like Sizzla, Cocoa Tea, Louie Culture, Mikey General, Capleton, and others, it seems Luciano is the label's number one artist, a fact attested to by Burrell's presence as manager on his 1996 visit to L.A.

RAS issued their first work together here as a CD called *Moving Up* (still as Luciana) in 1993. Although his sound and spirituality were still evolving, crucial cuts like "Chant Out" and "Poor and Simple" signaled the emergence of a new voice in the world of reggae. The title track, a reggae rework of the theme from the TV sitcom "The Jeffersons" was at once a nod to pop culture and a restatement of Luciano's working-class background and determination to improve his life.

One Way Ticket (VP) was quite simply the best reggae release of 1995. Many of the previously mentioned 1994 Xterminator singles and guest spots from Lady G, Cocoa Tea, and Charlie Chaplin as well as other major songs like "(Must) Raggamuffin" and the pop-crossover "Turn Your Life Around" propelled this new artist to a position of immediate respect. The combination of Burrell's electro-Nyahbingi riddims and Luciano's return to the righteous and revolutionary themes of reggae's more militant time electrified the music and signaled the Jamaican roots renewal still flourishing today.

His next release, *Where There Is Life* (Island Jamaica) had a smoother pop feel, veering dangerously close at times to rhythm and blues. Why major labels want to turn good roots singers

into so-so pop singers remains a mystery as time after time—Richie Stephens being a major case in point—they lose their original audience while failing to find that major market niche. Perhaps this was just a natural evolution for Xterminator, who's always tinkering with the sound to get it just right. Luciano pulled the disc out of the fire with the songs "It's Me Again Jah," "Who Could It Be," and the combination record "(We're All) In This Together" with Louie Culture and Terror Fabulous, retaining his momentum while sustaining his original vision.

It seemed with all of this that Luciano's time had come. But to him, "I say it's not even my time in that sense. It's a time for righteousness, a time for consciousness, a time for positive vibes. So we have seen a change not only in the music fraternity but also in the media. People are more willing to play positive tunes and seek out positive artists and do interviews.

"We can see a positive renaissance right throughout humanity. Speakers coming out, Million Man March, and so on. So we agree that there was a decadence after Bob Marley, a transition. So now we realize that the pendulum has swung and we have a positive upgrowth for music and the whole portion of humanity. So it's a situation like this where whosoever will may come. If I have this talent and ability then let me use it in a positive sense.

He attributes his success to his "connection with the infinite one" and ability to move forward in times of adversity. In his unique mystical syntax he sums it up. "Putting aside negative thoughts and toxic thoughts and just go positive! To reflect and meditate and have a little time for myself and God my creator. The connection has to be there with the infinite one. If you just allow people to draw you here and push you there you become a robot. All my contribution, my spiritual[ity] comes from within."

Two of a number of Xterminator singles recorded in '94 and '95 shed some light on this side of Luciano as well. One, "Ain't Giving Up," with DJ Charlie Chaplin, put to rest rumors of his early retirement, which he refers to as a "sabbatical." Another, with Chaplin and DJ Josie Wales, is 1994's "Rebel with a Cause," is one of Luciano's hottest rockers that pretty well defines the man himself.

Of another singer of his generation who sadly has already passed, the gentle-voiced Garnett Silk, Luciano says, "He's my brother and my friend. He's like a forerunner. When I observe life, me have to at least try and learn something from everything that happens around me. With this attitude in life I always seem to get through, being more vigilant and careful about my steps. At times when people get their blessing they overlook it then, so they deal with it with sacrilege, they don't respect that talent.

"Jah has a hand in everything that happens," he continues, "and Garnett Silk moving on has to a certain extent awakened the consciousness of the people 'cause they realize now you have to show your musical contributors more love and more respect, have time to deal with what they're saying, listen carefully to the contents and see what you can do. So I realize that they are appreciating me in a positive sense and I feel good and I'm happy to know that at least this—what

LUCIANO. Photograph by Jan Salzman; © 1997 Phantom Photos

has happen to Garnett Silk has jolt mankind, especially in Jamaica, to the consciousness to at least appreciate the positiveness in the music while they have it, while they can."

Silk is not the only artist whose praises Luciano sings. "Bob Marley has been very instrumental in getting me to see life in a very spiritual aspect, lyrically and otherwise." One of his early singles for Sky High was a medley of Bob Marley tunes. "Dennis Brown has been very instrumental also in vocal style. I could go on and on and say that Stevie Wonder— anyone really who has contributed positively in life has made an impact on my life."

Another interesting avowed influence is Louise Bennett, Jamaica's beloved Miss Lou, who helped Jamaicans see the beauty of their own intricate and poetic patois. "'Cause she has worked forward into my consciousness that I can be proud of my culture, I can be proud of myself." Other names mentioned are "Mr. Beres" Hammond ("a trailblazer" with whom he cut the also as yet uncollected Xterminator 7-inch "No Gabbon"), Admiral Tibet, Burning Spear, and Israel Vibration. "Jamaica has been blessed with lots of positive people who have come and made a positive contribution to the music fraternity."

The basic lesson learned from all of them, whether philosophical or technical, for Luciano boils down to "the more natural the better. The humility, the simplicity, and the love, these are the essence of life and once we abide by these principles of love and understanding then we'll find happiness, we'll find peace of mind. Vanity is one of the stumbling blocks to spiritual growth and to a certain extent I see where many spirits or souls have come and made a positive contribution but they have allowed vanity to corrode their minds and they're not here with us and no doubt they have to rebirth and come again over and over. If we can identify the essence of life being love in the core of our beings then we can find that happiness and

that peace of mind. Who knows, you might find immortality if you keep seeking."

In 1997 Jet Star in England released *Jet Star Reggae Max: Luciano,* a compilation of singles including some Freddie McGregor productions but mainly drawing from the Xterminator recordings. It includes "Psalm 24" with dub poet Mutabaruka, "Bounty Lover" with dancehall queen Lady G, and crucial cuts like "Wicked Haffe Run Way," "Jah Is Alive," and "That's the Way Life Goes." Part of a series that generally comprises Greatest Hits packages of classic singers like John Holt, Dennis Brown, and others, it's interesting that a singer as new as Luciano would already be considered for such a series.

Early that same year Island Jamaica issued *Messenger* (it had been available in England some time previously). Serious and contemplative songs like "Life," "Carry Jah Load," and "Messenger" as well as "How Can You" and "Never Give Up My Pride" showed Luciano's sound and style still growing, and message music predominates his lyrical output. No artist is better situated at present to carry on the conscious works of reggae's forbears.

Even so, throughout his career some have attempted to fit him into the mold of a romantic singer. "They've worked hard!" he exclaims. "But I say to myself seeing where I'm coming from I know there are many souls and many people out there who want an alternative life other than this fighting, killing, robbing, cheating, and backbiting. So I say with this it is my duty, I owe it to life to use this talent in a positive way. And hope that at the end of the day humanity will get enlightened and inspired to spiritual growth."

At the time the Jamaican public seemed to pass over the conscious artists the international audience embraced. But, says, Luciano, "Even in Jamaica—even though they may get careless at time, you may see them exercise some recklessness, in terms of when politics is coming about or in time when you have flood or hurricane—

these are the times I realize they are willing to listen to some positive music. So I always say to myself there is a time and place for everything. But just continue in your line of positiveness and all will be well. Because Jah is on your side when you're positive. The whole universe is behind you when you're doing something for the uplift of humanity."

For this kind of work the Jamaican phrase "nuh bettah nuh man" is applicable. Says Luciano, "I did this song with Louie Culture and Terror Fabulous, 'We're All In This Thing Together.' Is like baking a cake; even if you mix all ingredients properly and churn your butter or whatever, if you don't oil your pan, cake might burn! Everything is important and no man work is more important than the other one. It is true observation that I have come to understand: everyone plays an important part. So is just like the pebble, the pebble that go together to form the brick. No one him big that can boast 'pon a small, 'cause it takes a combination of pebbles to make that brick. Is a spiritual work."

CHAPTER 33

Homegrown:

Reggae in America

In every town in America you can check the local club listings and find a thriving reggae scene that includes "homegrown" reggae bands, visiting dignitaries from Jamaica and the international reggae scene, and shops selling records, tapes, CDs, stickers, and papers. These gathering places unfold even more information in the form of fliers and knowledgeable shop owners and clerks who can tell you where to check for the best reggae music in the area. Current concerts, upcoming events, and what nights are "reggae nights" in the local clubs are also provided by reggae radio, often only on college stations but in some cities on commercial and noncommercial stations.

As the "information superhighway" expands, many of the bands themselves have websites and you can step from the local to the international at the click of a mouse. Reggae survives through public support in the form of sales of concert tickets, compact discs, records, and cassettes, and local radio also helps keep the music alive. Over the years the bands themselves have developed a strong network that enables groups from outside the area to plug into club circuits and mini-tours that help spread the music and the message. Innumerable publications large and small fuel this growing underground.

One of the earliest U.S. reggae artists— the first if we don't count Annette's cover of Byron Lee's "Jamaican Ska."—would have to be American soul singer Johnny Nash, who scored several early seventies AM radio hits with rock steady and reggae songs. Nash was heavily influenced by Bob Marley, who was under contract to him as a writer and one of the hits was a version of Marley's "Stir It Up." Others include the self-penned "I Can See Clearly Now," "Hold Me Tight," and a reggae arrangement of Sam Cooke's "Cupid." Nash recorded in Jamaica using now legendary session musicians.

Paul Simon also recorded in Jamaica and emerged with crossover hits "Me and Julio Down by the Schoolyard" and "Mother and Child Reunion." Listen to them today and you'll clearly hear a very Jamaican sound. These records plus hit covers from England like Eric Clapton's "I Shot the Sheriff," Blondie's version of the John Holt/Paragons hit "Tide Is High" and the reggae-influenced Police opened the door for a wider acceptance of the reggae sound in the U.S.

Some of the first American reggae bands, like the Shakers, captured the pop feel of the earliest forms of the music heard in this country. Other early U.S. reggae bands include Juice, whose *Domestic Reggae* was issued in 1980,

the Fabulous Titans, and the Hoovers. One of the first in a long line of American singers to travel to Jamaica to record was Martha Velez, whose 1976 album *Escape from Babylon* was produced by Bob Marley. All but two tracks from that disc are now available on the CD *Angels of the Future/Past* (Sire).

Blue Riddim focused on the musical roots from which the pop styles were derived and was the first American band to play Jamaica's Reggae Sunsplash. Some of today's bands are inspired by the groups that get the most airplay—Steel Pulse, Third World, Bob Marley and the Wailers, and England's UB40. Others draw from a diverse selection of roots and dancehall, while some create their own style.

Generally classified within the so-called "local band" sound as well are many singers and players from Jamaica, Barbados, Guyana, Belize, Dominica, and other islands, as well as from Africa itself. Often a "homegrown" band will have one or more members who grew up in these locations, joined with American players who've grown to love the music and want to make it their own. Clinton Fearon and the Boogie Brown Band operate out of Seattle. Fearon is one of the original Gladiators, making great roots music in the United States.

An increasing number of international artists have roots in America as well as Africa or Jamaica: both Alpha Blondy and reggae-jazz saxophonist Courtney Pine have done time in American reggae bands. Cutting edge dancehall artists such as Shinehead, Born Jamericans, and Shaggy combine Jamaican heritage with American roots. Some early U.S. reggae bands like Killer Bees are still playing. Some bands like Northern California's Inka Inka, who exemplified homegrown roots, are no longer together.

Groups like Neon Prophet and Shagnatty from Arizona; Local Hero from Tulsa, Oklahoma; Michigan's Universal Xpression from Dearborn and Jah Kings from Kalamazoo; and Seattle's Ganja Farmers join Wisconsin's Natty Nation,

West Virginia's Rasta Rafiki, and Salt Lake City's I-Roots on the new American reggae playing field. Maryland's Jah Works and Abou Smith, Ark Band from Columbus, Ohio, and Chicago's Roots Rock Society have all issued independent CDs. Ohio's Groovemaster, Philadelphia's Spirit and Irie Vibration, and Texas's Irie Time, and Iya and Ipso Facto from Minneapolis are but a few keeping the music alive in their own hometowns while recording and releasing product available around the world.

The South provides its share of reggae with the likes of Ben Hunter, Irie Vibrations, the Elements, and the Shepherd Band from Louisiana; Monty Montgomery, Ashadu, and King Errison (moonlighting from his night job as Neil Diamond's drummer) from Georgia; and Lamb's Bread from Jericho, Vermont. North Carolina has become a virtual hive of reggae with releases from One Tribe, Ras Alan and the Lions (from the reggae-friendly town of Zionville), and Gurneyman.

From Texas we have Urban Roots, Root 1, and Ragga Massive out of Austin and Rashani from Dallas among many. Houston's Tony XPress, the Barrister of Roots Rock Reggae, does triple duty as a private investigator, car mechanic, and reggae singer. Zion, a reggae group based in Ore City, records in San Marcos and mixes in Austin. Their lead singer is Carlton Pride, son of country-and-western legend Charley Pride.

All styles collide in reggae and American reggae breaks down barriers in your own hometown. Just as we've seen the country-and-western styles of Reggae Cowboys and Austin's I-Tex (whose brilliant "Skank Across Texas" was the highlight of their independent cassette release *Border Crossing*), a multitude of U.S. reggae groups fuse soul, funk, and reggae, like Indiana's Citizen X.

With its large Jamaican population, New York City is a major haven for reggae with labels like VP, Clocktower, and Bullwackies. The city bustles with independents like Nami, whose 1988 LP *Stand and Be Counted* was issued on the Jamaa Zima label and distributed by VP. More recently Rising Lion featuring Danny Dread has been mashing up the Big Apple. The East Coast has also been the scene of a couple of major crossover attempts in the '90s. The Fugees scored chart action with reggae-influenced records and invited Ziggy Marley and the Melody Makers—along with the I-Threes—to perform with them at the Grammy awards ceremony. Worl-A-Girl also mixed hip-hop, rhythm and blues, and reggae for a shot at the charts.

Ranking Pulse mix hip-hop and reggae for a sound as sought after in Jamaica as in the States. Another band from New York is Ithaca's John Brown's Body, whose home-flavored recordings have the sound of the seventies. With a slightly different lineup they were previously known as Tribulation. New Jersey boasts King Benj-I and Jamaican-born Rula Brown, who operates a label issuing records from Jamaica and the U.S. Tony Nicholson shows that Motor City can keep reggae rolling, with his 1994 CD *Help Myself* featuring a mix of love songs and conscious cuts like "Garvey" and "Never Give Up."

From Massachusetts Black Rebels record in French, English, Wolof, and Cape Verde Creole (the core group was formed in Senegal and the drummer is from Jamaica). Massachusetts is also headquarters for Heartbeat Records, a label whose imprint has guaranteed quality since its earliest days. It's also seen a rash of independent releases like Danny Tucker's *True to the Root* on Twigzee Dee. Tucker perhaps speaks for many of those roped together here as American reggae with his song "I Come from Jamaica." Anyone who spent time in Boston from the '80s on should be familiar with Mystic Jammers, whose Lions Eye label and store and shows helped keep the reggae vibe alive on the East Coast.

Washington, D.C., home of the RAS label, is also home base for a one-man international reggae movement, the astounding Earl "Englishman" Briscoe. His Mighty Roots label has spread his reggae near and far and his group, like many of the bands mentioned in this section, doubles as an instant touring band for visiting performers from Jamaica. At one point they also functioned for about a year as Ras Michael's Sons of Negus. Vermont's Trippa and the Bottom Lion issued the independent CD *I Am* in 1995.

Miami, Florida, a short hop from Jamaica and a jumping-off point for travelers to the island, has a large Jamaican population and Jamaicans from producer Joe Gibbs to bassist Robbie Shakespeare have made it their home. It's no surprise that Miami's nightlife scene is ripe for reggae and it has spawned magazines, clubs, labels (like Upstairs Music, which releases CDs by Ken Boothe, Bob Andy, and instrumentalist Tony Greene), and bands galore. The mid-nineties saw a rush of product from there, including Riot Squad's *Soul Searching* on Ikus.

Among Florida's standouts are Beniah, Bigga, and Axx of Jahpostles, a Portland parish Jamaican band who relocated many years ago and backed the likes of Burning Spear and Garnett Silk before releasing their own work. Philip Leo and Midnight Blue have CDs from the Sunshine State. Other reggae bands from Florida include Boca Raton's H.I.M. Orchestra, Miami's Nori Nori, and Hollywood's Lenval "Shayar" Jarrett.

Hawaii is a hotbed for reggae, with groups like Ho-Aikane, One Foundation, Ras Inando, Roots Natty Roots, and The Toy(e)s, whose humor-laden herb anthem "Smoke Two Joints" has probably gotten more commercial airplay than most Jamaican reggae. Some have adopted—and others rejected—the tag "Jawaiian" for their music. Christian Hawaiian reggae is evoked in a series of releases from Bob Riley and the Fisher's Jairus Trust. Transplanted Californian Jack Miller is now a full-fledged Hawaiin reggae act, as is label-mate Marty Dread. One of the island's best-known groups is Missioniriez. Independent studios flourish, sustaining artists like Daniel Rae Costello. The Anthology *Hawaii Reggae International* features some of the best reggae from the island.

Southern California has Wendy Shaw, a native of Chicago who records in Jamaica, head-lining shows and playing festivals here. Her independent CDs *Through the Flames* and *Sing Out* (both on the Issachar label) reveal a sophisticated singer with rootical backing reminiscent of Marcia Griffiths and other great ladies of Jamaica. Wendy has moved well beyond the local tag to record in England with Mad Professor.

Boom Shaka honed their skills clubbing in L.A. for years, eventually becoming one of southern California's hardest bands. They have played, recorded, and toured for over a decade and issued four CDs to date, *Creation* (Moving Target), *Best Defense* (Liberty), *Freedom Now* (Stone Mountain), and their most recent and best, *Rebel-Lion* (Shanachie). They can always be counted on for thoughtful songs and energetic performances.

Jah Mark and the Soul Shakers are an exciting band whose live performances bristle with rhythm and commitment. They've issued two full-length independent CDs (*Love Power* is the latest, on the Banana Boat label) and appeared on several anthologies. Jah Mark, an artist with a paintbrush as well as a guitar, once lived in Tokyo, where the band headlined shows in the late eighties.

Other excellent southern California reggae has been recorded and released by Swelele, Jah Bandis, Urban Dread, the AKB band (featuring Jamaican keyboardist extraordinaire Pablove Black), and Ruff Soundz International, who double as a backing band on recordings by Jah Bull, Zema, and others. Zema herself issued her first reggae album in 1987, recorded at Channel One in Jamaica. Her latest release, *Stranger at the Gates* (Melchezdek), is a warm and inspiring set of songs based on scripture.

Woolton "Jah Bull" Harrison is a Jamaican DJ who worked alongside Junior Reid on Hugh Mundell's Sound System and who, like Reid and Mundell, recorded for Augustus Pablo. There are enough scattered singles and anthologized tracks to make an excellent Pablo-produced Jah Bull album, but to date his only CD is *Press Along Rasta* (Bull Don Records), recorded in the main at Rough Sounds in Southern California where Jah Bull is based. The disc also includes one track cut at Harry J's studio in the '70s. Jah Bull has also served at times as part of Ras Michael and the Sons of Negus's "drum core."

Mark Tyson, a guitarist who clubs in L.A. and who issued an independent CD with his Blue Nile band, also plays guitar for Ras Michael and the Sons of Negus. Jumbalaya issued a good late '80s CD and their lead singer Keidi has produced solo work and side projects and writes a local column called "Rasta Perspective." He has also played in bands such as the Superiors with guitarist Tony Chin.

For many years Anthony Doeman's Bass and Drum label made Los Angeles a righteous pocket for Rastafari with a record shop and studio; he has now returned to Jamaica where the label thrives. Dennis Scorcher (of the early group the Scorchers) has sustained a shop through great tribulation including destruction by earthquake, fire, and riots. Ras David from Santa Barbara, Root Awakening from Santa Cruz, and Romy Dee and Humble Soul from Venice are only a few of the artists who have played, recorded, and issued music in southern California.

Northern California has contributed groups like Redwood City's Dub Nation, who combine African and Native American themes within their spiritual and ecological concerns. Massawa, from Whitehorn, Junglez Apart from Berkeley, and San Francisco's Jah Big have all issued discs. Oakland's Native Elements, San Francisco's Dub Addxx and Culture Canute and the Iration Band, Concord's dancehall-based Culcha Society, San Jose's Yardies, and San Diego's Cardiff Reefers, Creed, Common Sense, and Christafari also have independent releases available, as do Ishmael and the Peacemakers. Other California bands include Cosmo, Culcha Society, Rootstock, and Crucial DBC to name only a few.

The Pacific Northwest offers O'Brien, and Oregon's Jah Levi and the Higher Reasoning have created an entire industry that includes live shows, a solar-powered recording studio and vibrant Nyahbingi Theocracy releases. They now distribute Ijahman Levi's product in America. Seattle offers Queen Ekanem, Azeem, and Urge to Merge. Alric Forbes, an original member of Yabby You and the Prophets who also did a stint with the Gladiators and along with Clinton Fearon formed the late eighties band the Defenders, issued two solo CDs on his own I and I Pride label before his untimely passing from leukemia in 1998. Washington provides a home base for the ethnically diverse Jumbalassy from Bellingham, who put out three CDs in the '90s.

In the end it doesn't matter where you're from. Without assistance from a major label Makka's *Seeds* has it all—original songs, unlikely covers, professional graphics, and international sounds. Jah Malla, whose 1981 Atco debut pulled roots from diverse sources, isn't simply an "American" reggae band. Murder City Players may have a well-known home, but as evinced by their Nighthawk CD their sound is aimed at the world.

For this reason I tend to think of "local bands" as international. All bands are local bands— the Wailers, like the Beatles, were considered provincial on arrival in London but soon made their urban competitors sit up and take notice. The tiny island of Dominica, for instance, has contributed more than its share of reggae bands and singers such as Tex Joseph, based for many years on the U.S. West Coast, and Lazo, who has lived and performed in Canada for many years. Some of the best reggae today doesn't come from Kingston, though much of the best reggae today is informed by the music that has.

Some American reggae blends modern rock guitar tones and driving reggae rhythms for a unique style not quite like anything that comes from Jamaica or England. Big Mountain, who gained international airplay with a cover of Peter Frampton's "Baby, I Love Your Way" incorporated Tony Chin and Santa Davis from the Soul Syndicate band and got airplay where no reggae band has gone before.

Native American reggae includes Nasio Fontaine from Dominica, who has eerily mastered the sound of Bob Marley. Casper Loma-Da-Wa bridges two completely different styles of traditional music, three if you count his dancehall influences. Casper hails from Hopiland, where Rasta, reggae, and roots penetrated long ago. Native Roots from Albuquerque combine a militant Native American stance with reggae for a double dose of roots.

Proof that independently released reggae has come into its own is the rapidly growing Reggae Ambassadors Worldwide (RAW) organization. Originally a loosely knit coalition of independent artists, producers, radio DJs, writers, and just plain committed reggae fans, RAW has grown to over a thousand members in a few short years. Membership allows access to an extensive mailing list of contacts that enables you to make connections with "locals" from around the world to further your own project—and help you further theirs.

The RAW organization is a sign that networking works in reggae. Members offer in-house product discounts, trade information, and tips and help make the whole world local. Their annual conference has become a must-attend for hundreds of bands, singers, and members of the growing reggae business community. A two-CD set titled *Reggae Ambassadors Worldwide* is the first of a number of projected releases showcasing members of the organization. For more information write to: Reggae Ambassadors Worldwide, 1057 South Denver Street, Salt Lake City, Utah, 84111. Or visit them on the web at: http://www.coolcrew.comRAW/index.html.

In my column for *Beat* magazine I have reviewed upward of 5,000 independent CDs with contact information on each of the bands. Another U.S. magazine, *Reggae Report,* issued a cassette-only sampler called *Reggae USA* on ROIR in 1989. More recently, the two-volume CD *Dread in America* on the Natural Mystic label offers another selection of homegrown U.S. reggae. As its roots have reached around the world, reggae has captured America.

CHAPTER 34

Instrumental Reggae:

The Players of Instruments

Jamaican musicians created reggae. Ska began as instrumental music and the same players cut solo sides and backed singers and groups. Lynn Taitt and the Jets were particularly prolific in the ska and rock steady eras, their trademark sound backing vocalists and cutting sides like "Napoleon Solo" that were hits alongside them. A sharp ear will recognize Taitt's playing on some early Johnny Nash hits too. Their early album, *Rock Steady Greatest Hits,* is difficult to find. In 1997 Lynn Taitt recorded his first CD of all new material, *New Oldies,* which also sounds superb.

Another early guitarist who's experienced a recent revival is Ernest "Ernie" Ranglin. Ranglin's guitar work is present in ska and prevalent in the rock steady and reggae eras backing Jimmy Cliff and others. A jazz CD *Below the Bassline* reworks reggae songs in sophisticated style with the help of Idris Muhammad and Monty Alexander. Reissues of early instrumental solo material, much of it in a Wes Montgomery style, include a Studio One set and proto-lounge classic *Mod Mod Ranglin*. *Tribute to a Legend* (1997) features mainly interpretations of Bob Marley songs in Ranglin's smooth and easy style. Though more jazz than reggae, *Memories of Barber Mack* from Island in the same year features a nice reworking of Keith and Tex's "Stop That Train." His latest, *In Search of the Lost Riddim* (Palm Pictures) was recorded in Senegal with members of Baaba Maal's band.

In the "classic" reggae era a scattering of albums by Joe Gibbs and the Professionals, Bobby Ellis, and Tommy McCook have been slowly edged out by dub. A nice (and dubby) Aggrovators instrumental album is one of the few selections that's survived in the CD format. Guitarists like Bobby Aitken and Hux Brown may find their names set in increasingly smaller type and even dropped out on reissues but the wise collector checks the lineup on classic albums to find those players whose identity cuts across the music no matter whose name is on the record.

Things have changed somewhat in the nineties as contemporary soloists have found their own recording outlets. Though some of the early instrumental albums will be harder to find they are well worth searching out. A few things to check for include solo albums by ska players like Don Drummond, Tommy McCook, and Roland Alphonso on which they're given a chance to stretch out and solo.

Another alumni of the Alpha Boys Catholic School was trombonist Rico Rodriguez. A significant ska session player, he relocated to

England in the late sixties and subsequently played on many of the British reggae records, backing Dandy Livingston, Greyhound and others. In the mid-seventies he issued *Man from Wareika,* then returned to ska, playing on many Two Tone records. He recently released a CD recorded in Tokyo playing reggae and ska with Japanese musicians.

Roy Richards played harmonica ("mouth organ" as Dennis Brown says) on many ska and reggae recordings. Two albums, one from Studio One and one from Dynamic, feature his distinctive style up front. Another Studio One instrumentalist is Sugar Belly, whose home-made bamboo saxophone, played in a mento style, sounds like nothing else from Jamaica. An interesting early jazz-reggae fusion album (now available on compact disc from Esoldun) is *Negril.* The disc is an outgrowth of the sessions that produced Joe Higgs's *Life of Contradiction* and features Peter Tosh and Eric Gale on guitars, as well as Cedric IM Brooks and Family Man Barrett.

One of the musicians who helped lay the foundation, Jackie Mittoo, not only can be heard in the background of other artists records and featured on countless Coxsone version sides, he also issued many keyboard albums that are as fully reggae as any vocal or dub. Mittoo was house arranger for Studio One in the crucial early days of reggae and (with bassist Leroy Sibbles) created many of the original rhythms tracks (or "riddims") that dominate the music to this day. He played piano and organ for the Soul Brothers and Soul Vendors, both Studio One house bands, as well as in the original lineup of the Skatalites from the time he was a teenager.

In the last few years of his life Mittoo, who had emigrated to Canada and helped found another burgeoning reggae scene there, received credit and—even more rare—compensation for one of his early works. His instrumental "Full Up" was reworked to "Pass the Kutchie" by the Mighty Diamonds and then as "Pass the Dutchie" for Musical Youth. After a court battle Jackie Mittoo was recognized as the original writer. He passed away at the beginning of the '90s. In 1995 Heartbeat issued the essential *Tribute,* a two-CD set of Mittoo's best and best known.

Pablove Black has played on more crucial reggae cuts than he can remember—including as backing keyboardist on Jackie Mittoo's *Showcase*—and has two fine solo albums as well, one for Coxsone from the early days and one recorded in the late '80s in an eight-hour time block he got in a tradeoff for some backing tracks. He is also featured on many classic reggae cuts including Horace Andy's "Skylarking." He is still actively touring and recording today.

Winston Wright played with most of the major studio bands of the seventies and eighties including Lynn Taitt and the Comets, Tommy McCook and the Supersonics, the Dragonaires, the Aggrovators, Revolutionaries and Roots Radics at one time or another. He was in Toots and the Maytals live band, and toured with Ken Boothe, Jimmy Cliff, and others. He has released a number of solo albums featuring his distinctive keyboard style.

Just as Skatalite Tommy McCook can be heard on half the ska, rock steady, and reggae records of the seventies (and is featured as a soloist on records that do and don't put his name above the title), Dean Fraser is a name you'll find listed on the backs of at least half the reggae records recorded in the eighties and nineties. Fraser stepped to the fore from Lloyd Parks's We the People band at the 1981 Bob Marley Memorial Sunsplash, playing a rendition of Marley's "Redemption Song" to an awed audience that required he return the next night and play it again. The hit record that resulted led to a career that has paralleled his "backing man" status. He is one of today's most recorded studio musicians and arrangers and tours with the likes of Luciano.

The saxophone seems drawn to reggae and considering how neglected it's become in jazz, rhythm and blues, and rock it deserves a big welcome. Besides Dean Fraser, Roland Alphonso, and Tommy McCook there are current reggae sax releases from Tony Greene, Courtney Pine, and Arthur Tappin. A recent project from Saxsemilla includes work with Michael Rose, the Mighty Diamonds, and "Deadly" Headley Bennett.

Some of Jamaica's earliest instrumentalists now have archival reissues, including Carlos Malcolm's Afro-Jamaican rhythms and the Sonny Bradshaw Quintet. "Backing" bands like the Dragonaires and the Dynamites often cut instrumentals issued on singles or anthologies. The unsung heroes of any style of music are the musicians.

Jamaican session players like Bobby Aitken, Winston "Bo Peep" Bowen, Tony Chin, Earl "Chinna" Smith, Hux Brown, Willie Lindo, Clinton Fearon, Jackie Jackson, Fully Fullwood, Lloyd Parks, Derrick Barnett, Robbie Shakespeare, Val Douglas, Vin Gordon, "Deadly" Headley Bennett, Robert "Nambo" Robinson, David Madden, Chico, Bobby Ellis, Herman Marquis, Dirty Harry, Dean Fraser, Junior Chin, Zoot Simms, Gladstone Anderson, Jackie Mittoo, Robbie Lyn, Neville Hines, Franklyn "Bubbler" Waul, Harold Butler, Bernard "Touter" Harvey, Ossie Hibbert, Keith Sterling, Winston Wright, Ansel Collins, Winston Grennan, Denzil Engle, Leroy "Horsemouth" Wallace, Sly Dunbar, Mickey "Boo" Richards, Santa Davis, "Seeco" Patterson, Sticky Thompson, and Skully—and many more unnamed—are as important as engineers like George Raymond, Soljie, Barnabas, Chemist, Scientist, Phillip Smart, Syd Bucknor, Fabian Cooke, and others.

Sometimes an individual contributes in many ways, like Clive Hunt, who plays clarinet, sings, and produces (presumably not all at the same time). As with singers, DJs, and even groups, there are far too many great players to name much less treat in the depth they deserve. All have played their part to make some of the most interesting and innovative music in the world.

And don't neglect the dubs. Sometimes on Jamaican records the engineer, mixer, and producer are all the same person, and sometimes a name you don't hear as often like Byron Smith, Ernest Hoo Kim, or Errol Thompson is working the board. Many of the unsung are also artists. Dub is still an instrumental form of music, though it is differentiated from "instrumental" records by the distinctive style of the mix. Even the voice is featured as a musical instrument in dub.

It's in dub you'll find the work of the great Jamaican "backing" bands like Skin, Flesh and Bones and the Revolutionaries. Often these so-called backing bands have both instrumental and dub releases available—Derrick Harriot's Crystalites, Lee Perry's Upsetters, and the Aggrovators, who recorded as such mainly for Bunny Lee, are three such groups. Soul Syndicate backed others and issued CDs with vocals and instrumentals. Though the Roots Radics went on to become a vocal group, they cut hundreds of backing tracks and dubs. Even the digital wunderkind of today like Steely and Clevie, Mafia and Fluxy, and Dave Kelly are showcased in dub.

One artist-producer active in instrumental and dub music (and as a producer in vocal and DJ records as well) is melodica-keyboard maestro Augustus Pablo. Born Horace Swaby, his distinctive piano and organ playing beds literally thousands of reggae records from the seventies on. His solo career is equally impressive, beginning with early recordings compiled on *This Is Augustus Pablo* and the 1972 hit "Java" for Clive Chin.

Pablo's trademark use of the melodica, a small, hand-held plastic instrument that fingers like a keyboard but is blown into through a mouthpiece (and thus, like the harmonica is regulated by breathing), made it an instrument of note in reggae. Others who played it on records include Joe White and Glen Brown, both well-known singers in their own right. But Pablo mastered the "Far East" style, which takes its name from a Don Drummond record on which he plays a minor key lead against major chords, the key element in the sound and indeed, when translated to vocals, in much of reggae. It's a style Bob Marley utilized too, and it's perhaps no coincidence Pablo played on some Perry productions of the Wailers.

Pablo produced many great records for such up-and-coming artists as Hugh Mundell, the late Jacob Miller, Delroy Williams, Yami Bolo, Jah Bull, Junior Reid, and Junior Delgado, usually recording them at early stages of their careers. He's issued uncountable sides on his own Message and Rockers International labels. Because, like King Tubby and Lee Perry, his own name became a selling point internationally, listeners must be selective when picking through albums and CDs "by" Augustus Pablo— some are instrumental, some are dub, some are are others' productions of Pablo, some his own productions of himself, some his productions of other singers or collections featuring many different artists, often in a "showcase" style (meaning vocal and dub).

The remarkable thing is all are good— undoubtedly the reason a cult following has given his name international cachet. A careful examination should distinguish the instrumentals from the dubs and anthologies. The crucial Pablo releases are his mid-seventies shots with King Tubby at the controls. The dub CD *King Tubby Meets the Rockers Uptown* is essential. It's as if the man was born to be dubbed. On his instrumental releases he displays a mastery of melody, a keen sense of production, and a flair for the uncommon nuance. Two of the best (and more accessible) strictly instrumental releases are *East of the River Nile* from the late '70s and *Blowin' with the Wind* from 1990.

As with many other reggae artists, Rastafarian thought and imagery permeates Pablo's work from cover art to song titles and undoubtedly the music itself. Pablo is much more likely to put a color picture of His Imperial Majesty Haile Selassie I on the front cover and a small photo of himself on the back of his own records, though they're often altered in international release. He lists the producer as Selassie and himself as co-producer. The titles—"Golden Seal," "Ethiopia," "Seven Winds from Zion," "Ark of the Covenant"—show that even these instrumentals are message music.

Pablo's own productions retain a mystical feel, and historically fascinating work with Derrick Harriot, Perry, and others exists on scattered anthologies. Pablo himself, like Yabby You, has followed the lead of Clement Dodd and Prince Buster in reissuing a great many of his 45s, so even some early works can be found on 7-inch at "as new" prices. The singles have the once uniquely Jamaican feature of dub-version flip-sides and his own productions demonstrate that he learned a thing or two from the other geniuses he worked with in the '70s.

CHAPTER 35

Dubbing Is a Must

Dub music was born in King Tubby's cramped mixing studio and forged in the dance in the early seventies, helping to birth the first DJ movement with it. Stripping the backing track to the heavy crash of bass and drums, he mixed in bits and pieces of vocals and other instruments swathed in echo and sounding like pieces of the Mir space station floating away. It was at once a mating of roots and technology, space and vibration, and the ratio of signal to noise. The concept was simple, remixing existing master tapes into entirely new musical entities. The genius with which it was done made it one of the only new musical discoveries of the twentieth century. Though attempts have been made to incorporate it into dance, trance, and ambient music, dub stands alone.

Osbourne "King Tubby" Ruddick built speakers and repaired electronics, but the mixdown studio he installed in his home studio in Waterhouse on Drumallie Avenue in Kingston became the center of the universe for what eventually entered popular music as the remix. He created the "dub plate," which featured the "dub" or "version," an artful rhythm-heavy retelling of a recording with slap-back echo effects, pulling instruments in and out, whacking them with reverb, and sending them on their way. Originally Tubby's special rhythm mixes were made only for sound system use.

The popularity of dub in the dance was enhanced by its use as a backing track for DJs and singers and that function of dub made possible the eventual evolution of dancehall music. The dub rhythm tracks or "riddims" were often the most popular side of the single and soon there were entire King Tubby albums such as *The Dubmaster* and *Roots of Dub*—both essential releases—as well as Tubby dub discs of Augustus Pablo and others. It's important to remember that dub is not just instrumental reggae or rhythm tracks but creative use of the multitrack masters to make entirely new music.

Duke Reid utilized Tubby's mixing genius and the classic *Treasure Isle Dub* LPs are among the finest dub—rock steady dub at that. Because the earliest Jamaican recordings were done on single-track tape decks there really is no ska dub. King Tubby utilized the new technology to create an innovative new style of Jamaican music. Over some of these riddims U Roy swept in the DJ era, which continues today.

"Tubby was a genius, man," says U Roy. "I start playing his sound after I stop playing for Sir George and I really love King Tubby for one reason. He was the man who took me to Duke Reid. We use to play a lot of Duke Reid and Coxsone music on the sound. At that time version was just coming in. You hear the vocal and after that we play the dub style, so people used to think we have something on the amp that take the sound out."

"Tubby used to build his own amplifiers. If he buy something he'd develop on it. He'd put them up and do a lot of different things to his equipment. Sometimes you would pass this man house like two o'clock in the morning and you would hear some Dizzy Gillespie music playing—he's working on some amplifier."

King Tubby and U Roy are the best-known exponents of the dub and DJ style, respectively. But imagine U Roy's own introduction to dub. "The first time I see Tubby come with this dub he say to me okay, this is the vocal and this is the version. I said wha'd you mean? So he put it on and play it and I hear the same rhythm come in but no vocal in the rhythm and say what?!"

One producer who greatly benefited from Tubby's innovations was Bunny Lee. Lee recorded his basic tracks with the Aggrovators, often cutting vocals at Tubby's mixing studio, then turned the masters over to Tubby for the mix, and the B-side remixes kept Lee and the Aggrovators on top. Less prolific producers such as Glenmore Brown made superb roots recordings and Tubby gave back equally superb dub versions. His dubs with strings for Harry Mudie are among the most unusual.

After King Tubby's death—shot with his own gun in an attempted robbery at the gate of his studio in 1989—his name became fair game and there are an absurd number of records and CDs billed as King Tubby, some of which he had minimal or no hand in. One of his finest works, *Treasure Isle Dub,* appears on the market with his name nowhere to be seen. (See the discography for recommended and representative selections.) Though his genius stamps all dub and his work remains its finest proponent where dub is concerned, King Tubby is only the beginning.

Early crucial dub proponents also include Lee "Scratch" Perry, mixing in his own Black Ark studio, Ernest Hookim at Channel One, and the seminal Keith Hudson. Lovers of dub have their own favorites. The spacey, slow hypnotic style of the Prince Far I, a seventies DJ who also produced and mastered dub, also had some very effective dubs made of work he did for other producers. Far I led dub down passageways strewn with deep-voiced biblical verses and mystical allusions. After his passing his voice has been sampled, flown in, and repositioned time and again for other producers, most notably Dub Syndicate.

Joe Gibbs and Errol Thompson (the Mighty Two) recorded hundreds of hard-driving versions still available only on 7-inch single B-sides, where dub was allowed to flourish. They also issued a series of increasingly "gimmicked" sound-effect-laden tracks (*African Dub*) recently reissued on CD. With all the changes in the music in recent years these recordings sound even better today.

Tubby brought a number of young people "into the mix" who went onto careers of their own as dubmasters, including Scientist, Phillip Smart, and Prince Jammy. The latter wasn't content to dub it up but went on to become a producer of note in the dancehall era, spawning other producers in his wake like Bobby Digital in the same way Tubby spawned more dub. As each student's style emerged, Tubby's legacy spread.

Overton "Scientist" Brown was in his teens when he began mixing in Tubby's studio and the series of albums issued under his name in the early eighties are pure representations of the time. Not only do they have extremely eighties titles like *Scientist Encounters Pac-Man* and *Scientist Destroys the Space Invaders,* they contain the early work of the Roots Radics, often with a fluctuating lineup that might include Earl "Chinna" Smith on guitar or Santa Davis on drums as well as Bingy Bunny, Flabba Holt, and Style Scott.

It's Scientist who helped us realize what a great band they really were.

Right after Scientist came Chemist, who dubbed up Roy Cousins among others for some early '80s albums. Though not as prolific as Scientist he went on to produce his own dub albums, making the transition from real-time drummers like Leroy "Horsemouth" Wallace and Style Scott (and what was essentially an early Roots Radics lineup) to Steely and Clevie and Danny Brownie's digital wizardry in the late eighties.

In New York the Bullwackie's studio mastered dub just as they had mastered their own sound in reggae. The Bullwackies sound began with a "basement" feel but evolved into a distinctive sound utilizing the talents of Jamaican-born engineers, musicians, and performers like Clive Hunt and Fabian Cooke. Recently Lloyd "Bullwackie" Barnes has begun reissuing these classic recordings and it's become possible to find some of their long out-of-print catalog. Another of King Tubby's students, Phillip Smart migrated to New York and helped forge the East Coast reggae sound. Just as Jammy had done, he began as a mixer but went on to become a respected producer.

Like ska, dub took on a life of its own twenty years after inception and the proliferation of dub today, particularly from the U.K., is astounding. The form has suffered in the land of its birth in recent years—the digital tracks of dancehall are just not as exciting as hard hard riddims laid down by hook or by crook when the music was young. A new trend in dancehall singles is the remix, borrowed back from the dance music remix inspired by dub, with several singers and DJs dubbed on one track. But the free-form creativity that launched the sound in the seventies has taken on a new direction and dimension in England in recent years.

Early U.K. innovators include Jamaica's Jah Shaka, whose legendary sound system dances gave way to a series of striking dub productions that made this music accessible to a new generation of dub lovers. Guyana's Mad Professor kept the movement alive by sticking to the roots and dubbing up Jamaican originators like U Roy and Lee Perry and English innovators alike. Dub Judah brought a very personal feel to the U.K. approach to dub, making penetrating, meditative music that newer groups attempt to assimilate.

Gussie Prento, also called Gussie P., is responsible for some excellent dub releases. His A-Class studio has recorded many luminaries like Johnny Clarke, and dub albums *Raw Rub a Dub in a Fashion, Rubble Dub,* and *Burial* are all excellent. The former contains "Who's Safe," a spine-tingling mix of Martin Luther King's "Mountaintop" speech with dub. As an added bonus, they generally feature hilarious cartoon cover art.

Norman Grant of the Twinkle Brothers has been instrumental in creating an atmosphere for dub as well as reggae in his adopted home. His *Dub Massacre* series and others are as much a part of the Twinkle sound as the corresponding vocal albums. Dennis "Mixman" Bedeau, or Blackamix, has created some innovative and resonant sound from his own studio and productions. All these producers release vocal albums with very dubby backgrounds and dub releases without compromise that will stand the test of time.

The rising tide of technology has worked in dub's favor too. Once the exclusive property of Jamaican "big studio" producers like Duke Reid, by the late seventies it was firmly in the hands of independent producers like Bunny Lee, who operated for years without his own studio in conjunction with master mixers like King Tubby and his students Scientist and Prince (later to be King) Jammy. Over the last twenty years a shift in the availability of and improvement in equipment has put the means of production in the hands of the people. One result of this is that, in the words of Pablo Moses, "Dubbing is a must."

Any talk of forging new territory in dub would have to include mention of the delightfully innovative Dub Syndicate, aided and abetted by Adrian Sherwood, who also produces the "new roots" outfits like African Head Charge and the New Age Steppers. Incorporating Jamaican players Style Scott and at times Flabba Holt and Frankie Waul and headed by U.K. visionary Skip McDonald, Dub Syndicate's series of brilliant dub and vocal releases extend dub to include sampling (allowing them the luxury of lead singers such as the late Prince Far I and Jim Morrison), effects, and a sense of the traditional values of dub that tie all these innovations together.

Armagideon, Black Roots, and the Dub Crusaders as well as newcomers like High Tech Roots Dynamic and New World Order are extending the realm of dub while staying true to the origins of the style. Labels like Nubian and Nomadix in England can always be counted on for far-reaching dub. As Nubian's *Roots Cultivatas: Dub Out West* anthology puts it, "Only the bass and drum on the culture vibe will survive." Another interesting crossbreed is the Royal Kushite Philharmonic Orchestra, which seeks to re-integrate dub and instrumental music.

Alpha and Omega exemplify the seamless connection between dub and the "new roots" music of the U.K. Some of their albums are vocal, some vocal and dub, and some pure dub, and all have a gentle, righteous feel to the music and the lyrics. From the Ethiopic album graphics to the textured tones, their mixes and dub-plate remixes present a seamless integrity of sound. Whether issued on their independent A&O label or through Greensleeves in England or ROIR in the U.S., Alpha and Omega always deliver spiritually edifying musically resonant works.

In the nineties home studio capability is creating a whole new wave of dub. Dub Specialists, Dub Liberation (dubbing up Rod Taylor), Dub Nation, and the Dub Factory are just a few of the latest wave. The Bush Chemists, Shotgun Rockers, Inner State Sound System, and Dub Crusaders join groups like Black Roots who issue vocal and dub product on anthologies like the three-volume *Dub Out West,* exploring the outer reaches of dub.

Dub has also gone international, with one of the more interesting contributors being Ryan Moore's Twilight Circus in Dub. His series of slow and steady dub releases have been coming out in the Netherlands over the last few years. Drummer for the Legendary Pink Dots and the Tear Garden on the side, he's also a one-man dub band and recently managed to tour the U.S. He has a good grasp on the once-elusive concept of dub and each succeeding recording improves on the last.

One of the best things about the new interest in dub is the massive amount of product being reissued, in some cases issued for the first time in America. There are dozens of King Tubby CDs to choose from, but watch out. Like Lee Perry, King Tubby's name is often used to sell product he had nothing to do with. In this case it's a good idea to look for the name of producer Bunny Lee, as some of Tubby's best work was done with "Striker"'s masters.

Paradoxically, some of Tubby's best work appears without his name above the title (or in the fine print). But there's plenty of great dub Tub never laid his hand on. Dub is an acquired experience and a learn-as-you-go addiction, but for those who've learned to love it there is no greater music in the world.

CHAPTER 36

Dub Poets

Just as dub inspired the DJ style, a phenomenon that spread from Jamaica to England and beyond is dub poetry. Jamaica's beloved Miss Lou, Louise Bennett, is the god-mother of the movement as her inspired reevaluation helped Jamaicans realize the beauty inherent in their own natural style of speaking. Her *Jamaican Labrish* (Sangster) is among a handful of books integral to understanding the Jamaican way of speech and thought. The live performance CD *Yes M'Dear* (Sonic Sounds) and the 1983 Island album *Miss Lou Live* illustrate how she uses patois to effect what she calls "Colonization in Reverse."

The proliferation of small theater and independent poetry publications in Jamaica will astound anyone who walks into a stationery store in Kingston and sees the acceptance given to poetry even in middle-class society. Perhaps this should be no surprise from a country that puts such a high priority on its National Dance Theater, long headed by Professor Rex M. Nettleford. Shakespeare and the Bible have had a profound influence on reggae song lyrics, as have Jamaica's wealth of folk sayings and proverbs.

The dub poets who blazed a trail through reggae have generally been of a militant variety. England's Linton Kwesi Johnson, beginning with his first release as *Poet and the Roots,* took aim at the hypocrisy and social repression in London with cuts like "Sonny's Lettah" about police brutality. He has recorded and toured with and without dub backing, often provided by Dennis "Bluebeard" Bovell in his post-Matumbi days, and remains an influential voice for the oppressed. A 1998 two-CD set, *Independent Intravenshan* (Island) collects some of his best-known work.

In 1983 Benjamin Zepheniah came with *Rasta,* a self-produced album on the Upright Records label. Born in Jamaica and raised in Birmingham, England, he presents an outspoken and uncompromising stance. He chastised politicians, the apartheid government of South Africa, and economic oppression. He returned in 1990 with *Us an Dem,* produced by Paul "Groucho" Smyrkle for Mango Records.

Also based in England, Kendell Smith deals with police brutality, African liberation, and the phenomenon he dubs "Dry Land Tourist" on 1988's *Time Running Out* (Ariwa). Produced by Mad Professor and backed by Robotics, Black Steel, and the Ariwa crew, Smith takes an individual approach. His readings, bedded by Mad Professor's own brand of dub, are energetic and believable.

Oku Onoura (born Orlando Wong) issued his first single, "Reflections in Red," on the 56 Hope Road label in 1979 after serving seven years of a ten-year sentence for armed robbery. Early eighties singles "What a Situashan" and "Dread Times" were followed by the albums *Pressure Drop* and *Bus Out.* On both discs he is backed by his band AK7. He is also the author of *Echoes,* a book of poems containing many of the lyrics of his songs. Defiant struggle against oppressive society is the hallmark of all his work, a "poetry for the people" dedicated to tearing down walls and educating the underdog.

Jamaica's Mutabaruka, with his startling shock of white hair striping his dreadlocks, had a similar effect as he took the high ground with a moral tone that sometimes made his own audience uncomfortable. Backed by the Roots Radics and others, working with singers like Gregory Isaacs, Dennis Brown, and Ini Kamoze, Muta has melded poetry, reggae, and social consciousness into a career unlike that of any other performer. A list of his albums appears in the selected discography.

Another early dub poet, Michael Smith, whose life was cut short after recording and releasing the album *Mi C-Yaan Believe It* on Mango in 1982, blazed a fiery trail for those to come. I saw him live on one occasion in Jamaica and can testify to his powerful presence. His album was also produced by Dennis Bovell and Linton Kwesi Johnson.

Women have made their own place in dub poetry, from the Rasta reasoning of Washington, D.C.'s Sister Farika, whose 1993 cassette-only release *Rainbow Dawning* (Mighty Roots, distributed by RAS) is one of the genre's finest entries, to the defiant resistance and sophisticated free verse of Canada's Lillian Allen. Her *Condition Critical* came out on Redwood Records in 1987. Jamaican-born Jean Binta Breeze made *Tracks,* produced by Dennis Bovell and Linton Kwesi Johnson, issued on the latter's LKJ label in England.

Queen Majeda's 1993 CD *Conscious* (Heartbeat) covers a broad spectrum from "Man and the Environment" to "Earth Rightful Ruler."

A number of Rasta poets have used the form of dub poetry to educate, enlighten, and cleanse. Ras Tesfa, with *Voice of the Rastaman,* a 1985 Meadowlark release distributed by Shanachie; Ras Sam Brown, whose CDs *Teacher* and *History Past and Present* present an ancient message in a modern form; and Ras Pidow (with *Modern Antique*) and the *Rastafari Elders,* whose self-titled CD presents the works of Ras Headful, Ras Tawny, Pidow, Ras Marcus, Sista Bubbles, Bongo Shep, and Ras Bigga, have also mixed the Rastafarian perspective with dub and poetry to achieve a kind of poetic Grounation. The last four releases are all available from RAS.

The early nineties saw the emergence of new young dub poet Yasus Afari. Singles like "Teachings of Marcus" and "Pangs of Babylon" and combination records with Horace Andy and Black Uhuru brought him public attention. He has billed himself as "The Afromantic Honour Dread." The CDs *Mental Assassin* (Tappa) and *Dancehall Baptism* (RAS) are "edu-tainment."

Several recorded anthologies of dub poetry were issued by the Heartbeat label in the eighties. *Word Soun' Have Power* collects a number of "Reggae Poets" not otherwise mentioned here including Oliver and Malachi Smith, Tomlin Ellis, Glenville Bryan, and Navvie Nabbie, along with Binta Breeze and Mutabaruka. *Dub Poets Dub,* produced by Mutabaruka, strips that album down to the riddims. *Woman Talk: Caribbean Dub Poetry* gathers together Binta Breeze and Louise Bennett as well as Elaine Thomas, Anita Stewart, Afua, and Trinidad's Cheryl Byron.

It may be difficult to find in America, but Christian Habekost's *Dub Poetry: 19 Poets from England and Jamaica* (Michael Schwinn, West Germany) is an excellent anthology of some of the dub poets' poems including interview material and photos. A number of the poets anthologized are otherwise unknown. Many of the poets mentioned here have also published books of their own.

Poetry is an aspect of reggae that goes to the root of the best song lyrics. The startlingly placed image, resonant rhyme, and rhythmic language of Jamaica's patois cuts through all of reggae and provides some of the best moments in the music from the very beginning to today. In this combination of political acuity, religious philosophy, dance, theater, costume, and international concern simmers a potent brew that helps make reggae a powerful force in the world.

CHAPTER 37

Jungle and Beyond

To many, reggae begins and ends with Bob Marley, which is like saying rock and roll begins and ends with Elvis Presley. It's just not true. Like Elvis, Marley drew from a vast body of work in creating his style and those influences are now more apparent and available than ever. He was part of a large group of artists who were his contemporaries, like those interviewed in this book, who helped create reggae right alongside him, though they often did not share in the widespread public adulation Marley received.

He also inspired a widespread movement that grew with his passing. One of the most fascinating publications in reggae is the fanzine *Distant Drums,* which microscopically examines Marley's life and work from every angle. Wherever you travel in the world you will find rebel lyrics set to timeless riffs that continue to expand the concept. Like ska and dub, reggae is in the mainstream and the bloodstream. Reggae will never die.

Though it's been much disguised in the dancehall era, Rastafari culture has always been at the foundation of reggae, from the Nyahbingi drumming of Count Ossie and Ras Michael to the message in the music of Burning Spear, Bunny Wailer, Culture, Israel Vibration, and other reggae "supergroups." From the up-in-the-hills dread of Jamaica to the dreadlocked Rastaman in your own home town, the root of reggae has always been the message of peace and love first propounded by the early Rastafarians.

One phenomenon we can always be sure of in reggae is the continual return to the wellsprings for inspiration. Countless times reggae has reinvented itself by returning to rhythms, artists, styles, and songs that helped lay the foundation. Thus the branches nurture the roots.

Ska, dub, rock steady, and reggae in all its variations are continuously being rediscovered by new generations of fans. In the mid-seventies Channel One made their name by dredging up Studio One rhythms and giving them a modern sound. In the eighties and nineties Germain's Penthouse and Fatis Burrell's Xterminator labels did the same. Artists like the Skatalites, Derrick Morgan, Eric "Monty" Morris, and Justin Hinds were playing more in the late nineties than they had in the three decades previous.

We've seen consciousness return to the dancehall, ska carried on by the young, and enough Bob Marley tributes to weigh down CD bins around the world. So whatever happens to reggae in the future it's always a good idea to check your rearview mirror—they didn't call it the land of look-behind for nothing—to see what's coming. In reggae there are more will-bes than has-beens and many artists have been written off only to reemerge—or to have their songs, their rhythms, or their kids do it for them—bigger than ever.

As rap and hip-hop, originally inspired by the Jamaican DJ style, came back around to influence reggae, it manifested differently in different parts of the world. We've seen how the Jamaican dancehall scene flourished and the styles called raggamuffin and ragga took hold. In England the mix of hip-hop and reggae birthed ragga and jungle, and others reacted with what is being called drum and bass. Like dub, jungle is a remix, though often artists redo their original work in a jungle style.

In a way, jungle returns us to the triple-time beats of ska, where it all began. These hip-hop rhythms are overlaid—digitally, of course— on a collage of sound that often includes stops and starts, loops and samples and stepped-up rhythms. Singers and DJs contributions are sublimated to the overall effect of the sound. Drum and bass seeks to find a middle ground between this mishmash of sound and dub proper.

In a strange city, any reggae fan can feel immediately at home walking into a club and being assailed by the sights, sounds, smells, and good vibes that have come to represent reggae music. Though Jamaican patois is not exactly a universal language—it was in fact originally intended to be something of the opposite—its terms and tailorings have worked their way into an "I-niversal" culture that knows no geographical boundaries. At a concert in any city you can see Chicanos in tams, Asian-Americans with dreadlocks, black and white mixing freely in a spirit of love that ought to have been the byword of America but seems to be more comfortable with Jamaica's concept of "out of many people, one." The "one love" of Bob Marley and the one world of Marcus Garvey are only beginning to be realized in this time.

Often we lose sight of this greater purpose and just relax and enjoy the music—and maybe that's what it's really all about. Reggae stands in stark contrast to the racism and division propagated in many quarters of society today. Maybe it's not the answer to all our problems—maybe there is no answer to all our problems—but no one who enters a hall where reggae music is being played can deny it's creating an environment that nurtures understanding among all types of people: young, old, black, white, brown, yellow, rich, and poor alike. Reggae music and the powerful philosophy it represents attempt to break down the barriers and divisions that keep us apart—

what Bob Marley and Peter Tosh called the "isms and schisms"—and replace them with a "heartical" vibe that extends a hand from the deepest well of suffering to the world at large.

As such, this music has never been merely another form of entertainment. Ska, rock steady, reggae, rockers, dub, even dancehall and the jungle variations challenge the mind and call into question the world we live in—the "Babylon" system—in a seditious way made all the more powerful by the gracious Caribbean rhythms that sustain it. We can all stand to learn something from this pervasive music, which will continue long after style has dropped away and nothing but substance remains.

CHAPTER 38

I Shall Sing:

The Singers

The abundance and diversity of reggae singers is astounding. What other music has provided vocalists of the breadth of Slim Smith, Ken Boothe, Roy Shirley, Leroy Sibbles, Cornell Campbell, Delroy Wilson, Horace Andy, Johnny Clarke, and Freddy McKay? All from one small island—mostly one city's recording studios in a ten year time span! Add the ska and rock steady eras many began in and the list alone would be staggering. Hundreds of influential singers such as Ken Parker, Leroy Brown, Sam Carty, Billy Dyce, Jackie Parris, Patrick Alley, Enos McLeod, Winston

McAnuff, Milton Henry and an equal number of contemporary vocalists like Ken Bob, Brian and Tony Gold, Scion Sashay Success, Pad Anthony, Ras Shiloh, Doniki and Steady Ranks, and Glen Washington deserve to be treated.

There are obscure delights such as the soulful Fitz Major, whose gospel-rooted voice propels the buoyant "Our Country Needs Love" and poignant love ballad "Marie," Rosso's Lambert Douglas with at least a dozen great singles not on any album (as well as an excellent album), and hundreds of one- and two-hit wonders like African Youth who exist to collectors only as names and voices. A friend once told me about a Jamaican grade-school teacher of his who recorded a couple of singles in the sixties—he turned out to be "Bumps" Oakley. His "I Get a Lick" is a Studio One rock steady standard whose "riddim" is still versioned today.

Take Ras Karbi, who followed excellent singles including the brilliant "Promised Land" on Total Sounds with the 1984 album *Seven Seals* on Rockstone. For every Horace Andy or Leroy Smart there's at least one Patrick Andy or Howie Smart to sing in their style. Horace Andy himself got his last name because C.S. Dodd was looking for a "new" Bob Andy who got his first name because Dodd wanted a new Bob Marley.

Many early singers like Ernie Smith and Ken Lazarus recorded ska, rock steady, and reggae. Both of these pioneer singers have recorded and released records in the sixties, seventies, eighties, and nineties. Voices as varied as Shenley Duffus and Sheldon Walks may make only occasional appearances on older import anthologies but each has a distinctive style. Some, like Lloyd Jones, Dobby Jones, Leo Graham, and Levi Williams, are known only for a few tantalizing singles.

Singers with lengthy careers include some who charted in England like Dandy Livingston, Nicky Thomas, and Delroy Washington. In Jamaica

singing engineer Ruddy Thomas also recorded under the name Flick Wilson. Brothers Tinga and Roman Stewart have recorded singly and together. Rasta singers like Sang Hugh, Kiddus I, Gideon Jah Rubaal, and Judah Eskendar Tafari, and stylists such as Sammy Dread, Ashanti Waugh, Chuck Turner, Horace Martin, Glen Ricks, Winston Fergus, Wayne Jarrett, and Horace Ferguson make trying to sort it all out part of the joy of reggae.

Many women have contributed to reggae, though only a handful have achieved international acclaim. Early Treasure Isle artist Phylis Dillon and seventies singers Cynthia Richards, Marcia Aitken, and Merlene Webber are joined today by Sophia George, Sharon Forrester, Cynthia Schloss, Twiggy, and many others.

Often these artists can be heard in scattered duets and contributing backing vocals. Bunny Brissett, a fine solo singer in her own right, sings backup for a host of other artists including Marcia Griffiths and dancehall darling Angie Angel. From Maxine Brown and Sonia Spence to Pam Hall, women have made major contributions to reggae. Three anthologies may help in this area. Shanachie's *Holding Up Half the Sky: Women in Reggae,* Heartbeat's *Reggae Songbirds,* and Trojan's *I Shall Sing* features well- and lesser-known female singers.

The brief descriptions that follow attempt to provide a few key points to help sort out at least the most well-known singers, those you're most likely to find records by in perusal of a well-stocked store, or simply personal favorites. They are best used in conjunction with the appended discography. I have omitted those treated more fully in interviews, though some interview material is included.

Laurel Aitken

Laurel Aitken's earliest records were cut before ska, rock steady, or reggae had been conceived. In those days he was singing calypso and straight-up rhythm and blues, the Jamaican version of which became known as Blue Beat in England (where a label of that name issued select recordings in the style as well as ska and rock steady). He cut some major ska classics (including 1963's "Lion of Judah") in Jamaica before emigrating to England, where he became something of a father figure to the early sixties skinheads. He has continued to record and release records well into the nineties and has participated in each era's ska revival.

Bob Andy

One of Jamaica's most sensitive vocalists, Keith "Bob Andy" Anderson's understanding of American music informs his well-crafted songs and expressive delivery. Beginning with Coxsone Dodd at Studio One, like many other singers, he worked with the Paragons, cut duets with Marcia Griffiths, and recorded solo. He wrote songs that became instant Jamaican standards and are still being drawn upon today for updates, remakes, and "riddims."

Among his songwriting credits are such Marcia Griffiths standards as "Tell Me Now," "Truly," "Mark My Word," and "Feel Like Jumping." His own Studio One hits include "I've Got to Go Back Home," "Let Them Say," and "Too Experienced," the latter a mega-hit in the nineties for Barrington Levy as well. The Studio One album *Bob Andy Songbook* is one of the essential cornerstones of reggae.

He charted with Marcia Griffiths as Bob and Marcia in the U.K. in the early seventies and went on to record superb solo albums of distinction that utilize elements of rock, rhythm and blues, and jazz while remaining at the top end of the reggae spectrum. He left Jamaica for London, where he produced his own records and recorded with Mad Professor. He currently resides in Miami, where he continues to record and issue material that is informed, accessible, and a delight to hear.

Everton Blender

One of the best of the new young singers to emerge in the nineties, Blender begs comparison with the roots singers of the seventies while mixing it up in a modern style with producer Richard Bell's Star Trail Posse. Two Heartbeat CDs collect his best to date including singles like "Create a Sound," "World Corruption," and "My Father's Home" and combination cuts with DJs Culture Knox and Prezident Brown. In addition he's a forceful live performer, lending credence to the concept that reggae has a future as well as significant past.

Yami Bolo

Young Roots singer R.E. McClean, aka Yami Bolo, issued his first singles in 1986 but it wasn't till his late eighties-early nineties work with Augustus Pablo on cuts like "Ransom of a Man's Life" and "Struggle in Babylon" that people began to sit up and take notice. In the early nineties he was one of the only young singers to come with a cultural message. He can also sing a love song, but it's his serious cuts like "Joe the Boss" for Tappa Zukie, "Ease Up the Pressure" for Fatis Burrell, and "Glock War" on his own Yam Euphony label that mark him as an exceptional artist.

Barry Brown

Whether inviting you to "Nice Up the Dance" or "Cool 'Pon Your Corner," Barry Brown puts you at ease. He cut mid-seventies albums with Bunny "Striker" Lee that contain powerful material like "Mr. Money Man," "Trying Youthman," and "No Wicked Shall Enter the Kingdom of Zion." He also recorded for Dodd, Jo Jo Hookim, Niney the Observer, Prince Jammy, Sugar Minott, Tony Robinson, Ranking Joe, and a host of other producers throughout the seventies and early eighties without achieving the widespread international success he deserves. Several of his best albums were self-produced and no one is better at delivering a warning (like his burning "Jah Jah Fire") in a relaxed and somehow comforting style.

Dennis Brown

A stage show veteran "since I was nine years old," Dennis Brown began his career "with Byron Lee and the Dragonaires, one of the ace band in Jamaica. They used to call me the Boy Wonder. At the time I was very much American-orientated musically. I used to listen to people like Sam Cooke, Nat King Cole, Lou Rawls, the Temptations, you name them." He went on to become "resident vocalist for the Falcons" performing "the various top ten songs on the charts in Jamaica."

"One night while playing at a club called Tit for Tat, the managers of the band knew Coxsone Dodd, we call him Downbeat. He was passing through the club and he was impressed with my singing. The other guy called Noel Brown and Scotty (the DJ), they had a group called the Chosen Few. So we were invited, we got the opportunity to come down to Studio One to record. They did a Delfonics song called 'Break Your Promise' and I did a song by the Hollies called 'Love Grows.'" (Though he did record a Hollies song, "He Ain't Heavy" for Dodd, "Love Grows" was actually by the slightly more obscure Edison Lighthouse.)

The musicians at the time were "Jackie Mittoo, Leroy Sibbles, Bagga Walker plays bass—you had a guy who used to be Carlton and the Shoes, 'Love Me Forever' guy, he [Carlton Manning] was the guitarist there. Then you had Ernie Ranglin, Denzil Engle was playing percussion, Roy Richards who plays mouth organ and Miss Enid (of Keith and Enid)—they were the ones who did the background vocals on many songs you hear." Young Dennis Brown waxed numerous hits for Studio One, including "Your Love Is Amazing," "It's Impossible," and "Easy Take It Easy," gathered on the albums *No Man Is an Island* and *If I Follow My Heart*.

He also became part of the backup team. Background singers on Alton Ellis's classic "Sunday Coming," he says, were "myself, Horace Andy, and Larry Marshall. We did the background vocals on many of the songs. I used to freelance with the Heptones doing backup vocals. At one point I could be regarded as part of the Heptones, doing background vocals on people like Little Roy ["Righteous Man"] and quite a few other artists. I used to be paid as a background vocalist working with the Heptones before getting the opportunity for recording [solo].

"I should have started out with Derrick Harriot," the producer to whom he turned at age sixteen, "but I thought he was moving too slow. He was the one who gave me the Impressions song 'No Man Is an Island' to sing." Harriot produced Brown's third album, *Super Reggae and Soul Hits*. Dennis also recorded for Lloyd Daley, Herman Chin-Loy, and Phil Pratt. He then entered into a lengthy relationship with Joe Gibbs that eventually resulted in dozens of albums. "I was treated well at Joe Gibbs, I was like the ace artist there."

Among his hits for Gibbs was "Money in My Pocket," "Should I" (many years later also a hit for Richie Stephens), and "Cassandra" and albums such as *Visions, Wolves, and Leopards* and *Joseph's Coat of Many Colors*. In the early eighties he signed to A&M records with Gibbs and Errol Thompson producing and issued the crossover albums *Foul Play* and *Love Has Found Its Way* and the rootsier *Prophet Rides Again*. He retained good relationships with his producers, returning to them again and again throughout his lengthy career.

Some of his best recordings were done for Niney the Observer, often working out of Gibbs's studio. "I think that was where most of the greater songs came about because Niney and I, we used to share a house in Pembroke Hall. In the evenings we would sit down and try and

DENNIS BROWN. Photograph by John Skomdahl

write songs. We would go around to various clubs and see what the people would be dancing to and then we would come up with some idea of making records, what type of rhythms to make for people there." Two Heartbeat CDs, *Some Like It Hot* and *Open the Gate,* collect this impressive body of songs, including "Here I Come," "Westbound Train," "No More Will I Roam," and "Whip Them Jah Jah."

Brown recorded for numerous other producers including Alvin Ranglin, Gussie Clarke, Chinna Smith, and Mikey Bennett with hits like "Have You Ever" and "Sitting and Watching" for Sly and Robbie, "To the Foundation" for Gussie Clarke, and "Wildfire" in tandem with singer John Holt. He also produced for himself and others, issuing records on his own D.E.B. and Yvonne's Special labels. In recent years he has recorded for Prince Jammy, Freddie McGregor, and Junior Reid.

Though a classic reggae singer in the seventies, Brown's output in the eighties and nineties is staggering. He has recorded and released over eighty albums. Brown has an outstanding voice and can be militant (as on his work with Niney the Observer) or romantic at will. He's written hundreds of great songs, retaining an astonishing consistency considering the amount of recordings available. He is one of Jamaica's best-known and best-loved vocalists and songwriters.

Burning Spear

Long before the concept of ambient trance music invaded dub, Winston "Burning Spear" Rodney hypnotized and mesmerized listeners with his African roots chant style. Hailing from St. Ann's, his lyrics are full of the teachings of Marcus Garvey and social consciousness. Upliftment and improvement have never been far from his concerns. Once he went international, he remained true to these ideals while building a rock and jazz-inflected sound that is one of reggae's most sophisticated and enduring.

Spear began his career at Studio One releasing singles like "Door Peep," "Ethiopians Live It Out," and "Foggy Road," from which two albums worth of material was drawn. He later recorded two more as a trio for legendary roots producer Jack Ruby with backup singers Rupert Wellington and Delroy Hines. The album *Marcus Garvey* and concomitant dub *Garvey's Ghost* with cuts like "The Invasion" and "Slavery Days" are required listening. Though he returned to solo singing after these discs, these recordings cemented Spear's sound and he went on to lengthy stints with Island (who issued the Ruby discs) and Heartbeat, releasing albums for a few smaller labels (as well as his own label in Jamaica).

The Burning Spear sound beds his rough-hewn but superbly worked vocal instrument with tight band arrangements including horns, rock-tinged guitar solos, and hard-thumping rhythms rooted in the arena—a big reggae sound making him an always dependable concert attraction and one of the most consistent recording artists to emerge from Jamaica. With nearly forty albums spread out over three decades it's a genuine achievement that every one of them is worth owning and listening to. Spear had an ancient sound when he was still a young man and has aged with dignity—few reggae artists could pull off his "Play Jerry," a song about a Grateful Dead concert, without ever straying from the root of the music.

Junior Byles

Junior Byles is one of the most profoundly original singer-songwriters of the "classic" age of reggae who amazed and dazzled many with his delicious juxtaposition of symbolist poetry and melodic gentility. Though his work is now more widely available than at any previous time, he cannot be said to have benefited from his contributions to Jamaican music. The poverty and hunger he often sings about seem never to have been far from his often troubled life.

Recording first for Joe Gibbs as a member of the Versatiles, Byles also cut solo records for Winston "Niney" Holness and others, issuing singles on Thing, Micron, Lovepower, Well Charge, Clocktower, Hot Shot, Impact, Treasure Isle, Observer, Advance, Soul Beat, and Lee "Scratch" Perry offprints like Justice League, Wizzdom, and Orchid. Outstanding cuts include "Place Called Africa," "Long Way," "Remember Me," "Weeping," and the late eighties "Let Us Reason Now" issued on One in Three.

Much of his best work for the Upsetter is now available on a Heartbeat CD titled *Curly Locks*. In addition there are or have been four Trojan albums, two anthologies, and two originals from the seventies (one, *Jordan,* reissued by Heartbeat) plus a mid-eighties album on Nighthawk. The 7-inch singles include many uncollected songs and alternate takes, to the delight of serious collectors. Despite a reputation for erratic behavior, Byles recently performed his first show in the U.S. at the Sierra Nevada Festival in Marysville.

Al Campbell

Whether recording roots, the lovers rock style popular in England, or in a modern dancehall mode, the smooth-voiced Al Campbell can be counted on for a laid-back sound that seems to emerge effortlessly. In addition, throughout his three decades in the business he's produced, and provided harmony backing for, the Mighty Diamonds and written for Dennis Brown, Beres Hammond, Robert French, and Barrington Levy, among others. He's recorded for producers Phill Pratt, U Brown, Linval Thompson, Top Rank's E.J. Robinson, and Bunny Lee, for whom he also arranged and sang harmony.

In his own words, he's "always in the studio working. Whenever we go in the studio and see anybody having any problem we help them out. Although most of the songs we don't see our name on it, we don't get the credit still, but the work is there and we go on and do it, helping the music to get across."

Campbell produced a number of excellent albums, including his own superior *Working Man* with cuts like "Lightning and Thunder," "Jah Love," and "You Won't Be Jamming." In later days he also recorded for Live and Learn's Delroy Wright and Prince Jammy. Classic cuts include "Wicked a Go Feel It Now," "Rasta Time" and "Hypocrites," often backed by the power team of Sly and Robbie. "Other than dealing with people music is the best thing," he explains. "Sometimes even sweeter than food."

Cornell Campbell

Bunny Lee's ability to squeeze great music from young singers is clearly shown in his productions of the sweet-voiced soulful Cornell Campbell. A one-time member of the Uniques along with Jimmy Riley, Campbell was also lead singer for the Eternals. After a brief stint with Coxsone Dodd, Campbell entered into a vast body of work for Lee and later recorded for producers like Linval Thompson, Joe Gibbs, Roy Cousins, and Delroy Wright. Influenced by Sam Cooke and Slim Smith, he recorded love songs, covers, and serious Rasta tunes like "The Judgment Has Come."

Early hits like "Dance in a Greenwich Farm" and "Duke of Earl" established Campbell and later U.K. lovers hits (as well as a series of singles positing him as the "Gorgon" of the dancehall) sustained him throughout the seventies and eighties. A handful of singles from the nineties including remakes of his own hits and the stirring "Nothing Come Easy" (Dub Chemist, 1994) and "Ruff Corigan" (Ugly Man, 1996) show that he's still in peak form, but the Bunny Lee productions backed by the Aggrovators best represent Cornell Campbell.

Jimmy Cliff

Jimmy Cliff was reggae's vanguard. A hit-maker in Jamaica since his teenage years (which coincided with the ska era), he played New York in the early sixties. He starred in Perry Henzel's 1972 film *The Harder They Come* and contributed half a dozen songs to the soundtrack. Cliff tried his hand at soul singing American style (on the early album *Can't Get Enough of It*) but returned to reggae for a long and distinguished career. His bright, lilting pop style helped paved the way for the harder-edged Wailers and others.

His early Island records are filled with great songs: the poignant ballads "Sitting in Limbo" and "Many Rivers to Cross," the searing "Viet Nam," and the inspirational "You Can Get It If You Really Want," all produced by Leslie Kong. He went on to record for CBS, EMI, Warner Brothers, and MCA and toured extensively throughout the seventies, eighties, and nineties. He continues to appear in films, including *Bongo Man* and *Club Paradise* and has talked about starring in a sequel to *The Harder They Come*.

Cocoa Tea

Calvin Scott first recorded for the Little Willie label in the mid-seventies. As Cocoa Tea in the early eighties he recorded with the High Times band for Michael Chin and the Roots Radics for Junjo Lawes before scoring big with Jammy's productions backed by Steely and Clevie. He is one of the best singers of the dancehall era: as with Sugar Minott his name aptly describes his sweet singing style. But don't get him riled! When his anti-Gulf War "Oil Thing" 7-inch was banned from Jamaican airplay, he countered with the even harder "No Blood for Oil."

In the early nineties Cocoa Tea cut great albums for Fatis Burrell, Bobby Digital, and Mr. Doo, with the last two again utilizing Steely and Clevie and the former Sly and Robbie and the Firehouse Crew. He also recorded again for Junjo Lawes. Recommended cuts include "Rikers Island," "Africa, Here I Come," and one of the few outstanding pro-woman songs of reggae, "(She Wants A) Good Life." He also excels at combination records with DJs such as Shabba and Cutty Ranks. His latest CD, *One Way* (VP), is quite possibly his best.

Stranger Cole

Wilburn "Stranger" Cole says he gained his nickname because he didn't look like either of his parents. A great Jamaican songwriter, his ska hit "Ruff and Tuff" revived Duke Reid's career as a producer. He had sublime rock steady hits ("Down By the Trainline," "Last Flight to Reggae City") and made some monumental reggae records like "Lift Your Head Up High," though he once confided, "It's all rock steady to me. That's what we called it when I was coming up." He says paradoxically he took to performing because of a deep-set fear of being in crowds since viewing the riots at H.I.M. Selassie's visit to Jamaica. He found it less crowded on stage than in the audience.

Stranger cut duets with partner Patsy, pianist Gladdy Anderson, Ken Boothe, and others and established a lengthy solo career. He moved to Canada in the seventies, where he sang and recorded with the group Chalawa and then on his own. Some of his great records include "Black Son," "Teeth and Tongue," and the early "Bangarang" with Lester Sterling. It's a tribute to the man that two of his finest are 1963's "Stranger at the Door" and 1994's "Cast Them in the Fire." Many of his best records are available only on scarce Jamaican 7-inch or scattered anthologies—there is at present no representative collection of his work. His son Squiddley is now a much-in-demand studio drummer who has also toured and recorded with Ziggy Marley.

Carl Dawkins

Though he sings in a deeper range, Carl Dawkins is a soulful singer like his mentor Slim Smith.

Outstanding early seventies singles include "Baby I Love You" for Sir J.J., "Heavy Load" for Beverley's, and "Picture on the Wall" (as Ras Dawkins) with the Wailers. He did a stint in America in the late seventies (I saw him live with Ken Boothe and Delroy Wilson and his performance was super-charged). One great album for Harry J was followed after nearly a decade and a half by an excellent album on Abraham that included superb cuts like "Crossfire" and "Ecclesiastical Day."

Junior Delgado

Oscar "Junior Delgado" Hibbert hit with "Every Natty Wants to Go Home" cut as "Jooks" for Niney the Observer, and came back again and again with cuts like "Sons of Slaves" for Lee Perry and "Arm Robbery" for Joe Gibbs. He sang originally with the group Time Unlimited and recorded extensively for Dennis Brown's D.E.B. label. Imprisoned in England in the early eighties, he came fresh in the mid-eighties with a vast outpouring of material.

Some of his best work has been with producer-melodica wizard Augustus Pablo, including songs like "Nine Fence," "Riot in the Juvenile Prison," "Dub School," and the album *Raggamuffin Year*. His gruff delivery is underpinned with a formidable melodic presence and he is responsible for some admirable sufferer's songs. He continued with strong singles in the nineties such as "Disarm the World," "Gonna Be a Showdown," and "Awake Rastaman." *Fearless* (Big Cat, 1998) fuses roots and jungle in a unique and experimental manner while keeping Delgado's magnificent voice to the fore.

Dobby Dobson

Rich and elegant are two words used to describe Dobby Dobson. Beginning in the early sixties his lovers style got him hits, particularly "Loving Pauper" (later a hit for Gregory Isaacs as well),

which he cut for Duke Reid's Treasure Isle. He went on to produce himself (most notably the album *Oh God, Are You Satisfied*) and others including the Mediations. He had a hit again in 1994 with the Penthouse single "Last Thing on My Mind."

Eric Donaldson

His voice is high, his style is pop, and his records are perhaps a little old fashioned—when he tours he tends to play supper clubs rather than arenas—but Eric Donaldson has filled album after album with Jamaican hits. He's best known for penning (and winning Jamaica's Song Festival with) "Cherry Oh Baby," later covered by the Rolling Stones and still later UB40. Other standards include "Keep on Riding," "You Must Believe," "Right on Time," "Sweet Jamaica," and "Land of My Birth." His gentle delivery made covers from Van Morrison's "Warm Love" to John Lennon's "Watchin' the Wheels" his own. He had a resurgence in the early '90s when the "Cherry Oh Baby" riddim was rediscovered and versioned aplenty.

Donovan (Francis)

Recording only under his first name, Donovan filled two Mango albums with cultural and social consciousness near the end of the eighties. Both were produced by the late and legendary Jack Ruby who, says Donovan, was "an adventure and an experience" to work with. "He is a very creative person, always have some creative ideas. In a lyric him like the best all-time lyric."

From the same Port Maria area as the group Foundation, Donovan sang cabaret in Montego Bay hotels before hooking up with Ruby. A "total musician," Donovan says he "just sing whatever me feel. Although the main thing is me always try to keep it in a positive concept.

So if you even go soul or funk or calypso, it still a go maintain that message all the while."

Mikey Dread

Michael "Mikey Dread" Campbell defies categories and it is in fact such defiance that makes up the category of reggae singers in the first place. An early Jamaican radio DJ, he went on to his own productions and achieved airplay where no dread had gone before as a result of his work with the Clash. Sing-jay, singer, dub innovator, entrepreneur with his Dread at the Controls label, like England's Pato Banton and Jamaica's Eek-A-Mouse he's constructed a persona that sells records.

Errol Dunkley

Errol Dunkley's expressive vulnerability came through on rock steady heart-wrenchers like "Please Stop Your Lying," "The Scorcher," and "Do Right Tonight" for Joe Gibbs. Hit albums include *Darling Ooh* for Sonia Pottinger and *O.K. Fred*. The self-affirming "A Little Way Different," the roots anthem "Repatriation," and one of the best reggae Beatle covers of all time, "You Never Know," are among his signature tunes.

Clancy Eccles

Besides being a producer of note, Clancy Eccles recorded throughout the ska, rock steady, and reggae periods and later song titles read like populist manifestos including "Power for the People," "Hungry World" and "Mash Up the Country." Several collections on Jamaica Gold span his career with biographical notes. His rock steady recordings in particular exude charm.

Jackie Edwards

Romantic balladeer and formative songwriter, Jackie Edwards racked up hit after hit with solos and duets with Millie Small. He wrote "Keep on Running" for the Spencer Davis Group (and Island seemed to promptly bury his original version). He had a roots side too as evinced by a 1979 album for Harry J containing the magnificent songs "Get Up" and "African Language." He continued to release lovers rock-style tunes throughout the eighties and was recording again when he passed in the early nineties.

Alton Ellis

American soul singers have nothing on Alton Ellis, who stands beside Sam Cooke and Jackie Wilson as one of the all time greats. Beginning in the '50s as half of Alton and Eddie (he also recorded duets with his sister Hortense), Ellis started singing rhythm and blues but was king of the rock steady era. Hits for Duke Reid and Dodd are some of the biggest of the late sixties: "Willow Tree," "Breaking Up," "Pearl," "I'm Just a Guy," "Girl I've Got a Date," "Remember That Sunday," and "I'm Still in Love with You" (whose "riddim" also fueled Althea and Donna's "Uptown Top Ranking") are just a few.

Ellis cut some powerful reggae sides too (his "I Wanna Reggae with You" was as much an anthem in its day as his own "Rock Steady" was). He influenced many, particularly Dennis Brown and thus later singers once removed, like Frankie Paul and Luciano. He moved to England in the early seventies, where he arguably founded and was certainly a mainstay of the lovers rock style. A sweet and gentle man with a short body and a long face, he can still punch a song like no one else, as on the later scorcher "We a Feel It."

George Faith

Jamaican soul singer Earl "George Faith" George (he also released at least one record as George Earl) recorded for Alvin Ranglin,

Phil Pratt, and Bunny Lee, among others, but his big record was *To Be a Lover,* produced by Lee "Scratch" Perry and released on Mango in 1977. Though he did essentially the same style of soul cover for Perry, the dubby production and backing vocals from the Meditations and Diamonds make this an outstanding album with cuts like "Opportunity," "So Fine," and "I've Got the Groove."

Edi Fitzroy

Edi Fitzroy was born in Clarendon, Jamaica, in 1955. He attended West Indies Commercial Institute and was inspired to take up music by meeting Freddie Thorpe from South Africa. One of his first singles was 1980's "African Religion." Edi first recorded for Mikey Dread in the late seventies and came to prominence in 1982 with the outstanding album *Youthman Penitentiary.* He issued conscious roots singles in a modern style throughout the eighties and excellent albums in 1993 (*Deep in Mi Culture*) and 1994 (*Pollution*). He's at his best with haunting, chanted lyrics based in the realities of ghetto life.

Phillip Frazer

Beginning in the late '70s Greenwich Farm's Phillip Frazer cut roots records for Bertram Brown's Freedom Sounds, Don Mais's Roots Tradition, and other labels such as Black Solidarity, Cornerstone, Gorgon, and Mummy. Crucial cuts like "2000 Years" and "Righteous Works" were gathered on the essential *Come Ethiopians.* He continued to record and release singles in the '80s and '90s.

Owen Gray

Owen Gray's blistering soul-charged humanism made for some mighty seventies volleys like "Blazing Fire," "Give the Children Food" and

(for producer Clement Bushay) "Rizzla." He started in the late fifties with rhythm and blues heavy on the rhythm, some of which can be heard on U.K. Blue Beat and early Coxsone singles. Besides Coxsone he recorded for Prince Buster and Chris Blackwell but hit his stride with "Striker" Lee on cuts like "Bongo Natty" and "Look What You've Done." He continued his success in England with the lovers style. Much of his early and mid-period work is presently hard to find.

Half Pint

Variously listed on records as Lindon and Linford Roberts, like many Jamaican singers Half Pint gained his nom de plume from his physical aspect. Short of stature but big of voice, he came of age in the days of dancehall, recording first for Prince Jammy. Always an exciting performer live, he has pleased crowds in the Caribbean, England, and America for well over a decade.

Half Pint contributed one of reggae's great international anthems, "Greetings," cut with producer George Phang. Other outstanding cuts include "Level the Vibes," "Victory," "Winsome" (covered by the Rolling Stones as "Too Rude"), and "One in a Million," from the eighties, and "Substitute Lover" and "Freedom Fighter" in the nineties. The VP CD *Half Pint* is that rare commodity in reggae: a "best of" that truly contains the best.

Derrick Harriot

Double-threat Derrick Harriot is a respected producer who laid some of the groundwork for pop reggae with hits by artists such as Scotty and Joe and Tex. He is also a singer with a long history in the business beginning with Coxsone and Duke Reid and the ska and rock steady vocal group the Jiving Juniors. His own hits include "Message from a Blackman," "The Loser,"

"Solomon," and covers of "Eighteen with a Bullet" and "Some Guys Have All the Luck."

Harriot issued his productions on his own Crystal label, backed by his house bands the Chariot Riders and the Crystalites (who released some stirring if strange instrumentals like "Stranger in Town" and "Blackula"), and could always be counted on for effects-laden dubs with unusual changes. His productions and vocals are influenced by American rhythm and blues, particularly the sweet soul singers. He still operates an electronics shop (in the grand tradition of Jamaican producers) and video store in Kingston.

Joe Higgs

Often called the godfather of reggae, Joe Higgs helped lay the foundation for modern Jamaican music. His early recordings with Roy Wilson (as Higgs and Wilson) are among the best known pre-ska rhythm and blues to come from the island. They were produced in the late fifties by future Prime Minister Edward Seaga.

"When I started singing for Edward he was not into politics," says Joe. "He was a businessman. He produced my first record, 'O Manny O.' That was in 1958. My first five records were recorded for him." Higgs and Wilson also recorded for Coxsone at Studio One including the 45 "Mighty Man" and a ska version of "There's a Reward." The duo "started professionally in '58 and we lasted until 1964 when my partner went off to the United States."

After Wilson's departure Higgs recorded solo and "started doing work with Carlos Malcolm and the Afro-Jamaican Rhythms. Then I became the vocalist for the Soul Brothers led by Lynn Taitt and performed around the North Coast. Then I got back into recording."

Higgs cut singles like "Change of Plan" for Coxsone, "Burning Fire," and the superb "Mother Radio." He won the Jamaica Tourist Board song competition with "Invitation to Jamaica" issued

on his own Elevation label in 1972. Other great singles include "More Slavery" issued on Micron and Grounation, "Creation" released on Ethnic Fight in the U.K., "Let Us Do Something" issued in 1974 on Joe's own Elevation label, and "I Am the Song (the Prophet)" issued by Island in England. Island included the classic "World Is Upside Down" on their *This Is Reggae Music* anthology series.

His first released album was *Life of Contradiction* on the Micron label. It stands with Bob Andy's *Songbook* as a seminally sophisticated work combining reggae, jazz, and rhythm and blues influences to create a new texture that would have a profound effect on the best Jamaican music to follow, as would Higgs himself.

Higgs not only contributed some of the finest recordings of the early reggae era, but his selfless energy assisting young singers and groups coming up in yard sessions offering harmony instruction and musical tutelage has been credited by Bob Marley, Peter Tosh, and Bunny Wailer as well as the Wailing Souls. Of the Wailers he says simply, "I structured the harmony. I am the one who taught the Wailers the craft, who taught them certain voice technique.

"Who couldn't sing would learn how to be crafty, a lot of breath control technique. 'Cause as I've said before, you can only be as good as Sam Cooke if you are Otis Redding or you know what to do." Higgs is also the one who, when they were ready, took the Wailers to Studio One and introduced them to Clement Dodd.

I first saw Joe Higgs live in the early seventies as band leader for Jimmy Cliff. He penned the song "Dear Mother" on Cliff's *Follow My Mind* LP, sang harmony live, and stepped forward for some tunes of his own in the show. He also filled in as a member of the Wailers when Bunny Wailer left the group. "And even before then," he admonishes. "I've been paid to be a Wailers many times, like a sideman."

One thing he didn't get paid for was a hit song Peter Tosh had after leaving the Wailers: "Steppin' Razor." "I am the sole composer of this song," he explains. "In 1967 I had entered this song in the Jamaican Festival Contest. They said that it was the most appealing song—at the same time it was very, very subversive and therefore naturally not for their program. It was a very good record but [they felt] it wasn't appropriate for the occasion.

"But then Peter took the song—I don't really remember if I had given the song to him. He took the song and he recorded it and he never credited me for it. And then he proceeded to street talk it, 'I will give you something,' man-to-man street talk, bredren talk. Nothing ever came of it. I tried to get legal rights back for a long time." Eventually he was successful but the statue of limitations had run out and Higgs was never repaid for the profits from the hit.

Unity Is Power (1979), his second released album, showcases his forceful bearing on songs like "Devotion," "Neither Gold Nor Silver," and "Vineyard," and also contains "Sons of Garvey." He and Jimmy Cliff sang the latter song and "Sounds of the City" together on singles on Cliff's Sunpower label. The following year,

JOE HIGGS. Photograph by John Skomdahl

1980, saw the single "Talk to That Man" on Bunny Wailer's Solomonic label.

In 1985 his third album, *Triumph,* was issued on the Alligator label. "So It Goes" was released as a single from the album. Three years later the album *Family* came out on Shanachie. It featured new material and remakes of some of his classics. In 1990 came what was amazingly only the fifth album in his long career, *Blackman Know Yourself.* On this album he was backed by the Wailers band, which he says was "like meeting people who you've gone to school with and haven't seen them for years."

On the album he reprises a number of his best songs and a few others including Marley's "Small Axe" and "Sun Is Shining." "The intent was to record songs without compromise," he says. The year 1995 saw the release of a very different kind of disc. *Joe and Marcia Together: Roots Combination* paired the veteran singer with his daughter (who had previously recorded as Higgs and Twins). It's typical of Joe Higgs that at this stage of his career he would still be doing what he's done for over four decades: singing, writing, performing, teaching, and sharing music with the world.

Keith Hudson

Keith Hudson, artist and producer, scored an early '70s number one in Jamaica with Ken Boothe's "Old Fashioned Way." Ever innovative and experimental, Hudson voiced DJs like Big Youth, Dennis Alcapone, and U Roy as well as singers such as Delroy Wilson. His dub albums were early entries in the field and remain some of the more unusual.

Hudson's own songs and vocals were equally quirky, with some of the hardest 7-inch singles of the seventies like "Boost It Up" and "Smoke Without Fire" balanced by some of the strangest including "Black Belt Jones." No other Jamaican writer ever came up with anything remotely

resembling cuts like "Darkest Night on a Wet-Looking Road" or "Lost All Sense of Direction."

His album output was unique and sporadic as well. Fine early productions are gathered on Trojan's *Studio Kinda Cloudy. Flesh of My Skin Blood of My Blood* (1974) is a brooding and ultimately triumphant work, the closest thing to Gothic in reggae. The follow-up, *Torch of Freedom* was distributed by Virgin, which led to the first album for them, *Too Expensive* (1976). The opening song, "Smoking," was addictive and "Civilization" bridged rock and reggae in a completely different way than did Bob Marley.

Two legendary dub albums, *Pick a Dub* and *The Brand,* helped cement his cult status and his next vocal album, *Rasta Communication* was pure Hudson with cuts including "Felt We Felt the Strain," "Bloody Eyes," "I Won't Compromise," and "I'm Not Satisfied." The albums that followed showed Hudson unaffected by the changes in reggae of the early '80s because he was playing in a style entirely his own. Hudson passed over the smoky border he often sang about after a battle with lung cancer in 1984. One can only imagine what he would have done with a digital drum machine.

Ijahman (Ijahman Levi)

Trevor "Ijahman Levi" Sutherland issued two late seventies albums on Island/Mango. *Hail I Hymn* and *Are We Are Warrior* are deeply moving works. Levi's singing style and lyrical trajectory are gentle and haunting. Residing in England since his teenage years, he joined Island's roster then including Steel Pulse, Aswad, and of course Bob Marley and the Wailers. After a reportedly acrimonious parting with Island celebrated in "Mr. C.B." from *Inside Out,* he set up a cottage industry under the Tree Roots banner and continued to release discs for the next two decades.

The D.I.Y. movement had no stronger advocate in reggae than Ijahman Levi, who produced others (the album *Ijahman and Friends* collects some) for his label Jahmani, but remained the mainstay of his own assembly line. His large output is replete with the upliftment of his race ("Marcus Hero") and of humanity as a whole ("Fisherman and Singerman Are Friends," "High Price Crisis"). Wife Madge joined him for the lightly self-indulgent *I Do* and also appears as frequent subject matter in song.

Ijahman has a lone-voice-in-the-wilderness appeal that inspires devotion among followers or fans and a just-visiting-from-up-in-the-hills mystique that adds depth to well-loved songs like "Jah Heavy Load" and "I Art Jah Watchman." Ijahman records in Jamaica and issues product from London and New York. Excellent new work—contemplative, historical, and urgent (like 1994's *Black Royalties*)—continues to pour forth from Ijahman's Tree Roots.

Gregory Isaacs

One of the great Jamaican roots singers of the seventies, Gregory Isaacs morphed into eighties bad man and nineties virtual lounge act, though there were elements of his later manifestations in his early work, and reminders of his early genius are scattered throughout his later recordings. His first few records were made in the late sixties, a couple as lead singer for the short-lived Concords. Cuts like "Lover Is Overdue" and "My Number One" from the early seventies are only a few of the outstanding records he cut for producers Alvin Ranglin, Rupie Edwards, Ossie Hibbert, Sly and Robbie, and others. Self-productions appear on African Museum and the U.K. Virgin imprint.

Late seventies albums *Cool Ruler, Extra Classic,* and *Soon Forward* are essential. Though those albums contain Rastafarian themes and social consciousness cuts like "Universal Tribulation," "Mr. Cop," and "Black Man Tribulation," songs of deep integrity like "Poor and Clean" and indescribably delicious cuts like "No Speech Nor Language (Where the Voice Is Not Heard)," it was 1982's *Night Nurse* with the Roots Radics that brought him international adulation. His smooth lovers style oozed as the Roots Radics developed the changes in the music that brought us into the early eighties. With these records he and they helped change the sound of reggae at a pivotal time in its history.

Private Beach Party and *Red Rose for Gregory* were enormous sellers. The rise to the top drew heat from the street and the brilliance of his seventies records cannot be diminished by the near destruction of his talents with the help of cocaine. One of Jamaica's most impressive voices slipped to the point of caricature, though he contributed some of the great rehab reggae of all times including "Hard Drugs" and "Hard Road to Travel" with Mutabaruka from 1989's *I.O.U.*

Through all of this he established a career as a recording artist with a release schedule few if any have matched. There are plenty of hits like "Mind You Dis," "Rumors," "Ghetto Celebrity," and "Rude Boy Sadaam" to remind you this is the guy who cut "The Phillistines," "Black a Kill Black," and "Bad Da." He simply released too much product in the early nineties—amounting to an album a month for a while—for it to be easy for new fans to discover which ones were his outstanding records. (The discography highlights some personal favorites.)

Gregory is the latter-day king of the ultimately laid-back delivery. His smooth and expressive style, romantic moans, love groans, and the occasional whistle through his missing teeth send chills through the well-dressed ladies in the dance as they did in the days when he and the Roots Radics shook the scene in the seventies. The late eighties Music Works, Jammy's and Digital-B productions, though digital, contain some great later work. His early nineties recordings for the Xterminator label are magnificent.

Jah Shaka

Though best known as a producer and dub artist, Jah Shaka has issued several vocal albums. Largely responsible for the survival of a roots underground in London, he ran a sound system, set up his own Jah Shaka King of the Zulus label, and went on to produce some of the best reggae in England with homegrown talent and visiting dignitaries. In recent years he has produced a series of excellent albums for Horace Andy, Max Romeo, and Willie Williams, recording in Jamaica, where he was born. All of his music has a spiritual vibe and hypnotic power.

David Jahson

Natty Chase the Barber Away (1978) is not merely a good example of a late seventies reggae album. It contains shoots that run from the earliest days of the music to the latest. The track (used also for the "Clean Head Dread" version) is a stepped-up take on John Holt's "Ali Baba" from the Duke Reid days and one of the few "riddims" that show the direct lineage of reggae from ska. Co-producer Ian Lewis of Inner Circle makes full use of Sly and Robbie, Chinna Smith, Lester Lewis, Bernard "Touter" Harvey, Robbie Lyn, and, not the least, King Tubby on the mix. And the cover, a mock front page of the *Daily Dread News* showing Natty chasing Jonathan Baldhead away from Zion, is priceless. To my knowledge this is the artist's only LP.

Winston Jarrett

Winston Jarrett backed Alton Ellis as one of the Flames for Duke Reid and Coxsone and sang lead for the Rightous Flames after Ellis emigrated to England. He's recorded for major producers including Roy Cousins, Alvin Ranglin, and Lee Perry and high-point records include "Fear Not," "Zion," and "True Born African." Albums in the eighties and nineties on Culture Press, Nighthawk, and several for RAS maintain a roots everyman vibe emphasizing African origin, Rasta trajectory, and I-niversal vision.

Anthony Johnson

Recording for a variety of producers but almost exclusively at Channel One, Anthony Johnson peppered the early dancehall scene with roots and culture and irie vibes sung in what could be mistaken for a lovers rock style. His first hit, "Gunshot" for Jah Thomas, set his style of conscious lyrics over rhythms rolled out by the Roots Radics, We the People, Sly and Robbie and the High Times Band. Outstanding cuts include "I Saw Jah in My Vision," "Dreadlocks Queen," and "Know Yourself Mankind." An early '90s CD of covers like "Suspicious Minds" still includes roots cuts "Original Roll Call" and "External Fire."

Barbara Jones

Though the regrettable phrase "girl singer" that appears on the back of her first Trojan LP is more a comment on the time (1974) than a description, it oddly fits her early work, which has the haunting vulnerability of a young Leslie Gore or Ronnie Specter. Saddled with love songs like "Slim Boy" and "Changing Partners," she tore into an occasional standard like "Walk Through This World" like it was written just for her and out-sang soul man Joe Tex on his own "Hold on to What You Have Got." Both cuts were produced by Alvin Ranglin, for whom she recorded through the early eighties. She continues recording for various producers today and Jamaica Gold recently issued a CD compilation of GG's hits.

Frankie Jones

Greenwich Farm's Frankie Jones hit the ground running as Jah Frankie with the ineffable *Satta and Praise Jah,* a roots single and fiery album for Striker Lee with a stellar backing. His career was never this focused again and for every eighties single like "Chase Them Jah" there were several more like "Niceness Tonight" or "Prefer the Mother." The same held true for later albums produced by Brent Dowe, George Phang, and others: lovers rock with a once-in-a-while roots tune worth waiting for. Hookim brother Kenneth produced one combination LP and an excellent later album on Bullwackies fulfilled early promise.

Vivian Jones

Vivian Jones's debut, *Jah Works,* is a stunning Rasta tableau produced in England by Jah Shaka with ten perfect tunes, including "Depend on Jah," "Ites Gold and Green," and "Schooling." The album is a stripped-down, dub-soaked textbook use of throbbing hypno-rhythms and chanted vocals that is a fully satisfying deep drink from the well. Hints of this approach dot his later lovers albums. A selection of these with an occasional culture tune are gathered on a mostly self-produced Reggae Max greatest hits CD from Jet Star.

Pat Kelly

Pat Kelly took over as lead vocalist of the Techniques with the departure of Slim Smith. A falsetto singer of the first rank, Kelly had hits in the late sixties with Duke Reid and on the U.K. Gas label and later for Black Swan, Sunshot, and Pama, among many. Some of his best '70s singles were "How Long," "It's a Good Day," and "What Am I to Do." Most available albums are from the eighties and feature covers like "Try to Remember," "Angel of the Morning," and signature tunes such as "They Talk About Love" and "There Comes a Time." Kelly's voice is as expressive today as on his early work. He has recorded in the '90s for Joe Frasier, Mister Tipsy, and others.

Jennifer Lara

An underrated singer of the first class, Jennifer Lara cut many sides for Studio One in the early eighties, about half of which are collected on her first LP. She also sang backup and duets for and with many other artists there, particularly Johnny Osbourne. She went on to hits like "Midnight Confession" for Black Solidarity, singles on Jammy's and Volcano, and more duets with the likes of Devon Russell. She scored again at the end of the eighties with "If You Don't Know Me by Now" for Outernational, who have an unreleased LP by her "in the can." Let it out!

Barrington Levy

Barrington Levy is a one-man definition of the term *dancehall singer.* Along with Junjo Lawes, who produced his early recordings, he helped establish the sound of the eighties. Along the way he made some great records like "My Woman" for Joe Gibbs and "Mr. Money Man" for Channel One but it was two herb songs—"Collie Weed" and "Under Mi Sensi"—as well as the huge hit "Here I Come" that made him a reggae megastar.

Later hits include "Murderer" and a massive remake of Bob Andy's "Too Experienced" for Donovan Germain. A "best of" from Profile is a good place to start, drawing from various producers. It's Levy's style—powerful and singerly while catching up the rhythms of his day as few singers could—that make all his records worth hearing. He brings a touch of class to dancehall music.

Hopeton Lewis

Hopeton Lewis's 1967 "Take It Easy" is one of the finest examples of rock steady, a brilliant song and recording. Lewis can lay claim to several of the period's best records, including "Sounds and Pressure" (recorded the same day) and the calming "Cool Cool Collie." All these were cut at Federal Records for Richard and

Ken Khouri and arranged by Keith Scott. Lewis also had hits like 1970's Festival Song Winner "Boom Shacka Lacka" for Duke Reid in 1970. His soul-style delivery made the transition to reggae with 1971's "Grooving Out on Life."

His career includes the dread "Leaving Babylon" of 1975 and the serio-comic "Don't Take Your Guns to Town" for Lee Perry. Two fine CD collections illustrate both phases of his career. He released satisfying albums in the seventies and the eighties, offering originals like "Irie Reggae Feeling" and soulful covers. His 1973 cover of "City of New Orleans" is surpassed in scope only by the flip-side, his unique interpretation of Jimi Hendrix's "Wind Cries Mary." Recent live performances have been outstanding.

Little Roy

Little Roy's reputation as a revered roots singer started with some early Matador singles as the Little Roys, including the crucial cut "Bongo Niah." When the group disbanded he kept the name (his own was originally Earl Lowe). His early '70s singles "Hard Fighter" and "Tribal War" as well as "Black Bird" and "Prophesy" on the Earth label are well dread.

His mid-seventies debut LP *Tribal War* (an impossible album to find) was followed by *Columbus Ship* in 1978. He gathered songs from both on the 1990 album *Prophesy*, then released an album of all new material nearly as great as his early work, *Live On*. In the mid-nineties Pressure Sounds, the U.K. reissue imprint of On U Sounds, re-released the scarce *Tribal War* set as *Tafari Earth Uprising* and On U followed with a brand new album in 1996 that is every bit as good as his earlier work. It seems after all these years Little Roy is still the hardest fighter.

Carlton Livingston

The sweet, humble style of singer Carlton Livingston's early '80s records meshed perfectly with the shifting rhythms of Sly and Robbie just before they handed Channel One house band duties over to the Roots Radics. Carlton also recorded with the Jah Life players, including Paul Henton on bass and Donny Marshall on drums. His songs include the contemplative ("Rasta Get the Blame," "100 Weight of Collie Weed"), beatific ("What in Battle Sweeter Than Victory?"), and soothing (a category that includes many of his great love songs). A 1994 CD on Grapevine has an updated sound but plenty of good songs and Carlton's distinctive approach.

Fred Locks

Lead singer for rock steady's Lyrics, who recorded fewer than a handful of singles, mainly for Coxsone, including the impassioned "Hear Whey the Old Man Say," Fred Locks went on to become a mid-seventies legend. Singles like "Black Star Liners" and "Wolf Wolf," gathered on the album *True Rastaman,* achieved international cult status. Affiliated with the Twelve Tribes of Israel he recorded sparsely, releasing two albums in the eighties and two in the nineties, one produced by Xterminator. All take a serious lyrical approach. Though he's recorded love songs, "Everybody know about love," says Locks. "It's more important trying to teach people. It's the universal love that's important."

J.C. Lodge

If you never heard J.C. Lodge's "Telephone Love," you must have sat out the Gussie Clarke Music Works sound revolution of the late eighties (the track also fueled hits for Gregory Isaacs and others). Her breathy, sexualized delivery attained its peak with this dollar-a-minute ode to what is today called phone sex. Follow-ups like "Pillow Talk," "Hardcore Loving," and "Satisfaction" (though it featured a guest spot from DJ U Roy) were less stimulating. Lodge is a sophisticated stylist who recorded a crossover album for Tommy Boy before returning to RAS for several fine albums, including one produced by Mad Professor.

Jimmy London

Jimmy London sang with Keith Poppin in Rocking Horse, whose singles included "Rightous Man" and "Weeping and Wailing." As a solo singer his high range, smooth control and pop sensibilities brought success. Odd cover tunes like "'Til I Kiss You" or "Just Tell Her Jim Said Hello" are well worth wading through for cuts like "Got to Change Your Ways" (penned by Peter Tosh) and "Thank the Lord," both produced by Phil Pratt. The latter is on a 1996 CD compilation from Esoldun.

Lovindeer

After one album of socially conscious tunes released variously as *Ride Ride Ride* and *Serious Time,* Lloyd Lovindeer turned into a one-man cottage industry of topical tropical humor. His own label (The Sound of Jamaica) and publishing company (Prolific) issues songs he writes and produces including his jab at transport, "De Blinkin' Bus." A religious-comedy album (*One Day Christian*), and from the secular side *Why Don't We All Just Have Sex,* were topped by a series of singles concerning Hurricane Gilbert including "Gilbert—One Hell of a Blow Job."

Rita Marley

Wife of Bob Marley, mother of Ziggy Marley of the Melody Makers, and member of the I-Threes, Rita Marley has a lengthy recording career as a solo artist stretching back to her work with the Soulettes and the mid-sixties hit "Pied Piper." Her three albums, all issued in America by Shanachie, set a high standard, whether on reinterpretations of Wailers material like "Thank You Lord"

or on originals like "Good Girls Culture." "One Draw" is perhaps her best-known record in the U.S. She has also recorded under the name Ganette Mirum.

Larry Marshall

A string of Studio One hits like "Hokey Jokey," "Nanny Goat," "Mean Girl," "Press Along Nyah," and "Throw Me Corn" with partner Alvin Leslie (as Larry and Alvin) put Larry Marshall on the musical map, and the high quality of his songs and stately delivery have kept him there. Solo hits for Coxsone include "Thelma," "How Can I Go On," and "True Believer." "I Admire You" and "Can't You Understand" on Black and White and Amanda are only a couple of his fine later hits.

In the mid-eighties he remade early winners and added the likes of "Ark of Jah Covenant" and "Heavy Load Jah Children Carry." The albums *Presenting Larry Marshall* and *I Admire You,* both crucial, are available on CD reissue from Heartbeat. A singer's singer and a writer's writer, Marshall is a good example of the quality and diversity of Jamaican vocalists. The guy never made a bad record!

Freddie McGregor

Starting young is a way of life for Jamaican singers but few can boast they made their first records at seven years old—the age at which Freddie McGregor began recording with the Clarendonians for Coxsone. One of his earliest solo releases was "Why Did My Little Girl Cry" as Little Freddie in 1970. He recorded for Dodd throughout the seventies including the roots "Rastaman Camp," finally collected on the LP *Boby Bobylon* in 1980.

He went on to record for just about everyone; high points include "Big Ship" for Linval Thompson, "Leave Yah" on the High Music label, and "Oh Marcus" on Black Star Liner.

He has recorded for Niney the Observer (an excellent set now available as *Zion Chant*), Steely and Clevie, Xterminator, and Chinna Smith, with major co-productions with Dalton Brownie on his own Big Ship label and a lengthy stint with Gussie Clarke that included a marvelous version of Justin Hinds's "Carry Go Bring Come" with DJ Snaggapuss. McGregor can always be counted on for an excellent live show.

With at least two dozen albums including a crossover release on Polydor, several volumes of smooth versions of Jamaican classics for VP, and world tours headlining Reggae Sunsplash, McGregor has also become a producer of note for other artists. Though his stylish delivery has at times approached slick and some of his later productions edged toward the mechanical he has time and again returned with fine roots material like "Jah Never Fail I" from his late '90s *Masterpiece*.

Freddie McKay

In a country that has produced some of the most soulful singers of all time, none more greatly deserves the application of the term than the late Freddie McKay, who first hit with 1967's "Love Is a Treasure" for Duke Reid. The epitome of a sweet-sounding singer with a gravel voice, he could wring an emotive musical missive out of a woman's name, an ancient tune (two of his best for Coxsone were "Drunken Sailor" and "High School Dance"), or—finest of all—an original like "Rock a Bye Woman," "I'm a Free Man" or "It Get So Hot." Many of his early classics for Dodd are collected on the Studio One LP *Picture on the Wall.*

Throughout the seventies he issued gut-wrenching love songs like "Our Rendezvous," and "Sweet You Sour You" with its logical impasse ("If I sweet you it will soon sour you"), one of several singles issued on Shelter records in the U.S. The equally philosophical "What You Gonna Do" and lovers cuts like "Since I Met You"

were always balanced by serious songs like "Father Will Cut You Off" and "Cool Down Your Temper." From the former category songs like "Just a Little Bit," "Since I Met You," and "Marcia" and from the latter "It Deh Yah," "Nah Mek It Look So," and "Jah Love I" are among his best.

The showcase album, *Creation,* produced by Ossie Hibbert, and a "best of" produced by Alvin Ranglin, join the Coxsone disc as essential listening, though frustratingly unavailable—it's hard to find anything in print by him today. McKay issued several brilliant singles in the mid-eighties including "Paulette" on Clan Disc, "Set Me Free" on Ujama, and "You Doin' Fine" for Mister Tipsy. He died of a heart attack—some say a broken heart—after finishing his final album, *I'm a Free Man,* in 1986.

Jacob Miller

Jacob Miller recorded one song ("Love Is a Melody") for Coxsone Dodd at Studio One at the age of twelve; while still a teenager he voiced a half-dozen tracks for Augustus Pablo. In the mid-seventies he joined forces with Roger and Ian Lewis of Inner Circle and sang lead for the band as well as recording solo backed by the brothers with whom he also wrote. He had a readily identifiable quavering singing style that was one-third gimmick and two-thirds genius.

With Inner Circle and/or the Lewis brothers, Miller made some crossover records that were too disco for American reggae fans in the '70s, covered countless reggae tunes in his own "human echoplex" style, and contributed some of early reggae's finest moments, such as "Tired Fe Lick Weed in a Bush," "Forward Jah Jah Children," "Roman Soldiers of Babylon," "Suzie Wong," and "Tenement Yard." He also recorded for Joe Gibbs (including the brilliant "Shakey Girl"), did a fairly ridiculous Christmas album at Channel One, and delivered some stunning live performances, a few of which were fortunately captured on video.

Miller was in the upper echelon of seventies reggae singer. It's tempting to speculate what his career might have been like had it continued. His death in a car accident in 1980—a year before Marley's passing—stunned the reggae world and robbed Jamaica of one of its most intriguing talents. In recent years much of his previously unavailable work with Pablo and recordings produced by Tommy Cowan have become available in the U.S. for the first time and it's now possible to reassess this early and important figure.

Sugar Minott

Lincoln "Sugar" Minott started out in the late sixties singing with roots group the African Brothers, whose members included Tony Tuff and Derrick Howard, now known as Eric "Bubbling" Buddles. Their "No Bruk No Cup" was cut for Coxsone at Studio One. "So when I went solo I just went right back there," says Sugar. "I liked the vibe. There was not great financial return but the amount of knowledge you could acquire!" The opportunity to sing over Dodd's classic rhythms was, he adds, "my dream."

He recorded extensively for Dodd throughout the seventies though it wasn't till the late seventies that Coxsone issued his first album with several more eked out over the years. "Every now and then he bounces forth on some tapes and comes up with something but I don't really mind because that's like a stepping stone for me. I appreciate all that happened at Studio One and know that I worked with a lot of people like Jackie Mittoo, Pablove Black, Carlton and the Shoes—I was living in heaven musically."

Minott is perhaps the earliest and best of the dancehall singers who forever changed the face of reggae beginning in the early eighties. His nickname came from his sweet singing style, which also established him as a veteran of the lovers rock scene. Whether singing lovers rock or soul-flavored roots, he captured the crowd because, he says, "Me a try not to be a specialist. Me a sing all kinda songs. Political songs, lovers rock, dancehall, soul—I can identify with different kinda people."

Hits include "Mr. D.C.," "Hard Time Pressure," "Buy off the Bar" and "Herbman Hustling." Of the latter song he says, "It's like I could never do a show without doing that song. It's nice—I like doing it." Sugar made a point throughout his career of giving back to the people who put him on top. His Youth Promotions wing champions new young talent and his reputation as a producer challenged but never eclipsed his career as a singer. His Black Roots label serves as a production umbrella for his own and others' work.

An international reggae artist of stature, Minott puts the same spirit of building up community in his music. His late '80s album *African Soldier* is "specially dedicated to the freedom fighters in South Africa—an album dedicated to the fight against apartheid." For Sugar Minott music is a mission and he works at home and abroad "sharing the vibes and spreading roots and culture."

Though he produced many up-and-coming singers in the '80s and '90s (often, like Coxsone, waxing an artist's first records) and self-produced the bulk of his own bulky catalog, Minott has also worked with the best of the rest of the producers from the island including Niney the Observer, George Phang, Sly Dunbar, Donovan Germain, King Jammy, Bobby Digital, Phillip "Fatis" Burrell, and Tappa Zukie. In addition he has co-produced with the likes of Bunny Lee and Bullwackie's Lloyd Barnes. Sugar Minott is a major Jamaican singer who has worked tirelessly to advance the quality of the music in every facet.

Denroy Morgan

Jamaican-born and New York–based Denroy Morgan scored crossover American radio play in 1981 with *I'll Do Anything for You*, issuing an album of that title on Becket Records backed by the Black Eagles. A 1984 album on RCA, *Make My Day,* and a rootsier double-album set, *Stand Firm and Dub* (Rohit), followed. In the '90s his children, the group Morgan Heritage, applied their own combination of American influences with reggae. They produced Morgans triumphant return *Salvation* (VP) in 1998.

Derrick Morgan

A major singer of the ska era, Derrick Morgan began recording in Jamaica in the late '50s for Duke Reid's Treasure Isle with "Lover Man." He also had hits with Hi Life ("Fat Man") and Coxsone ("Leave Earth"). A stint with Prince Buster was followed by a series of records for Leslie Kong, which in turn led to a musical war with Buster's "Blackhead Chinaman" aimed at Morgan and Kong, with Morgan's "Blazing Fire" in response.

Having laid the groundwork for ska in Jamaica, Morgan went on to do the same in England with later "rude boy" songs like "Moon Walk." He had early sixties hits in England on Blue Beat, late sixties and early seventies hits on Crab and Third World (some produced by his brother-in-law, Bunny Lee), and issued records throughout the seventies, eighties, and early nineties.

A major retrospective of his early work on Trojan (*I Am the Ruler*) contains many of his best singles. A 1995 Heartbeat CD, *Ska Man Classics,* reprises his and others hits with Mafia and Fluxy augmented by a new generation of ska stylists. In 1997 Heartbeat issued another crucial collection of his work spanning several decades titled *Time Marches On.* He continues to tour extensively.

Eric "Monty" Morris

Though there is at present no album collecting the classic singles of Eric "Monty" Morris, that day is bound to come. Recorded mainly for Prince Buster, his hits include "Sammy Dead," "Money Can't Buy Life," "Penny Reel," "Solomon Gundy," and "Humpty Dumpty"—some of the most distinctive works of the ska era. He made a few later records like 1969's "No More Teardrops" and, from the seventies, "Hard Time in Babylon." A 1988 LP with Michael Enkrumah is not representative of Eric "Monty" Morris's important contribution to Jamaican music.

Pablo Moses

The album *Revolutionary Dream* (issued by United Artists in the U.S. as *I Love I Bring*), with cuts like "Corrupted Man," "Blood Money," and the completely unique and powerful "Give I Fe I Name" was the first in a long series of cultural attacks from Pablita (Pablo Moses) Henry. Moses was never a prolific singles artist (though the ones he released are all desirable, not least for the heavy dub versions) but issued nearly a dozen albums from the mid-seventies to the early nineties.

Always inspirational and uncompromising, as titles like "Dubbing Is a Must," "Pave the Way," "One People," and "I Am a Rastaman" show, Moses was produced on his first three albums by Geoffrey Chung, aided and abetted by Lee Scratch Perry on the early single "I Man a Grasshopper," and self-produced later albums issued on Mango, Alligator, RAS, Profile, and his own Humble label. Live performances reminiscent of the mighty Peter Tosh and an unswerving devotion to Rastafari typify Moses's career.

Judy Mowatt

Judy Mowatt sang lead for rock steady's Gaylettes whose "Silent River" is a masterpiece of Jamaica's first "golden age." Early seventies solo work included U.K. hits "Emergency Call" and "I Shall Sing." With Marcia Griffiths and Rita Marley she formed the I-Threes, recording and touring with Bob Marley and the Wailers after Peter Tosh and Bunny Wailer left the band.

Her solo career continued through all of this with singles and albums released on her own Ashandan label. *Black Woman* (1979) and *Only a Woman* (1982), both released in the U.S. by Shanachie, are front-line calls for equality that helped redefine woman's role in reggae. She received a Grammy nomination for 1986's *Love Is Overdue* for the same label. Though she produced many of her own records she has also recorded for Sonia Pottinger (as Julianne), Clive Hunt, Geoffrey Chung, Sly and Robbie, and others.

In 1992 Junior Reid produced Judy and Marcia (Griffiths) together on "Unconditional Love." Her most recent album, issued in Jamaica as *Life* and the U.S. as *Rock Me,* mixed elements of sampling, hip-hop, and dancehall to interesting effect. Though only the title song and one other cut are self-penned, she has written some superb songs such as "Slave Queen," the I Threes hit "Many Are Called," and "Joseph," her tribute to the late Bob Marley.

Junior Murvin

Murvin is not to be confused with Junior Marvin, longtime member of the Wailers Band. Junior Murvin's high falsetto soul delivery cut like a hot knife through Jello, and Lee "Scratch" Perry used it to great advantage on the track and album *Police and Thieves*. "Roots Train" and "Tedious" from the same LP ensured he was no one-hit wonder, but like a few other Black Ark artists Murvin never seemed to recapture the magic Scratch performed on him. He recorded several albums, among which late eighties entries *Apartheid, Muggers in the Street,* and *Signs and Wonders* are quite good but only *Police and Thieves* is essential.

Hugh Mundell

A protege of Augustus Pablo from the mid-seventies, the late Hugh Mundell DJed under the name Jah Levi and recorded the classic albums *Africa*

Must Be Free by 1983 and *Blackman Foundation* for Pablo while still in his teens. Mundell went on to produce his own albums *Arise* and *Time and Place* (as well as Junior Reid's first single) and recorded early eighties albums for Junjo Lawes and Prince Jammy. His minor-against-major style of singing and distinctive voice were enhanced by serious lyrics and spiritual themes. Says Junior Reid, "He teach me to be independent, 'cause he a guy always producing his own thing. That's how JR [Junior Reid's label] come about. Because of the seed that Hugh Mundell plant."

George Nooks

George Nooks has a singing career that spans two decades and doubles as DJ Prince Mohammed. As George Nooks he cut singles like "Tribal War" for Joe Gibbs in the late seventies and "You Too Greedy" for Tony Robinson. The Jimpy's album *Today* balances love songs with more serious material like "Fret Not Yourself." As Prince Mohammed he issued albums with Winston Riley, Tony Tam, and Joe Gibbs, the latter including his hit "Forty Leg (Inna Him Dread)." He is still actively recording.

Jackie Opel

Hailing originally from Barbados, Jackie Opel took Jamaica by storm in the sixties with a series of soul and ska chargers cut mainly for Coxsone, including "Cry Me a River," "I Am What I Am," "Solid Rock," and "The Lord Is with Me" as well as duets with Doreen Schaeffer ("Welcome You Back Home") and Hortense Ellis. Two Studio One collections gather mainly the tearjerkers—most of his best work is still found only on scattered 7-inch singles issued in the mid-sixties.

Johnny Osbourne

"My first recording was done at Studio One," says Johnny Osbourne, who went on to record with the Sensations for Winston Riley in the late '60s and to sing lead for Canada's Ishan Band in the seventies before returning to Coxsone for the essential *Truths and Rights* in 1980. He later recorded for Junjo Lawes, Prince Jammy, King Tubby, and Bobby Digital with hits like "Budy Bye," "Yo Yo," and "Me and You Nuh Live So." "Can't mek the new guy get me out," he says, "'cause I been in it too long. So whatever they're doing I try and just extend my capability fe create something around what is happening."

Tristan Palma

Tristan Palma ("Not Palmer," he told me emphatically) sang in a youthful reedy voice on early eighties recordings for Black Solidarity and DJ-turned-producer Nkrumah Jah Thomas. Linval Thompson and Tony Robinson both cut albums with him but the Thomas sessions capture him at Channel One using the Roots Radics and were mixed at King Tubby's with a very dubby feel. Several are currently available on CD and vinyl. Palma also issued singles on Power House and the fantastic Grimm Ben labels.

He's mainly known for love songs but now and then a serious tune like "Don't Wanna Be a Rude Boy" on Afro Eagle stands out. He scored with herb songs "Spliff Tale," "Collie Man," and 1982's *Joker Smoker*. In the '90s he sang in combination with Sanchez, Lady Junie, Dennis Brown, and Beenie Man. The year 1997 saw a self-produced CD, *Born Naked,* that showcases a mature singer still attuned to musical values that predate the dancehall era in which he came to prominence.

Lloyd Parks

With Wentworth Vernal (who recorded the sublime "The Rainbow" for Studio One), Lloyd Parks comprised rock steady's the Termites, whose hits were collected by Coxsone on *Do*

the Rock Steady. Parks also sang with a post-Slim Smith version of the Techniques. He started playing bass in the late sixties and became one of Jamaica's most in-demand players, providing bottom for Skin, Flesh and Bones, Joe Gibbs' Professionals, the Revolutionaries, and later his own We the People Band. Parks's Jamaican hits as singer and songwriter include "Slaving," "I Man a Mafia," "Officially," and (for Lee Scratch Perry) "Professor Ironside." His solo LPs are pleasant reminders of the influence of American soul music on early reggae.

Frankie Paul

Frankie Paul is another dancehall-era singer who manages to escape being tagged dancehall because he keeps his musical standards high. Though he's put out so many albums from the early eighties to today tht it's difficult to recommend a selection, some of his great singles would have to include "Ites Gold and Green" on Freedom Sounds, "Anne Go Rope in Marget" on Youth Promotion, and the massive "Thu Sun-Peng" for Junjo Lawes, as well as "No Sizzling" on Skengdon, "Warning," on Vena and 1991's controversial "Crowning of the Browning."

F.P., as he's often called, is partially sighted and wears glasses as thick as bottle bottoms, but he's one of the most romantic singers of his era, almost single-handedly keeping lovers rock alive for the last decade. He can do a dead ringer impression of Dennis Brown, and has done it on cuts like "Promise Land," "Children of Israel," and "Whip Them Jah." Brown of course used to do pretty good impressions himself, including Alton Ellis and John Holt, and if F.P., Brown, and Luciano ever sing together I defy you to tell who's singing which part.

Dawn Penn

Though she recorded a handful of singles in the sixties Dawn Penn would have pretty much been considered a one-hit wonder for her "You Don't Love Me" for Coxsone had not fate, in the form of Steely and Clevie, stepped in. They recut her hit digital style for a Heartbeat CD of Studio One covers featuring the original singers. Months after its release, a remix surfaced on the East Coast club scene and "No, No, No" with its U Roy stinger intro captured American radio. An album of the same title followed. If Penn is a one-hit wonder, at least she has the satisfaction of having done it twice.

Lee Perry

One of Jamaica's greatest producers, Lee "Scratch" Perry is to reggae what dada is to art. As a vocalist he was produced by C.S. Dodd (early recordings collected on the LP *Chicken Scratch*) and Joe Gibbs (some cuts available on *Intensified Rock Steady*), both of whom employed him as arranger, talent scout, and engineer, and both of whom he later attacked in song. His own vocals pepper his greatest period of productivity at the Black Ark studio, some captured on *Roast Fish and Corn Bread* and the recent *Arkology* anthology of his productions.

After the no-longer-mysterious end to his home studio ("I burned the Black Ark," he says succinctly on *Live at Maritime Hall*), he developed a new style of performance poetry that dished word salad brilliant and banal, voicing his own and others' productions with scatological humor, dadaistic juxtaposition, and amusing asides. In the late '90s he toured with Mad Professor and Robotics and his performances were equally brilliant.

Keith Poppin

Keith Poppin was a member of the group Rocking Horse who recorded for Lloyd Campbell, with whom he had the later hit

"Same Thing for Breakfast." His instantly memorable voice could handle soulful ballads, sweet love songs, and the studio sermons that served seventies reggae so well. Two mid-seventies albums for producer Phil Pratt, though currently out of print, showcase his memorable vocal twists and turns on songs like "Envious," "Ho Lord," "Who Are You," and "Tell Why Do." Uncollected cuts like "Hopscotch," "Is It Too Late," and "Some a Dem a Go Shame" would fill another. He resurfaced in the early '90s with the single "God Is Standing By."

Maxi Priest

England's hit-maker Maxi Priest typifies the smooth lovers rock style, but whatever style he sings in he's polished and professional, both live and on record. He scored in the U.S. with a late eighties cover of Cat Stevens's "Wild World." In the '90s he hit with duets with Beres Hammond and Shaggy and a cover of Bob Marley's "Waiting in Vain" with jazz guitarist Lee Rittenour.

Prince Alla

Keith "Prince Alla" Blake (also spelled Allah and sometimes Ras Allah) is a rootical Rastafarian singer whose songs reflect his biblical vision of righteousness, Ethiopian origins, and everyday ghetto life. Essential works like "Gold Diver" and "Bosrah" are gathered on the Tappa Zukie production *Heaven Is My Roof* and equally important recordings for Freedom Sounds are collected on Blood and Fire's *Only Love Can Conquer*. A 1996 CD produced by Jah Shaka shows him still in excellent form.

Prince Buster

Cecil Campbell—"Prince Buster"—must have issued hundreds of singles from the early sixties through the early eighties with subject matter ranging from "Fowl Thief," "Gun the Man Down," and "Al Capone" in the ska days to the more philosophical "Belief Kill Belief Cure" and "Time Longer Than Rope." Buster is a pivotal figure in the early days of Jamaican music, from the sound systems to reggae, producing himself and others. "Earthquake on Orange Street," "Wash Wash," and "Ten Commandments" are only a few of his hits.

Michael Prophet

A protégé of Yabby You—hence the name Prophet—Michael Haynes recorded three albums for the producer beginning in 1977 before moving on to Junjo Lawes, with whom he cut a similar number of discs. After three more for Delroy Wright he began producing himself. His trajectory from songs like "Praise You Jah Jah," "Prayer of the Upright," "No Friend in This Time," and "Serious Reasoning" to the "Sexy Mama" and "Bull Talk" of his later career parallels the decline of reggae music from the seventies to the nineties with an occasional glimpse, like "Mother Africa" and "Rich Man Poor Man," of the roots artist still buried deep inside.

Jack Radics

As the '90s dawned a whole new set of faces and voices stepped to the fore. Jordan Bailey had recorded without much attention in the eighties but when he morphed into Jack Radics and began singing from the back of his throat, his lovers and soul covers style drew attention. He recorded for nearly every major '90s producer with singles on Roof International, Penthouse, Shocking Vibes, and others. His 1993 combination record with Chaka Demus and Pliers, a reworking of "Twist and Shout" that draws heavily on Shaggy's "Oh Carolina" formula, got U.S. airplay in 1993. But who knows what his real voice sounds like?

Ras Midas

The early '80s are dotted with releases from artists who'd been around a long time but finally got the show on the road just in time to see the music do a spinning turn. Roots man Ras Midas (born Lorenzo Nembhard) started singing in the sixties. A classic African chant record "Kude a Bamba" was issued by Black Swan in the U.K. and Mango in the U.S. in 1976; it was anthologized and widely played. In 1978 he issued "Can't Stop Rasta Now" on the Jahwax label.

Rastaman in Exile (1980) was thoughtful, educational, and apocalyptic. It boasted backing by Gladdy Anderson, Ranchy McLean, Jimmy Becker (who played harmonica for the Wailers), and Marcia Griffiths. In live shows his super-energized performance put him up with the majors. He relocated to Santa Cruz, California, where he issued *Stand Up Wise Up*, again with an all-star lineup including Andy Bassford on guitar, Sly and Robbie, and Ansel Collins. In '96 he returned with an equally fulfilling CD, mainly backed by his own band the Bridge. This is an excellent singer and songwriter with serious, thought-provoking songs.

Reggae George

"Reggae George" Daley contributed a handful of singles and fine roots albums in the early eighties, one produced by Prince Far I and one by Jah Woosh. Tender on tracks like "Jah Sweet Love" and "This Old World" and militant on "Stop Push the Fire," "Fight on My Own," and the outstanding 12-inch "Three Wicked Men," he recorded at Channel One with players who eventually became the Roots Radics. A cultural vibe dominates his recordings.

Jimmy Riley

Martin "Jimmy" Riley was a member of the Uniques, harmonizing with and writing songs for a singer he idolized, the late Slim Smith. He penned a number of tunes that are today considered "Slim Smith songs" such as "Love and Devotion," "Give Me a Love" and "This Little Boy's Lost." He worked briefly with Lee "Scratch" Perry, including "Sons of Negus" under his own name and "Rasta Train" and "Yagga Yagga" as Lee and Jimmy. Bunny Lee issued solo singles by him under the name Martin Riley as early as 1970 in England. He also recorded for Striker Lee under the name Jimmy Wonder.

Deeply affected by the death of Slim Smith, he laid low for a few years but by the mid-seventies he issued crucial singles like "Prophecy" on Max Romeo's Romax label. *Majority Rule* (1978; aka *Tell the Youths the Truth*) is one of the outstanding albums of its time and was issued on Burning Sounds, Makossa, and Trojan as well as the Camille label under the title *Superstar.* A series of Taxi singles led to the Mango album *Rydim Driven.*

From this point Riley produced himself; the album *Put the People First* (Shanachie), with cuts like "Poor Immigrants," is one of the best reggae records of the early '80s. He set up a record shop in Miami but by the early '90s was making the rounds of the new studios working with some of the best contemporary producers, and issued singles on Heavy Beat, Digital-B, Star Trail, Mister Tipsy, Ugly Man, and Observers. Riley always ropes in high-quality backing singers like Al Campbell, Derrick Lara, and Leroy Sibbles.

The CD *20 Classic Hits* barely scrapes the surface, though it includes crucial cuts like "It's So Hot" and "My Woman's Love." His latest releases, *Love Fa Real* (produced by Willie Lindo) and the self-produced *Attention Attention,* are in keeping with his earlier career, with a new generation of players like Danny Brownie, Computer Paul, and Steely and Clevie joining Sly and Robbie and others. A classic "old school" singer and songwriter, Jimmy sails into the '90s like he'd just begun.

Lloyd Robinson

With a couple of ska singles issued on the U.K. Blue Beat label in 1962, a crucial Coxsone standard ("It Deep"), a major early score for Harry J ("Cuss Cuss"), and singles for Duke Reid and others stretching into the late seventies, it's hard to believe that Lloyd Robinson never released an album. There are plenty of good singles—"Love Will Conquer" and "Rocky Road," from 1977 are just a couple—to fill one. On top of that he was half the singing team of Lloyd and Devon (Russell) who cut rock steady's "Bum Ball" and likewise half of Lloyd and Glen. Many of his records, like "Death a Come" for Matador and "King of the Worm" seem to have been issued only as (blank label) PREs, although he also has records on Mighty Cloud, Prophets, and Taxi.

Max Romeo

In a way, Max Romeo's trajectory was the opposite of reggae's—he started with slackness and went on to become a front-line singer for righteousness. Born Max Smith, the name Romeo fit well with early singles like "Raindrops" and "Close to Me," parodies of popular songs with crude sexual lyrics, and of course his huge late sixties smash "Wet Dream," a schoolboy's delight that became an underground hit in England. By 1971, still in his early twenties, that was all behind him and singles like "Let the Power Fall" were pointing him—and reggae—in a new direction.

Those early records were produced by Bunny Lee. Romeo first recorded for Ken Lack as lead singer for the Emotions and was briefly a member of the Hippy Boys, who were to become the Upsetters and in their final manifestation the Wailers Band. By 1975 the album *Revelation Time,* aka *Open the Iron Gate* (credited to several producers but recorded at Lee Perry's fabled Black Ark studio), with cuts like "Warning, Warning," "Tacko," and "Three Blind Mice," solidified the "new" Max Romeo.

The album that followed, *War in a Babylon,* produced by Perry and released by Island Records, made it clear even to Americans that reggae was more than the latest musical fad. Over twenty years later it's still one of the ten best reggae albums ever made. Max Romeo seemed destined to be one of reggae's strongest voices with everything—poetry, politics, surrealism, and sanctification—pressed into one package.

Subsequent releases were increasingly softer. His self-productions lacked the genius of Perry's aural assaults. By 1981's *Holding Out My Love to You,* co-produced by Keith Richards, the once-formidable Maxie had been seriously sidelined. As the decade turned again he was living in New York and released a promising album titled *Transition* with Lee Perry. In 1992 Max Romeo returned full force with *Far I Captain of My Ship,* produced in Jamaica by England's Jah Shaka.

The albums that followed were nearly as impressive—Tappa Zukie produced *Cross or the Gun,* with some updates and new cuts like "Rev. Cavalero" and "Trigger Happy Babylon" that might have been recorded by the Max Romeo of old. The Jah Shaka follow-up *Our Rights* was also a powerful set, with cuts like "Woe Be Unto Them" that rivaled the Maxie, Scratch, and Niney the Observer singles "Coming of Jah" and "Rasta Band Wagon." Taken all together Max Romeo's contribution to reggae is incalculable and indispensable.

Sanchez

Kevin "Sanchez" Jackson, former lead singer for Sunday choirs at Rehoboth Apostolic Church in St. Catherine, went on to become one of dancehall's best singers. His first hit was 1987's "Lady in Red" and cover and love songs predominate his career. Though Sanchez has suffered at times from inferior material and lackluster production

in the hands of the right producer—and he's worked with almost all the modern ones—he has made some impressive records and at his worst is merely pleasant.

Bim Sherman

A unique artist with a readily identifiable sound, Bim Sherman cut some fine and unusual Jamaican singles like "Blacker Sound" and "Mighty Ruler" in Jamaica before relocating to England. There he hooked up with progressive English producer Adrian Sherwood and issued a series of experimental albums exploring the borders of reggae. As a result his work is something of an acquired taste. He is also prominent in Sherwoods *Singers and Players.*

Roy Shirley

Roy Shirley is a true Jamaican original, a stylistic innovator of the highest order. He first recorded for Leslie Kong in 1964. He sang with a group called the Leaders that included Joe White and Ken Boothe. No album or CD available collects his ska singles, though you may find one or two on scattered anthologies. He briefly sang in the Uniques with Slim Smith. Roy Shirley is said to have "invented" rock steady in 1966 with the song "Hold Them," the first record produced by Joe Gibbs. It and other early works can be found on anthologies. Bunny Lee got his first hit off Roy Shirley as well, with the dazzling "Music Field."

Shirley made some astounding reggae records like "Dance up the Reggae," "Stop Your Fussing and Fighting," "Rasta Love," and "Action Speaks Louder Than Words." A soul singer who elongates and emphasizes portions of the songs that might be mere flourishes for lesser vocalists, he makes Solomon Burke seem straitlaced and Al Green underemotive. Roy Shirley *is* the High Priest of Soul. The only CDs presently available are later recordings or medleys of early hits, all fascinating but none with the impact of singles like "The Prophet," "Joe Frazier," or the uplifting "Prayer from the Priest." It's artists like this who are the reason the 7-inch 45 is still a highly sought-after commodity. A three-minute performance by Roy Shirley on videotape from Reggae Sunsplash 1982 is a stunning display of performance art genius.

Garnett Silk

More than anyone else it was Garnett Silk who pointed the dancehall toward a return to consciousness, and his tragic accidental death in a gun-related gas explosion nudged it in that direction. Horace Andy is right to note his own influence on the singer, and Silk's influence on his contemporaries and those who've come after is enormous. He was one of the shining lights of the early '90s, with cuts like "Zion in a Vision" reminding us that reggae began as message music and is still at its best when delivering the goods.

Earl Sixteen

We know how old he was when he entered show business. Earl "Sixteen" Daley is unique among Jamaican singers in being more of an album than a singles artist. He recorded for Derrick Harriot and Bunny Lee and turned in first-class albums for Coxsone Dodd, Lee Perry, Earl Morgan of the Heptones, Augustus Pablo, Mikey Dread, Mad Professor, Anthony Dehaney (now known as Bunny Gemini), and Roy Cousins. It's not by chance one is titled *Songs for a Reason*—they all contain carefully crafted well voiced conscious roots music with outstanding cuts like "Western Man," "Mighty One,""Changing World," and "Repatriate Your Mind." There isn't an album I wouldn't recommend; the Perry production *Phoenix of Peace* is brilliant from start to end.

Leroy Smart

An orphan who attended the legendary Alpha Boys School and worked as a gardener and shoemaker before entering show business, Leroy Smart developed a bad-boy reputation that's dogged his career and nurtured an intensely brooding, powerful, and expressive voice unlike anything else in or out of reggae. He sang on the Tippertone sound system among others and waxed discs like "Mother Liza," "Ballistic Affair," and "Badness No Pay," recording over thirty albums in the three decades of his career.

Named Best Male Vocalist in Jamaica five times, "Mr. Smart" as he was known early in his career, or "The Don" as he is now referred to, came up the hard way in the toughest ghetto areas of Kingston. A magnificent performer who gives 110 percent every show, his temperament, like his music, is ruled by strong emotions that make his songs, whether romantic or cultural, stark human statements. Conscious lyrics and message songs predominate.

High points include his work at Channel One with songs like "Pride and Ambition" and "Without Love," albums such as *Superstar* for Bunny Lee, and self-productions like "Stop Criticizing" on his own World Wide Success label. He has remained not only active but in top form, recording for Jammy's, Star Trail, and others throughout the eighties ("Prophecy a Go Hold Them," "Talk of the Town") and nineties ("Talk Bout Friend," "Time Longer Than Rope," and "Bad Boy Learn").

Slim Smith

A soulful singer of the first rank, Keith "Slim" Smith died young after achieving legendary status as one of Jamaica's greatest vocalists. He fronted both the Techniques and Uniques and recorded solo for Coxsone Dodd (with hits like "Rougher Yet," "Born to Love," "You Don't Care," and "The New Boss"), Duke Reid ("What Kind of Love"), and Sonia Pottinger

("The Time Has Come"). The bulk of his work with and without backing vocalists was done for Bunny "Striker" Lee.

"Little Did You Know," "Blinded By Love," "Don't Tell Your Mama," and "Everybody Needs Love" are only a few of his major hits. His recordings have been repackaged endlessly with Techniques and Uniques recordings being issued as Slim Smith and vice versa. Later versions of the Techniques and Uniques sans Smith slightly cloud the issue, but his unmistakable voice helps clear things up.

Wayne Smith

Wayne Smith's "Sleng Teng" is the record that kicked off the digital age in 1986. The track is a slowed-down preset rock rhythm from a Casio keyboard. Its use on Smith's record and subsequent development is what made Prince Jammy King. When the riddim returned in the mid-nineties so did Smith, voicing versions for various producers.

Barrington Spence

Sounding like Ken Boothe without the rough edges, he had the right producer (Tony Robinson), label (Trojan), and time (1975), but somehow Barrington Spence didn't set the musical world on fire, though he remained a *Star in the Ghetto* (title of a 1982 LP). The Trojan album, *Speak Softly,* had three singles issued—"Let Locks Grow," "Jah Jah Train," and "Darling Dry Your Eyes." Later great singles "Natty Dread a No Witness in a Babylon" (Jackpot) and of course the serious "Serious Joint" are roots classics.

Richie Stephens

A big booming voice and a straight-across delivery weren't all Richie Stephens had going for him when the '90s dawned. A Mister Tipsy cover of Dennis Brown's "Should I" on a riddim that also well served Beres Hammond's "Step Aside" all but cried out Next Big Thing. Dennis Star, Jammy's, and Top Rank each took a run with good result. So did Tuff Gong—who had him doing "Ole Man River," for Pete's sake— and Motown. Clifton "Specialist" Dillon delivered *Pot of Gold* (1993) to Motown, but it wasn't. Mid-nineties singles like "Fight Back" with Garnett Silk returned the man to the masses and 1997's *Special Work of Art* for Penthouse displays maturity and takes chances—Richie Stephens is back.

Nadine Sutherland

I first saw Nadine Sutherland perform with the Wailers when she was thirteen years old. She had already won RJR's Best Female Vocalist and the Jamaica Arts Best Upcoming Artists Awards. From the girlish charm of her first album *Until* to 1997's womanly *Nadine* (in the hands of producer Phillip "Fatis" Burrell), she can make you feel nice ("Turn Off the Lights") or give you some advice ("Don't Throw Pearls"). Hits include "Wicked and Wild" for Germain and "Action" with Terror Fabulous.

Rod Taylor

Roots singer Rod Taylor's late seventies Freedom Sounds singles "Ethiopian Kings" and "In the Right Way" and 1980's Dread at the Controls 12-inch "His Imperial Majesty" will endure. He recorded for Nigger Kojak, Ras Adabra, Prince Hammer, King Culture, Manzie, and others. He issued numerous albums from the late seventies on, including 1980's *Where Is Your Love Mankind* for Junjo Lawes. His most recent release is a 1993 production by England's Robert Tribulation.

Linval Thompson

In all of music there is probably no more fearful combination of words than singing producer, but in Jamaica many singers and DJs have gone on to produce. Linval Thompson first recorded for Bunny Lee in the mid-seventies with cuts like "Cool Down Your Temper," "Long Long Dreadlocks," and the burning "Jah Jah Dreader Than Dread." Often the Aggrovators flip-sides with snatches of Linval's voice floating by topped the chant-vocal A-sides, but Thompson's workmanlike vocals have an almost hypnotic charm.

For his Thompson Sound label Linval produced himself and others, generally recording at Channel One with Sly and Robbie and mixing down at King Tubby's. He was right at home with the early dancehall rhythms of the Roots Radics as the styles began to change and worked with a variety of artists, including the Viceroys and the Wailing Souls. His 1988 Mango album *Starlight* with standout cuts "Look Like It's Gonna Rain" and "Mercy" was produced by Sly and Robbie. Over the years he also worked with Lord Koos, Colin Sampson, Jah Thomas, Prince Jammy, Prince Jazzbo, and Tappa Zukie.

Tony Tuff

Winston "Tony Tuff" Morris began his career as lead singer for the African Brothers. For Yabby You he cut "Warrior No Tarry Yah" in 1978 and the first of two albums for Grove/Island. His early singles are studded with titles like "Deliver Me" (Channel One), "Oppressor" (High Note), "Practice What You Preach" (Black Link), and "Never Trouble Trouble" (Black Solidarity). Adept at the new style as well as the old, he demonstrated, through his later career as a dancehall singer, his ability to (in the words of a 1993 single) "Move with the Crowd." No matter the style, Tony Tuff gives every song a strong performance. Unlike some better-known singers, his music is always fleshed out, not sketched in.

Wayne Wade

Another protégé of Yabby You, Wayne Wade hit straight out of the gate with "Black Is Our Color," issued on Mango in the U.K. in 1977. The album of the same name was followed by a string of singles including "Fire Fire," the title of his second album. Roots themes predominate his early work, with outstanding titles like "Poverty in the Ghetto," "Gang War," and "There Must Be a Change." Later recordings for Delroy Wright and Linval Thompson include such disparate material as "Disco Lady" and "Down in Iran." The early '90s found him working with producer Willie Lindo.

Sylford Walker

With producer Joe Gibbs, Sylford Walker cut top form mid-seventies singles like "Burn Babylon" and "Jah Golden Pen," which can be found on various artists anthologies. An album issued by Greensleeves in 1988, *Lamb's Bread,* collects Glen Brown productions such as "Cleanliness Is Godliness" and "Eternal Day," originally released on 7-inch on South East Music. Later singles on E.B.T. Rock and Sir Clough retain conscious themes.

Dennis Walks

Dennis Walks (Dennis Vassel) had two major late sixties hits for producer Harry Mudie, "The Drifter" and "Heart Don't Leap," both contained on his debut *Meet Dennis Walks.* His lovers style dovetailed with Mudie's pop approach (he was one of the few producers to use strings effectively in reggae), making the album and the riddims standards. Walks went on to record for Bunny Lee, Joe Gibbs, and Prince Jazzbo, with standout singles like "Almighty I," "Waste Time in a Babylon," and "Navel String." He was still issuing singles in the early '90s, including "You Could a Deal" on Mandingo, and he remains a fine if oddly underrecorded singer.

Merlene Webber

One of Jamaica's great female vocalists, Merlene Webber had hits on Lloyd Campbell's Spiderman label, generally covering American country and soul hits, including "Once You Hit the Road," "No More Running," and "First Cut" in the early seventies. Backed by Tit for Tat club house band Skin, Flesh and Bones, she cut an album for the same producer that's hard to find but well worth seeking out. She also recorded with her sister Cynthia (a good singer in her own right) as the Webber Sisters.

Joy White

The earliest single I have by Joy White was recorded under the name Little Joy and the Fireflies. In the mid-seventies Joy White was something of an anomaly—a militant woman singer with records like "Black Am I," "Check Your Daughter," "Dread Out Deh,"and "Come on Natty Dread." By 1979's *Sentimental Reasons,* for up-and-coming producer Donovan Germain (with two tracks produced by Lloyd Campbell), she was singing mostly love songs. In either style, she is superb.

K.C. White

In the early seventies K.C. White was lead vocalist for Tommy McCook and the Supersonics. He scored with "Anywhere But Nowhere" and "First Cut Is the Deepest." He relocated to the U.S. and recorded for Bullwackies. Jamaican recordings from Channel One and Harry J were also issued on U.S. labels Love People and Puff. White produced an anthology of younger artists in the '90s.

Delroy Williams

There are two Delroy Williamses—as if trying to sort out Delroy Wilson, Delroy Washington, Roy Wilson, and Willie Williams wasn't enough.

One was raised in England and had a U.K. hit with a reggae cover of Billy Joe Royals "Down in the Boondocks" in the seventies. He returned with a 1990 CD *You Sexy Thing* on Trojan.

The other Delroy Williams was a protégé of melodica master Augustus Pablo beginning in the early eighties. Singles on Message and Rockers led up to 1982's *I Stand Black,* revealing a relaxed vocal approach that could be compared to Ijahman or more obviously to Hugh Mundell. The gentle, almost free delivery dovetails with Pablo's production sensibility and they continued with *Darkness with Fire.* A later release produced by Michael Taylor and Byron Whitley is also very nice.

Willie Williams

Willie Williams first recorded for Studio One in the mid-sixties. He ran a sound system in Kingston, set up his own record label and migrated to Canada. After 1980's *Messenger Man,* Coxsone Dodd brought Williams back into the studio in time-honored tradition to sing over an old Studio One rhythm track. The result, "Armagideon Time," was covered by the Clash in the early '80s and has become one of reggae's signature tunes.

Besides the Studio One *Armagideon Time* album a mid-eighties "clash" LP with Barry Brown, backed by Black Roots and mixed by Peter Chemist, and *Unity* were his main releases. In the '90s he resurfaced with two magnificent albums for Jah Shaka, *Natty with a Cause* and *See Me.* He is a consistent roots artist who swam against the tide in the dancehall era without being washed out to sea.

Delroy Wilson

Along with Ken Boothe, Delroy Wilson represents the soulful side of reggae. Delroy started out in the ska era with Studio One at age thirteen. Coxsone Dodd himself wrote his first hit,

"Spit in the Sky," and managed the young vocalist. From the ska jumpers like "Lion of Judah" and "I Shall Not Remove" to the rock steady and reggae of "Trying to Conquer Me," "Riding for a Fall," and "True Believer," Wilson's Coxsone output is among the best work from that "best of" studio.

He next went to Bunny Lee, with whom he eventually recorded a large amount of work including "Cool Operator" and "Better Must Come." Other producers for whom he recorded include Sonia Pottinger ("Nothing from Nothing," "Conference Table"), Jack Ruby ("Things in the Dark," "I Saw You Pack Your Things"), Keith Hudson ("Place in Africa"), Gussie Clarke, Niney the Observer, Jo Jo Hookim, Prince Jammy, and Blackbeard. Major albums include *Good All Over* for Coxsone, *Sarge* for Lloyd Charmers, and *Who Done It* with Bunny Lee.

With every changing style Delroy Wilson came again, making him one of the few singers to issue popular records in the ska, rock steady, reggae, rockers, steppers, lovers rock, and dancehall styles. By the time of the latter he was often reprising early hits with young DJs, including "Run for Your Life" with Beenie Man for Penthouse, "Some Like It Hot" with Culture Brown for Sonic Sounds and "Have Some Mercy" with Bounty Killer for Carib. When Delroy Wilson died a few years ago, the world of reggae lost one of its most soulful voices.

Yabby You

Vivian Jackson got the name Yabby You from the opening chorus to his first single, "Conquering Lion," with the Ralph Brothers—future Prophet Alric Forbes and singer Bobby Melody—on which the trio chants "Be You, Be Yabby Yabby You." With Forbes and Dada Smith as Yabby You and the Prophets, he issued singles throughout the mid-seventies on his own Prophets label, including "Judgment Time," "Bosrach," and

"Run Come Rally." Their recordings are characterized by heavy rhythms voiced and mixed at King Tubby's, engaging harmonies, and apocalyptic lyrics.

Jackson was something of an anomaly in Kingston's Rastafarian community, an outspoken Christian who used Rasta imagery in his songs. A combination of malnutrition and work-related illnesses from making Dutch Pots in a Kingston gully bank (an occupation that worked its way into his songs), as well as arthritis, severely damaged his health. But it didn't stop Yabby You and the Prophets from becoming a major force in Jamaican music in the seventies.

The group released singles on the Vivian Jackson label, such as "Jah Vengeance," "Fire in Kingston," "Judgment on the Land," and "Love Thy Neighbor." Several seventies albums collect Yabby You and the Prophets including the essential *Conquering Lion* and *Deliver Me from My Enemies. One Love, One Heart,* aka *The Yabby You Collection* boiled the hits down to one album. In the early eighties and nineties, Yabby You returned with new works consistent with his early sound and message.

Yabby You produced numerous other artists, with singers Michael Prophet, Tony Tuff, Wayne Wade, and DJs Trinity and Dillinger among them, issued on the Prophets and Vivian Jackson labels. In the early eighties he toured with the Gladiators. At a legendary show at L.A.'s now defunct Music Machine, Jackson hobbled to the stage on crutches, laid them down on the steps, and danced with wild abandon for his all-too-brief set, then picked up his crutches and hobbled backstage.

A career-spanning double-CD set from Blood and Fire gathers his best work as a singer and producer with informative liner notes, photos, and interview material from Steve Barrow and Dave Katz. The same label reissued the recommended and previously hard-to-find *Prophecy of Dub* with King Tubby.

The same year Yabby You issued *Jah Will Be Done,* reprising songs and restating major themes from his oeuvre with an all new set of Prophets.

Earl Zero

Earl Zero, who later changed his name to Earl Love, was born Earl Johnson in Kingston, Jamaica, in 1953. He penned "None Shall Escape the Judgment in This Time," a major hit for Johnny Clarke. Mid-seventies singles "Rightous Works" and "Please Officer" established the chanting style that became his trademark on later records like "Shackles and Chain," "Pure and Clean," and "Come Away," all backed by the Soul Syndicate and released by Freedom Sounds. He toured the U.S. in the early eighties, exhibiting a joyful persona and showcasing his serious, thoughtful songs. His 1981 Epiphany album *Visions of Love* was recently reissued on CD.

CHAPTER 39

Vocal Groups and Bands

Some ska groups, including Toots and the Maytals, Bob Marley and the Wailers, and Justin Hinds and the Dominoes, went on to major hits in the rock steady and reggae eras. The sheer quantity of Jamaican vocal groups is astounding. Hundreds of groups like the Africans, Almighty Stone, Belltones, Bleechers, Blue Bells, Jaylads, Mello Larks, Mellow Lads, Mellows, Mighty Travellers, Velvet Shadows, Versatiles, and the Vibrators released 7-inch singles or have anthologized tracks. Groups as diverse as the Charmers, Chosen Few, Cimmarons, Fantells, Melodies, Rulers, Scorchers,

Slickers, Spanishtonians, Tartans, Termites, Three Tops, Untouchables, and Valentines deserve attention, as do the astonishing number of labels on which they appeared and the studios from which they emerged.

Duos, once a highly popular configuration, include Alton and Eddie, Asher and Trimble, Bongo and Bunny, Chuck and Dobby, Joe White and Chuck, Higgs and Wilson, Rudy and Sketto, and Stranger and Ken, Stranger and Gladdy and Stranger and Patsy. Many of the great solo performers, like Ken Boothe, Alton Ellis, Joe Higgs, and Stranger Cole, started singing in duos and trios, or the more common cluster from which the groups emerged. Members change, singers regroup, vocalists from one group leave and join another, and sometimes one group goes through several names. Here and there one group survives for decades with essentially the same lineup.

As in any form of music, many groups recorded one album and faded from the scene. Two random examples are the Uplifters, whose King Culture LP *We're Moving* was recorded at Harry J, Channel One, and Joe Gibbs's studios and includes exquisite tunes like "Jah Jah Give I Strength" and "Mighty Ruler," and Unique Vision, a self-contained band formed by students of the Salvation Army School for the Blind and Visually Impaired. Many unlisted groups, including Hot Rocks, Identity, Isis, Kotch, Nagasa, Native, and Undivided Roots issued albums. The eighties and nineties have seen fewer groups but contain an interesting array of contributors such as Mystic Eyes, Fire Facts, and Brown, Eagle and Spear.

The Abyssinians

The original lineup of Bernard Collins and brothers Donald and Linford Manning provided a number of foundational hymns for reggae and Rastafari. With lyrics informed by the teachings of the Ethiopian World Federation Orthodox Church and strong, simple rhythms recorded at Studio One, Joe Gibbs, Harry J., and Channel One, they offer up ethereal harmonies on songs like "Declaration of Rights," "This Land Is for Everyone," and their classic "Satta Massagana." Internal problems split the band after several fine albums. In the nineties two completely different versions of the group toured, one with lead singer Bernard Collins and two harmony singers, and one with the Manning brothers minus Linford but including Carlton, the former lead singer of Carlton and the Shoes.

Althea and Donna

Althea and Donna's international hit "Uptown Top Ranking" was followed by a superb album of the same name produced by Karl Pitterson. "The West (Is Gonna Perish)," "Make a Truce," and "If You Don't Love Jah" are only a few of the great tracks. Sly and Robbie, Chinna, Touter, Scully and Tommy McCook, Vin Gordon, and Herman Marquis on horns—it's a wonder this has not yet been reissued on CD. It was the duo's only album together.

Aswad

U.K.'s Aswad stretched their pop reggae style into a career that's spanned two decades. Their early eighties Island releases with cuts like "Three Babylon" and "Warrior Charge" showed them capable of innovative roots stylings. By the nineties the three members left standing, Brinsley Ford, "Drummie" Zeb, and Tony Gad, concentrated on love songs and dance cuts while continuing to tour successfully and issue recordings at a breakneck pace.

Cables

Recorded in the late sixties, the Cables' *What Kind of World* is a picture-perfect Studio One album whose rhythms are still returned to today—

Kasheif Lindo hit in 1997 with a new version of the title track done in a modern, digital style. Keble Drummond, Elbert Stewart, and Vincent Stoddart made up the trio whose hits, including the sublime "Baby Why," were collected on their sole Studio One LP. A second album for Harry J is extremely hard to find. Drummond also did some solo work.

Carlton and the Shoes

The British lovers rock tradition was founded on soulful cuts like Carlton and the Shoes' "Love Me Forever" and "Never Give Your Heart Away," both contained on their Studio One LP *Love Me Forever*. In addition the trio, led by Carlton Manning and including his brother Linford, who later co-founded the Abyssinians, inspired that group with cuts like "Forward Jerusalem" and "Happy Land." A later album with Carlton providing his own backing vocals also contains a mix of love songs like "Sincerely Yours" and more serious works like "Arise Abraham" and "Send Us Moses."

Chalice

One of a very small number of self-contained bands to emerge from Jamaica, seven-piece Chalice stormed the early eighties with a series of albums and exciting live performances that tagged them as their generation's answer to Third World. Rock dynamics and theatrical presentation made for exciting stage shows. They recorded a series of albums with standout songs including "Good to Be There" and "I'm Trying."

Clarendonians

From Clarendon (as the Westmorlites were from Westmoreland, the Kingstonians from Kingston, and so on), Peter Austin and Ernest Wilson scored a series of number one ska and rock steady hits for Studio One in the sixties with songs like "You Can't Be Happy," "Sho Be Do Be," and "Rudie Gone a Jail." They later added a very young Freddie McGregor to the lineup. The Clarendonians helped define and give continuity to the transition from ska to rock steady in theme, style, and content.

McGregor went on to build a formidable solo reggae career (see separate listing). Austin issued singles such as "Juvenile Delinquent," and Wilson scored with "Undying Love," "Money Worries," and "Story Book Children" for Coxsone and "I Know Myself" for Channel One, continuing to record through the '80s and '90s, including 1986's *Love Revolution* (Natty Congo) and a series of early '90s singles on Techniques. A 1992 CD found the original duo remaking their hits with an all-star musical backing that included Leroy "Horsemouth" Wallace on drums, Winston "Bo-Peep" Bowen on guitar, and Bertram "Ranchie" McClean on bass.

Congos

The Congos prefigure Israel Vibration for ethereal harmonies and even surpass them in lyrical excursions through a universe unbounded by semiotic considerations. Held in high regard for their work with Lee "Scratch" Perry on the legendary *Heart of the Congos,* they were quintessentially a trio consisting of Cedric Myton, Roydell ("Congo Ashanti Roy") Johnson, and Watty Burnett. They seem to survive in any form that includes Myton.

Backing vocals were beefed up by the Meditations in the Black Ark sessions for producer Lee Perry. From then on the group has been self-produced, beginning with the excellent *Congo Ashanty*. Myton and Burnett were the Congos for 1979's *Image of Africa,* interestingly on the Congo Ashanty label. In the early '80s Myton, Devon Russell, and Lindburgh Lewis recorded *Face the Music* as the Congos, issued on Go-Feet. The same label released a limited remix of the Perry disc in this period.

Congo Ashanti Roy made some excellent solo records, including 1984's *Level Vibes* and *Berlin Wall* with Annette Brissett. Some of Watty Burnett's sides for Scratch can be found on scattered anthologies—they're worth searching for. He issued a great dub album in 1997 titled *King Tubby Meets Lee Scratch Perry* on Shanachie. Myton continues to issue Congo albums. The latest, *Natty Dread Rise Again* (RAS), features his wife, Yvonne, on harmonies. Myton and Burnett toured as the Congos in 1998.

Count Ossie and the Mystic Revelation of Rastafari

Oswald "Count Ossie" Williams played a style of African drumming called Buru at Nyahbingi grounations in Wareika Hill. These gatherings drew some of Jamaica's great musicians, and Ossie and his group of hand-drummers interacted with jazz horn players and eventually studio rhythm sections to create music that beats at the very heart of reggae. Many consider the Ossie-backed Folkes Brothers hit "Oh Carolina" (produced by Prince Buster) to be the first reggae record.

Ossie's recorded output includes some of the most traditional and experimental music ever waxed in Jamaica. The two-record set *Grounation* with soloist Cedric "IM" Brooks resembles improvisational field recordings and are unlike anything else you've ever heard. *Tales from Mozambique* extends the African pulse in the Rastafarian dialectic. A recently issued Harry Mudie CD, *Remembering Count Ossie,* collects recordings from the '50s and '60s—some never before available—with saxophonist "Big Bra" Gaynair and Rico Rodriguez on trombone.

Culture

A classic call-and-response vocal trio with Joseph Hill doing the calling and Albert Walker and Kenneth Paley responding, Culture cut two outstanding albums for Joe Gibbs at the end of the seventies and followed up with several equally fine discs for Sonia Pottinger. The latter were released on Virgin in the U.K. and helped propel Culture to international status, where they remain to this day, issuing on average an album a year over a twenty-year span.

Hill's militant lyrics, forceful and witty delivery, and ability to change with the times (they've been backed by everybody from Sly and Robbie to a digital chip) have kept Culture on top. Hill has recorded as Culture without Walker and Paley, with Walker and another singer, and with Walker alone; as great as the harmonies sound on the early records, it really doesn't seem to matter—Hill just covers the other harmonies himself on record or has them sketched in live.

Culture's sound today is very forward and contemporary without pandering to trends. The emphasis is as always on social criticism, Rastafarian worldview, and irie reggae vibes. Whether singing about "Innocent Blood" or "Crack in New York," Joseph Hill delivers penetrating commentary with a high moral tone to a rhythm you can dance to. No group was ever better named.

Dingles

From one of reggae's best-known groups to one of the least, though not for lack of talent. The Dingles are a roots harmony trio composed of Selvin Stewart, Logan Davis, and Cyril Shakes also known, in reverse order, as Planky, Blinks, and Stone. Along with Lambert Douglas and others, they record almost exclusively for Clive Francis's Rudwill and Rosso labels, funded with proceeds from his shoe store.

The Dingles started out in the seventies as the Dingle Brothers with the Caribbean 7-inch "Got to Leave This Land" and also recorded a one-off ("I Don't Care") for Clancy Eccles. Their one album, *Happiness*—cut at

Channel One and Treasure Isle and backed by the Revolutionaries—is highly recommended. They are still active today; when I visited with Francis in Jamaica in the early '90s he had spent the previous day recording with them. They have enough excellent uncollected singles to fill at least one more LP.

Ethiopians

Beginning as a trio in the ska days, the Ethiopians slimmed down to a duo for a series of rock steady hits for Coxsone Dodd and Sir J.J. After the death of Stephen Taylor, lead singer Leonard Dillon continued to record as the Ethiopian, contributing some of reggae's most refined records. It's possible the Ethiopians made more Jamaican 7-inch singles than any other group. They had massive hits in the ska and rock steady eras and made many great reggae records as well.

Along the way they recorded for most of the great Jamaican producers, including Dodd, Reid, Mrs. Pottinger, Lloyd Daley, Prince Buster, Joe Gibbs, Lee Perry, and Niney the Observer. Early massives include "Train to Skaville," "I'm Gonna Take Over Now,""Stay Loose, Mama," and "Hong Kong Flu." "The Whip" (with the equally hip flip-side "Cool It Omega") is one of rock steady's defining moments. They made excellent records like "Everything Crash" for Sir J.J. and "Gate of Zion" for GG's Alvin Ranglin. Leonard Dillon's voice got richer as it matured and his most recent recordings are as desirable as his earliest. Many of his songs are conscious sufferer's tunes, like the haunting "Let Me Blow My Smoke" from *Owner Fe the Yard* or the righteous "Nuh Follow Babylon" from *Slave Call*. He has earned a place in the upper echelon of Jamaican music.

Gaylads

The Gaylads—B.B. Seaton, Delano Stewart, and Maurice Roberts—began singing ska for Coxsone Dodd but had the majority of their hits in the rock steady era for a variety of producers including Dodd and Sonia Pottinger. They became a duo when Stewart left to pursue a solo career and had many top singles for Leslie Kong and others. When Seaton went solo, Roberts re-formed the group as the Gayladds, issuing an excellent showcase (half vocal/half dub) LP on United Artists in 1979. They later changed their name to Psalms and cut a 1992 CD produced by Bunny Wailer.

Gladiators

The early to mid-seventies belonged to the Gladiators, then a trio consisting of Albert Griffiths, Gallimore Sutherland, and Clinton Fearon, who not only sang but were a self-contained band backing other singers in the studio. They started out with Coxsone in the rock steady days with cuts like "Hello Carol," "Downtown Rebel," and the dreader "Jah Go Before Us," "Roots Natty Roots," and "On the Other Side." Several albums for Virgin produced by Tony Robinson helped usher in the age of reggae with cuts like "Stick a Bush," "Looks Is Deceiving," and "Dreadlocks the Time Is Now."

A 1980 album produced by Eddy Grant was a little too slick for roots lovers but the group bounced back with excellent discs for the American Nighthawk and Heartbeat labels. In the later years they became Albert Griffiths and the Gladiators as first Sutherland and then Fearon moved on. Griffith's voice and songwriting remain strong and there is fine work on the later records. A new collection from Studio One days was issued by Heartbeat in 1998.

Heptones

What's not to love about the Heptones? Leroy Sibbles has one of Jamaica's finest voices, rich, full-bodied, and expressive—he's a born singer who has written many outstanding tunes and contributed some of the classic Studio One bass lines that form the infrastructure of reggae. Earl Morgan and Barry Llewelyn are natural harmony singers with excellent songs of their own. They started out "listening to all of them R&B stuff," says Sibbles. "We grew up," Earl Morgan adds, "on the Motown thing." As influences they name "the Drifters, Platters, Ink Spots," and of course the Impressions.

The trio sang dozens of hits, including "Ting a Ling," "Fatty Fatty," and "I Hold the Handle" for Coxsone, whom Sibbles calls "a wicked, wicked man." Also, he says, "We did harmonies for a lot of people, including Bob Andy, Freddy McKay, Ernest Wilson, Delroy Wilson, Ken Boothe, and Marcia Griffiths. Earl is the one who came up with the idea for the name," Sibbles explains, a bit of wordplay resulting from the chance discovery of a discarded bottle of Jamaican health tonic. "Hep mean lively and tone is music, so it sounded like lively music."

The Heptones could charm ("Love Won't Come Easy"), disarm ("Sweet Talking"), or alarm ("Haven't You Any Fight Left") when recording for Dodd. Equally compelling were their reggae versions of rock standards—"Sea of Love," "Only Sixteen," "Suspicious Minds," even "Ob-La-Di-Ob-La-Da" somehow were transformed into Heptones vehicles. They later recorded for Duke Reid, including "Let's Build Our Dreams" with John Holt. With Harry J they cut Llewelyn's "Book of Rules," "Country Boy," and "Mama Say." *Night Food* (Island) and *Cool Rasta* (Trojan) are top-selling albums from this period. The group had, says Barry Llewelyn, "the golden touch," releasing "pure hit songs."

With Lee "Scratch" Perry producing, they recorded *Party Time* (Mango). All three speak highly of Perry, whom Sibbles says is "fun to be with." They issued singles with Prince Buster, Joe Gibbs, Alvin Ranglin, Gussie Clarke,

Randy's, and others. When Leroy departed for Canada and a solo career, Morgan and Llewelyn regrouped with Naggo "Dolphin" Morris to make hits for Channel One. They issued over a dozen self-produced albums with this lineup on labels like Vista, Greensleeves, Jackal, Jamrock, Celluloid, and Burning Sounds.

In the mid-nineties Sibbles, Morgan, and Llewelyn reunited, toured, and recorded *Pressure* (RAS). "Sometimes you just have to do a thing," says Llewelyn. "That's the work of the Almighty," is how Sibbles puts it. "People make plans but Jah is the original plan setter." Still in excellent form, the trio is stunning live and cuts like "Are You Coming with Me" rival their earlier work. Everything they've ever done shows class.

Justin Hinds and the Dominoes

The simple "country" harmonies of the Dominoes intertwine with Justin Hinds's pure unadorned vocals to create one of the most distinctive sounds in Jamaican music, and one that has cut across the ska, rock steady, and reggae eras with a purity that is always refreshing. Hinds's lyrics, drawing on the rich folk tradition of Jamaica, biblical prophecy, and poetic thoughtfulness are among reggae's most evocative. This thread runs from their earliest version of "Carry Go Bring Come" to Hinds's later solo work like "Almond Tree."

The Dominoes—Dennis Sinclair and Junior Dixon—provide the classic two-part support harmony, echoing the refrain like a church choir approving the preacher's remarks. The backing tracks may change over the years, from the early Treasure Isle ska recordings like "The Higher the Monkey Climbs" and "Once a Man, Twice a Child" to the Sonia Pottinger rock steady productions and the punchy reggae of Jack Ruby's Black Disciples, but the trio just shifts the tempo and delivers the goods as if leaning into a turn on a country bus.

Many (though certainly not all) Treasure Isle productions can be found on import CD. Ruby produced two fine albums that should never have been allowed to go out of print, *Jezebel* and *Just in Time* (both issued originally on Mango). Hinds's aching delivery wrings pathos from cuts like "Help Your Falling Brother" and Spotlight" and the upful "Natty Take Over" and "Let Jah Arise."

Besides new material Hinds reworked his own hits in each successive musical form. There are ska, rock steady, and (more than one) reggae versions of "Carry Go Bring Come"— and they all sound good. *Travel with Love* (1984) included excellent new material and 1990's *Know Jah Better* (both on Nighthawk) showcased Hinds without the Dominoes and contained introspective tunes like "Picking Up Chips" and "Know Jah Better."

In the late nineties Justin Hinds seemed to pop up everywhere. Having never before played Los Angeles he played three times, with a band that included "Deadly" Headley and Vin Gordon on horns. He also sings and plays as a member of Wingless Angels, a Nyahbingi group produced by Keith Richards, and contributed "Sitting in Babylon" to Mutabaruka's *Gathering of the Spirits* on Shanachie.

Inner Circle

A self-contained band, Inner Circle was always a tight, slick reggae unit. They were Jacob Miller's band and backed this truly original singer's all-too-brief career live and on record. With him brothers Ian and Roger Lewis wrote some of his most memorable material, including "Forward Jah Jah Children" and "Tired Fe Lick Weed in a Bush," They can be seen working on a tune with Miller in the film *Rockers* (a young Tommy Cowan scribbles down the lyrics as they call them out).

Other members who passed through the band included Philip Thompson and Charlie Roberts on vocals; Chinna Smith on guitar; Mike Chung on keys, guitars, and vocals; and a series of drummers including Lloyd Adams, Horsemouth Wallace, and Rasheed McKenzie. In later years they added Michael Sterling on lead guitar and vocals and Lancelot Hall on traps.

Inner Circle did some disco in the seventies, which didn't sit well with hardcore reggae fans. After Miller's death the group reformed with Carlton Coffie, a good writer and singer. Bernard "Touter" Harvey, one-time Wailers keyboardist, rounded out the already well-rounded lineup.

"Bad Boy," the theme song to the "reality-based" TV show *Cops,* gave them a new identity. To their credit they never became a Jacob Miller revival band, and they continue to write and perform new original material. Their ear for the commercial hook and their wealth of musical and songwriting talent carries them through to this day. Live and on record they are dynamic, mixing in modern elements (yesterday disco, today dancehall) without ever losing their professional edge. In 1998 they toured with a new lead singer.

Israel Vibration

One of the most inspirational reggae trios ever to be seen in a live setting, Israel Vibration powered by the Roots Radics became one of the international sensations of the '80s and '90s. Cecil "Skelly" Spence, Lacelle "Wiss" Bukgin, and Albert "Apple" Craig met in a children's hospital. "We got together from we had polio," explains Wiss, who says the trio "ended up in the same polio institution back in Jamaica. We was always the best of friends from that age coming up."

The future members of Israel Vibration sighted up Rastafari and began to grow dreads. Wiss continues, "The society fight against I and I because of I and I belief. And them reject

ISRAEL VIBRATION (LEFT TO RIGHT): CECIL SPENCE ("SKELLY"), ALBERT CRAIG ("APPLE"), AND LACELLE BUKGIN ("WISS"). Photograph by Jan Salzman; © Phantom Photos

I and I, them reject to give us any aid, [or to] help while they help the rest, then push us out so we end up in the bush sleeping. Sleep in the dirt every night. Go through that for a whole heap a month. Some rugged, tough life, you know? Lay among the donkey and the goat and the cow and ass and birds and trees. And that's how the whole inspiration really develop from that stage."

To hear them tell it their early recording career wasn't much different. Skelly says in those days the group "Mek good records but we never have good producers. Producers a rip-off the business all the while." Says Apple, "Whole heap a obstacles we overcome but the work never finish." In fact, he told me in the late eighties, "we just ready, mon. We don't work yet." They went on to a long career, resulting in many fine albums with RAS Records. With leg braces, crutches, and canes the trio toured incessantly throughout their recording career. Their work grew better over the years—tighter harmonies and stronger songs mark their later releases. Live recordings and dubs all maintain high standards of quality. At present Apple is persuing a solo project and

Wiss and Skelly are said to have a new Israel Vibration CD ready for release.

Jamaicans

Known today as an important early producer and the "voice of Sunsplash," Tommy Cowan was lead singer of the rock steady and early reggae group the Jamaicans, whose members included Martin Williams and Norris Weir, who went on to a later solo career. They won the Jamaican Song Festival Competition of 1967 with "Ba Ba Boom." Another major hit was "Things You Say You Love." Nearly all of their best-known work is collected on Jamaica Gold's *Ba Ba Boom Time* with a wealth of photos and informative historical liner notes.

Jayes

They issued only a handful of singles but two of them were "Pretty Looks," the definitive Channel One update of Barry Llewelyn's classic, and "Rightous Man Satta" on Well Charge. Two 12-inch disco mixes remake the Viceroy's "Yaho" and Curtis Mayfield by way of the Techniques' "Queen Majesty" on Hit Bound. Their two albums, *Unforgettable Times 1* and *Unforgettable Times 2,* are extremely forgettable collections of American oldies, though also produced by Ernest and JoJo Hookim.

Jolly Brothers

One magnificent album for Lee Perry issued by Roots Records in England and one adequate release on United Artists produced in the main by Lloyd "Prince Jammy" James constitute the entire output of the Jolly Brothers. The trio was composed of Winston Edwards, Clevian Lewis, and Willis Gordon on the latter; Clevian is Cleveland and Willis Leonard on the former. An English CD offers two of the Perry tracks plus dubs. Good songs from the Perry album include "Cool Down," "Brotherly Love," and "Babylon a Fight Rasta." The crucial cut "Conscious Man" occurs on every named selection and as a 7-inch single on Magnum and a Ballistic 12-inch with variant versions.

Kingstonians

The Kingstonians, and the solo work of lead singer Jackie Bernard, represent for many the first of the golden age of Jamaican music. Ska, with the relentless intensity that continues to attract new young listeners daily, slowed and shifted the emphasis from the horns to vocals and guitar. During the rock steady phase the bass and drums pushed forward as well and the result—reggae—made rock steady's stay a short one. The Kingstonians lone album available at this writing covers rock steady and early reggae productions from Derrick Harriot. These include the essential "Singer Man" and an updated version of "Winey Winey" originally done for Sir JJ. Uncollected hits include the rapid rock steady "I Need You Tomorrow" and the slow reggae "Ups and Downs." Bernard's solo career is replete with such excellent cuts as "Another Scorcher" (backed by another great rock steady group, the Tennors), "Burst Style," "Roots Music," and "Jah Jah Way." Anthologies and collector's singles are at present the only way to find most of these and the rest of the Kingstonians' output.

Knowledge

Roots quintet Knowledge issued a couple of brilliant singles on Tappa Zukie's Stars label in the late seventies and followed with an album produced by him. *Hail Dread* somehow got released on A&M in America, where it promptly faded from view. At the time the group included lead singer Anthony Doyle, Michael Samuels, Delroy Folding, Earl McFarlane, and Mike Smith. Flash forward to the '90s, when once again several roots singles from Knowledge appeared, this time produced by Roy Cousins on his Tamoki-Wambesi label. The album *Stumbling Block* soon followed with these and other crucial tunes. Some must have been in the hopper for years, since they are engineered by Ernest Hookim at Channel One.

Byron Lee and the Dragonaires

Byron Lee and the Dragonaires hold a unique position among Jamaican groups. In the first place Lee was not a singer but a bandleader and early Jamaican producer of note, with many important hits from Toots and the Maytals, Eric "Monty" Morris, The Blues Busters, Eric Donaldson, and others. From the early sixties he also cut instrumental and vocal "asides," versions of his own and others' top hits (as well as popular American tunes) with his house band the Dragonaires.

So many great Jamaican singers and players passed through this band that it's a whole separate college of music like (though not along the same lines of) Coxsone's Studio One. A Dynamic house producer, Lee had many U.K. hits, played the New York World's Fair with Jimmy Cliff as lead vocalist in 1962, and issued a huge catalog of records and recently CDs, often mixing instrumentals and "cover" vocals by respected singers fronting the band. His work spans early ska, rock steady, and reggae and he is one of the few early producers still issuing new work today.

The main thing to be aware of with Lee is the collection of his essential early productions on Rhino's sadly deleted *Jamaican Ska*. The Blues Busters, the Charmers, and the pre-Dragonaires Ska Kings cuts as well as the scarce stereo mix and informative liner notes from Hank Holmes make this a crucial find, albeit at present in the used bin. Jamaica Gold's *Byron Lee and the Dragonaires Play Dynamite Ska with the Jamaican All Stars* double-CD set also features Stranger and Patsy, Ken Boothe, and the Charmers, and incredible cuts like "If You Act This Way" from the Maytals and Keith and Ken's timely "The Beatles Got to Go," all of which show Lee in top form.

There are, however, an abundance of Lee releases on the market that are slightly watered-down "uptown" productions of reggae hits utilizing great players in charted territory with fine singers like Ken Lazarus, Keith Lyn, and Barry Biggs on board. They freely mix hotel and sometimes elevator reggae with the "Theme from Doctor Zhivago," "My Sweet Lord," and presumed originals like "Pum Pum on a String." Eric Donaldson and the Maytals even re-recorded their own hits in slightly tepid Byron Lee versions.

There are also a vast number of strictly instrumental—in fact, downright easy listening—albums that should be celebrated by the burgeoning new lounge culture. The covers of the '90s *Soft Lee* series ought to clue you that these versions of "Never on Sunday," "Bridge Over Troubled Waters," and "Chariots of Fire" are background music to make out to. At that they're not much different from his '70s U.K. release *Tighten Up* or 1985's *Wine Miss Tiny* with their loving front cover homages to butt, bosom, and belly. The music was a bit livelier then (as on 1975's *Disco Reggae*—also available on 8-track tape!—or the recently reissued *Reggae Blast Off*) but the polished-till-the-soul's-scrubbed-out feel is the same.

Still, in an age that's learning to appreciate Martin Denny, Les Baxter, and Esquivel (much less the Three Suns and the theramin), can Byron Lee be far behind? He's never been afraid to branch out, having released songs in every style from ska, rock steady, and reggae to "carnival," "jump up," and even 1997's Socarobics, whose cover photo of a topless workout modestly conceals offending portions with his and the band's name. Can a Byron Lee dancehall disc with an orchestrated version of Buju Banton's "'Til Shiloh" be far behind?

Link and Chain

One of the chain of groups linked to producer Jack Ruby, this vocal trio exchanged members with Earth's Last Messengers, which became Earth Messengers and then Jah Messengers, and Rightous Foundation, which became Foundation. Their eventual lineup comprised Paul "Mirror" Williams on lead and Dwight "Tweety" Campbell and Trevor "Kashah" Douglas on harmonies. Their first album, 1990's *New Day*, was Ruby's last issued production. The follow-up, 1992's *S.T.O.P.*, was produced by Fatis Burrell.

Matumbi

England's Matumbi was a pop-lovers-reggae group that garnered radio airplay with "After Tonight," "Brother Louie," and a unique interpretation of Bob Dylan's "The Man in Me." After several late seventies albums founder Dennis "Blackbeard" Bovell went on to a solo career as a dub-roots producer and artist in his own right. Somewhat overlooked today, the group has no CDs in print at this writing.

Maytones

Though the vocal trio was the main embodiment of mid-seventies reggae, a few duos stand out. Like the Ethiopians, the Maytones began as a trio, with producer Alvin Ranglin as their third member. The Maytones—sometimes called the Mighty Maytones—were composed of lead singer Vernon Buckley and harmonizer Gladstone Grant. "Judgment a Come," "Boat to Zion," and "Serious World" are only a few of the fine songs they recorded, mainly for Ranglin's GG's label, though they also recorded for Coxsone, Sidney Crooks, Duke Reid Junior, A. Doeman, and Buckley himself. Their vocal style is humble, their lyrical focus righteous, and their recordings well worth seeking out. *Funny Man* on Jamaica Gold is a good CD sampler.

Melodians

Brent Dowe, Tony Brevett, and Trevor McNaughton made some of rock steady's most delicious harmony records, cutting sides like "Lay It On" for Coxsone and "Last Train," "Come on Little Girl," and "Everybody Bawling" for Duke Reid. With Sonia Pottinger they did "Little Nut Tree" and "Swing and Dine," both gathered on the album *Pre-Meditation*. Leslie Kong took them to new heights with "Sweet Sensation," "Rivers of Babylon," and "Rock It with Me," all contained on the Mango LP *Sweet Sensation*.

They released albums in the late seventies and early eighties but never strayed far from their rock steady roots. Brevett had some minor solo hits like "Don't Get Weary" and "Words of Prophecy" and Dowe some majors like "It Was Love," "Down Here in Babylon," and "Rightous Works" as well as a Trojan LP, *Build Me Up*, produced by Sonia Pottinger. "Rivers of Babylon" has been covered by Joe Higgs and Boney M and David Lindley covered "Rock It with I." Retrospective CD collections have been issued by Heartbeat and Trojan.

Mighty Diamonds

The consummate Jamaican vocal trio, the Mighty Diamonds have exactly what it takes to make it work. Lead singer Donald "Tabby" Shaw could weave a melody through a crowded football stadium; Fitzroy "Bunny" Simpson offers support vocals that would hold down any self-respecting doo-wop group, and Lloyd "Judge" Ferguson has as fine a natural falsetto as ever graced a soul side. Add that the three have sung together since their early teens and among them written dozens of what are now considered reggae standards and you have one of the most professional and hardest-working acts in the business.

They credit DJ Jah Lloyd—then producer Pat Francis—with founding the band. Their earliest record, "before we ever made a name," says Judge, was cut for singer-producer Stranger Cole. "Squiddley Cole, my nephew, is his son" explains Tabby. Their first album, produced by

Jo Jo Hookim with brother Ernest on the mixing board at Channel One in the mid-seventies, is one of reggae's finest. "Shame and Pride," "I Need a Roof," "Why Me Black Brother, Why," and of course *Right Time*—the eventual title track—are only some of the highlights. It's close to the first and undoubtedly the best showcase of the then newly emerging "rockers" style. The follow-up, *Deeper Roots,* with a crucial Ernest Hookim dub issued in the same sleeve, was another "rockers" triumph.

"Dem days was more like acoustic," says Bunny of the Channel One sessions, which included musicians like Sly Dunbar, Lloyd Parks,

MIGHTY DIAMONDS (LEFT TO RIGHT): DONALD SHAW ("TABBY"), FITZROY SIMPSON ("BUNNY"), AND LLOYD FERGUSON ("JUDGE"). Photograph by John Skomdahl

Ranchie McClean, Ansel Collins, and Sticky Thompson. "Live drums, live keyboards, live organ. Everything was just a natural. I think we need back some a dem things right now inna the recording field because the whole field gone electronic." Judge agrees: "It kinda get more artificial now." Today, says Bunny, "one man play everything and it lacks a form of togetherness."

A crossover album co-produced by Allen Toussaint in the late seventies seemed ill conceived, but the trio more than made up for it with a series of Gussie Clarke-produced releases that recaptured their roots and set the young producer on a trajectory that eventually took reggae into the nineties. The Diamonds were one of reggae's most dependable touring acts at a time when few Jamaican groups toured America. They have served as musical ambassadors for a generation and their live shows are never less than excellent.

From the Clarke sessions emerged a song, "Pass the Dutchie," that revamped a Jackie Mittoo keyboard solo from Studio One and was covered with a few alterations to disguise the herb references by the U.K.'s Musical Youth. When the credits were sorted out everybody made money and the process of naming the original rhythm or "riddim"—in this case "Full Up" after the Mittoo solo—became de rigueur. The Diamonds blithely reclaimed the tune with "Pass the Knowledge," beginning the cycle again.

The Mighty Diamonds issued albums throughout the seventies, eighties, and nineties, including live recordings from Jamaica's Reggae Sunsplash and from Europe and Japan. According to Judge they have released 39 albums. They always worked with the finest musicians. Sly and Robbie appear on their first album and throughout their recordings with Gussie Clarke.

One reason for the Mighty Diamonds' continued success is that they never issued anything that was less than technically excellent.

They have recorded for producers Joe Gibbs, Delroy Wright, and DJ-turned-producer Tappa Zukie among others and cut albums with DJs Trinity and U Roy. They scored again with Germain's Penthouse in 1993 with a remake of their own "Tell Me What's Wrong." At this writing they are set to release a new album with Gussie Clarke. Their songs focusing on Black History and social consciousness are among reggae's finest. "And remember," says Bunny, "Diamonds are a girl's best friend."

Misty in Roots

England's Misty in Roots never approached the international record sales of Aswad or Steel Pulse but they developed a large following in the U.K. and Europe, touring and issuing records from the late seventies through the late eighties. Though they didn't crack the American market their records were available on their own People Unite label on import. Kaz records has recently reissued their catalog on CD.

Morgan Heritage

Una, Gramps, Lukes, Mr. Mojo, and Peter—five New York-born sons and daughter of singer Denroy Morgan—accomplished the near impossible for an American-based reggae group. An appearance on Jamaica's 1995 Reggae Sunsplash led to the major-label album *Miracle* (MCA), produced by Lee Jaffe and daddy Denroy. With Bobby "Digital" Dixon, *Thank You Jah* accomplished a second miracle—a return-to-roots crossover from American reggae to one of the best Jamaican albums of the year.

One Calling (1998), produced with Prince Jammy, blends both styles and features a guest appearance from Denroy. "He spotted the talent from we were toddlers," says Una of her father. "He said this one's gonna play this,

this one's gonna play that." Says brother Peter, "If Daddy did have guns in the house maybe he would have a gunman, if he was a doctor maybe we would be doctor. But it was music. We just deal with music." In 1998 the group produced their father's return CD *Salvation,* and the various-artist *Family and Friends.*

Morwells

Eric "Bingy Bunny" Lamont cut several roots singles with percussionist Bongo Herman as Bongo and Bunny, including the Nyahbingi "Know for I" in the early seventies. In 1973 he and independent producer Maurice "Blacka" Wellington (a friend since early youth) formed the Morwells. They issued dozens of reality tunes in the mid-seventies, including "You Got to Be Holy," "Cut Them Down," and "Cold Cold World." They released albums into the early eighties, honing their harmonies on cuts like "Don Morwell," "Kingston 12 Tuffie," "Wish I Could Fly," and "Educate Your Mind."

Wellington produced sessions for Joe Gibbs, including early Culture tracks. Lamont, who learned guitar from sometime group member Louis Davis, played with Joe Gibbs and the Professionals, a later lineup of the Revolutionaries and the group that replaced them as Channel One's house rhythm section, the Roots Radics. Bass player Flabba Holt also came to the Roots Radics from a stint with the Morwells.

Two fine dub albums are part of the group's legacy. Bingy Bunny put out two solo albums in 1982, *Bingy Bunny and Morwells* (Park Heights) and *Me and Jane* (Cha Cha). He died of cancer on the last day of 1993. His influence as a guitarist is still being felt today. In 1996 Night Nurse Amy Wachtel put together *Tribute to Bingy Bunny* (RAS), which includes some Morwells material. Blacka Morwell went on to produce the late Nicodemus and others. Most of the Morwells' best work is not available on CD.

Mystic Revealers

One of the last self-contained bands to emerge in the '90s, Mystic Revealers blend disarmingly sweet pop vocals with uncontrived lyrics bent on correcting the faults of the world. "As youngsters coming up we were exposed to this consciousness and it's what inspired us," says lead Revealer Billy Mystic. "The most sincere man that you find is the Rastaman because he doesn't worship silver and gold."

"Reggae music has always been crying out against injustice," he explains, "because it came out of a people that were in a social condition where they feel helpless and when you feel helpless sometimes all you can do is sing about the problem and pray for redemption." To date the group has released a half dozen CDs and toured extensively.

Naturalites

Formed in 1982, U.K. roots conglomerate Naturalites issued three albums after their stunning 12-inch debut, "Picture on the Wall." Core singer-songwriters Ossie Samms and Percy McLeod craft fine material like "Rasta Youth," and "What About the Africans" from 1987's *Marvelous.* Their third outing is more in the lovers vein.

Paragons

The Paragons were the leading vocal group of the rock steady era, with major hits for Duke Reid's Treasure Isle like "On the Beach," "Tide Is High," "Only a Smile," "Happy Go Lucky Girl," and others, mostly collected on their first album *On the Beach.* The trio consisted of John Holt, Howard Barrett, and Tyrone Evans. Some early recordings for Studio One feature Bob Andy as well. U Roy rode the rhythms to fame a little later, and Blondie covered "Tide Is High" for a hit in the U.S. and U.K. They re-formed with Holt (for Mango and Bunny Lee) and without him (the CD *Heaven and Earth*); his solo career surpassed the well-named trio.

Pioneers

The Pioneers epitomize the innocence of the rock steady era with singles like "Dem a Laugh" for Joe Gibbs and a steady stream of Beverley's 45s such as "Mother Rittie" and "Samfie Man" for Leslie Kong. The amorphous lineup included George Agard (or Dekker, brother of singer Desmond), Sydney Crooks, and Jackie Robinson. Other early members are said to have included Dennis Walks and Glen Adams.

By the early seventies the Pioneers had relocated to England, where they recorded for Trojan. Their later sound is pop to the max, with covers of Elton John and Percy Sledge mixed with originals penned mainly by Agard. He and Robinson issued solo singles; Crooks went on to produce a number of other artists. The Trojan *Longshot Kick the Bucket* CD is representative: the early stuff is best.

Roots Radics

The Roots Radics began as the last of Jamaica's great studio bands, heir to the studio throne of the Aggrovators, whose early seventies "flying cymbal" sound led the rockers charge, and of the Revolutionaries, whose militant steppers style made the mid-seventies a golden age for reggae. The core pairing of Earl "Flabba" Holt on bass and Eric "Bingy Bunny" Lamont on guitar began with the Morwells. By the end of the seventies the lineup included Style Scott on drums and Dwight Pickney on lead guitar. They worked for Harry J, Joe Gibbs, and Gussie Clarke, eventually taking over as Channel One house band when Sly and Robbie toured with Peter Tosh and later Black Uhuru.

Besides studio work they were initially Bunny Wailer's backing band. Bunny wasn't touring in those days and they wound up touring and recording with Gregory Isaacs on some of his biggest hits and the most brilliant shows of his international career. By the early eighties the sound of reggae began to change again and Roots Radics had a lot to do with the changing style. They can be heard backing Yellowman, Eek-A-Mouse, Wailing Souls, Itals, Charlie Chaplin, Israel Vibration, and dozens of others.

But Roots Radics was more than just a backing band and eventually recorded on their own with Bingy Bunny singing lead. Several keyboard players have been active members of the band—Gladdy Anderson, and Steely (of Steely and Clevie) Johnson are featured on the early dub disc *Radical Dub Sessions* and Max Middleton on their early album *Freelance*. Earl Fitzsimmons toured with them on keyboards and is featured on *Hot We Hot* and *Forward Ever, Backward Never.* Richard "Tee Bird" Johnson took over on *World Peace Three* and subsequent tours and releases.

With the death of Bingy Bunny in 1994 the band added Steve Golding on rhythm guitar. Style Scott, who also drums for England's Dub Syndicate, was replaced by Carl Ayton for the 1996 release *Radically Yours,* on which everyone but Tee Bird contributes lead and backing vocals. Roots Radics continue to back other artists live and in the studio. They have played on so many records from the '70s through the '90s that it would be impossible to list them all. In a time when digitally programmed tracks have become predominant they remain a major link to the original roots reggae sound.

Junior Ross and the Spears

A handful of singles and an album for Tappa Zukie, all recorded in the mid-seventies, would indicate minor status if the songs themselves weren't major contributions—"Babylon a Fall," "Send Me Over There," "Judgment Time," and "Bow Down Babylon" are some of the dreadest tunes of their time. Sly and Robbie, "Chinna" Smith, and Augustus Pablo were aided and abetted by Deadly Headley Bennett and Vinnie Gordon, recorded at Channel One by Scientist, and mixed at King Tubby's by Jammy. The disc was reissued in 1992 (though only on vinyl) and remains a roots reggae classic.

Royals

The Royals' early Coxsone 7-inch "Pick Up the Pieces" is one of those Studio One gems it would be hard to imagine the world without. Roy Cousins took the group through several incarnations that included members of the Jayes and Heptones, with the best early work collected on an album of the same title that features a remake of the tune. Cousins is also a Jamaican producer of note whose U.K. Kingdom and Tamoki Wambesi imprints contain many fine releases, particularly anthologies and dub. *Nexus Dub,* issued in the mid-nineties, is a tour de force of Jamaican studios and engineers that samples the mixing talents of every major dub master from the late sixties through the late seventies.

Ruffy and Tuffy

Ruffy and Tuffy made their film debut in the movie *Rockers* at the age of eleven. Twin brothers Otis and Omar Newton appeared with Bob Marley and the Wailers at Reggae Sunsplash the following year. They recorded for Augustus Pablo in the late eighties, issuing singles the "Take One Step," "Harm No One," and "Danger Zone" on the Rockers label. "Message music we a deal with," says Ruffy, "no too much slackness." Their goal is to "Open the people them mind. Can't take the gang bang business, just strictly reality."

Their self-produced debut album, *Climax,* contains the single "If the Third World War Is a Must." Says Tuffy, "I and I want I and I black bredder dem to aware of what's going on in the world. That's why we really stress

world peace because that's the main cry for everyone right now. No one want to be a part of that bomb blasting. Just love and unity." Concerning their career he continues, "We don't voice out for too many producers—just ourselves and Augustus Pablo." Of their commitment to Rastafari he says, "I and I are not afraid of spreading Selassie-I message."

Silvertones

For Duke Reid they cut rock steady versions of American soul classics like "Midnight Hour" and "True Confession." For Coxsone they contributed the sublime early reggae "I Want to Be There" and "Burning in My Soul." Sonia Pottinger? The magnificent "Gun Fever." A fine album for Lee "Scratch" Perry included "Rejoice Jah Jah Children." "African Dub" on Black Eagle, "When Knotty Come" on Clocktower—surely the Silvertones were one of Jamaica's finest vocal groups who could turn in a great performance no matter who the producer.

Slickers

A group formed by Sydney Crook's brother Derrick, best known for a song written by Delroy Wilson's brother Trevor, "Johnny Too Bad." Other outstanding '70s singles include "Fussing and Fighting" issued on the U.K. Punch label in 1971, 1972's "9 Millie" on Tuna, "Man Beware" (Pressure Beat), "I A Dread" (Jupiter), 1975's "Dread Selassie" on Black Cat, and "St. Jago De La Vega" (Afrik, 1977). Ten years after "Johnny Too Bad" they recorded the album *Break Through* for Earl Chin and Tad Dawkins at Harry J (with Sylvan Morris) and Black Ark with Lee "Scratch" Perry.

Sly and Robbie

Though best known as producers and one of reggae's supreme backing bands, Sly and Robbie did release one album on which they are the featured vocalists, *Remember Precious Times.* The "riddim twins" played on a major portion of the greatest reggae of the seventies and eighties and didn't slack up in the '90s. They backed Peter Tosh, Black Uhuru, and many others live and on record. Their latest release, *Friends,* features Simply Red's Mick Hucknall covering Gregory Isaacs's "Night Nurse." A recent anthology, *La Trenggae,* explores Latin-Reggae fusion.

Soul Syndicate

Another great Jamaican studio group who went on to record several vocal albums, Soul Syndicate backed Philip Frazer, Earl Zero, Freddie McGregor, and others. They were also Big Youth's Ark Angels. Integral elements include guitarists Earl "Chinna" Smith, who later formed his own High Times label and band, and Tony Valentine Chin. Fully Fullwood and Santa Davis went on to back Peter Tosh and with Tony Chin beefed Big Mountain's rhythm section. Maxie Edwards drummed for them when they recorded for Epiphany and keyboards have been passed from "Touter" Harvey to Richard Johnson (now in the Roots Radics) and Keith Sterling, who's played for just about everyone. Recent live shows as the Fully Fullwood Band feature Jawge (of the Unknown Band) on keyboards.

Starlights

Proving the conscious/slack dichotomy didn't start with dancehall, Stanley Beckford's Starlights sang about love ("Hold My Hand,") sex (their calypso-tinged "Soldering"), and conscious themes ("Born Again Rasta," "Dip Them Jah Jah Dip Them") with equal fervor in the mid-seventies. The Heartbeat CD *Soldering* collects all these and more. The calypso connection permeates their sound: Beckford also fronted Stanley and the Turbines, whose '70s recordings in that style are collected on CDs from Jamaica Gold (*Big Bamboo,* 1992) and Esoldun (*Africa,* 1995).

Tamlins

Backstage with the Tamlins (courtesy of Al Campbell), who join voices in harmony beautifully, John Holt says, "That sounds great! Now put a lead on it." When he adds his voice it's magnificent and may also show why the Tamlins are often thought of as a backing group—for Peter Tosh's later albums and tours as well as many others in the studio—instead of the fine harmony trio they are. The original lineup of Junior Moore, Winston Morgan, and Carlton Smith cut "Sentimental Reason" as the Hamlins for Studio One. With Derrick Lara replacing Morgan they survive into the present. Their biggest hit to date was with a Randy Newman song, "Baltimore," for Sly and Robbie's Taxi label.

Techniques

The Techniques started in the late ska days and made rock steady hits for Duke Reid with Slim Smith, Winston Riley, Franklyn White, and Freddie Waite. At one time or another their lineup featured Pat Kelly, Bruce Ruffin, Jackie Parris, and Marvin Brooks, all of whom went on to solo careers. Others who passed through include Tyrone Evans (of the Paragons), Ernest Wilson (of the Clarendonians), Dave Barker (of Dave and Ansel Collins), and Lloyd Parks (who started with the Termites). Hits include "You Don't Care" (with Kelly on lead), "Little Did You Know" (with Slim Smith), and Curtis Mayfield's "Queen Majesty." Riley became a producer of note with his Techniques label and Waite fathered and formed the English group Musical Youth.

Tennors

One of the sweetest vocal groups to grace rock steady, the Tennors had a massive hit with much-versioned "Pressure and Slide" for Studio One and the popular "Ride Your Donkey," an independent release. Early members include Maurice Johnson, George "Clive Tennors" Murphy, and Milton Wilson. With Ronnie Davis singing lead they cut magnificent tunes like Festival Song "Hopeful Village" and a cover of Paul Simon's "Only Living Boy in New York," retitled "Weather Report," for Treasure Isle.

Singles issued on the U.K. Crab label included "Baff Boom." The 1970 reggae tune "My World," with its chorus "I'm living in a world I created for myself," summed up the sixties good and bad. Ronnie Davis went on to sing backup in the Itals and now fronts his own trio. In 1998 Nighthawk issued the Tennors only CD to date, the eighteen-track *Rock Steady Classics*.

Third World

Third World introduced a sophisticated mix of black American music with Jamaican reggae and found favor with a series of Island albums, including 1977's *96 Degrees in the Shade* and the following year's *Journey to Addis* featuring the hit "Now That We Found Love." A slick live act heavy on harmony and percussion made them crossover favorites. In the early eighties they scored again with "Try Jah Love" with Stevie Wonder.

Early core band members included Cat Coore and Ibo Cooper, originally members of Inner Circle, with Bunny Ruggs later taking the bulk of lead vocals. Percussionist Irwin "Carrot" Jarrett, bassists Richie Daley, vocalist Prilly Hamilton, and drummers Carl Barovier, Cornell Marshall, and Willie Stewart have all played in the band at various times.

Third World went on to record for CBS and Mercury/Polygram, eventually setting up their own Third World Productions. They have remained a popular draw headlining shows in the U.S. and recently celebrated twenty-five years in the business with a major retrospective. Bunny Ruggs released a solo album, *Talking to You* (Shanachie), in 1995, though he continued to sing lead for the band. Ibo and Willie departed in the late '90s. In late 1998 original member Cat Coore also left the band. The 1995 two-CD set *Reggae Ambassadors* provides an excellent selection drawn from their lengthy career.

Toots and the Maytals

If pure raw energy could be captured and encoded it wouldn't stand a chance against the early records of Toots and the Maytals. Frederick "Toots" Hibbert, Raleigh Gordon, and Jerry "Mathias" McCarthy sang with wild abandon, gospel fervor, and a deep-seated desire that turned despair into joy and wickedness into wisdom before your very ears. Beginning in 1962 they pounded out a stunning series of records at Studio One, singing live with the Skatalites backing, many collected on the recently reissued *Never Grow Old*.

The trio next worked for Prince Buster with whom they cut one of the most manic records ever made, "Dog War" aka "Broadway Jungle." They won Jamaica's Festival Song Contest in 1966 with "Bam Bam," produced by Byron Lee; in 1969 with "Sweet and Dandy," produced by Leslie Kong; and in 1972 with "Pomp and Pride," produced by Warwick Lyn. Albums produced by Kong, including *From the Roots*, contain some of their finest work. Other early hits include the punk anthem "Monkey Man," "Do the Reggay" (the first song to use the word), and "54-46 That's My Number," about Toots's stay in prison on a Ganja bust.

Signed to Island Records, the Maytals (as their early records tagged them) became one of the first international reggae groups with albums like *Funky Kingston* and *Reggae Got Soul* that featured Hibbert's soulful vocals and an unbeatable lineup of players, including Jackie Jackson on bass, Hux Brown on guitar, and Winston Wright on organ. They opened for rock acts like the Rolling Stones and played ice skating rinks and clubs across Europe and America, breaking ground and sowing seeds the reggae world still reaps today.

In the late seventies Toots's voice got even warmer and more mellow and on albums *Just Like That* and 1981's *Knock Out* it displays a richness easily comparable to the great American soul singers. A songwriter of great depth—scan 1971's "One Eyed Enos," 1974's "Screwface Underground," or 1981's "Careless Ethiopians"—Toots Hibbert is a musical icon and Jamaican national treasure. Though he continued to tour, first with Raleigh alone on harmonies and then with female backup singers, Hibbert released only one more studio album in the eighties, 1988's *Toots in Memphis*.

Island's superb two-CD set *Time Tough* draws from the entire career of Toots and the Maytals and gathers works from many labels, producers, and time periods. It is an excellent introduction and reminder of the trio's place in a music they helped to create. Hibbert's first new disc in a decade, *Recoup* (Artists Only), includes a cover of Leon Russell's "Back to the Island," a leisurely stroll through early hits, .some soca, and a few cuts featuring the original trio. He returned with *Ska Father* for the same label in 1998, reprising early hits, adding new work (like the engaging "Do You Believe," and offering a cover of the Kinks' "You Really Got Me." His rich and mellow voice is one of Jamaica's finest.

Twinkle Brothers

The Twinkle Brothers recorded for Leslie Kong, Duke Reid, Phil Pratt, and Bunny Lee and worked the North Coast hotel circuit. In 1975 they released their first album, *Rasta Pon Top*. The band consisted of lead singer Norman Grant (who started out playing drums and then switched to guitar), Ralston on guitar and vocals, Derrick Brown on bass and vocals, and percussionist Karl Hyatt with Eric "Zacky" Bernard on keyboards and Bongo Asher on congas. *Do Your Own Thing* (1977, Carib Gems) included the classic "Jah Army."

Signed to Virgin Records they released *Praise Jah* with Ralston's "Jahoviah" and "Keep on Trying." *Love* of 1979 (also a 10-inch LP—those were the days) included "Watch the Hypocrites" and 1980's *Countryman* contained the anthem "Since I Threw the Comb Away" and the rousing "Never Get Burn." The group toured and live shows were genuine events. At the beginning of the eighties Norman Grant moved to England and set up the Twinkle label, issuing new albums by the band, which often consisted of Norman and musicians like Black Steel or producer Jah Shaka.

Ralston relocated to Northern California, where he is involved touring and recording with his wife, Della. He still contributes tracks to Twinkle Brother projects and the brothers toured together with Della Grant in the midnineties. The Twinkle label now has over fifty releases, including *Don't Forget Africa, Babylon Rise Again, Equality and Justice,* and *New Songs for Jah*. Most are available on CD. Norman has also produced records for a bevy of "Twinkle" artists, including Phillip Parkinson and E.T. Webster, that share the clean, crisp sound and forward-looking lyrics of the Twinkle Brothers own work.

Uniques

After the death of Slim Smith a good deal of the material he recorded with the Uniques was released under his name, clouding an already confusing issue. The practice of artists, backing bands, and groups recording for different producers under different names has at times made several groups seem like one and at others one like several. The Uniques first recorded in the ska era with a most unusual lineup that included Smith and Franklyn White, both members of the Techniques, and Roy Shirley, a vocalist so distinctive it's hard to imagine him in a harmony group.

That version of the group didn't last long. Even though the Techniques successfully made the transition from ska to rock steady and Smith, like Shirley, made it as a solo artist, he reformed the group in 1967 with Jimmy Riley and Lloyd Charmers, who had success with his group the Charmers, as a solo artist singing mainly romantic ballads and later in his career with a slack group (Lloydie and the Lowbites), and as a significant producer of Ken Boothe and others. This lineup proved viable and was responsible for most of the well-known Uniques hits.

Though Smith's magnificent voice and spirited delivery fronted the trio, their secret weapon was Jimmy Riley, who penned many of the classic tunes like "My Woman's Love" and "Love and Devotion." Their biggest hits were "My Conversation," a riddim still being versioned, and a cover of the Buffalo Springfield's "For What It's Worth," retitled "Watch This Sound." Many of these were done for Bunny Lee and are now available on a new collection from Pressure Sounds. Long after the group separated, and after Smith's death, Jimmy Riley and Cornell Campbell recorded an album's worth of material for Joe Gibbs as the Uniques, continuing the cycle for another spin. Recent 7-inch singles present a version of the group featuring Jimmy Riley, Cornell Campbell, and Al Campbell.

Upsetters

If the foundation of reggae is bass and drum it could easily be argued that brothers Aston and Carlton Barrett laid the cornerstone. They were Max Romeo's bass player and drummer in a band called the Hippy Boys, which also featured Leroy Brown on lead vocals at one time (he and Max Romeo both also sang in the Emotions). The Hippy Boys practiced in Robbie Shakespeare's room when he was growing up (his brother was a member of the band at the time). When they recorded for the Upsetter (Lee Perry) they naturally became the Upsetters, which they remained (with the inevitable changes in lineup) until, as the backup band for Bob Marley and the Wailers, they became the Wailers Band.

You could probably call any seventies Lee Perry album an Upsetters album, and the same goes for many Perry-produced anthologies. I have included in the discography only those albums that are mainly instrumental and feature the group not as a backing band but as a playing unit. Interestingly this includes one album not produced by Perry (*Good Bad and the Upsetters*) and one that contains some of his productions but is really a Glen Brown and the Upsetters album (*Upsetters A Go Go*). For a more complete listing check the Lee "Scratch" Perry entry in the Billboard Books *Encyclopedia of Top Producers*.

Viceroys

Like many Jamaican vocal trios the Viceroys had a fluctuating lineup even on their late sixties Studio One recordings on which they were first called the Voice Roys. On single they were produced at various times by Lloyd "Matador" Daley, Lee "Scratch" Perry (the rollicking "Take Your Hand from Me Neck"), Derrick Morgan, Sidney Crooks, and Sly and Robbie, among others. In the '70s they also recorded under the name the Interns, waxing the classic "Nothing Is Impossible" for Winston Riley and the album *Detour* with Phil Pratt, also released under the titles *Do We Have to Fight* and *Consider Yourself*.

The early eighties saw two albums produced by Linval Thompson, *We Must Unite* and *Brethren and Sistren,* and a return to Riley for the 1984 album *Chancery Lane.* Members at various times included Wesley Tinglin, who sang lead and wrote most of the group's material, Neville Ingram, Linval Williams, Daniel Bernard, and two singers who went on to solo careers, Norris Reid and his later replacement Chris Wayne. In 1995 Heartbeat released a seventeen-track CD of their recordings for Coxsone titled *Ya Ho.*

Well Pleased and Satisfied

The distinctive lead vocals of Ephraim "Jerry" Baxter joined on harmony by David Paul Johnson and Hugh Lewis made for one of the late seventies finest vocal trios. Their songs were strictly Jamaican with themes like "Pickney a Have Pickney," "Fast Mouth One," "Barberman Bawling," and the stirring "Sweetie Come from America." They issued two self-produced albums on the Burning Sounds label in England. After their breakup Baxter released two ten-inch singles on the Ball of Fire label.

CHAPTER 40

DJs of the Seventies

(And a Few Outside)

The DJ (or deejay style) is only tangentially related to what we call DJs (or "disc jockeys") in America, who are generally regarded as "selectors" in Jamaica. But the early Jamaican DJs, birthed in the dancehall long before there was a separate style that took that name, did begin by imitating American radio record spinners' "jive talk" and that influence can be heard in the early word-slinging of King Stitt, Charlie Ace, U Roy, (the Jamaican) Jerry Lewis, and others. Other forerunners—including country and western "talking blues" and jazz innovators like Fats Waller, whose covers of standards often included his own amused commentary—slipped into the musical spaces between the melody as written.

The Jamaican DJ began as a sound system phenomenon, a man on a microphone haranguing the crowd over a popular record, creating excitement and drawing people to the dance. Early innovators include Count Machuki, Prince Pompadou, and others who didn't record, recorded very little, or recorded only in their later years. It was U Roy who woke the town to tell the people about DJ. After the success of U Roy came a first wave of DJs that included I Roy, Big Youth, Dennis Alcapone, and others. By the mid-seventies a whole new set of names were invoking the dancers and cutting records released in Jamaica and the U.K. The DJs stole the day as the eighties "dancehall" era took over the charts, and a new generation of DJs ply their trade today, influenced by hip-hop and rap, itself an outgrowth of the original Jamaican DJ style.

This section briefly summarizes the careers of some of the pioneers whose work inspired rap and dancehall DJs (who are covered more briefly in Chapter 23, "Wicked Inna Dance: The Dancehall Invasion," since there are so many more of them). I have included some later DJs, mainly those who extend the cultural themes of the seventies even when working in a modern style. Like the sections on singers and vocal groups, this is in no way intended to represent a complete or even comprehensive treatment.

The early DJs innovated over rhythms that were strikingly original and often created a body of work much more enduring than some of today's flash artists who record over digital rhythms that lack the integrity of the so-called "golden age" of the seventies. Some of these originators are in danger of being passed by in the tide of new releases from younger and often less talented chatters. Lest we forget, here are some of the DJs who first sketched out the style.

Charlie Ace

Known for his colorful "Swing-A-Ling" sound system truck from which he played and sold records in the ghetto of Kingston, Charlie Ace was one of the earliest DJs on record. Conscious themes predominate his work, with high points like "Father and Dreadlocks" for Studio One over the Larry Marshall "Throw Me Corn" riddim. Most of his records are from the very early seventies on Giant, GG's, Scorpio, High Note, and of course his own Swing-A-Ling label. There is at present no album or CD of his work available.

Dennis Alcapone

When U Roy hit big with a series of Treasure Isle singles, Dennis "Alcapone" Smith (sometimes billed as just Al Capone) wasn't far behind. Tagged the "young" U Roy, he came with a series of singles for Coxsone gathered on his crucial Studio One LP and followed up with the likes "My Voice Is Insured for Half a Million Dollars" for Duke Reid. When he moved to England he took on a second career as Jamaica's DJ ambassador, recording a huge body of work in the U.K. and keeping his name alive there long after other early DJs faded from the scene. In 1992 he issued a new album produced by the king of the second wind, Bunny Lee.

Dr. Alimantado

Emerging in the mid-seventies with a series of singles that included "Can't Conquer Natty Dreadlocks" and "I Killed the Barber," the outrageous Winston "Dr. Alimantado" Thompson came like a wild man with a dazzling sense of humor. Although his "Gimme Mi Gun" could have been an NRA theme song, it was a finely reasoned argument that benefited from the use of the backing track to Gregory Isaac's "Thief a Man." After recording "Born for a Purpose" he was run down by a bus, recovering to cut

"Still Alive" over the same rhythm. He recorded for Lee "Scratch" Perry (including the boastful "Best Dressed Chicken in Town") and others before relocating to England for a series of self-produced albums and dub releases.

Big Joe

Though somewhat overlooked today, Big Joe had some crucial 7-inch releases in Jamaica in the early seventies, like "Jah Jah Help Us" on Winro, a string of mid-seventies blasts such as "Show Them Love" on Mummy and "Set Your Face at Ease" on Mudie's (for whom he cut several great singles), and some great late seventies releases on Gorgon, Burning Sounds, and others. He also issued at least one album, *Keep Rocking and Swinging* for Bunny Lee, though it is now long out of print.

Big Youth

Beginning in the early seventies Manley Buchanan—Big Youth—brought a sense of joy and wisdom to the DJ fraternity. His infectious voice and cultural perspective brightened a scene that might otherwise have taken itself too seriously, and the quality of his work, much of it released originally on 7-inch singles on his own Negusa Nagast label, set high standards for his contemporaries and those who followed. A few highlights include "I Pray Thee," "Hell Is for Heroes," "Political Confusion," and "Pope Paul Feel It." He issued albums on Trojan and Front Line throughout the seventies and Heartbeat in the eighties. On many of his later albums he sings in addition to DJing. His most recent release, produced by Junior Reid, finds him still exploring cultural themes.

Brigadier Jerry

Though he rose to prominence in the early eighties, Brigadier Jerry, like DJ Charlie Chaplin, got his start on U Roy's Stur-gav Sound System and kept to the high ground while other DJs of his era gathered in shallow pools. His recordings, like the outstanding "Jah D." for Tappa Zukie, are characterized by innovation, imagination, and cultural integrity. Inspired by the best of the seventies he has himself provided inspiration for the likes of Sisters Carol and Nancy (the latter really is his sister).

Charlie Chaplin

Longtime chatter for U Roy's Stur-gav Hi-Fi, Chaplin began making records in the late eighties and went on to record a string of RAS releases backed by Roots Radics. His output is characterized by conscious lyrics and fluid melody lines. He has worked with a variety of producers, including Roy Cousins, Prince Jammy, and Phillip Burrell, and in combination with singers as diverse as Andrew Tosh and Cocoa Tea. Recommended releases include *Take Two* and *Too Hot to Handle*.

Dillinger

Lester "Dillinger" Bullock was in the right place at the right time—as a '70s sound system DJ just when they became as hot in the studio as the dance, he had the chance to record for Coxsone Dodd, Jo Jo Hookim, and other great producers. Hit singles led to international record contracts and two albums with Mango. His excesses were also the excesses of his time: the regrettable hit "Cocaine in My Brain" smacks of the seventies. He did some excellent later tracks like the follow-up "Marijuana in My Brain" and the over-the-top "Fernando Sancho" from *Hard Core Dillinger*. As with other artists of his era, many of his best singles remain uncollected: there is no one truly representative CD.

Clint Eastwood

Robert "Clint Eastwood" Brammer came along a little later—you can probably tell by the fact that he took a cowboy actor's name instead of a gangster's. He straddled the late seventies roots vibe and early eighties slackness with cuts like "Whip Them Jah" on Belmont and the later "Sex Education." He was one of the first DJs to pair up, in his case with General Saint. DJ duets were a natural since the next man could always jump in when the first ran out of ideas or breath. Eastwood and Saint had a minor hit with a DJ cover of Queen's "Another One Bites the Dust."

I Roy

If he were starting out today Roy "I Roy" Reid would probably be called a sing-jay: his bouncy '80s recordings little resemble '90s dancehall. I Roy was in fact a ruling sound system DJ with sets including King Tubby's, and his "uptown" delivery made for some big early seventies records that led to numerous albums released in the U.K. His name was derived from the great U Roy, but like contemporary Big Youth he developed a style of his own.

The talking style was so hot there was room for plenty more, including contemporaries like Trinity and Dillinger with more of a "ghetto vibe." A legendary 45 clash between I Roy and Prince Jazzbo sparked singles like "Straight to Jazzbo's Head" on Bar Bell and "Jazzbo Ha Fe Run" for Lee Perry's Black Ark label. Gussie Clarke, Alvin Ranglin, Bunny Lee, and Harry J all produced quality records for the gruff but melodic DJ. Most of his later discs (including many for Virgin) were self-produced. I Roy displayed versatility—compare 1973's "Space Flight" on Attack with the following year's "Orthodox Rock." It allowed him to cop enough styles into his mix to keep it going with consistent releases throughout his career, and he has continued to record and issue sporadic new works.

In the late eighties he and former rival Jazzbo buried their musical hatchet and united for a CD. I Roy has many great uncollected seventies cuts with producers Joe Gibbs, Harry Mudie, and Channel One. A 1997 CD selection from the British Blood and Fire label and a 1991 Virgin sampler between them represent both his roots and rockers sides.

Jah Lloyd/Jah Lion

Patrick Francis started out singing with the Mediators and made solo records before settling into his DJ career as Jah Lloyd, occasionally Jah Ali, Prince Francis, and (when recording for producer Lee "Scratch" Perry) Jah Lion. *Columbia Collie* and *The Humble Lion* are two of the outstanding DJ albums of the '70s. He produced records for the Mighty Diamonds, Heptones, and others, as well as top-flight dub, but he will mainly be known for cuts like "Soldier and Police War" over Junior Murvin's "Police and Thieves."

Jah Stitch

Mid-seventies sound system DJ Melborne "Jah Stitch" James waxed some outstanding 7-inch singles like "Natty Dread in Demand" and "Berry the Barber," mainly for Bunny Lee, backed by the Aggrovators, who he introduces player by player on the lively "Aggrovators Knock Them Out" from 1977. Though he issued three albums in England he will be known here mainly for the standard-setting *Original Raggamuffin* compilation. It includes some of his finest raw performances, such as the autobiographical "No Dread Can't Dead" and the celebratory "Give Jah the Glory."

Jah Thomas

Nkrumah Jah Thomas had hits with Channel One in the mid-seventies, including "Dress with Split," and a big-selling U.K. single and album on Greensleeves in '78, *Stop Your Loafin',* but came into his own with early '80s productions of himself and others such as Tristan Palma and Anthony Johnson on his Midnight Rock label (named after his first hit for GG's Alvin Ranglin). His DJ style is bright and bouncy, with serious songs like "Black Starliner" outnumbered by lighter material such as "Joker Smoker." He was generally backed by the Roots Radics. In recent years he has consolidated early productions and issued fine dub CDs.

Jah Woosh

As early as 1973's "Cripple Skank," Neville "Jah Woosh" Beckford was mashing up the dance and hits included "Shine Eye Gal" from 1975, "Set Up Yourself Dread" from '76 and 1978's "Marcus Say." Two excellent Trojan albums, *Dreadlocks Affair* and *Religious Dread,* were self-produced, as were most of his later works, though he also recorded for Creation Rebel and Dennis "Mixman" Bedeau in the U.K. "Omega Dollar," which kicks off his first Trojan LP (on which he is backed by the Mighty Cloud Band), is one of the all-time great DJ diatribes. Honorable mention goes to *Marijuana World Tour,* on the back of which he thanks Doctor Pablo for "six ounces of Jamaican Collie consumed during the recording."

King Stitt

A Coxsone sound system DJ of the first rank, King Stitt, also known as "The Ugly One," did not have a successful recording career for Dodd, though he worked for him for decades. His great records were done for Clancy Eccles and include "Dance Beat," a glorious history of the early sound system days; "Fire Corner," which documents rivalry among producers; and "Vigorton Two," which celebrates a health tonic and takes a jab at Coxsone at the same time. His "Herbman Shuffle" is one of the great marijuana anthems.

Lone Ranger

Anthony "Lone Ranger" Waldron cut his teeth on some of the sturdiest of Studio One riddims, presented in a showcase style as *On the Other Side of Dub.* Whether serious ("Noah in the Ark") or tongue in cheek ("Apprentice Dentist") he's always in high gear. Another album for Coxsone was engineered and mixed by Dodd himself. Only in Jamaica could a guy called Lone Ranger issue a single called "Frankenstine" on the Spider Man label and have a big hit with "Barnabas Collins" (an ode to the *Dark Shadows* vampire). *M16* is critical Channel One. He returned in 1994 with the 7-inch "Badd Badd Boy" on Dynamic.

Prince Far I

He was born Michael James Williams and first recorded as King Cry Cry, but the world came to know him as Prince Far I. Gravel hardly describes his deep, haggard "voice of thunder," so rich in texture it continues to be sampled and pressed back into service years after he was murdered in a home-invasion robbery. Early on he recorded for Bunny Lee, Coxsone, and Enos McLeod, who gave him the name Prince Far I. His debut LP, *Psalms of Dub,* produced by Lloydie Slim, is perhaps the best musical interpretation of Bible verses ever recorded.

His next album, *Under Heavy Manners* for producer Joe Gibbs, remains one of reggae's enduring DJ classics, his sense of humor never so apparent as on the classic boxing match "Big Fight," which pits Babylon against dreadlocks. Babylon doesn't stand a chance. His version of "Deck of Cards" surpasses those of cowboy Tex Ritter and DJ and game show host Wink Martindale.

Prince Far I developed a worldwide following—you might even say cult—and issued many albums in the U.K. on the Virgin and Trojan labels. Experimental without ever losing his roots (something many have tried and failed at), he produced most of his own records as well as an excellent album for Reggae George.

Roy Cousins and Adrian Sherwood produced him as well, and Dub Syndicate and others have utilized existing vocals to build new songs.

Prince Hammer

Though not as prolific as Princes Far I or Jazzbo, Prince Hammer (Beres Simpson) had a series of late '70s singles, including "Orthodox Rock" for Crazy Joe and "Never See Come See" on I.S.D.A., as well as 45s on Soul Beat, Belva, and Gold Cup. *Bible* (1978) was filled with Rasta imagery and impeccable timing. Produced by Blacka Morwell it featured liner notes by Linton Kwesi Johnson. Simpson went on to produce others, including Rod Taylor. On the Roy Cousins-produced CD *Respect I Man,* recorded in 1989, and later Sonic Sounds 7-inch "Jah Rastafari," Prince Hammer still packs a wallop.

Prince Jazzbo

A series of Bongo Man singles (an early Coxsone imprint) clued collectors to Prince Jazzbo (Linval Carter), "Crabwalking" over Horace Andy's Skylarking chief among them. In 1990 Studio One swung the vault door open with *Choice of Version* containing "Imperial I" and "Jah Dread." The mid-seventies "Bag a Wolf," "Youth in Service" and "Freedom" all appeared on 7-inch on English labels.

Like many other Jamaican artists his best album was done with Lee Perry. *Natty Pass Through Rome,* as it was titled in England (*Ital Corner* on the U.S. Clocktower label), is essential. By the third song, "Prophet Live," you are caught and held while the dub that follows pummels you mercilessly. This is a hard, hard record.

So was the self-produced *Kick Boy Face,* containing the burning "Church Is a Rome," "Straight to I Roy's Head," and "Every Nigga Is a Winner." Jazzbo is one of the outstanding "classic" DJs who wisely turned his talent and earnings back into the music industry, setting up his own Ujama label, releasing his own productions and later works like "Naw Flex Right," his answer to Cobra's smash "Flex."

A 1989 album with I Roy recalled their dueling singles feud from the '70s and contributed "Live Together," whereby the two old word warriors make peace. In the early '90s *Wise Shepherd* reprised some early hits and offered up some new material. An odd 1982 Coxsone album called *Battle of the DJs Dance Hall Style* contains an incredible "live" Jazzbo toast over a Burning Spear dub plate (the same track the original single was cut over).

Ranking Joe

The late seventies saw a whole new batch of DJs who came slightly after the wave that included Big Youth, I Roy, and Alcapone but preceded what we think of as the "dancehall" era. Joseph "Ranking Joe" Jackson recorded for Tony Robinson at Harry J's and Errol Thompson at Joe Gibbs after working his way up through the sound systems (originally as Little Joe to distinguish himself from the DJ Big Joe), including El Paso and Stur-gav. Hit singles include "A You Mr. Fennigan" and a blistering "Weak Heart Fade Away" over Jr. Byles's "Fade Away." "Tribute to John Lennon," recorded after that singer's murder, is one of the more amazing such records ever made. Ranking Joe still tours and put out a new single with another early DJ, Scotty, on his own label in the early '90s.

Ranking Trevor

For many, 1978 was a ranking year, with records from Ranking Rueben, Ranking Superstar, Ranking Toyan (later trimmed to Toyan), Ranking Fish Eye, Ranking Magnum, and Ranking Starcky. Even established singer Devon Russell became Ranking Devon for a while in the late '70s. Ranking Trevor rose above the pack with numerous singles on Channel One and its subsidiaries Well Charge and Hit Bound, some collected on the album *In Fine Style.* Though it's not on the album "Three Piece Chicken and Chips" was probably the best. He also did a churning chat over Yabby You's "Jah Vengeance" and later recorded for Gussie, Morwell Esq., and (with Nickademous) Papa Roots.

Scotty

I defy any dancehall DJ to be as wild as Scotty, who dressed for stage shows as a schoolboy complete with lunch box and knee socks. David Scott sang with the Federals and the Chosen Few but will be best remembered for "Draw Your Brakes," found on the soundtrack to *The Harder They Come,* and "Skank in Bed," an answer record to Lorna Bennett's "Breakfast in Bed." The latter is right up there with Ike and Tina Turner's "I Think It's Gonna Work Out Fine" and Bo Diddley and his maraca-man Jerome Green's "Say Man" as one of the greatest musical comedy duets of all time.

His only album, *Schooldays,* which contains the bulk of his singles for Derrick Harriot, originally issued on Crystal (and some on Songbird in the U.K.), was reissued in the late '80s as *Unbelievable* with the addition of five vital tracks including the brain-numbing "Monkey Drop." A pared-down version appeared in JA as *Draw Your Brakes: The Best Of.* But happily it isn't, as Scotty returned to recording in the late eighties and has issued more than an album's worth of uncollected great new material on a variety of labels since.

Shorty The President

Of his two albums for Bunny Lee and a dozen singles for Joe Gibbs and others, mostly cut in the early to mid-seventies heyday of DJ, his best record still remains "The President a Mash up the Resident," over the rhythm track to the Uniques' "My Conversation." Turning a seventies DJ loose on a sixties rock steady rhythm was a

formula for success that worked for U Roy and Scotty—interestingly, '90s DJ Shaggy tearing loose on "Oh Carolina" had similar results.

Sir Lord Comic

One of the earliest and certainly one of the most innovative DJs, Sir Lord Comic plied his trade in the days of ska and rock steady with such ground-breaking work as "Ska-ing West" and "The Great Wuga-Wuga." Though there are no Sir Lord Comic albums or CDs, his work can be found scattered on anthologies of early Jamaican music (such as the boxed set *Trojan Story*); if humor, timing, and taste are among your DJ requirements, they're worth searching out.

Trinity

Know today as singer Junior Brammer, Trinity made his name as a DJ in the late seventies, first voicing rhythms for the Hookim brothers at Channel One. The smash "Three Piece Suit" for Joe Gibbs and singles like "No Makeup in Zion" for Vivian Jackson followed. He recorded for a variety of producers, including Gussie Clarke and Donovan Germain as early in their careers as his, with albums for Linval Thompson and many others including the excellent LP *Trinity Meet the Mighty Diamonds* issued on Gorgon.

Every complaint you hear about dancehall DJs today—the shift away from conscious lyrics, questionable talent, and potential inability to endure—was said of Trinity and Dillinger when their generation began to imitate U Roy and Big Youth. His response was the Mummy 7-inch "No Like It, Bite It." A kind of walking newspaper, Trinity's lyrics commented on the events of his day on singles like "Shaolin Temple," based on the popular *Kung Fu* TV show; "Jamaican Dollar," "Eventide Home," about the fire that also inspired Yellowman's first hit; and "Miss Lou Rock" dedicated to the woman—Louise Bennett—who made patois palatable.

U Brown

A top-ranking sound system DJ who began recording in the mid-seventies, Huford Brown (U Brown) cut his first album, *Satta Dread,* for Bunny "Striker" Lee. Though neither his name nor his picture was prominently featured on the disc, it was issued in England on the Klik label and led to two late seventies albums on the Virgin label, *Mr. Brown Something* and *You Can't Keep a Good Man Down,* which contained the hit "Weather Balloon."

By 1979's *Repatriation,* Brown took over production duties and went on to produce himself and others, issuing records in Jamaica on his own Hit Sound label and internationally on a variety of labels throughout the eighties. Though he clearly owes a debt to U Roy for his name and style, U Brown has managed to survive, riding an ever-changing array of rhythms. An excellent compilation appeared in 1997 on Blood and Fire titled *Train to Zion.*

U Roy

Before Big Youth, before Scotty, before Alcapone, there was U Roy. Before I Roy, Dillinger, Trinity, Ranking Joe, long before Yellowman, Charlie Chaplin, or Lieutenant Stitchie, U Roy reigned supreme. If not the first Jamaican DJ on record, he was and still is the best. His expert timing, classy lyrics, one-in-a-million voice, and musical foresight put him in a category all his own, often imitated but never duplicated.

When he connected with Duke Reid in the early days of King Tubby's studio, a legend was born. On disc after disc he kept the legend alive through the years as reggae and the DJ style he helped originate grew and changed. With a continuous output from 1970 to the present, he has revived the interest of one-time fans and introduced new young audiences to his always unique sound.

With U Roy the DJ style was never a gimmick but a natural extension of the music. The same voice that cut through a classic Paragons or Diamonds track can soar through relatively new tunes from Horace Ferguson's "Great Stone" to Mad Professor productions. U Roy could always deconstruct an old standard to create a new one. The magnificent voice that called dancers over dub plates to a sound-system truck many years ago still pulls crowds from their tables and onto the dance floor with seeming effortlessness today.

Taking on the singers with friendly jibes and stingers, he parodied and defied the accepted rules of music, answering back the coy lyrics of his day while leaving enough bare dub showing through to spin the brain at greater than 45 rpm. And a consciousness permeated his work that put him above those who jumped on the DJ phenomenon as his records rose on the charts. And it was all in fun—everybody loved U Roy.

He delivered like a great comedian who doesn't have to lower himself or his audience to make his point. And like Brother Dave Gardner, the all-but-forgotten Southern comedian of the late '50s and early '60s, there was a serious thought behind each humorous remark. The tracks he chose to work with didn't hurt. He covered nearly every song on the Paragons' *On the Beach* LP for Duke Reid, giving rock steady a second life, and he deejayed over early reggae classics by the Diamonds, Gladiators, John Holt, Johnny Clarke, Horace Andy, and others. U Roy mined the early gold of reggae's greats and added his own sparkle to the shine.

Born Ewart Beckford and named U Roy by a cousin who had trouble pronouncing his first name, U Roy at one point held chart positions one, two, and three at the same time on the Jamaican hit parade. Much of his work was ground-breaking: check the early multilayered overdubs on the Lee Perry-produced "Earthquake" (from the *Trojan Story, Volume 2*). Possessing one of the most distinctive voices that ever recorded, his early records defined the upward limits of the DJ style. Those who came after him have yet to top those limits.

His first single, "Rightous Ruler," featured a talking introduction from Peter Tosh and was recorded in a different style than the U Roy we know today. John Holt tells the story of hearing him chat over a Paragons track at a sound system and bringing him to Treasure Isle. The confluence of Duke Reid, King Tubby, and U Roy broke the new style wide open. We're still feeling the ramifications today.

After his early work with Duke Reid (gathered on the albums *U Roy* and *Version Galore*),

he cut a series of discs for Tony Robinson issued on Virgin Records in the late seventies. *Dread in a Babylon, Natty Rebel, Rasta Ambassador,* and *Jah Son of Africa* are all classics. He continued to make excellent records throughout the eighties, including *Line Up and Come, Music Addict,* and *The Originator*. He worked with Bunny Lee, King Attarney (with whom he cut an album over classic Mighty Diamonds rhythms), Prince Jazzbo, and others.

In the late eighties and nineties U Roy hooked up with Neil "Mad Professor" Frazier for a series of albums that didn't just recall his early greatness but expanded on his repertoire

U ROY. Photograph by John Skomdahl

and abilities. *True Born African, Smile a While,* and *Babylon Kingdom Must Fall* are among the finest DJ records done anywhere at any time. "Working with Professor is like workin' with Duke Reid," says U Roy. "Duke Reid is a man who know what he want and when Duke tell you seh okay, this all right, then that all right— you don't have to worry, that all right. Professor have the same kind of vibes—good vibes."

For those considering a career as a DJ, U Roy offers a tip on timing, advising you not to "clash" with the vocal you chat over: "It's best you say something before him or immediately after him, but don't come in the same time," he advises. "Whatever you do, just do it in time." For a surprising number of people it was U Roy, not Bob Marley or Jimmy Cliff, who convinced them that reggae was worth checking out. His music will be around as long as reggae is played.

Josey Wales

The era (early eighties) and producer (Junjo Lawes) of his first single, "Baby Come Home (With Joseph)," flag Joseph "Josey Wales" Sterling as a dancehall DJ, but his style and cultural focus make him one of the last of the classics. In the late eighties when lyrics reached an all-time low, he came with cuts like "Culture a Lick" and "Slackness Done," spearheading the eventual return to conscious considerations. "Respect the Woman" (1993) is, along with Cocoa Tea's "Good Life," one of the few outstanding defenses of the feminine gender in dancehall.

In the early '90s Josey Wales was shot twice in the back in a barroom holdup. The tale he lived to tell, "Bush Wacked," is an odd combination of country western and dancehall in which he relates the story of the robbery with beautiful vignettes like "When I woke up in the hospital/Luciano was at my bedside playing his guitar." It was a hit in Jamaica in 1997. That this would happen to an artist who took his stage name from a Clint Eastwood cowboy flick and whose biggest-selling album was called *The Outlaw* is kind of spooky.

Tappa Zukie

Like the dancehall music of the early eighties, the DJ style of the early seventies grew out of the sound systems that had been running in Jamaica since the forties. David "Tappa Zukie" (originally "Tapper Zukie") Sinclair was one of the first-wave DJs inspired by U Roy. He cut his debut single—"Jump and Twist," released on the Ethnic label—as King Tapper in England. While there he recorded the material eventually released on his first album, *Man Ah Warrior,* which included the classic "Message to Pork Eaters" and the incredibly bizarre "Archie, the Rednose Reindeer."

One of his earliest Jamaican singles was "Father, Father," issued on the Ivanhoe label. A mid-seventies string of 45s like "Quarter Pound of Ichens," "Pontious Pilot," and "Natty Dread Don't Cry" and the legendary album *M.P.L.A.* put him in the first rank of Jamaica DJs and cemented his international following. He went on to become a major producer of hits for Horace Andy, Prince Alla, Knowledge, and Junior Ross and the Spear, issuing records on his own Stars, New Stars, and Tappa labels. His hit single "Oh Lord" became an early dancehall rallying cry.

As Tapper Zukie he released a series of late seventies albums, including *Tapper Roots* and *Peace in the Ghetto* on Virgin, but his relationship with the label deteriorated to such a degree that none of them is presently available. Today Tappa Zukie is one of JA's best-known producers, scoring hits again and again, often with roots artists neglected by others. He voiced a number of excellent singles in the '90s, including "Stout Heart" and "Rastaman Camp," and had a major retrospective and new CD released by RAS records.

Selected Discography

These listings include only a fraction of the incredible amount and variety of music recorded and released from Jamaica, much less internationally. To this date more records come out of Jamaica weekly than from anywhere else in the world. And this has been going on for four decades! A recent flood of vinyl reissues, compilations, and previously unreleased material indicates the golden age of reggae releases is in the present, not the past.

An asterisk indicates that the recording is available on CD (compact disc) format. The lack of an asterisk should not be construed to indicate that it isn't on CD, only that I haven't actually seen it in that format. Two asterisks indicate a recommended or representative selection on CD. A plus sign indicates a recommended selection that is not yet—to my knowledge—available on CD. Because CD reissues come out at an astonishing rate, hopefully the bulk of records listed will eventually be issued in that format.

This selected discography does not include 7-inch Jamaican singles, which are really the heart of any reggae collection since they include unreleased cuts, B-side dub mixes, and otherwise unavailable material, generally with a heavier bass sound than the later album and CD versions. They have also reached the point of collectibility as to be price-prohibitive to the average music lover and would require a separate book to detail the intricacies of their issue points, time periods, release dates, label copy, and matrix detail. Twelve-inch "disco-mix" singles are also not included.

Most Jamaican records don't include dates. I have included them when present and indicated eras (for example, "mid-1970s") when internal clues allow certainty. Where more than one label or date are present, the later entry represents a reissue; sometimes a reissue is indicated when the original label information is not available, to avoid confusing the release date with that of the original recording (when known). For the same reason I have tried wherever possible to indicate the era in which something was recorded when it differs radically from the release date. Thus a date in parentheses followed by an era (such as "(1997), 1970s" indicates seventies recordings issued in 1997.

ABYSSINIANS

Arise (Virgin, 1978; 1990**)

Forward on to Zion (Clinch, circa 1976)

Forward (Alligator, 1980)

Reunion (Artists Only, 1998*)

Satta Massagana (Jam Sounds, 1978; Heartbeat, 1993**)

1995 Plus Tax (Clinch, mid-1990s*)

AITKEN, LAUREL

Blue Beat Years (Moon Ska, 1995**)

High Priest of Reggae (Blue Beat, 1969)

It's Too Late: Personal Selections, 1961–84 (Unicorn, U.K., 1989*)

Ringo the Gringo (Unicorn, 1990)

Rise and Fall: Personal Selections, 1960–85 (Unicorn, 1989*)

Ska with Laurel (Rio, 1965)

With the Skatalites During the Long Hot Summer of 1963 (Unicorn, 1990)

ALCAPONE, DENNIS

Ba-Ba Ri-Ba Skank (Esoldun, France, 1992*), featuring Lizzy

Belch It Off (Attack, U.K., 1974)

Dread Capone (Third World, U.K., 1976)

Forever Version (Studio One, 1971; Heartbeat, 1991**)

Guns Don't Argue (Trojan, U.K., 1971)

Investigator Rock (Third World, 1977)

My Voice Is Insured for Half a Million Dollars (Trojan, 1989+), 1970s

Universal Rockers (RAS, 1992*)

ALIMANTADO, DR.

Best Dressed Chicken in Town (Greensleeves, 1978**)

Born for a Purpose (Greensleeves, 1987**), 1970s recordings

King's Bread (Ital Sounds, 1979)

Love Is (Keyman Records)

The Privileged Few (Keyman, 1980s*)

Reggae Review (Keyman, 1985)

Sons of Thunder (Greensleeves, 1981), reissued as Born for a Purpose with the addition of "Still Alive"

(Tell Me Are You Having A) Wonderful Time (Keyman, 1988)

ALPHA & OMEGA

Almighty Jah (Greensleeves, U.K., 1992*)

Daniel in the Lions Den (Greensleeves, early 1990s, includes "King and Queen"**)

Dub Plate Selections (A&O, U.K., 1995*)

Iries in Roots Meets Alpha & Omega (Buback, 1990s*)

Sound System Dub (ROIR, 1995**)

Voice in the Wilderness (A&O, 1996**)

ALTHEA AND DONNA

Uptown Top Ranking (Virgin, 1978+)

ANDY, BOB

Andywork (I-Anka, 1991), compilation of Andy's songs by other artists recorded in Jamaica, 1970–74*

Bob Andy's Song Book (Studio One, 1972**)

Freely (I-Anka, 1988*)

Friends (I-Anka, 1983*)

Hanging Tough (VP, 1997**)

Lots of Love and I (Sky Note)

Music Inside Me (Sound Tracks, 1975)

Retrospective (I-Anka, 1986)

Songs of Bob Andy (Jove, 1993), by other artists

ANDY, BOB, AND MARCIA GRIFFITHS

Pied Piper (Harry J, 1971)

Really Together (I-Anka, 1987)

Sweet Memories (Nectar, 1997*), early 1970s recordings

Young Gifted and Black (Harry J, 1971)

ANDY, HORACE

Best of Horace Andy (Studio One, 1974+)

Best of Horace Andy (United Artists, 1979+), Clement "Coxsone" Dodd productions; not the same album as above

Best of Horace Andy (Culture Press, 1985), produced by Bunny Lee

Big Bad Man (Rockers Forever, 1987)

Clash of the Andys with Patrick Andy (Thunderbolt, 1985)

Confusion (Music Hawk, 1985)

Dance Hall Style (Wackies, 1983, reissued 1997)

Don't Stop (Island in the Sun, 1985)

Earth Must Be Hell (Atra, U.K., 1988), with Winston Jarrett and the Wailers

Elementary (Rough Trade, 1985)

Everyday People (Wackies/Tachyon, 1988)

Exclusively aka Dance Hall Style (Solid Groove, U.K., 1982)

Fresh (Island in the Sun, 1987)

From One Extreme to Another (Beta, U.K.), with John Holt

Get Wise (Hot Disc)

Good Vibes (Blood and Fire, 1997*), Bunny Lee

Haul and Jack Up (Live & Love, 1987)

Hits from Studio One and More (Rhino, U.K., 1995*)

In the Light/In the Light Dub (Hungry Town, 1977; Blood and Fire, reissue 1996**)

Jah Shaka Meets Horace Andy (Jah Shaka, U.K., 1993**)

Life Is for Living (RAS, 1995**), Mad Professor

Mr. Bassie (Heartbeat, 1998**), 1970s Studio One recordings

Natty Dread a Weh She Want (VP, 1979)

Prime of Horace Andy (Music Club, 1998*)

Pure Ranking (Clocktower, early 1980s)

Roots and Branches (RAS, 1997*), produced by Mad Professor

Rude Boy (Shanachie, 1993*)

See and Blind (Heartbeat Europe, 1998*)

Seek and You Will Find (Blackamix, U.K., 1985)

Seek and You Will Find the Dub Pieces (Blackamix, 1985)

Shame and Scandal (Midnight Rock, early 1990s)

Showcase (Tad's, 1983)

Sings for You and I (World Enterprises, 1985)

Skylarking (Studio One, 1972+)

Skylarking: Best of Horace Andy, Vol. 1 (Melankolik, 1997**)

You Are My Angel (Trojan, 1973, CD reissue 1996*)

ASWAD

Crucial Tracks (Mango, 1989), compilation

Distant Thunder (Mango, 1988)

Don't Turn Around (Mango, 1993), compilation

Firesticks (Mango, 1993), compilation

Hulet (Mango, 1979*)

Jah Shaka Meets Aswad in Addis Ababa Studio (Jah Shaka, 1985)
Live and Direct (Mango, 1983)
New Chapter of Dub (Mango, 1982)
Next Frontier (Mesa, 1995*)
Not Satisfied (CBS, 1982)
On Top (Simba/EMI, 1986)
Rebel Souls (Mango, 1984)
Renaissance (Stylus, 1988)
Rise and Shine (Mesa, 1994*)
Rise and Shine Again (Mesa, 1995*), remixes
Roots Rocking: The Island Anthology (Island Jamaica, 1997**), 2-CD set
Showcase (Island, 1981**)
Too Wicked (Mango, 1990*)
To the Top (Mango, 1986*)

BARKER, DAVE
Monkey Business (Trojan, 1997*)
Prisoner of Love (Trojan, 1970; reissue 1995*), featuring the Upsetters; produced by Lee Perry
See also Dave and Ansel Collins

BEES, ANDREW
Militant (RAS, 1995*)

BIG YOUTH
Chanting Dread Inna Fine Style (Heartbeat, 1983)
Dreadlocks Dread (Front Line, 1978; 1990**)
Everyday Skank: Best of Big Youth (Trojan, 1980*)
Higher Grounds (JR, 1995)
Hit the Road Jack (Trojan, 1976)
Isaiah First Prophet of Old (Caroline, reissue 1997*)
Jamming in the House of Dread (Live in Japan) (Danceteria, 1990)
Live At Reggae Sunsplash (Sunsplash, 1984)
A Luta Continua (The Struggle Continues) (Heartbeat, 1986*)
Manifestation (Heartbeat, 1988)
Progress (Negusa Nagast)
Reggae Phenomenon (Trojan, 1977; 1990)
Rock Holy (Negusa Nagast, 1980)
Natty Cultural Dread (Trojan, 1976)
Screaming Target (Trojan, U.K., 1973; 1989**)
Some Great Big Youth (Heartbeat, 1981)

BLACK UHURU
Anthem (Island, 1984**)
Black Sounds of Freedom (Greensleeves, U.K., 1981;1986**), Jammy's remix of the first album, Love Crisis
Black Uhuru (Virgin, 1979), reissue of Showcase with 1 added track
Brutal (RAS, 1986)
Chill Out (Island, 1982)
Guess Who's Coming to Dinner (Heartbeat, 1983), same as Black Uhuru
Iron Storm (Mesa, 1991*)
Liberation: The Island Anthology (Mango, 1993**), 2-CD compilation
Live in New York (Rohit, 1988)
Love Crisis (Jammy's, 1977)
Mystical Truth (Mesa, 1992*)
Now (Mesa, 1990*)
Positive (RAS, 1987)
Red (Mango, 1981**)
Reggae Greats (Island, 1984)
Showcase (D-Roy, 1979)
Sinsemilla (Mango, 1980**)
Strongg (Mesa, 1994*)
Tear It Up Live (Island, 1982), also released as a video
Unification (Five Star General, 1998*)

BLENDER, EVERTON
Lift Up Your Head (Heartbeat, 1994)
Piece of the Blender: The Singles (Heartbeat, 1996)

BLONDY, ALPHA
Apartheid Is Nazism (Shanachie, 1987), with the Solar System
Best of Alpha Blondy (Shanachie, 1990)
Cocody Rock (Shanachie, 1988), with the Solar System
Dieu (World Pacific, 1994*), with the Solar System
Jah Glory (Syllart, mid-1980s), with the Natty Rebels
Jerusalem (Shanachie, 1988), with the Wailers
Masada (EMI, 1992**)
Prophets (Capitol, 1989*)
Revolution (Shanachie, 1989), with the Solar System
Yitzhak Rabin (Tuff Gong, 1998*)

BLUES BUSTERS
Behold (Trojan), late 1960s

BOLO, YAMI
Born Again (RAS, 1996*)
Cool and Easy (Tappa, circa 1993**)
Fighting for Peace (RAS, 1994*)
He Who Knows It Feels It (Heartbeat, 1991*)
Jah Love (VP, 1998*)
Jah Made Them All (Greensleeves, 1989+), Augustus Pablo
Put Down the Weapons (Yam Euphony, 1998+)
Ransom (Greensleeves, 1989+), Junior Delgado
Star of Love (VP, 1995)
Up Life Street (Heartbeat, 1992*)
Wonders and Signs (Super Power, 1997)
Yami Bolo Meets Lloyd Hemmings (RAS, 1994*)

BOOTHE, KEN
Acclaimed (Upstairs Music, 1996*)
Black, Gold and Green (Trojan, 1973+)
Blood Brothers (Trojan, 1978; K&K CD, 1996*)
Call Me (Rohit)
Disco Reggae (Phil Pratt, late 1970s)
Don't You Know (Tappa, 1988)
Everything I Own (Trojan, 1974+)
Everything I Own (Trojan, 1997**), not the same album as above
Freedom Street (Trojan, 1971, CD reissue 1997**)
Great Ken Boothe Meets B.B. Seaton and the Gaylads (Jaguar, 1971)
I'm Just a Man (B. Lee, early 1980s)
Imagine (Park Heights, late 1980s)
Ken Boothe Collection (Trojan, 1987**), compilation
Let's Get It On (Trojan, 1974)
Live Good (United Artists, 1978+)
Man and His Hits (Studio One, 1970)
Memories (Abraham*)
Mr. Rock Steady (Studio One, 1968+)
More of Ken Boothe (Studio One, 1968)
Power of Love (New Name, mid-1990s)
Reggae for Lovers (Generation, 1979)
Sings Hits from Studio One and More (Rhino, U.K., 1995*)
Talk to Me (VP, 1990)
Two of a Kind (Tuff Gong, late 1980s), with Tyrone Taylor, produced by Jack Ruby
Who Gets Your Love? (Trojan, 1978)

BRIGADIER JERRY

Hail H.I.M. (Tappa, 1993**), produced by Tappa Zukie

Jamaica Jamaica (Jah Love Muzik, 1985)

Live At the Controls (Vista, U.K., 1983), live sound system recording

On the Road (RAS, 1990*)

BRISSETT, BUNNY

Better Safe Than Sorry (Rockers), 1995

BROWN, BARRY

Barry (Vista, U.K.), early 1980s, produced by Niney

Barry Brown and Johnny Clarke Sing Roots and Culture (Roots Records, U.K., recorded early 1980s, CD issue 1992**)

Barry Brown: Artist of the 1980s (TR, 1980)

Barry Brown Showcase (Third World, U.K., mid-1970s), Bunny Lee

Barry Brown Showcase (VP), late 1970s, Prince Jammy

Barry Brown Superstar (Bunny Lee, mid-1970s)

Best of Barry Brown (Culture Press, 1984+)

Best of Barry Brown (JA Classics, mid-1990s*), not the same as above album

Cool Pon Your Corner (Trojan, 1980)

Far East (Channel One mid-1970s, CD reissue mid-1990s**)

I'm Not So Lucky (Black Roots, 1980)

Love and Protection (Prestige, 1996*)

Mr. Moneyman (originally issued mid-1970s, Esoldun CD, 1993**)

More Vibes of Barry Brown (King Culture, Canada), with Stamma Rank

Roots and Culture (Uptempo, U.K.), with Willie Williams

Same Sound (Chart Street, 1991)

Show-Down, Vol. 1 (Empire, 1983), with Little John

Stand Firm (Justice/VP), mid-1970s

Step It Up Youthman (Paradise/Third World)

Vibes of Barry Brown (Sonic Sounds/Gorgon)

BROWN, DENNIS

Africa (Celluloid), 1970s

Beautiful Morning (World Records, 1992)

Best of Dennis Brown, Part 1 (Joe Gibbs circa 1980)

Best of Dennis Brown, Part 2 (Joe Gibbs circa 1980)

Best of Dennis Brown, Vol. 1: Africa (Esoldun France, 1995*)

Best of Dennis Brown, Vol. 2: Traveling Man (Esoldun, 1995*)

Blazing (Shanachie, 1992)

Brown Sugar (RAS, 1988+)

Cosmic Force (Heartbeat, 1993*)

Could It Be (VP, 1996*), produced by Bunny Gemini

Crown Prince (World Records, mid-1990s*)

Death Before Dishonor (Tappa, 1989)

Dennis (Burning Sounds, 1996), 1970s

Dennis Brown (Observer), mid-1970s

Dennis Brown in Concert (Ayeola, 1987)

Exit (Trojan, 1986), King Jammy

Foul Play (A&M, 1981), Joe Gibbs/crossover

Friends for Life (Shanachie, 1992*)

General (VP, mid-1990s*)

Give Praises (Tappa, early 1990s*)

Good Vibrations (Yvonne's Special, 1989*)

History (World Enterprise, 1986), same as The Exit

Hit After Hit (Rocky One), reissues 1970s Joe Gibbs productions*

Hold Tight (Live & Learn, 1986)

I Don't Know (RAS, 1995*)

If I Follow My Heart (Studio One, 1971)

Inseparable (J & W, 1987)

Joseph's Coat of Many Colors (Laser, U.K., 1980)

Just Dennis (Trojan, 1975)

Kollection (RAS, 1991*)

Legit (Shanachie, 1993*), with Cocoa Tea and Freddie McGregor

Light My Fire (Heartbeat, 1994**), Alvin Ranglin

Limited Edition (VP, 1993)

Live At Montreux (Laser, 1984)

Love and Hate: Best of Dennis Brown (VP, 1996*)

Love Has Found Its Way (A&M, 1982)

Lovers Paradise (Classic Sounds, 1994*)

Love's Gotta Hold On Me (Joe Gibbs, 1984)

Milk and Honey (RAS, 1996*)

Money in My Pocket (Trojan, 1981)

My Time (Rohit), 1970s, Niney productions

No Man Is an Island (Studio One, 1970; CD reissue 1997**)

Nothing Like This (RAS, 1995*)

Open the Gate (Heartbeat, 1995**), companion to Some Like It Hot

Over Proof (Shanachie, 1991*)

Prophet Rides Again (A&M, 1983)

Reggae Max (Jet Star, U.K., 1997*)

Revolution (Yvonne's Special)

Sarge (CPI, 1990)

Satisfaction Feeling (Tad's)

Slow Down (Shanachie, 1985)

So Long Rastafari (Observer), 1970s

Some Like It Hot (Heartbeat, 1992**)

Spellbound (Joe Gibbs, 1990)

Stage Coach Showdown (Joe Gibbs mid-1970s)

Super Reggae and Soul Hits (Trojan, 1972), Derrick Harriot

Superstar (Micron), mid-1970s

Temperature Rising (VP, 1995*)

Unchallenged (VP, 1990*), Gussie Clarke

Victory Is Mine (RAS, 1991*)

Visions (Shanachie, 1988), reissues 1977 Joe Gibbs production

West Bound Train (Third World, 1977)

Words of Wisdom (Shanachie, 1990**)

Wolf and Leopard (EMI, 1977)

Wolves and Leopards (Joe Gibbs, 1978)

Yesterday Today and Tomorrow (Joe Gibbs, 1982)

You Got the Best of Me (Saxon, U.K., 1995)

BURNING SPEAR

Appointment with His Majesty (Heartbeat, 1997**)

Burning Spear (Studio One, 1973+), Coxsone Dodd

Chant Down Babylon: The Island Anthology (Island Jamaica, 1995**), career-spanning 2-CD label retrospective

Dry and Heavy (Mango, 1977), produced by Jack Ruby

Farover (EMI, 1982)

Fittest of the Fittest (Heartbeat, 1983)

Hail H.I.M. (Burning Spear, 1980; Heartbeat, 1994**)

Harder Than the Best (Island, late 1970s compilation)

Jah Kingdom (Mango, 1991*)

Live (Island, 1977)

Live in Paris Zenith '88 (Slash, 1988), double album

Love and Peace: Burning Spear Live (Heartbeat, 1994*)

Man in the Hills (Island, 1976; Mango reissue CD**), Jack Ruby

Marcus Children (Burning Spear, 1978), reissued as Social Living

Marcus Garvey/Garvey's Ghost (Island, 1975–76; Jack Ruby), 1987 CD combines album and dub album originally released separately**

Mek We Dweet (Mango, 1990*)

Mistress Music (Slash, 1988)

100th Anniversary (Island**), same as Marcus Garvey/Garvey's Ghost

People of the World (Slash, 1986)

Rasta Business (Heartbeat, 1995*)

Reggae Greats (Mango, 1984)

Resistance (Heartbeat. 1985)

Rocking Time (Studio One, 1974; Buddah, 1976)

Social Living (Blood & Fire, reissues 1980 LP on CD**)

World Should Know (Heartbeat, 1983*)

BYLES, JUNIOR

Beat Down Babylon (Dynamic, 1972)

Beat Down Babylon: The Upsetter Years (Trojan, 1987), compilation

Curly Locks: Best of Junior Byles and the Upsetters, 1970–76 (Heartbeat, 1997**)

Jordan (Heartbeat, 1988+), reissues second album, originally on Micron

Rasta No Pickpocket (Nighthawk, 1986)

When Will Better Come, 1972–76 (Trojan, 1988)

CABLES

Baby Why (Harry J), early 1970s, scarce

What Kind of World (Studio One, 1970; Heartbeat, 1991**)

CADOGAN, SUSAN

Hurt So Good (Trojan, 1975; 1995*), Lee "Scratch" Perry

CAMPBELL, AL

Ain't That Loving You (Jamaica Sounds), mid-1970s

Ain't Too Proud to Beg (Live & Love), late 1980s

Al Campbell Collection, 1972–75 (Angella)

Bad Boy (CSA, 1984)

Bounce Back (Free World*), mid-1990s

Dance Hall Stylee (Narrows), late 1980s

Diamonds (Burning Sounds), early 1980s

Fence Too Tall (Live & Learn, 1987)

Forward Natty (Live & Learn, 1985)

Freedom Street (Top Rank, JA; Londisc, U.K.), early 1980s

Gee Baby (Phil Pratt, 1975)

It's Magic (Free World*), mid-1990s

Loving Moods of Al Campbell (Music Force), early 1980s

Mr. Lovers Rock (Sonic Sounds, 1980)

More Al Campbell: Showcase LP (Ethnic)

Natty Too Tall (Live & Learn/RAS*)

Other Side of Love (Greensleeves, 1981)

Rainy Days (Hawkeye, 1978)

Rasta Time (Esoldun, 1992**), early 1970s cuts

Shaggy Raggy (Sampler), late 1980s

Sly and Robbie Present (Rhino, U.K.**), compilation

Talk About Love (Al Campbell Music, 1991)

Working Man (JB, 1980+)

CAMPBELL, CORNELL

Boxing (Star Light, U.K.), early 1980s, Bunny Lee

Boxing Around (Joe Gibbs, 1982)

Collection: 20 Magnificent Hits (Striker Lee)

Cornell Campbell (Trojan, 1973), Bunny Lee

Cornell Campbell Meets the Gaylads (Culture Press, U.K., 1984), with Sly and Robbie; Roy Cousins

Dance Inna Greenwich Farm (Grounation, U.K., 1975)

Fight Against Corruption (Vista Sounds, 1983), "Striker" Lee

Follow Instructions (Mobiliser, 1983), Tappa Zukie

Gorgon (Klik/Angen, 1976+), Bunny Lee

Inspector General (Imperial, 1979)

Money (Live and Learn, 1983), Delroy Wright

New Boss (Lee's, 1984)

Reggae Sun (Amo), but for a few cuts the same as Gorgon on Klik

Ropin' (Justice), Bunny Lee

Silver Jubilee: 25 Classic Cuts (Rhino, U.K.*)

Stalowatt (Third World, U.K., 1978)

Superstar (Micron+), Linval Thompson

Sweet Baby (Burning Sounds, 1983), Linval Thompson

Sweet Dancehall Collection (JA, 1995**), Bunny Lee

Tell the People (CSI, 1994*)

Turn Back the Hands of Time (Third World, 1977)

What's Happening to Me? (Joe Gibbs)

Yes I Will (Micron), Bunny Lee

CARLOS, DON

Day to Day Living (Shanachie, 1983), Junjo Lawes

Deeply Concerned (RAS, 1987*)

Don Carlos and Gold/The Gladiators: Showdown (Empire, 1984)

Ease Up (RAS, 1994*)

Ghetto Living (Tamoki Wambesi, 1983, CD reissue 1990*)

Harvest Time (Negus Roots, 1982)

Just a Passing Glance (RAS, 1994**), Doctor Dread

Never Run Away (Kingdom, U.K., 1984), with Gold

Pass Me the Lazer Beam (World Enterprize+), produced by Bunny Lee

Prophecy (Blue Moon, U.K.), reissues 1981's Suffering

Pure Gold (Vista Sounds, 1983), Bunny Lee

Rasta Brothers (Vista, 1985), with Anthony Johnson and Little John

Raving Tonight (RAS, 1983), with Gold

7 Days a Week (RAS, 1998**)

Spread Out (Burning Sounds, 1983)

Suffering (Negus Roots, 1981), "Showcase" style, includes dubs

Time Is the Master (RAS, 1992*)

CARLTON AND THE SHOES

Love Me Forever (Studio One, 1978+)

This Heart of Mine (Quality Records, 1980)

CHALICE
Blasted (Pipe, 1981; 1998*)
Live (Reggae Sunsplash, 1981)
Up Till Now (RAS, 1987)

CLARENDONIANS
Best of the Clarendonians (Studio
   One, 1968+)
Can't Keep a Good Man Down
   (King's Music, 1992*)
Freddie McGregor and the
   Clarendonians:Early Years
   (Rhino, U.K., 1996)

CLARKE, JOHNNY
Authorized Rockers (Virgin, U.K.,
   1991**), CD compilation
Authorized Version (Virgin, 1976)
Don't Stay Out Late (Rhino, U.K.*),
   compiles Bunny Lee
Don't Trouble Trouble (Attack, U.K.,
   1989+), compilation
Dreader Dread 1976–79 (Blood and
   Fire, 1998), compilation
Enter in to His Gates with Praise
   (Attack, 1989), compilation
Girl I Love You (Justice), mid-1970s
Give Thanks (Ariwa, U.K.), mid-1980s
I Man Come Again (Black Music),
   mid-1980s
Johnny Clarke Meets Cornell
   Campbell (Vista, U.K., 1983)
Lovers Rock, Vol. 5 (Third World), late
   1970s
Originally King in the Arena (Third
   World), mid-1970s
Originally Mr. Clarke (Clocktower)
Out of the Past (Third World), late
   1970s
Put It On (Vulcan, U.K.), mid-1970s
Rasta Nuh Fear (Ujama/Tuff Gong)
Reggae Archives (RAS, 1991*), recorded
   early 1980s
Reggae Party (Vista, 1984)
Reggae Rebel (Circle, 1982)
Rock with Me (JA, 1995*)
Rock with Me Baby (Abraham**)
Rockers Time Now (Virgin, 1976)
Satisfaction (Third World, mid-1970s),
   Lee/Tubby/Aggrovators
Show Case (Third World, mid-1970s),
   half vocal half dub
Sings in Fine Style (Abraham**)
Sly and Robbie Present the Best of
   Johnny Clarke (Vista, 1985)
Super Star (Jackpot), mid-1970s

Sweet Conversation (Third World),
   late 1970s
Think About It (Super Power), 1990
Twenty Massive Hits (Striker Lee, 1985)
Up Park Camp (Justice), mid-1970s
Wondering (Imperial)
Yard Style (Ariwa, 1983)

CLIFF, JIMMY
Another Cycle (Island, 1971)
Brave Warrior (EMI, 1975)
Breakout (JRS, 1992*)
Can't Get Enough of It (Veep, 1968)
Cliff Hanger (CBS, 1985)
Follow My Mind (Warner Brothers,
   1975)
Give Thanks (Warner Brothers, 1978)
Give the People What They Want
   (Sonic Sounds; MCA, 1981)
Hanging Fire (CBS, 1988)
Harder They Come Original
   Soundtrack Recording (Island,
   1973**)
House of Exile (EMI, 1974)
I Am the Living (MCA, 1980)
Images (Vision, 1989*)
In Concert: The Best of Jimmy Cliff
   (Reprise, 1976**)
Jimmy Cliff (Trojan, 1976), same as
   Wonderful World
Live, 1993 (Lagoon, 1993*)
Many Rivers to Cross (Island, U.K.,
   1978)
Music Maker (Warner, 1974)
Pop Gold (Island International)
Power and the Glory (CBS, 1983)
Reggae Greats (Island, 1984),
   compilation
Special (CBS, 1982)
Struggling Man (Island, 1974)
Two Worlds (Beverleys)
Unlimited (Reprise, 1973)
Very Best of Jimmy Cliff (Island,
   1975+), double album set
Wonderful World, Beautiful People
   (A&M)

COCOA TEA
Authorized (RAS, 1992*), Gussie
   Clarke
Can't Live So (Shanachie, 1994),
   Gussie
Come Again (Super Power), Jammy's
Good Life (VP, 1994**), Fatis Burrell
Holding On (VP), with Home T. and
   Shabba Ranks; Gussie

I Am the Toughest (VP)
Israel's King (VP, 1996), Fatis Burrell
Kingston Hot (RAS, 1992**), Junjo
   Lawes
Love Me (Digital-B, 1995*), Bobby
   Dixon
Marshall (Jammys), Michael Chin
Mr. Cocoa Tea (Cornerstone), Chin
One Up (VP, 1993), Fatis
One Way (VP, 1998*), Fatis
Replay (Gone Clear, 1997*)
Rikers Island (VP, 1990), Mr. Doo
Rocking Dolly (RAS, 1991*), Junjo
Settle Down (Cornerstone)
Sweet Love (RAS, 1994), Junjo
Sweet Sweet Cocoa Tea (Blue
   Mountain, 1985)
Whe Dem a Go Do . . . Can't Stop
   Cocoa Tea (Volcano)

COLE, STRANGER
Capture Land (Chalawa, Canada,
   early 1980s)
First Ten Years (Camelot, Canada,
   early 1980s)
Forward in the Land of Sunshine
   (Canada, 1976)
No More Fussing and Fighting
   (Scorcher, 1986+)
Patriot *aka* No More Fussing and
   Fighting (Stranger Cole, 1982)

COLLINS, DAVE AND ANSELL
Double Barrel (Big Tree, 1970)
In the Ghetto (Trojan, 1976)

CONGOS (CEDRIC MYTON & THE CONGOS)
Best of Congos, Vol. 1 (Tafari Records)
Congo Ashanty (Congo Ashanty; CBS,
   1979+)
Face the Music (Go Feet, 1981)
Heart of the Congos (Black Art, in
   more than one mix; Go-Feet
   [remix]; restored mix on CD from
   Blood & Fire, 1997**)
Image of Africa (Congo Ashanty, 1979)
Natty Dread Rise Again (RAS, 1997*)

COUNT OSSIE
Grounation (MRR, 1973+), with
   Mystic Revelation of Rastafari,
   2-record set
Man from Higher Heights (Vista
   Sounds, U.K.), mid-1970s

Remembering Count Ossie: A Rasta "Reggae" Legend (Moodisc, 1996**), recordings from the 1950s–'60s

Tales of Mozambique (Dynamic, 1975+), with Mystic Revelation of Rastafari

CULTURE
Africa Stand Alone (April, 1978)
Baldhead Bridge (Laser, 1980+)
Cultural Livity (Live) (RAS, 1998*)
Culture (Joe Gibbs, 1981)
Culture At Their Best: Stronger Than Ever (Rocky 1, 1990)
Culture At Work (Blue Mountain, 1986)
Culture in Culture (Music Track, Heartbeat, 1991*)
Cumbolo (High Note, Front Line, 1979; Shanachie, 1989**)
Good Things (RAS, 1989)
Harder Than the Rest (Virgin, 1978+)
International Herb (Virgin, 1979+)
Lion Rock (Sonic Sounds)
Nuff Crisis! (Blue Mountain, 1988; Shanachie, 1989)
One Stone (RAS, 1996**)
Peel Sessions (Radio One, 1987)
Production Something (Heartbeat, 1998**), 1970s Pottinger productions
Roots and Culture: Culture and Don Carlos (Jah Guidance), 1980s
Too Long in Slavery (Virgin, U.K., 1990**), Pottinger, 1970s
Trod On (Heartbeat, 1983**), Sonia Pottinger, 1970s productions
Trust Me (RAS, 1998**)
Two Sevens Clash (Lightning, 1978; Shanachie CD, 1988**)
Strictly Culture: Best of Culture, 1977–79 (Music Club, 1994**)
Three Sides to My Story (Shanachie, 1991*)
Vital Selection (Virgin, 1981)
Wings of a Dove (Shanachie, 1992*)

DAVIS, RONNIE
Come Straight (Nighthawk, 1997), with Idren
Incredible Ronnie Davis Sings for You and I (Jamaica Sound+), 1970s
Wheel of Life (Upstairs, 1983)

DAWKINS, CARL
Carl Dawkins (Harry J+), mid-1970s
Motherland Africa (Abraham), early 1990s

DEKKER, DESMOND
Black and Dekker (Stiff, 1980)
Compass Point (Stiff, 1981)
Double Dekker (Trojan, 1974+), double album set
First Time for a Long Time: Rare and Unreleased, 1968–71 (Trojan, 1997*), compilation
Israelites (Beverley's, 1969; UNI, U.S.), Leslie Kong
Israelites (Trojan, 1981), same producer and era, different selections
Israelites (Crab, U.K.), title song the same otherwise different
Israelites (Bulldog, 1985), title song same o/w diff from all above
King of Ska (Trojan, 1991), contemporary remakes
Music Like Dirt (Trojan, 1992*)
Officially Live and Rare (Trojan, 1987), compilation of Kong cuts
Original Reggae Hitsound of Desmond Dekker and the Aces, 1969–71 (Trojan, 1985), compilation
Original Rude Boy (Music Club, 1997*)
Rockin' Steady: Best of Desmond Dekker (Rhino, 1992**)
Shanty Town Original (Drive, 1994*), compilation
Twenty Greatest Hits (Streetlite, 1988*), Kong
Writing on the Wall (Trojan, 1998**), 1960s recordings

DELGADO, JUNIOR
Another Place in Time (Vision, 1994*)
Augustus Pablo and Jr. Delgado Showcase (Rockers, 1992), vocal/dub
Dub School: A Junior Delgado Showcase (Buffalo, 1989), vocal/dub
Effort (DEB, 1979)
Fearless (Big Cat, 1998**)
It Takes Two to Tango (Fashion, U.K., 1986)
Movin' Down the Road (Live and Love)
One Step More (Mango, 1988**)
Raggamuffin Year (Mango, 1986+)
Stranger (Skengdon, 1986)

DILLINGER
Badder Than Them (A&M, 1980)
Best of Live (Trojan, 1988)
Bionic Dread (Mango, 1976)
Blackboard Jungle (Culture Press, 1984)
CB 200 (Mango, 1976)
Corn Bread (Vista, 1983)
Dillinger Verses Trinity (Burning Sounds, 1978)
Hard Core Dillinger (Third World, 1978)
Join the Queue (Oak Sound, 1982)
Killer Man Jaro (Esoldun, 1992)
Live At the Music Machine (Jamaica Sound, 1979)
Marijuana in My Brain (Jamaica Sound, 1979)
Ranking Dillinger (Abraham*), late 1970s
Ready Natty Dreadie (Studio One, 1975+)
Say No to Drugs (Lagoon, 1993)
Superstar (Weed Beat), late 1970s
Talkin' Blues (Jamaica Sound, 1979)
Three Piece Suit (Esoldun, 1993**), Bunny Lee, 1970s
Top Ranking Dillinger (Third World, 1977)

DILLON, PHILLIS
One Life to Live (Treasure Isle)

DINGLES
Happiness (Rosso)

DOBSON, DOBBY
Best of Dobby Dobson (Super Power)
Sweet Christmas (Top Ranking)
Oh God, Are You Satisfied (United Artists, 1978+)

DONALDSON, ERIC
Come Away (Dynamic, 1982)
Eric Donaldson (Dynamic, 1971)
Keep On Riding (Dynamic, 1975)
Kent Village (Dynamic, 1979; Rhino, U.K., CD reissue 1995*)
Right On Time (Dynamic, 1985)
Very Best of Eric Donaldson (Rhino, U.K.**), 1990s compilation

DONOVAN
Banzani-! (Mango, 1989*)
World Power (Mango, 1988*)

DOUGLAS, LAMBERT
Living Man (Rosso)

DREAD, MIKEY
African Anthem (Big Cat, 1997*)
African Anthem Revisited (RAS, 1991*)
Beyond World War III (Big Cat, 1997*)
Come to Mikey Dread's Dub Party (ROIR, 1995*)
Obsession (Rykodisc, 1992)
Profile (RAS, 1991*)

DUBE, LUCKY
Captured Live (Shanachie, 1991*)
House of Exile (Shanachie, 1992**)
Prisoner (Shanachie, 1990*)
Rastas Never Dies (Polygram, 1989)
Serious Reggae Business (Shanachie, 1996**), compilation
Slave (Shanachie, 1988)
Taxman (Shanachie, 1997**)
Think About the Children (Polygram, 1989)
Together As One (Celluloid, 1989)
Trinity (Tabu, 1995*)
Umadakeni (Celluloid), mid-1980s
Victims (Shanachie, 1993*)

DUB SYNDICATE
Classic Selection, Vols. 1–3 (On-U Sound, 1989–94**)
Echomania (On-U, 1993*)
Ital Breakfast (On-U, 1996*)
Mellow and Collie (Lion & Roots, 1998)
One Way System (Danceteria)
Research and Development (On-U, 1996)
Stoned Immaculate (On-U, 1991**)
Tunes from the Missing Channel (On-U)

DUNKLEY, ERROL
Aquarius (NIA, 1990)
Darling Ooh (Attack, U.K., 1972; 1991 reissue**)
In a Different, Different Style (Easy Street, 1984)
Militant Man (Lovella, U.K.)
Nostalgia (Gargonites, 1983)
O.K. Fred (Celluloid France)
Please Stop Your Lying (Rocky One, 1996**), late 1960s–early 1970s
Sit and Cry Over You (Shelly Power)

EARTH AND STONE
Kool Roots (Cha Cha, 1979; Pressure Sounds, 1996**), album and dub combined

EARTH MESSENGERS
Ivory Towers (Mango, 1989)

EASTWOOD, CLINT
Best of Clint Eastwood (Culture Press, 1984)
Death in the Arena (Cha Cha), circa 1979
Jah Lights Shining (Jamaica Sound)
Love and Happiness (Burning Sounds), early 1980s
Reggae Sun (Amo, 1980)
Sex Education (Greensleeves, 1980)
Step It in a Zion (Live & Love)
Two Bad DJ (Greensleeves, 1981), with General Saint

ECCLES, CLANCY
Feel the Rhythm: Jamaican Ska, Rock Steady and Reggae, 1966–68 (Jamaica Gold, 1997*)
Joshua's Rod of Correction (Jamaica Gold, 1996*)
Nyah Reggae Rock, 1969–70 (Jamaica Gold, 1997*)

EDWARDS, JACKIE
African Language (Harry J, 1977+)
Best of Jackie and Millie (Small) (Trojan, 1970)
By Demand (Trojan, 1967)
Come On Home (Trojan, 1966)
Come to Me Softly (Third World)
I Do Love You (Trojan, 1972)
Jackie and Millie (Trojan), late 1960s
Let's Fall in Love (Third World), late 1970s
Love and Affection (Abraham), 1970s
Most of Wilfred "Jackie" Edwards (Trojan, 1963)
Paradise (Carl's)
Premature Golden Sands (Trojan, 1967)
Reggae Sun (Amo, 1980)
Sincerely (Trojan, 1978)
Singing Hits from Studio One and More (Rhino, U.K., 1995*)

EEK-A-MOUSE
Assasinator (RAS, 1983)
Black Cowboy (Sunset Blvd., 1995*)
Bubble Up Yu Hip (Thompson Sound), late 1970s
Eek-A-Nomics ((RAS, 1988)
King and I (RAS, 1987)
Live At Reggae Sunsplash (Sunsplash, 1984), with Michigan and Smiley
Mouse-A-Mania (RAS, 1987*)
Mouse and Man (Shanachie, 1983)
Mouseketeer (Shanachie, 1984)
Skidip! (Greensleeves, 1982)
U-Neek (Island, 1991*)
Very Best of Shanachie, 1990*)
Wa-Do-Dem (Greensleeves, 1981)

ELLIS, ALTON
Alton and Hortense Ellis (Heartbeat, 1990**), late 1960s
Alton Ellis Greatest Hits (Third World)
Best of Alton Ellis (Coxsone)
Cry Tough, 1966–68 (Heartbeat, 1993**)
Family Vibes (All Tone, 1992)
Here I Am (Angella, 1988)
Legendary, 1967–71 (All Tone**)
Love to Share (Third World, 1979)
Many Moods of Alton Ellis (Tele-Tech)
Mr. Skabeena (Cha Cha, 1980), with the Heptones
Mr. Soul of Jamaica (Treasure Isle)
My Time Is Right (Trojan, 1990)
Set a Better Example (Half-Way Tree, 1989)
Showcase (Studio One, 1980)
Sings Rock and Soul (Coxsone)
Slummin' (Abraham)
Still in Love (Trojan, 1977; reissue 1995)
Sunday Coming (Heartbeat, 1995**), reissues late 1960s Studio One LP
25th Silver Jubilee (High Note, 1984)

ETHIOPIANS
Clap your Hands (Lagoon, 1993*), J.J. Johnson
Dread Prophesy (Nighthawk, 1985), with the Gladiators
Engine '54: Let's Ska and Rock Steady (Jamaica Gold, 1992*), 1968
Everything Crash (Studio One, 1980)
No Baptism (Crystal, 1991), Derrick Harriot, 1960s–'70s
Open the Gate of Zion (GG's, 1978)

Owner Fe De Yard (Heartbeat, 1994**), Dodd
Reggae Power (Trojan, 1969)
Sir J.J. and Friends (Lagoon, 1993*), Johnson
Slave Call (Third World, 1977; Rohit, 1988; Heartbeat, 1992**)
World Goes Ska (Trojan, 1992*), compilation

FAITH, GEORGE
Bunny Lee Presents: "Soulfull" George Faith (Hollywood)
Like Never Before (Virgo Stomach), early 1980s
Loving Something as Earl George (GG's)
One and Only as Earl George (Burning Sounds)
Since I Met You Baby (GG's)
Straight to the Heart (EAD)
To Be a Lover (Mango, 1977+), Lee Perry production

FASHEK, MAJEK
I and I Experience (CBS Nigeria, 1989)
Prisoner of Conscience (Tabansi, Nigeria; Mango, 1989*)
Rainmaker (Tuff Gong, 1997*)
Spirit of Love (East/West, 1991*)

FITZROY, EDDIE
Check for You Once (Musical Ambassador, 1982)
Coming Up Strong (Sun Power), circa 1986
Deep in Me Culture (Massive Music, 1983**)
Eclipse (RAS, 1988)
Pollution (Bromac), mid-1980s
Youthman Penitentiary (Alligator, 1982+)

FOUNDATION
Flames (Mango, 1988**)
Heart Feel It (Mango, 1989**)
One Shirt (Mango, 1995*)

FRANKLYN, CHEVELLE
Serious Girl (Mesa, 1995)

FRAZER, PHILLIP
I and I in Inity (Drum & Bass), late 1980s, with Tristan Palmer
I Who Have Nothing (Tuff Gong)

Loving You (Silver Camel)
Never Let Go (Roots Tradition, 1992)
Rightous Works (Redemption Sounds+), late 1970s
Sharp Like a Razor (Roots Tradition, 1994)

GAYLADS
Best of the Gaylads (Studio One), late 1960s
Over the Rainbow's End: Best of, 1968–71 (Trojan, 1995*)
Soul Beat (Studio One+), late 1960s

GENERAL, MIKEY
Stronger Rastaman (VP, 1995)

GEORGE, SOPHIA
For Everyone (Pow Wow, 1989)
Fresh (Jet Star, 1986)

GLADIATORS
Babylon Street (Jam Rock), circa 1982
Back to Roots (Stunt Sound, 1982)
Bongo Red (Heartbeat, 1998**), 1970s Studio One productions
Country Living (Heartbeat, 1985)
Dreadlocks the Time Is Now (Virgin, 1990**)
Full Time (Nighthawk, 1993*)
Gladiators (Virgin, 1980), produced by Eddy Grant
Gladiators and Israel Vibration Live (Genes, 1990*)
Gladiators By Bus (Jam Rock, 1982)
In Store for You (Heartbeat, 1988)
Naturality (Virgin, 1978)
On the Right Track (Heartbeat, 1989)
Presenting the Gladiators (Studio One, 1979+)
Proverbial Reggae (Virgin, 1978)
Reggae to Bone (Jam Rock, 1982)
Serious Thing (Nighthawk, 1984)
Storm (Musidisc, 1994*)
Sweet So Till (Virgin, 1979)
Symbol of Reality (Nighthawk, 1982)
Trenchtown Mix-Up (Jam Rock, 1981)
U.S. Tour E.P. (Nighthawk, 1983)
Valley of Decision (Heartbeat, 1991*)
Vital Selection (Virgin, 1981**)

GRAY, OWEN
Battle of the Giants Round One: Owen Gray and Pluggy Satchmo (Echo)

Best of Owen Grey ((Super Power*), mid-1990s
Call On Me (Techniques), late 1980s
Dreams of Owen Gray (Trojan, 1978)
Fire and Bullets (Trojan, 1977+)
Forward On the Scene (Third World, 1978+)
Get On Board (Gees)
Hit After Hit After Hit, Vols. 1–3 (Abraham), 1980s; Vol. 4 (Echo)
Instant Rapport (Bushay, U.K.), 1989)
Little Girl (Vista, 1984)
None of Jah-Jah's Children Shall Ever Suffer (Imperial Records)
Ready, Willing and Able (Park Heights, 1988)
Something Good Going On (Bushay), 1980s
This Is Owen Grey (Pama, 1988)

GRIFFITHS, MARCIA
Carousel (Mango, 1990*)
I Love Music (Mountain Sound, 1986)
Indomitable (Penthouse, 1993)
Land of Love (Penthouse, 1995**)
Marcia (VP, 1988)
Marcia Griffiths at Studio One (Studio One+), 1970s
Naturally (High Note, 1978)
Rock My Soul (Tuff Gong; Pioneer, 1984)
Steppin' (1979; Shanachie, 1991**)
Sweet Bitter Love (Trojan, 1974)

HALF PINT
Classics (Hightone, 1994*)
Classics in Dub (Hightone, 1995*)
Greetings (Power House, 1986)
In Fine Style (Sunset, 1984)
Half Pint (VP, 1997**), Best Of
Joint Favorites (Greensleeves, 1986), with Michael Palmer
Legal We Legal (Artists Only, 1998*)
Money Man Skank (Jammys, 1983)
One Big Family (Power House, 1989)
One in a Million (Greensleeves, 1984)
Pick Your Choice (VP, 1993)
Victory (RAS, 1987)

HAMMOND, BERES
A Day in the Life (VP, 1998*)
Beres Hammond (Charm; VP*), late 1980s
Beres Hammond/Barrington Levy (Live & Learn*), 1980s

Beres Hammond and Mikey Zappow
Meet in Jamaica (Rhino, U.K.,
1995*)
Collectors Series (Penthouse, 1998**)
Expression (Heartbeat, 1995*), with
Derrick Lara
From My Heart with Love (Rocky
One), 1970s, Joe Gibbs
Full Attention (VP, 1993**)
Getting Stronger (Heartbeat, 1997**),
Star Trail
Have a Nice Weekend (VP), 1980s,
Willie Lindo
In Control (Elektra, 1994**)
Irie and Mellow (Rhino, U.K.*), Willie
Lindo, 1980s
Just a Vibes (Star Trail, 1991), same as
Expression with Derrick Lara
Love Affair (Penthouse,**), early 1990s
Love from a Distance (VP, 1996*)
Putting Up Resistance (RAS, 1996**),
reissues Tappa Zukie LP
Red Light (Heavy Beat)
Soul Reggae (Water LIlly, 1976)
Sweetness (VP, 1993)

HARRIOT, DERRICK
Best of Derrick Harriot (Trojan), late
1960s
Best of Derrick Harriot and the
Crystalites (Trojan), late 1960s
Derrick Harriot and the Jiving Juniors:
The Donkey Years, 1961–65
(Jamaica Gold, 1993)
Float On (Charmers), late 1970s
Greatest Reggae Hits (Trojan, 1975)
Psychedelic Train (Trojan), mid-1970s
Rock Steady Party (Trojan), late 1960s
Sensational Derrick Harriot sings
Jamaican Rock Steady-Ska
(Jamaica Gold, 1993**)
Skin to Skin (Sarge), 1980s
Songs for Midnight Lovers (Trojan,
1981)

HEPTONES
Back On Top (Vista, 1983)
Best of the Heptones (Studio One,
Buddah, 1976)
Better Days (Celluloid), with Naggo
Morris
Big and Free (Trenchtown)
Black Is Black (Studio One)
Changing Times (Celluloid, 1986),
with Naggo Morris
Cool Rasta (Trojan, 1976+), Harry J

Freedom Line (Studio One)
Good Life (Greensleeves, 1979), with
Naggo
Good Vibes (Classic Sounds*)
Heptones (Studio One)
Heptones On Top (Studio One)
In a Dance Hall Style (Vista, 1983),
Naggo
In Love with You (United Artists, 1978)
King of My Town (Jackal), Naggo
Legends from Studio One (Trenchtown)
Mr. "T" (Esoldun, 1991), Dolphin
Morris
Night Food (Mango, 1976**)
Observers Style (Esoldun, 1994*)
On the Run (Shanachie, 1982), Naggo
One Step Ahead (Sonic Sounds,
1981), Naggo
Original Heptones (Trenchtown)
Party Time (Mango, 1977**), produced
by Lee Perry
Place Called Love (Moving Target,
1987), Naggo
Pressure (RAS, 1995**)
Sea of Love (Heartbeat, 1997**),
Studio One tracks
Street of Gold (Jamrock, 1981), Naggo
Swing Low (Burning Sounds,
1997**), reissues 1985 Burning
Sounds LP
Trench Town Experience (Trenchtown)
22 Golden Hits (Trenchtown)

HIGGS, JOE
Blackman Know Yourself (Shanachie,
1990**), with the Wailers
Family (Shanachie, 1988*)
Joe and Marcia Together: Roots
Combination (Macola, 1995)
Life of Contradiction (Micron, 1975;
Esoldun reissue, 1991**)
Triumph (Alligator, 1985)
Unity Is Power (One Stop, 1979+)

HINDS, JUSTIN AND THE
DOMINOES
Early Recordings (Esoldun, 1991*),
1960s
From Jamaica with Reggae (High
Note), late 1960s
Jezebel (Island, 1976+)
Just in Time (Mango, 1978+)
Justin Hinds (Jwyanza, 1990), sans the
Dominoes
Know Jah Better (Nighthawk**),
slightly different version of above

Ska Uprising (Trojan, 1993**), 1960s
This Carry Go Bring Come (Rhino,
U.K.*)
Travel with Love (Nighthawk, 1984)

HOLT, JOHN
All Night Long (Ikus, 1997)
Best of and the Rest of (Action Replay,
1994*)
Born Free (Live and Love)
Children of the World (VP*)
Classic Touch (World Enterprise), with
Slim Smith
Disco Showcase (Taurus)
Dusty Roads (Trojan, 1974)
Everytime (Ikus, 1992)
For Lovers and Dancers (Trojan, 1984)
Greatest Hits (Studio One, 1972)
Greatest Hits (Prince Buster), not the
same as above album
Greatest Hits Collection (Rohit), 1980s
Here I Come Again (Rohit*), 1980s
Holt (Sonic Sounds), Blackbeard
Holt (Trojan, 1972), Bunny Lee; not
the same as above album
Holt Goes Disco (Trojan, 1978)
If I Were a Carpenter (Live and Love,
1989)
In Demand (Dynamic, 1991*),
compilation
John Holt Story (John Holt, 1997**)
Just a Country Boy (Trojan, 1978)
Just the Two of Us (CSA, 1982)
Kiss and Say Goodbye (Abraham*)
Let It Go On (Trojan, 1978)
Like a Bolt (Treasure Isle)
Live in London (Sonic Sounds), early
1980s
Love I Can Feel (Studio One, 1971;
Trojan, 1974, with 2 extra songs)
My Desire (World Enterprises), 1980s
Showcase (SP, 1977)
One Million Volts of Holt (Rhino, U.K.
1995*)
One Thousand Volts of Holt (Trojan,
1973)
1000 Volts of Holt (Trojan, 1987*),
compilation
Paragons and Friends (Studio One),
late 1960s–early 1970s
Pledging My Love (Striker Lee), mid-
1970s
Police in Helicopter (Greensleeves,
1983**)
Reggae Christmas Hits Album (Trojan,
1986)

Reggae Max (Jet Star, 1996**)
Reggae Peacemaker (Classic Sounds*),
    early 1990s
Roots of Holt (Trojan, 1977)
Sings for I (Trojan, 1974)
Slow Dancing (Moodies)
Solid Gold (THI, 1982)
Still in Chains (Trojan, 1973)
Super Star (Weed Beat, 1976)
Sweetie Come Brush Me (Volcano,
    1982)
Time Is the Master (Moodisc, 1974)
3000 Volts of Holt (Trojan, 1977)
20 Golden Love Songs (Trojan), 1970s
20 Super Hits (Sonic Sounds, 1990*)
2000 Volts of Holt (Trojan, 1976;
    Vol. 2, Trojan, 1997**)
3000 Volts of Holt (Trojan; Vol. 3,
    Trojan, 1997**)
Up Park Camp (Channel One, 1977,
    reissue 1997**)
Vibes (Leggo, 1985)
Why I Care (Redman, 1989)
Wild Fire (Tad's, 1985), with Dennis
    Brown
World of Love (Weed Beat, 1977)

HUDSON, KEITH
Black Morphologist of Reggae (Keja),
    same as From One Extreme
Entering the Dragon (Magnet)
Flesh of My Skin, Blood of My Blood
    (Atra, 1974+)
From One Extreme to Another (Joint
    International)
Nah Skin Up (Joint International)
Playing It Cool (Joint International,
    1981)
Rasta Communication (Greensleeves,
    1979)
Steaming Jungle (Disc Disc, 1982)
Too Expensive (Virgin, 1976+)
Torch of Freedom (Atra, 1975; alternate
    covers: N.Y., U.K.)

I ROY
Best of I Roy (GG's, 1977)
Black Man Time (Jamaica Gold,
    1994*), 1970s
Cancer (Virgin, 1979)
Can't Conquer Rasta (Justice), 1970s,
    Bunny Lee
Crisus Time, Extra Version (Virgin,
    1976; reissue 1991**), and 6 extra
Crucial Cuts (Virgin, 1983**),
    compilation

Doctor Fish (Hot Disc)
Don't Check Me with No Lightweight
    Stuff (Blood & Fire, 1972–75**)
Dread/Bald Head (Klik, 1976+),
    Bunny Lee
General (Virgin, 1979), included
    additional dub album
Heart of a Lion (Virgin, 1978),
    co-produced with Harry J
Lyrics Man (Witty, N.Y.), 1980s
Many Moods of I Roy (Trojan, 1974)
Presenting I Roy (Gussie, 1977; Trojan)
Soundsystem Anthology (Kings Music,
    1993*)
Straight to the Heart (Esoldun, 1991)
Sunset at Moonlight City (Imperial,
    Canada), 1980s, with Derrick
    Morgan
Sunshine for I (Esoldun, 1992*)
Ten Commandments (Virgin, 1980),
    picture disc
World On Fire (Virgin, 1979)

I-THREES
Beginning (EMI, 1986)

IJAHMAN (IJAHMAN LEVI)
Africa (RAS, 1984)
Are We a Warrior (Mango, 1979+)
Beauty and the Lion (Jahmani, 1996**)
Black Royalties (Jahmani, 1994*)
Culture Country (Jahmani/Tree Roots,
    1987)
Forward Rastaman (Jahmani, 1987)
Haile I Hymn (Chapter I) (Mango,
    1978+)
Ijahman and Friends (Jahmani, 1988)
Ijahman and Madge: I Do (Jahmani,
    1986)
Ijahman Live: Reggae On the River
    USA (Jahmani, 1996)
Ijahman Over Europe Live (Jahmani,
    1988)
Inside Out (Jahmani, 1989)
Kingfari (Jahmani, 1992*)
Lion Dub Beauty (Jahmani, 1996*)
Love Smiles (Jahmani, 1991)
On Track (Jahmani, 1991)
Tell It to the Children (Tree Roots,
    1988)
Two Double Six 701 (Jahmani, 1994*)

INNER CIRCLE
Bad Boys (RAS, 1991*), EP
Bad Boys (Atlantic, 1993**)

Bad to the Bone (RAS, 1992*)
Best of Inner Circle (Mango, 1992**),
    featuring Jacob Miller
Black Roses (RAS, 1990*)
Blame It On the Sun (Trojan, 1975)
Everything Is Great (Island, 1979)
Heavy Reggae (Starapple), 1970s,
    Tommy Cowan
Identified (Vision, 1989)
New Age Music (Island, 1979)
One Way (RAS, 1987)
Ready for the World (Capital, 1977)
Reggae Greats (Island, 1985)
Reggae Thing (Capitol, 1976+),
    self-produced
Rock the Boat (Trojan, 1974), Tommy
    Cowan

ISAACS, GREGORY
All I Have Is Love (Abraham+),
    mid-1970s, Sydney Crooks
All I Have Is Love, Love, Love (Tad's,
    1986)
Best of, Vols. 1–2 (Heartbeat,
    1992**), GGs
Blood Brothers (RAS, 1994*), with
    Dennis Brown
Boom Shot (Shanachie, 1991*)
Call Me Collect (RAS*), early 1990s,
    Xterminator
Come Along (Live and Love), late
    1980s, Jammys
Come Closer (Declic, 1994*)
Consequence (Scorpio, 1989; Rohit,
    1990*)
Cool Ruler (Virgin, 1978+)
Cool Ruler Soon Forward Selection
    (Virgin, 1990**)
Cooyah (New Name, 1990)
Crucial Cuts (Virgin, 1983+)
Dance Curfew (Acid Jazz, 1997*),
    Dread Flimstone, U.K.
    production
Dance Hall Don (Shanachie, 1994*),
    with 6 DJs
Dancing Floor (Heartbeat, 1990*)
Do Lord (Xterminator, 1998*)
Dreaming (Heartbeat, 1995*), Alvin
    Ranglin
Early Years (Trojan+), 1970s cuts
Easy (Tad), mid-1980s
Encore (Kingdom, 1988)
Extra Classic (Conflict; Echo, 1980+)
Feature Attraction (VP), early 1990s
Gilbert (Firehouse, 1988), produced
    by King Tubby

Gregory Isaacs Meets Ronnie Davis
(Plant, 1979)
Hardcore (RAS, 1992*)
Heartbreaker (Rohit, 1990)
Hold Tight (Heartbeat, 1997*), Mafia
and Fluxy inna U.K. style
Holding Me Captive (VP, 1993)
I Am the Investigator (Esoldun, 1995*)
In Person (GG's+), circa 1974
Judge Not (Greensleeves, 1984), with
Dennis Brown
Lee Perry Presents Gregory Isaacs
(Rhino, U.K.*)
Let's Go Dancing (Jammys, 1989)
Live (Island, 1985)
Live at Maritime Hall (Artists Only,
1998*)
Live at the Academy, Brixton (Rough
Trade, 1984)
Lonely Days (Jamaica Gold, 1992*),
GG's 1970s tracks
Lonely Lover (PRE, 1980)
Looking Back (RAS, 1995**),
compilation, Gregory's selection
Lovers Rock (Charisma, 1981+),
1970s, double album
Maximum Respect (CSI, 1994*)
More Gregory (Mango, 1981**),
self-produced
Mr. Cool (VP, 1996*)
Mr. Isaacs (Micron+), mid-1970s,
Gregory Isaacs production
Mr. Love (Caroline**), late 1970s
compilation
My Poor Heart (Heartbeat, 1994*),
Star Trail
New Dance (EAD), late 1980s
Night Nurse (Mango, 1982+)
No Contest (Greensleeves, 1989), with
Dennis Brown
No Intention (VP, 1990)
No Surrender (RAS, 1992*)
Not a One Man Thing (RAS, 1995*)
Once Ago (Virgin, 1990**)
One Man Against the World (VP,
1996*)
Out Deh! (Mango, 1983)
Pardon Me! (RAS, 1992*)
Prime of Gregory Isaacs (Music Club,
1998*)
Private Beach Party (RAS, 1988+),
Gussie Clarke
Reggae Best (Esoldun, 1993*)
Reggae Greats: Gregory Isaacs Live
(Mango, 1984)
Reggae It's Fresh (Tad's, 1989)
Reggae Jammin' (Essex, 1992*)

Reserved for Gregory (Exodus, U.K.),
late 1980s
Rudie Boo (Star Trail, 1992*)
Showcase (Taxi), 1970s
Sensational Gregory Isaacs (Vista),
recorded late 1960s–early 1970s
Sly and Robbie Present Gregory Isaacs
(RAS, 1987**), Showcase reissue
Soon Forward (Virgin, 1979+)
State of Shock (RAS, 1991*)
Talk Don't Bother Me (Rohit, 1987)
Too Good to Be True (RAS, 1989)
Two Bad Superstars (Burning Sounds,
1984+), Gussie
Unforgettable (Rohit), late 1980s
Unlocked (RAS, 1993)
Victim (C&E), 1980s
Warning (Serious Business), late 1980s
Watchman of the City (Rohit, 1987)
Willow Tree (Jamaica Gold, 1992**),
1970s, GG's
Yesterday (VP, 1997*)

ISRAEL VIBRATION
Best of Israel Vibration (Sonic Sounds),
1978–80, Tommy Cowan
Feelin' Irie (RAS CD EP, 1996*),
4 mixes
Forever (RAS, 1991*)
Free to Move (RAS, 1996*)
Israel Vibration IV (RAS, 1993**)
Live Again (RAS, 1997)
On the Rock (RAS, 1995*)
Praises (RAS, 1990*)
Same Song (Top Ranking, 1978; RAS,
1996**), Tommy Cowan
Strength of My Life (RAS, 1988)
Unconquerable People (Israel Vibes,
1980, RAS, 1996+), with T. Cowan
Vibes Alive (RAS, 1992*)
Why You So Craven (Arrival; RAS,
1991*), 1970s, Junjo Lawes

ITALS
Brutal Out Deh (Nighthawk, 1981+)
Cool and Dread (Nighthawk, 1988)
Early Recordings, 1971–79
(Nighthawk, 1987**)
Easy to Catch (Rhythm Safari, 1991*)
Give Me Power (Nighthawk, 1983)
Modern Age (RAS, 1998*)
Rasta Philosophy (Nighthawk, 1985)

JAH LION
Columbia Collie (Mango, 1976**)

JAH LLOYD (JAH LION)
Black Moses (Virgin, 1979)
Herbs of Dub (Teem, 1996)
Humble One (Virgin, 1978+), 1974–76

**JAH MESSENGERS (FORMERLY
EARTH'S MESSENGERS)**
Jah Messengers (Heartbeat, 1993*)

JAH SHAKA
Kings Music (Jah Shaka, 1984)
Message from Africa (Jah Shaka, 1985)
Message from Africa (Jah Shaka, 1988)

JAH STITCH
Original Raggamuffin, 1975–77 (Blood
and Fire, 1996*)

JAH THOMAS
Dance Hall Connection (Silver Camel,
U.K., 1983)
Dance Hall Stylee (Midnight Rock),
early 1980s
Dance On the Corner (Midnight
Rock), early 1980s
Jah Thomas Meets Scientist in Dub
Conference (Munich, 1996*)
Nah Fight Over Woman (Midnight
Rock), early 1980s
Stop Yu Loafin' (Greensleeves, 1978+),
produced by Jo Jo Hookim
Tribute to Reggae King Bob N. Marley
(Midnight Rock, 1981)
Tristan Palma Meets Jah Thomas in
Disco Style (Munich, 1996*)

JAH WOOSH
Best of (Rhino, U.K., 1993*)
Chalice Blaze (Original Music, 1996*)
Dreadlocks Affair (Trojan, 1976+)
Dub Plate Specials (original Music,
1992)
Jah Woosh Meets Mixman: Fire Inna
Blackamix (Blackamix, 1993)
Marijuana World Tour (Original
Music+), produced by Creation
Rebel
Religious Dread (Trojan, 1978+)
Sing and Chant with Jah Woosh
(September), 1980s
Sinsemilla Song (Original Music, 1990)
Some Sign (Sky Juice), late 1980s
We Chat You Rock (Trojan, 1991*),
with I Roy

JAHSON, DAVID
Natty Chase the Barber (Top Ranking, 1978)

JAMAICANS
Ba Ba Boom Time (Jamaica Gold, 1996**)

JARRETT, WINSTON
Jonestown (Nighthawk, 1989**)
Kingston Vibration (RAS, 1991**)
Rocking Vibration (Culture Press, 1984)
Solid Foundation (Heartbeat, 1991**)
Too Many Boundaries (RAS, 1995*)
Tribute to Bob Marley (Original Music*), early 1990s

JAYES
Unforgettable Times (E&J, 1979; Vol. 2, 1980)

JOHNSON, ANTHONY
Gunshot (Midnight Rock), early 1980s
I'm Ready (Rusty International, U.K.), early 1980s
Reggae Feeling (Live and Learn, 1982)
Robert French Meets Anthony Johnson (Midnight Rock), late 1980s
Togetherness (Prestige, 1993*)
Want More Loving (Black Link), 1980s
Yah We Deh (Jammys, 1985), showcase stylee half vocal half dub

JOHNSON, LINTON KWESI
Bass Culture (Mango, 1980)
Dread Beat and Blood as Poet and the Roots (Virgin, 1990**)
Forces of Victory (Mango, 1979)
In Concert with the Dub Band (Rough Trade)
Independent Intravenshan (Island, 1998*)
Making History (Mango, 1984)
Reggae Greats (Mango, 1984)
Tings An' Times (Shanachie, 1991*)
LKJ in Dub (LKJ)
LKJ in Dub, Vol. 2 (LKJ, 1992)

JOLLY BROTHERS
Conscious Man (Roots, U.K.+), late 1970s, produced by Lee Perry
Conscious Man (Roots CD EP, 1992**)
Consciousness (United Artists, 1978)

JONES, BARBARA
Best of Barbara Jones (Trojan, 1976)
Don't Stop Loving Me (GG's, 1979)
For Your Eyes Only (Jamaica Gold, 1994**)
Will It Last Forever (GG's, 1982)

JONES, FRANKIE
Best of Frankie Jones, Vol. 1 (Trojan, 1986)
Dance Cork (World Enterprise), early 1980s
Hell in the Dance (Live & Learn, 1986)
Old Fire Stick (Power House), 1980s, produced by George Phang
Satta an Praise Jah (Third World, 1977+)
Show-Down, Vol. 4 (Empire, 1984), with Michael Palmer; Kenneth Hookim production
Them Nice (Sunset, 1985), produced by Brent Dowe
Two New Superstars (Burning Sounds, 1985), with Patrick Andy
Who Nuh Hear Me Yet (Wackies), 1980s

JONES, VIVIAN
Bank Robbery (Ruff Kutt), late 1980s
Iyaman (Imperial House, 1994), with Iauwata and Jah Wayne
Jah Works (Jah Shaka+), circa 1986
Jet Star Reggae Max (Jet Star, 1997*)
Jamaica Love (Virgo Stomach), late 1980s
King (Imperial House, 1992)
Strong Love (Imperial House), circa 1990

KAMOZE, INI
Here Comes the Hotstepper (Columbia, 1995*)
Ini Kamoze (Island, 1984*)
Lyrical Gangsta (East/West, 1995*)
Pirate (Mango, 1986)
Shocking Out (RAS, 1988*)
Statement (Mango, 1984)

KELLY, PAT
Best of Pat Kelly (Vista, 1983)
Classics (Super Power), 1980s
Cry for You No More (Blue Moon, 1988)
Lonely Man (Burning Sounds+), late 1970s

Man and His Hits (World Enterprise)
One Man Stand (Third World, 1979)
Ordinary Man (Body Music), late 1980s
Pat Kelly Sings (Pama, 1969)
So Proud (Chanan-Jah+), 1980s
Soulful Love: The Best of Pat Kelly, 1967–74 (Trojan, 1997**)
Srevol (Ethnic), 1980s
Sunshine (Imperial, 1980)
Talk About Love (Terminal, 1975)
20 Golden Hits (Striker Lee*)
20 Magnificent Hits, early 1980s
Wish It Would Rain (Joe Gibbs, 1980+)

KING STITT
Dance Hall '63 (Studio One), mid-1990s
Fire Corner (Trojan, 1969)
Reggae Fire Beat (Jamaica Gold, 1996**)

KINGSTONIANS
Sufferer (Attack, 1970; 1991+)

KNOWLEDGE
Hail Dread (A&M, 1978+)
Stumbling Block (Tamoki-Wambesi+), 1990s
Words, Sounds and Power aka Hail Dread (Tappa), late 1970s

LARA, DERRICK
Right On Time (Taxi)

LARA, JENNIFER
Studio One Presents Jennifer Lara (Studio One), early 1980s

LEE, BYRON AND THE DRAGONAIRES
Carnival Experience (Dynamic, 1979)
Come Fly with Lee (Soul), 1960s
Disco Reggae (Mercury, 1975)
Jamaica's Golden Hits, Vols. 1–3 (Jamaica Gold, 1992)
Jump Up (Atco, 1966)
Only a Fool (Jamaica Gold, 1993)
People Get Ready, This Is Rock, Rock Steady (Jamaica Gold, 1993*)
Reggae Hot Shots, Vol. 1 (Jamaica Gold, 1995*)
Reggay Blast Off (Trojan, 1980; Jamaica Gold, 1993**)
Reggay Eyes (Jamaica Gold, 1993*)

Reggay International (Creole), late
    1970s
Soft Lee, Vols. 1–6 (Dynamic)
Soul-Ska! (Echo, U.K.), mid-1960s
Wine Miss Tiney (Dynamic, 1985)

LEVY, BARRINGTON
Barrington (MCA, 1993**)
Broader Than Broadway (Best of)
    (Profile), early 1990s
Collection (Time 1), 1980s
Divine (RAS, 1994), produced by Jah
    Screw
Doh Ray Me (JB, 1980)
Englishman/Robin Hood (Greensleeves,
    1991**), 1979–80, reissues 2 LPs
Here I Come (Time 1, 1985; RAS,
    1995**), produced by Jah Screw
Hunter Man (Burning Sounds), 1979,
    Junjo Lawes
Living Dangerously (Navarre, 1998*)
Love the Life You Live (Time 1, 1989),
    Paul Love (Jah Screw)
Money Move (Power House), George
    Phang
Open Book (Tuff Gong), late 1980s
Poorman Style (Clocktower; Trojan,
    1982)
Prison Oval Rock (Garand; RAS, 1991*)
Reggae Vibes (Rocky One*), early
    1980s
Shine Eye Gal (Burning Sounds), 1979
Teach Me Culture (Live & Learn,
    1983*)
Time Capsule (RAS, 1996*), 1980s
Turning Point (Profile, 1992)

LEWIS, HOPETON
Dynamic Hopeton Lewis (Dragon,
    U.K., 1975)
All Night Bubblin' (Boss Records, 1985)
Grooving Out On Life (Jamaica Gold,
    1993**), early 1970s
Take It Easy (Merritone, 1967,
    K&K**), mid-1990s reissue

LINK AND CHAIN
New Day (RAS, 1990**), produced by
    Jack Ruby and Stephen Stewart
S.T.O.P. (RAS, 1992*), Fatis Burrell

LITTLE ROY
Columbus Ship (Copasetic, 1981)
Live On (Tafari, 1991)
Longtime (On-U, 1996**)

Prophesy (Tafari, 1990)
Tafari Earth Uprising (Pressure
    Sounds**), mid-1990s reissue
Tribal War (Tafari, 1975)

LIVINGSTON, CARLETON
Best of Carlton Livingston (Abraham,
    1984**)
Emotions (Grapevine, 1994**)
Fret Them a Fret (Live & Learn)
100 Weight of Collie Weed
    (Greensleeves, 1984)
Rumors (Bebo, 1985)
Soweto (Bebo, 1982+)
Trodding Through the Jungle
    (Dynamite, 1984)

LOCKS, FRED
Culturally (Tan-Yah*), early 1990s
Love and Only Love (Regal, U.K.),
    early 1980s, with Creation Steppers
Nebuchadnezzar King of Babylon
    (Revelations), 1980s, with Steppers
Never Give Up (VP, 1998**)
True Rastaman (Reggae
    Bloodlines/Vulcan**), mid-1970s

LODGE, J.C.
Love for All Seasons (RAS, 1996)
Revealed (RAS, 1985)
Selfish Lover (VP, 1990), Gussie
    Clarke
Special Request (RAS, 1995)
To the Max (RAS, 1993)
Tropic of Love (Tommy Boy, 1991)

LONDON, JIMMY
Hold On (Esoldun, 1996*)
It Ain't Easy Living in the Ghetto
    (Burning Sounds)
Welcome to My World (Burning
    Sounds)

LONE RANGER
Badda Dan Dem (Studio One, 1982)
Barnabas Collins (GGs, 1980)
Collections (Greensleeves, 1994*)
Hi-Yo Silver, Away (Greensleeves,
    1982)
Learn to Drive (Bebo, 1985)
M16 (Hitbound, 1982**)
On the Other Side of Dub (Studio
    One, 1981; Heartbeat, 1991**)
Rosemarie (Techniques), mid-1980s

LOVINDEER
Best of Lovindeer (TSOJ*), 1980s
De Blinkin' Bus (TSOJ, 1982)
One Day Christian (TSOJ, 1989)
Ride Ride Ride (Wildlife), late
    1970s
Serious Times (Pye), same as above
Why Don't We All Just Have Sex
    (TSOJ), late 1980s

LUCIANO
After All (VP, 1995)
Jet Star Reggae Max (Jet Star, 1997*)
Messenger (Island Jamaica, 1996*)
Moving Up (RAS, 1993*)
One Way Ticket (VP, 1994**)
Shake It Up Tonight (Big Ship,
    1994)
Stuck on You (Sky High, 1993),
    with Presley
Where There Is Life (Island Jamaica,
    1995*)

MARLEY, BOB, AND THE WAILERS
African Herbsman (Trojan, 1973),
    half the Lee Perry sessions
African Herbsman (Fame), Perry
    selections differing from above
All the Hits (Rohit, 1990*), Bunny
    Lee and others
Babylon By Bus (Island, 1978; Tuff
    Gong**), 2 albums on one CD
Best of Bob Marley and Peter Tosh
    with the Wailers (URTI, 1981),
    7 of 10 songs from the Leslie
    Kong Sessions or Shakedown
Best of Bob Marley and the Wailers
    (Studio One), late 1960s
Best of Bob Marley and the Wailers
    (Studio One/Buddah), late 1960s,
    completely different from Jamaican
    album above (later issued here)
Best Rarities of Bob Marley (Time
    Wind), Lee Perry productions
Birth of a Legend (Calla; CBS, 1977,
    1990*), issued as both a single
    and double album these 20 tracks
    have been endlessly recycled
Blackout (Splash), 199 cuts culled
    from Perry and Kong
Bob Marley aka Soul Shakedown Party
    or Shakedown (Slam, 1988)
Bob Marley and the Wailers (Hammer,
    1981), Shakedown scrambled
Bob Marley and the Wailers aka Soul
    Rebel (Magnum, 1978)

Bob Marley and the Wailers *aka* Soul Revolution, Part 2 (Exclusive Picturedisc)

Bob Marley and the Wailers: The Box Set (Island), repackages the 9 original Island albums (excluding Babylon by Bus), late 1980s

Bob Marley 50th Birthday Commemorative (Trojan, 1995**), 5 CD singles, 5 mixes—dubs, DJ, vocals, instrumentals—of each song

Bob, Peter Bunny and Rita (Jamaica Records, 1985), JAD sessions

Burnin' (Island, 1973; Tuff Gong**)

Catch a Fire (Island, 1973; Tuff Gong**)

Chances Are (Cotillion, 1981), from the JAD sessions

Complete Wailers, 1967–72, Part 1 (JAD, 1998**), 3-CD rarities set; first of projected 3 vols.

Confrontation (Island, 1983**), also issued as a picture disc

Crying for Freedom (Time Wind), "memorial" box set containing the Lee Perry Sessions and the Leslie Kong sessions

Early Music (Calla), vol. 2 of Birth of a Legend when issued separately

Early Years, 1969–73 (Trojan, 1993**), 4-CD boxed set includes Rasta Revolution, African Herbsman: In the Beginning and Soul Revolution, Vol. 2 (the dub set)

Essential Bob Marley (Design), combines Shakedown with Jamaican Storm

In Memorium (Trojan, 1991), 3-record set includes the Lee Perry and Leslie Kong sessions

In the Beginning (Trojan, 1983), includes some uncommon tracks

Jamaican Storm (Accord, 1982), material from JAD sessions

Kaya (Island, 1978**)

Lee Perry Sessions (Konexion), African Herbman and Rasta Revolution

Legend (Island, 1984**), compilation

Lions Domain (Collector's Edition), live in London, 1978 bootleg

Live (Island, 1975; Tuff Gong**)

Marley, Tosh, Livingston and Associates (Studio One), 1960s

Natty Dread (Island, 1974; Tuff Gong**)

Natural Mystic (Avid, 1995), tracks from Perry and JAD sessions

Natural Mystic: Legend Lives On (Tuff Gong, 1995**), compilation

Exodus (Island, 1977**)

Greatest Hits of Bob Marley (Babylon), 12 from the Perry sessions

Marley (Phoenix, 1982), 10 selections from the Perry sessions

Natty Dread (Island, 1974; Tuff Gong**)

Nice Time (Esoldun, 1991*), All the Hits plus dub of same

On the Wings of Memory (Telstar, 1988*), pretty standard selection

One Love (Heartbeat, 1991**), crucial 1960s Studio One recordings

Rasta Revolution (Trojan), Soul Rebels plus "Duppy Conqueror"

Rastaman Vibration (Island, 1976**)

Rebel Music (Island, 1986**), compilation

Reggae (Classic Sounds, 1992*), Kong/Perry/JAD

Reggae Greats: The Wailers (Island/Mango, 1981), early compilation

Reggae Rebel (Surprise Records), 10 tracks from the Perry sessions

Return to Dunn's River Falls (Compose, 1989), mixes tracks from the Perry and Kong sessions

Roots (Blue Moon*), early recordings

Shakedown (Ala, 1982), Leslie Kong productions

Simmer Down (Heartbeat, 1994*), One Love, disc one

Slave Driver (Creative Sounds, 1991*), compilation

Songs of Freedom (Tuff Gong, 1992**), 4-CD set

Soul Almighty (Creative Sounds, 1991), Perry and JAD sessions

Soul Almighty: Natural Mystic II (Avid, 1995*), mainly from the Perry sessions with 3 JAD sessions tracks

Soul Almighty: The Formative Years (JAD, 1996*), with interactive CD

Soul Captives (Ala), same tracks as Shakedown

Soul Rebel (New Cross), material from JAD sessions

Soul Rebels (Receiver, 1988**), Perry sessions as originally issued in the, U.K. by Trojan including original front cover

Soul Revolution (URTI), actually pretty much African Herbsman

Soul Revolution, Part 2 (Maroon), produced by Lee Perry

Soul Revolution, Parts 1–2 (Trojan, 1988), 14 tracks from the Perry Sessions, Soul Revolution, Part 2, plus 2 with corresponding dubs

Survival (Island, 1979**)

Talkin' Blues (Tuff Gong, 1991**), collects mid-1970s rarities

Uprising (Island, 1980; Tuff Gong**)

Upsetter Record Shop, Part 1 (Esoldun, 1992), nonstandard

Upsetter Record Shop, Part 2 (Esoldun, 1992)

Wailing for the Last Time: The Final Performance; recorded live at Stanley Theater, Pittsburgh, 9/23/80 (Rasta Records), bootleg also issued as Bob Marley's Last Performance

Wailing Wailers (Studio One; Heartbeat, 1994*), One Love, disc 2

Wings of Reggae (Time Wind), memorial box set collecting Birth of a Legend, Shakedown, and Perry sessions

20 Greatest Hits (Black Tulip), selects from Coxsone and Perry

INTERVIEWS

Bob Marley in Conversation (Tabak, 1993*)

Bob Marley Interviews (Tuff Gong), early 1980s

OF RELATED INTEREST

The Wailers Tribute to Carly Barrett (Atra, 1987)

Jimi Hendrix, Bob Marley, Percy Sledge (Curcio Italy), 6 from Kong

Marley Family Album (Heartbeat, 1995*)

Marley Magic: Live in Central Park (Tuff Gong, 1997)

See also Peter Tosh, Bunny Wailer, Wailers band

MARLEY, DAMIAN "JR. GONG"
Mr. Marley (Tuff Gong, 1997*)

MARLEY, JULIAN
Lion in the Morning (Tuff Gong, 1997*)

MARLEY, KYMANI
Dear Dad (VP, 1997*)
Ky-Mani (Shang, 1997)

Like Father Like Son (Rhino, U.K., 1997*)

MARLEY, RITA
Harambe (Shanachie, 1982)
We Must Carry On (Shanachie, 1991)
Who Feels It Knows It (Shanachie, 1981)

MARLEY, ZIGGY, AND THE MELODY MAKERS
Conscious Party (Virgin, 1988*)
Fallen Is Babylon (Elektra, 1997*)
Free Like We Want 2 B (Elektra, 1995*)
Hey World (EMI, 1986)
Jahmekya (Virgin, 1991*)
Joy and Blues (Virgin, 1993*)
One Bright Day (Virgin, 1989*)
Play the Game Right (EMI, 1985)
Time Has Come: Best of (EMI, 1988)

MARSHALL, LARRY
Come Let Us Reason (King's Music, 1992*)
Dance with Me Across the Floor (Conqueror Records, 1988)
I Admire You (Java, 1975; Heartbeat, 1992**)
Presenting Larry Marshall (Studio One, 1973; Heartbeat, 1992**)
Throw Me Corn (Original Music+), mid-1980s

MATUMBI
Best of Matumbi (Trojan, 1977)
Matumbi (EMI, 1981)
Point of View (EMI, 1979)
Seven Seals (EMI, 1978)

MAYTONES
Best of the Mighty Maytones (Burning Sounds, 1983)
Boat to Zion (Burning Sounds, 1979)
Funny Man (Jamaica Gold, 1993**)
Greatest Hits (GG's, 1977)
Hard Time (Tabansi), late 1970s
Keep the Fire Burning (Third World), circa 1974
Madness (Burning Sounds, 1976), A. Ranglin
Natural Feeling (Drum & Bass), early 1980s
One Way (GG's, 1979)

Only Your Picture (D Music, 1981)
Showcase (Funky Hut), late 1970s
Tune in and Rock (Pioneer International), late 1970s

MCGREGOR, FREDDIE
Across the Border (RAS, 1984)
All in the Same Boat (RAS, 1986)
Big Ship (Thompson Sounds, Greensleeves, 1982)
Boby Bobylon (Studio One, 1980; Heartbeat, 1991**)
Carry Go Bring Come (Pow Wow, 1994*), Gussie Clarke
Come On Over (RAS, 1983)
Don't Want to Be Lonely (Studio One), recorded 1968–76; 1987
Forever My Love (RAS, 1995*)
Freddie McGregor (Polydor, 1987)
Freddy McGregor (Tuff Gong, 1979)
Hard to Get (Pow Wow, 1993*)
I Am Ready (Studio One, 1982)
Jamaican Classics, Vols. 1–3 (VP, 1991–96)
Legit (Shanachie, 1993*), with Cocoa Tea and Dennis Brown
Live At Town and Country Club London England (Gold Disc, 1990)
Love At First Sight (Joe Gibbs, 1982)
Mr. McGregor (Observer, 1979), same as Freddy McGregor
Now (Steely & Clevie, 1991)
Push On (Big Ship, 1994*)
Rumors (Gone Clear, 1997*)
Zion Chant (Heartbeat, 1994**)

MCKAY, FREDDIE
Best of Freddie McKay (GG's, 1977+)
Creation (Plant Music, 1979+), Ossie Hibbert
Fire Is Burning (Amethyst)
Harsh Words (Gorgon+)
I'm a Free Man (Uptempo, 1986)
Lonely Man (Dragon, 1974+)
Picture On the Wall (Studio One, 1971+)

MEDITATIONS
Deeper Roots: Best of the Meditations (Heartbeat, 1994**)
For the Good of Man (Heartbeat, 1988), without Ansel Cridland
Greatest Hits (Shanachie, 1984)
Guidance (Tad's, 1980)

Message from the Meditations (Double-D, New York, 1976; Wild Flower, Jamaica, 1977; UA, 1978; Makossa, 1981; Liberty, 1981+)
No More Friend (Greensleeves, 1983)
Return of the Meditations (Heartbeat, 1992*)
Reggae Crazy: Anthology, 1971–79 (Nighhawk, 1998*)
Wake Up (Sound Proof, JA; Double-D, 1977; Third World, U.K., 1978+)

MELODIANS
Irie Feeling (RAS, 1983)
Pre-Meditation (Sky Note), mid-1980s
Sweet Sensation (Harry J, 1977)
Sweet Sensation (Mango, 1980), compilation; not the same as above
Swing and Dine (Heartbeat, 1992**)

MIGHTY DIAMONDS
Backstage (Music Works, 1983), produced by Gussie Clarke
Bust Out (VP, 1993), produced by Junior Reid
Changes (Music Works, 1981), Gussie
Deeper Roots and Dub (Virgin, 1979; Caroline, 1997**), Jo Jo Hookim
Get Ready (Rohit, 1988), Gussie
Go Seek Your Roots (Virgin, 1990*), Hookim
Heads of Government (Germain)
I Need a Roof aka Right Time (J&J), recorded 1975
Ice On Fire ((Virgin, 1977), Allen Toussaint/Marshall Sehorn
If You Looking for Trouble (Live & Learn, 1986), Delroy Wright
Indestructible (Alligator, 1982+), Gussie
Ital Selection (Virgin, 1981), compilation
Jam Session (Live & Learn, 1990*)
Kouchie Vibes (Burning Sounds, 1984)
Leaders of Black Countrys (Tappa; Mobiliser, 1983)
Live (Genes, 1992*), with Mutabaruka
Live in Europe (Greensleeves, 1989)
Live in Tokyo (Overheat, 1985)
Moment of Truth (Mango, 1992*)
Never Get Weary (Live & Learn, 1988)
Paint It Red (RAS, 1993*)
Pass the Koutchie (Bad Gong), early 1980s
Patience (Tassa, 1991*)
Planet Earth (Virgin, 1978)

Real Enemy (Greensleeves, 1987),
    Gussie
Reggae Street (Shanachie, 1981)
Right Time (Virgin, 1976; Shanachie,
    1983+)
Roots Is There (Shanachie, 1982),
    Gussie and Germain
Speak the Truth (RAS, 1994*)
Stand Up to Your Judgment (Channel
    One, 1978)
Struggling (Live & Learn, 1985)
Tell Me What's Wrong (J&J), mid-1970s

MILLER, JACOB
Dread, Dread (United Artists, 1978;
    Liberty reissue, 1985)
Greatest Hits (RAS), same as Mango
    Reggae Greats
I'm Just a Dread (Rocky One, 1994)
Jacob "Killer" Miller (Top Ranking,
    1978; RAS, 1987)
Jacob Miller and the Inner Circle Band
    and Augustus Pablo (Esoldun,
    1992)
Jacob Miller Meets Fatman Riddim
    Section, 1978–79 (Esoldun, 1995*)
Killer Rides Again (VP*)
Mixed Up Moods (Top Ranking, late
    1970s; Esoldun, 1993*)
Natty Christmas (Top Ranking, late
    1970s; RAS, 1990*), with Ray I
Reggae Greats: Jacob Miller and Inner
    Circle (Mango, 1984**)
Wanted (Top Ranking, 1979)
Who Say Jah No Dread (Greensleeves,
    1992**), recorded 1974–75

MINOTT, SUGAR
A True (Arrival, 1985)
African Soldier (Heartbeat, 1988+)
Black Roots (Mango, 1979+)
Breaking Free (RAS, 1994*)
Buy Off the Bar (Power House, 1988)
Ghetto Child (Heartbeat, 1989)
Ghettology (Trojan, 1979+)
Give the People (United Artists, 1979)
Good Thing Going (Heartbeat, 1982)
Happy Together (Heartbeat, 1991*)
Herbman Hustling (Heartbeat 1998**),
    reissues early 1980s recordings
Hit Man (Black Roots, 1992)
In the Residence (Black Roots, 1994)
International (RAS, 1996*)
Leader for the Pack (Black Roots, 1985)
Live Loving (Studio One, 1978)
Mr. Fix It (VP, 1990+)

More Sugar Minott (Studio One),
    1980s
Musical Murder (VP, 1996*)
Run Things (VP, 1993*)
Rydim (Power House), mid-1980s
Showcase (Studio One, 1979;
    Heartbeat, 1992**)
Smile (VP), late 1980s
Sufferer's Choice (Heartbeat, 1983)
Sugar and Spice (Taxi; RAS, 1986)
Sugar Minott and the African Brothers
    (Uptempo, 1987)
Sugar Minott Collection (Rhino, U.K.,
    1995*)
Sugar Minott Collector's Collection,
    Vol. 1 (Youth Promotions, 1992;
    Heartbeat, 1996**)
Sugar Minott Story (Uptempo, 1997*)
Sweeter Than Sugar (Hummingbird),
    1980s
Touch of Class (Jammys, 1990)
Wicked a Go Feel It (Wackies, 1984)

MISTY IN ROOTS
Chronicles (Kaz, 1994**)
Earth (People Unite, 1983; Kaz, 1995*)
Forward (Kaz, 1989)
Live At the Counter Eurovision (1979;
    Kaz, 1990)
Music-O-Tunya (1985; Kaz, 1995*)
Wise and Foolish (1981; Kaz, 1995*)

MORGAN, DERRICK
Conquerer (Vista, 1985)
Feel So Good (Attack, 1975)
Forward March (Beverley's), early 1960s
I Am the Ruler (Trojan, 1992**)
In the Mood (Magnet, 1974)
Moon Hop (Unicorn, 1990)
Ride the Rhythm (LA, U.K., 1990)
Ska Man Classics (Heartbeat, 1995*)
Time Marches On (Heartbeat, 1997**)

MORGAN HERITAGE
Miracle (MCA, 1994*)
One Calling (VP, 1998*)
Thank You Jah (VP, 1997**)

MORWELLS
Best of the Morwells (Nighthawk,
    1981)
Cool Runnings (Bushays, 1979)
Crab Race (Burning Sounds, 1978)
Kingston 12 Tuffie (Carib Gems, 1980)
Presenting (Morwell Esq, 1975)

MOSES, PABLO
A Song (Mango, 1980)
Charlie (Profile, 1990)
Confessions of a Rastaman (Free
    World Music, 1993*)
I Love I Bring (United Artists, 1978+)
In the Future (Alligator, 1983)
Live to Love (Rohit, 1987)
Mission (RAS, 1995*)
Pave the Way (Mango, 1981)
Reggae Greats (Mango, 1984)
Revolutionary Dream aka I Love I
    Bring (Jam Sounds, 1975)
Tension (Alligator, 1985)
We Refuse (Profile, 1990*)

MOWATT, JUDY
Black Woman (Ashandan, 1979)
Life aka Rock Me (Judy M, JA)
Look at Love (Shanachie, 1991*)
Love Is Overdue (Shanachie, 1986)
Mellow Mood (Tuff Gong, 1975)
Mr. Dee J. (Ashandan, 1982)
Only a Woman (Shanachie, 1982+)
Rock Me (Pow Wow, 1993)
Working Wonders (Ashandan;
    Shanachie, 1985)

MUNDELL, HUGH
Africa Must Be Free by 1983/Augustus
    Pablo: Africa Dub (Greensleeves,
    1990**), 1978 LP and dub album
    reissued on one CD
Arise (Network, 1991*), self-produced
Blackman's Foundation (Shanachie,
    1983+), Pablo/Mundell production
Jah Fire (Arawak), produced by Prince
    Jammy
Mundell (Greensleeves, 1982; 1992*),
    produced by Junjo Lawes
Time and Place (Mun-Rock, 1980),
    self-produced; Pablo arranged

MURVIN, JUNIOR
Best of Junior Murvin (Sunset, 1985),
    Junjo Lawes
Apartheid (Greensleeves, 1986)
Muggers in the Street (Greensleeves,
    1984)
Police and Thieves (Mango, 1977**)
Signs and Wonders (Live & Learn, 1988)

MUSICAL YOUTH
Different Style (MCA, 1983)
Youths of Today (MCA, 1982)

MUTABARUKA

Any Which Way . . . Freedom (Tuff Gong; Shanachie, 1989)
Blakk Wi Blak . . . k . . . k . . . (Shanachie, 1991*)
Check It (Alligator, 1983)
Melanin Man (Shanachie, 1994*)
Mystery Unfolds (Shanachie, 1986)
Outcry (Shanachie, 1984)
Ultimate Collection (Shanachie, 1996**)

MUTE BEAT

Flower (Overheat, 1987*)
In Dub (ROIR, 1996*)
Still Echo (Overheat, 1987**)

MYSTIC REVEALERS

Jah Works (RAS, 1993*)
Space and Time (RAS, 1995*)
Young Revolutionaries (RAS, 1991*)
This One's for Jah (Mesa, 1997*)

NATURALITES

Marvelous (Realistic, 1985; CSA, 1989**)
Naturalites in Ites (Realistics Music Society, 1989)
Picture On the Wall (1985; CSA, 1989**)

NOOKS, GEORGE

George Nooks (Correct, 1997)
Today (Jimpy's), early 1980s

ONOURA, OKU

Bus Out (Zola & Zola, 1993*)
Pressure Drop (Heartbeat, 1984; Zola & Zola, 1993**)

OPEL, JACKIE

Best of Jackie Opel (Studio One), 1960s
Cry Me a River (Studio One), 1960s
Love to Share (Top Deck, 1998+)
Memorable (WIRL), late 1960s

OSBOURNE, JOHNNY

Come Back Darling (Techniques, 1969), with the Sensations
Cool Down (VP, 1989)
Dancing Time (Londisc, 1984)
Fally Lover/Never Stop Fighting (Greensleeves, 1992*), reissues 2 albums from the early 1980s

Folly Ranking (Positive Sounds, 1980)
In Nah Disco Style (Cha Cha, 1981)
Never Stop Fighting (Greensleeves, 1982)
Nightfall Showcase (Munich, 1997*)
Nuh Dis (Come Ya Fe Drink Milk) (Serious Business, 1989), produced by King Tubby
Reality (Selection, 1984)
Reggae On Broadway (Vista, 1983), Jammy's
Rougher Than Them (Digital-B, 1989)
Sexy Thing (Esoldun, 1994*)
Truths and Rights (Studio One, 1980; Heartbeat, 1992**)
Warrior (Black Joy, 1981)
Water Pumping (Shanachie, 1983)

PALMA, TRISTAN

Born Naked (I & I Foundation, 1997*)
Joker Smoker (Shanachie, 1982), Jah Thomas
Nice Time (Jam Rock, 1982), with Toyan, produced by Tony Robinson
Settle Down Girl (Trojan, 1983), Linval Thompson
Showcase (Midnight Rock; Abraham*), early 1980s, Jah Thomas
Touch Me, Take Me (Abraham)
Tristan Palmer Meets Jah Thomas in Disco Style (Munich, 1996*)

PALMER, MICHAEL

Angella (Vista, 1984)
Ghetto Living (Bebo's, 1985)
I'm So Attractive (Jammy's, 1985)
Lick Shot (Powerhouse, 1984)
Pull It Up Now (Greensleeves, 1985)
Star Performer (Tonos , 1984)

PARAGONS

Golden Hits (Esoldun, 1992*)
Heaven and Earth (Prestige, 1993*)
On the Beach (Treasure Isle, 1968)
Original Paragons (Treasure Isle, 1990)
Paragons (Mango, 1981)
Paragons Return (Third World), Bunny Lee

PARKS, LLOYD

Girl in the Morning (Trojan, 1975)
Jeans, Jeans (TAD, 1985)
Loving You (Trojan, 1976)
Officially (Attack, 1974)
What More Can I Do (Parks, 1983)

PAUL, FRANKIE

A We Rule (RAS, 1997*), 1980s, Jazzbo productions
Be My Lady (Joe Gibbs, 1984)
Best in Me (VP*), early 1990s, Xterminator
Can't Get You Out of My Mind (Rohit), mid-1980s
Come Back Again (VP, 1996*), Bobby Digital
Dance Hall Duo (RAS), mid-1990s, with Pinchers
Detrimental (Rohit), mid-1980s
Don Man (Heartbeat, 1993*)
Double Trouble (Greensleeves, 1985), with Michael Palmer
Freedom (RAS), mid-1990s
Get Closer (Profile, 1990*)
Hard Work (RAS, 1994*)
Heartical Don (Super Power), Prince Jammy
I've Got the Vibes (Digital-B, 1995)
Jammin' (VP, 1991)
Let's Chill (VP), early 1990s
Love Affair (Techniques), 1980s
Pass the Tu-Sheng-Peng/Tidal Wave (Greensleeves, 1988**), mid-1980s, Junjo Lawes productions, 2 albums on one CD
Sara (Live & Love), Prince Jammy
Should I (Heartbeat, 1991*)
Slow Down (VP), 1980s, produced by Hugh "Redman" James
Still Alive (Jammy's, 1985)
Strange Feeling (Techniques, 1983)
Timeless (Tan-Yah), early 1990s
True (Black Scorpio, 1988)
Veteran (VP, 1991), Steely and Clevie
Warning (RAS, 1987)

PENN, DAWN

No, No, No (Atlantic, 1994*)

PERRY, LEE "SCRATCH"

Battle of Armageddon (Trojan, 1986)
Blood Vapour (LA, 1990), produced by Mike Brooks and Jah Lion
Chicken Scratch (Heartbeat, 1989+), produced by C.S. Dodd
Dub-Net Philosophy (Fotofun, 1997*)
Dub Messenger (Tassa, 1990*), Bullwackie
Excaliburman (Seven Leaves, 1989)
From the Secret Laboratory (Mango, 1990)

History, Mystery, Prophecy (Mango, 1984*)

Hold of Death (Rhino, U.K.), Mike Brooks/Jah Lion

Introducing Lee Perry (Esoldun, 1995*), Niney the Observer

Live At Maritime Hall with Mad Professor (2B1, 1997**)

Lord God Muzick (Heartbeat, 1991*)

Message from Yard (Rohit)

Mystic Warrior (Ariwa, 1989), with Mad Professor

Mystic Miracle Star (Heartbeat, 1982), with the Majestics

Quest (Abraham)

Return of Pipecock Jackxon (Black Star Liner, 1980)

Roast Fish, Collie Weed and Cornbread (Lion of Judah, 1978+)

Satan Kicked the Bucket (Bullwackies, 1988*)

Smokin' (VP*), 1990s, produced by Melvin "Munchie" Jackson

Soundz from the Hotline (Heartbeat, 1992*)

Technomajikal (ROIR, 1997*)

Upsetter and the Beat (Heartbeat, 1992*), C.S. Dodd

PIONEERS

Battle of the Giants (Trojan, U.K., 1970)

Feel the Rhythm (Mercury, U.K., 1976)

Freedom Feeling (Trojan), early 1970s

Greatest Hits (Pioneer International)

Greetings from the Pioneers (Joe Gibbs), late 1960s

I Believe in Love (Trojan), early 1970s

I'm Gonna Knock On Your Door (Trojan, 1974)

Long Shot (Trojan, 1969)

Long Shot Kick de Bucket (Trojan, 1997**), compilation

More Reggae for Lovers, Vols. 1–4 (Vista, 1985)

Pusher Man (Trojan, 1978)

Roll On Muddy River (Trojan, 1977)

Yeah (Trojan), 1970s

POPPIN, KEITH

Envious (Sunshot, 1975)

Pop Inn (Burning Sounds), mid-1970s

PRIEST, MAXI

Bonafide (Charisma, 1990*)

Intentions (Ten, 1986)

Man with the Fun (Virgin, 1996*)

Maxi (Ten, 1988)

Maxi Priest (Virgin, 1988)

You're Safe (Ten, U.K., 1985)

PRINCE ALLAH

Best of Prince Alla (Redemption Sounds), mid-1970s

Heaven Is My Roof (Stars, 1976; Tappa)

Jah Children Gather Round (Jah Shaka, 1996*)

King of the Road (Ital International, 1982)

Only Love Can Conquer, 1976–79 (Blood and Fire, 1996**)

Ras Allah Showcase (Vista, 1984)

PRINCE BUSTER

Big Five (Blue Beat, 1972, Mellodisc, 1988)

Fabulous Greatest Hits (Melodisc, 1967)

Golden Oldies (Prince Buster), 1960s

Judge Dread (Prince Buster, 1967; Melodisc, U.K. reissue)

King of Ska (Quattro, 1992**)

On Tour (Westmoor, 1967; Skank, 1988*)

Prophet (Melodisc, 1994**)

She Was a Rough Rider (Blue Beat, 1968; Skank, 1988)

Ten Commandments (RCA), late 1960s

Wreck a Pum Pum (Blue Beat, 1968)

PRINCE FAR I

Black Man Land (Virgin, 1990**), compilation

Free from Sin (Trojan, 1979)

In the House of Vocal and Dub (LJ*)

Jamaican Heroes (Trojan, 1980)

Livity (PRE, 1981)

Long Life (Virgin, 1978)

Message from the King (Virgin, 1978)

Musical History (Trojan, 1983)

Musical Revue with the Suns of Arqa (Danceteria), recorded 1982

Psalms for I (Carib Gems, 1976+)

Showcase in a Suitcase (PRE, 1980)

Spear of the Nation (Kingdom, 1984; Tamoki Wambesi)

Under Heavy Manners (Joe Gibbs, 1977+)

Voice of Thunder (Trojan, 1981)

PRINCE HAMMER

Bible (Virgin, 1978)

Respect I Man (Tamoki-Wambesi-Dove), early 1990s

PRINCE JAZZBO

Choice of Version (Studio One, 1990)

Head to Head Clash (RAS, 1989), with I Roy

Ital Corner (Clocktower), circa 1976

Kick Boy Face (Third World, 1976)

Wise Shepherd (Ujama, 1993)

PRINCE MOHAMMED

Bubbling (Techniques), early 1980s

No One Remembers Africa (Unity House)

People Are You Ready (Ballistic, 1978)

"?" Inna Him Head (Joe Gibbs, 1978)

PROPHET, MICHAEL

Bull-Talk (Greensleeves, 1992)

Cease and Settle (Live & Learn, 1994*)

Cease-Fire (Live & Learn, 1985; Move)

Certify (Burning Sounds, 1983)

Get Ready (Passion, 1991), with Ricky Tuffy

Gun Man (Jah Guidance)

Gunman/Righteous Are the Conqueror (Greensleeves, 1991*)

Jah Love (Live & Learn)

Know the Right (Vivian Jackson)

Love Is an Earthly Thing (CSA, 1983)

Loving You (Jam Rock), mid-1990s

Michael Prophet in Disco Style (Vivian Jackson, 1982)

Righteous Are the Conqueror (Greensleeves, 1980)

Serious Reasoning (Island, 1980)

Settle Yu Fe Settle (Live & Learn, 1986)

PSALMS

Up Front (RAS, 1992*)

RADICS, JACK

Affairs of the Heart (Sony, 1996*)

I'll Be Sweeter (VP)

Open Rebuke (Heartbeat, 1994*)

Radical (Shanachie, 1992*)

Something (VP*), Top Rank

What About Me (RUNN, 1994*)

RANKING JOE

Best of Ranking Joe (TR, 1978)
Dub It in a Dance (Trojan, 1980)
Natty Superstar (Joe Gibbs; Blue Moon, 1988)
Saturday Night Jamdown Style (Greensleeves, 1980)
Tribute to John Lennon (Tads), early 1980s
Weakheart Fadeaway (Greensleeves, 1978)

RANKING TREVOR

In Fine Style (Virgin, 1978)

RAS MICHAEL AND THE SONS OF NEGUS

Dadawah: Peace and Love (Trojan, 1975+)
Disarmament (Trojan, 1983)
Freedom Sounds (Dynamic, 1974; Rhino, U.K. CD reissue*)
Irations of Ras Michael (Top Ranking, 1977), compilation
Kibir-Am-Lak: Glory to God (Rastafari, 1978; Greensleeves, 1991; VP; Esoldun, 1994*)
Know Now (Shanachie, 1989*)
Lion Country (Zion Disc, JA, 1998**)
Love Thy Neighbor (Jah Life, 1984)
Mediator (High Times, 1993)
Movements (Ras Michael & the Sons of Negus, 1978)
New Name (Reggae Best (Esoldun, 1994*), compilation
Nyahbinghi (Trojan, 1974)
Promised Land Sounds (Lion Gates, 1980)
Rally Round (Shanachie, 1985**), compilation
Rastafari (Top Ranking, 1978)
Rastafari in Dub (Top Ranking, Grounation, 1979; ROIR CD reissue*)
Rastafari and Dub (Esoldun, 1992*)
Revelation (Trojan, 1982)
Tribute to the Emperor (Trojan, 1976)
Zion Train (SST, 1988), with HR

RAS MIDAS

Loving Vibration (Worldwide Music, 1996*)
Rain and Fire (Harry J, 1979+)
Rastaman in Exile (Skej, 1980)
Stand Up Wise Up (JML, 1989)

REGGAE GEORGE

Fight On My Own (Sky Juice)
Mix Up (Trojan, 1982)

REID, JUNIOR

Big Timer (VP*), recorded mid-1980s
Boom Shack a Lack (Greensleeves, 1985)
Junior Reid and the Bloods (RAS, 1995*)
Listen to the Voices (RAS, 1995*)
Long Road (Big Life/Cohiba, 1991)
Mini-Bus Driver (Negus Roots, 1982), with Voice of Progress
One Blood (JR, Big Life/Mercury, 1989**)
Original Foreign Mind (Sunset; Black Roots, 1985)
Progress (JR, 1990)
True World Order (JR, 1997*)
Visa (JR, RAS, 1994*)

CLASH ALBUMS (one side Junior Reid)
Double Top (Tamoki Wambesi), 1980s, with Cornell Campbell
Face to Face Clash (Sunset), 1980s, with Leroy Smart
Firehouse Clash (Live & Learn, 1986), with Don Carlos
Two of a Kind (Tamoki Wambesi), 1980s, with Teezy

RILEY, JIMMY

Attention, Attention (Blue Mountain*), mid-1990s
Give Love a Try (Live and Love), 1980s, produced by King Jammy
Jimmy Riley (Makossa, 1980)
Love Fa Real (Heavybeat*), mid-1990s
Magic (Omar*), late 1980s
Majority Rule (Makossa, 1978; Burning Sounds+)
Put the People First (Shanachie, 1982+)
Reggae Superstar (Camille), same as Majority Rule
Rydim Driven (Mango, 1981)
Tell the Youths the Truth aka Majority Rule (Trojan, 1979)
20 Classic Hits (Sonic Sounds**), compilation
World for Everyone (Blue Mountain, 1985)

ROMEO, MAX

Cross Or the Gun (Tappa*), early 1990s
Dream (Dynamic, 1970)

Every Man Ought to Know (Impact, 1972)
Fari: Captain of My Ship (Jah Shaka, 1992**)
Freedom Street (Island in the Sun), mid-1980s
Holding Out My Love to You (Shanachie, 1981)
I Love My Music (Solid Groove, 1982)
Let the Power Fall (Dynamic, 1971+), Bunny Lee
Love Message (Romeo), with guests
Max Romeo Meets Owen Gray at King Tubby's Studio (Culture Press, 1984), produced by Bunny Lee
On the Beach (Esoldun, 1992), 1970s, Bunny Lee
One Horse Race (Island in the Sun, 1985)
Open the Iron Gate (United Artists, 1978; Liberty, 1978+)
Our Rights (Jah Shaka, 1995*)
Reconstruction (Mango, 1977)
Revelation Time aka Open the Iron Gate (Black World, 1975)
Transition (Rohit*)
War in a Babylon (Island, 1976**)
Wet Dream (Pama, 1970)

ROOTS RADICS

Forward Ever, Backwards Never (Heartbeat, 1990*)
Freelance (Kingdom, 1985)
Hot We Hot (RAS, 1989)
Radically Radics (RAS, 1996*)
World Peace Three (Heartbeat, 1992*)

ROSE, MICHAEL

Be Yourself (Heartbeat, 1996*)
Bonanza (Japanese-only release), early 1990s
Dance Wicked (Heartbeat, 1997*)
Last Chance (Ruff Cut), mid-1990s
Michael Rose (Heartbeat, 1995*)
Nah Carbon (RAS, 1996*)
Party in Session (Live) (Heartbeat, 1998*)
Proud (BMG, 1990)
Selassie I Showcase (Melodee, 1997*)
Taxi Sessions (Taxi)
Voice of the Ghetto (VP, 1995)
See also Black Uhuru

ROSS, JUNIOR, AND THE SPEARS

Babylon Fall (Tappa+), mid-1970s

ROYALS
Israel Be Wise (Ballistic, 1978)
Moving On (Kingdom, 1981)
Pick Up the Pieces (Magnum, U.K.,
   1977; Ballistic, U.K., 1979+)
Royals Collection (Trojan, 1983)
Ten Years After (Ballistic, 1978)

RUFFY AND TUFFY
Climax (Ikus, 1988)

RUGGS, BUNNY
Talking to You (Shanachie, 1995*)

RUSSELL, DEVON
Darker Than Blue (Sweetest, 1993)
Prison Life (Tamoki Wambesi), late
   1980s
Roots Music (Studio One, 1982)
Three the Hard Way (Uptempo,
   1996), with Willie Williams and
   Nitty Gritty

SANCHEZ
Bring Back the Love (World
   Enterprise, 1992)
I Can't Wait (Digital-B, 1991)
In Fine Style (Exterminator, 1990)
Loneliness (Techniques, 1988)
Number One (RAS, 1989)
One in a Million: Best Of (VP, 1997)
Sanchez (Vena, 1987)
Sweetest Girl (Rohit, 1988)
Wild Sanchez (Greensleeves, 1989)

SCOTTY
Draw Your Breaks (Crystal, 1992)
School Days (Trojan, 1972)
Unbelievable Sounds (Trojan, 1988**)

SHERMAN, BIM
Crazy World (Century, 1992*)
Crucial Cuts, Vols. 1–2 (Century*),
   compilations 1970s–'90s
Danger, 1975–79 (Century, 1984)
Miracle (Mantra), mid-1990s
Reality (Century, 1992*), with Dub
   Syndicate

SHIRLEY, ROY
Black Lion Negus Rastafari (Roots,
   1995)
Control Them, Vol. 1 (Gallup*), 1990s

Good News (GG's), 1980s
Return of the High Priest (Weed Beat,
   1982)

SHORTY THE PRESIDENT
Fire Fire (Charmers, 1978)
High Ranking (Live and Love), 1970s

SILK, GARNETT
Garnett Silk & the DJ's Rule Thing
   (Rhino, U.K.), early 1990s
Gold (Charm, 1993**)
It's Growing (VP, 1992**)
Journey (VP, 1998*)
Live in Concert (Power Play), early
   1990s
Love Is the Answer (VP)
Lord Watch Over Our Shoulders
   (Greensleeves, 1995)
100% Silk (VP**), early 1990s
Silky Mood (VP, 1995)

SILVERTONES
Silver Bullets (Trojan, 1996**), reissue
   of 1970s Lee Perry cuts

SIXTEEN, EARL
Babylon Walls (Ariwa, 1992**)
Julia (Wambesi)
Not for Sale (Next Step, 1993+)
Phoenix of Peace (Seven Leaves,
   1993**), Lee Perry
Reggae Sound (Dread At the Controls,
   1981)
Rootsman (Rhino, U.K.*)
Shining Star (Vista, 1983)
Showcase (Studio One)
Songs for a Reason (Vista, 1983)
Songs of Love and Hardship
   (Kingdom, 1984)
Special Request (Tamoki Wambesi)
Them a Raiders (Rockers
   International+)

SKATALITES
African Roots (United Artists, 1978;
   Moon Ska, 1997**)
Ball of Fire (Island Jamaica, 1997*)
Best of the Skatalites (Studio One+),
   late 1950s–early 1960s
Celebration Time (Studio One), late
   1950s–early 1960s
Foundation Ska (Heartbeat, 1997**),
   supreme compilation

Greetings from Skamania (Shanachie,
   1996*)
Hi-Bop Ska (Shanachie, 1994*)
Legendary Skatalites aka African Roots
   (Jam Sounds)
Scattered Lights (Alligator)
Ska Authentic (Studio One), late
   1950s–early 1960s recordings
Ska-Voovie (Shanachie, 1993*)
Stretching Out (Danceteria/ROIR,
   1986, 1997*)

SLICKERS
Break Through (Tads), early 1980s

SLY AND ROBBIE
Friends (East/West, 1998*)
Language Barrier (Island, 1985)
Meet King Tubby (Esoldun, 1991)
Remember Precious Times (RAS,
   1992*)
Rhythm Killers (Island, 1987)
Silent Assassin (Island, 1989*)
Skatalites with Sly and Robbie and
   the Taxi Gang (Vista, 1983)
Sting (Moving Target, 1986)
Summit (RAS, 1988), produced by
   Phillip Burrell
Syncopation (Joe Gibbs, 1982)

SMART, LEROY
Ballistic Affair (Conflict+), mid-1970s,
   Jo Jo Hookim
Bank Account (Powerhouse, 1985)
Barry Heptones Meets Leroy Smart
   Showcase (Struggle, 1978)
Best of Leroy Smart (Channel One+)
Don of Class (World Wide Success,
   1988)
Dread Hot in Africa (Burning Sounds),
   late 1970s
Everytime (RAS*), 1990s
Face to Face Clash (Sunset. 1985),
   with Jr. Reid
Get Smart (Gussie), late 1970s
Harder Than the Rest (Tads)
Impressions of Leroy Smart (Burning
   Sounds, 1978+)
In London Clinker (Attack, JA)
Jah Loves Everyone (Burning Sounds,
   1978)
Leroy Smart & Friends (Esoldun,
   1995*)
Leroy Smart Showcase (Shuttle,
   1985)

Let Everyman Survive (GGs, 1979;
    Jamaica Gold, 1993*)
Live Up Roots Children (Striker Lee,
    1985+)
Musical Don (Skengdon, 1988)
On Top (Jah Life)
Private Message (RAS, 1993*)
Propaganda (Burning Sounds, 1979+)
Prophecy a Go Hold Them (Life
    Time), 1980s
She Just a Draw Card (WWS, 1982)
She Love It in the Morning (GGs,
    1983)
Showcase Rub a Dub (GGs, 1979)
Style and Fashion (Nura, 1983)
Superstar (Third World, 1977)
Talk 'Bout Friend (VP, 1992*)
Temptation (Blue Mountain, 1985)
Too Much Grudgefulness (Jah Life),
    1980s
Vintage Classics (GRAS, 1995*)

SMITH, SLIM

Best of the Uniques, (Trojan, 1994*),
    Slim Smith and the Uniques
Born to Love (Studio One; Heartbeat,
    1991**)
Early Days (Clocktower; Total Sounds)
Everybody Needs Love (Pama, 1969;
    1989)
Forever (Rhino, U.K., 1995*), Slim
    Smith and the Uniques
Just a Dream (Clocktower, 1972)
Late and Great Slim Smith (Micron)
Light (Abraham)
Memorial (Trojan, 1980)
Rain from the Skies (Trojan, 1992**)
Time Has Come (Pama)
20 Rare Grooves (Rhino, U.K.*)
24 Super Hits (Striker Lee)
Very Best of Slim Smith (Pama)

SOUL SYNDICATE

Famine Downtown (Epiphany, 1977;
    1994*)
Friends & Family (Epiphany, 1977;
    1994*)

SOUL VIBRATIONS

Black History/Black Culture (Aural
    Tradition, 1991**)

SPENCE, BARRINGTON

Speak Softly (Trojan), early 1970s
Star in the Ghetto (Circle, 1982)

SPENCE, SONYA

In the Dark (High Note), mid-1970s,
    Sonia Pottinger

STARLITES

Soldering (Heartbeat, 1993*)

STEEL PULSE

Babylon the Bandit (Elektra, 1985)
Caught You (Island, 1980)
Earth Crisis (Elektra, 1984)
Handsworth Revolution (Mango,
    1978)
Rage and Fury (Mesa, 1997*)
Rastafari Centennial: Live in Paris
    (MCA, 1992*)
Rastanthology (Wise Man Doctrine,
    1996*)
Reggae Greats (Mango, 1984; 1995*)
Sound System: The Island Anthology
    (Island Jamaica, 1997**)
State of Emergency (MCA, 1988)
Tribute to the Martyrs (Mango:
    1979)
True Democracy (Elektra, 1982)
Vex (MCA, 1994*)
Victim (MCA, 1991*)

STEPHENS, RICHIE

Miracles (VP, 1995*)
Pot of Gold (Motown, 1993*)
Richie Stephens (RAS, 1991*)
Sincerely (VP, 1991*)
Special Work of Art (Penthouse,
    1997*)
Winner (Greensleeves, 1998*)

SUTHERLAND, NADINE

Nadine (VP, 1997**)
Until (Tuff Gong, 1985)

TAMLINS

Love Divine (Heartbeat, 1989)
Red Rose (Vista, 1983)

ROD TAYLOR

If Jah Should Come Now (Little Luke,
    1983)
Liberate (Word, Sound and Power,
    1993)
Lonely Girl (King Culture)
One in a Million (Plexi, 1989)
Where Is Your Love Mankind
    (Greensleeves, 1980)

TECHNIQUES

Classics (Techniques)
I'll Never Fall in Love (Techniques)
Little Did You Know (Treasure Isle)
Run Come Celebrate (Heartbeat,
    1993**)
Unforgettable Days (Techniques)

TERMITES

Do the Rock Steady (Heartbeat, 1991*)

TETRACK

Let's Get Started/Augustus
    Pablo/Eastman Dub (Greensleeves,
    1990*)

THIRD WORLD

All the Way Strong (Columbia, 1983)
Arise in Harmony (Island, 1980)
Best of Third World (Columbia Legacy,
    1993*)
Committed (Mercury, 1992*)
Hold on to Love (Columbia, 1987)
Journey to Addis (Island, 1978)
96 Degrees in the Shade (Island, 1977)
Prisoner in the Street (Island, 1980)
Reggae Ambassadors (Mercury**),
    3-CD retrospective
Reggae Greats (Mango, 1985*)
Rock the World (CBS, 1981)
Sense of Purpose (Columbia, 1985*)
Third World (Island, 1976)
You've Got the Power (Columbia, 1982)

THOMPSON, LINVAL

Cool Down (Clocktower), late 1970s
Ease Up (Taxi), mid-1980s
Follow My Heart (Burning Sounds),
    late 1970s
Have to Be Sure (Rhino, U.K., 1995*),
    mid-1970s recordings
I Love Jah (Burning Sounds), late
    1970s
I Love Marijuana (Trojan, 1978;
    1996*)
Linval (Vista), late 1970s
Long Long Dreadlocks, 1976–79
    (Esoldun, 1995**)
Look How Me Sexy/Baby Father
    (Greensleeves, 1982, 1983; 1995*)
Rescue Lover (Glory Gold), early 1980s
Love Is the Question (Burning
    Sounds), late 1970s
Rocking Vibration (Vista, 1983)
Six Babylon (Clocktower), late 1970s

Starlight (Mango, 1988**)
Stay a Little Bit Longer (Micron), mid-1970s

TIBET, ADMIRAL
Come Into the Light (Live and Love)
Excitement (VP, 1995*)
Leave People Business (Techniques+)
Reality Time (Digital B/VP)
Separate Class (VP, 1991*)
Things That You Do (Super Powers, 1997**)
Time Is Going to Come (Rhino, U.K.)
Two Good to Be True (Digital-B, 1989), with Thriller U
War in a Babylon (RAS, 1987+)
Weeping and Mourning (Melodee, 1994**), Bobby Digital productions

TOOTS AND THE MAYTALS
An Hour Live (Genes, 1990*)
Best Of (Trojan, 1979)
Bla Bla Bla (Esoldun, 1993**)
Do the Reggae, 1966–70 (Attack, 1988)
Don't Trouble, 1968–80 (Esoldun, 1995*)
From the Roots (Trojan, 1970+)
Funky Kingston (Island, 1975; Trojan, 1976+)
In the Dark (Dragon, 1974+)
Just Like That (Mango, 1980)
Knock Out! (Island, 1981)
Life Could Be a Dream (Studio One, 1992), 1960s
Live at Hammersmith Palace (Island, 1980)
Live At Reggae Sunsplash (Sunsplash, 1983)
Monkey Man (Trojan, 1970+)
Never Grow Old (Studio One, 1966; Heartbeat, 1997**)
Original Golden Oldies, Vol. 3 (Fab), late 1960s
Pass the Pipe (Mango, 1979*)
Recoup (AO, 1997*)
Reggae Collection, 1970–85 (Essex, 1992*)
Reggae Got Soul (Island, 1976+)
Reggae Greats (Mango, 1985*)
Roots Reggae (Dynamic, 1974)
Sensational Maytals (WIRL), mid-1960s
Sensational Ska Explosion (Jamaica Gold, 1993**), 1960s
Slatyam Stoot (Dynamic, 1972)
Sweet and Dandy (Beverley's, 1969+)

Time Tough: The Anthology (Island Jamaica, 1996**)
Toots in Memphis (Mango, 1988**)
Toots Presents the Maytals (State Records, 1977)
Very Best Of (Music Club, 1997*)

TOSH, ANDREW
Make Place for the Youth (Tomato, 1989–91*)
Original Man (Heartbeat, 1994*)

TOSH, PETER
Best Of: Dreads Don't Die (EMI, 1996*)
Bush Doctor (Rolling Stone Records, 1978+; Trojan, 1990)
Captured Live (EMI, 1984)
Equal Rights (Columbia, 1977**)
Honorary Citizen (Columbia Legacy, 1997**), 3-CD set
Island Zoro (Excitable Boot, 1979)
Legalize It (Columbia, 1976**)
Mama Africa (Intel-Diplo; EMI, 1983)
Mystic Man (Rolling Stone Records, 1979+; Trojan, 1990)
No Nuclear War (EMI, 1987*)
Toughest (Capital; Parlophone, 1988*), compilation
Toughest (Heartbeat, 1996**)
Wanted: Dread and Alive (Rolling Stone, 1981)

TRINITY
African Revolution (GG's, 1979; Jamaica Gold, 1993*)
Bad Card (Joe Gibbs, 1981)
Have a Little Faith (Micron), late 1970s
Rock in the Ghetto (Trojan, 1979)
Three Piece Suit (Joe Gibbs+), late 1970s
Trinity Meet the Mighty Diamonds (Gorgon), late 1970s
as Junior Brammer: Hold Your Corner (Live and Learn, 1987)

TUFF, TONY
Best of Tony Tuff (Tad's)
Come Fe Mash It (Volcano, 1983)
Keep the Faith (Black Scorpio, 1988)
Ketch a Fire (Music Master, 1985)
Presenting Mr. Tuff (Black Roots, 1981)
Render Your Heart (CSA, 1984)
Reggae in City (Stateline, 1981)
Sailing (Park Heights), mid-1980s

Tony Tuff (Grove/Island, 1980)
Tuff Selection (Grove/Island, 1982+)
Wha We a Go Do (Top Rank, 1984)

TWINKLE BROTHERS
All Is Well (Twinkle, 1990)
All the Hits, 1970–88 (Twinkle, 1988*)
All the Hits, Vol. 2, 1971–91 (Twinkle, 1991*)
Anti-Apartheid (Twinkle, 1985)
Babylon Rise Again (Twinkle, 1991)
Breaking Down the Barriers (Twinkle, 1987)
Burden Bearer (Twinkle, 1984)
Chant Down Babylon (Twinkle, 1995*)
Countrymen (Virgin, 1980)
Crucial Cuts (Virgin, 1983)
Do Your Own Thing (Carib Gems, 1977*)
Don't Forget Africa (Twinkle, 1992*)
Enter Zion (Twinkle, 1984*)
Equality (Twinkle, 1994*), Free Africa (Virgin, 1990**), compilation
Higher Heights (Twinkle, 1992+)
Live in Warsaw (Twinkle, 1989)
Love (Virgin, 1979)
Me No You (Twinkle, 1981)
New Songs for Jah (Twinkle, 1989*)
Other Side (Twinkle, 1995*), mid-1990s
Praise Jah (Virgin, 1979+)
Rasta Pon Top (Grounation, 1975; Vista, 1984)
Rasta Surface (Jah Shaka)
Rastafari Chant (Twinkle, 1989)
Respect and Honor (Twinkle, 1987)
Right Way (Jah Shaka, 1984)
Since I Throw the Comb Away (Sunsplash, 1984)
Twinkle in Poland (Twinkle, 1988)
Twinkle Love Songs (Twinkle, 1987)
Twinkle Sample, Vol. 1 (Twinkle), circa 1990
Twinkle Sample, Vol. 2 (Twinkle), early 1990s
Twinkle Talent Spotting, Part 1 (Twinkle, 1992)
Underground (Twinkle, 1982)
Unification (Twinkle, 1990)
Wind of Change (Twinkle, 1990)

U BLACK
Westbound Thing a Swing (Third World, 1977)

U BROWN

Jam It Tonight (CSA, 1983)
Mr. Brown Something (Virgin, 1978)
Ravers Party (Trojan, 1982)
Repatriation (Hit Sound, 1979)
Satta Dread (Klik, 1976+)
Superstar (Culture Press, 1984)
Train to Zion (Blood and Fire, 1997**)
Tu Sheng Peng (Vista, 1983)
You Can't Keep a Good Man Down
    (Virgin, 1978)

U ROY

African Roots (Celluloid, 1977),
    Bunny Lee
Babylon Kingdom Must Fall (RAS,
    1996**), Mad Professor
Best of U Roy (Sonic Sounds, Live
    and Love), same as African Roots
Crucial Cuts (Virgin, 1983),
    compilation
Dread in a Babylon (TR, Jamaica;
    Virgin, 1975; 1990**)
Dubbing to the King in a Higher Rank
    (King Attarney, 1977)
Jah Son of Africa (Virgin, 1978), Tony
    Robinson
Line Up and Come (Tappa, 1987)
Love Is Not a Gamble aka Love
    Gamble (TR; Stateline, 1980)
Music Addict (RAS, 1987)
Natty Rebel (TR, Jamaica; Virgin,
    1976)
Natty Rebel, Extra Version (Caroline,
    1991**)
Original DJ (Caroline, 1995**),
    compilation
Originator: Nuroy (Carib Gems, 1980;
    Super Power, 1990), late 1970s,
    Bunny Lee production
Rasta Ambassador (TR; Virgin, 1977;
    Caroline, 1991*), Prince Tony
Rock with I (RAS, 1992*), Bunny Lee
Seven Gold (Ujama), mid-1980s
Smile a While (RAS, 1993*), Mad
    Professor
Super Boss (Esoldun, 1992), double
    album compilation of Duke Reid
True Born African (RAS, 1991*), Mad
    Professor
U Roy (Attack, 1974+)
Version Galore (Duke Reid, circa
    1970; Trojan, 1972; Virgin, 1978+)
Version of Wisdom (Caroline, 1990*)
With Words of Wisdom (Virgin,
    1979), same as U Roy on Attack

U ROY AND FRIENDS

DJ Masterpieces (Vista)
Teacher Meets the Student (Sonic
    Sounds, 1992), with Josey Wales
With a Flick of My Musical Wrist:
    Jamaican Deejay Music, 1970–73
    (Trojan, 1988)

UB40

Guns in the Ghetto (Virgin, 1997*)
Labour of Love (Virgin, 1983*)
Labour of Love II (Virgin, 1989*)
Little Baggariddim (A&M, 1985)
Promises and Lies (Virgin, 1993*)
Singles Album (Graduate, 1980)

UNIQUES

Absolutely the Uniques (Clocktower;
    Trojan, 1969)
Give Thanks (Joe Gibbs, 1980)
Showcase, Vol. 1 (Jackpot; Third
    World), Bunny Lee
Watch This Sound (Pressure Sounds,
    1998**)
See also Slim Smith

UPSETTERS

Best of Lee Perry and the Upsetters,
    Vols. 1–2 (Pama, U.K.), 1960s
Eastwood Rides Again (Trojan, 1970;
    reissued 1995)
Good Bad and the Upsetters (Esoldun,
    1993), reissues 1970s U.K. album
    produced by Bruce Anthony with-
    out the involvement of Lee Perry
Return of Django (Trojan, 1969)
Upsetter (Trojan, 1969)
Upsetters a Go Go (Heartbeat, 1995**)
Upsetters in dub
Blackboard Jungle Dub (Clocktower*),
    mid-1970s
Super Ape (Island, 1976)
Return of the Super Ape (Upsetters)

WADE, WAYNE

Black Is Our Color (Vivian Jackson,
    1977)
Fire Fire (Vivian Jackson, 1978)
Poor and Humble (Live and Learn,
    1982)
Respect Due Always (FJ, 1989)

WAILER, BUNNY

Blackheart Man (Island, 1976**)

Crucial! Roots Classics (Shanachie,
    1994**)
Dance Massive (Shanachie, 1992*)
Gumption (Shanachie, 1990*)
Hall of Fame (RAS, 1995**), 2-CD set
Hook, Line and Sinker (Solomonic,
    1982)
In I Father's House (Solomonic, 1980)
Just Be Nice (RAS, 1993*)
Liberation (Shanachie, 1988**)
Live (Solomonic, 1983)
Marketplace (Solomonic, 1986)
Protest (Island, 1977; Solomonic)
Retrospective (Shanachie, 1995**)
Rock and Groove (Solomonic, 1981)
Roots Radics Rockers Reggae
    (Shanachie, 1983)
Rootsman Skanking (Solomonic, 1986)
Rule Dance Hall (Solomonic, 1987)
Sings the Wailers (Mango, 1980*)
Struggle (Solomonic, 1979)
Time Will Tell (Shanachie, 1990*)
Tribute (Solomonic, 1981)

OF RELATED INTEREST
Never Ending Wailers (RAS, 1993*)

WAILERS BAND

I.D. (Atlantic, 1989)
Jah Message (RAS, 1994*)
Majestic Warriors (Tabu/A&M, 1991*)

WAILING SOULS

All Over the World (Chaos, 1992*)
Baby Come Rock (Joe Gibbs, 1983),
    Junjo Lawes
Best of the Wailing Soul (Sunset, 1985)
Fire House Rock (Volcano, 1981;
    Greensleeves), Junjo
Inchpinchers (Greensleeves, 1983;
    1992*)
Kingston 14 (Live and Learn, 1987)
Lay It On the Line (Live & Learn,
    1986*)
Live On (Zoo Entertainment, 1994*)
Psychedelic Souls (Pow Wow, 1998**)
Reggae Ina Firehouse (Live & Learn,
    1991*)
Soul and Power (Studio One, 1984),
    early 1970s
Stranded (Shanachie, 1984)
Stormy Night (Rohit, 1990)
Tension (Pow Wow, 1997*)
Very Best of the Wailing Souls
    (Greensleeves, 1987; Shanachie,
    1990*)

Wailing (Jah Guidance), early 1980s
Wailing Souls (Studio One, 1976+)
Wild Suspense (Mango, 1979; Island
    Jamaica, 1995**)

WALKER, SYLFORD
Lamb's Bread (Greensleeves, 1998)

WASHINGTON, DELROY
I-Sus (Virgin, 1976)
Rasta (Virgin, 1977)

WEBBER, MERLYN
Once You Hit the Road (Jama)

WELL PLEASED AND SATISFIED
Give Thanks and Praise (Burning
    Sounds), late 1970s
Love Train (Burning Sounds), late
    1970s

WHITE, JOY
Sentimental Reasons (Germain
    Revolutionary Sounds, 1979)

WHITE, K.C.
Showcase (Love People)
Try a Little Happiness (Puff)

DELROY WILLIAMS
Darkness with Fire (Rockers), 1982
I Stand Black (Rockers)
Two Timer (Island in the Sun)

WILLIAMS, WILLIE
Armagideon Time (Studio One, 1982;
    Heartbeat, 1992**)
Messenger Man (Jah Muzik, 1980)
Natty with a Cause (Jah Shaka, 1992*)
See Me (Jah Shaka, 1993*)
Unity (Black Star, 1987)

WILSON, DELROY
Best of Delroy Wilson: Hit After Hit
    (Empire, 1984)
Best Of (Studio One, United Artists,
    1978; Liberty)
Best Of: Original Twelve (Heartbeat,
    1991**)
Better Must Come (Trojan, 1972+)
Dance with Me (Top Priority), 1980s,
    with Donna Marie

Dean of Reggae (Mister Tipsy), late
    1980s
Dancing Mood (Studio One**), 1960s
    ska
Go Away Dream (Black Joy), late 1970s
Good All Over (Studio One)
Greatest Hits (TR), mid-1970s
Greatest Hits (Jaguar), mid-1970s;
    different from above
Greatest Hits (Jamaica Gold, 1992*),
    different from above
I Shall Not Remove (Studio One+)
Living in the Footsteps (Joe Gibbs,
    1981)
Looking for Love (Phil Pratt)
Lovers Rock (Burning Sounds)
Money (Clocktower), mid-1970s
My Special Dream (World Enterprise,
    1989)
Nice Times (Jamaica Sound), mid-
    1970s
Prophecy (Gorgon), mid-1970s
Reggae Classics (Londisc)
Sarge (Charmers)
Special (RAS, 1993*)
Straight from the Heart (VP), late 1980s
Super Mix Hits (Pioneer International)
True Believer in Love (Carib Gems),
    Bunny Lee/Aggrovators
24 Super Hits (Sonic Sounds, 1990*)
Unedited (Hulk), late 1970s
Who Done It (Third World+), mid-
    1970s
Worth Your Weight in Gold (Burning
    Sounds, 1984)

ERNEST WILSON
Love Revolution (Natty Congo, 1986)

WINGLESS ANGELS
Wingless Angels (Island Jamaica,
    1997*)

YABBY YOU
African Queen (Clappers, 1982)
Chant Down Babylon Kingdom
    (Nationwide, 1978; Yabby You**)
Conquering Lion (Vivian Jackson,
    1975+)
Deliver Me from My Enemies (Vivian
    Jackson; Grove, 1977+)
Fleeing from the City (Shanachie,
    1985; 1991**)
Jah Jah Way (Island, 1980)
Jah Will Be Done (Prophet, 1997*)

Jesus Dread, 1972–77 (Blood and Fire,
    1997**), 2-CD set
King Tubby Meet Vivian Jackson
    (Yabby You), same as Conquering
    Lion
New Roots Reggae (Yabby), early 1990s
One Love, One Heart (Shanachie,
    1983), compilation
Prophecy (WLN), early 1990s, with
    Michael Prophet and Wayne Wade
Ram-A-Dam (Lucky, U.K., 1976)
Yabby the You Man (Peacemaker,
    1995*)
Yabby You Collection (Greensleeves,
    1984), same as One Love/Heart

ZAP POW
Jungle Beat (Esoldun, 1992*), recorded
    1970–72
Reggae Rules (Rhino, 1980)
Revolution (Trojan, 1976)
Zap Pow (Mango, 1978)

ZERO, EARL
In the Right Way (Student, U.K.+),
    early 1980s
Only Jah Can Ease the Pressure
    (Freedom Sounds), same LP as above
Visions of Love (Epiphany, 1981;
    1998**)

ZUKIE, TAPPER
Blackman (Stars), 1980s
Deep Roots (RAS, 1996*)
From the Archives (RAS, 1995**)
Living in the Ghetto (Stars)
Man Ah Warrior (Klik, 1975; Mer,
    1977+)
Man from Bosrah (Stars, 1977)
MPLA (Klik, 1976)
Peace in the Ghetto (Virgin, 1978)
People Are You Ready (Stars, 1983)
Raggamuffin (Tappa, 1983)
Tapper Roots (Virgin, 1978)
Tappa Zukie International (New Star,
    1978+)

Compilations

PRE-SKA
Caribbean Island Music (Nonesuch,
    1972)
Churchical Chants of the Nyabingi
    (Heartbeat, 1983*)

Drums of Defiance: Maroon Music from the Earliest Free Black Communes of Jamaica (Smithsonian Folkways, 1992*)

From Boogie to Nyabinghi (Esoldun, 1993*)

From the Grass Roots of Jamaica (Dynamic)

Jamaican R&B: The Dawn of Ska (Sequel, 1993)

Up You Mighty Race: Recollections of Marcus Garvey (Garvey)

SKA

Note: Despite release dates all contain original 1960s ska.

Birth of Ska (Trojan, 1972), Duke Reid productions

Calypso, Ska, Jump-Up (Studio One)

Club Ska '67 (Island+)

History of Ska Blue Beat and Reggae (Esoldun, 1992*)

History of Ska: Golden Years, 1960–65 (Studio One+)

History of Ska: Golden Years, 1966–69 (Studio One+)

Intensified! Original Ska, 1962–66 (Island/Mango, 1979**)

Intensified! Original Ska, 1963–67 (Island/Mango, 1980**)

It's Shuffle 'n Ska Time (Jamaica Gold, 1994*)

Jamaica Beat (Esoldun, 1992*), Duke Reid productions

King Edwards Presents Ska Volution (King Edwards, 1989), mid-1960s

Man About Ska-Town (King Edwards, 1989), mid-1960s recordings

Monkey Ska: 20 Classic Ska Tracks from the Sixties (Trojan, 1993*)

Original Club Ska: Authentic Jamaican Beat (Heartbeat, 1990**)

Original Ska Explosion (Carib Gems), recorded 1960–62, Duke Reid

Real Jamaica Ska (Epic, 1993*)

Rebel Music: An Anthology of Reggae Music (Trojan, 1989**)

Roots of Reggae: Ska (Rhino, 1996**)

Rudies All Around: Rude Boy Records, 1966–67 (Trojan U.K.)

Scandal Ska (Mango, 1989**)

Ska After Ska After Ska (Heartbeat, 1998**)

Ska a Go Go (Studio One)

Ska-Ba-Dip: The Essential King Edwards (King Edwards. 1989), mid-1960s recordings

Ska Bonanza: The Studio One Years (Heartbeat, 1991**)

Ska Down Jamaica Way (Top Deck), 1962–66

Ska-Lutations from King Edward (King Edwards, 1989), mid-1960s

Ska Spectacular, Vol. 1 (Charley, 1993*)

Ska Strictly for You (Studio One)

Ska's the Limit, 1959–64, Vol. 1 (Island), 40 years

Skatalites and Friends: Hog in a Cocoa (Esoldun, 1991*), Duke Reid

Skatalites and Friends at Randys (VP, 1998**)

Skatalites Plus (Treasure Isle)

This Is Jamaican Ska (Coxsone)

This Is Ska: 16 Original Ska Classics (Music Club, 1997*)

Top Sounds from Top Deck (Westside, 1998*)

Treasure Ska (Treasure Isle, 1989)

Tribute to the Skatalites (Esoldun, 1991*), Duke Reid productions

NEW SKA

American Skathic, Vols. 1–4 (Jump Up), 1990s Midwest ska

Land of the Rising Ska: Nihon Ska Danso (Moon Ska, 1997), anthology of contemporary Japanese ska

Latin Ska, Vols. 1–2 (Moon Ska)

Let's Ska Again (Charly, 1989), first crest of the third wave

New York Beat: Breaking and Entering (Moon Ska, 1998*)

New York Beat: Hit and Run (Moon Ska, 1985; 1998*)

Ska Beats (ROIR, 1989+), sampling, triple-time-beat acid house ska

Ska: The Third Wave, Vols. 1–2 (Shanachie)

Skankin' Round the World (Moon, 1989)

Skarmageddon, Vols. 1–3 (Moon Ska)

This Are Two Tone (Chrysalis, 1983), second wave compilation

ROCK STEADY

Bobby Aitken Presents Rocksteady Original and Red Hot, 1966–67 (Next Step, 1993**)

Ba-Ba Boom Time, 1967–68 (Trojan, 1988)

Catch This Beat: The Rock Steady Years, 1966–68 (Island, 1980+)

Clement 'Coxsone' Dodd: Musical Fever, 1967–68 (Trojan, 1989+)

Dance All Night (Trojan, 1991**)

Depth Charge (Esoldun, 1992*), Duke Reid productions

Duke Reid's Treasure Chest (Heartbeat, 1992**), 2-CD set

Explosive Rock Steady: Joe Gibbs's Amalgammated Label, 1967–73 (Heartbeat, 1992**)

Feel Like Jumping: Rock Steady and Reggae from Jamaica, 1966–68 (Receiver, 1989)

Flo and Eddie Rock Steady (Epiphany, 1982; 1998*)

Get in the Groove: Roy Shirley, Stranger Cole, Ken Parker (Rocky One, 1996**)

Get Ready Rock Steady (Coxsone), mid- to late 1960s

Midnight Confession: Duke Reid's Greatest Rocksteady Moods (Esoldun, 1993)

Mojo Rock Steady (Heartbeat, 1994**), Coxsone

More Hottest Hits from Treasure Isle (Heartbeat, 1994**)

Put On Your Best Dress: Sonia Pottinger's Rocksteady, 1967–68 (Attack, 1990)

Reflections of Rock Steady (Micron, 1990*), 1960s, early Bunny Lee

Rock Steady Beat (Treasure Isle), late 1960s, Duke Reid productions

Rock Steady Coxsone Style (Coxsone)

Rock Steady Intensified! (WIRL)

Roots of Reggae: Rock Steady (Rhino, 1996**)

Rudies All Round: Rude Boy Records, 1966–67 (Trojan, 1993*)

Rusty Dusties: Reggae and Soul Hits of the Sixties (Wild Flower)

Soul of Jamaica / Here Comes the Duke (Trojan, 1997*), reissue

Top Rock Steady (Esoldun, 1992*)

Unearthed Gold of Rock Steady (Rocky One*)

Wake Up Jamaica: Sweet Rock Steady and Reggae Harmonies (Trojan, 1994*)

Selected Reggae Anthologies, by Producer

GLENMORE BROWN
Boat to Progress Vocal Collection, 1970–74 (Greensleeves)
Dubble Attack Dee-Jay Collection, 1972–74 (Greensleeves)

ROY COUSINS
Herb Dust, Vol. 1 (Kingdom, 1983+)
History of Tamoki Wambesi (Tamoki Wambesi*)
Sunsplash Showcase (Kingdom, 1981)
Visions of Reggae (Tamoki Wambesi), early 1980s

LLOYD DALEY
From Matador's Arena, 1969–70, Vols. 1–3 (Jamaica Gold, 1995*)
Lloyd Daley's Matador Productions, 1968–72 (Heartbeat, 1992**)

C.S. "COXSONE" DODD
All On the Same Rhythm (RAS, 1988)
All Star Top Hits (Coxsone)
Battle of the DJ's Dancehall Style (Coxsone)
Big Bamboo (Attack, 1974+)
Blue Beat Special (Coxsone)
Dance Hall Session (RAS, 1987)
Freedom Sounds (Studio One; Bamboo, U.K.)
Fire Down Below: Scorchers from Studio One (Heartbeat, 1990**)
Full Up: Best of Studio One, Vol. 2 (Heartbeat, 1985)
Grooving At Studio One (Heartbeat, 1996*)
Jamaica All Stars, Vols. 1–2 (Studio One), 1960s–'70s
Jamaica Today: the Seventies (Studio One)
Real Authentic Sound of Studio One (RAS), recorded late 1980s
Reggae Christmas from Studio One (Heartbeat, 1992*)
Reggaematic Sounds (Studio One)
Respect to Studio One (Heartbeat, 1994**), double CD set
Ride Me Donkey: Solid Gold from Jamaica (Studio One)
Sales Conference (Studio One)
Scorcha from Studio One (Studio One)
Solid Gold, Coxsone Style (Heartbeat, 1992**)
Soul Defenders At Studio One (Studio One)
Sounds of Jamaica: Top Ten (Studio One)
Sounds of Young Jamaica: A Collection of 12 Original Big Hits, Vol. 1 (Studio One)
Studio One Showcase, Vols. 1–2 (Studio One)
Studio One Various Artists, Vol. 3 (Studio One)
Swing Easy (Studio One)

CLANCY ECCLES
Clancy Eccles Presents His Reggae Review (Heartbeat, 1990*)
Clancy Eccles and Friends: Fatty Fatty, 1967–70 (Trojan, 1988)
Herbman Reggae: (Trojan, 1970)
Jamaica Reggae: 12 Golden Hits (Clan Disc, 1972)
Kingston Town: 18 Reggae Hits (Heartbeat, 1993*)

EDWARDS, RUPIE
Conversation Stylee (Tads+)
Hit Picks (Trojan, 1975+)
Irie Feelings: Chapter and Version (Trojan, 1990)
Let There Be Version (Trojan, 1990)

JOE GIBBS
DJ Originators, Vols. 1–2 (Rocky One, 1995*)
Heptones and Friends, Vols. 1–2 (Attack), early 1970s
Irie Reggae Hits (Joe Gibbs), early 1980s
Jackpot of Hits (Joe Gibbs, 1968)
Joe Gibbs Revive 45s, Vols. 1–2 (Rocky One*), 1970s
Mighty Two: Joe Gibbs and Errol Thompson (Heartbeat, 1992**)
Original DJ Classics, Vols. 1–2 (Rocky One), circa 1994
Reggae Christmas (Joe Gibbs, 1982)
Reggae Hits (Blue Moon, 1982)
Reggae Hits of the 1980s (Joe Gibbs, 1983)
Reggae Masterpiece (Joe Gibbs, 1980)
Rock Steady to Reggae: The Early Years, Vols. 1–3 (Rocky One**)
Spotlight on Reggae, Vols. 1–3 (Rocky One, 1990)
Top Ranking DJ Session, Vols. 1–2 (Joe Gibbs, 1979, 1982)
Uncle Sam Goes Reggae (Joe Gibbs, 1980), delightful cover
United Dreadlocks, Vols. 1–2 (Joe Gibbs), late 1970s
Wonderful World of Reggae (Joe Gibbs, 1980)

NORMAN GRANT
Age of Reggae, Parts 1–2 (Twinkle, 1987+)

DERRICK HARRIOT
Riding the Musical Chariot (Heartbeat, 1990*)
Riding the Roots Chariot (Pressure Sounds, 1998*), 1970s recordings
Step Softly: Rock Steady and Reggae, 1965–72 (Trojan, 1988)
Those Reggae Oldies (Crystal+), 1964–75

JOJO HOOKIM
Hit Bound! The Revolutionary Sound of Channel One (Heartbeat, 1989**)
Well Charged: Channel One (Pressure Sounds, 1996**)

KEITH HUDSON
Studio Kinda Cloudy (Trojan, 1988), 1967–72

HARRY J
Reggae Gold (Gold Rush), early 1980s
Return of the Liquidator: 30 Skinhead Classics, 1968–70 (Trojan, 1991**)
What Am I to Do (Harry J, 1970)

JAH SHAKA
Hits from the House of Jah Shaka: The Message, Parts 1–2 (Jah Shaka)
Message from Africa (Jah Shaka), mid-1980s

LESLIE KONG
Best of Beverley's Records (Trojan, 1981+)
King Kong Compilation (Mango, 1981+)
Leslie Kong's Connection (Jet Star, 1997**), 1969–71

BUNNY LEE

Best of Reggae, 1968–74 (Micron)

Creation Rebel (Esoldun, 1995*)

Dreadlocks in Jamaica (Attack), mid-1970s

Jumping with Mr. Lee, 1967–68 (Trojan+)

Lovers Rock, Vols. 1–3, 5 (Cardinal)

Now This Is What I and I Call Version (Trojan, 1989), 1969

Reggae Legends (Rohit), early 1980s

Straight to I Roy's Head (Esoldun, 1995*)

Straight to Prince Jazzbo's Head (Esoldun, 1995*)

Striker Lee Presents: Oldies Keep Swinging (Sonic Sounds*), 1970s

BYRON LEE

Jamaica Ska (Rhino, 1980+)

Byron Lee and the Dragonaires Play Dynamite Ska with the Jamaica All-Stars (Jamaica Gold, 1993**)

WILLIE LINDO

Reggae Hits of the Century (Heavy Beat)

MAD PROFESSOR

Ariwa Hits '89 (Ariwa, 1989)

Ariwa Posse (Ariwa)

Ariwa 12th Anniversary Album (Ariwa, 1992)

Roots Daughters, Vols. 1–2 (RAS, 1988–90**)

This Is Lovers Reggae, Vols. 1–3 (RAS, 1991–93*)

FREDDIE MCGREGOR

Best of the Best, Vol. 5 (RAS, 1995*)

Big Ship Ole Fung Reggae Ska, Vol. 1 (Greensleeves, 1997*)

HARRY MUDIE

Let Me Tell You Boy (Trojan, 1988+)

Mudies Mood (Moodisc, 1987+)

Reggae History A–Z (Moods International, 1985+)

(Mutabaruka) Gathering of the Spirits (Shanachie, 1998*)

NINEY THE OBSERVER

Blood and Fire, 1971–72 (Trojan, 1988**)

Bring the Couchie, 1974–76 (Trojan, 1989**)

Hard Works from the Observer All-Stars (Heartbeat, 1992*)

Legends of Reggae Music (Rohit), mid-1980s

Niney the Observer Presents the All Stars Turbo Charge (Heartbeat, 1991*)

Observation Station (Heartbeat, 1990**)

Truths and Rights Observer Style (Heartbeat, 1994*)

Turbo Charge (Heartbeat, 1991*)

Vintage Classics (Rohit), mid-1980s

AUGUSTUS PABLO PRODUCTIONS

Classic Rockers (Rockers; Island Jamaica, 1995**), 1970s recordings

Classic Rockers 2 (Rockers, 1989)

DJ's of the 1970s and 1980s (Big Cat, 1997*)

Pablo and Friends (RAS, 1992*)

Rockers All-Star Explosion (Alligator, 1984)

Rockers International (Message), late 1980s

Rockers International 2 (Greensleeves, 1992)

Rockers International Showcase (Ryko, 1991*)

Rockers Showcase, Vol. 3 (Message, 1987)

Rockers Story (RAS, 1989)

LEE "SCRATCH" PERRY

Archive Series (Rialto, 1998*), 1970s recordings

Arkology (Island Jamaica, 1997**), 3-CD set

Battle Axe (Trojan, 1972; 1995**)

Black Ark Presents: Rastafari Livith Initually (Justice League, 1998), 1970s recordings

Build the Ark (Trojan, 1990), 3-record set

Complete UK Upsetter Singles Collection, Vol. 1 (Trojan 1998**), 1970s

Give Me Power, 1970–73 (Trojan, 1988)

Heart of the Ark, Vol. 2 (Seven Leaves+)

Larks from the Ark: 18 Crucial Tracks from Lee Perry, Artist and Producer (Nektar Masters, 1995**), selected from above 2 albums

Magnetic Mirror Master Mix (Anachron, 1989)

Open the Gate (Trojan, 1989), 1970s, 3-record set

Out of Many the Upsetter (Trojan, 1991), 1970s

People Funny Boy (Trojan, 1994**)

Produced and Directed by the Upsetters (Pressure Sounds, 1998**), 1970s

Public Jestering (Attack, 1990**)

Reggae Greats (Mango, 1985)

Scratch and Company (Clocktower)

Scratch Attack (RAS, 1988*)

Scratch On the Wire (Island, 1979)

Some of the Best (Heartbeat, 1985**)

Turn and Fire (Anachron), mid-1970s recordings

Upsetter Collection (Trojan, 1981)

Upsetting the Nation (Trojan, 1993)

Version Like Rain, 1972–78 (Trojan, 1989)

Voodooism (Pressure Sounds, 1996)

Wizdom 1971–1975 (Ascension, 1998*), 1970s

Words of My Mouth (Trojan, 1996**)

SONIA POTTINGER

Musical Feast: Mrs. Pottinger's High Note and Gay Feet Label (Heartbeat, 1991**)

Old Hits of the Past (High Note), 1970s

Reggae Song Birds: 17 Great Tracks from the High Note Label (Heartbeat, 1996**)

Reggae Train: More Great Hits from the High Note Label (Heartbeat, 1996**)

Time to Remember: Oldies But Goodies (High Note), 1970s

PRINCE JAMMY

King Jammy: A Man and His Music, Vols. 1–3 (RAS, 1991**)

King Jammy Presents Dub Plates (Melodie, France)

Sleng Teng (Jammys, 1985)

PRINCE JAZZBO

All Round (Ujama), late 1980s

Sure Shot (Ujama, 1987)

Veteran DJ Jamboree (RAS, 1991*)

ALVIN RANGLIN

Atlantic 1 (Horse, 1975+), Alvin Ranglin Productions

Holy Ground: Alvin Ranglin's GG
Records (Heartbeat, 1990**), 1970s
Reggae Flight 404 (Trojan+), 1970s

WINSTON RILEY

14 Carat Gold (Techniques), 1970s
Best of the Best, Vol. 6 (RAS, 1995*)

DUKE REID

Depth Charge (Esoldun, 1992*)
Duke Reid's Midnight Hour (Rhino,
U.K., 1994*)
Greater Jamaica (Treasure Isle, 1969;
Jet Star, 1997*)
Hottest Hits (Treasure Isle, 1979+)
Hottest Hits, Vol. 2 (Treasure Isle,
1979+)
Here Comes the Duke (Treasure Isle)
More Hottest Hits (Heartbeat, 1994**)
Soul Music for Sale (Treasure Isle,
1968; Jet Star, 1997**)
Soul of Jamaica (Trojan, 1968)
Soul to Soul: DJ's Choice (Trojan, U.K.),
early 1970s
Version Affair, Vol. 1 (Esoldun, 1992*)

JACK RUBY

Crucial Records Presents Jack Ruby
(Clappers, 1980)
Jack Ruby Hi-Power Live (Clappers,
1982)

B.B. SEATON

Sunshine Reggae Revival, Vol. 1 (Soul
Beat, 1995*)

SLY AND ROBBIE

Bam Bam It's Murder (Mango, 1982*),
produced by Sly with Lloyd Willis,
son Lee, and Herbie Harris
Crucial Reggae (Taxi, 1984)
DJ Riot (Mango, 1990)
Electro Reggae (Mango, 1986)
Friends (East/West, 1998*)
La Trenggae (VP, 1998*)
Punishers (Mango, 1993)
Ragga Pon Top (Pow Wow, 1983),
associate producer Gitsy
Sound of the 1990s (Taxi, 1990)
Speeding Taxi (Sonic Sounds, 1993)
Taxi (Taxi, 1981)
Taxi Connection: Live in London
(Taxi, 1986)
Taxi Fare (Taxi, 1987)

Taxi Gang (Taxi, 1984)
Taxi Wax (Taxi, 1984)
Taxi X-Mas (RAS, 1991)
Two Rhythms Clash (RAS, 1990)

PHILIP SMART

Singing for the People (Tan-Yah),
mid-1990s

LINVAL THOMPSON

Jah Jah Dreader Than Dread (Munich,
1997**)
2 Sexes Clash (CSA, 1990)
Negrea Love Dub (Trojan, 1978)

TAPPA ZUKIE

Best of the Best:, Vol. 1 (RAS, 1993**)
Massive Resistance (RAS, 1994**)
Old Time DJ Come Back Again (RAS,
1994*)

Compilations by Various Artists and Producers

Absolute Reggae (Eva, 1991*)
African Museum All-Stars (African
Museum), 1970s .
An Even Harder Shade of Black
(Pressure Sounds**), 1970s
Atra 10 Track (Atra, 1988)
Babylon a Fall Down (Trojan, 1991**),
1970s
Bamboo Fence and Curry Goat 82–84
(Black Solidarity, 1998)
Be Thankful (Attack, 1991*)
Best of Jamaica Gold, Vols. 1–2
(Jamaica Gold, 1994*)
Best of the Best (RAS**), 1990s series,
multiple vols.
Beyond the Front Line (Caroline,
1990*)
Big Blunts: 12 Smokin' Reggae Hits
(Tommy Boy, 1994*)
Black Echoes D.E.B. Special (Gorgon,
1978+)
Black Slavery Days (Clappers, 1982)
Brand New Second Hand (Ryko,
1992*)
Bubbling Hot: Strictly Lovers Rock
(IRS, 1995*)
Calling Rastafari (Nighthawk, 1982+)
Chatty Chatty Mouth Versions
(Greensleeves, 1993**)

Classic Reggae in a 1990s Style (RAS,
1994*)
Clocktower Classics (Abraham, 1990**)
Clocktower Records Presents Reggae
and Fire and Water, 1974–79
(Abraham, 1998+)
Cool Runnings: Music from the
Motion Picture (Chaos, 1993*)
Club Reggae (Trojan), 1970s, multiple
vols.
Creation Rockers, Vols. 1–6 (Trojan,
1979+)
DJ Legends of the 1960s and 1980s
(Blue Beat, 1990*)
Dread in America (Natural Mystic,
1995*), 2-CD set
Essential Reggae Jams (K-Tel, 1997**)
Family Album (Jah Life+)
Fashion Statement: The Fashion
Records Story (RAS, U.K., 1995**)
Feelin' High (Columbia House,
1975**)
First Family of Reggae (Shanachie,
1991*)
Fly African Eagle: The Best of African
Reggae (Shanachie, 1997**)
Funky Chicken (Trojan, 1970*), early
funk/reggae barnyard fusion
Funky Reggae Crew: Strictly Hip-Hop
Reggae Fusion (Warner Brothers,
1989*)
Grapevine/Dynamite Records Vault
Classics, Vols. 1–2 (RAS, 1995*)
Greensleeves Sampler (Shanachie,
1990*)
Groove Yard (Mango, 1989*)
Happy Families: A Compendium of
Reggae Hits (Shangri-La, 1984)
The Harder They Come Original Movie
Soundtrack (Mango, 1972**)
Hawaii Reggae International (Dub
Machine, 1991*)
Heartbeat Reggae Now (Heartbeat,
1993*)
Heartbeat Reggae Roundup (Heartbeat,
1991*)
Heathen Chant Continuous Mix
(RUNN), mid-1990s
Heavyweight Sound (Blood and Fire,
1995**)
H.I.M. Haile Selassie I Centenary,
Vol. 1 (Surr Zema), U.K. new
roots with Dub Judah, others; also
available in dub
History of Jamaican Vocal Harmony:
The Great Reggae Trios (Munich,
1996**)

Hold Me Strong: Love Songs Jamaican Style, 1972–76 (Trojan, 1989)

Holding Up Half the Sky: Women in Reggae: Roots Daughters (Shanachie, 1996**)

Ital International Presents Various Artists (Ital International, 1990)

Jah Son Invasion (Wackies, 1982)

Jammin' (Island, 1989*)

Jungle Hits, Vols. 1–3 (Street Tuff, 1995*)

Keep on Coming Through the Door: Jamaican Deejay Music, 1969–73 (Trojan, 1988)

Knotty Vision (Nighthawk, 1983+)

Legend (Atra, 1980), featuring Augustus Pablo and others

Live & Learn Smashing All-Stars (CSA, 1986)

Lovers Mood, Vols. 1–3 (VP, to 1996*)

Lunatic Soundtrack (Mango, 1991*)

Many Moods of Love, Vols. 1–2 (RUNN)

Massive Three: A Collection of British Reggae Hits (Mango, 1989*)

Natty Queen Divas (Tuff Gong), late 1990s

Natty Rebel Roots (Virgin, 1990*)

Now Sound: Reggae (Island, 1975)

Now This Is What I and I Call Version (Trojan, 1989)

Peeni Waali (Shanachie, 1991*)

Phase One Collectors Edition (Phase One+), 1970s

Power of the Trinity: Great Moments in Reggae Harmony (Shanachie, 1997**)

Pressure Drop (Mango, 1988+), 7-record set

Psalms for Solomon (Blackamix, 1995**)

Psalms of Drums: The Black and White Story (Pressure Sounds, 1996**), 1970s, Carlton Patterson/King Tubby

Real Authentic Sampler, Vol. 3 (RAS, 1994*)

Rebel Music: An Anthology of Reggae Music (Trojan, 1979+)

Record Factory Presents Singers On Top (Melodie, France), mid-1990s

Reggatta Mondatta: A Reggae Tribute to the Police (Ark, 1997*)

Reggae All Night Long (Trojan, 1991*), 2-vol. compilation

Reggae All Star (Freedom Sound), early 1980s

Reggae Ambassadors Worldwide, Vol. 1 (Tronic 1, 1995), 2 CDs gather recordings from members of the ever-growing RAW network

Reggae Best: Rasta Reggae (Esoldun, 1995*)

Reggae Culture: More Heartbeat Reggae Now (Heartbeat, 1994*)

Reggae for Kids, Vols. 1–2 (RAS, 1992, 1997*)

Reggae from Around the World (RAS, 1988+)

Reggae Gold (VP, 1994, 1995, 1996, and more**)

Reggae Greats (Mango), mid-1980s compilations of product mainly deleted from Mango catalog; includes Strictly for Rockers, Strictly for Lovers, anthologies of groups, and more

Reggae Jamdown: The RAS Tapes (Rykodisc, 1990*)

Reggae On Mango (Mango, 1988*)

Reggae On the River: The Tenth Anniversary (Earthbeat, 1994*)

Reggae Report Presents Reggae USA (ROIR, 1991)

Reggae Revolution (Esoldun, 1990*)

Reggae Rockers (Black Joy), early 1980s

Reggae Roots: The RAS Records Story (RAS, 1995*)

Reggae Sunsplash Live (MCA, 1993*)

Reggae Superstars of the 1980s (Rohit)

Reggae Under Cover (Relativity, 1994*)

Reggaemania: The Best of Reggae (Milan, 1996*)

Rewind! Part 1: The DJs (RAS, 1990*)

Rewind! Part 2: The Singers (RAS, 1990*)

Rhythm Come Forward, Vols. 1–3 (Columbia/Legacy, 1993*)

Rightous Reggae Jams (K-Tel, 1997*)

Rockers Original Soundtrack (Mango, 1979**)

Roots and Culture (Cha Cha), 1970s, Channel One

Roots and Culture (Music Club, 1993*)

Roots Rock Reggae (Creole, 1978+)

Roots Tradition from the Vinyard (Munich, 1997**), Freedom Sounds

R.O.R.X: Tenth Annual Reggae On the Rocks (What Are Records, 1997**)

Run 4 Cover: Songs for a New Generation (EBS), mid-1990s

Seventeen North Parade (Pressure Beat, 1998**)

Sky High Presents All Stars (Sky High, 1988)

Smashing Superstars (Jah Life, 1981+)

Soul Defenders at Studio One (Heartbeat, 1991**)

Soulful Reggae (Trojan), 1970s

Sounds and Pressure, Vols. 1–3 (Pressure Sounds**), 1970s

Strictly for Rockers (Mango, 1985**)

Sufferer's Choice (Attack, 1988+)

Take a Ride (RAS, 1991*)

Thirty Years of Jamaican Music On the Go (Rhino, U.K.**), 1960s–'70s

This Is Reggae Music, Vols. 1–5 (Mango, 1990*)

This Is Reggae (Music Club, 1998*), 1960s, 1970s

Tighten Up (Trojan), 1970s, multiple vols.

Tougher Than Tough: The Story of Jamaican Music (Mango, 1993**), 4-CD retrospective

Trojan Story (Trojan, 1972+), 3-record set

Trojan Story, Vol. 2 (Trojan, 1971–82+), 3-record set

Twenty Reggae Classics, Vols. 1–3 (Trojan, 1984–88+)

Urban Beat Reggae (Heartbeat, 1996*)

Waterhouse Revisited, Chapters 1–2 (Outa/Hightone, 1994*)

Wiser Dread (Nighthawk, 1981+)

With a Flick of My Musical Wrist: Jamaican Deejay Music, 1970–73 (Trojan, 1988+)

Word Sound 'Ave Power: Dub Poets and Dub (Heartbeat reissue, 1994*)

Young Lions Pride Compilation (Young Lions, 1996*)

Dancehall Selections

ANTHONY B.

So Many Things (VP, 1996*)

Universal Struggle (VP, 1998*)

ADMIRAL BAILEY

Born Champion (Live and Love, 1989)

Science Again (Rohit, 1989)

Think Me Did Done (Live and Love, 1987)

BANNER, SPANNER
Chill (Island Jamaica, 1995*)
Now and Forever (RAS, 1994*)

BANTON, BUJU
Inna Heights (VP, 1997*)
Mr. Mention (Penthouse, 1991)
Stamina Daddy (Techniques, 1991)
'Til Shiloh (Loose Canon, 1995*)
Voice of Jamaica (Mercury, 1993*)

BANTON, MEGA
Money First (Relativity, 1995*)
New Year New Style (Shanachie, 1994*)

BANTON, PATO (UK)
Collections (IRS, 1994*)
Mad Professor Captures Pato Banton (RAS, 1990*)
Mad Professor Recaptures Pato Banton (RAS, 1990*)
Never Give In (IRS, 1988)
Universal Love (RS, 1992*)
Visions of the World (RS, 1989)

BEENIE MAN
Blessed (Island Jamaica, 1995*)
Dis Uni Fi Hear (Hightone, 1994*)
Maestro (VP, 1996)
Many Moods of Moses (VP, 1998*)

BORN JAMERICANS
Kids from Foreign (Delicious Vinyl, 1994*)

BOUNTY KILLER
Ghetto Gramma (Greensleeves, 1997*), produced by Prince Jammy
My Xperience (VP, 1996*), Scare Dem production

BROWN, FOXY
Foxy (RAS, 1989)
My Kind of Girl (RAS, 1990)
Whip Appeal (VP, 1991)

CAPLETON
Alms House (RAS, 1993*)
Gold (Charm, 1991*)
I Testament (Def Jam, 1997**)
Prophecy (African Star/Rush, 1997*)

CHAKA DEMUS AND PLIERS
All She Wrote (Mango, 1993**)
Bad Mind (Pow Wow, 1992*)
Ruff This Year (RAS*)

CHAPLIN, CHARLIE
Cry Blood (RAS, 1991*)
Free Africa (Sonic Sounds, 1987), produced by George Phang
Old and New Testament (RAS, 1992*)
One of a Kind (Trojan, 1983), produced by Roy Cousins
Presenting Charlie Chaplin (Kingdom, U.K., 1982), roy Cousins
Quenchie (Tamoki-Wambesi, 1992*), reissues One of a Kind
Red Pond/Chaplin Chant (Tamoki Wambesi, 1991*), reissues 2 early LPs
Sound System (Arrival, 1984), produced by Junjo Lawes
Too Hot to Handle (RAS, 1994*)
Two Sides of Charlie Chaplin (RAS, 1989)

DIRTSMAN
Acid (Supreme, 1988)

GANZIE, TERRY
Heavy Like Lead (Profile, 1994*)
Outlaw: 'Nuff Reward (VP), 1994, produced by John John

GENERAL DEGREE
Degree (VP, 1997*)
P'N'S' (VP), late 1990s

GENERAL ECHO
Slackest LP (Techniques, 1979)
Twelve Inches of Pleasure (Greensleeves, 1980)

GENERAL TREES
Every Thing So So (Black Scorpio), late 1980s
Kingstonian Man (CSA, 1988), "Black Scorpio"
Nuff Respect (Shanachie, 1987*), produced by Maurice Johnson
Ragga Ragga Raggamuffin (Rohit), Bobby Digital
Younger Horseman (Sunset), late 1980s

KING KONG
Trouble Again (Jammys, 1986)

KULCHA KNOX
Praise Jah Again (Karaing, 1997)

LADY ANN
Vanity (GG's, 1983)

LADY G
God Daughter (VP, 1995)

LADY SAW
Best of Raw (VP, 1998*)
Collection (Diamond Rush, 1997*)
Give Me the Reason (VP, 1996*)
Passion (VP, 1997*)

LIEUTENANT STITCHIE
Bangarang (Shanachie, 1995**)
Governor (Atlantic, 1989*)
Great Ambitions (Super Power, 1987+)
Rude Boy (Atlantic, 1995*)
Wild Jamaican Romances (Atlantic, 1991*)

LITTLE JOHN
Best of Little John (RM), 1980s
Boombastic (Heartbeat, 1990*)
Early Days (Jah Bible), early 1980s
Give the Youth a Try (Live & Learn, 1983)
Reggae Dance (Midnight Rock), 1980s
Showcase '83 (EAD)
True Confession (Power House, 1984+)
Youth of Today (Skengdon, 1986)

LITTLE LENNY
All the Girls (Grapevine, 1995*)
Gun in a Baggy (RAS, 1990)
Is My Name (VP), early 1990s

MACKA B (UK)
Buppie Culture (RAS, 1990*)
Discrimination (RAS, 1994*)
Here Comes Trouble (Ariwa, 1994*)
Hold Onto Your Culture (RAS, 1995*)
Looks Are Deceiving (RAS, 1990*)
Natural Suntan (RAS, 1990*)
Peace Cup (RAS, 1991*)
Roots Ragga (RAS, 1993)
Sign of the Times (RAS, 1986*)

Suspicious (RAS, 1998*)
We've Had Enough (RAS, 1990*)

MAD COBRA
Bad Boy Talk (Penthouse), early
    1990s
Exclusive Decision (VP, 1996*)
Goldmine (RAS, 1993*)
Hard to Wet (Columbia, 1993*),
    contains "Flex"
Milkman (EMI, 1996*)
Spotlight (VP*), early 1990s
Step Aside (RAS, 1992*)
Venom (Greensleeves, 1994*)

MINOTT, ECHO
What the Hell (Jammys, 1987)

NICODEMUS
Dancehall Giant (Positive Sounds
    Massive, 1996*)
Nice Up the Dance (Clappers, 1983)

NINJAMAN
Artical Don (VP), early 1990s
Bad Grand Dad (VP), 1990s
De Man Good (ACT III), 1991–92
    picture disc
Hollow Point Bad Boy (Greensleeves,
    1994*)
Kill Them and Done (Tassa, 1991*)
Move from Here (VP, 1990*)
My Weapon (VP), 1990s
Nobody's Business But My Own
    (Shanachie, 1993*)
Original Front Tooth Gold Tooth Gun
    Pon Tooth Don Gorgon
    (Greensleeves, 1993*)
Out Pon Bail (Gold Disc, 1990)
Run Come Test (RAS, 1993*)
Settle All Scores (Gone Clear, 1997)
Superstar (Witty)
Target Practice (VP, 1991*)
2 for 1 (RAS, 1994**)

NITTY GRITTY (U.K.)
Nitty Gritty (Witty), 1980s
Turbo Charged (Greensleeves, 1986)

PAPA LEVI
Back to Basics (Ariwa, 1994*),
    produced by Mad Professor
Code of Practice (RAS, 1990*),
    produced by Mad Professor

Lion Ain't Sleeping (Bright Soul, 1990)
Trouble in Africa (Jah Records)

PAPA SAN
Fire Inna Dancehall (Melodie, France),
    early 1990s
Gi Mi Di Loving (Melodie), early 1990s
Pray Fi Dem (RAS, 1993*), produced
    by Prince Jazzbo
Rough Cut (Pow Wow, 1992)
Style and Fashion (Pow Wow, 1989)
System (Pow Wow, 1990*)
Clash, Vols. 1–2 (Fashion), early
    1990s, with Tippa Irie
Prince Jazzbo (Linval Carter)

PINCHERS
Bad Caesar (Yammie, 1989)
Bandalero (Pow Wow, 1991*)
Can't Take the Pressure (Blue
    Mountain, 1986)
Got to Be Me (Live and Love), late
    1980s, Jammys
Mass Out (RAS, 1987)
Pinchers with Pliers (Scorpio, 1988)
Two Originals (Melodie, France), late
    1980s, with Tweetie Bird

RANKING ANN (U.K.)
Slice of English Toast (Ariwa), late
    1980s
Something Fish Going On (Ariwa),
    late 1980s

RANKS, CUTTY
Die Hard (Penthouse, 1991), with
    Tony Rebel
From Mi Heart (Shanachie, 1992)
Lethal Weapon (Penthouse, 1991)
Retreat (Gold Disc, 1991)
Six Million Ways to Die (Priority, 1996*)
Stopper (Profile, 1991*)
20 Man Dead (Charm, 1991)

RANKS, SHABBA
A Mi Shabba (Epic, 1995*)
As Raw As Ever (Sony, 1991*)
Best Baby Father (Blue Mountain, 1989)
Golden Touch (Two Friends)
Just Reality (VP, 1990)
Mr. Maximum (Pow-Wow, 1991*),
    with guests
No Competition (Radikal, 1993**),
    with guests

Original Hardcore (Gone Clear, 1997*)
Rappin with the Ladies (VP, 1990)
Rawer Than Ever (Epic, 1991*),
    interview
Rough and Ready, Vol. 2 (Sony, 1993*)
Star of the 1990s (Super Power)
X-tra Naked (Epic, 1992*)

REBEL, TONY
If Jah (VP, 1997**)
Meets Garnet Silk in a Dancehall
    Conference (Heartbeat, 1994*)
Rebel with a Cause (Penthouse, 1992*)
Rebellious (RAS, 1992*)
Vibes of the Time (Sony, 1993*)

RED RAT
Oh No It's Red Rat (Greensleeves, 1997*)

SHAGGY
Boombastic (Virgin, 1995*)
Midnite Lover (Virgin, 1997*)
Pure Pleasure (Greensleeves, 1993*)

SHINEHEAD
Real Rock (Elektra, 1990*)
Rough and Rugged (African Love), late
    1980s
Sidewalk University (Elektra, 1992*)
Troddin' (Elektra, 1994*)
Unity (Elektra, 1988)

SISTER CAROL
Black Cinderella (1984; Heartbeat,
    1995*)
Call Mi Sister Carol (Heartbeat, 1994**)
Jah Disciple (RAS, 1989)
Lyrically Potent (Heartbeat, 1996**)
Mother Culture (RAS, 1991*)
Potent Dub (RAS, 1997*)

SISTER NANCY
One, Two (Techniques), early 1980s

SIZZLA
Black Woman and Child (Brick Wall,
    1997*)
Burning Up (RAS, 1995*)
Praise Ye Jah (Xterminator, 1997*)

SMITH, WAYNE
Sleng Teng (Greensleeves, 1986)
Wicked Inna Dance Hall (Rohit)

Youthman Skanking (Black Joy),
circa 1985

SNAGGAPUSS
Line Up All the Girls Dem
(Outa/Hightone, 1994*)
Reggae Funky (VP, 1995)
Whap Dem Merlene (Shocking Vibes),
mid-1990s

SNOW
12 Inches of Snow (East/West, 1993*)

STEPHENS, TANYA
Big Things a Gwan (RUNN, 1996*)
Too Hype (VP, 1997*)

TENOR SAW
Fever (Blue Mountain, 1986)
Tenor Saw and Nitty Gritty (Power
House)
Tribute to Tenor Saw (Tuff Gong,
1985), includes interviews
Wake the Town (VP, 1989)

TERROR FABULOUS
Lyrically Rough (Greensleeves, 1995*)
Yaga Yaga (VP, 1994*)

TIGER
Bam Bam (RAS, (1988*)
Claws of the Cat (Columbia, 1993*)
Mi Name Tiger (RAS, 1987*)
New Brand Style (RAS, 1995*)
Touch Is a Move (Mango, 1990*)

THUNDER, SHELLY
Fresh Out of the Pack (Mango, 1989*)

TUCKER, JUNIOR
Ooh Child (Esoldun, 1992*)
Love of a Lifetime (VP)
Secret Lover (VP)
True Confession (VP, 1996*)

WALES, JOSEY
Cowboy Style (Greensleeves, 1994*)
Ganja Pipe Is Harmless (Live &
Learn), mid-1980s
Na Lef Jamaica (Mango, 1986)
No Way Better Than Yard
(Greensleeves, 1984)

Outlaw (Greensleeves, 1983; Live &
Learn*)
Two Giants Clash (Greensleeves,
1984), with Yellowman

YELLOWMAN
Bad Boy Skanking (Greensleeves,
1982)
Divorced (Burning Sounds, 1983)
Duppy Or Gunman (Volcano,
1982)
Freedom of Speech (RAS, 1997*)
Girls Them Pet (Taxi), mid-1980s
Hotter Reggae (Jam Rock, 1982)
King Yellowman (CBWS, 1984)
Live (Reggae Sunsplash, 1983)
Live At Aces (Jah Guidance, 1982)
Man You Want (Shanachie, 1993*)
Message to the World (RAS, 1995*)
Nobody Move Nobody Get Hurt
(Shanachie, 1984)
One in a Million (Shanachie, 1989)
Party (RAS, 1991)
Rambo (Moving Target, 1986)
Reggae On Top (Pow Wow, 1993*)
Reggae On the Move (RAS, 1992*)
Rides Again (RAS, 1988)
Sings the Blues (Rohit, 1988)
Supermix (Volcano, 1982), with
Fathead
Them Mad Over Me (Channel One,
1982+)
Yellow Like Cheese (RAS, 1987)
Yellow, the Purple, the Nancy
(Greensleeves, 1983)
Zungguzungguguzungguzeng
(Shanachie, 1983)

DANCEHALL COMPILATIONS
Another Dimension: Nanny Goat Style
(Penthouse, 1994)
Awakening (RAS, 1996*), produced
by Phillip "Fatis" Burrell
Black Scorpio All Stars (Melodie*),
mid-1990s
Blend Dem (Pow Wow, 1995*)
Bogle (Mango, 1992*)
Bogle Mania: 14 Jamaican Dance-Floor
Hits (Greensleeves, 1993)
Captain of Your Ship: New Dancehall
Shots from Black Scorpio
(Shanachie, 1992*)
Culture Vibes: The Best of Conscious
Dancehall Reggae (Scratchie/Mercury,
1997**)
Dance Hall Hits (Penthouse, 1993)

Dancehall Queen: Original Motion
Picture Soundtrack (Island
Jamaica, 1997**)
Dancehall Roughneck (Heartbeat,
1993*), produced by Observer
Dancehall Style, Vols. 1–4 (Profile,
1989–93+)
DJ Clash, Vols. 1–2
(Greensleeves/Shanachie, 1983)
East Coast Meets Fat Eyes (EC, 1996*)
Exterminator Dance Hall Revue
(ROIR, 1991)
Fire Burning (Penthouse)
Five Star General (Penthouse)
Good, the Bad, the Ugly and the Crazy
(Columbia, 1994*)
Greensleeves Sampler, Vols. 1–20 to
date (Greensleeves)
Handle the Ride (VP, 1996*)
Jah Screw Presents: Dancehall Glamity
(Heartbeat, 1993*)
Jam Down Vibrations (Scratchie, 1996*)
Jamaica a Go Go (Mango, 1990*),
original soundtrack
Joyride (VP, 1995*), produced by
Dave Kelly
Killa Sound (Outa/Hightone, 1993*)
Love Punany Bad: Slackness in the
Dancehall (Priority, 1995*)
Mash Up the Place! The Best of Reggae
Dancehall (Rhino, 1995**)
Me Gone Buck Wild: Reggae Dance
Hall Killers (Shanachie, 1991*)
Nice Up Dancee (Rykodisc, 1991*)
Ninja Turtle, Parts 1–3 (Penthouse)
Operation D, Vols. 1–4 (Stingray),
mid-1990s, Bobby Digital Dixon
Penthouse Celebration, Parts 1–3
(Penthouse), live
Penthouse Party Mix (Penthouse, 1994)
Platinum Reggae (Artists Only, 1998*)
Producer's Trophy: Roof International
(Outa/Hightone, 1994**)
Producers Trophy: Fitzmar Productions
(Outa/Hightone, 1994*)
Producers Trophy: Jahmento Records
(Outa/Hightone, 1994*)
Ram Jam a Gwan (Heartbeat, 1994*),
produced by Richard Bell
Ragga Culture, Vol. 2 (Mixman, U.K.,
1992–93*)
Ragga Mania, Vols. 1–4 (Chemist),
mid-1990s
Ragga Ragga Ragga (Greensleeves),
1990s; multiple vols.
Ragga Sun Hit (Decclic), mid-1990s,
French dancehall

Ram "Dancehall" (Island, 1989*)
Reggae Ambassadors, Vols. 1–2 (Penthouse, 1990)
Reggae Gold, 1994, 1995, 1996, 1997 (VP*)
Reggae Hits (Jet Star), mid-1980s to present, multiple vols.
Reggae, 1990 (Penthouse, 1990)
Rude Bwoy Reggae (Priority, 1995*)
Selectors Choice (Outa/Hightone, 1992*)
Shark Records: In the Belly of the Whale (Outa/Hightone, 1994*)
Sound Boy Killing (Shanachie, 1994*)
Stalag 17 (Jammys, 1985)
Stalag 18, 19, 20 (Techniques), mid-1980s
Strictly Riddim: Dancehall Reggae, Vol. 1: The Singers; Vol. 2: The DJs (Priority, 1990*)
Strictly the Best (VP), 1990s, multiple vols.
Super Star Hit Parade (World Enterprise/Greensleeves), multiple vols.
Ten to One (Jammys, 1985)
This Is Dancehall (Continuum), late 1990s, multiple vols.
Thursday Night Juggling (Two Friends), early 1990s
Top Ten, Vols. 1–3 (World Enterprise, 1989), Jammy productions
Total Togetherness, Vols. 1–8 to date (VP, 1991–97*)
What a Bam Bam! Women in Reggae: Dancehall Queens (Shanachie, 1996*)
What One Riddim Can Do (Germain, 1987)
World of Digital-B (Mesa), 1990s
X-Rated Gang, Vols. 1–2 (RUNN), 1990s, continuous mix by Mixmaster Mighty Mike of Irie-FM

Instrumental

AGGROVATORS
Instrumental Reggae (RAS, 1992**), featuring Bobby Ellis and Tommy McCook

ALPHONSO, ROLAND
Best Of (Studio One)
Roll On (Wackies)
Strictly for You (Studio One)

BENNETT (DEADLY HEADLY)
25 Years from Alpha (On-U)

BLACK, PABLOVE
Mister Music (Studio One), 1970s
Charcoal Charlie (Tamoki Wambesi, 1989)

BLACK STEEL
Jungle Lion (Ariwa, 1988)
Lion in the Jungle (Ariwa, 1996*)

CRYSTALITES
Blockbuster Reggae Instrumentals (Crystal, 1990)
Undertaker (Crystal, 1970)

DRUMMOND, DON
Best of Don Drummond (Studio One)
Greatest Hits (Treasure Isle)
In Memory of Don Drummond (Studio One)

ELLIS, BOBBY
Bobby Ellis and the Professionals Meet the Revolutionaries (Third World, 1977)
Green Mango (Attack), mid-1970s, with Tommy McCook as Bobby and Tommy
Shaka (Dublab, 1984)

FRASER, DEAN
Black Horn Man (Joe Gibbs), early 1980s
Dean Fraser (WKS)
Dean Plays Bob (RAS, 1994*)
Dean Plays Bob, Vol. 2 (RAS, 1996)
Moonlight (VP)
Mystical Sax (Esoldun, 1992*)
Raw Sax (Clef, Canada*), mid-1990s
Sings and Blows (Shanachie, 1990*)
Taking Chances (RAS, 1992)
Verdict (VP, 1995*)

GIBBS, JOE AND THE PROFESSIONALS
State of Emergency (Joe Gibbs, 1980)

JAZZ JAMAICA
Skaravan (Hannibal, 1996**)

McCOOK, TOMMY
Brass Rockers (Striker Lee), mid-1970s, with the Aggrovators
Cookin' (Trojan, 1975), with the Aggrovators
Tommy McCook (Attack, 1974)
Superstar Disco Rockers (Weed Beat, 1977)

MITTOO, JACKIE
Evening Time (Studio One, 1967), with the Soul Vendors
Hot Blood (Attack, 1977)
In Cold Blood (Third World, 1978)
Jackie Mittoo (United Artists, 1978; Liberty, 1985)
Jackie Mittoo in London (Studio One, 1967)
Jackie Mittoo Showcase (Sonic Sounds, 1978)
Keep On Dancing (Coxsone, 1969)
Key Board King (Third World, 1976)
Macka Fat (Studio One, 1970)
Now (Studio One, 1969)
On Tour (Studio One), 1960s, with the Soul Vendors
Original (Third World, 1979)
Reggae Magic (CTL, 1972)
Showcase (Studio One, 1983)
Showcase, Vol. 3 (Jackie), mid-1980s
Tribute to Jackie Mittoo (Heartbeat, 1995**)
Wild Jockey (Bullwackies), 1980s

PABLO, AUGUSTUS
Augustus Pablo at his Very Best (Abraham*), 1970s recordings
Authentic Golden Melodies (Rockers International, 1992)
Blowing with the Wind (Shanachie, 1990**)
Dubbing in a Africa aka At His Very Best (Abraham)
Earth Rightful Ruler (Message), 1980s
East of the River Nile (Message, 1978; Shanachie**)
Eastman Dub (RAS, 1988*)
Heartical Chart (RAS, 1993*)
King David's Melodies (Alligator, 1983)
King Selassie I Calling (Rockers), mid-1990s
Live in Tokyo Japan (Rockers International, 1997*)
Original Rockers, Vols. 1–3 (Rockers), recorded in the 1970s

Red Sea (Black Underground, 1998+)
Rising Sun (Shanachie, 1986)
This Is Augustus Pablo Heartbeat, 1986**), recorded 1970
Thriller (1975; Echo, 1980)
See also Augustus Pablo productions in compilations and Pablo in dub

RANGLIN, ERNEST ("ERNIE")
Be What You Want to Be (Konduko, 1984)
Below the Bassline (Island Jamaica Jazz, 1996**)
In Search of the Lost Riddim (Palm Pictures, 1998*)
Memories of Barber Mack (Island, 1997*)
Mod Mod Ranglin (K&K, 1996** 1960s
Ranglin Roots (Water Lilly, 1976)
Sounds and Power (Studio One, 1997*), 1960s
Tribute to a Legend (Kariang, 1997**)

RICHARDS, ROY
Roy Richards (Studio One)
Roy Richards (Dynamic, 1977)

RODRIGUEZ, RICO
Blow Your Horn (Trojan, 1969; 1996)
Man from Wareika (Island, 1976)
Rising in the East (Jove, 1996*)

ROSE, WINSTON SAXTON
Sounds of Freedom (Roots, U.K., 1995*)

ROUGH SOUNDS INTERNATIONAL
Close Encounters (Rough Sounds, 1995*)

TAITT, LYNN
I'm in the Mood for Moods: New Oldies (Twolyn, 1997**)
Rock Steady Greatest Hits (Merritone+), 1967, with the Jets

TAPPIN, ARTURO
Java (Saxroots)
Strictly Roots Jazz (Saxroots)

UPSETTERS
Best of Lee Perry and the Upsetters, Vols. 1–2 (Pama)

Eastwood Rides Again (Trojan, 1970; 1995**)
Return of Django (Trojan, 1969; 1995**)

WRIGHT, WINSTON
Who Done It (Third World)

VARIOUS-ARTIST INSTRUMENTALS
Best of Studio One, Vol. 3: Killer Instrumentals (Heartbeat, 1988)
Blow Mr. Hornsman: Instrumental Reggae, 1968–75 (Trojan, 1988+)
Check the Winner 1970–74 (Greensleeves), Glenmore Brown production
Jazz Jamaica (Studio One), late 1960s
Magnificent Fourteen: 14 Shots of Western Inspired Reggae (Trojan, 1990+)
Melodica Melodies (Trojan, 1981+), includes Augustus Pablo, Joe White and Glen Brown
Music Is My Occupation: Instrumentals Produced by Duke Reid, 1962–65 (Trojan+)
Negril (Esoldun, 1992**)
Run Rhythm Run: Rock Steady and Reggae Instrumentals from Treasure Isle (Heartbet, 1996**)
Shufflin' On Bond Street: Jamaican R&B and Ska Instrumentals, 1959–66 (Trojan, 1989+)

Dub

ABYSSINIANS
Declaration of Dub (Heartbeat, 1998**)

AGGROVATORS
Aggrovators Meet the Revolutionaries at Channel One, Vols. 1–2 (Gorgon), mid-1970s, dub-bedded Tommy McCook-driven instrumentals
Reggae Stones Dub (Abraham, 1997), 1970s

DR. ALIMANTADO
In the Mix, Parts 1–5 (Keyman, 1985–89)
King's Bread Dub (Ital Sounds, 1979)

BADAWI
Bedouin Sound Clash (ROIR, 1996*)
Jerusalem Under Fire (ROIR, 1997*)

BLACK UHURU
Brutal Dub (RAS, 1986*), dubs Brutal LP
Dub Factor (Mango, 1983), dubs Chill Out LP
Iron Storm Dub (Mesa, 1992), dubs Iron Storm
Jammy's in Lion Dub Style (Jammy's, 1981+), dubs Love Crisis LP
Love Dub (Rohit), late 1980s, dubs no known release
Now Dub (Mesa, 1990*), dubs Now
Positive Dub (RAS, 1987*), dubs Positive
Strongg Dubb (Mesa, 1994*), dubs Strongg
Uhuru in Dub (CSA, 1982), remix of Jammy's in Lion Dub Style

BURNING SPEAR
Living Dub, Vol. 1 (Burning Spear, 1982; Heartbeat, 1993*)
Living Dub, Vol. 2 (Heartbeat, 1993*)
Living Dub, Vol. 3 (Heartbeat, 1997*)

CHEMIST
Dub Mixture (Kingdom, 1984+)
Dub Prescription (KIngdom, 1984)
Formula, Vol. 1 (Blue Mountain, 1989)

CLARKE, JOHNNY
Johnny in the Echo Chamber (Attack, 1989)

COUSINS, ROY
Force of Music Liberated Dub (Ballistic, 1979+)
International Heroes Dub (Tamoki Wambesi+), early 1980s
Kings and Queens of Dub (Tamoki Wambesi+)
Nexus Dub (Tamoki Wambesi**)

CULTURE IN DUB
Culture Dub (High Note, 1978)
Culture in Dub (Sky Note, U.K., 1978), not the same album as above
Culture in Dub: 15 Dub Shots (Heartbeat, 1994*), Sonia Pottinger
Stoned (RAS, 1997)

DELGADO, JUNIOR, IN DUB
Dance a Dub (Big Cat, 1997**)

DODD, C.S., IN DUB (STUDIO ONE)
African Rub a Dub (Studio One), 1970s
Better Dub from Studio One (Studio
One)
Bionic Dub (Studio One)
Dub Specialist: 17 Dub Shots from
Studio One (Heartbeat, 1995*)
Dub Store Special (Studio One)
Hi Fashion Dub Top Ten (Studio One)
Ital Dub (Studio One)
Juk's Incorporation (Studio One)
Juk's Incorporation, Vol. 2 (Studio
One)
Mello Dub (Studio One)
Roots Dub (Studio One)
Sample Dub (Studio One)
Zodiac Dub (Studio One)

GIBBS, JOE, AND ERROL
THOMPSON (THE MIGHTY TWO)
African Dub, Chapters 1–5 (Joe
Gibbs), mid- to late 1970s
African Dub: The Series, Parts 1–2,
3–4 (Rocky One, 1994**)
Earthquake Dub (Joe Gibbs), mid-
1970s
Majestic Dub (Joe Gibbs), 1980

HARRIOT, DERRICK, IN DUB
More Scrub-A-Dub (Crystal, 1975)
Scrub-A-Dub (Crystal, 1974)
Sinsemilla Dub (Crystal, 1980)

HOOKIM, ERNEST AND JO JO,
IN DUB
Don't Underestimate the Force, the
Force Is Within You (J&L), early
1980s
I Came I Saw I Conquered (Channel
One, 1978)
Seducer Dub-Wise (Hitbound, 1982)
Vital Dub: Strictly Rockers (Well
Charge, 1976+), dubs the Mighty
Diamonds' Right Time album track
for track

HUDSON, KEITH, IN DUB
Brand (Joint International; Pressure
Sounds, 1997**), mid-1970s dub
Pick a Dub (Blood & Fire reissue,
1994**)

ISAACS, GREGORY, IN DUB
Come Again Dub (Danceteria), 1990s,
Xterminator
Slum Dub (Burning Sounds, 1978+)

IMPACT ALL STARS
Forward the Bass (Blood & Fire, 1998*)

ISRAEL VIBRATION IN DUB
Israel Vibration in Dub (RAS, 1990)
Israel Dub (RAS, 1996*)
I.V. Dub (RAS, 1994*)

JAH SHAKA IN DUB
Brimstone and Fire (Jah Shaka, 1983)
Commandments of Dub, Chapters
1–10 (Jah Shaka, 1980–91+)
Dub Salute, Vols. 1–5 (Jah Shaka,
1995*)
Far-I Ship Dub (Jah Shaka, 1992+)
Jah Shaka Presents: Dub Master, Vol. 1
(Mango, 1989)
New Testaments of Dub, Part 1
(Greensleeves)

JAH THOMAS IN DUB
Jah Thomas Meets Scientist in Dub
Conference (Munich, 1996*)

PRINCE JAMMY (LATER KING
JAMMY)
Black Uhuru in Dub (CSA, 1982)
Black Uhuru's Love Dub (Rohit)
Computerized Dub (Greensleeves,
1985)
Dub War (Vista, 1985)
Dubbing in the Back Yard (Black Music)
In Lion Style Dub (Third World, 1977+)
Kamikaze Dub (Trojan, 1979; 1996**)
Prince Jammy Destroys the Invaders
(Greensleeves, 1982)
Strictly Dub (Arawak), early 1980s
See also Black Uhuru in dub

KING TUBBY
Bionic Dub (Esoldun, 1995*)
Creation Dub (Esoldun, 1995*),
1973–77, Bunny Lee/Aggrovators
Crossfire (Esoldun, 1992*), Fatman
Dangerous Dub (Greensleeves, 1996**),
reissues 1981 LP and more
Dancehall Style Dub (Abraham,
Canada*), 1970s, Clocktower
productions

Dub Basket (Rhino, U.K.*), Rupie
Edwards
Dub from the Roots aka Dubmaster
(Live and Love+), mid-1970s
Dubmaster (Clocktower+), Bunny
Lee/Aggrovators mid-1970s
Freedom Sounds in Dub, 1976–79
(Blood & Fire, 1996**)
Harry Mudie Meets King Tubby's in
Dub Conference (Moodisc, Vol. 1,
1976; Vol. 2, 1977)
I Am the King, Vols. 1–3 (Sprint)
Jah Thomas Meets King Tubby in the
House of Dub (Munich, 1996*)
King At the Controls (Tads), 1970s
King Tubby Meets Lee Perry: Megawatt
Dub (Shanachie, 1997), Watty
Burnett productions
King Tubbys Meets Rockers Uptown
(Yard Music**)
King Tubby Meets the Aggrovators at
Dub Station (Attack+), B.Lee
King Tubby Meets the Upsetter
(Celluloid+)
King Tubby on the Mix, Vols. 1–2
(Original Music, 1991*), recorded
in the early 1970s
King Tubby Surrounded by the Dreads
at the National Arena (Studio
Sixteen), Winston Edwards
King Tubby the Dubmaster with the
Waterhouse Posse (Vista)
King Tubby Upset the Upsetter (Third
World+), late 1970s
King Tubby versus Channel One
(Bumb), 1970s
King Tubby's Controls (Abraham,
1990), 1970s compilation
King Tubby's Prophecy of Dub (Blood
& Fire, 1995**), Yabby You
King Tubby's Special, 1973–76
(Trojan, 1989**), double album
Laser Rock (Esoldun, 1992*)
Majestic Dub (Jet Star+), Bunny
Lee/Aggrovators
Memorial Dub (Rhino, U.K.*), early
1990s
Morwell Unlimited Meet King Tubby:
Dub Me (Blood & Fire, 1997**),
mid-1970s, Blacka Morwell
productions
Penwood Walk (Esoldun, 1992*)
Prophet of Dub (Prophets, 1976),
Yabby You
Psalm of the Time Dub (Tamoki-
Wambesi), Roy Cousins
Roots Dub (Esoldun, 1992*)

Roots of Dub (Clocktower/Abraham**),
Benny Lee/Aggrovators
Rub a Dub (Esoldun, 1992*)
Shalom Dub (Klik, 1975+),
B.Lee/Aggrovators
Shining Dub (Esoldun, 1992*)
Sly and Robbie Meet King Tubby
(Culture Press, 1985)
Treasure Isle Dub, Vols. 1–2 (Esoldun,
1993**), both vols. on 1 CD
Yah Congo: King Tubby and Professor
at Dub Table (ROIR, 1995**)

OF RELATED INTEREST
Channel One Meets King Tubby's in
the House of Dub (AG*), 1990s
Dub Gone Crazy: The Evolution of
Dub at King Tubby's, 1975–79
(Blood and Fire, 1994**)
Dub Gone 2 Crazy (Blood & Fire,
1996**), Bunny Lee, Tubby, and
Jammy
If Deejay Was Your Trade: The Dreads
at King Tubby's, 1974–77 (Blood
and Fire, 1994**), dub-mix DJ
anthology
King Tubby's Meets Scientist at Dub
Station (Burning Sounds, 1996*)
King Tubby's Meets Scientist in a
World of Dub (Burning Sounds,
1996)
Rockers Meets King Tubby's in a Fire
House (Shanachie, 1980)
Rod of Correction Showcase (Abraham)
30 Years of Rude Boy Dance Hall Dub
(Rhino, U.K., 1996*)
Tribute to King Tubby's (Star), early
1990s
Twin Spin (Fatman*), 1990s release,
mixed by Tubby and others
Two Big Bull in a One Pen Dubwise
(Firehouse)
Unleashed Dub from King Tubby's
Studio (Fatman, 1991*), mixed by
Tubby, Scientist, Professor, Jammy
and Pat Kelly

MAD PROFESSOR
Black Liberation Dub, Chapter 1 (RAS,
1994*)
Black Liberation Dub, Chapter 2: Anti-
Racist Dub Broadcast (RAS, 1995*)
Black Liberation Dub, Chapter 3:
Evolution of Dub (RAS, 1996*)
Bob Andy's Dub Book As Revealed to
the Mad Professor (I-Anka, 1989*)

Dub Me Crazy, Parts 1–12 (RAS,
1985–92**)
It's a Mad Mad Mad Mad Mad
Professor (RAS, 1994**)
Lost Scrolls of Moses (RAS, 1993*)
Mystic Warrior in Dub (RAS, 1990*),
with Lee Perry
Stepping in Dub-Wise Country
(Ariwa, 1987)
True Born African Dub (RAS, 1992*)
Under the Spell of Dub (RAS, 1998**)

MIGHTY DIAMONDS IN DUB
Mighty Diamonds Dubwise (Music
Works), 1980s
Planet Mars Dub (Virgin, 1978)
Vital Dub (Channel One; Virgin,
1976+)

MIXMAN
African Gold Dub, Series 3 (Mixman,
1993**)
Dub Like Wildfire Dub, Series 2
(Mixman, 1992**)
New Dimension Dub Dub, Series 1
(Mixman, 1991*)

MORWELLS IN DUB
A1 Dub (Trojan, 1980)
Dub Me (Morwell Esq, 1975; Blood &
Fire, 1997**)

MYSTIC REVEALERS IN DUB
In Dub: Space and Dub (RAS, 1995*)

NINEY THE OBSERVER IN DUB
Dubbing with the Observer (Attack,
1975)
Observation of Life Dub (Carib Gems),
mid-1970s
Observer Attack Dub (ROIR, 1994*)

PABLO, AUGUSTUS, IN DUB
Africa Must Be Free by 1983 Dub: See
Mundell, Hugh
Beat Street Dub (Rockers), early 1990s
Dub Store 1990s (RAS, 1993*)
King Tubby Meets Rockers Uptown
(Clocktower, 1977; Shanachie**)
One Step Dub (Greensleeves, 1991)
Pablo Meets Mr. Bassie (Shanachie,
1991**)
Raggamuffin Dub (Rockers
International, 1990)

Raiders Dub (Yard Music, 1997**)
Rockers Come East (Shanachie, 1987)
Rockers Meets King Tubby Inna
Firehouse (Shanachie, 1982)

PERRY, LEE, IN DUB
Blackboard Jungle Dub (Upsetters,
Clocktower, 1973+)
Cloak and Dagger (Black Art, 1978)
Kung Fu Meets the Dragon (Justice
League, 1995), circa 1975
Lee "Scratch" Perry Meets Bullwackies
in Satan's Dub (ROIR), 1988
Megaton Dub (Seven Leaves, 1983)
Megaton Dub 2 (Seven Leaves, 1983)
Mystic Warrior Dub (Ariwa, 1989),
with Mad Professor
Revolution Dub (Anachron), recorded
mid-1970s
Rhythm Shower (Upsetter, 1973+)
Super-Ape (Island, 1976**)
Upsetter in Dub (Heartbeat, 1997**)

POTTINGER, SONIA, IN DUB
Culture Dub (High Note), 1978
Culture in Dub (Sky Note)
Culture in Dub: 15 Dub Shots
(Heartbeat, 1994*)
Dub Expression (High Note+), 1970s
Dub Over Dub: 27 Track Dub
Extravaganza (Heartbeat, 1996**)
Medley Dub (High Note+), late
1970s

PRENTO, GUSSIE ("GUSSIE P.")
Burial Dub (Digikal, 1986), U.K.
Fashion crashers
Raw Rub a Dub Inna Fashion (Top
Notch), 1980s, contains "Who's
Safe?"
Rubble Dub: MCs Choice (Top
Notch), 1980s

PRINCE FAR I IN DUB
Cry Tuff Dub Encounter, Chapter 1
(Danceteria/ROIR*), CD reissue
Cry Tuff Dub Encounter, Part 2
(Virgin, 1979)
Cry Tuff Dub Encounter, Chapter 3
(Pressure Sounds)
Cry Tuff Dub Encounter, Chapter 4
(Trojan, 1981)
Dub to Africa (Pressure Sounds),
recorded 1979, with the Arabs
Dubwise (Virgin, 1991)

REVOLUTIONARIES

Dutch Man Dub (Burning Sounds+)
Gold Mine Dub (Greensleeves, 1979+), Jah Lloyd
Green Bay Dub (Burning Sounds+), late 1970s, Linval Thompson
Jonkanoo Dub (Cha Cha, 1978+), "Produced by Channel One"
Outlaw Dub (Trojan, 1979+), Linval Thompson
Reaction in Dub (Cha Cha+), Jo Jo Hookim
Revival (Cha Cha, 1982), "Produced by Channel One"
Revolutionaries Sounds (Well Charge, 1976+), Jo Jo Hookim
Revolutionaries Sounds, Vol. 2 (Ballistic+), Jo Jo Hookim, Channel One, 1976
Top Ranking Dub (Top Ranking*), Music Force Production

ROBOTICS

Man and Machine (Ariwa, 1985**)
My Computer's Acting Strange (Ariwa, 1986+)
Strictly Automatic (as the Electro-Robitic Dub Orckestra) (Ariwa, 1984), Mad Professor

ROOTS RADICS IN DUB

Hot We Hot Dub (ROIR, 1989)
Live At Channel One Kingston Jamaica (Live & Love*), 1980s
Radical Dub Session (Solid Groove), early 1980s
Radification (Cha Cha, 1982)

ROSE, MICHAEL, IN DUB

Big Business Frontline (Heartbeat, 1996*)
Dub Wicked (Heartbeat, 1997*)

SCIENTIST

Crucial Cuts, Vols. 1–2 (Kingdom, 1983, 1986+)
Dub in the Roots Tradition, 1976–79 (Blood and Fire, 1996**)
Dubbin with Horns (Burning Sounds, 1996)
Heavyweight Dub Champion (Greensleeves, 1980)
High Priest of Dub (Kingdom, 1982; Tamoki Wambesi)
Introducing Scientist (JB, 1980)

King of Dub (Kingdom, 1987*)
People's Choice (Kingdom, 1983)
Repatriation Dub (Tamoki-Wambesi*)
Scientific Dub (Clocktower), circa 1980
Scientist in Dub, Vol. 1 (Jah Guidance)
Scientist Encounters Pac-Man (Greensleeves, 1982+)
Scientist Meets the Space Invaders (Greensleeves, 1981)
Scientist Rids the World of the Evil Curse of the Vampires (Greensleeves, 1982; 1990**)
Scientist Wins the World Cup (Greensleeves, 1982)

SLY AND ROBBIE IN DUB

Dubs for Tubs: A Tribute to King Tubby (Rohit)
Master of Ceremony "Dub" (Imperial), early 1980s
See also Revolutionaries, Black Uhuru in dub, and others

TWILIGHT CIRCUS IN DUB

Bin Shaker Dub (M Records, 1997*)
Dub Plate Selection (M Records, 1998**)
Other Worlds of Dub (M Records, 1996*)
Twilight Circus in Dub, Vol. 1 (M Records, 1995*)

TWINKLE BROTHERS IN DUB

Dub Massacre, Parts 1–6 (Twinkle, 1982–94)
Dub Pack: Old Cuts (Twinkle, 1991)
Dub Plate (Twinkle, 1995*)
Dub with Strings (Twinkle, 1992*)

BUNNY WAILER IN DUB

Bunny Wailer's Dubd'sco, Vols. 1–2 (Solomonic), 1978–81

YABBY YOU IN DUB

Beware (Grove, 1978; ROIR**)
King Tubby/Yabby You Hits of the Past, Vols. 1–2 (Vivian Jackson)
King Tubby's Prophecy of Dub (Prophets, 1976; Blood & Fire, 1995**)
Yabby You and Michael Prophet Meets Scientist At the Dub Station (Yabby You, 1991*)

Yabby You Meets Mad Professor and Black Steel in Ariwa Studios (RAS, 1993)
Yabby U Meets Sly and Robbie Along with Tommy McCook (WLN)
Yabby You and Michael Prophet Vocal and Dub (Vivian Jackson)
Yabby You Meets Sly and Robbie at the Mixing Lab (Vivian Jackson)
Yabby You Meets Tommy McCook in Dub: Sound of the Seventies (Peacemaker*)

YELLOWMAN IN DUB

A Feast of Yellow Dub (RAS, 1990*)

TAPPA ZUKIE IN DUB

Escape from Hell (Stars, 1977)
Tappa Zukie in Dub (Stars, 1977; Blood and Fire, 1995**)

VARIOUS-ARTISTS DUB

African Roots, Acts 1–5 (Bullwackies+), late 1970s–early 1980s
African Rubber-Dub (Cartel), 1980s, Bim Sherman
A.K.A. Dub (Lush Records, 1997)
Bag-O-Wire (Klik, 1975+) Sydney Crooks
Bald Head Justice (Top Ranking), late 1970s
Big Ship Classic Dub (VP, 1992), produced, arranged, and mixed by Freddie McGregor and Dalton Browne
Black Foundation Dub (Gussie), late 1970s, Augustus "Gussie" Clarke
Black Magic Dub (Burning Sounds), late 1970s
Chalice Dub, Part 1 (Reggae On Top, 1995*)
Concrete Dub (Concrete Jungle, 1976)
Creation Dub (Wackies, 1977+)
Cultural Dub (Harry J, 1978)
Dial M for Murder (Express), 1970s, Phil Pratt
Dub Chill Out (Music Club, 1996**)
Dub for Daze, Vol. 1 (RAS, 1996*), Jim Fox
Dub for Daze, Vol. 2 (RAS, 1997*), Scientist
Dub from Jamaican Roots: Studio 1 Band Meets High Times Band (Original Music, 1996*), produced by Jah Thomas

Dubs from the South East (Pantomime, 1991+), 1969–76, produced by Glenmore Brown, mixed by King Tubby

Dub Justice (Attack, 1990+), Bunny Lee/Aggrovators

Dubmission, Parts 1–2 (Quango), Tomas masterminds 1990s remix anthology

Dub of the 1970s (Atra, 1988+)

Dub or Die, Vols. 1–2 (Roir), late 1980s

Dub Out West, Parts 1–3 (Nubian**)

Dub Revolution: UK Roots High Steppin' to the Future (ROIR, 1994*)

Dub the Millennium: Manasseh Meets the Equaliser (Hollywood Records/Acid Jazz, 1996*)

Dub the Generals (Wackies, 1997*)

Dubwise (Dread At the Control), Mikey Dread in dub

Ghetto Dub (Revolver), Bim Sherman

Ghettology Dubwise (Black Roots, 1980), Sugar Minott in dub

Heavy Metal Dub (Clocktower), early 1980s

Herbs of Dub (Jet Star), 1970s, Jah Lloyd productions with King Tubby

H.I.M. Haile Selassie I Centenary Dub, Chapter 1 (Surr Zema, 1993)

History of Dub (Munich, 1995**)

I Shall Sing (Trojan, 1991+)

In the Red Zone: The Essential Collection of Classic Dub (Shanachie, 1997**)

I Wah Dub (More Cut/EMI, 1980), Dennis "Blackbeard" Bovell

Jah Works International (ROIR, 1996*), new alternative dub

Jamaica Super Dub Session (Bullwackies)

Java Java Dub (Impact, 1989), Clive Chin

Kaya Dub (Kaya, 1975)

King of Dub (Clocktower), Bunny Lee Aggrovators

KTW Dub (Clappers, 1982), produced by bass man Junior Dan

Leggo Dub (Cash & Carry), 1970s

Live & Learn Dub (Live & Learn, 1985), Delroy Wright

Meditation Dub (Techniques), mid-1970s, Winston Riley

New Dimensions Dub (Blackamix)

More Scrubbing the Dub (Crystal), Derrick Harriot

Phase One Dub-Wise, Vols. 1–2 (Phase One), Roy Francis

Raiders of the Lost Dub (Island, 1981)

Rasta Dub, 1976 (Micron+)

Rasta Dub, 1977 (Micron+)

Reggae Gi Dem Dub (Negusa Nagast), 1970s, Big Youth in dub

Rockers Almighty Dub (Clocktower)

Scrub-A-Dub (Crystal, 1974+), Derrick Harriot

Sensi Dub, Vols. 1–5 (Revolver)

Serious Dub (Mango, 1987+)

Slum in Dub (Burning Sounds), 1970s, dubs Gregory Isaacs

Sound of Macka Dub (Clocktower)

Star Wars Dub (Burning Sounds), Phil Pratt

Techniques in Dub (Pressure Sounds, 1997), Winston Riley

Towering Dub Inferno (ROIR, 1990**)

Tough Guys in Dub (Top Ranking International), Fatman

21st Century Dub (Roir)

Universal Dub (Zola & Zola, 1997*)

Words in Dub (Jah Marcus)

Xterminator Dub (RAS, 1996**), dubs Phillip Burrell's Awakening

Zion Dub (Carls), late 1970s

Index